Ford Madox Brown

Pre-Raphaelite Pioneer

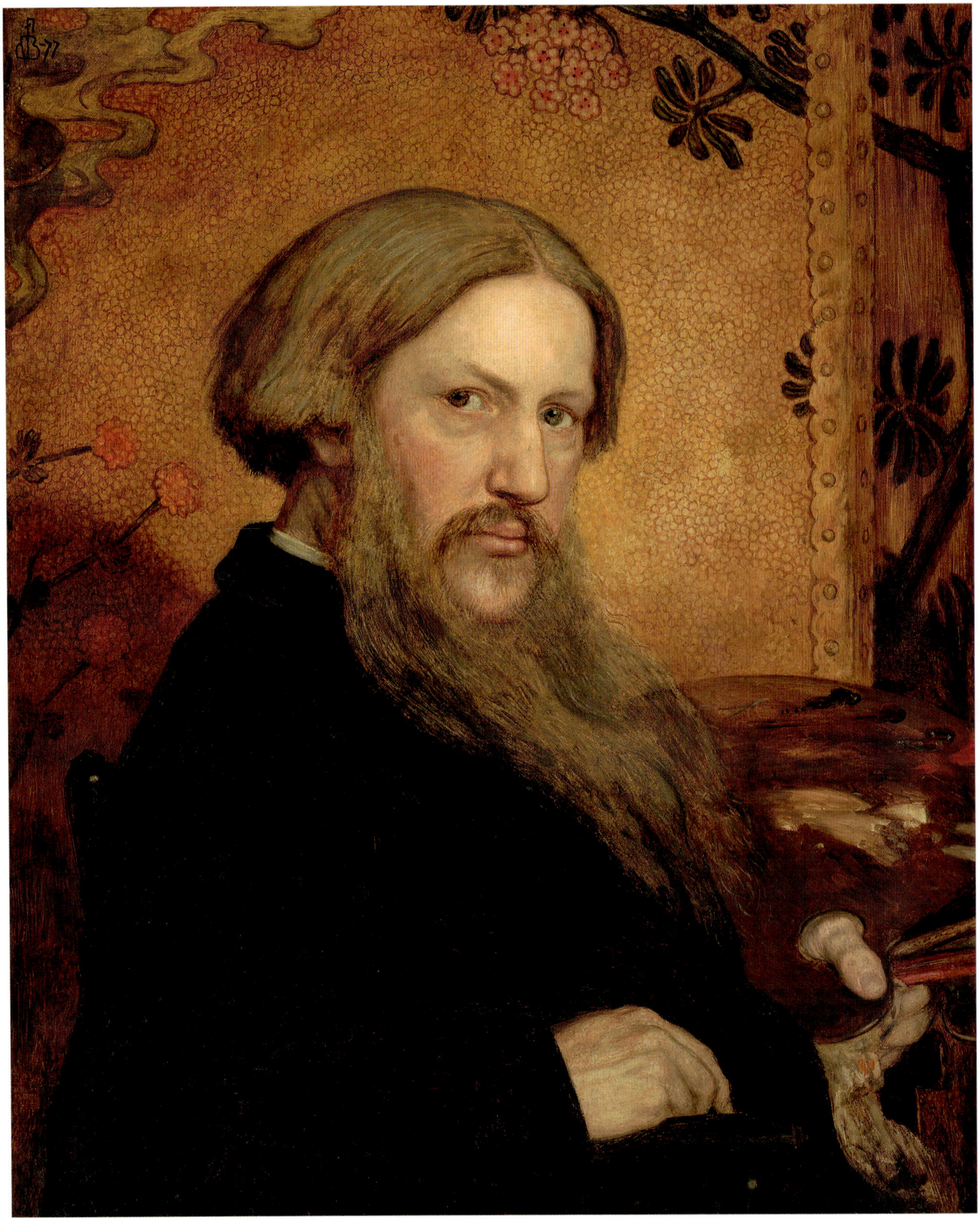

Ford Madox Brown

Pre-Raphaelite Pioneer

JULIAN TREUHERZ

With contributions from
ANGELA THIRLWELL and KENNETH BENDINER

PHILIP WILSON PUBLISHERS in association with MANCHESTER ART GALLERY

Published on the occasion of the exhibition

Ford Madox Brown: Pre-Raphaelite Pioneer

Manchester Art Gallery
24 September 2011 – 29 January 2012

Museum of Fine Arts, Ghent
25 February – 3 June 2012

Manchester Art Gallery
Mosley Street
Manchester M2 3JL
Tel: +44 (0) 161 235 8888
www.manchestergalleries.org

Published by Philip Wilson Publishers, an imprint of I.B.Tauris & Co Ltd
in association with Manchester Art Gallery

Philip Wilson Publishers
6 Salem Road
London W2 4BU
www.philip-wilson.co.uk

ISBN 978-0-85667-700-7 (Hardback)
ISBN 978-0-901673-80-0 (Softback)

Distributed in the United States and Canada exclusively by:
Palgrave Macmillan, 175 Fifth Avenue, New York NY 10010

Designed by Caroline and Roger Hillier
The Old Chapel Graphic Design
www.theoldchapelivinghoe.com

Printed and bound in China by Everbest

Manchester Art Gallery

MANCHESTER CITY COUNCIL

Manchester Art Gallery Trust

The Zochonis Charitable Trust

MSK GENT

Front cover: *Detail of cat. 58,* The Last of England

Back cover: *Detail of cat. 14,* Manfred on the Jungfrau

Frontispiece: *Ford Madox Brown,* Self-portrait, *1877.*
Harvard Art Museums, Fogg Art Museum,
Bequest of Grenville L. Winthrop, 1943.185

CONTENTS

FOREWORD AND ACKNOWLEDGEMENTS

Manchester Art Gallery is renowned for its collection of major works by the Pre-Raphaelites, which are perennially popular with our visitors. People know and love the Victorian vision of the world they present, but how well are they really understood? It is sometimes overlooked that when the gallery became a public institution as part of Manchester Corporation in 1882, the Pre-Raphaelites were the cutting-edge experimental artists of their day. At the time, their work was being shown and celebrated in Europe alongside that of the Impressionists and Symbolists.

Of all the Pre-Raphaelites, the one most closely associated with Manchester is Ford Madox Brown. In 1878 the city commissioned him to create a series of murals for Waterhouse's new Town Hall. The murals represent Brown's characteristically radical attempt to convey the commercial, scientific and political events of local history in a place of public assembly and ceremony. They emphasize the dignity of the common citizen and are firmly rooted in the democratic rather than aristocratic tradition. Brown even proposed to the city fathers that he include the Peterloo massacre, but though it was nearly sixty years after the event this proved too sensitive a subject. Even so, procuring the services of Brown proved to be a major coup for the city. His sequence of paintings sparked a revival in mural painting and made Manchester an admired leader of public art patronage.

It took Brown over thirteen years to complete the murals, and for six of these he took up residence in the city. Even after leaving for London in 1887, Brown visited Manchester at intervals, and he continued to work on the murals until not long before his death in 1893. While in Manchester, he contributed to many aspects of city life. Passionately engaged in social reform as well as art, he was involved in founding a labour exchange to help the unemployed and produced furniture designs for an early job-creation scheme. He inspired local artists, such as Frederic Shields, with whom he formed a close friendship, and he worked with a group of young artists who assisted him in painting the large-scale decorations commissioned from him for the temporary structure which housed the 1887 exhibition for Queen Victoria's Jubilee. Brown's presence in the city also stimulated art collecting, public and private. The brewer Henry Boddington, for example, became a major collector of his work, building a special gallery for it in his home in Wilmslow. In 1885 Brown's masterpiece, *Work*, was the first Pre-Raphaelite painting to be purchased by the recently instituted City Art Gallery. Today it is still one of the highlights of Manchester's collection.

It seems surprising therefore, that despite a wealth of exhibitions devoted to the Pre-Raphaelites around the world in the last three decades there has been no comprehensive solo examination of Brown's work since the pioneering exhibition held in Liverpool, Birmingham and here at the Manchester Art Gallery in 1964–65.

In recent years, Manchester Art Gallery has mounted a series of exhibitions that have reassessed the cultural history of the nineteenth century through its art: *Pre-Raphaelite Women Artists*, *Black Victorians*, *Art Treasures in Manchester: 150 Years On* and *Holman Hunt and the Pre-Raphaelite Vision*. In view of their success, I was delighted when Julian Treuherz, former Director of the Walker Art Gallery in Liverpool (and for many years Keeper of Fine Art at Manchester Art Gallery) accepted our invitation to curate an exhibition re-examining Ford Madox Brown's significance. Julian has judiciously chosen a selection of works which look at all aspects of Brown's career and reveal what a radical and inventive artist he was.

Brown's direct and penetrating eye made him a pioneer of original ways of seeing, even within the Pre-Raphaelite circle. Of an older generation than the others, and never a member of the Brotherhood, from the 1840s onwards he brought a breath of fresh air into academic historical and literary subjects by introducing sunlight and realism. In his major landscape paintings, he observed the range of colour as well as tone in shadows, anticipating the open-air effects of the Impressionists. He painted a modern British landscape of workaday fields and urban back gardens, rather than conventionally grand or picturesque scenery. His great set pieces, *Work* and *The Last of England*, unique in their day, have become icons of socially-engaged art, both for their subject matter and their lack of preaching, sentimentality and condescension: an attitude relevant both then and now.

An exhibition of this nature cannot be achieved without the great generosity of lenders and especially those private collectors who have agreed to part with their pictures for both venues. Our institutional colleagues too have been extremely accommodating to our project lending significant numbers of key public attractions and I am particularly indebted to:

Aberdeen Art Gallery & Museums; Ashmolean Museum, University of Oxford; Atkinson Gallery, Sefton Musuems and Galleries, Southport; Birmingham Museums & Art Gallery; The Trustees of the British Museum; Bradford Museums and Galleries; The Forbes Collection, New York; Culture and Sport Glasgow, Glasgow City Council; Maidstone Museum & Bentlif Art Gallery; National Museums Liverpool; Manchester Metropolitan University Special Collections; Amgueddfa Cymru – National Museum Wales; National Portrait Gallery, London; Society of Antiquaries of London; National Trust; William Morris Gallery, London Borough of Waltham Forest; Tate, London; Tullie House Museum & Art Gallery, Carlisle; Victoria and Albert Museum, London; Yale Center for British Art, Paul Mellon Fund; The Whitworth Art Gallery, The University of Manchester.

I would also like to extend my thanks to Professor Kenneth Bendiner, author of the first full-length art historical study of Brown, and to Angela Thirlwell, writer of an acclaimed biographical account of the artist and his relationships with women, for their stimulating contributions to the catalogue.

We are delighted to be able to enter into a professional partnership with the Museum of Fine Arts in Ghent and I must extend my thanks to the Director, Robert Hoozee, for taking this exhibition to Belgium where Brown's work will be seen for the first time alongside that of his tutors and contemporaries from his years of study there.

In times when it is becoming increasingly difficult to organise such ground-breaking exhibitions I am continually pleased and gratified by the support given to us by our benefactors and I must extend particular thanks to the Zochonis Charitable Trust and Manchester Art Gallery Trust, without whose generosity this exhibition would not have been possible.

Maria Balshaw
Director of Manchester City Galleries

AUTHOR'S ACKNOWLEDGEMENTS

My first thanks go to Mary Bennett, who curated the Ford Madox Brown exhibition in 1964–65 and has devoted a lifetime of expertise to the artist, culminating in her magnificent catalogue raisonné. I am indebted to her for generously allowing me to use the catalogue before publication. I am also grateful to my colleagues at Manchester Art Gallery, especially Sara Holdsworth for inviting me to curate the exhibition, to Virginia Tandy and Moira Stevenson for supporting the project, and to Tim Wilcox and Rebecca Milner for all their help. I am also grateful to the following: Martin Beisly, Heather Birchall, Stephanie Boydell, Judith Bronkhurst, Lorne Campbell, Karien Cremer, Robin Croft, Mark Chadwick, Peter de Figueiredo, Germaine Denn, Julia Dudkiewicz, Christopher Forbes, Melanie Gardner, Alastair Grieve, Pat Hardy, Colin Harrison, Robert Holden, James Holland, Anthea Jarvis, Jane Kennedy, Reyahn King, Laura MacCulloch, John Maddison, Jennifer Melville, Julie Milne, Jane Munro, Victoria Osborne, Harriet Owen-Hughes, Sandra Penketh, the late Tessa Sidey, Alison Smith, Oliver and Janet Soskice, Michael Stammers, Guilland Sutherland, Virginia Surtees, Angela Thirlwell, John Thirlwell and Fiona Woolley.

Julian Treuherz

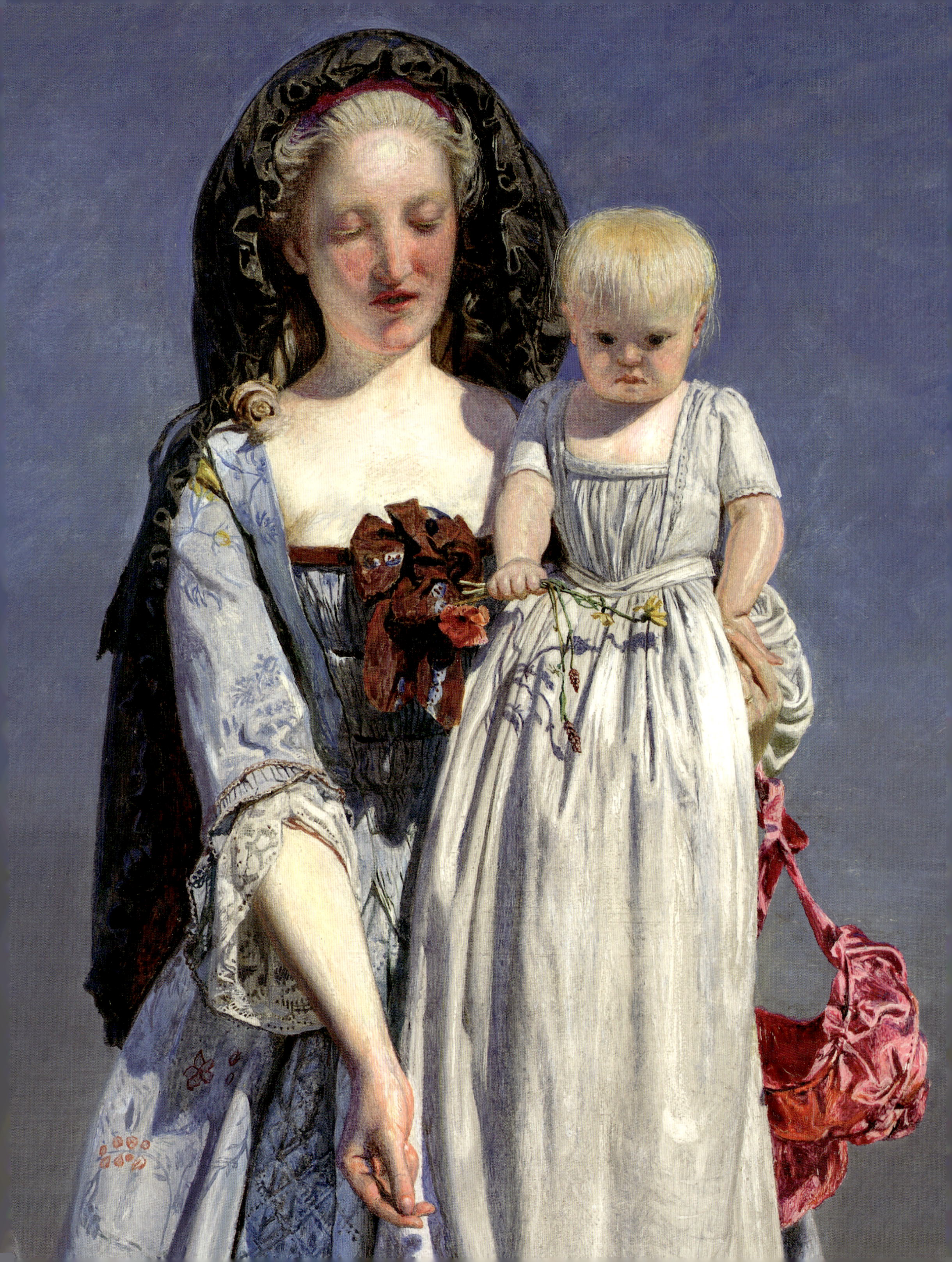

Ford Madox Brown – Pre-Raphaelite Pioneer

JULIAN TREUHERZ

In 1845 Ford Madox Brown, in his early twenties, travelled across Europe to Italy with his first wife Elisabeth and their young daughter Lucy. Elisabeth was suffering from consumption and had been recommended to winter in a mild climate. After seven months in Rome her health worsened, and the family left for England. Tragically Elisabeth died in Brown's arms as they were crossing Paris by carriage.

Brown came back a changed man. He was deeply affected by the loss of his wife, and had to send his 'sweet Lucy'[1] to board with his aunt so that he could pursue his career as a painter. But his artistic outlook had also been transformed. The pictures he painted on his return, influenced by what he had seen on his journey, made him a pioneer of Pre-Raphaelitism. Before the style had a name, before the Pre-Raphaelite Brotherhood was founded, he began to paint pictures influenced by fourteenth- and fifteenth-century art, the period before Raphael. He did so not through direct imitation or pastiche, but by assimilating what he had seen and combining it with his own style.

This was typical, for everything Brown did was touched with originality. He received a thorough training in the principles of academic art, only to spend his life subverting them. He created a new kind of history painting arising directly from the social and political ideas of his time. He brought natural-looking sunlight to historical and literary subjects, and took realism to unusual extremes of detail. His repertoire of forms included clashing colours, restless juxtapositions, confrontational poses, agitated movement, and grimacing faces, challenging accepted ideas of beauty. His later work, although it embraced the newly fashionable aesthetic style, combined it with his own forceful and expressive inventions. The character of Brown's art was summed up by his friend Charles Rowley:

> Some of Ford Madox Brown's really powerful designs have passages so queer, so exaggerated and wanting in control, that even his best friends "cannot abide them." This vigorous originality is part of the price one has to pay for his abounding and lasting power.[2]

Brown's oeuvre includes many contrasting styles and subjects: Pre-Raphaelite and aesthetic, historical and modern, grand and intimate, melodramatic and factual, tragic and comic. 'Vigorous originality' is the thread that runs through his career. It was what he admired in others, and what he sought in his own work.

Listen to Brown's revealing account of his visits to the Nazarene artists in Rome, Overbeck looked like

> some figure of the fifteenth century. When he spoke to me it was with all the humility of a saint. Being so young at the time, I noticed this the more. He had some five or six cartoons on view … I noticed that where any of the naked flesh was shown, it looked exactly like wooden dolls or lay figures. I heard him explain that he never drew these parts from nature, on the principle of avoiding the sensuous in religious art. In spite of this, nevertheless the sentiment was so vivid, so unlike most other art, that one felt a disinclination to go away. One could not see enough of it. To-day, more than forty years after, when coming suddenly

Fig. 1
Detail of cat. 49, The pretty baa-lambs

on one of these designs in a print-shop window, I again experienced the same sensation. Cornelius was different: short, with red hair and eyebrows, and keen eyes under. When I called at his studio he was showing his large cartoon of 'Death on the Pale Horse' (fig. 2). Some twenty years ago I saw this cartoon again in London and it produced on me exactly the effect it did at first. Full of action and strange character, it was everything the reverse of that dreadful commonplace into which art on the Continent seems to be hurrying back. But Cornelius was no commonplace being.[3]

Fig. 2
Peter von Cornelius, Death on the Pale Horse (The Four Horsemen of the Apocalypse)*, 1846. Kupferstichkabinett, Staatliche Museen zu Berlin*

Art that was vivid even in its imperfection, art that was unlike other art, art that was the reverse of commonplace: these were the qualities that made an impression on the young Brown, and which marked him for life.

Brown's upbringing and education set him apart from his contemporaries: although born of British parents, he was brought up in Northern France and received his formal art education at the academies of Bruges, Ghent and Antwerp. This was an unusual but not unique route for an English art student; the Belgian academies had a good reputation and they were a cheaper option than Paris. Nevertheless when he first came to London, it made him something of an outsider in the insular English art world, where most artists were trained at the Royal Academy Schools.

Brown's first two masters, Albert Gregorius at Bruges

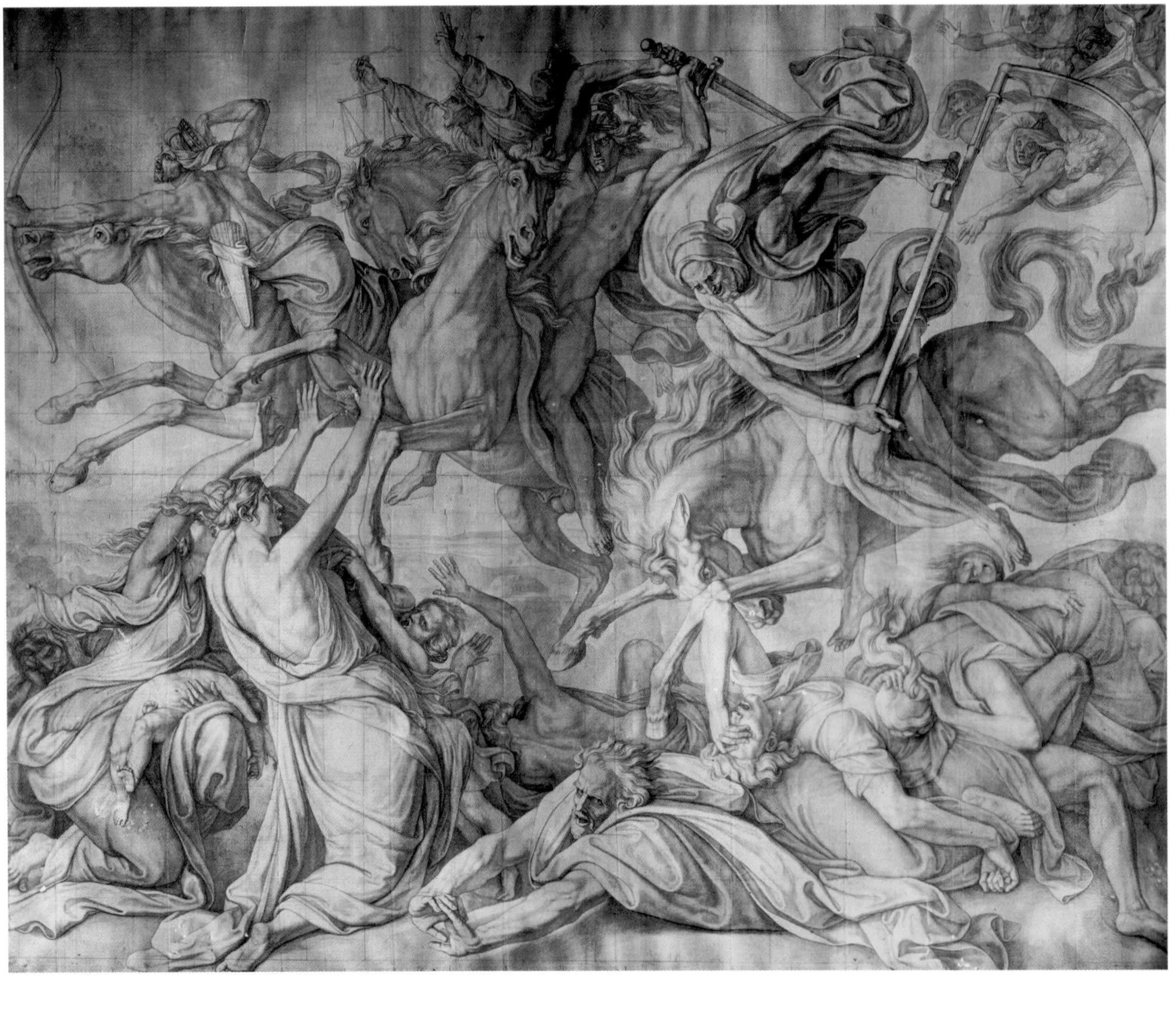

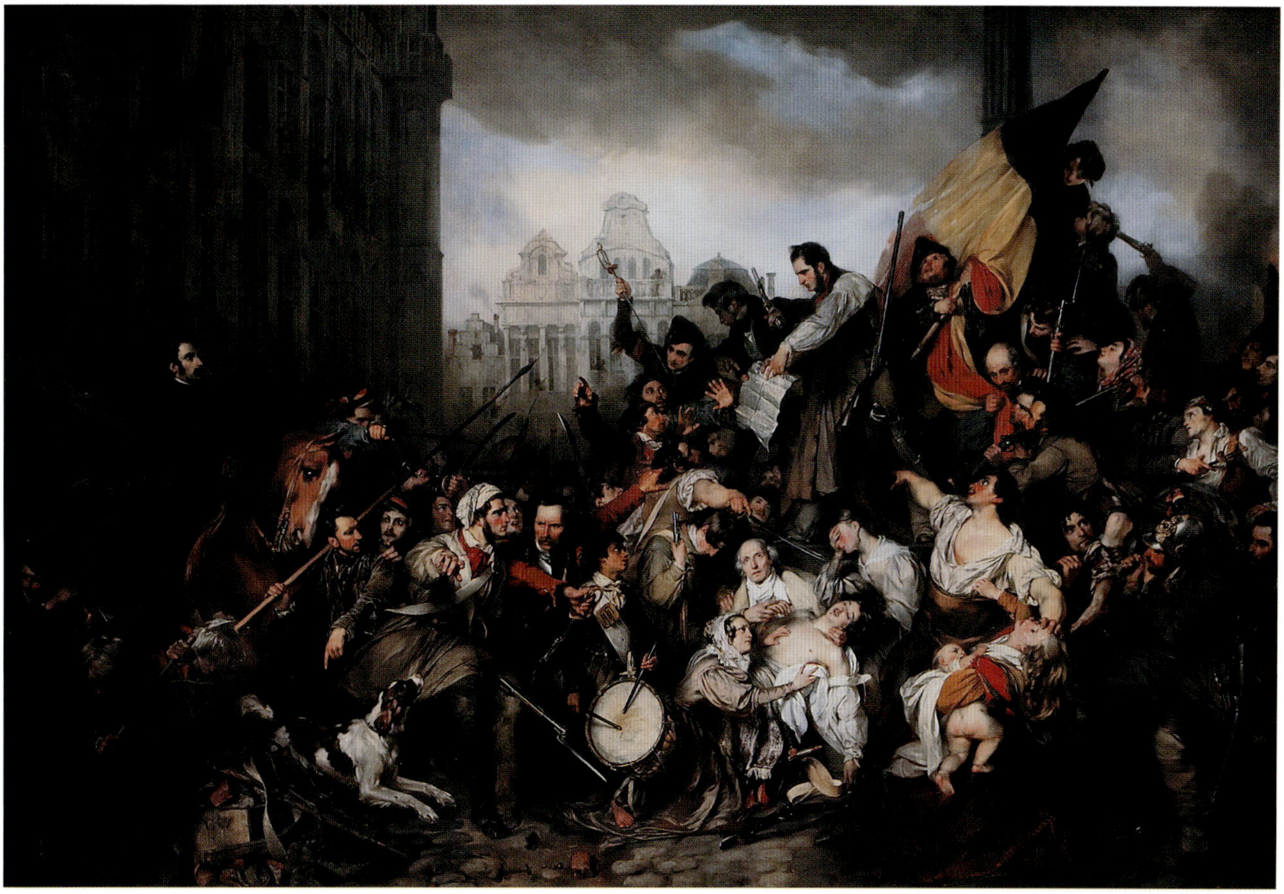

Fig. 3
Gustav Wappers, Episode from the Events of September 1830, *1835. Musées royaux des Beaux-Arts de Belgique, Brussels*

and Pieter van Hanselaer at Ghent, were former pupils of the French neoclassical painter Jacques-Louis David, and from them he learned to draw in a rigid impersonal style. His third teacher, at Antwerp, was Gustav Wappers, leader of the Belgian Romantic school. Before Wappers, the Antwerp Academy had already established a reputation for instruction by absolute rule, with an emphasis on drawing and on archaeological exactitude. Discipline was strict and Brown would have had to work hard from dawn to dusk.[4] (A very different routine prevailed at the Royal Academy Schools where Hunt and Millais had studied.) The aim of the training was to produce history paintings, grand, multi-figured compositions with subjects drawn from myth, literature and history, telling stories of great deeds and uplifting moral exemplars. The students produced by this system were expected to go on to decorate the public buildings of Europe. Brown was to reinvent history painting in accordance with his own ideas, but he remained a history painter and a narrative painter at heart. The thoroughness of his training meant that although he rejected the academic rules, he was able to do so from a position of knowledge, in contrast with Rossetti for example, who never completed his artistic education. Rossetti often drew badly and his ignorance of mural technique proved disastrous, whereas Brown was an accomplished draughtsman, and knew about fresco and other methods of mural painting.

Brown must have learned a great deal from Wappers's *Episode from the Events of September 1830* (fig. 3), which had caused a sensation when exhibited in Brussels in 1835.[5] This vast canvas glorified the recent revolution and the new-found independence of Belgium. It has a pyramidal composition showing a crowd writhing with gesticulating figures who react to the announcement of the proclamation 'Aux citoyens de Bruxelles!'. At the apex of the pyramid is the Belgian flag, inspired by Delacroix's *Liberty leading the People* (Louvre, Paris). The crowd includes portraits of political figures and artists, including Wappers himself, as well as people from all social classes, each displaying their emotions. The French painter Jules Breton, who studied with Wappers, remarked on his master's technique of painting figures with individual expressions to show their reactions to events, considering the tearful eyes and gaping mouths of Wappers's figures a vulgarism.[6] Perhaps it was from the shouting demonstrators in Wappers's crowd that Brown first learned his curious habit of painting people with their mouths open. Brown's unconvincing efforts to show characters in the act of speaking consort strangely with his otherwise faultless ability to depict natural-looking people.

In the 1850s, Brown began work on his masterpiece, *Work* (cat. 61), a large and complex composition which, like *Episode from the Events of September 1830*, dealt with vital political issues rather than edifying generalisations, represented all social classes, and included portraits of real people as well as equally life-like fictional characters. Yet whatever the two paintings had in common, *Work* was a radical departure in style and character from the romanticism of Wappers. Nevertheless, Brown was in a way true to his master's ideas. Although Wappers maintained the system of teaching by rule, realising its value for students, in practice he was less rigid; in an interview he stated that he encouraged bold conceptions and inspiration in his pupils, implying that the academic rules were there to be broken.[7]

While in Belgium, Brown would have had ample opportunities to see the work of the early Flemish and Dutch schools, known for realism and fine detail. This may also have encouraged him to challenge the prescriptive rules, the ideal proportions and the hierarchical compositions he was being taught. Some of the paintings he could have seen, by artists such as van Eyck and Hans Memling, may have left traces on his later work (see cats. 32, 56).[8] At any rate, his earliest pictures made in Antwerp and shortly afterwards in Paris show him breaking away from the academic yoke. In paintings such as *The Execution of Mary Stuart* and *Parisina* (cats. 13, 38) Brown distorted the proportions of the figures to express their extreme emotional states, while in the scenes from *King Lear* (cats. 17–22), he experimented with a new style of drawing, abandoning the soft shading and modelling required of academic draughtsmanship. Thus began a process of looking afresh at all he had been taught.

The most significant result of this process was Brown's three great paintings of modern life, painted in the Pre-Raphaelite style and dating from the 1850s, *An English Autumn Afternoon*, *The Last of England* and *Work* (cats. 50, 58, 61). Their originality lies in their reinvention of history and landscape painting for the mid-nineteenth century: instead of elevated generalities, they presented viewers with an accumulation of highly particularised, ordinary, momentary details; and instead of moral exemplars, myths, heroic stories or ancient associations, they embodied some of the great issues of the mid-Victorian age – class and social inequality in *Work*, emigration in *The Last of England*, and the transformation of landscape and leisure in *An English Autumn Afternoon*.[9] The status of these paintings was recognized by a few perceptive critics when they were first exhibited: *The Last of England* was considered 'a most noble historical picture'[10] and *Work* secured 'Mr. Brown's place amongst true historical painters'.[11] Only *An English Autumn Afternoon* did not receive as much attention as the others; its particularity made more of an impression than its general significance, although Rossetti referred to its intensely English character.[12] But all three turned upside down the accepted norms of history painting. Nothing quite like them had previously been seen in British art, not even the modern-life subjects of the other Pre-Raphaelites, which dealt with more personal, less political issues.

It had already been accepted at the Royal Academy that history painting need not be set in the distant past – West and Copley in the eighteenth century and Wilkie in the early nineteenth century had depicted recent events with the grandeur of traditional history painting.[13] Brown did something more. Rather than recreate deaths, battles or proclamations, he painted the ordinary and the mundane. This was normally the territory of genre painting, the intimate and charming everyday-life scenes that were so popular with the early Victorians. The street characters in *Work*, the emigrants in *The Last of England*, the middle-class couple looking over a view of orchards and back gardens in *An English Autumn Afternoon* might have been material for genre painting, but Brown transformed them into something powerful and serious through exceptionally intense and vivid presentation.

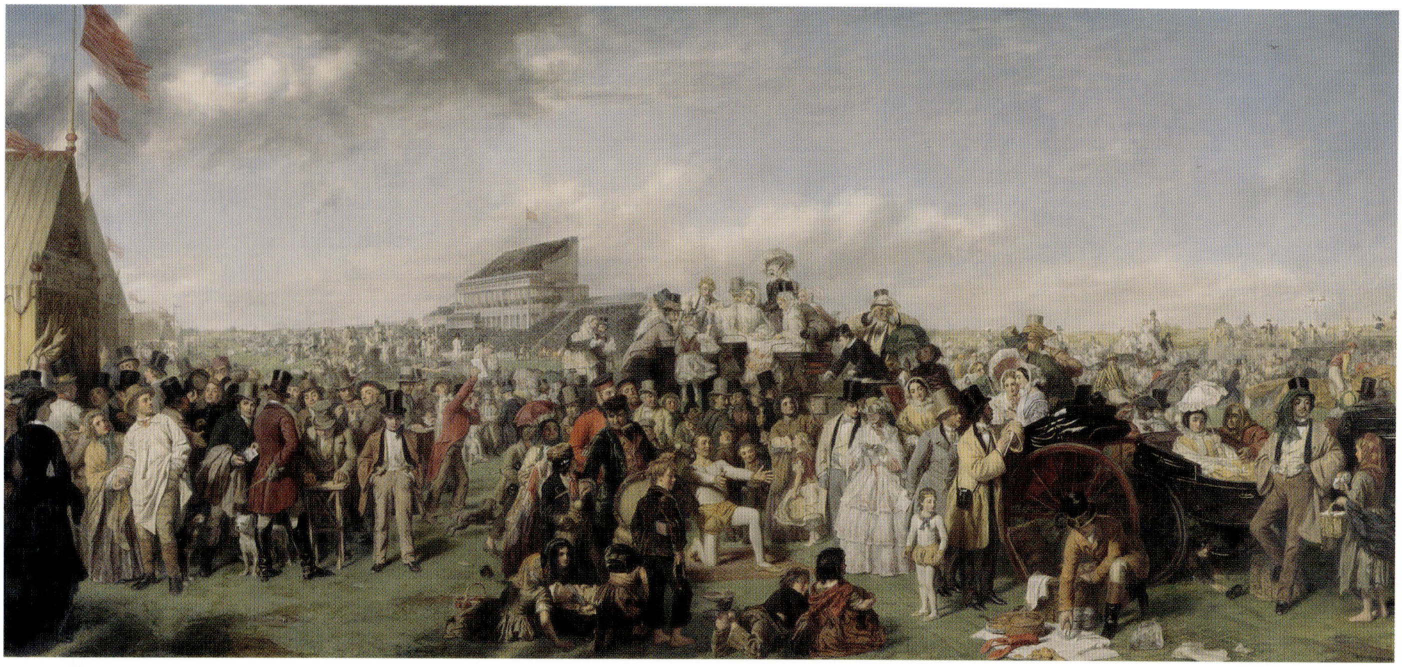

Fig. 4
William Powell Frith, The Derby Day*, 1893–94 (replica of work originally painted 1858). Manchester City Galleries*

Brown was one of a number of artists who turned to serious contemporary subject matter in the early 1850s. His first ideas for modern subjects dated from 1852; Holman Hunt started work on *The Awakening Conscience* (Tate) early in 1853, and Millais's series of drawings on modern love and marriage date from 1853–54.[14] Prior to this, in 1850, writers in the Pre-Raphaelite journal *The Germ* had made the point that artists could treat subjects of the present day with seriousness, rather than with the lightweight approach of the genre painter.[15] Earlier still, in his Paris Salon reviews of the 1840s, Baudelaire had called for artists to represent 'the heroism of modern life.' At the Royal Academy W.P. Frith also took up the idea with *Life at the Seaside* (1854, Royal Collection) and *The Derby Day* (fig. 4), showing modern, fashionably dressed crowds. Many critics initially greeted these pictures with disdain. In size and number of figures, they set out to rival history paintings, but their content was not elevated; they were works of social observation and entertainment rather than social criticism. They were also visually conservative, with compositions articulated by triangles and diagonal lines in the academically approved manner; with figure groups occupying a clearly defined space spread across the centre of the painting, and the individual characters clearly modelled with light and dark shading.

Brown brought into play a completely different visual language that broke the academic rules. *Work* dispensed with a traditional hierarchical composition so that it is not immediately apparent which are the most important figures; incidents are spread all over the picture, from top to bottom, and there is no clear centre, no aerial perspective, and no differentiation of focus, so that the eye restlessly moves across the surface, confused by a jumble of minute details and clashing colours all of equal weight. *The Last of England* at first looks more like a genre painting than a history; the protagonists are clearly indicated, but the subsidiary figures are teasingly half-hidden in a condensed space, and where their faces are visible they have grotesque expressions that break the rules of decorum. *An English Autumn Afternoon* does not look like a history either. Its oval form was usually associated with elegant vignettes in books or with decorative paintings set into panelled rooms; the unpretentious landscape has no obvious picturesque or ancient associations, hence Ruskin's question as to why Brown had painted such an ugly subject, and the artist's blunt repartee 'Because it lay out of a back window.'[16]

In these paintings, Brown was in tune with the trends of European realism. In the 1840s Adolph von Menzel painted views of shabby back yards seen from rear windows (fig. 5); and depicted a nondescript landscape in *The Berlin-Potsdam Railway* (1847; Nationalgalerie, Berlin). Gustave Courbet's panoramic *The Painter's Studio* of 1854–55 (fig. 6) is curiously similar to *Work*; it is a 'real allegory', an assemblage of figures representing people and ideas of importance to the artist, including workers, beggars, a poor Irishwoman, ragged children, dogs, middle-class onlookers and intellectuals.[17] Work is also a 'real allegory', although Brown's use of sharp detail and vivid sunlit colour was unlike Courbet's traditional *chiaroscuro* technique, with its deep shadows, and quite different from anything to be found in European art.

Fig. 5
Adolph von Menzel, View over Back Yards, *1844. Nationalgalerie, Staatliche Museen zu Berlin*

Brown returned to an apparently more orthodox form of history painting towards the end of his career, in the twelve murals of the history of Manchester in the city's Town Hall. For these, he had to paint scenes from the past, requiring the kind of detailed research into historical personages, costume, furniture and setting that he had been taught to do in Belgium (and that he had carried out for his early historical subjects such as *The Body of Harold* and *Chaucer*, cats. 23, 34). Nevertheless, the murals also continued Brown's subversion of traditional history painting. The compositions with empty centres or steeply foreshortened viewpoints, the anti-heroic narrative, the abundance of engaging details and humorous asides took Brown's anti-academicism even further than before. His emphasis on the role of ordinary people and on the random and accidental forces in history has been interpreted as reflecting the new ideas about the nature

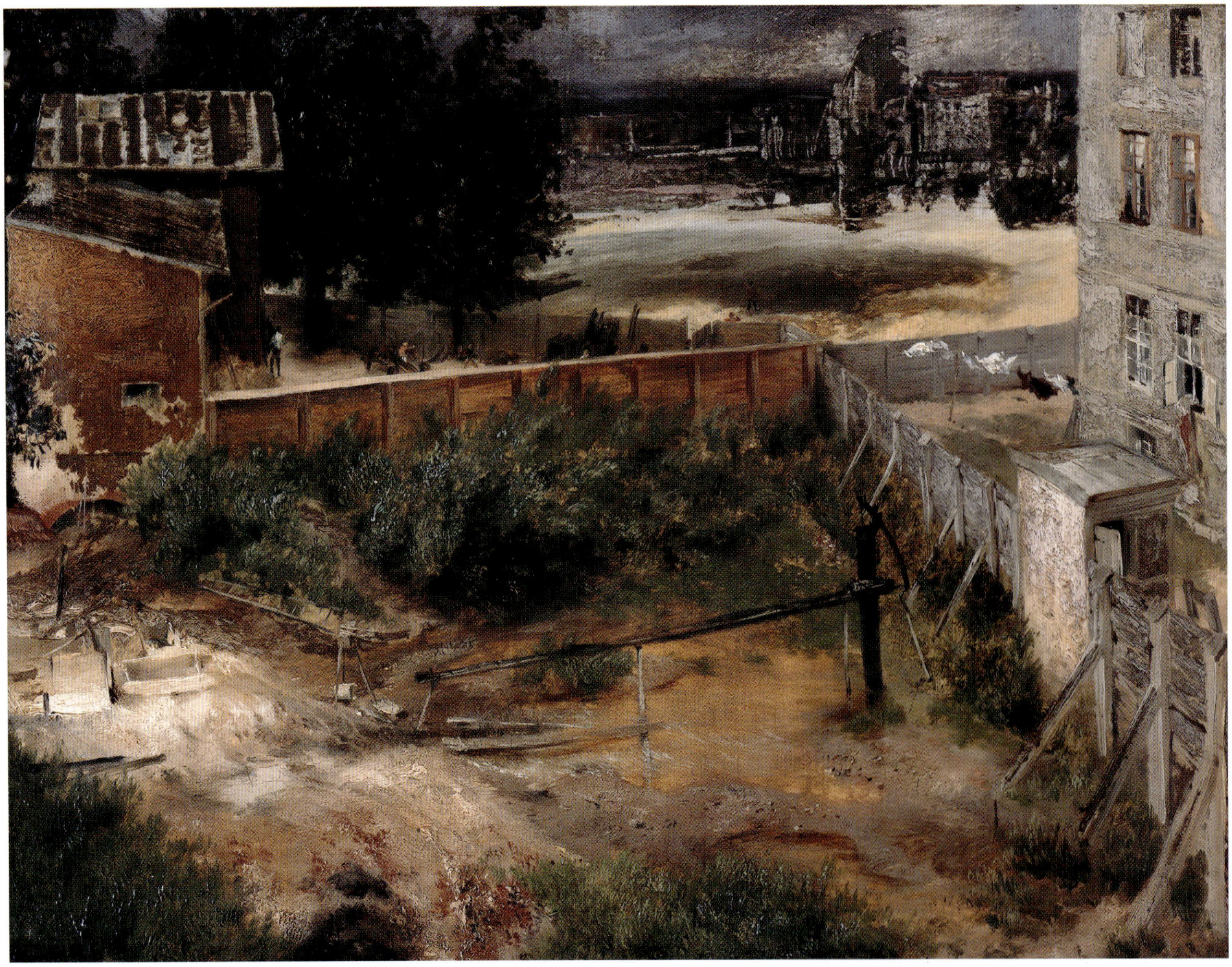

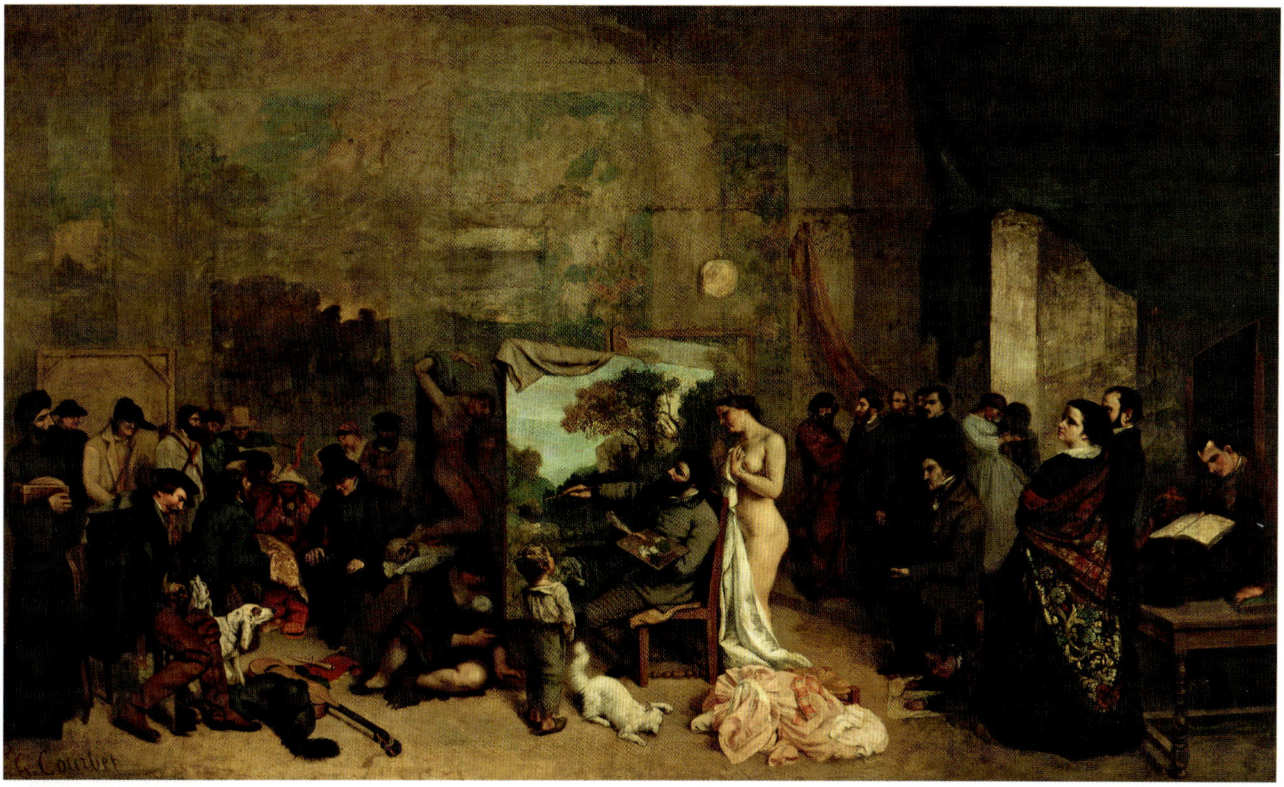

Fig. 6
Gustave Courbet, The Painter's Studio. A real allegory summing up seven years of my artistic life, *1854–55. Musée d'Orsay, Paris*

of history evident in the writings of Carlyle, Macaulay and Bakhtin.[18] But in the murals, the anti-academic elements are allied to a sure sense of design, a respect for the architectural setting and an understanding of how to work on a large scale, recalling the lessons that Brown had learned in Belgium.

One feature that gives Brown's modern subjects their particularly lifelike quality was his use of realistic effects of light, unparalleled in any traditional history painting. *Work*, for example was painted in 'hot July sunlight',[19] and includes objects in shade and reflected light as well as direct sunlight. While in Belgium and Paris, Brown came to dislike the artificial studio light in which he had been taught to paint. His *Manfred on the Jungfrau* (cat. 14), begun in Antwerp and finished in Paris in 1841, was in his own words 'a first, though not very recognisable attempt, at an out-door effect of light'.[20] Regrettably, it is now impossible to tell what it looked like originally, because Brown later repainted it. But in 1845, Brown's journey to Italy brought him in contact with the work of the early Italians, and with the light of Italy itself, and his art took a new direction.

Most of the paintings Brown had made before his journey were dark in tonality, but those done in the first few years after his return were quite different, with pale colours and even lighting, almost eliminating the use of black in the shadows. This almost shadowless style was a feature Brown had observed in fourteenth- and fifteenth-century Italian (and indeed Flemish and German) art and he reproduced it in *The First Translation of the Bible* (cat. 33). His most ambitions painting of this period was *Geoffrey Chaucer reading the 'Legend of Custance' to Edward III and his Court* (see cat. 34). It was, he wrote, 'the first [picture] in which I endeavoured to carry out the notion, long before conceived, of treating the light and shade absolutely, as it exists at any one moment, instead of approximately, or in generalised style.'[21] Most of the figures in *Chaucer* were painted indoors, but Brown arranged the blinds of his studio to admit sunlight, and he painted the landscape background from a study of a real landscape that he had previously sketched out of doors (cat. 48).

He took this further in later pictures. For *Work*, he went to the trouble of rigging up his large canvas on a special cart and trundling it out into the street, in order to paint the background directly without an intervening sketch; but the elaborate painting of the figures was done several years later, in the studio. However, before this, for *The pretty baa-lambs,* (cat. 49) he not only took the canvas out of doors but painted the whole thing, landscape and figures, in the open air. This was standard for a sketch but unprecedented for an exhibition picture of this kind. In similar landscapes with figures, painted at around the same time, Hunt and Millais completed the landscape parts out of doors, but left blank white patches for the figures, which were painted later in the studio, under different light.[22] Brown's procedure gave *The pretty baa-lambs* a convincing atmospheric unity, avoiding the disjointed effect sometimes found, where the figures seem to have been cut out and pasted on to a separate background. He also captured the effects of sunlight with particular accuracy: he showed the shadows on the grass and clothing as coloured (an innovation usually associated with the French Impressionists twenty years later) and painted the woman's face unflatteringly flushed in the heat. It is not surprising to learn from Brown's diary that he himself suffered from a fever twice while working on the painting out in the sun.

Brown's interest in 'treating the light and shade absolutely, as it exists at any one moment' became a kind of fixation. 'Subjects, according to their nature, require different effects of light' he wrote in the catalogue to his 1865 exhibition.[23] His catalogue entries read like notes from a scientific experiment to explore a range of effects: 'Sunlight not too bright, such as is pleasant to sit in out of doors', 'just after sunset,' '3 P.M., when late in October the shadows already lie long, and the sun's rays ... are preternaturally glowing,' 'the peculiar look of *light all round* which objects have on a dull day at sea,' 'under the glow of twilight'.[24] Artificial light was also explored, for example gaslight in the portrait of *William Michael Rossetti* and a combination of firelight and an oil lamp in *Waiting* (cats. 88, 56). In a lecture given in the 1870s and '80s on 'The Latest Phase of Painting in Europe', he described natural lighting as a thread that had been dropped after the early Italian period, and not taken up again until the middle of the nineteenth century: 'Til the year 1851, such works would all have been painted with strong dark shadows down one side, as the models appear in what is called a finely lighted studio, that is a square room with one light to it from the north'. He continued, 'I care not who began the reform first, but with this expiring falsity goes out the last hindrance to pure realism in painting'.[25] He did not mention in the lecture his own pioneering role in this process.

Brown's visit to Italy brought him into contact with the great altarpieces and fresco cycles of Florence and Rome, with their overall high key and bright colour, which can only be properly appreciated at first hand. He described the works he painted after his journey as 'the pouring out of the emotions and remembrances still vibrating within me of Italian Art.'[26] But Northern European art had also made a strong impression: on the way to Italy, he had stopped at Basel, where he had admired the Holbeins, and in his portrait of James Bamford (cat. 29), he attempted 'a *Holbein of the 19th century.*'

In the 1840s the High Renaissance was still regarded as the greatest period in art, and its visual language of monumental and idealised forms was canonical. Fourteenth- and fifteenth-century Italian and Northern European painting was regarded by all but a very small number of connoisseurs as flawed and primitive. It required a particularly open mind to see positive qualities – sincerity and truth – in what most people regarded as faults: naiveté, angularity, disregard of anatomy and imperfect perspective. Brown was in advance of public taste in his admiration for early art, but he was not the only British artist who went to Italy and on returning painted in a new archaic-looking style. The Scottish painter William Dyce was briefly in Rome in the 1820s, earlier than Brown, and he too met the Nazarenes there. When he returned his palette lightened and he painted Madonnas and Dante subjects with idealised figure types derived from Perugino and the young Raphael, not so very different from the revivalist works of the Nazarenes. Brown's originality was to assimilate what he had seen into his own style, using individualised, portrait-like faces and idiosyncratic English subjects of his own invention: *Oure Ladye of Saturday Night* (cat. 28) celebrates the English ritual of bath night, whilst *Chaucer* and *The First Translation of the Bible* depict the flowering of English language freed from French and Latin domination.

Brown's direct contact with early Italian art was a formative influence on the development of Pre-Raphaelitism. In March 1848, just under two years after he returned from Italy, he

Fig. 7
Dante Gabriel Rossetti, The Girlhood of Mary Virgin, *1848-49. Tate*

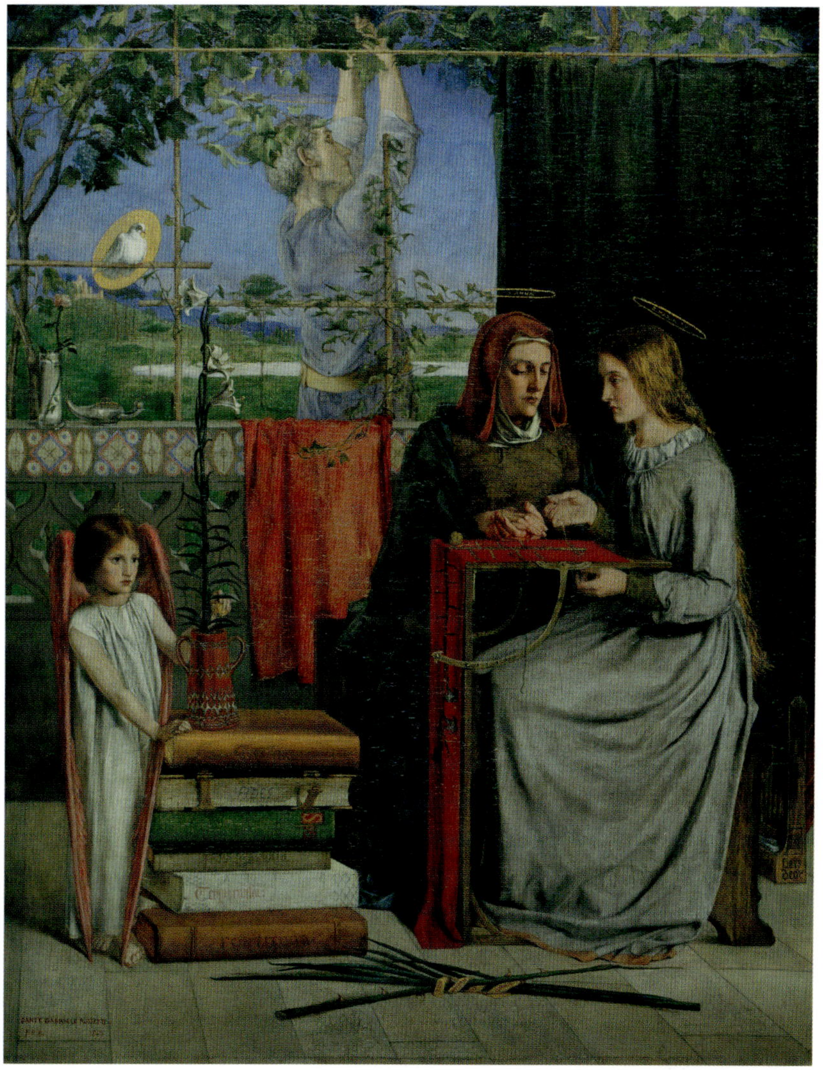

received an enthusiastic letter from the young Rossetti, who had seen some of Brown's paintings in exhibitions. Rossetti praised these 'glorious works' that 'have successively raised my admiration and kept me standing on the same spot for fabulous lengths of time',[27] and asked if Brown would give him lessons. The older artist at first thought it was a practical joke, but when he realised Rossetti was serious, Brown took him on as a pupil, and set him the task of copying *The Seraph's Watch* (cat. 27), one of the paintings that represents most directly Brown's reaction to Italian and Nazarene painting. Rossetti did not stay long as a pupil, but a close friendship developed, and Brown was introduced to Rossetti's friends Millais and Holman Hunt.

The younger men must have been in considerable awe of Brown and his experience; they were scarcely out of art school, and had never visited Italy, whereas Brown had not only been there and seen the works of Giotto, Masaccio and Fra Angelico at first hand, but had also shown several paintings in the London exhibitions. In the autumn of 1848, Rossetti, Hunt and Millais, along with four of their friends, formed the Pre-Raphaelite Brotherhood, with the aim of reforming British art by bringing to it the sincerity and seriousness that they had, with Brown's help, learned to see in art of the period before Raphael. One of the first paintings exhibited after the Brotherhood was founded, Rossetti's *The Girlhood of Mary Virgin* (fig. 7), displays the same pale, fresco-like colour scheme as Brown's post-Italian work, as well as similar details such as the pile of books from *The First Translation of the Bible* and the palms and thorns placed in the foreground, akin to the crown of thorns in *The Seraph's*

Watch. Rossetti's next painting, *Ecce Ancilla Domini!* (Tate) was also in a pale-coloured, deliberately archaic style.

Despite Brown's close associations with the young Pre-Raphaelites in the early years, he never joined the Brotherhood itself. He was almost certainly invited, but seems to have refused because he was older than the others, and did not feel inclined to join a secret society that he saw as a silly boyish venture. There was also a disagreement about the role of models in subject paintings. It was generally accepted by both Brown and the members of the Brotherhood that it was preferable to paint from friends and family than from professional models, who could appear, in Brown's words, 'stiff and feelingless'.[28] It was common practice to seek out someone who had an affinity with the character being represented; a typical example was Brown's choice of Rossetti to sit for Chaucer, a modern poet for a medieval poet, and one who in Brown's view resembled the historical portraits of Chaucer. But the members insisted that a model once found should be portrayed absolutely literally, without adaptation. Brown refused to accept this inflexible principle. He had more experience of using professional models than the others, and continued to use paid models when it suited him, although later he tended to use a mixture of friends, family and ordinary people spotted in the street.

Brown was not a member of the Brotherhood, but he continued to be closely associated with it; he and the members met frequently, they visited each other's studios and discussed the paintings they were engaged on. Although an admiration for archaic simplicity was the starting point of the Brotherhood, in the first three or four years after 1848 it developed in a different direction. Under the influence of Ruskin's 'truth to nature,' minutely painted naturalistic detail and vivid colour came to be hallmarks of the Pre-Raphaelite style. Brown's work developed in the same way. *Chaucer*, which he planned in Italy, was completed in London after the foundation of the Brotherhood, between 1848 and 1851. The sharp all-over focus, the variety of instantaneous facial expressions and vivid array of textures, including fur, damask, silk and velvet were a move away from the pale colours and gentle archaism of *The First Translation of the Bible*, which Brown had painted before he met Rossetti, towards something more like the early works of Hunt and Millais; although the huge size of *Chaucer* (the original version is in the Art Gallery of New South Wales, Sydney; fig. 58, p. 130) was much larger than anything attempted by them.

It is not possible to say that any one artist originated this change in the Brotherhood's style, and it is likely that it came about through mutual discussion and experimentation, for the Brotherhood had no clear programme. But Brown certainly learned from the younger artists, just as they had learned from him. He seems to have been impressed by what he called the 'microscopic detail'[29] in Hunt's work. He adjusted his palette to make it even brighter after seeing the vivid colours of the Pre-Raphaelite pictures at the 1851 Royal Academy Exhibition, where *Chaucer* was also on view.[30] Finally, when Millais showed him how to use a wet white ground to give extra brilliance to parts of a picture, he adopted the technique for *Jesus washing Peter's Feet* (cat. 75), although the results were not entirely successful.[31]

Once he had started in this direction, Brown took Pre-Raphaelite realism to extreme lengths. He was a perfectionist and his diary is full of examples of labouring for days over small details, struggling to get them right – such as the plaid shawl worn by his second wife Emma in *The Last of England*, or the lilac leaves in *Stages of Cruelty* (cat. 60). He observed the imperfections of Emma's face with quasi-scientific accuracy: she had an abnormally short upper lip which made it difficult for her to close her mouth.[32] Many of Brown's drawings show her with her mouth open and the teeth protruding, but when she closed her mouth, the muscles on her lower jaw and chin became tense; this can be seen by comparing the drawing of her for *The Last of England* with the painting (cats. 4, 58). As for *Work*, Rossetti felt that Brown was spending too long over its 'excessive elaboration', particularly over things 'which are far from beautiful in themselves - for instance the flowing waistcoat of a potboy on which Brown has lately been spending some weeks of his life' (fig. 71, p. 190); he feared that Brown's way of working 'may result in his producing one work where he might produce three equally good.'[33]

In contrast to Brown's larger, more complex paintings where his labour was clearly displayed in the sheer amount of detail, his small landscapes look effortless. But their lyrical and poetic effects were hard-won. He had intended to paint and sell them quickly as a way of making money, but his obsession with accurate detail meant that they took far longer than anticipated. Each time he went back to the site to finish one of them off, he was frustrated when he found that everything had changed, the light, the colour, the clouds, the shadows: 'one feels the want of a life study such as Turner devoted to landskape & even then what a botch is any attempt to render it.'[34] These paintings earned him little in relation to the time spent on them, yet they are among his finest achievements, each one showing a quite different aspect of landscape from the other, and owing nothing to the stock formulae of most Victorian landscape paintings.

'Absolutely without regard to the art of any period or country, I have tried to render this scene as it would appear',[35] wrote Brown of *The Last of England*. Here we have a declaration of unmediated realism, as though the artist were a neutral recording instrument like a camera. He would have felt that the statement applied to much of his work of the 1850s. And in a sense it is true that Brown's penetrating eye could see through artifice and convention. His pictures of children generally avoid the sentimentality of most Victorian child subjects, seen for instance in the watercolours of his friend and admirer Frederic Shields (fig. 8) and he was also able to depict poor people without condescension, such as the migrant labourers on the bank in *Work*, painted from real people that Brown had found in the street. Yet Brown would have been the first to admit that the artist was not a passive imitator of reality: *The Last of England* was an invention, showing a scene 'as it would appear' not as it did appear; and during the painting of *Work*, in a particularly ecstatic mood, he wrote in his diary, 'I worked at the navvies – the pot boy a triumph, the mortarman perfection & the ragged child upsetting the barrow & getting cuffed, all creations'.[36]

In the 1860s, Pre-Raphaelitism developed in new directions. Just as Brown had learned from Hunt and Millais in the early 1850s, during the 1860s his work changed through his close friendship with Rossetti and William Morris. Brown's style moved away from hard-edged realism, with its jarring colours and sharp details, and embraced aestheticism. His work softened and became more decorative, his compositions were articulated by sweeping lines and rippling draperies and he used richer and more harmonious colours. He experimented with Rossetti's bust-length portrait format, and later took up coloured chalks for portrait drawings, also following Rossetti. The women in *Downstream* and *Byron's Dream* (cats. 83, 85) have the voluptuous proportions of Rossetti's later models, and a portrait of the mature Emma was entitled *Thinking* (cat. 94), like Rossetti's day-dreaming beauties. But Brown only painted a very few works that wholeheartedly followed aestheticism, for he remained committed to narrative. Although decorative qualities pervade works like *Cordelia's Portion* (cat. 79), every detail of gesture and facial expression contributes to the story, and *Cromwell on his Farm* (cat. 87) harks back to the thoughtfulness and symbolic realism of his earlier histories. Similar quirky and expressive qualities are seen in the many designs for stained glass Brown made for Morris, Marshall, Faulkner & Co., which formed a large part of his output in the late '60s and early '70s (cats. 101–7).

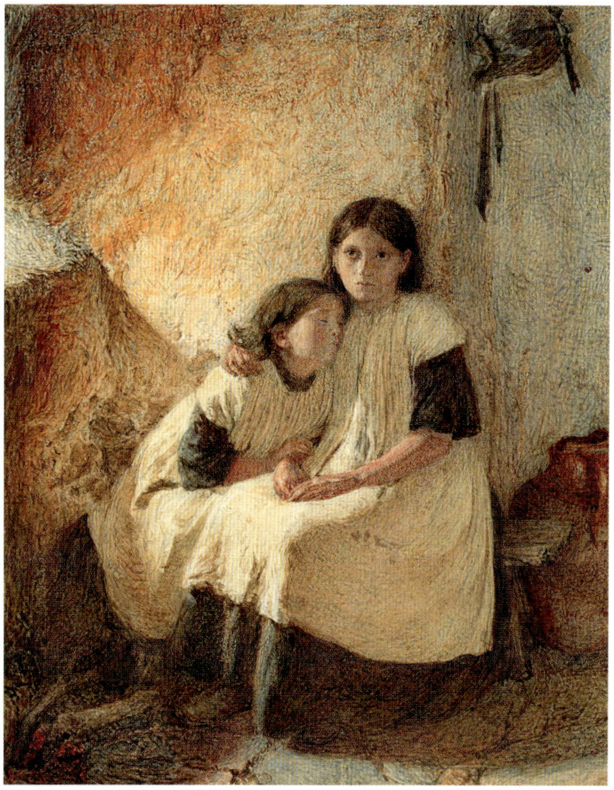

Fig. 8
Frederic Shields, The Orphans, *1862. Manchester City Galleries*

Brown's refusal to join the Brotherhood in 1848 was in character with his independent nature, perhaps inherited from his grandfather, Dr. John Brown, a leading Edinburgh physician, whose unorthodox methods antagonised the medical authorities. Throughout Ford Madox Brown's life, he set himself against the establishment, and was suspicious of coteries. He was angry at his treatment by the Royal Academy. In 1851 *Chaucer* was hung without its frame and where it could not be seen for reflections. In 1852 *The pretty baa-lambs* was placed two feet from the floor next to a door jamb and *Jesus washing Peter's Feet* was hung too high to be properly seen. Brown refused to accept the apology of Francis Grant, speaking on behalf of the other Academicians, who assured him of their admiration for it.[37] In 1854 all Brown's submissions were rejected. No wonder that later the same year, when no-one would buy his pictures and he was almost without money to support himself and his family, he wrote in his diary 'What chance is there for me out of all the Bodies, Institutions, Art unions & accademies & Commissions of this country, Classes sects or cotteries, Nobles dealers patrons rich men or friends. Which one takes an interest in me or my works. Is it encouraging to go on?'[38]

This was a constant preoccupation; he bore a grudge against the Royal Academy and later took against the Grosvenor Gallery and the watercolour societies for not inviting him to exhibit. In Manchester he believed that Agnews, the art dealers who dominated the local scene, had advised local collectors against buying his work, and he thought that most of the Manchester newspapers were prejudiced against him. He did not mellow. In 1892 he went to a banquet in honour of art and literature given by the Lord Mayor of London, attended by many Royal Academicians. As there were a number of vacant places, Holman Hunt invited Brown to sit next to him, where he could also converse with other artists, but 'dear old "Bruno"' declined with a "Thank you, I would rather sit here" and remained isolated, speaking to no-one.[39]

Yet he did not stand entirely apart from groups and he was certainly not antisocial. In the late 1860s he was famous for the parties he and his wife gave, which were attended by a wide circle of London's artistic Bohemia. He also became involved with several avant-garde groups that set up in opposition to the art establishment. He was one of the chief founders of the Hogarth Club in 1858, a society for artists, friends and patrons mainly from the Pre-Raphaelite circle, that combined social activities with exhibitions. He then intemperately resigned when the club refused to exhibit his furniture designs on the grounds that they were not fine art, but was soon persuaded to rejoin. He became an active partner in Morris, Marshall, Faulkner and Co., and not just as a designer: at the early meetings, because of his seniority, he was the natural choice for chairman and took the lead in insisting on business-like procedures such as proper accounts and agreement on the ownership of designs.[40] Although in 1886 he refused Walter Crane's invitation to join the proposed Arts and Crafts Exhibition Society, in 1888 he took part in the society's inaugural exhibition. Brown came to be regarded as a pioneering senior figure by the younger members of the Arts and Crafts movement. They admired the simple furniture he designed for Morris (cats. 112–15), and the later artisan's furniture he showed at the Manchester Jubilee Exhibition, which prefigured the fashion for cottage furniture in the 1890s and 1900s (fig. 38, p. 56). His Manchester murals were regarded as a model for the collaboration between artist and architect in the decoration of public buildings. In 1893, the last year of his life, Brown accepted an invitation to exhibit with the Brussels avant-garde exhibiting society Les XX (The Twenty), which in addition to showing the work of its own members, such as Ensor, Khnopff and Van de Velde, invited artists from other countries to show with them, seeking to represent all the advanced trends in Europe. Among those invited over the period 1884 to 1893 were Cezanne, Monet, Gauguin, Redon, Whistler and Van Gogh; the organisers evidently wanted to include Pre-Raphaelitism, and although a number of British artists including Walter Crane took part, Brown was the only senior figure to exhibit there, sending in versions of *Cordelia's Portion* and *Romeo and Juliet*, and the portrait of Emma (cat. 94).[41]

Brown's anti-academic, anti-authoritarian stance in art was a part of his general attitude to society. His political views were a contradictory mixture: 'In his early days he was nearly a Whig; in later life he was by temperament a good deal of a 'Tory of the old school,' but his intellect made him a Socialist of an extreme type', wrote his grandson.[42] Brown's views on the place of Britain in the world can be deduced from *Waiting*, a glorification of motherhood but also an acknowledgement of the soldier husband's role in defending Britain in the Crimea; and from *Walton-on-the-Naze* (cat. 55), a dreamlike idyll of a Britain protected from French invasion by British military defences, and also by the Artist's Rifles Corps, a volunteer company that Brown himself joined at the time. Cosmopolitan in his artistic interests, he was also a fervent supporter of English values, and of English literature. This was a theme that ran through his art, in his subjects inspired by Chaucer, Shakespeare and Byron; in his worship of Hogarth; and in paintings such as *Waiting: An English Fireside*, *An English*

Autumn Afternoon, The English Boy, and indeed in *Work*, where he made a hero of the 'British excavator, or *navvy* ... at least as worthy of the powers of an English painter, as the fishermen of the Adriatic, the peasant of the Campana or the Neapolitan lazzarone.'[43]

But his national pride was compromised by his bitter experience of the class system, as expressed by several outbursts in his diary. 'To what pitch is England destined to soar in the History of the world. Externally a far shining glory to all the earth and an example, internally a prey to snobbishness and the worship of gold & tinsel – a place chiefly for sneaks and lacqueys ... The deepest pondering alas brings me back to old & nothing original conclusions that the Aristocracy of this Country presses with Torpedo influence on all classes of men and works, commerce alone is free from all their intermeddling and thoroughly successful. In all else be it war, literature, art or science we are great if great in *spite* of them – and the depressing influence of established authority taking precedence of merit & justice.'[44] Brown's dislike of the aristocracy and of the inequalities of the class system, and his general sympathy with the underprivileged, were also expressed in a less virulent form, in his paintings – not only in *Work*, but also in *The Body of Harold* and *Spirit of Justice*. The normal hierarchies of society were reversed in *Jesus washing Peter's Feet* and in many of the Manchester murals: Brown depicted the linen-draper Crabtree as a scientific hero, and in *The Opening of the Bridgewater Canal*, gave the bargee's wife greater prominence than the Duke (cats. 129, 136).

On the other hand Brown was not a card-carrying Socialist and never joined William Morris's Socialist League. His socialism took the form of practical help for the poor, such as his teaching at the Working Men's College in London or the Labour Bureau he founded in Manchester to alleviate unemployment; his attitude was a liberal, left-leaning humanitarianism. Unlike William Morris, Brown did not see it as his role to change society. He used his art as social comment, but not as simplistic propaganda. His paintings express important ideas, but ideas were not enough. 'Pictures must be judged first as pictures,' he wrote, 'a deep philosophical intention will not make a faire picture ... I should be much inclined to doubt the genuineness of that artist's ideas who never painted from love of the mere look of things'.[45]

1 *Diary*, p. 66.
2 Rowley 1911, p. 94.
3 Brown 1888 i, pp. 48–49.
4 Rabin 1973, pp. 6–15.
5 Brussels 2005, pp. 58–59.
6 Rabin 1973, pp. 12–13.
7 *Art Journal* 1846, p. 153.
8 Newman and Watkinson 1991, p. 8.
9 See catalogue entries for discussion of these issues.
10 Lushington 1856.
11 Palgrave 1865.
12 D.G. Rossetti 1856.
13 Benjamin West, *The Death of Wolfe*, 1770, National Gallery of Canada; J.S. Copley, *The Death of Major Pierson*, 1783, Tate; David Wilkie, *Chelsea Pensioners Reading the Waterloo Despatch*, 1822, Apsley House, London.
14 Bronkhurst 2006 , I, p. 165; Rosenfeld and Smith 2007, pp. 84–93.
15 Germ no. 3, March 1850, p. 121; no. 4, May 1850, p. 170.
16 *Diary*, p. 144.
17 The comparison was first made by Kenneth Clark in Clark 1960, p. 170.
18 Codell 1994.
19 Brown 1865, description of *Work*.
20 Brown 1865, no. 42.
21 Brown 1865, no. 1.
22 Bronkhurst 2006, I, p. 147.
23 Brown 1865, description of *Work*.
24 The extracts from Brown 1865 refer to *Chaucer, Oure Ladye of Saturday Night, An English Autumn Afternoon, The Last of England* and *The Hayfield*.
25 V&A Box 36, Lecture 3, pp. 11-12.
26 Brown 1865, no. 3.
27 D.G. Rossetti *Correspondence*, I, p. 58.
28 Germ no. 2, Feb 1850, p. 71.
29 Hunt 1905 I, p. 127.
30 Hueffer 1896, p. 77.
31 Hunt 1905 I, p. 278.
32 Information from Denis Lanigan, who describes her condition as 'Class II Division I malocclusion secondary to mandibular retrognathia combined with absolute shortness of the upper lip leading to lip incompetency.'
33 Rossetti *Correspondence*, 2, pp. 229–30.
34 *Diary*, p. 145.
35 Brown 1865, no. 14.
36 *Diary*, p. 114.
37 Hunt 1905, I, p. 318.
38 *Diary*, pp. 96–97.
39 Hunt 1905, 2, pp. 382–84.
40 Harvey and Press 1991, pp. 47–48.
41 Laughton 1967, pp. 372–79.
42 Hueffer 1896, p. 401.
43 Brown 1865, description of *Work*.
44 *Diary*, p. 98.
45 Brown 1865, no. 11.

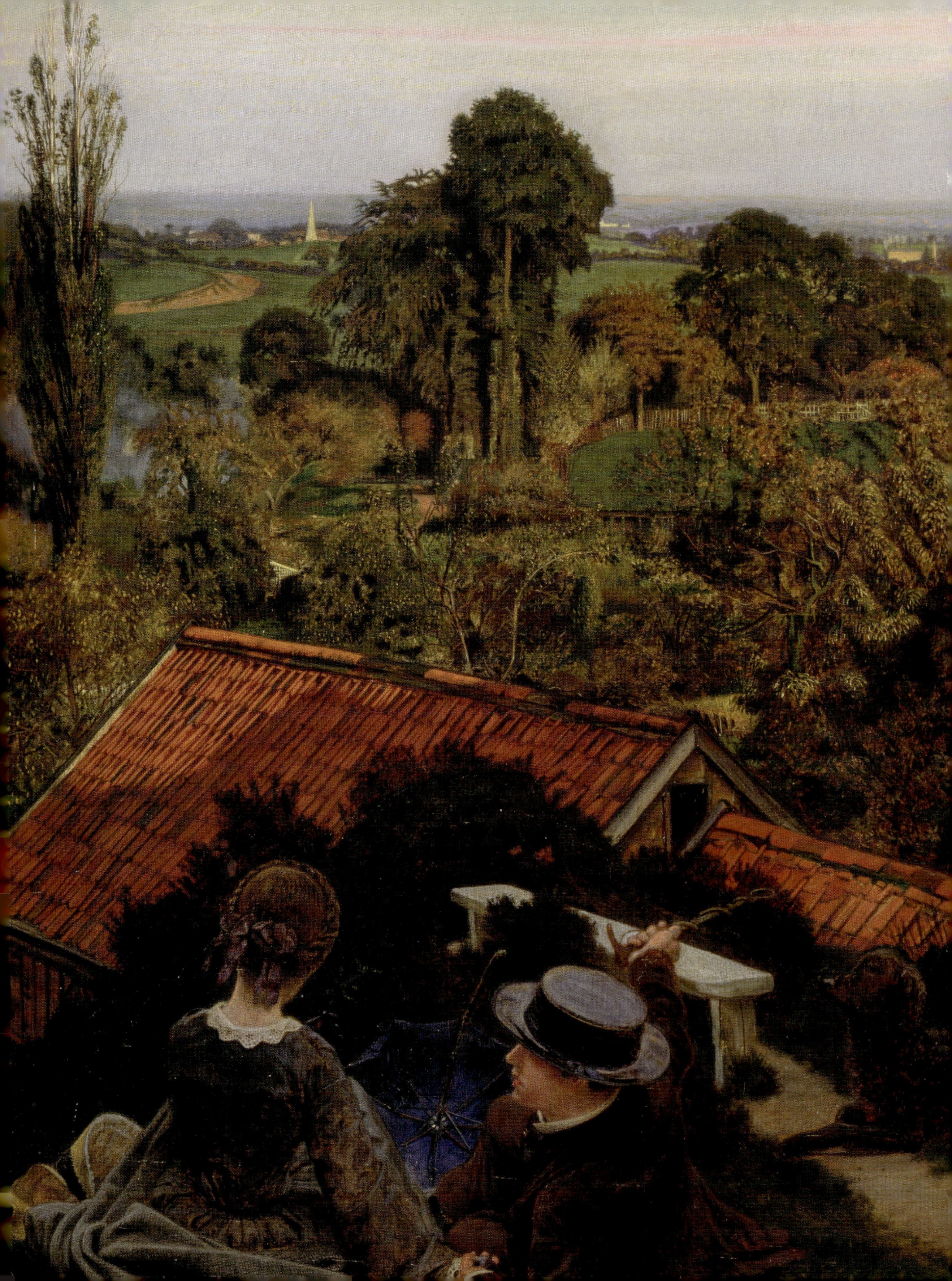

The Game of Life
Ford Madox Brown – a character study

ANGELA THIRLWELL

For very many years Ford Madox Brown's life was not a game. It was late nights, labour intensive brushstrokes, relentless industry, intellectual effort, no proper recognition, family deaths, and grinding money worries. But for a few glorious years during his mid-forties he enjoyed new exuberance, a public profile, a healthier income and a position at the centre of London's Bohemian life.

In 1865 he staged an innovative retrospective exhibition, one of the first artists ever to do so. William Gladstone, then Chancellor of the Exchequer, paid a surprise visit and shook Brown by the hand.[1] The show and the gesture brought him unexpected fame and attracted new buyers. He wrote the catalogue himself, sold over two thousand copies at sixpence each, and more than three thousand people paid a shilling to gaze at a hundred pictures of half a lifetime. The exhibition was shaped like an autobiography, leading the visitor ever onwards to the heart of the show, Brown's great canvas *Work* (cat. 61). Inviting Victorians to look at a mirror image of their own stratified society, it was also a monument to his own career of unremitting artistic labour. The show signalled the beginning of a new phase of life for Brown. He moved with his wife Emma, daughters Lucy and Cathy and son Oliver, from London's rural Highgate to fashionable and expensive Fitzrovia. At 37 Fitzroy Square his salon and his parties would become a focus for London's intelligentsia over the next decade.

One evening soon after moving he felt buoyant enough to play the popular Victorian parlour game 'My Favourite Things'.

Fig. 9
Detail of cat. 50, An English Autumn Afternoon, Hampstead – Scenery in 1853

The record of the game survives in the Morgan Library, New York. On the left are the standard questions posed in the neat blue ink of another hand. Brown's answers flow down the opposite column in his large, free, emphatic black script, characteristic of his most confident moods, signed and dated at Fitzroy Square, 2 October 1866 (fig. 10).

In his imposing new home with 'the most extraordinary pictures on the walls', its shabby chic and suspiciously oriental divan,[2] Brown played this miniature game of life in a light-hearted spirit, sometimes with transparent honesty, sometimes with teasing opacity. Guests and family members present that night would have recognised not only the irony but also a kind of inner truth in those quick-fire responses. At the distance of nearly a century and a half, it is more difficult to distinguish his mischief from his sincerity. Who is your Favourite Queen? 'Jezebel'[3] – seems provocative. Favourite Artist? 'Afraid to say' – coy. Favourite Costume? 'Bathing dress' – daring. Favourite Dislike? 'Onions' – bathetic.

His first three answers to questions about his favourite King, Queen and Hero are all drawn from the Bible, specifically the Old Testament. Two responses further down the list citing Peter as his Favourite Name, and Star of Bethlehem, *Ornithogalum spicatum monspelliensium*,[4] as his Favourite Flower, refer to the New Testament. One of the lily family, the Star of Bethlehem, according to Gerard's *Herbal* of 1597, grows 'in sundrie places which lie open to the aire' and can easily be overlooked. Like a rayed star, the flower is named after the star of Christ's nativity. The back of its white perianth segments is striped with green, the leaves have white lines and look grassy and inconspicuous.[5] In the Victorian language of flowers it is associated with the idea of hope. Taller lilies, the symbol of purity, often featured in Pre-Raphaelite art, most notably in *The Girlhood of Mary*

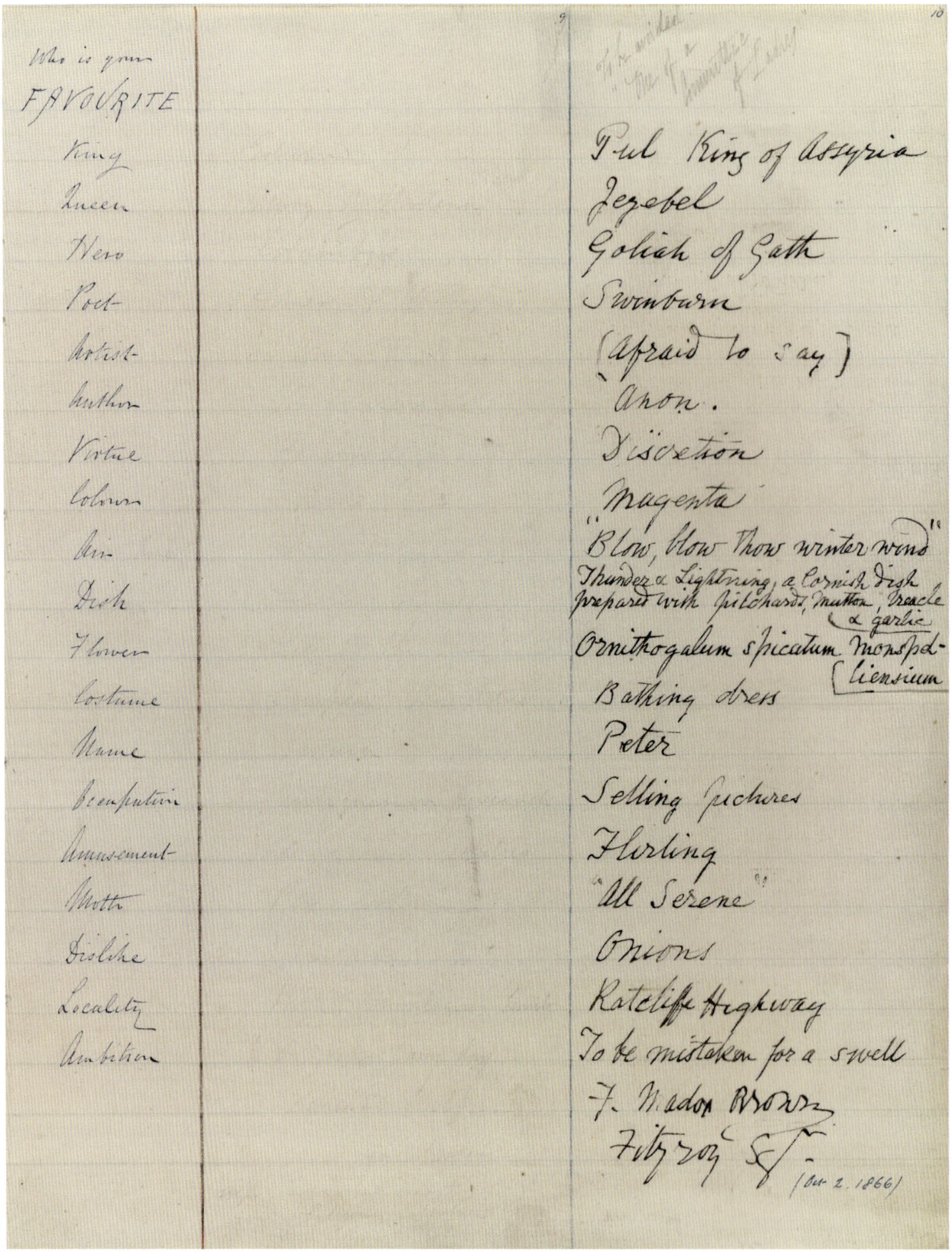

Fig. 10
Ford Madox Brown, List of Favourite Things, *2 October 1866. The Pierpont Morgan Library, New York. Bequest Gordon N. Ray, 1987.*

Who is your	
FAVOURITE	
King	Pul King of Assyria
Queen	Jezebel
Hero	Goliath of Gath
Poet	Swinburne
Artist	(Afraid to say)
Author	Anon.
Virtue	Discretion
Colour	Magenta
Air	"Blow, blow thou winter wind"
Dish	Thunder & Lightning, a Cornish dish prepared with pilchards, mutton, treacle & garlic
Flower	Ornithogalum spicatum monspelliensium
Costume	Bathing dress
Name	Peter
Occupation	Selling pictures
Amusement	Flirting
Moth	"All Serene"
Dislike	Onions
Locality	Ratcliffe Highway
Ambition	To be mistaken for a swell
	F. Madox Brown
	Fitzroy Sqr-
	(Oct 2.1866)

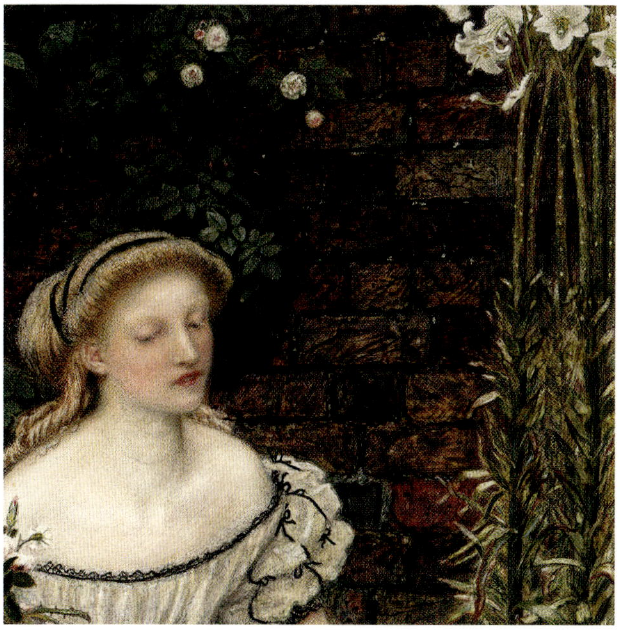

Fig. 11
Ford Madox Brown, detail of cat. 93, The Nosegay

Virgin (fig. 7, p. 17) and *Ecce Ancilla Domini!* (Tate) by Brown's one-time student, Dante Gabriel Rossetti. Brown's own lilies can be seen in the right hand roundel of his *The First Translation of the Bible into English* (cat. 33) and growing against the wall in *The Nosegay* (fig. 11).

'Peter' is perhaps a tacit memory of his noble and hyper-realistic picture *Jesus washing Peter's Feet* (cat. 75). This had won a £50 prize at the Liverpool Academy of Arts in 1856 but a year later was shockingly skied[6] at the Manchester Art Treasures Exhibition. Religion was not a factor in Brown's mature spiritual life although he always recognised the power of religious subjects in art. Seeing Giotto's iridescent frescoes in the Arena Chapel in Padua on his way south to Rome with his frail wife Elisabeth in 1845 was an indelible memory which he always venerated.[7] Many of his most daring pictures such as *Oure Ladye of Saturday Night, The pretty baa-lambs, Waiting* and *'Take your Son, Sir!'* (cats. 28, 49, 56, 57) were modern interpretations of the Virgin and Child theme he saw so many times in Italy.

As a young man Brown observed conventional religion. He took his eldest child Lucy to church. He married twice in church, first his cousin Elisabeth Bromley on 3 April 1841, and after her death from tuberculosis, secondly Emma Hill on 5 April 1853, but only after the birth of their love-child Cathy in 1850. Of course, there were no Register Office weddings at that time but it is significant that by the 1870s both Brown's daughters married without benefit of clergy. By this time Brown himself had abandoned Christianity although he always continued to paint religious subjects.[8] *The Coat of Many Colours, Elijah and the Widow's Son, The Entombment,* as well as *The Baptism of Edwin* and *The Trial of Wyclif* (cats. 76–78, 118, 125) in his great series of murals for Manchester Town Hall, all provided him with the scenes of drama and high emotion that he relished.

Like his friend and son-in-law, William Michael Rossetti, who married Lucy, Brown became a confirmed agnostic[9] (if not an atheist) before the term was invented – as William said of his own position.[10] Nevertheless, when the craze for spiritualism and table rapping was at its height during the mid-1860s and Dante Gabriel Rossetti was trying to contact his dead wife Lizzie Siddal, Brown and William attended séances with professional mediums. Although Brown had no belief in an afterlife,[11] he even hosted séances at 37 Fitzroy Square where lowered lamps and dying firelight cast the sitting room into sepulchral gloom. Only afterwards did his eleven-year-old son Oliver (Nolly) confess to his half-sister Lucy that it was he who had encouraged the rappings from the other world and had made the table move.[12] Brown kept faith with his agnosticism so that when he died in 1893 his funeral took place without religious ceremony in the unconsecrated section of St Pancras Cemetery at East Finchley. The American freethinker Moncure Conway, in whose honour Conway Hall in London was later named, gave a moving and entirely secular address reported in the national and international press.[13]

Although he moved to agnosticism, Brown knew his Bible. The Old Testament characters he named as his Favourites, Pul the usurping King of Assyria[14] (fig. 12) (inspired perhaps by A.H. Layard's work on Assyrian archaeology),[15] Jezebel the Bible's harlot queen (whose sexual reputation is still debated today),[16] and the Philistine, Goliath of Gath, were all of legendary dimensions. Only a few months before playing the parlour game, Brown had made a vigorous cartoon of *David and Goliath* for a stained glass design (fig. 13).[17] Choosing the usually demonised Philistine as his Favourite Hero was humorously perverse. Why didn't Brown identify with the puny but wily David who defeated the burly giant? Brown himself

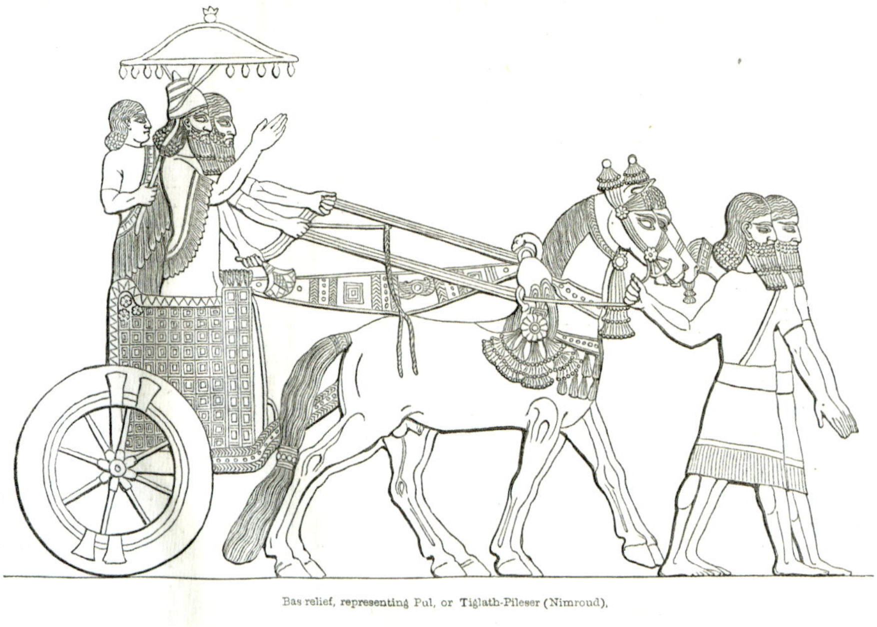

Fig. 12
Bas relief of King Pul *from A.H. Layard,* Discoveries in the Ruins of Nineveh and Babylon, *1853. University of Liverpool Library*

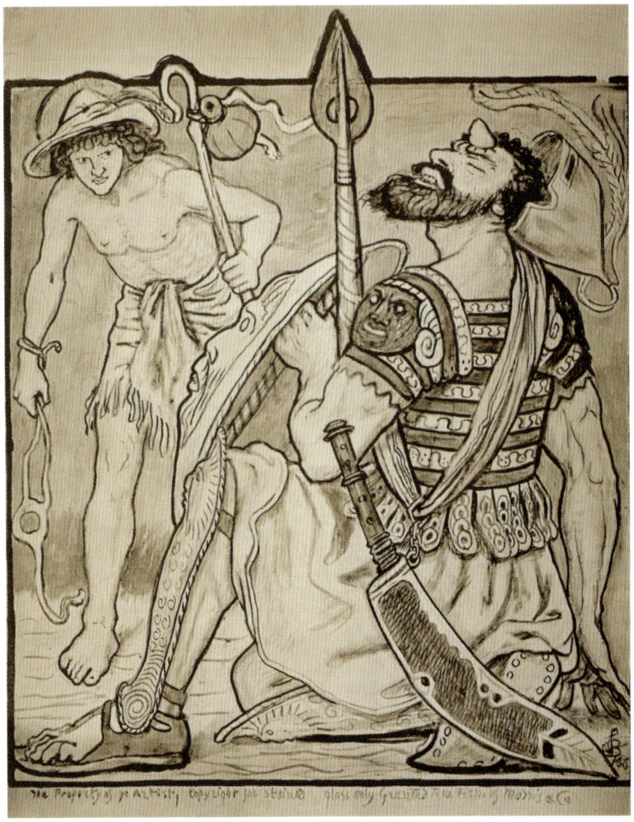

Fig. 13
Ford Madox Brown, stained glass cartoon for David and Goliath, *1866, from Harold Rathbone,* The Cartoons of Ford Madox Brown, *1895*

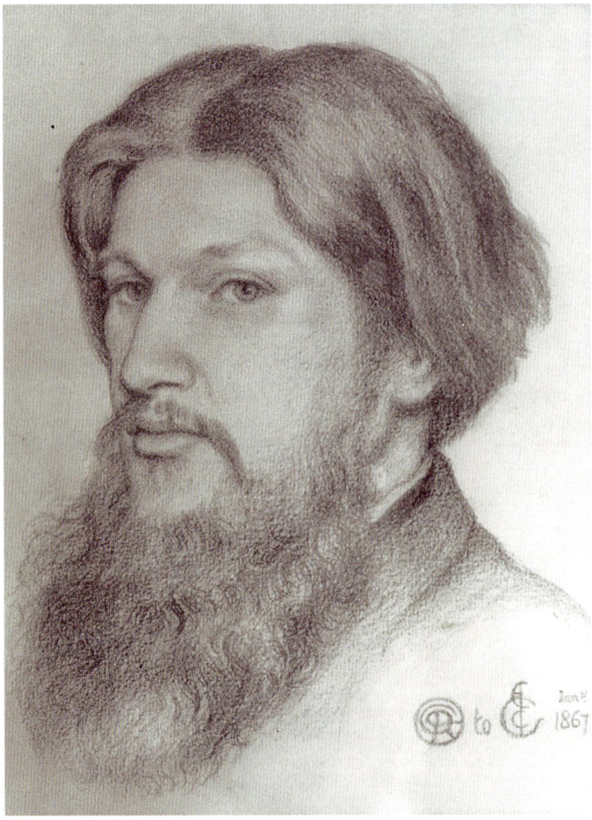

Fig. 14
Dante Gabriel Rossetti, Ford Madox Brown, *31 January 1867. Private collection*

was a small man with a big presence. His passport issued by the Belgian Legation in London[18] recorded that he was just 1 m 71 cm tall (just over 5 ft 7 in), at least a foot shorter than Goliath even according to the most conservative estimates recorded in the Dead Sea Scrolls or by the historian Josephus. As a young man Brown had a delicate physique, an oval face, chestnut hair and blond beard[19] (cat. 1), but by 1866 he had new magnetism and authority. His second wife Emma cut his hair blunt and square and he kept his beard long so that he looked like a pocket-sized Goliath or King Pul (fig. 14).

In his heyday, Brown was known as the handsomest man in London and the best conversationalist.[20] The poet Swinburne, sixteen years his junior and an *enfant terrible* even in Bohemian circles, was one of the regular guests at Brown's parties. During the parlour game Brown avowed that Swinburne was his Favourite Poet (fig. 15). Swinburne's admiration for Brown's talented student, the stunning young Anglo-Greek, Marie Spartali – 'She is so beautiful that I want to sit down and cry'[21] – may have been one of the factors which encouraged Brown's painful obsession with her (fig. 16). By 1866, the date of the parlour game, Brown's extensive and idiosyncratic diary which he had kept for over twenty years, with the exception of one four-year black hole, had collapsed. Now he only recorded the dates he gave art lessons to Marie, each session denoted with a single word, simply the name of the woman he loved without hope – 'Spartali'. At New Year 1867 Brown enlisted Swinburne to write an *Ode on the Insurrection in Candia* (Crete), one of Marie's favourite political causes. Swinburne's verse was limpid and musical. Brown's passion for Marie drove him to awkward, anguished poetic expression in a series of sonnets he wrote and re-wrote in a private notebook.[22] Although he practised it, poetry was not his art.

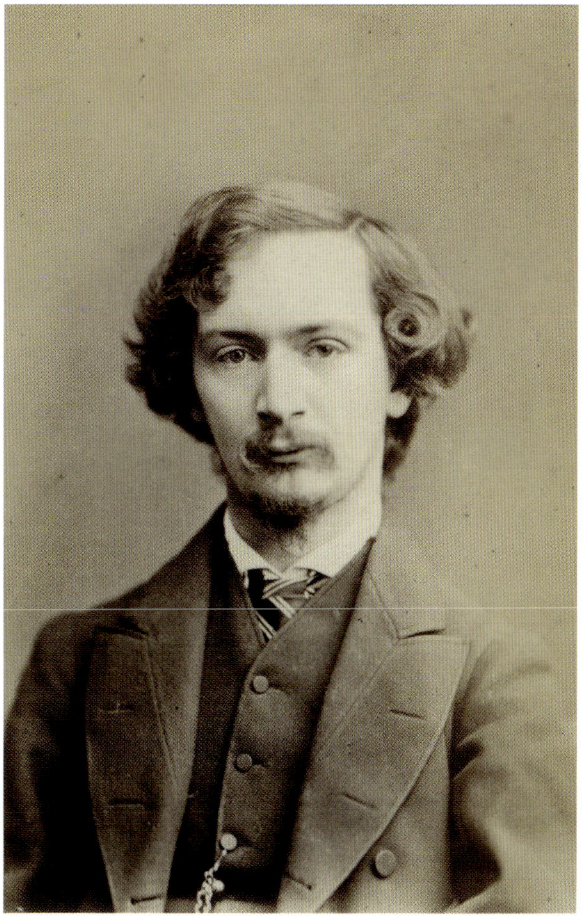

Fig. 15
Algernon Charles Swinburne, photograph by London Stereoscopic Company, c.1865. National Portrait Gallery, London

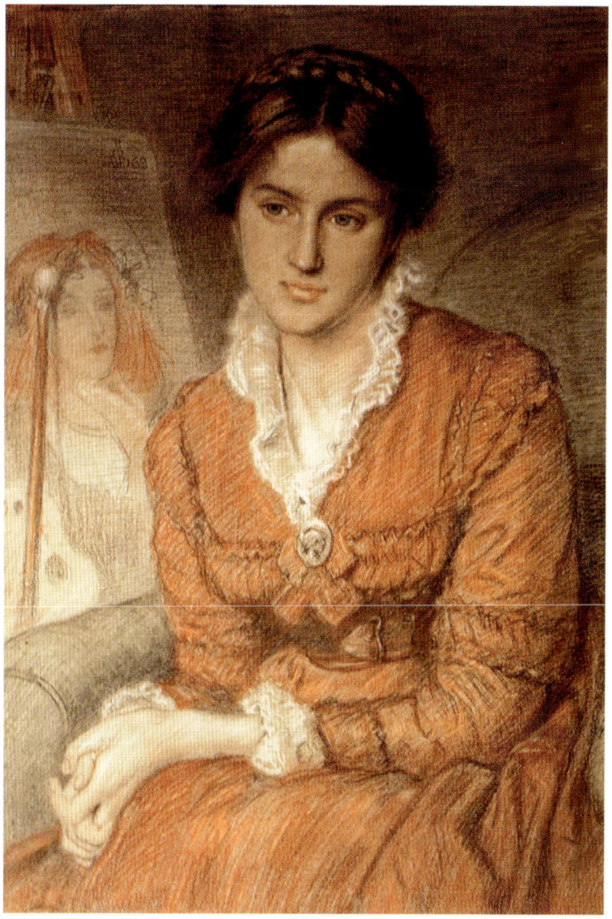

Fig. 16
Ford Madox Brown, Marie Spartali at her easel, *1869. Private collection*

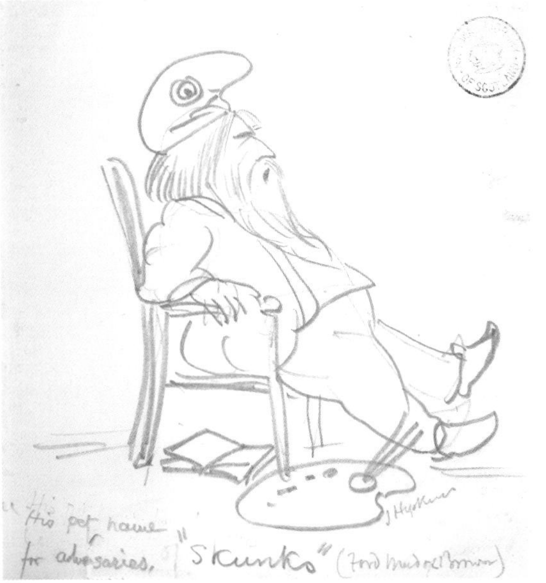

Fig. 17
John Hipkins, Caricature of Ford Madox Brown. *National Library of Scotland, Edinburgh*

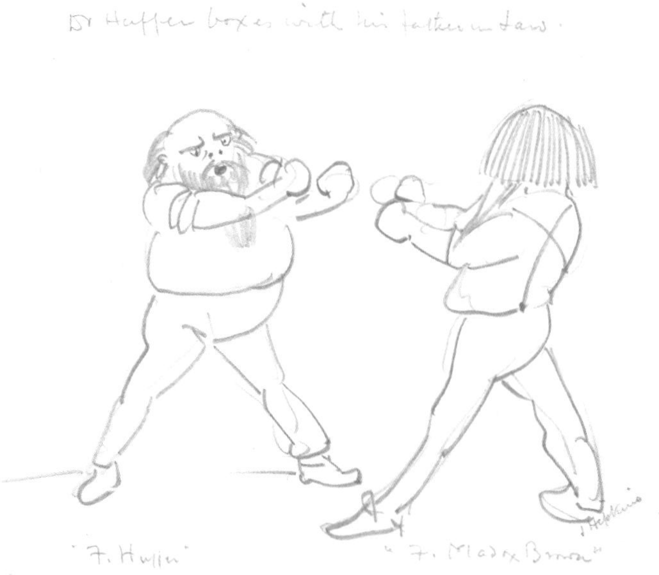

Fig. 18
John Hipkins, Ford Madox Brown boxing with Frank Hueffer. *National Library of Scotland, Edinburgh*

When the quizmaster asked him to name his favourite artist, Brown refused to say, tactfully avoiding giving offence to any fellow-painters who were in the room. He also ducked out of naming his favourite author. For these silences alone, he could boast that his Favourite Virtue was 'Discretion' which indeed he did manage to show on this occasion, although everyone knew that discretion was hardly part of his nature. Always outspoken, he was so scathing about enemies that caricaturist John Hipkins showed him decrying them with his favourite epithet – 'Skunks! His pet name for adversaries' (fig. 17).

Although Brown agreed with good humour to play the sedentary, indoors parlour game of 'Favourite Things' in autumn 1866, he was not a 'games player' in any conventional, all-weathers, sporty sense. However, he doodled a scene from a cricket match[23] on a letter he received from picture buyer Frederick Craven in 1866 and twenty years later showed a boy practising batting in *Chetham's Life Dream* (cat. 131), one of his most lyrical frescoes for Manchester Town Hall. In 1884, he depicted a lacrosse player sauntering to a match along Manchester's evocative *Platt Lane* (cat. 152).[24] Brown did take part in at least one boxing bout when he faced up to Frank Hueffer, his strapping son-in-law who married Cathy. A German immigrant, Frank became music critic of *The Times*. Hipkins observed Brown in characteristic belligerent pose taking up the gloves against his vastly superior opponent (fig. 18).

This was the stance of a lifetime for Brown, who felt himself embattled against the world of art critics and the art establishment. He was a man who would never play social games to advance his professional career, nor act the sycophant to dealers like Ernest Gambart or to opinion-makers such as John Ruskin. He simply refused to toady. Ruskin, who had no temperamental affinity with Brown, enraged the artist by belittling his luminous landscape, *An English Autumn Afternoon* (cat. 50). After staying up all night, eating strawberries and discussing art, Brown was smoking a pipe in Rossetti's studio, when Ruskin, Rossetti's powerful patron, dropped in. Brown recorded the incident with rich irony in his diary (the characteristic eccentric spelling is all his own):

> I smoke, he talkes divers nonsense about art, hurriedly in shrill flippant tones – I answer him civilly – then resume my coat & prepare to leave. Suddenly, upon this he sais "Mr Brown will you tell me why you chose such a very ugly subject for your last picture." I dumbfounded at such a beginning from a stranger, look in his face expectant of some *qualifiycation* ...

Ruskin pressed on:

> What made you take such a very ugly subject, it was a pitty for there was some *nice* painting in it. I, from his manner coupled with the knowledge of his having *praised* the subject to Gabriel a few days before, being satisfied that he intended impertinence replied contemptuously "Because it lay out of a back window" & turning on my heel took my hat & wished Gabriel goodbuy. Ruskin seemed by this time in high dudgeon & would not look at me as I left the room.[25]

The colours in *An English Autumn Afternoon* are alive with October tints. The vivid blue of the man's boater and of the umbrella upturned between the two young people is vividly contrasted with the warm terracotta rooftops lying like a splayed letter W across the centre of the picture. And on the right, the eye is drawn to a roan pigeon sitting on the dovecote, these rusty tints all within the spectrum of magenta the colour which Brown named his Favourite.

Magenta suited Brown's new brio on the night he played the parlour game in 1866. It was a startlingly modern pigment, only recently invented and named after the Battle of Magenta, on 4 June 1859, one of the decisive moments during the Second Italian War of Independence when the French-Sardinian alliance defeated superior Austrian forces. Brown loved France where he had been brought up and whose language he always spoke. He retained French friends all his life. His socialist views were so close to the Communards in 1871 that he employed an anarchist exile, Jules Andrieu, to teach Oliver French and Latin. Through the Andrieu connection, it is likely that Rimbaud and Verlaine attended Brown's London salon.[26] Among the glamorous personalities invited to his parties during the early 1870s, the only ban was on Royal Academicians, Brown's *bêtes noires*. His grandson Ford Madox Ford remembered: 'He hated all Academicians, all Cabinet Ministers, all Officials, all Tories, all Whigs and the *Times* newspaper ... All Academies – except the *Académie Française* – were anathema'.[27] Equal to Brown's love of France was his loathing of tyranny; he identified with the Italian struggle for independence from Austria. Thus, for Brown the radical, the choice of magenta as his Favourite Colour held many layers of political associations as well as practical applications.

Unlike traditional artists' pigments made from natural substances, magenta was one of the earliest to be made by chemical extraction. Aniline was first extracted from heated indigo in Germany in 1826. In London, in the mid-1850s, William Henry Perkin attempted to synthesize quinine from aniline and found that one of the products of the reaction was violet. Three years later he patented mauve – French for mallow flower – under the name *mauveine*, the first synthetic dye in the world. In the year of the Battle of Magenta, François Emmanuel Verguin synthesized another brilliant new colour, similar to the fuchsia flower, which he patented as *fuchsin*. These discoveries began the vogue for scintillating, off-beat, deep purply pinks with hints of blue and burgundy known as fuchsia, solferino (named after another bloody battle in the same campaign for Italian independence) and magenta.[28]

When you look at some of Brown's major paintings, you can see how magenta had been spicing his palette for years although previously he would have made it with pigments such as alizarin crimson, white and ultramarine. Hints of fuchsia, mauve, crimson and magenta fluttered in Emma's bonnet ribbons as well as on her lips when she posed on bitter wintry days as the emigrating wife for *The Last of England* in 1852 (fig. 19).[29] Similar tones can be seen in the bonnet of the

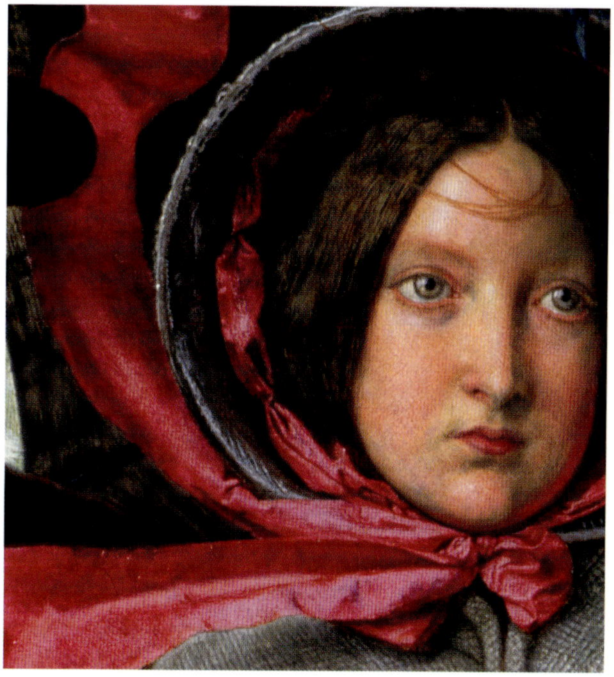

Fig. 19
Magenta ribbon on Emma's bonnet, detail of cat. 58, The Last of England

little blonde child (modelled by Brown and Emma's daughter Cathy) on the outside left of the picture, in the deep maroon skeins in the grey deck-rope slung across the foreground, and in the solferino purple cabbage on the left, suspended from that rope.

In *The Last of England* the relationship of husband and wife is central to the picture's enduring charge. When Brown began his first studies for the figure of the emigrating wife in December 1852, Emma was still Miss Hill, although their daughter Cathy was already two years old. Probably 'working from self in the looking glass',[30] Brown copied his own face for the figure of the husband who 'broods bitterly over blighted hopes and severance from all he has been striving for. The young wife's grief is of a less cantankerous sort … The circle of her love moves with her.'[31] The circle of that love is personal as well as universal, for the infant hand clasped beneath Emma's shawl belongs to their second child, Oliver, born in wedlock, eighteen months after Brown and Emma's marriage at St. Dunstan-in-the-West on Fleet Street.

Emma became Brown's most emblematic model. She could embody so much more than herself, slipping easily into role as an ancient British princess, a modern Madonna or an Everywoman figure. But she sulked if he asked her to pose once too often.[32] Their relationship had begun in frank physicality in 1848/49, but in spite of Brown's susceptibility to other women and Emma's increasing alcohol dependence – when 'E.D.' (Emma drunk) began to litter his diary entries – it became one of mutual understanding. She was a natural, instinctive mother and spent many evenings round the fireside telling fairy tales or singing. Sometimes they sang duets together and filled the house with harmony. When Brown played the game of Favourite Things, he chose 'Blow, blow thou winter wind' as his Favourite Air.[33] Perhaps this was one of Emma's most often performed songs, sung to Thomas Arne's melodic setting, specially written for the production of *As You Like It* at Drury Lane in 1740 and still popular today.

> Blow, blow, thou winter wind,
> Thou art not so unkind
>   As man's ingratitude:
> Thy tooth is not so keen,
> Because thou art not seen,
>   Although thy breath be rude.
> Heigh-ho, sing heigh-ho, unto the green holly.
> Most friendship is faining, most loving mere folly:
> Then, heigh-ho, the holly.
> This life is most jolly.

The conflicts in the song, between the harshness of winter, the sting of human ingratitude but the determination to sing 'heigh-ho' in spite of everything, to proclaim that 'life is most jolly' are a direct reflection of Brown's stoicism. Whatever life threw at him – lack of recognition, personal loss, particularly the death of three sons, one newborn by his first wife Elisabeth in 1842, Emma's second son baby Arthur in 1857, and in 1874 at less than twenty, Oliver already a poet, novelist and painter of distinct promise – Brown remained controlled. The death of this 'golden boy' implicitly recalled 'Golden Lads and girls all must/ As chimney-sweepers, come to dust', in the 'Dirge for Fidele' from Shakespeare's *Cymbeline*. Shakespeare's plays, especially *King Lear*, with its theme of tragic endurance, fascinated Brown throughout his life. In Paris with Elisabeth in 1844, as a very young man he had made a series of pen-and-ink drawings inspired by the play. His prime interest was in psychological interaction, which he conveyed in vivid shorthand through exaggerated facial expressions and contorted body language. When viewed in sequence like a strip cartoon, the sketches build up to a powerful narrative drama. His energetic pen-strokes highlighted profound thematic contrasts: youth against age, parent against child, insubordination against authority, female against male, weakness against strength, loving-kindness against ruthlessness, and man against the elements as in 'Blow, blow thou winter wind' (cat. 22). His Favourite Air was not lightly chosen.

After Oliver's death, he would stare into desolation. There was no remedy in false gods, only in absolute fortitude and the salvation of work. 'We are strangely calm, after our wont, and indeed, my belief; it is of no use arguing with the whirlwind. There is nothing for it but to patch up what remains of hope in other directions and get to work again – but the savour is gone, unless in the work for itself,' he told his friend and patron, George Rae, the Birkenhead banker.[34] So in the two decades left to him after Oliver's death, he undertook his most strenuous project, a great public commission to paint twelve murals in Manchester Town Hall. At the end of his life

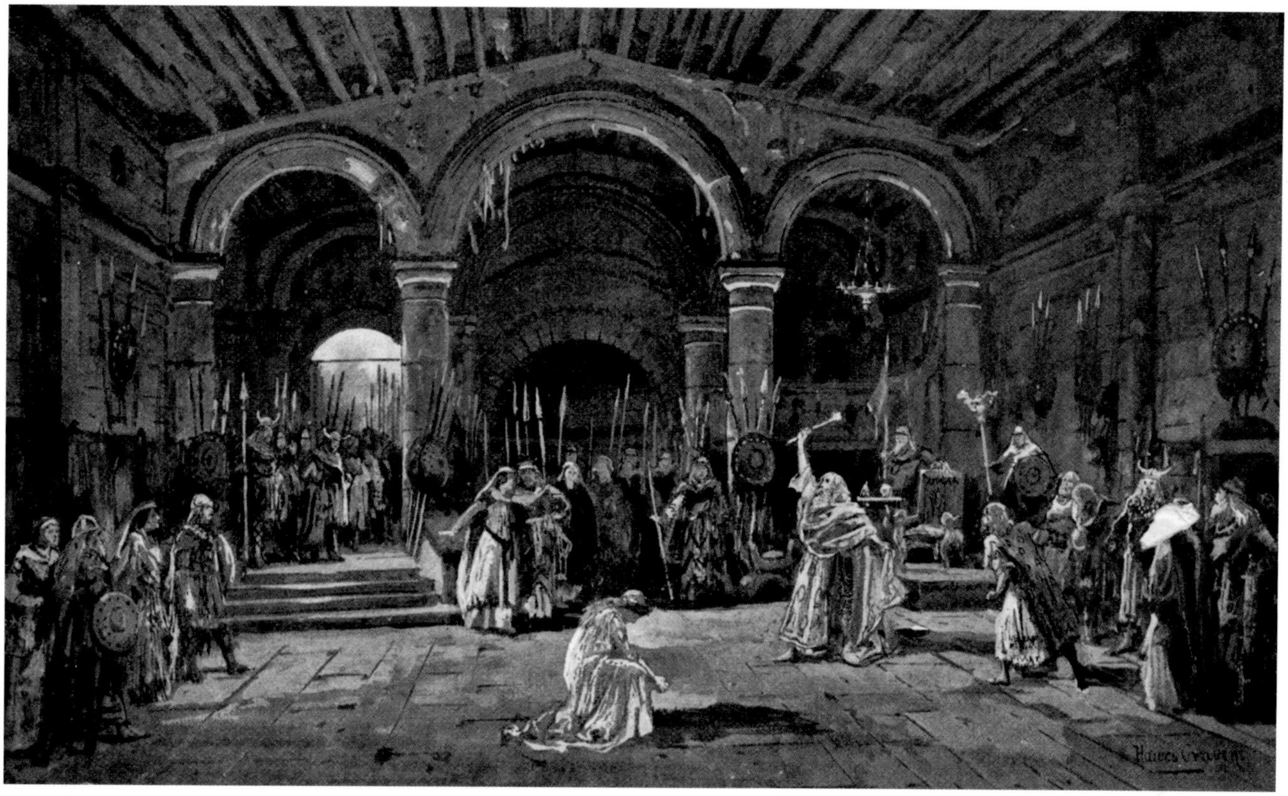

Fig. 20
Set for King Lear *designed by Ford Madox Brown, from Souvenir Programme, Lyceum Theatre London, 1892. Private collection*

Brown's thoughts came back to Shakespeare when in 1892 Henry Irving commissioned him to design three majestic sets for his production of *King Lear* at the Lyceum. Irving had always admired Brown's treatment of the play, including paintings such as *King Lear* (cat. 36), and in his dressing room hung in homage a print of *Cordelia's Portion* (cat. 79), unmistakeably based on Brown's drawing of half a century earlier (cat. 17). For this production Irving naturally turned to Brown who by now cultivated a Lear-like personal image. Theatre critics had often noted Irving's extreme gestures on stage. Perhaps his acting style attracted him to Brown's dramatic *King Lear* pictures with their psychological intensity (fig. 20).

Brown's art was sustained by high culture. But a man can't live on culture alone. He drank, smoked and enjoyed a good meal. By 1866 he could look back on 'Onions' as his chief 'Dislike' which he associated with depression and with the lean times. After Elisabeth's death in 1846 and well into the early years of his relationship with Emma, he had felt frantic and pursued, trying to make an artistic career support both himself and his child Lucy (cat. 6), whose compelling gaze was a constant reminder of Elisabeth. Then he continually berated himself as 'a very swine … a beast & a sleepy brute'.[35] He suffered a range of physical and psychosomatic disorders, toothache, facial swellings, insomnia, and low-grade infections. In fact he was sliding into clinical depression, 'broken in spirit and but a melancholy copy of what I once was'.[36] As he learnt to live with his melancholia he could even joke about it. Like Churchill who had his Black Dog, Brown would refer almost affectionately to his 'mulligrubs'.[37]

In 1847 he had forced himself to begin what he called the 'Diary of my Painting' in which he frequently itemised the hours and minutes he put in each day at his work. There were days when he made up his mind 'to do much work & did nil',[38] but when things went well he recorded nine hours, ten hours, eleven hours.[39] He laboured so long that his eyes couldn't see the colours in the end. In those years, he had no commercial success and was desperate about money. He considered suicide or emigration to India.[40] When he sold a picture such as a version of *Waiting* (cat. 56) modelled by

Emma, he felt temporarily uplifted and 'went & laid out a lot of money for Emma & chicks.'[41] Finances were a problem throughout his career. Even as he became more successful, following his 1865 exhibition, it was with considerable feeling that he cited his Favourite Occupation as 'Selling Pictures'.

In the early days, trying to make a living as an artist in London, he was constantly 'low & dejected', never felt happy – and the studio at 20½ Clipstone Street swarmed with rats so large that they made off with a mutton chop.[42] After a little break at St Albans with Emma who was pregnant with their second child in August 1854, he noted his negative mood on their return home as 'lazy; sad, nervous, stupid state again, hopes gone, unspeakably flown, onions for supper.'[43] As ever, his phases of low self-worth were exacerbated by humble onions. Salt beef made him vomit[44] but seafood was a treat, especially when dining with Dante Gabriel Rossetti 'off a lobster' in London, [45] or fresh soles from Mr Banger's catch at Pegwell Bay in Kent, 'which he assured me had been *hopping in the pan*.'[46]

Far more idiosyncratic was his Favourite Dish, 'Thunder and Lightning, a Cornish dish prepared with pilchards, mutton, treacle & garlic', a mischievously outlandish meal, which guests at his table may have dreaded. Even Rick Stein, restaurateur and authority on cooking fish, finds pilchards challenging. 'They have that sort of flavour that initially makes you think "How could anyone eat that?"'[47] Brown spent at least one significant summer in the West Country. This holiday, in 1871, marked a turning point in Brown's emotional life. His beloved pupil, Marie Spartali, had just left his orbit to marry a sensationally unsuitable penniless American widower with three children. After Marie's departure, Brown invited another exotic young woman to join the family group in Lynmouth. This was Mathilde Blind, a German intellectual, writer and radical feminist who would be part of Brown's life until his death (fig.46. p. 70). Petite, dark and intense, in her vivid striped silks, Mathilde, the Continental revolutionary whirled in on Brown's summer painting party with a storm of talk and German argument. 'Thunder and Lightning' on the table at Lynn Cottage that summer represented the *Sturm und Drang* of emotions.

In romantic Lynmouth where Shelley had once honeymooned with his first wife, Harriet Westbrook, Mathilde tracked down an old woman who remembered the poet. She immediately involved Brown in her Shelley mania. 'I am going to draw her [Mary Blackmore]', he wrote to his friend the artist Frederic Shields, and 'Miss Blind is to make an article about her.'[48] His pencil sketch of the old woman who had once known Shelley still survives.[49] The Pre-Raphaelites idealised the Romantic poets and although Brown was never an official member of the Brotherhood, he shared their admiration for Romantic literature. In their 1848 'List of Immortals' they included Byron and Wordsworth, but Keats and Shelley merited even higher status, in the same bracket as Homer, Dante and Chaucer.[50] Brown painted pictures inspired by Byron, notably *Manfred on the Jungfrau*, *The Corsair* and *Byron's Dream* (cats. 14, 82, 85), as well as *The Dream of Sardanapalus* (Delaware Art Museum), *Jacopo Foscari* (William Morris Museum, Walthamstow), and *Don Juan found by Haidée* (National Gallery of Victoria, Melbourne).

One of the most original satellite writers connected with the Romantics was opium addict and essayist Thomas De Quincey. When Brown cited 'Ratcliffe Highway', noted for its vice and crime, as his Favourite Locality it was probably with De Quincey in mind. Ratcliffe Highway (now renamed simply The Highway, in Docklands just east of the Tower of London) was the scene of two sensational and apparently motiveless multiple murders in 1811. 'On Murder considered as one of the Fine Arts' (1827) was a bravura performance essay by De Quincey based on an ironic, dramatic retelling of the Ratcliffe Highway murders, which he expanded in 1839 and 1854,[51] and which became almost as famous as his *Confessions of an English Opium-Eater*. De Quincey's taste for glamorizing the astonishing blood-thirstiness of these notorious murders began the tradition of elegant crime writing, fed into the work of Dickens and Poe, and more recently continues to inspire Peter Ackroyd in his novels *Hawksmoor* and *Dan Leno and the Limehouse Golem*.[52] Brown's close friend, Dante Gabriel Rossetti, appropriated the idea of the murderer as an artist. When witnessing a butchered body pulled out of the Seine, he imagined the killer silently joining the crowd:

> You fancy him –
> Smoking an early pipe, and watching, as
> An artist, the effect of his last work.[53]

Brown's taste for the off-beat, his sense of humour and his

position as an unconventional Bohemian, might have tempted him to name Ratcliffe Highway as his Favourite Locality, naughtily anticipating the frisson of shock or recognition that other players of the parlour game would register. 'For the final purpose of murder, considered as a fine art,' claimed De Quincey coolly, 'is precisely the same as that of Tragedy, in Aristotle's account of it, viz. "to cleanse the heart by means of pity and terror."' De Quincey's astonishing insouciance in equating murder with artistry, and indeed with Aristotle's classic theory of tragic catharsis, would have amused and intrigued Brown. He enjoyed brilliant writing such as De Quincey's and described his own elegant murder scenes in *Ehud and Eglon* (fig. 21) and *The Death of Sir Tristram* (cat. 98).

This image of *Sir Tristram* based on Malory's *Morte d'Arthur* showed the dangerous outcome of passion unrestrained. Although an intensely moral man, Brown was never averse to 'Flirting' which he named as his Favourite Amusement, at the moment when his obsession with Marie Spartali was at its most ardent and hopeless. It is doubtful whether his wife Emma would have laughed at this frank boast. She might have looked more favourably on his 'Favourite Ambition – To be mistaken for a swell'. Originally slang, a 'swell' became popular during the nineteenth century to denote a fashionably or stylishly dressed person. Brown may have been ambitious to be mistaken for a swell either in self-mockery, or to deflate the pretensions of the middle classes. At the centre of London's Bohemia, Brown didn't care a pin about appearances, but liked nice clothes whenever he could afford them. An early portrait drawing by Millais (fig. 22) showcases Brown as a bit of a dandy, an image also seen in his mature self-portrait (frontispiece).

Bravado and flippant humour characterize some of his answers in the parlour game, as evidenced by 'Flirting' and 'To be taken for a swell'. In similar risqué vein is 'Bathing Dress' which he gives as his Favourite Costume – though whether female or male bathing dress is unclear. Brown certainly enjoyed water. He had a penchant for Turkish baths and installed a shower bath at home which he used daily. One of his most beautiful pictures is the liquid landscape, *Walton-on-the-Naze* (cat. 55). It was a vivid memory of a

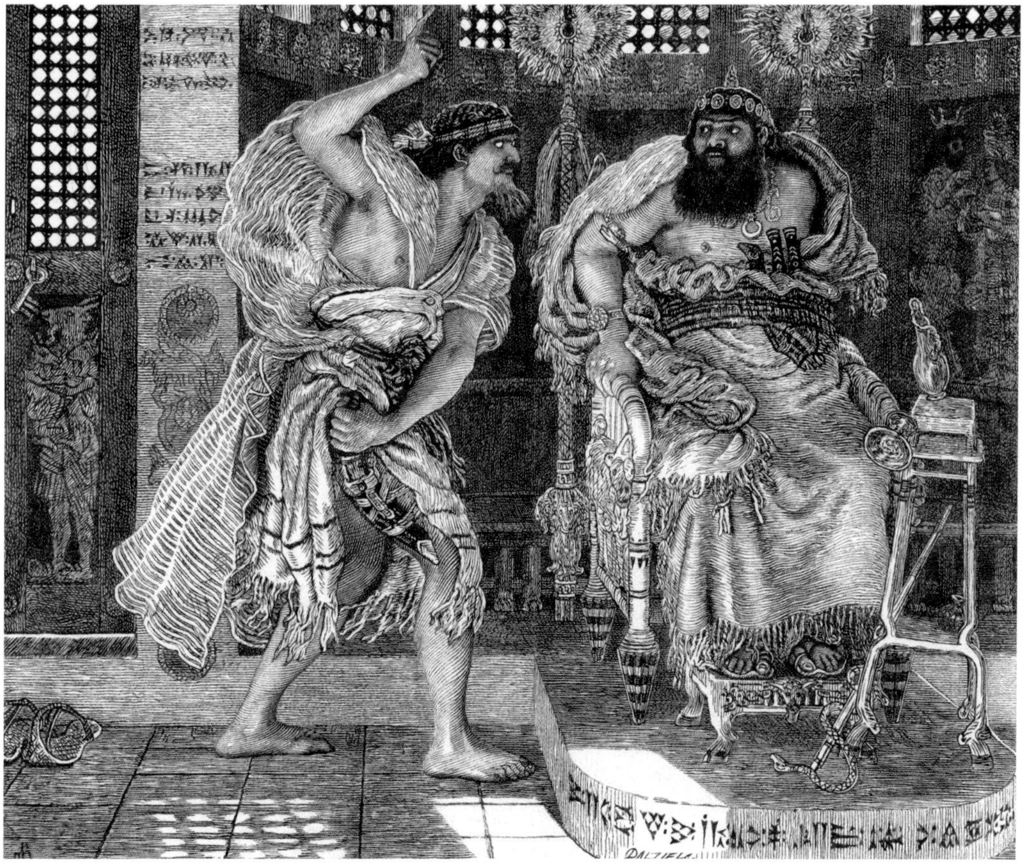

Fig. 21
Ford Madox Brown, Ehud and Eglon, *1865, from Dalziel's* Bible Gallery, *1881. Victoria and Albert Museum*

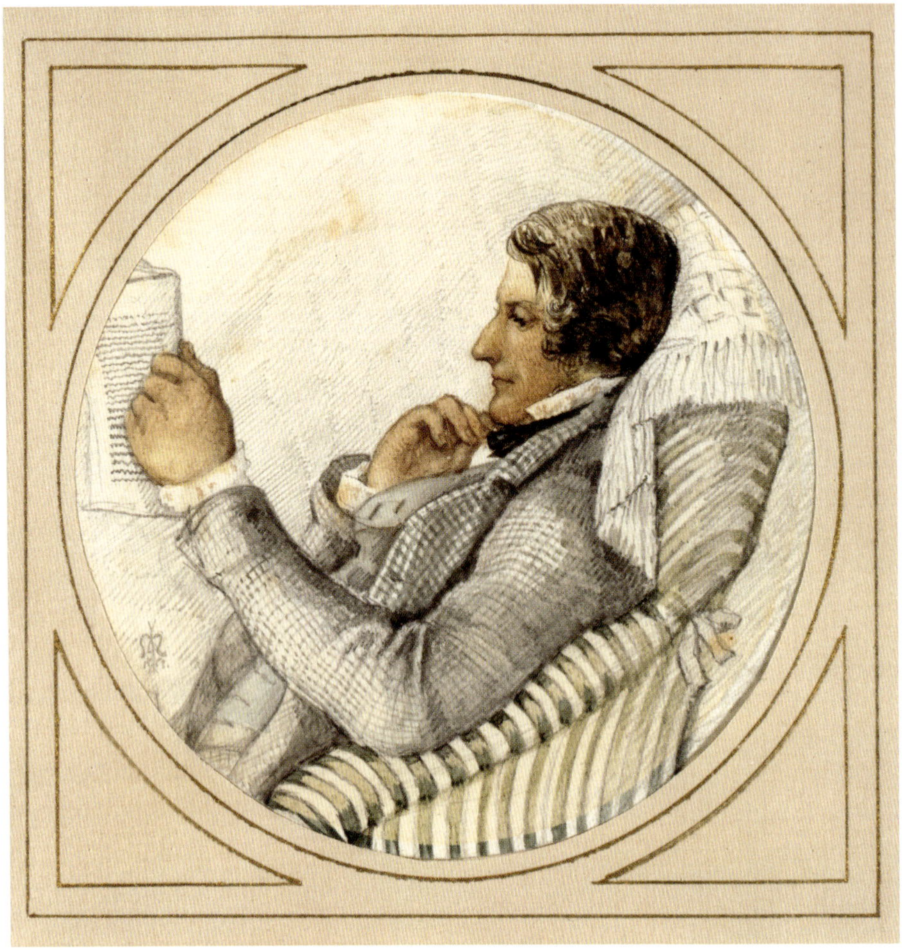

Fig. 22
John Everett Millais, Ford Madox Brown reading, *1853. Ashmolean Museum, Oxford*

summer holiday on the Essex coast. In the right hand corner Brown, Emma and Cathy are absorbed into the natural scene, within the embracing arc of the rainbow. Painted in super-naturalistic detail, with Emma's hair streaming down after swimming, maybe their bathing dresses had been left outside the picture frame.

If Victorians, even Bohemian ones, hesitated to display their bathing costumes, they were far less shy about their zeal for cataloguing the creatures of the natural world. One of the abiding passions of the age was the craze for lepidoptera which makes it no surprise that the parlour game questioner asked Brown to name his Favourite Moth. By this stage of the game he was in party mood and had had enough of accurate answers. So he just replied 'All Serene' which was a popular music-hall phrase short for 'it's all serene'. Dickens noticed that if a comedian dropped the catchphrase 'It's all serene' into his patter the whole audience would roar with laughter.[54] Brown's answer was an in-joke of the day.

Decoding the parlour game provides us with a cross-section of Brown's personality on one day in October 1866. Played like a sharp-shooting, free-association exercise, his answers are sometimes serious, sometimes playful, often both. He reveals and conceals himself at the same time, offering an insight into his quirky individuality. This once overlooked document challenges a common image of the artist as gouty, morose and prickly. It gives us instead a more authentic, upbeat, exhilarated Ford Madox Brown.

1 NML, Rae papers, FMB to George Rae, 18 March 1865.
2 The interior of 37 Fitzroy Square as observed by diarist Jeannette Marshall, daughter of Brown's friend the surgeon John Marshall, in Zuzanna Shonfield, *The Precariously Privileged: A Professional Family in Victorian London* (Oxford, 1987), p. 86.
3 FMB would have known the engraving of Jezebel from the *Bilderbibel* or *Bible Pictures* by Julius Schnorr von Carolsfeld published in Germany in 1851 and in England in 1855 (and several later editions). The Dalziels'

Bible Gallery for which FMB drew his illustrations in 1864 and 1865 was modelled on the *Bilderbibel*.

4 According to the RHS Lindley Library, *monspelliensium* is used in the names of a few plants that grow in S.W. Europe and may derive from the French town, Montpellier. On the other hand, FMB may have invented the word *monspelliensium* as 'franglais' for 'my spelling'. He was always aware of his own eccentric spelling, probably the result of being brought up in two languages, English and French.

5 Information from Geoffrey Grigson, *The Englishman's Flora*, London, 1975.

6 'skied' – i.e. the picture was hung high above 'the line' which marked the optimum eye-level view of the gallery visitor.

7 *Diary*, p. 171.

8 In the 1860s FMB worked on religious subjects in response to the commission to provide designs for *Dalziel's Bible Gallery*, eventually published in 1881.

9 The word 'agnostic' was coined in 1869 by T.H. Huxley, biologist and science educationalist.

10 W.M. Rossetti 1906, I, p. 122

11 'Neither Mathilde [Blind] nor Madox Brown envisaged an afterlife': UBC, Holman Hunt to WMR, 15 April 1894.

12 WMR unpublished *Séance Diary*, UBC, 15 December 1866, and note added later, 2 April 1868, and on microfilm at the Bodleian. See also Thirlwell 2003, chapter 3.

13 Thirlwell 2010, pp. 248–49.

14 See Kings II, 15–19: 'Pul the king of Assyria came against the land: and Menahem gave Pul a thousand talents of silver, that his hand might be with him to confirm the kingdom in his hand.' Pul is now identified with King Tiglath-Pileser III.

15 FMB 1865, no. 67, *Ehud, and Eglon King of Moab*: 'The costume and accessories of this cartoon are taken from Assyrian and Egyptian remains of a remote period … the evidence of our eyes, as may be readily seen by the Assyrian remains … which we have in the British Museum.' See also Brown's *Sardanapalus*, which shows a relief panel based on Assyrian sculptures Brown may have seen in the British Museum, or as engravings in A.H. Layard's books on his Babylonian discoveries. I am grateful to Dr Laura MacCulloch for making this connection.

16 See Lesley Hazleton, *The Untold Story of the Bible's Harlot Queen* (New York, 2009).

17 In 1872 FMB made a second cartoon of *David and Goliath* for a stained glass window in Jesus College Chapel, Cambridge (Bennett 2010, 2, p. 516, C185).

18 This passport was probably issued in 1845, Hueffer 1896, p. 39.

19 Ibid.

20 Thirlwell 2010, pp. 98–100.

21 Robertson 1931, p. 13.

22 The exercise book containing FMB's sonnets to Marie Spartali is in the House of Lords Record Office, Stow Hill Papers STH/BH/2/3–6. Some of the poems, in the same or slightly alternative versions, are in General MS Bound, CO199 no 155, Manuscripts Division, Department of Rare Books & Special Collections, Princeton University Library.

23 V&A, Craven to FMB 28 November 1866.

24 Lacrosse was only imported to England in 1867 from Canada where it was played by Native Americans. Manchester is a stronghold of the game today.

25 *Diary*, p. 144.

26 'Through the Andrieu connection': see *The Diary of W.M. Rossetti 1870–1873* Odette Bornand, ed. (Oxford, 1977), p. 195, WMR's entry 4 May 1872, and see Bornand's note 1 referring to the probable connection made by Jules Andrieu between Oliver Madox Brown and the French poets Rimbaud and Verlaine in 1872. See also discussion in V.P. Underwood's *Verlaine et l'Angleterre* (Paris, 1956), p. 84.

27 Ford Madox Hueffer, 'Nice People', *Temple Bar*, November 1903, p. 572.

28 For a biography of William Perkin, see Simon Garfield, *Mauve* (London, 2000).

29 FMB's use of magenta was noted approvingly by George Bernard Shaw. 'Madox Brown is more of a realist than Rembrandt … You can all but breathe his open air, warm yourself in his sun … Rembrandt would have died rather than paint a cabbage unconditionally green, or meddle with those piercing aniline discords of colour which modern ingenuity has extracted from soot and other unpromising materials. Madox Brown took to Paisley shawls and magenta ribbons and genuine greengrocer's cabbages as kindly as Wagner took to 'false relation' in harmony …' *The Saturday Review*, 13 March 1897, 'Madox Brown, Watts and Ibsen'.

30 'from self in the looking glass': FMB is known to have used this method when working on *The Prisoner of Chillon* in 1856, *Diary*, p. 167

31 FMB 1865, no. 14.

32 'found the little picture still faulty, made Emma sit to me again at which she sulked.' *Diary*, p. 126.

33 *As You Like It*, II, vii.

34 NML, Rae papers, FMB to George Rae, 16 November 1874.

35 *Diary*, p. 7.

36 *Diary*, p. 82.

37 *Diary*, p. 153.

38 *Diary*, p. 135.

39 *Diary*, p. 57.

40 *Diary*, p. 132.

41 *Diary*, pp. 90–91.

42 *Diary*, p. 6–7.

43 *Diary*, p. 86.

44 *Diary*, p. 189.

45 *Diary*, p. 163.

46 *Diary*, pp. 180–81.

47 'A Taste of Cornwall' by Claire Hopley, 2005, www.womans-world.co.uk

48 'I am going to draw [Mary Blackmore]': Hueffer 1896, p. 267, FMB to Shields, 26 July 1871.

49 The drawing by Brown survives: *Mary Blackmore*, (Bennett 2010, 2, p. 371, B6).

50 Hunt 1905, I, p. 159. The 'List of Immortals' was reprinted in *PRB Journal*, p. 107.

51 All contained in *Thomas De Quincey: On Murder* ed. Robert Morrison (Oxford, 2006).

52 For historical investigation of the Ratcliffe Highway murders see T.A. Critchley and P.D. James, *The Maul and the Pear Tree*, London 1971.

53 Dante Gabriel Rossetti, 'Poem at the Paris Station', 1849.

54 Eric Partridge, *A Dictionary of English and American catch-phrases: from the sixteenth century to the present day*, London, 1977, p. 12.

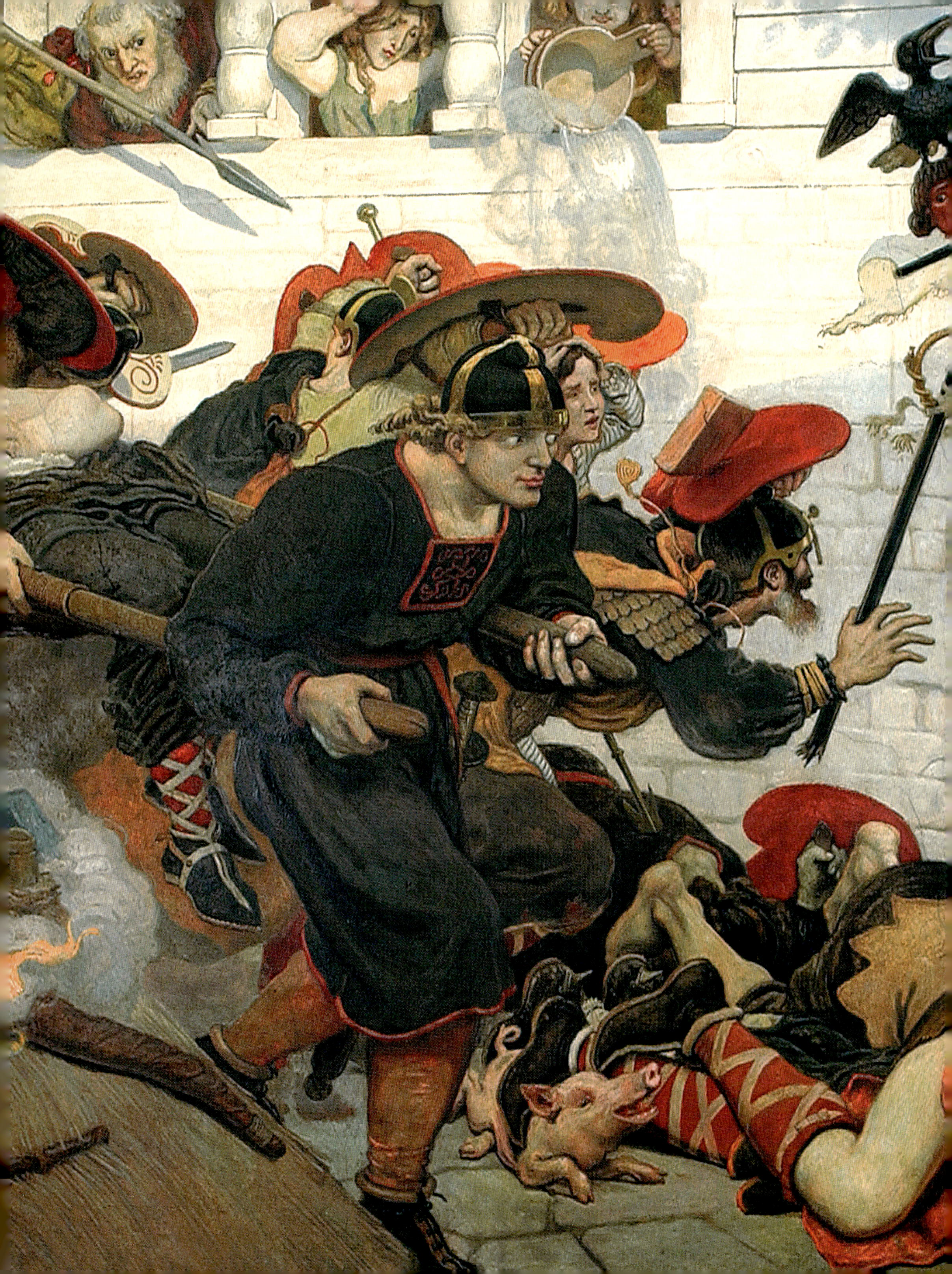

Ford Madox Brown's Humour

KENNETH BENDINER

There's something funny about Ford Madox Brown's Manchester Town Hall murals. Those large history paintings display Viking warriors who trip over pigs as they flee the city (fig. 23), an astronomer who drops his instruments at a key moment of scientific discovery (cat. 129), a great inventor in the textile industry trundled off in bed-linen to escape an angry mob of workers (cat. 133), and the teetotaler Duke of Bridgewater in a state of inebriation at the opening of the Bridgewater Canal (cat. 136). The entire set of murals, filled with naughty children and nagging wives, appears to undermine the dignity of Manchester, and this in the Town Hall, where one expects to see civic grandeur.

One might suppose that Brown held a grudge against the city: in one mural (cat. 127) a blind man with a muzzled dog announces anti-corruption laws, hardly a glorious vision of watchful municipal government. But these images represent only the most obvious and outlandish examples of a comic sensibility that runs throughout Brown's career. If you claim Brown's humour as a mode of attack, then you have to admit that he aimed his aggression at more than Manchester. His comedy is visible in all sorts of subjects: the life of Oliver Cromwell, ordinary family outings, the New Testament and Shakespeare's plays. Prior to late works such as the Town Hall murals, however, Brown usually kept his humour more quiet, marginal and sly. Even his best-known productions, *The Last of England* (cat. 58) and *Work* (cat. 61) include dashes of comedy while remaining serious reflections of modern social issues.

In the *Last of England*, a painting of the mass emigration of Britons in the nineteenth century, a Holy Family-like group of emigrants at the stern of a vessel bound for Australia stares somberly out of the canvas. Figures in the background react in various ways to the economic plight that has led them to seek a better life abroad. Brown represents them as comical grotesques, drunken and gap-toothed. In the catalogue of his one-man show of 1865, he described one of them as shaking his fist with 'curses at the land of his birth,' while 'his old mother reproves him for his foul-mouthed profanity'. On the ship's rail, just beneath the family in the foreground hang several cabbages, and at the back, a cabin boy takes turnips from a lifeboat aboard the vessel. Such vegetables, according to the artist, indicate that the voyage will be a long one. The swearing passengers and the humble vegetables wittily diminish the epic vision of modern British history. Brown noted in the 1865 catalogue that the *Last of England*'s cabin boy has voyaged so often to Australia that to him the whole affair of emigration is of little interest.[1] What some take as a development of momentous import to others seems just a routine incident.

A comic diminution of serious social concern also marks Brown's *Work*. That canvas, which served as the centerpiece of Brown's one-man exhibition in 1865, is one of the first major Western paintings to glorify common manual labourers, a daring enaction of social change in European art that looks forward to the muscular proletarian giants of twentieth-century communist imagery. Navvies boldly occupy the center of Brown's canvas, casting all else into shadow or background. It is a radical departure not just from the drunken or faceless peasants of Renaissance and Baroque art, but also from earlier nineteenth-century paintings of lower-class characters, where such people appear either as victims or neutral figures. Yet even in this groundbreaking

Fig. 23
Detail of cat. 120, The Expulsion of the Danes from Manchester, A.D. 910

painting, Brown introduces some comedy. A retarded boy, a hump-backed beer seller, philosophers who look like idlers, and a host of other less-than-magnificent types populate the crowded scene, along with amusing dogs and mischievous children. These subsidiary figures act as contrasts to the hard-working, confident navvies, a bitter social commentary, perhaps. But the surrounding figures also play comic roles that defuse some of the serious business of Brown's picture. He seems to mock most of these non-navvies, but not with the moralizing satire of William Hogarth (an artist whom Brown admired).[2] Brown's comedy here is different, more subtle, more marginal: it provides almost invisible little touches that offer something like Shakespearean comic relief, a respite from the artwork's grander themes. Brown added to the comedy in his written description of *Work*: 'Back in the distance we see the Assembly-room of the "Flamstead Institute of Arts", where Professor Snoox is about to repeat his interesting lecture on the habits of the domestic cat. Indignant pusses upon the roof are denying his theory in toto.'[3] (fig. 74, p. 192) Brown refused to keep his subjects straight-faced. If the comedy had appeared right in the foreground, as though central to his painting, the forceful socialist-like theme would completely crumble, and the common labourers would become a laughing stock. Brown managed to balance both perfectly.

Brown employed similar peripheral comedy in *Cromwell on His Farm* (cat. 87). The Puritan leader on horseback on his land in 1635 ponders his fate, God's design, and the future of the British nation. Will divine guidance sweep him to power? In contrast to these deep musings, at the lower right of the painting, a cook-maid calls the master to dinner. An everyday event invades the airy realm of Cromwell's concentration. What's more, as Cromwell rides through his fields, pigs and sheep gambol every which way: the estate is a riot of agricultural activity. The great man contemplates his place in the universe, but remains laughably unaware of his surroundings. Marginal humour acts like a punchline, as if the image were to be extended in time, with one viewing the dignified Oliver Cromwell first, and then, a moment later, seeing the humorous 'aside'. Brown's Cromwell remains an illustrious protagonist in the centre, a figure of respect. But the little comic events around the man tone down unquestioning adulation. With touches of amusement, Cromwell perhaps even seems more human.

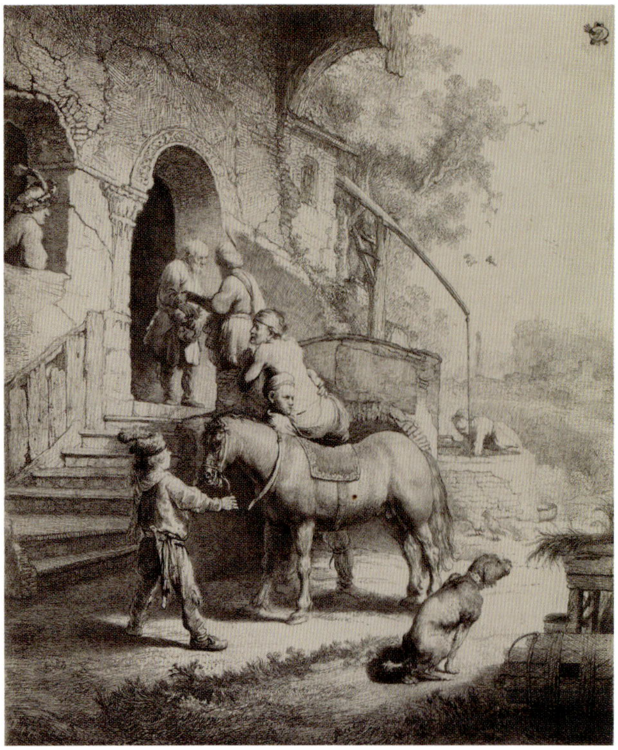

Fig. 24
Rembrandt van Rijn, The Good Samaritan, *1633. The British Museum, London*

It is hard, however, to retain dignity when surrounded by farmyard noises and Brown frequently deployed frisky animals to undercut his subjects. A woman in the middle distance feeds chickens in Brown's splendid landscape *An English Autumn Afternoon* (cat. 50). The domestic fowl (so different from the love-bird doves in the right foreground) form an unseemly contrast to the ecstatic vision of the English land and to the middle-class couple in the foreground, who contemplate the beauty of the scenery. Yet the commonplace chicken-feeding scene is so small that the viewer only half-remarks its presence, at least initially. In a similarly subtle vein, a large turkey, for no good reason, wanders into Brown's painting of an ordinary family's country excursion, *Out of Town* (cat. 54). The turkey tries to eat a child's bunch of grapes. Fowl even enter the precincts of Brown's religious pictures. In *Elijah and the Widow's Son* (cat. 77), the Biblical prophet has resurrected a young boy; the boy's mother kneels and clasps her hands in thankfulness; a miracle has occurred; and a hen in the right foreground flaps her wings while carrying a chick on her back. The hen and chick in some way allude to the

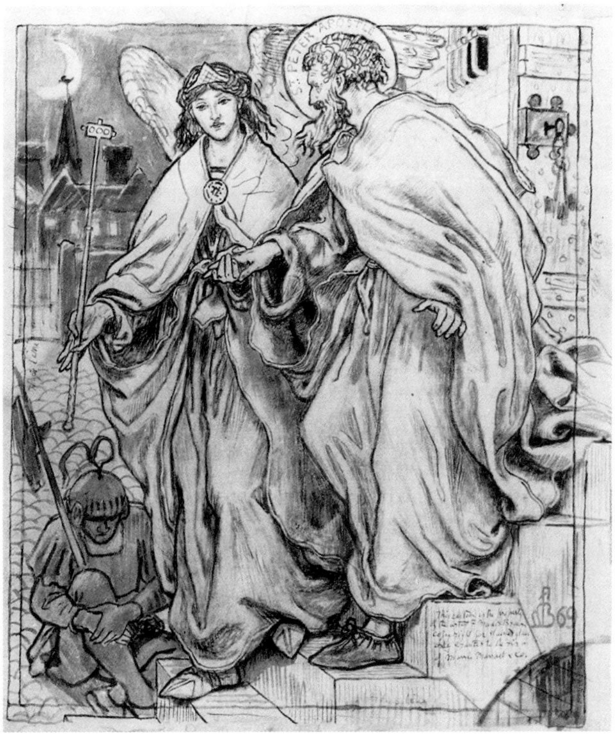

Fig. 25
Ford Madox Brown, stained glass cartoon for St. Peter delivered by the Angel, *1869. Private collection*

thankful mother and her reborn son, but they seem intrusive, distracting the viewer from the holy event. In the same way, in an etching of the *The Good Samaritan* by Rembrandt (fig. 24), a dog defecates in the foreground, while the figures of the New Testament parable further back in the scene engage in their good works. Rembrandt's outlandish dog, however, remains not only more vulgar than Brown's resurrection chickens, but also more prominent in the image. Brown's mother hen disturbs the important happening, but not so overtly as Rembrandt's animal. Nevertheless, in both images grand drama takes a beating, and is relieved by laughter. In another religious subject, the stained-glass design *St. Peter delivered by the Angel* (fig. 25), Brown discreetly manages to upset another miracle. The angel purportedly freed the apostle supernaturally; the iron prison doors opened in a miracle (Acts 12:1–19). In Brown's version a key rests in the prison door keyhole, hardly a sign of magical escape. The artist brings into question the higher reality of scripture. Perhaps the St. Peter design expresses Brown's atheistic leanings.[4] But the tiny questioning of the overall theme in the *St. Peter* falls well within the bounds of the artist's usual marginal humour. Brown evidently indulged his contrarian humour even in sacred imagery.

To return to secular subjects and animal antics, Brown's *Walton-on-the-Naze* (cat. 55) presents the back view of a pair of figures, male and female, who gaze upon a lovely landscape. On the right side of the painting, the gentleman points and 'descants learnedly on the beauty of the scene',[5] and at the left, a pair of mice appear, one of which stands up on its hind legs and gestures exactly as does the man at the right. The animal mimicry, though scarcely noticeable, just punctures the presumed exquisiteness of nature and those who would dilate upon beauty.

Art historians have given Brown's *The pretty baa-lambs* (cat. 49) a significant place in the development of Pre-Raphaelitism. It stands as one of the earliest portrayals of bright, natural sunlight in Pre-Raphaelite painting. But this Rococo pastoral subject gone realist (note the eighteenth-century costumes) also possesses some comedy, as the baby-talk title might suggest. The woman in the foreground directs her child to observe the 'pretty baa-lambs,' while the lady's maid dutifully gathers grass in a basket. Is the maid going to feed the animals from a basket? How understated and nearly invisible is this sly touch of Brownian humour. Once one finds this sort of muffled joke in a few of Brown's paintings, they seem everywhere in his art. He shows Romeo on a rope ladder at Juliet's balcony (fig. 26), but the young man's right foot has missed a rung, and no doubt he'll plunge to the ground in the next act. Isolde wails over her dead lover Tristram (cat. 98), but her little lap dog sits contentedly in the middle of the murder scene. A long-haired, beautiful, amorous, Rossetti-like woman in Brown's *Myosotis* holds a forget-me-not and seems lost in rapturous memory (fig. 27). But the forget-me-nots in the background are wilting, which implies that the woman's undying love will not last too long. Love, like angelic intervention, does not hold up under close inspection. Brown's John Wycliffe reads his translation of the Bible to John of Gaunt (cat. 33), but Gaunt appears bored and Wycliffe's Bible on the lectern is upside down. Even Brown's hero Geoffrey Chaucer does not escape. The poet reads his verse to an audience (cat. 34), but practically the only people who pay keen attention are a fool and a note-taking plagiarist.

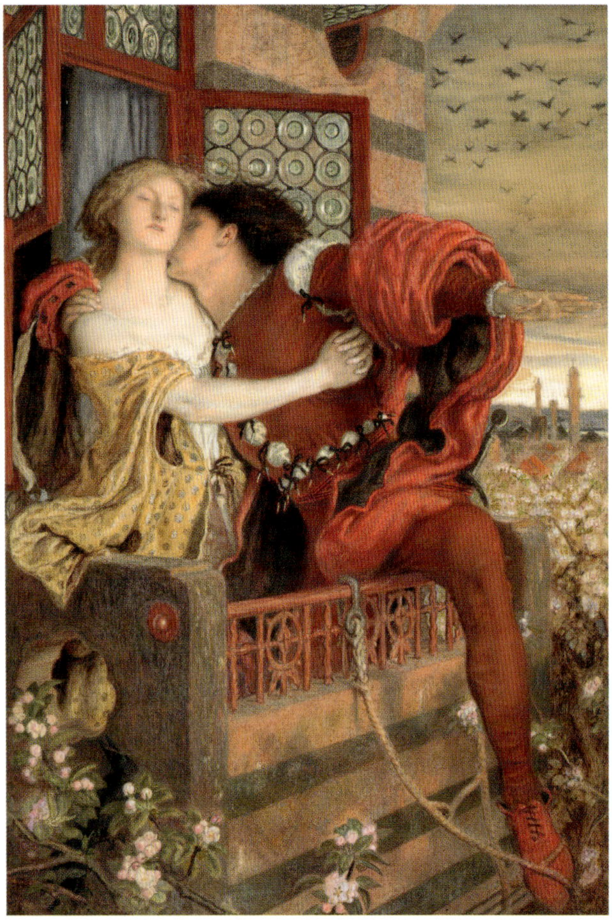

Fig. 26
Ford Madox Brown, Romeo and Juliet, *1867. The Whitworth Art Gallery, The University of Manchester*

Brown's marginal humour belongs to a certain strain in Western art. His comedy appears similar to that found in some well-known and revered paintings by the Old Masters. Raphael's *Sistine Madonna* (fig. 28), for example, displays the Virgin and Child and Saints in heaven with dignity and grandeur, but the little winged putti beneath the sacred figures look bored to tears. The magnificent, beautifully orchestrated deities receive a small kick in the pants by the *putti*, who find all this symmetrically balanced holiness tiresome. The august art of the sixteenth and seventeenth centuries frequently includes such wry asides. In Albrecht Dürer's woodcuts for the *Large Passion* and the *Small Passion* a ridiculously mannered dog, too frisky and fluffy to act seriously as a symbol of faithfulness, poses coyly in the Flagellation (fig. 29), wags his tail as Christ bears the cross, and wakes from a nap as Christ stands trial. Dürer's little dog is not so different from Brown's lapdog in *The Death of Sir Tristam*.

The comedy in medieval art, however, probably influenced Brown most. His taste for things Gothic and the archaizing doings of his acquaintances would have familiarized him with medieval marginal humour. In innumerable medieval manuscripts, one sees dignity and sacredness in the central illuminations and texts, but raucous humour in the margins. Dog-headed priests teach fox-headed students. Monkeys play organs. Small vignettes of monstrosities and folk tales and scatological activities crop up at the bottom of pages, and to the left and right of august visions of God.[6] We know that Brown and his Pre-Raphaelite friends consulted mid-nineteenth-century publications of medieval images.[7] Brown also visited the British Museum to see a French missal.[8] The Luttrell Psalter displays many marginal drolleries, including an image of a chick on the back of a hen (fig. 30), very like the fowl in *Elijah and the Widow's Son*. Brown's good friend Rossetti certainly studied medieval manuscripts closely. Rossetti's watercolour *Fra Pace* (1856; private collection) amusingly depicts a monk who uses a dead mouse as a model as he paints a manuscript border. In *The Wedding of St. George and the Princess Sabra* (1857; fig. 31, p. 42), Rossetti placed the severed head of the dragon in a little

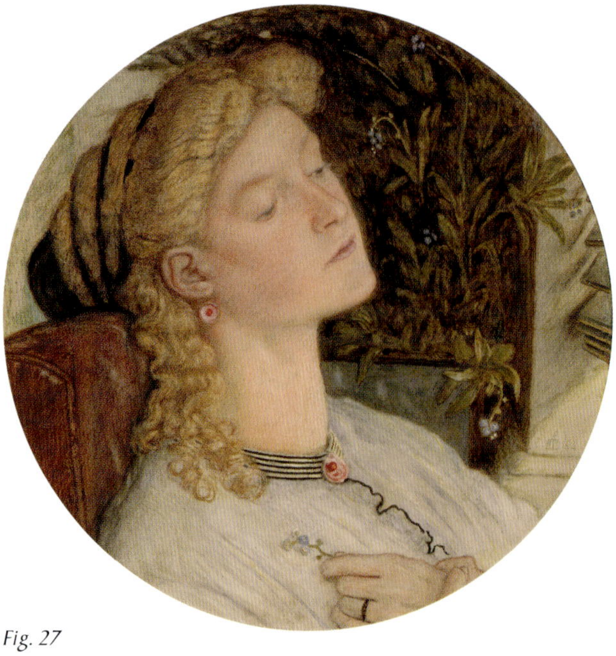

Fig. 27
Ford Madox Brown, Myosotis, *1864. Private collection/Albert Dawson Trust*

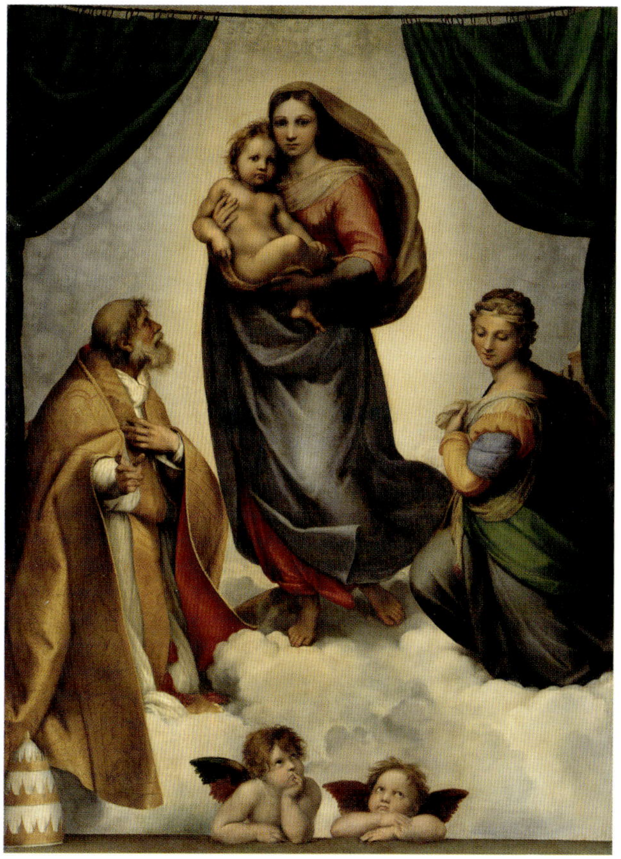

Fig. 28
Raphael, The Sistine Madonna, *1512/13. Gemäldegalerie Alte Meister, Staatliche Kunstsammlungen, Dresden*

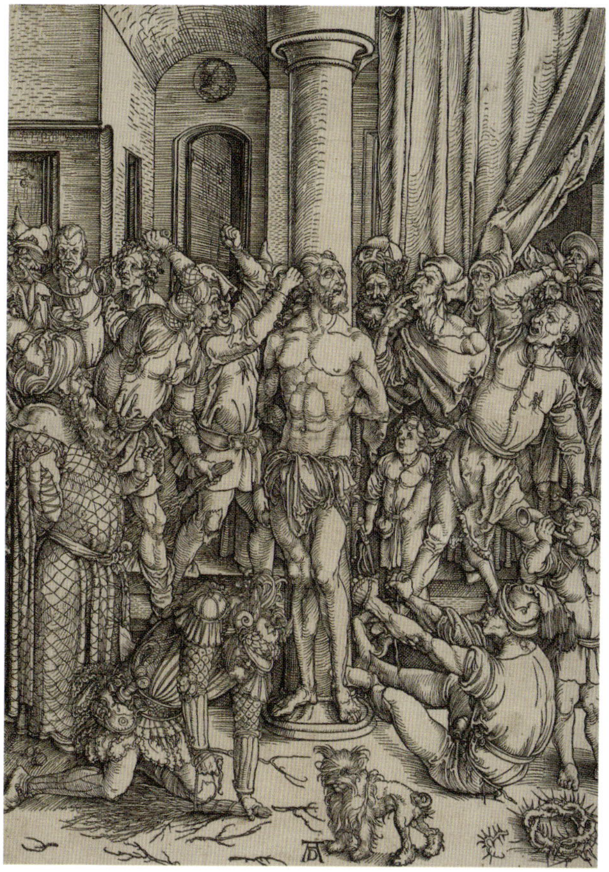

Fig. 29
Albrecht Dürer, The Flagellation from the Large Passion, *1497/1500. The British Museum, London*

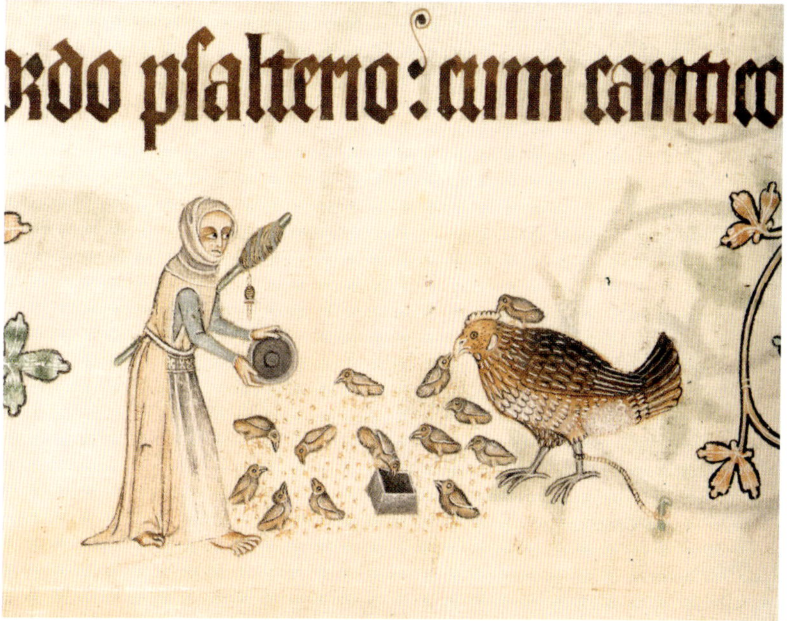

Fig. 30
Woman feeding a hen and chickens, *detail from the Luttrell Psalter, fol. 166v, 1525/35. The British Library, London*

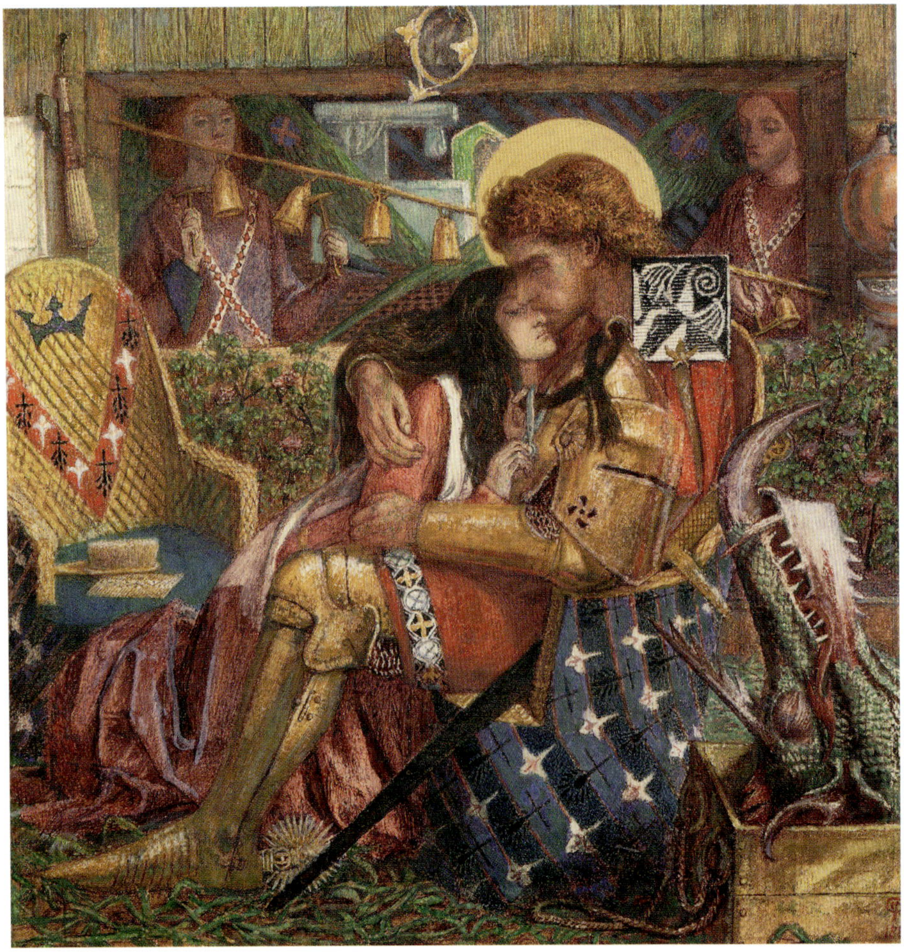

Fig. 31
Dante Gabriel Rossetti, The Wedding of St. George and the Princess Sabra, *1857. Tate*

wooden crate next to George's chair, as if it had been delivered by Fortnum & Mason for the occasion. How silly and how like the little jokes at the sides of Brown's works. Both these Pre-Raphaelites enjoyed their medieval chuckles. Even Rossetti, however, could not countenance some of Brown's grotesqueries. Rossetti wrote to Mrs. William Morris in 1879 about Brown's stained-glass window designs for the church of St. Editha, Tamworth (cats. 102–5):

> Really I must say they are inconceivable. Every figure (it is a long series) is passing one hand through the stone mullion of the window into the next panel of glass!! – each panel containing one figure. It is called the Story of St. Edith. I must say if this series was what reduced Top [William Morris] to desperation, I think every one wd have sympathized with him [in firing Brown from the Morris firm] if he had only shown the cartoons. However, if too public, the incident might have ended in a strait waistcoat for old B.[9]

Rossetti's irritation here is what one also finds in the remarks of several nineteenth-century commentators on Brown's art. A German critic in 1845 noted that there was something peculiar about Brown's *The Body of Harold brought before William the Conqueror* (cat. 23). Instead of dealing with the great historical significance of the Norman invasion of England, Brown had represented common soldiers complaining that Harold's huge body was really too heavy to lug around. The German critic remarked that 'something else than the enormous gigantic size of the adversary could have been exhibited; and the ridicule … could have been introduced as secondary in a poetical historical representation.'[10] William Butler Yeats in 1890 described Brown's *Baptism of Edwin* (cat. 118) as 'a picture that I cannot persuade myself to like chiefly, I think, because I have taken a violent hatred for

"Eadwins" himself, with his clerical beard, and because I do not know what he has done with his feet in that very small fount.'[11] And a critic in the *Saturday Review* in 1867 complained that Brown's 'energy is not accompanied by moderation and good taste', and noted that in *Cordelia's Portion* (cat. 79) 'there is an overcrowding and obtrusiveness of minor material which, though common in the [Pre-Raphaelite] school to which Mr. Madox Brown belongs, is a fault and a hindrance. What is the use of the dog's paws under the table?... and the dog's head does not easily explain itself; many spectators fail to see what it is'.[12] Are the dogs in *Cordelia's Portion* humorous distractions, or part of the overall clutter that makes the scene look realistic instead of artificially staged? Realism and humour can be intertwined. That certainly occurred to two further commentators on Brown's comedy, his son-in-law, William Michael Rossetti, and Brown's grandson, Ford Madox Ford.

In 1886, with Brown's approval, William Michael Rossetti published 'Ford Madox Brown: Characteristics' in the *Century Guild Hobby Horse* magazine, and there said of Brown that 'one of his most marked characteristics is that of combining with elevated subject-matter, and a passionate dramatic, and impressive general treatment, a considerable spice of the familiar, or even the grotesque or semi-grotesque. He will be dignified, but "stuck up" he will never be.' Rossetti cited as examples the Manchester murals, where 'the [Roman] general's wife has dyed her hair, and a small boy kicks out at a "nigger": if King Edwin is baptized in York, there is an old Saxon nobleman who cannot manage to kneel down without the aid of two crutches: if the Danes are driven out of Manchester, a sow and her litter bear their part in overthrowing the invader; and so on constantly in Brown's compositions.' Rossetti went on to liken Brown's humour to Shakespeare's, and to link him to Hogarth, but unlike the latter, noted Rossetti, Brown 'does not paint pictures of which the external aspect is mainly comic, satirical or burlesque: but he likes very much to call a spade a spade (pictorially) even when the main subject is of a highly elevated or exalted kind.' He added, 'While occupied with the large outlines of subject-matter large and grave, he can relish none the less what is peculiar in itself, or what, from familiarity of association, appears peculiar or even odd in relation to historic dignity; an interest which, being real and personal, neither disdains this subsidiary familiar element, nor forces that ampler dignified element into artificial and bloodless pomposity.'[13] Amid William Michael Rossetti's tortured prose, one can discern a realist interpretation of Brown's comedy: the funny parts deflate 'bloodless pomposity' and bring the grandiose subject down to the familiar world.

Ford Madox Ford in his biography of Brown explains the artist's humour similarly.

> In *Romeo and Juliet*, the *Don Juan*, and the *Cordelia's Portion* there are none of the touches of purposely bathetic humour that so strongly distinguishes Madox Brown's work. There are no girls with ducks under their arms to call the Cromwells from their grim musings to the immediate necessity of the dinner that waits.
>
> The frescoes [at Manchester Town Hall] on the other hand, are full of such episodes. Roman children kick litter-bearers, thurifers deride each other, pigs upset ferocious warriors, or children mock great scientists, and seem to utter the continual 'after all' of Nature herself.
>
> In his art Madox Brown's attitude toward life was two-fold.
>
> In the conception of his pictures he entirely identified himself with the hero of the picture, and seemed to become for the time a grim mystic, a passionate lover, or an abstracted scientist. But once the central idea was evolved and embodied, he sympathized with the unsympathetic outer world, the unconcerned, wondering child of the *Entombment*, or the laughing, ignorant cook-maid of the *Cromwell on his Farm*.[14]

This is the realist interpretation of Brown's humour, presented in the nineteenth century by two writers who knew the artist well and it is still valid today. The comic elements bring Brown's subjects down to earth with a bump. Realism figured prominently in the Pre-Raphaelites' art theory, and certainly remained a concern for Brown over many decades. His marginal humour tints Rococo pastoral fantasies, heroic historical melodramas, the worship of nature, and the desperation of economic woe just enough to make the themes seem more real, more believable, more true to normal experience. Brown's comedy chips away at the pedestals of the high and mighty, and makes the viewer question some of his subjects' pretensions. But there are other possible interpretations of Brown's humour if one takes into account the theories of humour espoused by several writers over time.

Aristotle and Plato generally disapproved of humour, in contrast to seriousness, which too often caused vulgarity and pain. But Aristotle apparently also saw comedy as catharsis: a means to unleash repressed emotions, which could be beneficial. He touched upon the power of humour to release the hidden features of the psyche, something that Sigmund Freud would take up in the twentieth century, and it perhaps applies to Brown's art if we analyze our emotional responses to his works.[15] At the time of the Roman Empire, Dio Chrysostom found a different sort of value in comedy as a way to reveal the false, the ugly and the sinful. He saw humour as a moral tool.[16] But do Brown's humorous works teach us moral truths? What good or evil becomes apparent with the vegetable mockery of emigrants, or the invasion of Cromwell's visions with ordinariness, or the stumbling love of Romeo, or the pigs who upset Vikings? Events are brought to understandable levels by these comic touches, maybe, but they do not add up to moralizing satire. Brown is not like Hogarth. Several commentators on comedy probed further into the psychological effects of humour. In the seventeenth century, the Earl of Shaftsbury claimed that humour and the laughter it provoked produced amiability in the viewer or audience. In the same period, Thomas Hobbes, in contrast, claimed that humour and laughter produced in the viewer or listener a reprehensible feeling of pride and superciliousness.[17] The viewer of Brown's works might ask themselves whether they feel more open and amiable or more proudly superior to the Vikings who trip over pigs or Cromwell called to dinner. Are the Vikings contemptible stupid brutes or just people who occasionally get into trouble? Does the laughter smack of disdain or fellowship? In either case, humour remains a contrast to seriousness, and certainly causes us to pause and re-think what we see, but aren't these essayists' descriptions of human psychology rather simplistic? Concepts of amiability and condescension don't possess enough breadth or depth to describe the viewer's mind. In the nineteenth century, Charles Baudelaire dissected the different kinds of humour in painting, especially pure fantasy humour as against reality-based humour (none of Brown's comedy seems set in otherworldly realms), but Baudelaire also took up Hobbes' view of humour, and saw at least some forms of laughter as symptomatic of humanity's inner demons.[18] Two other nineteenth-century writers on comedy gave more realist interpretations. Champfleury saw caricature as a means to liberate the artist from artificial ideals in art.[19] Yet for all his grotesquerie, can any of Brown's images be called 'caricatures'? His funny jabs are too peripheral and subtle. Again, he's not like Hogarth; Brown didn't portray big-nosed buffoons or outlandish fops. Ralph Waldo Emerson more simply saw comedy as the expression of the disparity between the ideal and things as they are.[20] Emerson's view seems most sensible in light of Brown's works, but Emerson fails to tackle the emotional forces embedded in humour and laughter. Freud's study of jokes, however, filled the gap, and took up the psychological aspects of comedy more fully than any previous theorist. Freud saw jokes as employing the same unconscious techniques of wish-fulfillment that he found in dreams: displacement, substitution, and indirect representation. In jokes (and humour in general), inhibitions break down, hostility against authority breaks out, and the freedom of childhood play is recaptured. In some kinds of humour, wrote Freud, the restraints of decorum, rationality and morality can be challenged, and free childhood pleasure attained through a kind of Aristotelian catharsis. In other forms of humour, the most abhorrent conditions become a bearable laughing matter, as something like Shaftsbury's amiability arises. Gallows humour exemplifies this kind of comedy.[21]

With Freud in mind, can't Brown's humour, no matter how sly and marginal, be seen as an attack on authority, on literature, government, religion, love, beauty, art and history? Perhaps his humour was some form of getting even. Could it have been a vituperative reaction to personal dissatisfaction, humiliation and lack of worldly success, or a path to find childish delight in opposing parental rule (throughout his adult life, he depended on the income from properties he inherited from his mother)? This is not wholly convincing. Humour appears in Brown's art long before he could claim to be a failure in the art world. His submission to the Westminster murals contest (cat. 23) was already fraught with comedy. We know little of the private world of his upbringing. But then again, this painter in England, born and trained abroad, a Pre-Raphaelite without membership of the Pre-Raphaelite Brotherhood, a founder of William Morris's decorating firm who was fired by Morris, a founder of the Hogarth Club who was forbidden to exhibit furniture designs at the club's exhibitions, might indeed have seen himself as a defamed outsider, a person ready to attack an unreceptive world. Brown certainly sometimes appeared cantankerous. Even his adoring grandchildren noted Brown's furious reactions to perceived enemies and insults.[22] His diary and letters frequently include outcries against Royal Academicians, John Ruskin, critics, and his pathetic financial state. In a letter of 1869 to the painter Frederic Shields, Brown wrote, 'However things look too threatening—nothing less than a combination of all England against one or two poor devils, even the Edit'r of the Athenaeum seems now to cut out anything [F.G.] Stephens attempts to write about me or any of my name.'[23] Some deep well of disgruntlement may explain Brown's humour, even if one accepts the realist interpretation of his comedy. Realism is aggressive. Realism destroys ideals. It tries to see the world without cosmetics or pretense or metaphor. Humour is a form of realism that can also respond to unconscious personal wishes and angry needs.

Whatever Brown might have had in mind, the viewer's response to Brown's humour demands attention. What happens when we see those anti-Professor cats on the roof of the Flamstead Institute of Arts in *Work*? What occurs when we notice the gesticulating mouse in *Walton-on-the-Naze*? We take a step back, laugh and reconsider the event depicted. Silliness invades the proposed serious subject and we're given an alternative reading. Brown's peripheral humour, once noticed, offers us not just the joy of upsetting authority, but an opportunity to stop and get a second opinion. With a tinge of modernist open-endedness, we become more active participants in the picture, able to decide the image's meaning for ourselves. Brown's humour engages the viewer and his opinions, inviting him to get involved. And as we stand before *The Last of England*, and take in the amusing details, an atmosphere of intimacy arises (Freud likened joke-telling to seduction). It's as if the painter had sidled up to us, gently poked us in the ribs, and whispered in our ear, 'Not to worry. If the ship goes down, there are plenty of lifeboats. The salad greens will be saved.'

1 Brown, 1865, no. 14, [Bendiner, 1998, p. 37]

2 Brown praised Hogarth for studying "nature unassisted' in Brown 1848), p. 531 .

3 Brown 1865, description of *Work*

4 See Mary E. Burtis, *Moncure Conway 1832–1907*,New Brunswick, N.J., 1952 and Warren Sylvester Smith, *The London Heretics, 1870–1914*, New York, 1968.

5 Brown, 1865, no. 27, [Bendiner, 1998, p. 139].

6 Lilian Randall, *Images in the Margins of Gothic Manuscripts*. Berkeley, CA, 1966 and Michael Camille, *Image on the Edge: The Margins of Medieval Art*,Cambridge, MA, 1992.

7 Treuherz 1984, pp. 153–69.

8 *Diary*, p. 85 (30 August, 1854).

9 Bryson and Troxell 1971, no. 97, Dante Gabriel Rossetti to Jane Morris, undated letter (probably 1878 or 1879).

10 Rabin 1978 p. 78 (Comments on *The Body of Harold* by Dr. Foerster, originally in the *Kunstblatt*, translated and published in the *Art Journal* in 1845, p. 127.)

11 W.B. Yeats, 'The Arts and Crafts: An Exhibition at William Morris's,' *Providence (Rhode Island) Sunday Journal*, 26 October, 1890, repr. in Stansky 1985, p. 273.

12 *Saturday Review*, March 1867, cited in Bennett 1988, p. 44.

13 W.M. Rosssetti, 1886, pp. 48–54.

14 Hueffer 1896, pp. 421–22.

15 Plato, *Republic*, 388e, *Plato's Republic*, trans. P. Shorey, Loeb Classical Library , Cambridge, MA, 1946, pp. 211–12. Plato, *Laws*, 816e, and *Philebus*, 49e, *Plato, Laws*, vol. II, trans. R.G. Bury, Loeb Classical Library, Cambridge, MA, 1925, p. 97, Plato, *The Statesman, Philebus, Ion*, Loeb Classical Library, Cambridge MA, 1925, p. 339. Aristotle, *Poetics*, 1449a, *Aristotle, The Poetics, Longinus on the Sublime, Demetritus on Style*, Loeb Classical Library Cambridge, MA, 1932, pp. 17–21. Aristotle, *Poetics I with the Tractatus Coislinianus*, trans. Richard Janko, Indianapolis, IN, 1987, pp. 43–46. Richard Janko, *Aristotle on Comedy* London, 1984.

16 Dio Chrysostomus, *Orations*, 2.4, Dio Chrisostum, trans. J.W. Cohoon, Loeb Classical Library, Cambridge, MA, 1932, p. 53.

17 Anthony Ashley Cooper, Earl of Shaftsbury, *Characteristics of Men, Manners, Opeinioins, Times*, J.M. Robertson, ed., Indianapolis, IN, 1964. Thomas Hobbes, *The English Works of Thomas Hobbes*, ed., William Molesworth London, 1839–45, III, pp. 27, 46. See also Stanley Grean, *Shaftsbury's Philosophy of Religion and Ethics*, Athens, OH, 1967, chap. 8.

18 Charles Baudelaire, *De l'essence du rire et generalment du comique dans les arts plastiques*, Paris, 1855.

19 Champfleury (Jules Husson), *Histoire de la Caricature* Paris, 1865.

20 R. W. Emerson, 'Comic Theory' (1843), in Paul Lauter, ed., *Theories of Comedy*, Garden City, N.Y., 1964, pp. 378–87.

21 S. Freud, *Jokes and their Relation to the Unconscious*, 1905, vol. III of the *Standard Edition of the Complete Psychological Works of Sigmund Freud*, trans. James Strachey, London, 1960.

22 See Hueffer 1896, pp. 247–51, 336, 381–82; Soskice, 1921, pp. 33–34. For other instances of cantankerous character, Newman and Watkinson, 1991, pp. 192–93.

23 Princeton, FMB to Frederic Shields, 6 February, 1869.

This essay includes some material previously published in Bendiner 1998.

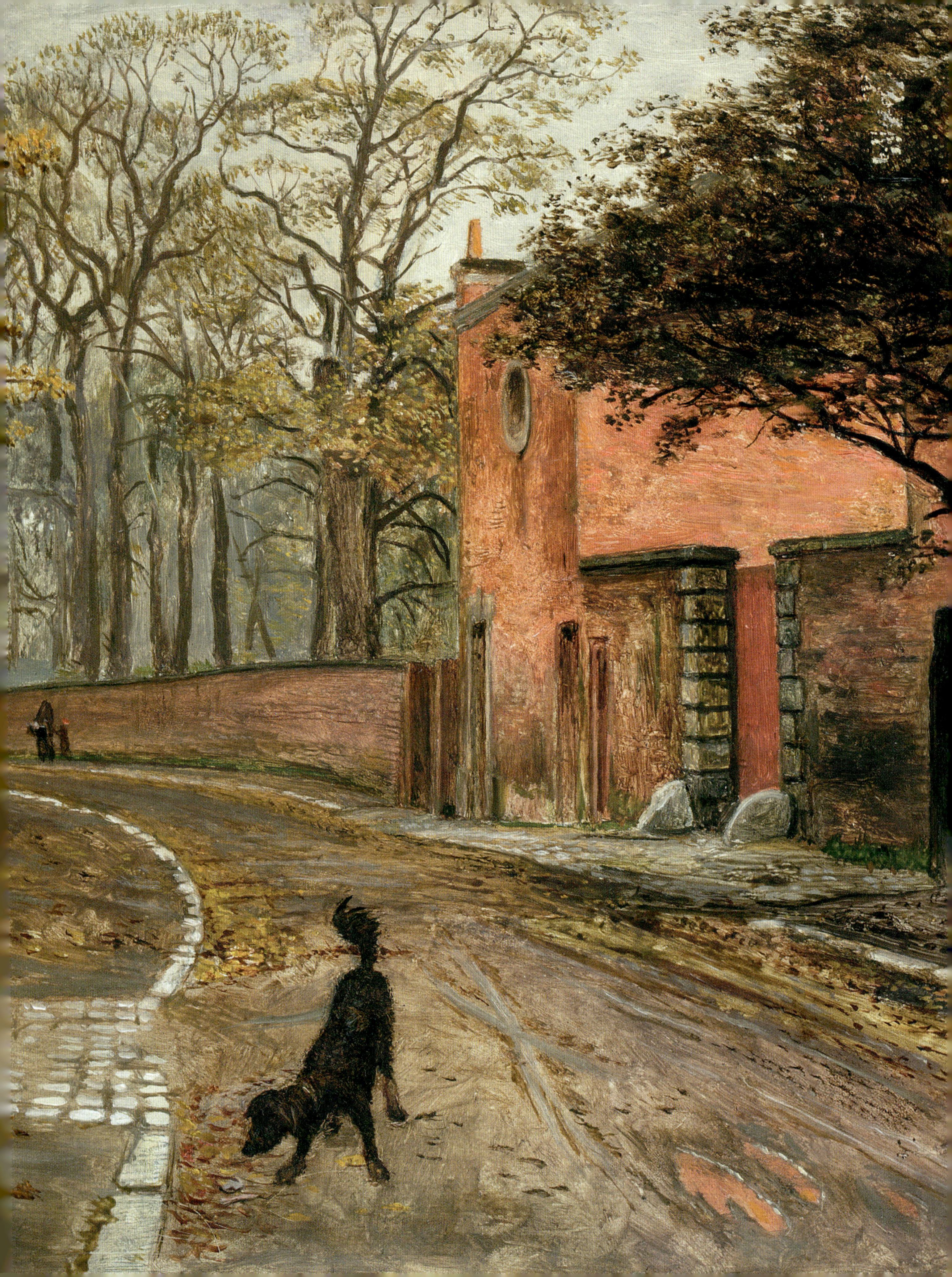

Ford Madox Brown in Manchester

JULIAN TREUHERZ

'What chance remains of a Common Council deciding reasonably on matters of art?'[1] Brown's despairing words about his experience of painting the murals in Manchester Town Hall between 1879 and 1893 (fig. 33) suggest an inevitable conflict between philistines and aesthetes. The truth was more complicated. The process of commissioning and supervising their execution was a convoluted and long-drawn-out saga, where artistic ideals and politics co-existed uneasily, mixed with bureaucratic inertia and occasional elements of farce. But although the city council as a whole was responsible, the credit for the murals rested with a few dedicated individuals with the drive and persistence to pursue their vision. Some of these were members of the council some not. And during the process, Brown made friends in Manchester, took part in social and cultural life and acquired a following in the city resulting in the purchase by the City Gallery of his masterpiece *Work*.

The opportunity of painting the murals was just what Brown needed at that moment in his career. He was in his late fifties. His training in Antwerp with Baron Gustav Wappers (fig. 3, p. 11) had equipped him to paint large mural compositions, and in his youth he had tried, but failed, to obtain a commission to paint murals in the Houses of Parliament. He had only ever painted one picture on the same scale as a mural, his vast *Chaucer*, much larger than the better known version in the Tate (cat. 34). *Chaucer* had been a commercial failure: it was never sold to a private collector but passed through the hands of dealers until Brown himself bought it back in 1863. He finally managed to sell it to the Art Gallery of New South Wales, Sydney in 1876, twenty-five years after its completion (fig. 58, p. 130).

Around 1875, when the possibility of the Manchester commission arose, Brown desperately needed work. He had never been a high earner; the 1850s, when he was producing what are now regarded as his greatest paintings, were years of poverty and hardship, and those works that he could sell

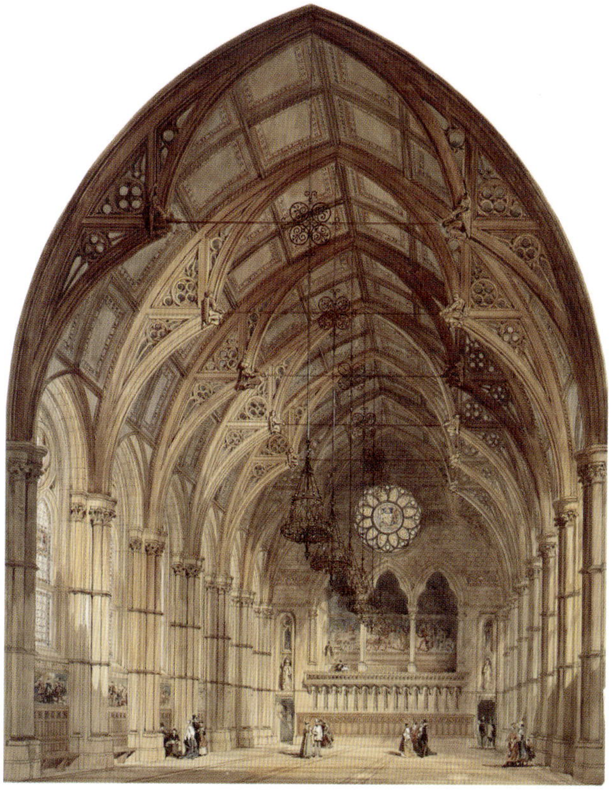

Fig. 33
Alfred Waterhouse, The Great Hall, Manchester Town Hall, *1868. Victoria and Albert Museum*

Fig. 32
Detail of cat. 152, Platt Lane

went for derisory prices. By 1865, when he held his one-man exhibition in London, the position had improved but from the later 1860s his earnings dropped back again. His outgoings had increased after moving from Highgate to Fitzroy Square in 1865 and to supplement his earnings he had to resort to the hack work of retouching portraits and to giving lectures. By the mid 1870s his most loyal patrons were no longer collecting;[2] he had recently suffered a personal tragedy in the death of his beloved son Oliver in 1875; and his wife's addiction to the bottle was a continuing problem. The Manchester commission offered the prospect of a change of scene, a steady income and the opportunity to realise his early artistic ideals.

Brown had no special connection with Manchester. His first recorded visit was in 1848 when he saw the annual exhibition at the Royal Manchester Institution (RMI) en route to the Lake District. He exhibited at the RMI in the early 1850s but was not a regular there. Two of his paintings had been in the great Manchester Art Treasures Exhibition of 1857 (cats. 53, 75): apart from the work of the Pre-Raphaelites, the only picture he remembered from his visit to that exhibition was the Wilton Diptych (National Gallery).[3] In the mid-1860s he had sold a few of his works to Manchester collectors. In many ways, Brown had stronger links with Liverpool where he had found an early patron in the tobacco merchant John Miller, purchaser of *Waiting* (cat. 56), and where he twice won the first prize at the Liverpool Academy, for *Jesus washing Peter's Feet* (cat. 75) in 1856 and for *Chaucer* in 1858. Through the support of Miller, Brown was introduced to local collectors such as George Rae, who in 1861 bought *An English Autumn Afternoon* (cat. 50).

The initial link between Brown and Manchester was the Manchester artist Frederic Shields (fig. 34). Born in Hartlepool, Shields had settled in Manchester about 1847, where he worked as a jobbing engraver but also studied at the city's School of Design. The budding artist came under the spell of the Pre-Raphaelites; his first sight of a painting by Brown, *King Lear* (cat. 36), seen at the RMI when he was about twenty, made a deep impression, and he later recalled that at the 1857 Manchester Art Treasures Exhibition *Jesus washing Peter's Feet* although 'hung at the very roof' still 'held me riveted'.[4] He engineered an introduction to Rossetti, and through him met Brown. Shields idolized his new friends and did everything he could to help them. He proved to be a stalwart promoter of Brown in Manchester: he introduced Brown to one of his own patrons, the Manchester calico printer Frederick Craven, who bought *The Nosegay* (cat. 93) in 1865. When another of Craven's commissions from Brown, *Elijah and the Widow's Son* (cat. 77), did not win the Heywood prize for the best picture at the RMI 1869 exhibition, Shields leapt to Brown's defence in the Manchester newspapers. And in 1874 when *Cromwell on his Farm* and *Henry and Millicent Fawcett* (cats. 87, 97) were on display at the RMI, Shields praised them extravagantly in a lecture to the Manchester Literary Club.

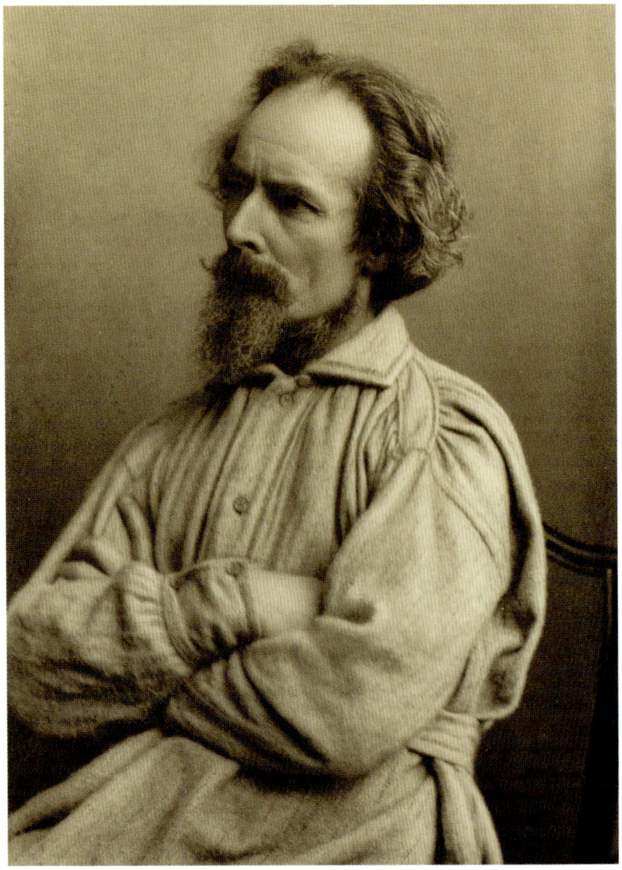

Fig. 34
Frederic Shields, photograph by Elliot and Fry, 1903, from The Life and Letters of Frederic Shields, *Ernestine Mills, ed., 1912*

It was probably through Shields that Brown met another Mancunian who became a close friend and supporter. This was the frame-maker Charles Rowley (cat. 150) who met Brown in 1875, when Rowley bought the monochrome cartoon for *Cordelia's Portion* (see cat. 79). Rowley stayed with Brown in

London and put Brown up on his visits to Manchester. Like Shields, Rowley regarded Brown as a neglected genius and wanted to help him. 'Anything legitimate I will do. I grieve to think that these men are so stupid that they cannot see that you perhaps the fittest man now on the planet, could do that for them which wd. be an honour to their city & to yourself.'[5] Shields and Rowley paved the way for Brown to get the murals commission, but the process was unexpectedly lengthy and hazardous.

Shields was an old acquaintance of Alfred Waterhouse, the architect of the new Town Hall; it was entirely Waterhouse's idea to have murals in his building. It was a personal enthusiasm of his, in pursuance of which he himself did not expect payment. Waterhouse designed spaces for mural paintings running right through the suite of ceremonial rooms fronting Albert Square as well as in the Great Hall, although in the event, only the panels in the Great Hall were filled. The murals were part of Waterhouse's extensive decorative programme that can be seen all over the Town Hall, including sculpture, armorials and symbolic emblems such as the bees, the interlaced strands of cotton and the cotton plants incorporated into tiles and decorative painting.

Yet Waterhouse must have been aware of the divergence between ideal and achievement in the recent history of mural paintings in British public buildings. On the one hand, murals were considered to be a good thing: they were a way of providing patronage for artists, they promoted history painting, still in theory regarded as the highest form of art, and they exposed the general public to art. On the other hand, the most ambitious recent British scheme, the murals in the Palace of Westminster, was generally regarded as a failure. With the honourable exceptions of Dyce and Maclise, the artists involved did not have the ability to design on the grand scale required, their works lacked conviction and many of them had faded, darkened or cracked within a few years of being painted. It was therefore bold if not rash of Waterhouse to plan murals in his new Town Hall. As the building itself neared completion, he sought advice widely on the murals before making recommendations to the Decorations and Furnishings Sub-Committee, formed in January 1876 to deal with the internal decoration.[6] On this committee he had an ally, Councillor Joseph Thomson, an Ancoats mill-owner, bibliophile and local historian who was 'most anxious to teach the people that Manchester has a history of which they may be proud ... something to brighten the age and quicken the pulse'. Thompson felt that the employment of Brown would relieve the scheme 'from the possibility of an Agnew-octopus embrace'.[7] Thompson took an active role on the committee, corresponding with artists and compiling a list of possible subjects for the murals.

At the April meeting of the subcommittee, Waterhouse put forward the names of Brown and Shields together with two lesser-known artists E.J. Gregory and John Dawson Watson but, nervous of the artists' lack of experience with murals, the architect had second thoughts. On the suggestion of Thompson, who had been to Belgium to look at carillons for the Town Hall, and of Beresford Hope, the British Minister at Brussels, Waterhouse went to Belgium to examine the paintings of two Belgian artists, Godfried Guffens and Jan Sweerts.[8] They had proven experience of mural paintings, having decorated the town halls of Ypres and Courtrai and the Antwerp Stock Exchange, and their names were put to the committee.[9] Rowley was scathing, writing to Brown 'None of the decoration Committee have any feeling for Art & I fear Waterhouse is no better.'[10] 'Can he be managed? That is the question ... These foreigners with their acres of work done & to be seen will I fear step in because they can show just what they can do.'[11] At the same time Waterhouse was grappling with the problem of selecting the best technique for the murals. Guffens and Sweerts had recommended waterglass, but the English artists were not in favour.[12] Other media considered included true fresco ('out of the question in this country, especially in Manchester' because of the damp), wax encaustic, oil on copper and even mosaic.[13] 'I have collected a great mass of evidence about the wall paintings but I must say that the more I talk to the painters, the more confused I become', wrote Waterhouse in December 1876, more than a little out of his depth.[14]

By the following summer, Waterhouse had devised a new plan recommending Brown and Shields to each paint six of the twelve murals in the Great Hall, while the other rooms were to be painted by a group of English artists including Walter Crane and W.F. Yeames (later to gain fame for *And when did you see your Father?*). But then another group, the Manchester Academy of Fine Arts, entered the fray, writing to the newspapers and sending a delegation to the Town Hall to demand that their members should paint the murals in the lesser rooms.[15]

At this, Brown very nearly lost patience, asking Waterhouse to inform the committee that if the 'group of nobodies' from Manchester were involved, he might withdraw altogether.[16] In the meantime, the Council was asking questions about the total cost of the murals in all of the rooms: 'Too absurd to think that the Council will stop at this paltry sum of £9000 for the decoration of the rooms … Yesterday we passed a Water Scheme to cost 3 millions but any flea-bite in the way of Art only irritates them', wrote Rowley.[17] But although the committee in December 1877 agreed that Brown and Shields should proceed with the Great Hall (leaving aside both the questions of the medium and the other rooms), the two artists were left in limbo for several months whilst a contract was being drawn up, leaving everyone, even the councillors uncertain: 'There is evidently a screw loose either on your side or the Committee's. Everybody thinks you and Shields are pegging away at the Manchester work. Now surely the matter will be cleared up.'[18]

In the meantime another bombshell was launched when William Axon, a distinguished local antiquarian and former City Librarian took exception to another aspect of the scheme, the subjects of the murals. Some time before, Councillor Thompson had drawn up a long list of about 250 possible subjects. From these Shields and Waterhouse selected what in their view was 'the most comprehensive epitome of the rise and progress of Manchester that can be compressed into 12 pictures' and after some discussion a list was approved in August 1878.[19] It was this list that Axon attacked in a long and pedantic letter to the Mayor, Abel Heywood.[20]

Axon's points are dealt with in detail in the catalogue entries for individual murals; he picked out a number of factual errors, and criticised the mythical or fanciful nature of several subjects, but his main objection was that some events – the baptism of Edwin at York, the trial of Wycliff in London and the John Kay incident in Bury – did not even take place in Manchester. This was undeniable, but Thompson and the artists felt that even in these cases the events were significant for the city, representing respectively the coming of Christianity, the beginnings of nonconformism, and the importance of machinery. Brown felt that Axon wrongly expected art to be '*documentary*, instead of as it should be *typical*, and calculated to arouse our sympathies for certain great ideas and beautiful phases of nature'.[21] The programme of the murals underlined the importance of Christianity, nonconformism, commercial integrity, philanthropy, education and science in Manchester's history; it included the textile industry, the basis of Manchester's nineteenth-century prosperity, albeit depicted in historical guise; and it had a more radical localist agenda, portraying Manchester and Mancunians as independent and anti-authoritarian.

Axon's criticism led to some adjustments in the subjects but politics rather than antiquarian pedantry caused a far more significant change in the programme. Shields and Brown wished to close the series with the Peterloo Massacre to represent the nineteenth century. This was an important event in itself, an opportunity to represent the conflict between radicalism and the forces of law, but the artists felt it had a wider significance as it led to the Reform and Free Trade movements which were crucial in the making of nineteenth-century Manchester. The artists also wanted Peterloo because it was 'dramatically pictorial.'[22] But they found themselves at the centre of a bitter political dispute. The committee rejected Peterloo as politically divisive. Shields wrote a private letter to Thompson fulminating against the Conservative councillors and 'their detestation of that outrage on the right of public meeting'. He accused them of suppressing free speech,[23] but it was to no avail. Various alternatives for contemporary subjects were considered for the last scene of the cycle, including the opening of the Manchester and Liverpool Railway; the arrival of first bale of cotton at the end of cotton famine; the reception of Walker and Richardson on their triumphant return from London after the repeal of the fustian tax; and the procession celebrating the passing of the 1832 Reform Bill enfranchising Manchester and Salford. In the end it was agreed to drop not only Peterloo but a subject depicting the Jacobite rising showing the Old Pretender reviewing the Manchester Regiment, and to close the series with the Bridgewater Canal and John Dalton subjects, representing transport and science. Thus, although numerous details in many of the paintings still convey the localist agenda, the radical element in the original programme was eliminated.

In the meantime, in July 1878 Brown, in London, had started work on the cartoon for *The Baptism of Edwin* (cat.118); the reason for beginning with the second rather than the first panel in the series was probably because for this scene the artist was able to recycle an existing composition, *The Baptism of St. Oswald*, a stained glass cartoon he had made in 1864 for St. Oswald's church, Durham.[24] It had been agreed that he and Shields would each be paid £275 per mural, half to be paid when Waterhouse had approved the cartoon, and the other half on completion. The Corporation was to pay for all colours and materials, and all cartoons, working drawings, studies and replicas remained the property of the artist.[25] These were an important source of extra income for Brown and he sold several to local collectors. But the medium was still undecided, and frustratingly remained so until almost the last minute. Finally in March 1879, just before Brown came up to Manchester to start work in the Town Hall, the committee approved Brown's own choice, the Gambier Parry Method of spirit fresco. Thomas Gambier Parry is today remembered, if at all, as the collector of the early Italian paintings in the Courtauld Gallery, but he was also a church decorator. He devised a method of wall-painting that he claimed was more resistant to damp than fresco: the pigments were mixed with a medium of copal varnish, wax and gum elemi and were then applied to a specially prepared wall surface. Unlike fresco, it could be retouched easily, and combined 'the richness and the resources of oil with the absence of shine, which is so valuable in fresco.'[26] The method had been successfully used by Gambier Parry at Highnam church, Gloucestershire, and by Frederic Leighton at Lyndhurst church, Hampshire.

At last Brown could begin painting on the wall, and in April 1879 he came up to Manchester to start work in situ. As the Great Hall was often in use for meetings, Brown worked in a canvas booth on a movable wooden platform built in front of the mural. He was initially exhilarated. 'I find it very comfortable here; the only thing about my box (for its like a box at the opera) being that it is far too comfortable, and I fear, not to be abandoned often enough to see the effect of one's work at a distance. At night, when I'm all alone, with an excellent gas stand, it is perfectly delightful, and by daylight I feel charmingly free from household worries.'[27]

The original idea was for him to make preparatory drawings and cartoons in London and to come up to Manchester for short periods, staying in temporary accommodation while working in the Great Hall. But the work took far longer than anyone had imagined. He found the Gambier Parry process 'for luminousness and rendering of the texture and colour of flesh is all anyone could desire,' yet it was hard work: 'My hours are from 10am to 10pm seven days a week – consequently no dinners or little trips to friends out of Manchester.'[28] He began to encounter technical problems, 'such as shadows cast at certain hours by the projecting piers on either side, and sunshine. These, of course, I manage to counteract, but the result is that time is wasted and the difficulty of obtaining the desired result increased.' By July he was writing to Shields, 'I am not so satisfied as I was with the Gambier Parry process. I find it keeps on drying and getting paler for three or four weeks, which makes it difficult to know what one's work will look like.'[29]

By the time he returned to London in September 1879 after finishing the first mural, he had tired himself out. 'What has come over me I don't know, I seem to have exhausted what little energy pertains to me while at Manchester, and here can only yawn and lie on the sofa.'[30] In November 1880, when two panels, the *Baptism of Edwin* and the *Romans*, were complete and he had just begun the third, the *Danes* (cats 118, 116, 120) he sent in a report to the committee asking for more money: 'It is quite impossible for me to carry them out in the time I had originally reckoned on'. This he stated was because he had to carry out so much historical research for them, and because they required 'all the finish of easel works', being 'so near to the eye of the spectator.'[31] Brown had always been a slow worker; his perfectionism and his tendency to get carried away and lose track of time were just the same problems that had led to his earlier paintings taking so long. The request was refused.

Increasingly irritable, he complained to the committee in January 1881 about the 'interruptions to which my work is constantly subjected.' 'I speak not of noise caused by what might be termed the legitimate use of the room I am painting in for Public Meetings, Flower Shows, Organ Recitals.... What I wish to draw your attention to is the quite novel employment of the Great Hall as cloakroom for dinner-guests, causing me again tonight a loss of five hours.' The draughts from the constant opening of doors were 'scarcely endurable', the rush of air 'intolerable', and he did not wish 'to be arrested in the very heat and excitement of artistic inspiration ... unless you can stand between me and such disturbance, I shall be forced to return to my natural sphere in London.'[32]

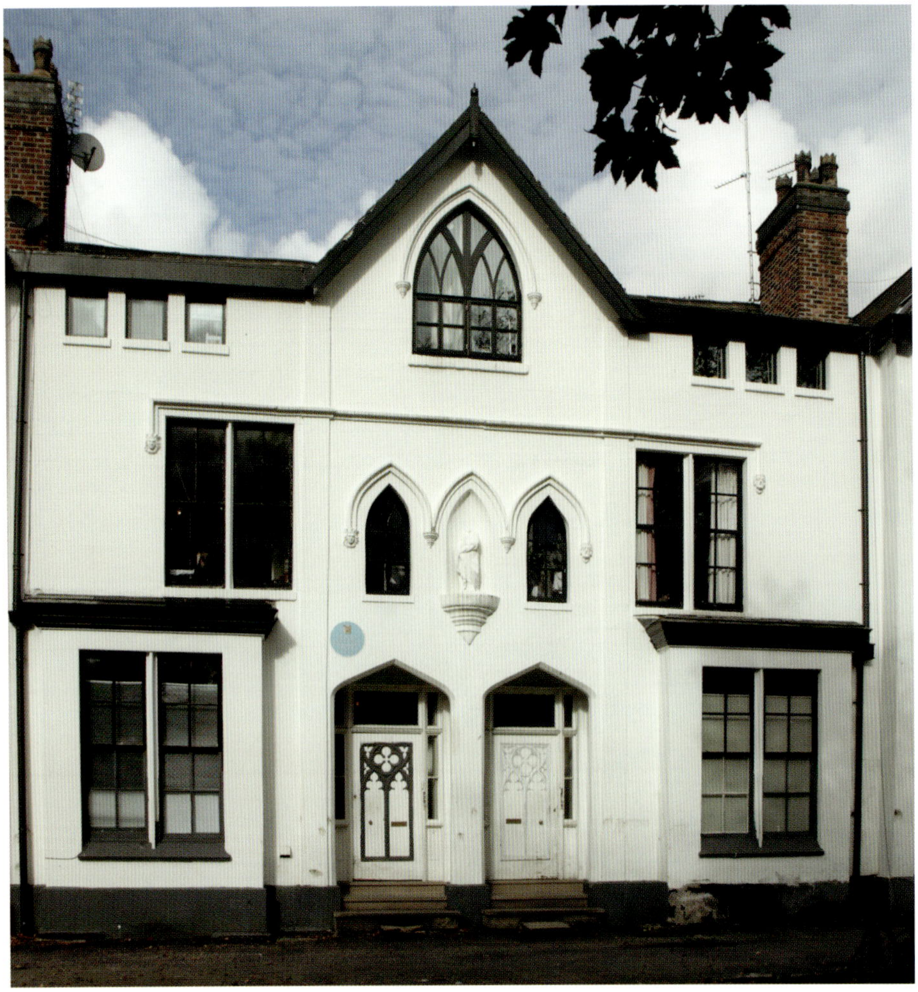

Fig. 35
3 Addison Terrace, Daisy Bank Road, Victoria Park, Manchester

In fact he did the opposite and decided to leave London altogether. 'Things look so gloomy here that I have come to the determination to get rid of this expensive house and take a small one at Marple or Hayfield, and there, if possible, live within my means ... I have written to Heywood about a studio in the Town Hall, and think this the time, now or never, to make a new start in life. With a painting-room in the Town Hall I might perhaps, get in with a fresh lot of clients, and things could not be worse than in London, and will certainly be cheaper.'[33] Rowley advised against Marple or Hayfield and in August 1881 Brown sold the house in Fitzroy Square and came to live in Manchester, at first renting Calais Cottage, Cleveland Road, Crumpsall, on the edge of the country north of the city, and in August 1883 moving to a more convenient inner suburb, Victoria Park, where he rented 3 Addison Terrace, Daisy Bank Road a house previously occupied by Sir Charles Hallé, founder of the Hallé orchestra (fig. 35).

Meanwhile, Shields had done nothing about starting on his share of the work. After several reminders, in May 1881 he withdrew on grounds of nervous ill health, writing in typically verbose terms that 'the varied distractions and noises of the Great Hall … would be so constantly provocative of intense suffering to my nervous system that I should break down.'[34] It is possible that Shields never really intended to carry out his part of the work, for already in December 1879, Rowley had written to Brown 'You will most probably have the whole 12 to do for I fancy Shields will cave in.'[35] Shields may well have considered himself outclassed; he certainly did not need the money as his colourful watercolours of children had made him prosperous. It was probably a good thing that Shields did not take part because the relentlessly heavy symbolism and hard outlines of his later murals at the Chapel of the Ascension in Bayswater (destroyed during the Blitz) would not have sat well with Brown's more engaging and lively style (fig. 36).

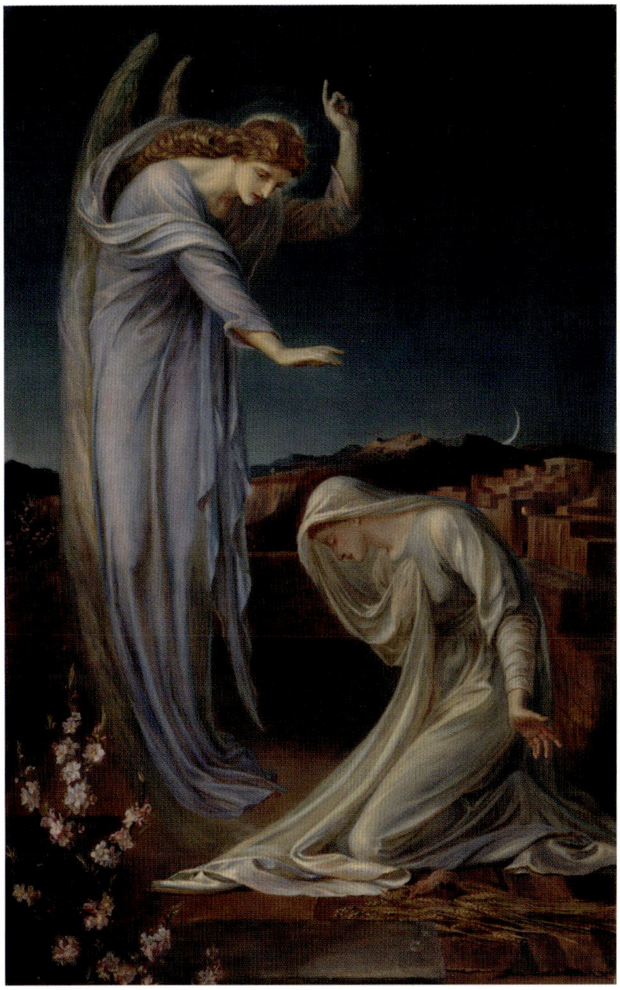

Fig. 36
Frederic Shields, The Annunciation (version of mural painting in the Chapel of the Ascension), *1894. Manchester City Galleries*

It was not until January 1884 that Brown was formally asked to paint all twelve panels, following the intercession of Waterhouse. A new contract was agreed. Brown was to receive £375 for each of the last six subjects as yet unpainted (£100 more than had originally been agreed for the first six) and he was to be paid an extra £100 retrospectively for each of the earlier ones. 'This is not very pleasing, but as nothing else seems to succeed I think it best to acquiesce. It is only five years more exile in this place'.[36]

Brown had been fifty-eight and full of hope when he first came to Manchester to start work on *The Baptism of Edwin* in April 1879. After initially staying with Rowley, he moved to a succession of lodgings, eventually ending up at Marshall Place, Cheetham Hill. But the artist's health was not good. In the first month he had two attacks of gout, and two falls. One evening, working late in his tent in the Town Hall, he fell between the platform and the wall, and the caretaker, assuming he had gone home, put out the lights, leaving poor Brown to feel his way all round the building until he managed to find his room.[37] Next, he fell in the street 'trying to alight from a bus in Lancashire fashion, while it was in motion.'[38] Later the following year Emma came to Manchester to stay with him: her fragile health and her drinking were a worry and he did not like leaving her alone in London where she was an increasing burden on his daughters. But though they made a resolution of 'total abstinence' it did not work.[39] Mathilde Blind also came, and when the Browns were in lodgings at Marshall Place, Cheetham Hill, Mathilde was installed nearby in York Place, her presence tolerated by Emma.

Brown's initial mood of elation did not last. 'This place certainly does *not* improve by length of acquaintance' he wrote in spring 1881, before temporarily returning to London to sort out his affairs before coming to live at Crumpsall. Yet life in Manchester was not without its compensations. One great pleasure was the music. He and Emma were regular attenders at Hallé concerts and they also went to recitals in private houses: once at a private party he stood throughout a recital of Brahms *Liebeslieder* despite suffering from gout, declaring afterwards 'That's what I call good music.'[40] But a special privilege of working in the Town Hall was hearing the organ in the Great Hall. 'I work till quite late & sometimes the organist, a splendid musician, steals in unperceived, & the organ, one of the finest in the world, pours forth wonderful strains in the scarce-lit hall, to one all alone as it would seem.'[41] The splendid musician was the Town Hall organist, James Kendrick Pyne (fig. 37), also the organist at Manchester Cathedral. He was keen on French organ music by Saint-Saens, Widor and Dubois, and he brought his friend Alexandre Guilmant to play in Manchester. One day Brown brought a pig into his tent in the Great Hall, to paint the escaping animal in the *Danes*. It caused a 'pigmentary predicament': 'The pig set up a series of hideous screams that pretty soon overpowered the loudest tones of the organ. What the maestro thought of the rivalry I don't know … but it was agony to me and probably to the pig.'[42]

Pyne and Brown became great friends; Brown recalled his visits to Pyne's house with its 'gorgeous William Morris wall-paper setting off the dark-hued cabinets, and well-known rare old instruments, spinets and harpsichords and Turkey carpets.'[43] Pyne later sold his collection of antique musical instruments to Henry Boddington, Brown's Manchester patron. Pyne also helped Brown sell works to the industrialist Benjamin Armitage. After Brown's return to London Pyne wrote to Brown, 'I have missed you enormously at the Hall and don't care so much for my practising now that you are not there to run in and chat with. I often go and look at the picture it is now quite an old friend.'[44] Here he was probably referring to the mural of *Wyclif* where he appeared as the Bishop of London (cat. 125). He was later to sit for the Duke in the *Bridgewater Canal* and his wife Agnes modelled for a court lady in the *Flemish Weavers* (cats. 136, 122, 148). She became friendly with Emma and got into terrible trouble with Brown once after Emma was found unconscious at home in Addison Terrace; he discovered that Emma had inveigled Mrs. Pyne into smuggling bottles of rum into the house. 'While her poor husband was playing the organ ... I told her that since seeing her, Emma had had to see the doctor who pronounced it to be spirits which if we could not intercept, death and a coroner's inquest would follow.'[45]

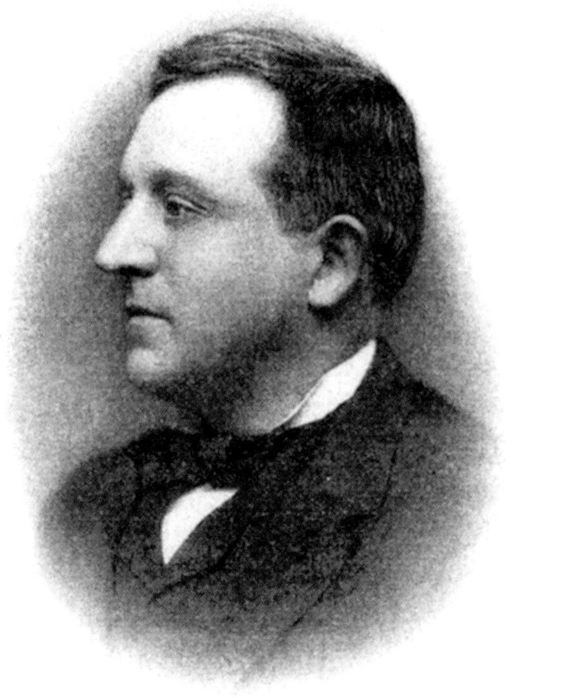

Fig. 37
James Kendrick Pyne, photograph from Manchester Faces and Places, *1891–92*

The Browns met the Lancashire dialect poet Edwin Waugh and he gave Emma, who loved to sing, a copy of his *Lancashire Songs*, a book of his poems set to music. In 1883, at Waugh's request, Brown made a sketch for an illustration in a book of his poems, but it was never published.[46] Other friends included Alexander Ireland, the Business Manager of the newspaper the *Manchester Examiner and Times* and his wife Annie, the biographer of Jane Welsh Carlyle. Brown regarded hostile newspaper reports as part of a conspiracy against him, and felt that notwithstanding his friendship with the Irelands, the *Examiner* had always been against him until they started to employ Rowley to write about him.[47] He acknowledged however that the *Manchester Guardian* was supportive. Its editor C.P. Scott commissioned a portrait of his daughter, and he and Brown became more friendly once the Browns had left Crumpsall for Victoria Park, which was nearer Scott's house in Withington. In May 1884 Brown showed the Scott children round the Town Hall, which they much enjoyed.[48]

After the Browns had moved to Victoria Park, a more fashionable area than Crumpsall, they were able to take a greater part in society. In February 1884 they gave a grand house-warming party, and they often had friends to stay. Annie Ireland warmly remembered the Browns' hospitality at Addison Terrace and recalled that in her room all the newest books and reviews were placed on the table by her bed. Once at a gathering of literary and artistic friends in her own house, Brown, she wrote, was so absorbed in what he was saying that when offered coffee by a servant, he took a cup and began putting lumps of sugar in, but went on putting them in without interrupting what he was saying, until the cup overflowed onto the carpet.[49] The Browns received many invitations. 'We were out at the Behrens last night with music. Mama had on a new plush and brocade dress,' wrote Brown to Lucy.[50] But towards the end of his time in Manchester he grew less inclined to go out into society. 'I have refused the Mayor's dinner, and I could show you half a dozen invitations to dinner with the best people, which we have recently refused. We are not rich enough to keep up with that sort of thing, but we are on friendly terms with the only few worth, or near enough for, knowing ... Many others I have dropped or cut.'[51] This may have been because of Brown's increasing suspicion of a conspiracy against him, but Emma's alcoholism must surely have played a part.

Brown also naturally became involved in the art life of Manchester. He lectured at the Manchester Literary Club, the Royal Manchester Institution and the Graphic Club. He attended their Conversaziones, and took part in their exhibitions. He presented prizes at art classes. He exhibited with the Manchester Academy of Fine Arts (the very same 'bunch of nobodies' that he had previously refused to work with), and was pleased when they elected him as an Honorary Member. He also became an Honorary Member of the Brasenose Club, one of the more cultured of the Manchester clubs. He went to Paris with Charles Rowley to buy casts for the new Art Gallery, recently opened in the RMI's building.[52] At the request of Rowley and Scott, Brown advised the Gallery on the colour schemes for an exhibition of the Bock collection of textiles.[53] Scott was a member of the Art Galleries Sub-Committee in 1885, when *Work* was bought by the gallery for its permanent collection, a singular honour of which Brown was proud. Yet he was not afraid to create a stir if he believed himself wronged. When asked to recommended artists to be invited to show at the opening exhibition of the new Art Gallery, he suggested various artists including Hunt, Moore and Poynter, but was enraged when the painter Val Prinsep, who was hanging the show, rejected his own *Waiting* on the grounds that it was not a recent work. At the opening banquet he with Emma and Mrs Pyne walked out ostentatiously just as Prinsep got up to make his speech.[54]

Perhaps Brown's closest friendship was with Rowley who fondly recalled the happy times together at his country cottage in Chapel-en-le-Frith. 'After the day's work, the simple meal, the quiet, and the glass of Scotch, he would look so radiant and talk so divinely we forgot ourselves and it was only my midnight remark "Come Brown, let's go to bed," that broke the spell and off we went.'[55] (It was also at Chapel-en-le-Frith, while the Browns and the William Michael Rossettis were holidaying there in August 1882, that Brown and Mathilde Blind had a tremendous row, exacerbating the tensions that she had already caused in the Brown family. They refused to speak to each other, although they became reconciled a few months later.[56])

Brown became involved in Rowley's philanthropic schemes. A city councillor for the New Cross ward in Ancoats, one of the poorest areas of the city, Rowley campaigned for baths, wash-houses and improved sewerage; and also for a public meeting place. This led to the building of the New Islington Hall, which opened in Ancoats in 1877 and became the base for Rowley's Ancoats Recreation Committee which from 1882 to 1889 organised events to bring cultural enrichment to the working class. Rowley persuaded leading artists, musicians and university lecturers to participate in a winter programme of free Sunday lectures, concerts and art exhibitions; Brown lectured there on 'Aesthetic Possibilities in Manchester' in December 1882, and allowed his paintings to be shown at the exhibitions. The committee also organised a series of 'at homes' where local residents mingled with distinguished guests such as William Morris, Bernard Shaw and G.K. Chesterton; but when it was decided to make a charge for refreshments the local element in the attendance dropped off. After 1889, this work was continued by another body organised by Rowley, the Ancoats Brotherhood, and later still by the University Settlement. Rowley himself seems to have lost interest in social improvement in the 1890s, but he continued his involvement in the art institutions of the city becoming chairman of the Manchester School of Art in 1890.

Rowley performed an important service for Brown, in bringing about his reconciliation with William Morris. Since the reorganisation of the Firm in 1874 had caused a complete rift between them, they had never spoken. Ten years later Morris lectured in Ancoats on 'Art and Plutocracy'. Brown did not attend but Morris came to look at the murals, and a year later through Rowley's encouragement Brown invited Morris to stay. 'As soon as they met they were at once quite as good chums as of old ... The old quarrel has no interest for us – the reconciliation was more important, and gave comfort not only to each of them but to all their friends', wrote Rowley.[57]

According to Rowley, 'one of Brown's most lovable qualities was his touching affection for suffering and distress. Whilst in Manchester he often took boys and girls who were badly shod in wintry weather and bought them shoes or clogs.'[58] This concern took a more organised form when the harsh winter of 1886 caused exceptional hardship among the working class. Brown, Rowley and few friends founded a Labour Bureau to help the unemployed find work. Brown himself spoke at a mass meeting for the unemployed held on 15 April 1886 at Pomona Gardens, attended by about 6,000 people. After the chairman of the meeting denounced the system of poor law relief as utterly inadequate to cope with the distress, Brown, who was received with cheers, gave a speech about the Labour Bureau, affirming his desire to see the scheme made compulsory throughout the country. So far in Manchester they had been able to give employment to not quite five per cent of those who had applied. He hoped to be able to do more. He condemned the charitable ladies who said that drink was the cause of it all (an echo of *Work*) and he refuted the statistical explanation, saying that it was unhelpful to be told that more people were starving a year ago. He urged Parliament to pay more attention to home interests and think less of Burma and Afghanistan. A joiner named Joseph Waddington then read letters of support, criticized the Mayor for his inaction and called for 'Justice not Charity'. A second meeting was held on 8 May, after which a procession was held, and the police made four arrests including Waddington. The men were freed on bail, but at a later court appearance fines were imposed. The defendants objected and were removed from the dock, but were then called back and informed that their fines had been paid and they were discharged.[59]

Their fines had been paid by C.P. Scott who had also provided them with counsel. Brown was closely involved in the affair. Concerned that Waddington, because of his record of haranguing 'everyone from the Mayor downwards', could not get work, Brown took the trouble to visit him at his home, noting that the 'Rienzi or the Masaniello of the Manchester unemployed' was 'a small rather sickly-looking young mechanic, hardly what you would expect as the leader of thousands of roughest men; who silently & cheerfully obey him'.[60]

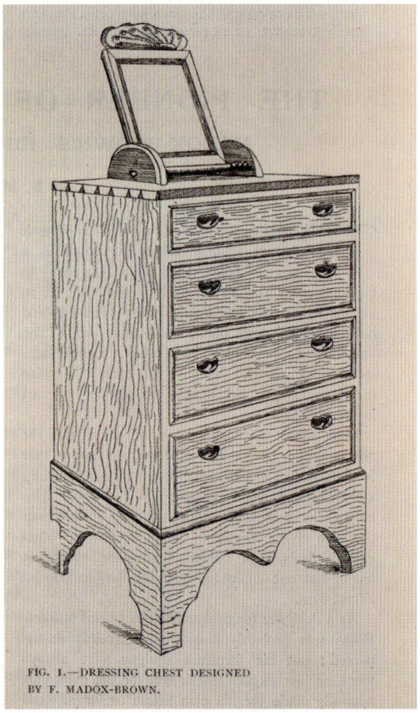

Fig. 38 Workman's chest of drawers designed by Ford Madox Brown, from The Artist, *1898*

To help Waddington, Brown employed him to make up his designs for inexpensive artisan's furniture, a scheme inspired by the model workmen's room shown at another philanthropic enterprise, the Manchester Art Museum (at first displayed at the Queen's Park Museum and then relocated to Ancoats Hall), the creation of Thomas Coghlan Horsfall (see cat. 151). In October 1886 Brown wrote to his daughter Lucy about his new idea, a 'Cottage Furniture Scheme': he was setting Waddington to 'make two or three things on my own account & we will either send them to the Jubilee Exhin. or exhibit them in a little shop Waddington has taken in Brook Street. I want to get up a small company of 10 Shareholders at £5 each, & hope that we may sell things (*as designed by me*) so as to keep Waddington in work.'[61] The company was never formed, and the only piece known to have come out of the scheme is a simple chest of drawers, originally stained green, with a mirror on top, and instead of handles, gilded recesses gouged from the fronts of the drawers.[62] An example was exhibited on Goodall's stand at the Manchester Royal Jubilee Exhibition (fig. 38).

No less than eight of Brown's paintings were exhibited at the Jubilee Exhibition, and *Work* was hung prominently in the first gallery, containing works mostly lent by Manchester collectors. Unfortunately some of Brown's exhibits at the Jubilee were skied, which Brown attributed to the malign influence of the chairman of the Fine Art section, William Agnew. Brown, perhaps trying to get his own back, published an article criticising the selection of the exhibition, which he felt had left out important artists including Haydon, Danby, Martin and Whistler.[63] Among Brown's exhibits was a watercolour version of *The Entombment*, lent by Henry Boddington, the Manchester brewer. This was one of three works by Brown sold to Boddington by Rowley. Over the next few years Boddington, who was a guarantor of the Jubilee Exhibition, purchased over thirty of Brown's pictures, including some from the Belgian and Paris periods that Brown had never sold. He also commissioned a group portrait of his

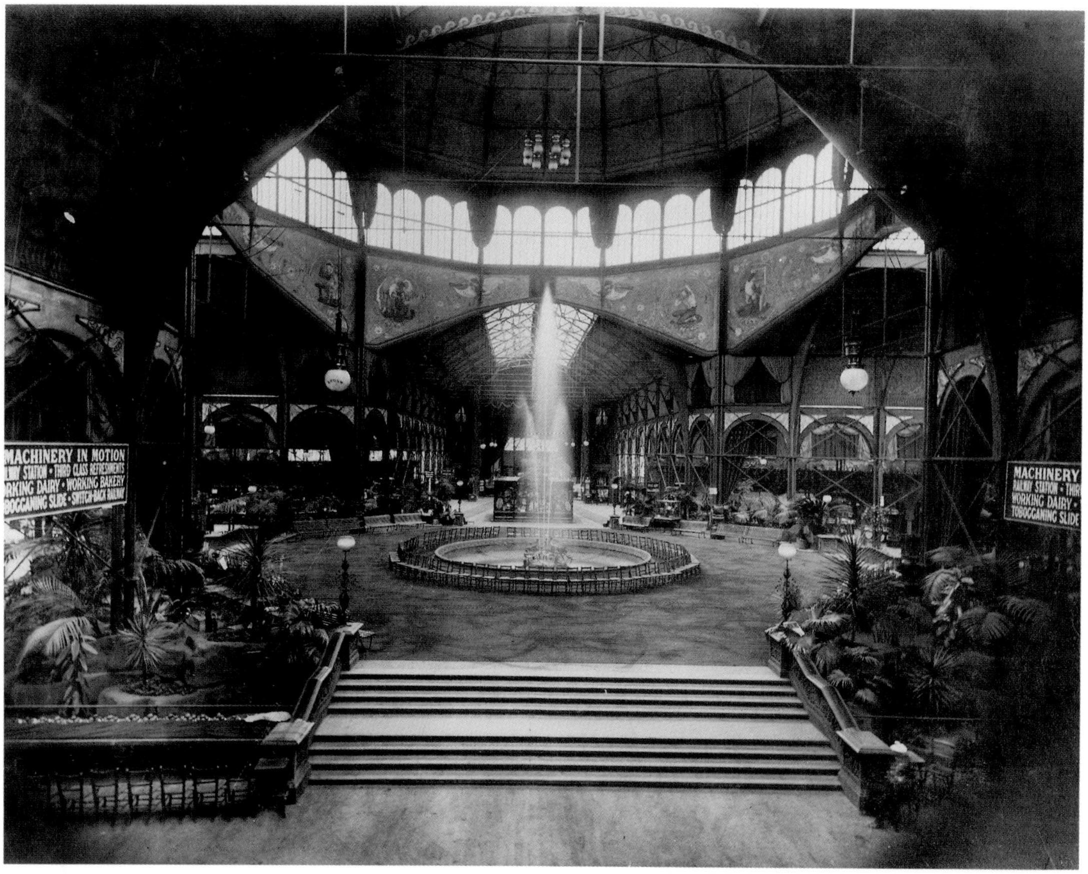

Fig. 39
Dome of the Manchester Royal Jubilee Exhibition, 1887. Photograph by H. Garside. Manchester Local Studies

family, later destroyed.[64] Boddington housed his collection in a special gallery built next to his house, Pownall Hall, Wilmslow. The main part of the house was decorated in advanced taste by the Century Guild, a group of craftworkers inspired by Ruskin and Morris. Its founder, A.H. Mackmurdo claimed that it was at his own suggestion that Boddington bought paintings by Brown.[65]

Brown made another, more prominent, contribution to the exhibition. In November 1886, whilst working on *John Dalton*, he was asked by George Faulkner Armitage, whose Altrincham firm was responsible for the interior decoration of the exhibition, to paint figure groups for the eight spandrels of the great domed space in the centre of the exhibition building. Brown was enthused by the task, despite the short notice, and, as group compositions would have been too complicated to do in the time, designed eight single figures of Lancashire workers, each accompanied by a winged spirit of Lancashire energy (see cats. 143-47). He recruited a group of assistants, including several women artists from Manchester, to paint them from his designs; the figures were on a vast scale, twelve feet high and the winged figures measured fourteen feet across (fig. 39). Brown went to a great deal of trouble over the commission, especially the installation and lighting of the paintings, which had to be done at the last minute: 'Thursday I spent on a swing scaffolding, putting the last touches to my work, at a height to 50 feet from the ground, hauled up by ten men with ropes. I was determined to do it … I underwent nothing like real danger, and could have had assistants go up for me. But they could not have done what I did … three men had fallen and been killed just before.'[66] These decorative paintings, the Boddington portrait and a portrait of the daughter of C.P. Scott (cat. 149), were the only substantial new commissions received while the artist was living in Manchester; this was disappointing to him, although his work on the murals took up so much of his time that he would have been hard pressed to take on more.

The Jubilee decorations were Brown's last Manchester undertaking before his return to London. In 1885 he had written to Shields of his intention to change from the Gambier Parry method to oil, because of the difficult conditions of painting in the Great Hall: 'to avoid the difficulties of working from models on the walls and have the luxury of working in my nice studio with the sun and trees in front of it.'[67] *Wyclif*, the last mural to be painted in the Gambier Parry method on to the wall, was left half-finished over the winter of 1885–86, and the committee of August 1885 approved of Brown painting the next panel, *Chetham*, in oil on canvas as an experiment. When completed, it was glued to the wall by the French process of *marouflage*. The next panel, *Dalton*, was painted in Brown's Manchester studio, on canvas, but using the Gambier Parry medium (cats. 125, 131, 142). However, there was now no need for Brown to stay in Manchester. He was worried about the effect of the damp Victoria Park house on Emma's worsening health, and he himself longed to be back in London. He moved in December 1887, to a new address, 1 St. Edmund's Terrace, Regent's Park. It was here that the last three murals, *John Kay*, *The Bridgewater Canal* and *Bradshaw* were painted in oil on canvas (cats. 133, 136, 132). Sadly, during this period, his son-in-law Franz Hueffer, Cathy's husband, died in January 1889, and Brown also lost his beloved Emma who died in October 1890 after a long illness.

The last three murals were not well received, and the ageing artist grew bitter at his treatment. While the boldly foreshortened compositions were startlingly original, especially considering Brown's age, the handling of paint and the figure drawing showed increasing signs of weakness due to his deteriorating health. Progress on *John Kay* was held up by another serious attack of gout, and while working on *Bradshaw*, Brown had a mild stroke which temporarily deprived him of the use of his right arm; the committee was unaware that Brown had painted much of it with his left hand. The reception of all three was marked by hurtful criticism. Imperfect drawing, confused figures and grotesque faces were censured in *John Kay* and the reaction to *The Bridgewater Canal* was worse: it was called a 'burlesque,' a 'caricature' and an 'insoluble riddle'.[68] The committee demanded that Brown should submit a drawing of the next and final subject in advance of starting it. Brown was deeply upset by this even though his supporters, including the women artists who had assisted him on the Jubilee decorations, came to his defence in the press.

Brown's reaction can be deduced from a letter to the *Manchester Guardian* signed with the initials of his grandson, F.H., but which doubtless recorded his own exasperation, as well as his artistic aims: 'Mr. Brown did not choose his subject, it was chosen for him ... and who but a municipal councillor would have desired such an impossibility of so great an artist?... Nevertheless, Mr. Brown was foolish enough to take upon him the colossal task of making a fine picture out of nothing, and he has done it in a way that no man, past or present, unless it be Hogarth, – ever has done. He has made a picture, it is true, that gives us something to reflect upon, and that is just what municipal councillors do not want. This picture is brimming over with life, and with English life too, it is at once a masterpiece of genre and of historic painting'.[69]

Brown ignored the request to submit a drawing of his last panel, *Bradshaw*, for advance approval and, after completing it, refused to allow the Mayor and a deputation to see it. He was then informed that Manchester would not accept or pay for it, and he threatened to sell it to someone else. Eventually, through the agency of Rowley he was persuaded to back down, and the committee agreed to accept it. 'It was a very painful conclusion to a happy connection with the artist,' wrote Thompson.[70]

Once the murals were completed, their merits were soon recognised, and they set an example for a younger generation of mural painters, many of whom would have read Brown's influential essay 'Of Mural Painting' published in 1893 by the Arts and Crafts Exhibition Society. The Manchester murals scheme came to be regarded as a model of the collaborative ideal of architecture and the fine arts, an idea initially associated with the Gothic Revival but taken over by the Arts and Crafts movement. When reproduced as a series of independent pictures, the theatricality and eccentricity of the murals tends to be exaggerated, but in situ, as an integral part of the Great Hall, the murals are a perfect complement to the architecture. Their warmly glowing colours are set off by their stone surrounds and by the sumptuous decoration of the roof, but they are far from mere background decoration. The bold movement and steep foreshortening of their compositions and their many engaging details command attention and tell their stories with wit and verve. 'It cannot be genius that is lacking to us,' wrote the Arts and Crafts teacher and philosopher W.R. Lethaby, 'An age that can produce Watts' *Physical Energy*, Madox Brown's Manchester paintings, and the Forth Bridge, should be able to produce anything'.[71]

1 Shields 1912, p. 223.
2 James Leathart of Gateshead and George Rae of Birkenhead; Thomas Plint had died in 1862.
3 *Diary*, p. 201.
4 Shields 1874–75, pp. 40–41, giving the incorrect date of 1849 for the RMI exhibition of *Lear and Cordelia*.
5 V&A, Charles Rowley to FMB, 14 December 1876.
6 MCL Town Hall Archive, General Purposes Sub-Committee, 4, p. 406; New Town Hall Sub-Committee 19 January 1876.
7 V&A, Joseph Thompson to unspecified (Charles Rowley?), 25 July 1875.
8 V&A, Joseph Thompson to Charles Rowley 21 July 1876.
9 MCL Town Hall Archive, General Purposes Sub-Committee, 4, p. 483; New Town Hall Sub-Committee 21 June 1876.
10 V&A, Charles Rowley to FMB, 8 July 1876.
11 V&A, Charles Rowley to FMB, 28 September 1876.
12 Waterhouse 1876–77, p. 135.
13 MCL Thompson papers, copy of report to Building Committee Chairman, 18 February 1879.
14 MCL Thompson Letters, Alfred Waterhouse to Joseph Thomson, 15 December 1876.
15 Manchester City News, 21 August 1877; MCL Town Hall Archive, General Purposes Sub-Committee, 5, p. 81; New Town Hall Sub-Committee, 15 August 1877; Decorations and Furnishings Sub-Committee, 2 August 1877.
16 Shields 1912, p. 222.
17 V&A Charles Rowley to FMB ,5 July 1877.
18 V&A Charles Rowley to FMB, 8 July 1878; see also Thompson to Rowley, 8 July 1878.
19 MCL, Town Hall Archive, Town Hall Committee, 1, FMB to Alfred Waterhouse, 15 June 1877, and Thomas Wrigley, Committee Clerk, to FMB, 22 August 1878.
20 MCL, Thompson papers, William Axon to Abel Heywood, 23 September 1878.
21 MCL, FMB to Alfred Waterhouse 1 October 1878.
22 V&A, Draft Memo by FMB and Frederic Shields, 6 March 1878.
23 MCL, Thomson papers, Frederic Shields to Joseph Thompson 7 March 1878.
24 Bennett 2010, 1, p. 290; the cartoon is in the Victoria & Albert Museum (C115).
25 MCL, Town Hall Archive, Town Hall Committee, 1, Report of Decorations Sub-committee 20 June 1877; approved by General Purposes Committee 1878; see also Report of Deputy Town Clerk 20 July 1881.
26 MCL, Town Hall Archive, Town Hall Committee, 1, 19 February 1879, Report by Waterhouse.
27 Hueffer 1896, p. 334.
28 Bodleian, FMB to F.G. Stephens, 1 June 1879.
29 Hueffer 1896, pp. 336–37.
30 Hueffer 1896, p. 337 (FMB to Charles Rowley, 17 September 1879).
31 MCL, Town Hall Archive, Town Hall Committee, 1, 17 November 1880 (2 November 1880).
32 V&A FMB to Abel Heywood (draft), 27 January 1881.
33 Hueffer 1896, p. 341: FMB to Charles Rowley, 29 January 1881.
34 MCL Town Hall Committee 1, Shields to Sir Joseph Heron 10 May 1881 (Report of Deputy Town Clerk, 20 July 1881).
35 V&A, Charles Rowley to FMB, 23 December 1879.
36 Hueffer 1896, p. 365.
37 Hueffer 1896, pp. 347–48.
38 Thirlwell 2010, p. 164.
39 Newman & Watkinson 1991, p. 178.
40 *Pall Mall Gazette* 11 October 1911: Obituary 'by one who knew him.'
41 Thirlwell 2010, p. 163.
42 Hueffer 1896, p. 346–47; UBC FMB to DG Rossetti 9 January 1881.
43 Brown 1889, p. 188.
44 V&A, J.K. Pyne to FMB, undated.
45 Newman & Watkinson 1991 pp. 178–79.
46 Bennett 2010 2, C.234; copy of Lancashire Songs, Stow Hill Papers, House of Lords.
47 Hueffer p. 358.
48 V&A C.P. Scott to FMB 4 March and 22 May 1884.
49 *Leicester Chronicle* 2 July 1892: 'Recollections and Studies by Mrs. Alexander Ireland.'
50 UBC, FMB to Lucy Madox Brown 2 February 1884.
51 Hueffer 1896, p. 381: FMB to Shields 22 May 1887.
52MAG, MAFA 1882–84.
53 Hammond 1934, p. 48.
54 Newman & Watkinson 1991, p. 182.
55 MCL, *Odds & Ends by As and Bs* (Mss of St. Paul's Literary and Educational Society), 41, pp. 132–35.
56 Thirlwell 2008, p. 216.
57 Rowley 1911, pp. 133–34.
58 Rowley 1911, p. 107.
59 *Manchester Examiner and Times* 16 April 1886; *Manchester Guardian* 16 April 1886, 8 May 1886, 10 May 1886.
60 JRL, FMB to M.H. Spielmann 9 May 1886.
61 UBC, FMB to Lucy Madox Brown, 5 October 1885.
62 Bennett 2010, 2, E.15. An example painted black is with the artist's descendants.
63 Brown 1888, ii, pp. 122–24.
64 Bennett 2010, 2, pp. 373-74, B8)
65 Evans 1985, p. 260.
66 Hueffer 1896, p. 378.
67 Hueffer 1896, p. 368.
68 Bennett 1, 2010, pp. 340–41.
69 *Manchester Guardian* 24 May 1892, letter signed F.H. [Ford Madox Hueffer].
70 MCL, Thompson papers, later note by Thomson on letter Waterhouse to Chairman, 18 February 1876.
71 Lethaby 1911, p. 251.

This essay includes some material previously published in Treuherz 1985.

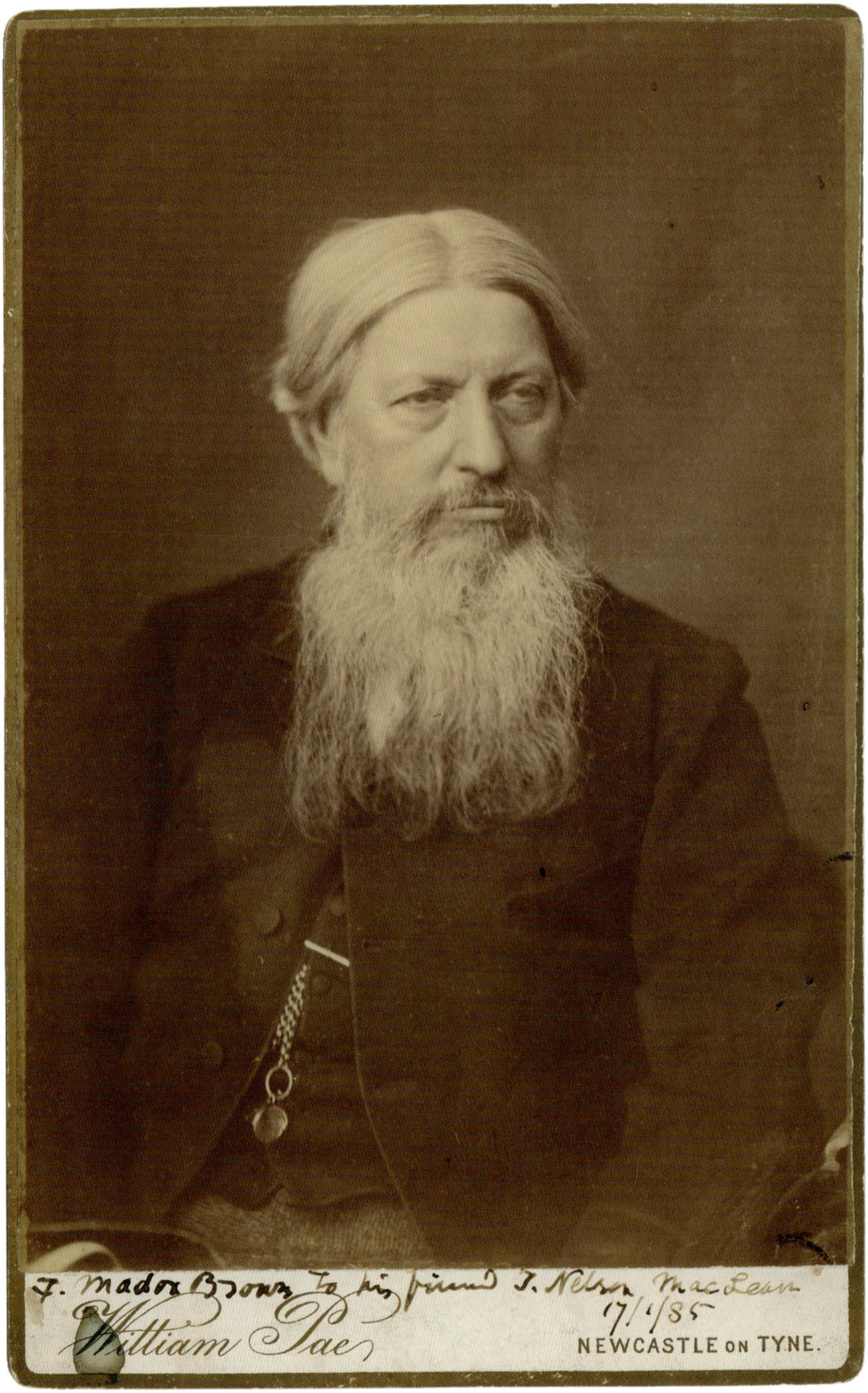
F. Madox Brown to his friend F. Nelson MacLean
17/1/85
William Pae
NEWCASTLE ON TYNE.

CHRONOLOGY

1821 16 April, Birth of Ford Madox Brown in Calais to Ford Brown, former ship's purser and Caroline Madox (married in 1818; their daughter Eliza born 1819).
Family lives in Calais but also moves to different towns in Northern France.

1825 Family lives briefly in Dunkirk.

1834 Ford Brown Sr. suffers a stroke. Family living in Dunkirk.

1835 From November, FMB studies at the Bruges Academy of Art under Albert Gregorius.

1836 From autumn, FMB studies at the Ghent Academy of Art under Pieter van Hanselaer.

1838 From winter, FMB studies at Antwerp Academy of Art under Gustav Wappers.
Exhibits *Colonel Kirke* at Brussels Salon, and *Job among the Ashes* at Ghent Salon (both works untraced).

1839 September, FMB's mother dies at Calais. He and his sister inherit properties in England, providing modest income. Father and sister join him in Antwerp.

1840 Meets Elisabeth Bromley who stays with Brown family in Antwerp after attending finishing school in Germany.
Death of Eliza, FMB's sister; he inherits her share of her mother's property.
The Giaour's Confession (untraced) exhibited at Antwerp Salon.

1841 3 April, marries Elisabeth Bromley at Meopham Parish Church.
May, exhibits for the first time at the Royal Academy, London: *The Giaour's Confession* (untraced).
Summer, FMB and Elisabeth move to Paris.
Paints *Manfred on the Jungfrau*.

1842 Birth of son, who dies after five days.
Death of FMB's father.
The Execution of Mary Stuart exhibited at Paris Salon.

1843 19 July, birth of Lucy, daughter of FMB and Elisabeth.
FMB still in Paris; works on Westminster murals competition.
Parisina rejected by Paris Salon.

1844 Summer, moves to England, staying with Bromley family at Meopham.
July, Westminster competition entries shown in second frescoes exhibition at Westminster Hall: *The Body of Harold brought before William the Conqueror* and *Adam and Eve*.
November, FMB moves to studio at Tudor Lodge, Albert Street, London. Elisabeth stays in Meopham.
December, enters *The Ascension* in altarpiece competition for St. James's, Bermondsey.

1845 Illness of Elisabeth.
August, family travel to Rome via Ostend, Antwerp, Aachen, Cologne, Basel. In Milan by 15 September; Florence end of September; arrive Rome 3 October.
Visit to studios of Peter Cornelius and Friedrich Overbeck in Rome.
Begins *The Seeds and Fruits of English Poetry* in Rome.
While in Rome, works exhibited in London: *Spirit of Justice* in third and final frescoes exhibition at Westminster Hall; *Parisina* in British Institution.

1846 Elisabeth's illness worsens. May, the Browns leave Rome and travel via Civitavecchia, Marseilles, Lyons and Paris.
5 June, Elisabeth dies in FMB's arms while crossing Paris by carriage.
FMB goes to England. Burial of Elisabeth at Highgate Cemetery. Daughter Lucy sent to stay at Helen Bromley's school at Gravesend.
FMB stays at various addresses in London, including Cheapside and Blackheath, mostly with relatives of Elisabeth.
Paints first version of *The Seraph's Watch* and portrait of *James Bamford*.

1847 FMB stays briefly at Kensington and Tudor Lodge. August, moves to studio at Clipstone Street, Bloomsbury.
Oure Ladye of Saturday Night rejected by Royal Academy but exhibited at Liverpool Academy.
The Seraph's Watch exhibited at British Institution, London.
September, begins to write Diary.
September, research into costumes for *Geoffrey Chaucer reading the 'Legend of Custance' to Edward III and his Court*, draws studies and begins work on large canvas.
November, stops work on *Chaucer*, commences *The First Translation of the Bible into English: Wycliffe reading his translation of the New Testament*.

1848 March, Rossetti writes to FMB asking to become his pupil and receives lessons May and June.

Fig. 40
Ford Madox Brown, photograph by William Pae, 1885. Rob Dickins Collection, Watts Gallery

July, visits Paris to see Dan Casey, fellow-student from Antwerp.

Exhibits *The First Translation of the Bible into English: Wycliffe reading his translation of the New Testament* at Free Exhibition, London, and at the Liverpool Academy.

May, resumes work on *Chaucer.*

September-October, FMB visits Manchester, Lake District (starts *Windermere*), Liverpool and Birmingham.

Autumn, formation of Pre-Raphaelite Brotherhood: members: Dante Gabriel Rossetti, John Everett Millais, William Holman Hunt, James Collinson, Frederic Stephens, Thomas Woolner, William Michael Rossetti.

November, starts *King Lear.*

December, first meeting with Emma Hill.

1849 Emma living in Hendon or Highgate.

From April, working on *Chaucer.*

Windermere rejected by the Royal Academy.

King Lear (Cordelia at the Bedside of Lear) and *The Infant's Repast* at Free Exhibition, London and Liverpool Academy.

December, moves to 17 Newman Street, London.

1850 Further work on *Chaucer.*

Contributions to *The Germ* include etching of *The Parting of Cordelia and her Sisters.*

11 November, birth of Catherine Emily, daughter of FMB and Emma.

1851 Takes one-year lease on house in Wellington Road, Stockwell, near Clapham Common; keeps on Newman Street studio.

Summer, paints *'The pretty baa lambs.'*

Learns to paint in wet white ground technique.

Exhibits *Geoffrey Chaucer reading the 'Legend of Custance' to Edward III and his Court* at Royal Academy.

Sells *The First Translation of the Bible into English: Wycliffe reading his translation of the New Testament* to Francis McCracken of Belfast.

Starts *Jesus washing Peter's Feet* and *Waiting.*

1852 Spring, moves briefly to Weedington Street, Kentish Town.

June, moves to lodgings at 33 High Street, Hampstead; leaves Newman Street Studio. Emma and Cathy living at Hendon.

June, begins *Work*: draws first design and starts painting background on full-size canvas out-of-doors in Heath Street, Hampstead.

June(?), headmaster at North London School of Drawing (until 1853).

July, Thomas Woolner leaves for Australia.

Summer, begins *An English Autumn Afternoon.*

October, designs *The Last of England.*

November, Emma and Cathy move to Highgate, and Emma attends school for young ladies.

The pretty baa-lambs and *Jesus washing Peter's Feet* exhibited at Royal Academy.

1853 5 April, marriage of FMB and Emma Hill at St. Dunstan-in-the-West (wedding attended by Thomas Seddon and D.G. Rossetti).

FMB and family move briefly to Woodside Cottage, Highgate North Hill, and then live at Hendon.

August 1853, move to 1 Grove Villas, Church End, Finchley; FMB retains painting room at 33 High Street, Hampstead for one year.

September–October, resumes work on *An English Autumn Afternoon.*

Large version of *Waiting* exhibited at Royal Academy and Royal Manchester Institution.

The Seeds and Fruits of English Poetry exhibited at Liverpool Academy.

1854 July, *King Lear* and *An English Autumn Afternoon* sold at auction for low prices.

Summer, sells works to D.T. White, London art dealer, including large version of *Waiting.*

September, starts *A Study on the Brent at Hendon* and *Carrying Corn*

1855 January, applies unsuccessfully for teaching appointment at the Government Schools of Design.

20 January, birth of Oliver Madox Brown, son of FMB and Emma.

January to April, resumes *Work*, makes designs for the figures.

Carrying Corn and two other works rejected by Royal Academy.

Geoffrey Chaucer reading the 'Legend of Custance' to Edward III and his Court and small version of *Waiting* exhibited in Paris at Exposition Universelle.

An English Autumn Afternoon exhibited at British Institution, London.

13 July, quarrels with Ruskin about *An English Autumn Afternoon.*

July, painting *The Hayfield.*

September, completes *The Last of England.*

September, move to 13 Fortess Terrace, Kentish Town.

Windermere exhibited at Royal Manchester Institution.

1856 January, hack work adding costumes and backgrounds to portraits for Dickinson Brothers.

March, commissioned by Dalziel Brothers to design wood-engraving of Byron's *The Prisoner of Chillon* for *Poets of the Nineteenth Century*, published 1857.

June, starts *Stages of Cruelty*.

July, first meeting with William Morris, who buys *The Hayfield*.

16 September, birth of Arthur Gabriel, son of FMB and Emma.

Paintings exhibited at Liverpool Academy include *Jesus washing Peter's Feet*, small version of *Waiting*, *The Last of England* and *A Study on the Brent at Hendon*. *Jesus washing Peter's Feet* wins £50 prize.

September, first meeting with Liverpool collector John Miller, who buys *Waiting*.

November, first meeting with Leeds collector Thomas Plint who commissions *Work*; Brown resumes work on the painting.

1857 FMB helps to organise Pre-Raphaelite exhibition at 4 Russell Place, Fitzroy Square, London. Exhibition opens June, includes several of FMB's works.

21 July, death of Arthur Gabriel, aged ten months.

31 October, visits Oxford where Rossetti, Morris, Burne-Jones and others engaged in painting murals in the Oxford Union.

From May, *Jesus washing Peter's Feet* and *The Hayfield* exhibited at Manchester Art Treasures exhibition.

An English Autumn Afternoon, *William Michael Rossetti* and *Windermere* exhibited at Liverpool Academy.

Helps organise Pre-Raphaelite Exhibition which goes to America, opens in October. Works by FMB include *King Lear*, *Oure Ladye of Saturday Night* and *An English Autumn Afternoon*.

1858 January, designs for chairs.

April, foundation of the Hogarth Club; FMB takes leading role and exhibits at Hogarth Club exhibition.

Meets Major Gillum and designs badge for his Boy's Home, Euston Road, London.

Teaches at Working Men's College, London (until 1860).

Geoffrey Chaucer reading the 'Legend of Custance' to Edward III and his Court wins £50 prize at Liverpool Academy; other works exhibited include *The Hayfield*.

1859 Submits furniture designs to Hogarth Club exhibition; rejected by the hanging committee; FMB removes all his work from the exhibition.

The pretty baa-lambs, *Out of Town* and *Windermere* exhibited at Liverpool Academy.

August–September, holiday in Walton-on-the Naze; paints Walton-on-the Naze.

First meeting with James Leathart of Gateshead, who commissions replica of *Work* and buys *The pretty baa-lambs*.

Joins Artists' Rifles Corps in response to threat of French invasion.

1860 FMB becomes chairman of Hogarth Club.

Paints *The English Boy* and *The Irish Girl*.

Walton-on-the Naze, *Southend*, *The English Boy* and *The Irish Girl* shown at Liverpool Academy.

1861 April, establishment of Morris, Marshall, Faulkner & Co. FMB a founding partner.

October, George Rae of Liverpool buys *An English Autumn Afternoon*.

December, Hogarth Club disbanded.

1862 From May, *The Last of England* and *An English Autumn Afternoon* shown at International Exhibition, London; bookcase designed and decorated by FMB amongst works exhibited by Morris, Marshall, Faulkner & Co.

First stained glass cartoons for Morris, Marshall, Faulkner & Co: *Crucifixion* and *Nativity* for All Saint's, Selsley, Gloucestershire, architect G.F. Bodley.

1863 Completion of *Work*.

November, commissioned by Dalziel Brothers to design Bible illustrations: designs later used for paintings of *The Coat of Many Colours* and *Elijah and the Widow's Son*.

1864 April, Marie Spartali becomes pupil of FMB.

May, first meeting with Frederic Shields.

November, starts *The Coat of Many Colours* for George Rae.

1865 FMB organises exhibition of his own work at 191 Piccadilly, opens 10 March with *Work* as the centrepiece.

April, stained glass design of *The Entombment*, later used for paintings.

July, first commission from Manchester patron Frederick Craven: *The Nosegay*.

November, moves to 37 Fitzroy Square, London. Gives fortnightly parties there for about seven years, attended by artistic society.

November, starts *Cordelia's Portion*.

1866 *The Coat of Many Colours* shown at Ernest Gambart's French Gallery, London.

1867 January, commissioned to paint *Romeo and Juliet* for Craven.

Cordelia's Portion shown at Dudley Gallery, London.

1868 *Work* and *The Coat of Many Colours* shown at Leeds Exhibition.

1869 February, publication of engraving of *The Traveller* in *Once a Week*.

Commissioned by Edward Moxon to illustrate *The Poetical Works of Lord Byron* edited by William Michael Rossetti, published in 1870.

Watercolour version of *Elijah and the Widow's Son* shown at Royal Manchester Institution.

1870 Publication of *The Poetical Works of Lord Byron* with six illustrations by Brown.

1871 Marie Spartali ceases to be Brown's pupil and marries William Stillmann 10 April 1871.

Summer, Mathilde Blind joins FMB and family on holiday at Lynmouth, Devon.

October, publication of engravings of *Downstream* in *The Dark Blue*.

1872 January, Sir Charles Dilke commissions portrait of *Henry and Millicent Fawcett*.

3 September, marriage of daughter Catherine to Franz Hueffer, music critic of *The Times*.

December, FMB tries unsuccessfully for award of Slade Professorship of Fine Art at Cambridge.

1873 March/April, William Brockbank of Manchester commissions *Cromwell on his Farm*.

Designs St. Edith stained glass.

17 December, birth of grandson Ford Madox Hueffer (later changed name to Ford Madox Ford).

1874 Early 1874, FMB suffering from severe attack of gout.

31 March, marriage of daughter Lucy to William Michael Rossetti.

5 November, death of son Oliver Madox Brown, aged nineteen.

Reorganisation of Morris, Marshall, Faulkner & Co. as Morris & Co. causing rift between FMB and Morris. FMB ceases to be a partner.

Cromwell on his Farm exhibited at Royal Manchester Institution.

1875 Visits Antwerp and Brussels in connection with plan for painting *Rubens' Ride*, never completed.

February, first purchase by Charles Rowley of Manchester: monochrome version of *Cordelia's Portion*.

First discussions with Waterhouse about possibility of commission for Manchester Town Hall murals.

Byron's Dream exhibited at Royal Manchester Institution.

1876 July, *Geoffrey Chaucer reading the 'Legend of Custance' to Edward III and his Court* purchased by Art Gallery of New South Wales, Sydney.

1877 February, begins *Self-portrait*.

June, Waterhouse recommends the Manchester committee to commission FMB and Shields each to paint six murals in the Town Hall.

1878 FMB and Shields commissioned to paint the Manchester Town Hall murals.

July, starts work on cartoon for *The Baptism of Edwin*.

1879 March, final approval of Gambier Parry process.

April–July, working in Manchester Town Hall on first mural to be painted, *The Baptism of Edwin*. Staying with Charles Rowley. Returns to London in September.

1880 Spring, moves to Manchester, lives in lodgings in Grafton Street and then Market Place.

Mathilde Blind living in York Place, Cheetham Hill.

April–September, paints *The Romans building a Fort at Mancenion*.

September, starts *The Expulsion of the Danes from Manchester* (completed March 1881).

1881 May, Shields withdraws from murals commission.

August, sale of Fitzroy Square house. FMB moves to Calais Cottage, Cleveland Road, Crumpsall, Manchester.

October, starts *The Establishment of the Flemish Weavers in Manchester* (completed May/June 1882).

1882 Death of Rossetti. FMB designs his grave at Birchington, Kent, completed 1884, and his memorial fountain at Cheyne Walk, London, unveiled 1887.

June, starts *Crabtree watching the Transit of Venus* (completed May 1883).

December, lectures on 'Aesthetic Possibilities in Manchester' at Ancoats.

1883 January, severe attack of gout, while in Manchester. February, moves to London, still suffering from gout, and stays with Mathilde Blind in Hampstead to recuperate.

April 1883, starts portrait of Madeline Scott.

July, starts *The Proclamation Regarding Weights and Measures* (completed March 1884).

August, moves to 3 Addison Terrace, Victoria Park, Manchester.

1884 January, new contract with Manchester raises FMB's fee and confirms that he is to paint all twelve murals.

February, house-warming party at 3 Addison Terrace.

October, painting *Platt Lane*.

1885 February, *Work* purchased by Manchester Art Gallery.

June starts work on the mural of *The Trial of Wyclif* (stops August).

August, approval given for change from Gambier Parry method to oil. Begins *Chetham* in his Manchester studio in oils (completed February 1886).

September, ending of rift between FMB and William Morris, who stays with FMB in Manchester.

October, attack of gout.

1886 March–August, completes *The Trial of Wyclif*.

Helps to organise Labour Bureau scheme to assist Manchester unemployed. April, speaks at mass meeting of unemployed at Pomona Gardens, Manchester.

October, employs Joseph Waddington, leader of unemployed, to make furniture.

November, starts *Dalton collecting Marsh-Fire Gas*, but interrupted by work on Jubilee Decorations.

December, starts work on decorations for Manchester Jubilee Exhibition.

1887 May, Manchester Jubilee Exhibition opens with FMB's decorations in the Central Hall. His exhibits include *Work* and workman's chest of drawers.

May–December, completes *Dalton collecting Marsh-Fire Gas*.

October, Henry Boddington, Manchester brewer, purchases large group of Brown's works and commissions family portrait (later destroyed).

December, moves back to London; purchases 1 St. Edmund'sTerrace.

1888 Joins Arts and Crafts Exhibition Society and exhibits furniture at inaugural exhibition in London (opens October).

October, starts *John Kay, Inventor of the Fly Shuttle* (completed April 1890).

Autumn–Winter, FMB suffers from gout and kidney trouble, and Emma from rheumatism.

1889 20 January, death of son-in-law Franz Hueffer.

1890 April, starts *The Opening of the Bridgewater Canal*

April, Emma severely ill.

11 October, death of Emma.

Catherine Hueffer and her children Ford Madox Hueffer (later Ford) and Juliet move in with FMB. Willam Michael and Lucy Rossetti and their children Olivia, Arthur, Helen, Mary and Michael move next door to 3 St. Edmund's Terrace.

1891 November, Shields begins fund to help FMB out of financial difficulties.

1892 January, FMB finds out about the fund. Initially offended, but persuaded to accept commission to paint replica of *The Trial of Wyclif*. (As this was unfinished at FMB's death, the Fund was used to purchase *Jesus washing Peter's Feet* for presentation to National Gallery; later transferred to Tate Gallery.)

March, *The Opening of the Bridgewater Canal* installed in Manchester Town Hall. Severe criticism. Brown requested to submit a preliminary drawing of next and final subject in advance for approval.

April, starts *Bradshaw's Defence of Manchester*.

November, Henry Irving's production of *King Lear* at Lyceum Theatre, London opens with sets designed by FMB.

Suffers stroke which leaves him without the use of his right arm (late 1892 or early 1893).

1893 April, refuses to allow Manchester Committee to inspect final mural *Bradshaw's Defence of Manchester*. Committee refuses to pay for it; FMB threatens to sell it to someone else, but persuaded to back down. Mural accepted and paid for by Manchester; installed September.

6 October, death of Ford Madox Brown. Buried in St. Pancras cemetery.

NOTES TO CATALOGUE

No attempt has been made in this exhibition catalogue to duplicate the comprehensive material about each work set out in Mary Bennett's recently published *Ford Madox Brown, A Catalogue Raisonné*, New Haven and London 2010. For full discussion of each work, together with complete listings of literature, provenance, exhibition history and critical reception, the reader is referred to Mary Bennett's catalogue.

The reference numbers in brackets below the titles refer to Mary Bennett's catalogue.

Sources are given for all direct quotations, and for selected key points but for complete sources see Mary Bennett's catalogue.

References in the endnotes have been abbreviated; full citations are given in the Bibliography.

The division into sections and the order in which entries appear in the catalogue is a compromise between a chronological and a thematic arrangement.

Titles are generally those under which the works were first exhibited; Brown was apt to vary his titles slightly for different exhibitions, and in some cases change them altogether. In the catalogue, alternative commonly used titles are given in brackets.

The dating of Brown's works is complex because he worked on many of his paintings over extended periods, and often had several pictures in progress at the same time. He also frequently retouched or repainted finished works at a later date; and although he recorded detailed progress on certain works in his diary, the diary is incomplete. The conventions here adopted are as follows: a hyphen between years indicates that the artist began the work in the first year and completed it in the second. A forward slash between years indicates that the work was painted either during the first year or the second or at some time between, but the exact dates are not known. Minor retouchings after a work was substantially completed are indicated by a date in brackets. For more detailed information on dates and on the progress of individual works, the reader is referred to Mary Bennett's catalogue.

Dimensions are given in inches, followed by centimetres in brackets, height before width.

Quotations from Brown's diary have been transcribed with their original misspellings and punctuation.

Brown's twelve murals in Manchester Town Hall are included in the catalogue even though strictly speaking they are not part of the exhibition.

Discussion of frame design has been restricted to the frames that are illustrated, which have been selected as a representative sample of Brown's frame designs.

Fig. 41 (opposite)
Detail of cat. 61, Work

CATALOGUE OF WORKS

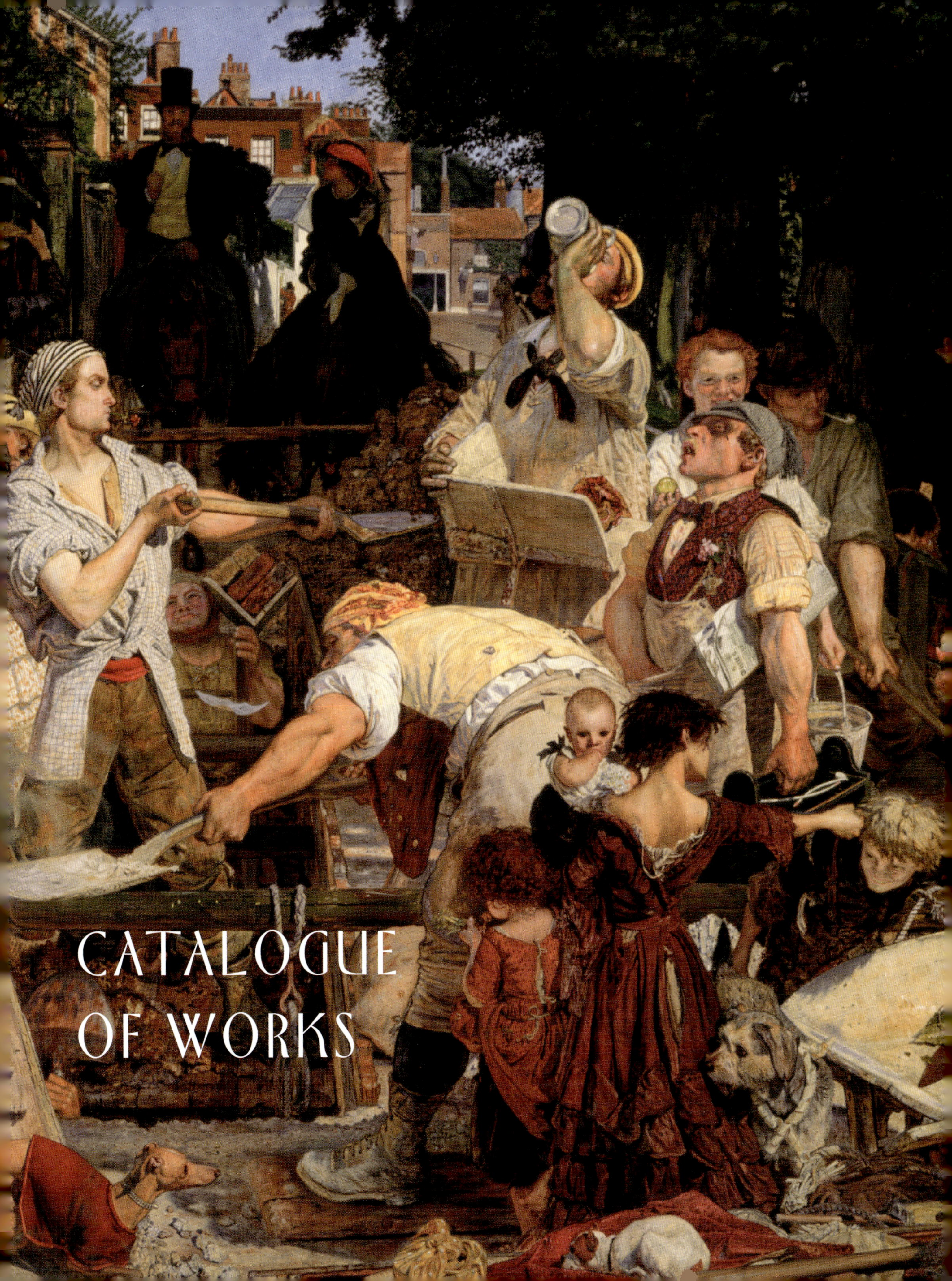

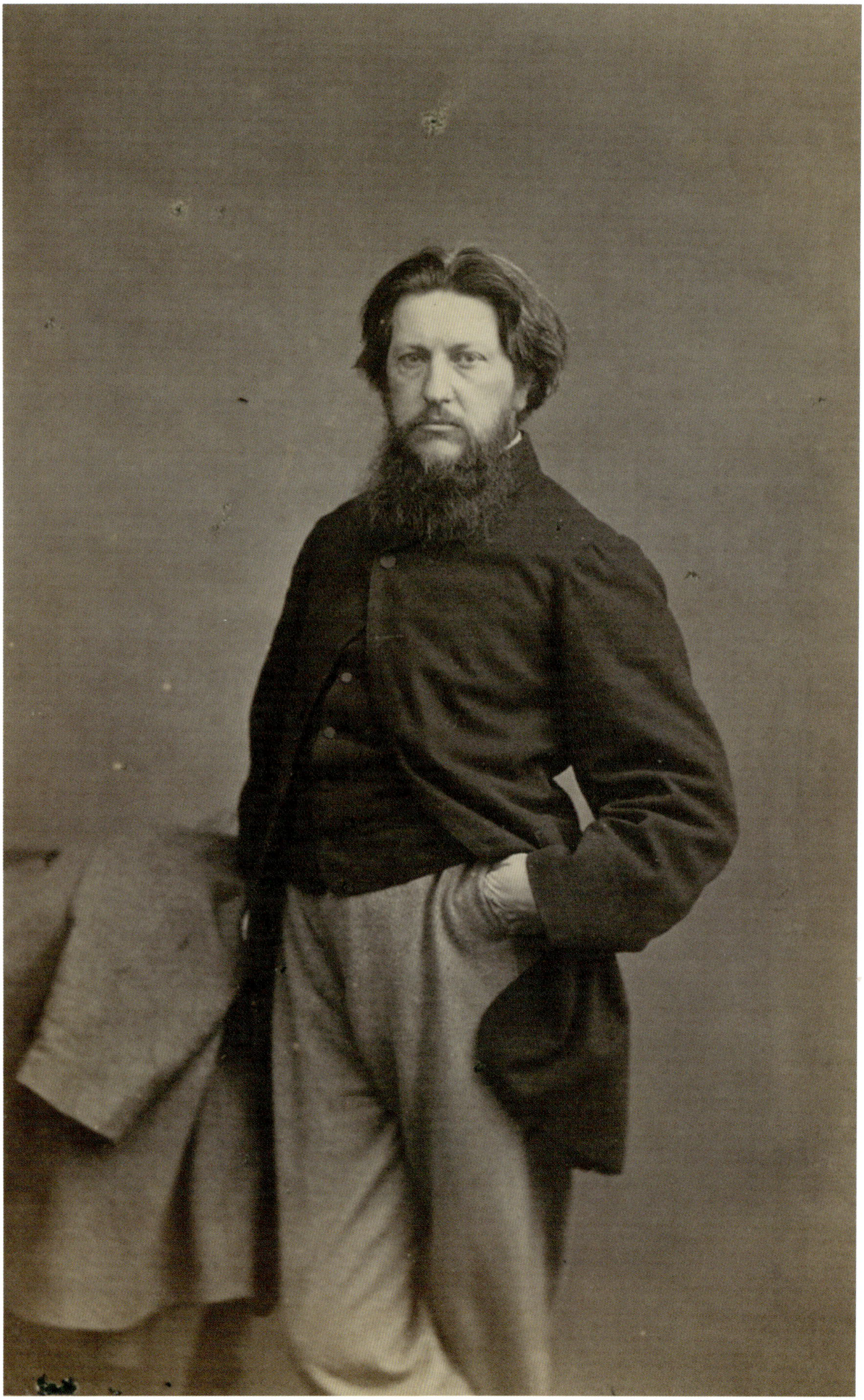

THE ARTIST AND HIS FAMILY

Ford Madox Brown's father, Ford Brown, was a ship's purser who lost his job at the end of the Napoleonic Wars and never found alternative work. Three years later in 1818 he married Caroline Madox, and the couple moved to France, living in genteel poverty in Calais, with periods spent in Dunkirk. Ford Madox Brown, the second child, was born in 1821. His parents inculcated in him a love of literature, art and science, and sent their son to study at the Fine Art Academies of Bruges, Ghent and Antwerp. He then spent a period in France before moving to London, where he began his career.

Brown's family life was marked by sadness. He was married twice, and had five children, three of them boys: all three died young. His first marriage, to his cousin Elisabeth (fig. 43), was cut short by his wife's early death. They married in 1841 and the following year they had a son, but he died aged only five days. Another child, Lucy, was born in 1843 but three years later, after only five years of marriage, Elisabeth died of tuberculosis. After her mother's death, Lucy was sent to stay with an aunt who kept a school.

Elisabeth had been Brown's social equal; his second wife, Emma, was a bricklayer's daughter (fig. 44). She first met Brown when she came to model for him. The couple lived together for several years before getting married, and their first child, Cathy, was born out of wedlock. The wedding took place in secret with only a few close friends present. Emma was illiterate, and Brown had to give her an education before she could meet

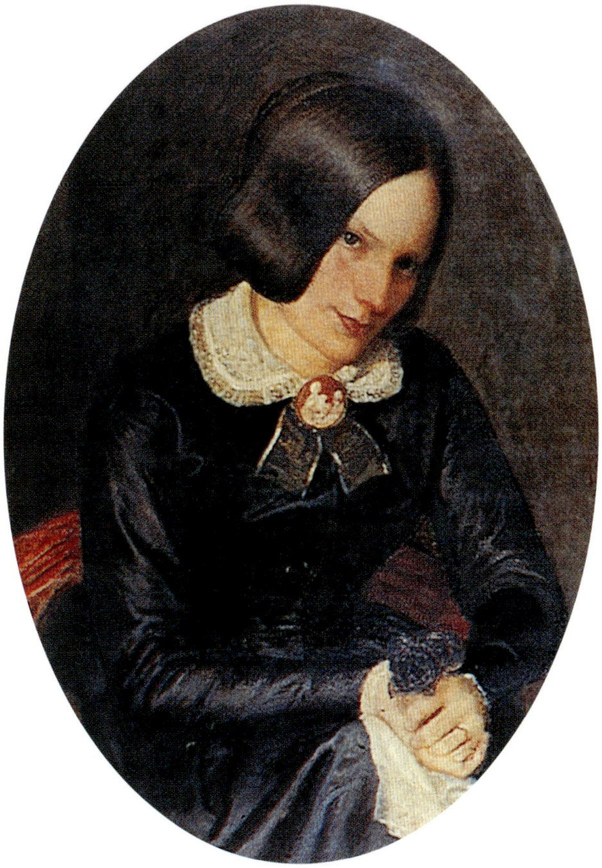

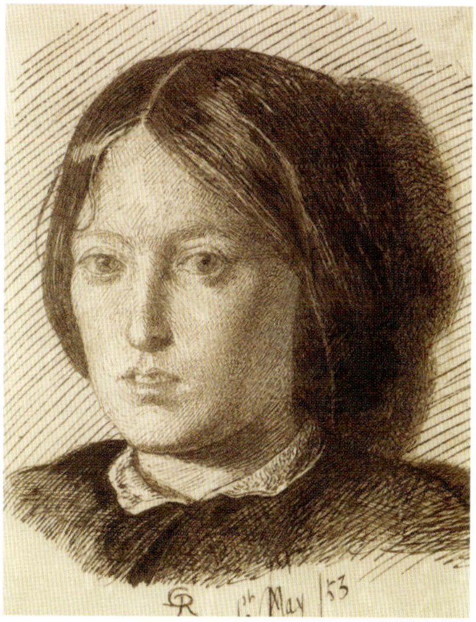

Fig. 42 (opposite)
Ford Madox Brown, photograph by W. & D. Downey, early 1860s. Rob Dickins Collection, Watts Gallery
Fig. 43 (left)
Ford Madox Brown, Elisabeth Madox Brown, *1845/46. Private collection*
Fig. 44 (above)
Dante Gabriel Rossetti, Emma Madox Brown, *1853. Birmingham Museums and Art Gallery*

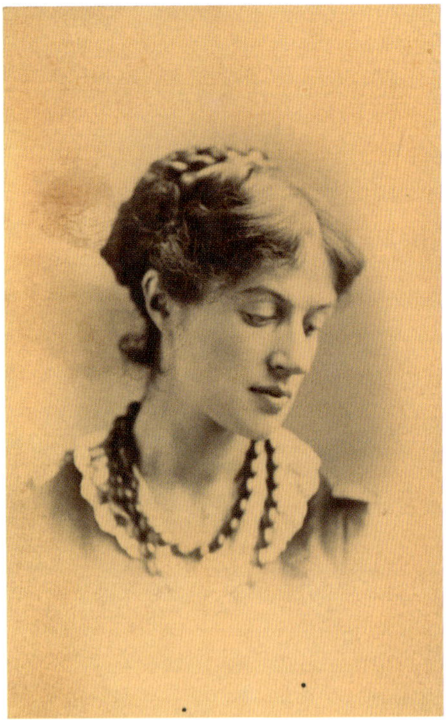

Fig. 45
Marie Spartali, photograph by Black of Boston, early 1880s. Princeton University Library

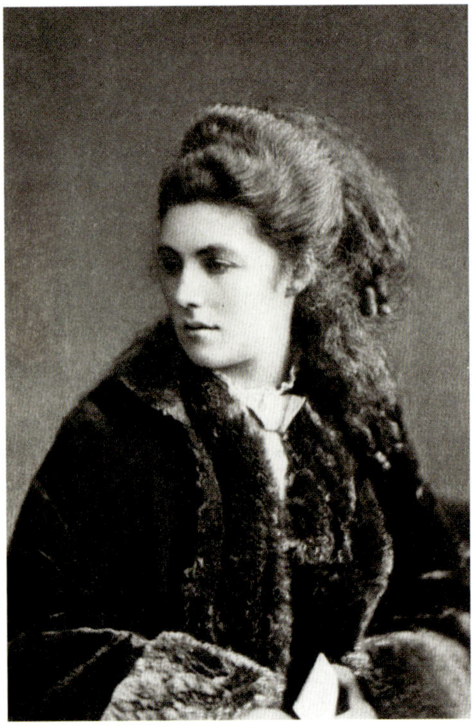

Fig. 46
Mathilde Blind, photograph, 1872/75, from Selection of the Poems of Mathilde Blind, *Arthur Symons, ed., 1897*

his wider circle of friends and relations. Their second child, Oliver, was born in 1855 and showed great promise as a writer and artist, but died in 1874, aged nineteen. Their third, Arthur, born in 1856, died aged only ten months.

The marriage survived against considerable difficulties. Emma drank too much; Ford could not sell his paintings easily, and for a time became depressed and reclusive. His style was uncompromising and uncommercial; he refused to paint obvious or conventionally beautiful subjects, and his obsession with fine detail meant that his paintings took a very long time to complete. The family never had enough money and occasionally Brown had to take on hack work retouching portraits based on photographs. His work was badly hung at the Royal Academy, and he eventually refused to exhibit there, thus denying himself an important way of getting his work seen.

Brown organised his own one-man exhibition in London in 1865, which barely covered its costs, although it was well-publicized and received praise from many critics. It also attracted a few new patrons. But Brown was disappointed that engravings were never made of his major paintings, which would have made them and him better known. He took offence easily and believed the establishment had conspired against him. But he could also enjoy his outsider status. In the mid 1860s and early '70s, when his work was selling better, he and Emma gave legendary parties for a bohemian circle of poets, artists, musicians and intellectuals.

Perhaps because of his wife's drinking, Brown took refuge in relationships with two other women, both considerably younger than he was. In the late 1860s Brown became infatuated with one of his pupils, the beautiful Greek artist Marie Spartali (fig. 45). It was a hopeless passion and ended when she married an American journalist in 1871. A close friendship then developed with the freethinking poet and feminist Mathilde Blind (fig. 46). It should not be assumed that these relationships were sexual: there is no evidence either way, and it is entirely possible that they were platonic.[1] They did however cause tensions within Brown's family. Despite this and Emma's continuing alcohol addiction, the marriage survived until her death in 1890. By this time, Brown was engaged in his last great work, the murals at Manchester Town Hall, which he finished just before his death in 1893.

1

SELF-PORTRAIT

(B31)
1844/5
oil on board, 8 × 5⅞ (20.3 × 15)
Peter and Renate Nahum, London

2

SELF-PORTRAIT

(B32)
1850, (1853)
black chalk, 9⅞ × 9⅛ (25 × 23)
signed and dated: *Ford Madox Brown etat 29. Sepr. 1850 / retouched Octr./53*
National Museums Liverpool, Walker Art Gallery. Purchased with the assistance of the Art Fund 1984

Despite the small size of these two self-portraits, they both vividly convey the artist's personality. The earlier of the two was probably painted for Brown's first wife, Elisabeth. He looks out of the picture with piercing eyes, inclining his head forward slightly and tensing his brows in concentration. He wears dark outer clothing but his tie-pin and a glimpse of blue and white striped waistcoat hint at the dandy. Brown's appearance is close to the description in the passport issued by the Belgian legation when he was aged twenty-four: chestnut hair, oval face, rounded chin and blond beard.[2]

He started the pencil self-portait about five years later. By this time he had shaved off his beard, and grown more luxuriant sideburns. The drawing shows how Brown's powers of observation had developed over the intervening period. Although the coat and cravat are only roughly blocked in, the drawing of the face and hair has been carried out with extraordinary fidelity and sensitivity to texture. The artist's searching gaze is conveyed by the asymmetrical shapes of his eyes, with the pupil of his right eye darker than his left, although farther from the spectator. Brown's technique was based on the thorough training he had acquired in Belgium and on his later study of Holbein. He began the pencil self-portrait when he was working on his large painting *Geoffrey Chaucer reading the 'Legend of Custance' to Edward III and his Court*, an immense investment in time and labour, which he hoped would establish his reputation (see cat. 34). He retouched the self-portrait drawing three years later, when he was depressed and struggling to make a living.

The intense self-scrutiny evident in both self-portraits had its written counterpart in the diary that Brown began to write in 1847, recording with great frankness his changing states of mind ranging from intense elation to black despair. But although self-analysis was a keynote of his diary, Brown made surprisingly few self-portraits; his only other independent self-portrait is a larger and more imposing oil of 1877 showing him in his maturity, with a flowing beard (frontispiece). But he also used his features for the emigrant in *The Last of England* (cat. 58), in *Cromwell on his Farm* (cat. 87) and in two of the Manchester Town Hall Murals (cats. 118, 125).

William Michael Rossetti, later to become Brown's son-in-law, described the artist's appearance as a young man: 'He was a vigorous-looking man, with a face full of insight and purpose; thick straight brown hair, fair skin, well-coloured visage, bluish eyes, broad brow, square and rather high shoulders, slow and distinct articulation. His face was good-looking as well as fine; but less decidedly handsome, I think, than it became towards the age of forty.... what struck us at first, more than his personal aspect, was his slow, deliberate, uniform voice'.[3]

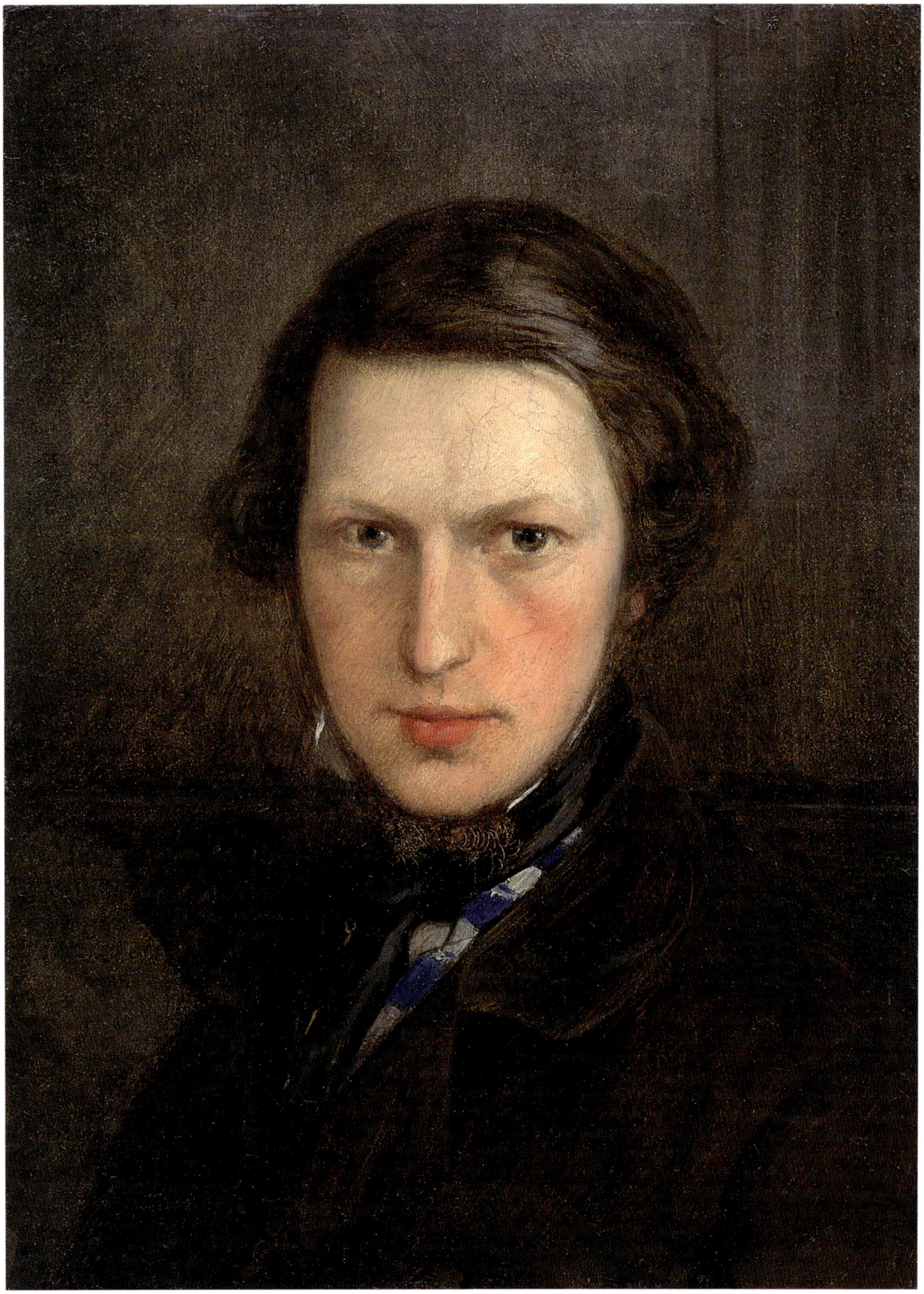

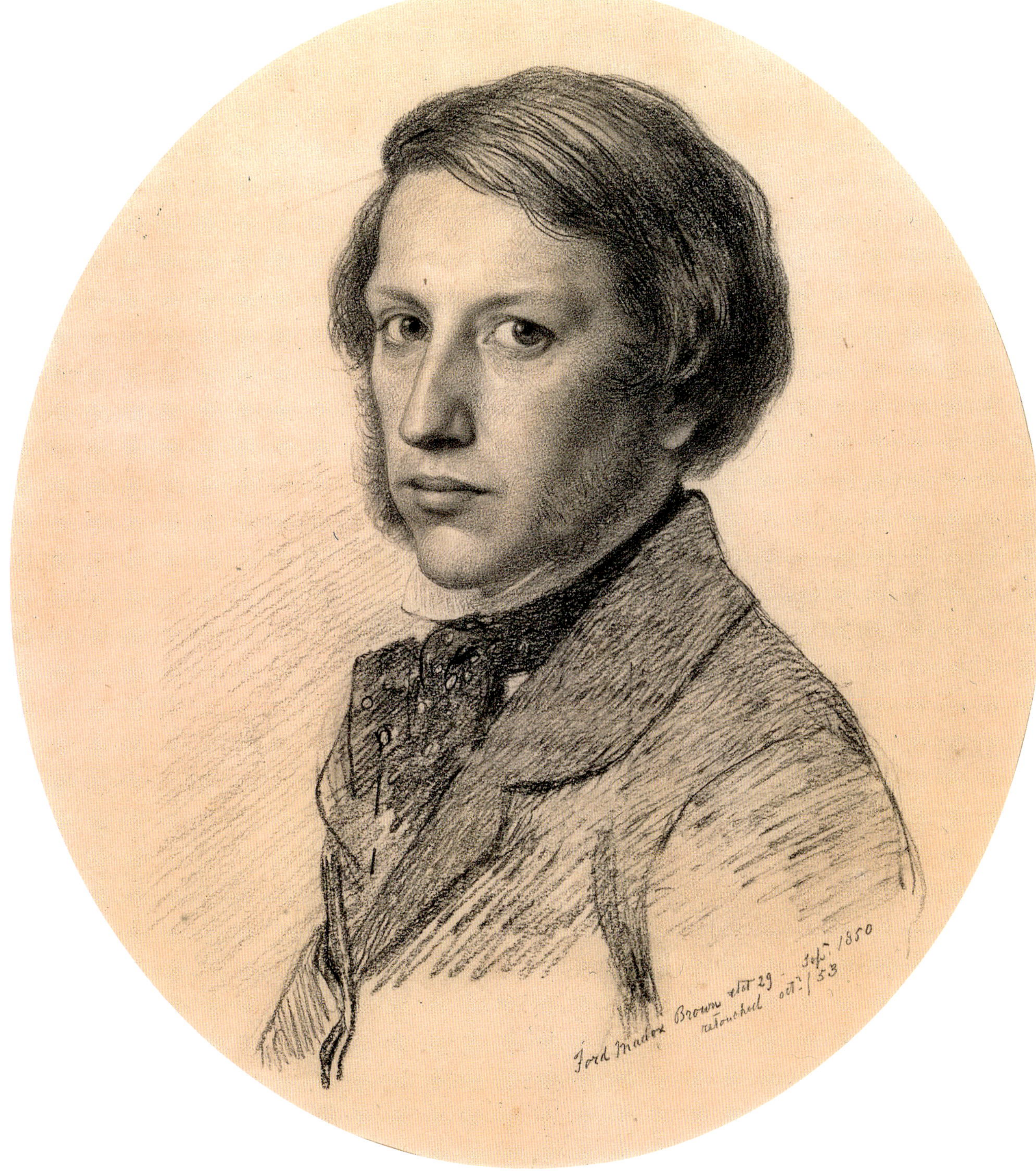

2

3

THE BROMLEY FAMILY

(B14)
1844
oil on canvas, 43 3/16 × 31 15/16 (117.4 × 81.1)
signed and dated: *F.M. BROWN / 1844*
Manchester City Galleries

Brown's first wife Elisabeth Bromley was also his cousin. She is seated at the front on the right with other members of her family. Next to her is her mother (the sister of Brown's mother), wearing a widow's cap. Elisabeth was two years older than her husband. She was well-educated and shared Brown's interest in literature and art. The landscape in the background is near Meopham, Kent, where Elisabeth's brother Augustus had a farm. Brown and Elisabeth had been married at Meopham parish church in 1841, and he painted this picture on a visit to Kent in 1844.

This type of portrait group, showing a well-to-do middle-class family in comfortable domestic surroundings, often depicted outdoors under a trellis of leaves, was widespread in Europe in the early-nineteenth century. It is often described as Biedermeyer portraiture because of its popularity in Vienna of the Biedermeyer period (1820s–40s). Brown would have seen examples during his studies in Belgium: one of the principal exponents in Belgium was Francois-Joseph Navez, Director of the Brussels Academy. This style of portrait is unique in Brown's work. He may have chosen the format because it was particularly appropriate to the circumstances of his wife's family, more settled and better-off than his own: the Bromleys were of ancient yeoman stock and had been in Kent since the early seventeenth century, whereas Brown's childhood was spent moving around between towns in Northern France.

The roses and the dog are traditional symbols of love and loyalty, and the ivy also indicates faithfulness. But they may have been included simply to suggest the prosperous and cultured milieu of the family evident from many other details. Elisabeth's mother is shown with her work-basket, while in front of Elisabeth is an album with green and gold binding, showing her cultural interests, and the roses are arranged in a Crown Derby porcelain vase. The gestures of the four people at the back indicate a lively conversation, but Elisabeth is lost in thought. Her health was delicate and she died of tuberculosis in 1846.

The identity of the four people at the rear is problematic. They are usually described as Elisabeth's brothers Richard (b. 1813) and Augustus (b. 1815) and their wives Clara and Helen. But Augustus died in December 1843, whereas the painting is dated 1844. In any case the man at the left appears more than two years older than the other. The portrait does not appear to commemorate a marriage, as the ladies are in formal evening dress, not wedding gowns.[4]

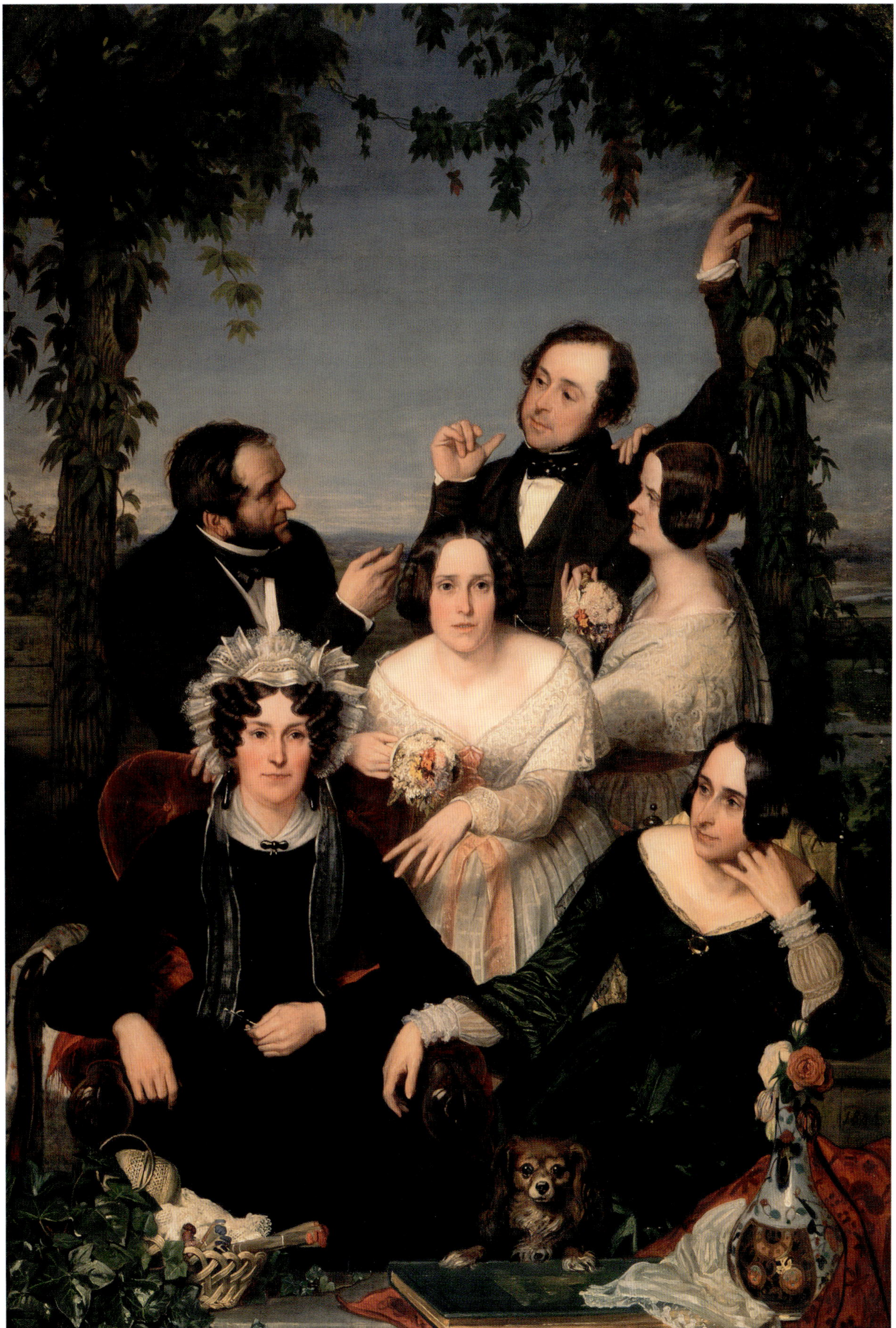

4

EMMA HILL
(Study for 'King Lear')

(A 51.3)
1848
black chalk, 4 1/16 × 3 7/8 (10.2 × 9.8)
signed and dated: *F.M.B. / Xmas /48*
Birmingham Museums and Art Gallery

4

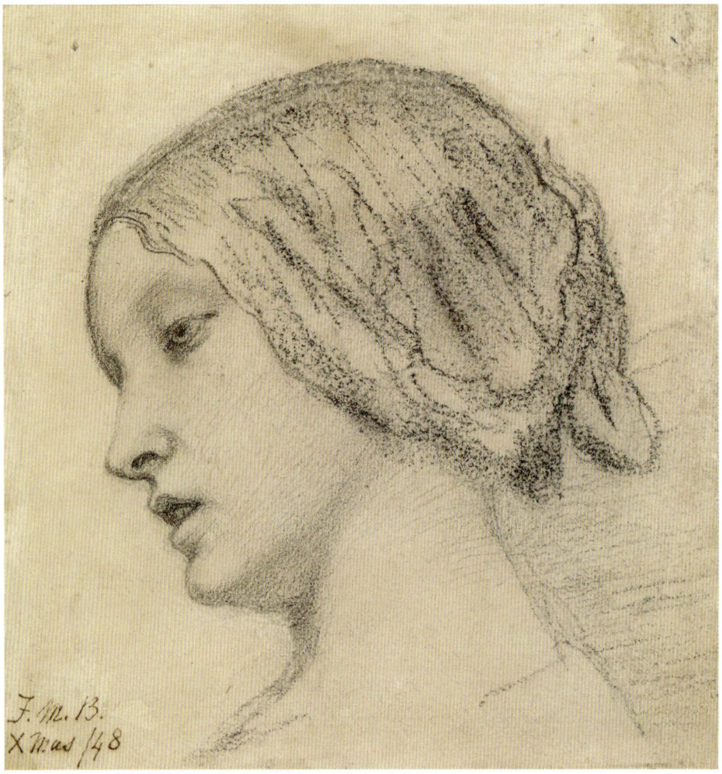

This is Brown's earliest portrait of Emma Hill, later to become his second wife. She first entered his life as a model: the drawing is similar to the head of Cordelia in *King Lear* (cat. 36) and is mentioned in Brown's diary on 13 January 1849 as a drawing of 'Miss Stone' (Stone was her mother's maiden name). By 10 February they were in love and Brown's diary recorded 'up late through foolery the night before. Began the veil of Cordelia, only laid in part of it when a girl as loves me came in & disturbed me'. By July Brown stopped referring to her in his diary as Miss Stone, and she was now 'E' or 'Emma.'[5]

Emma was described by William Michael Rossetti: she had 'a pink complexion, regular features and a fine abundance of beautiful yellow hair, the tint of harvest corn.'[6] Her most individual feature was the shape of her upper lip, drawn back to reveal her front teeth. This is seen in the drawing, but in the finished painting, which shows her in strict profile, her mouth is closed and her teeth hidden.

Emma's background was completely different from that of Elisabeth. She was the illiterate daughter of a bricklayer from Newent in Gloucestershire, and was probably nineteen when she met Brown. Although she and Brown lived together, intermittently at first, and had a child, born in 1850, they did not marry until 1853. By this time, she had been given an education, partly by Brown himself, and also through attending lessons in social and domestic skills.

5

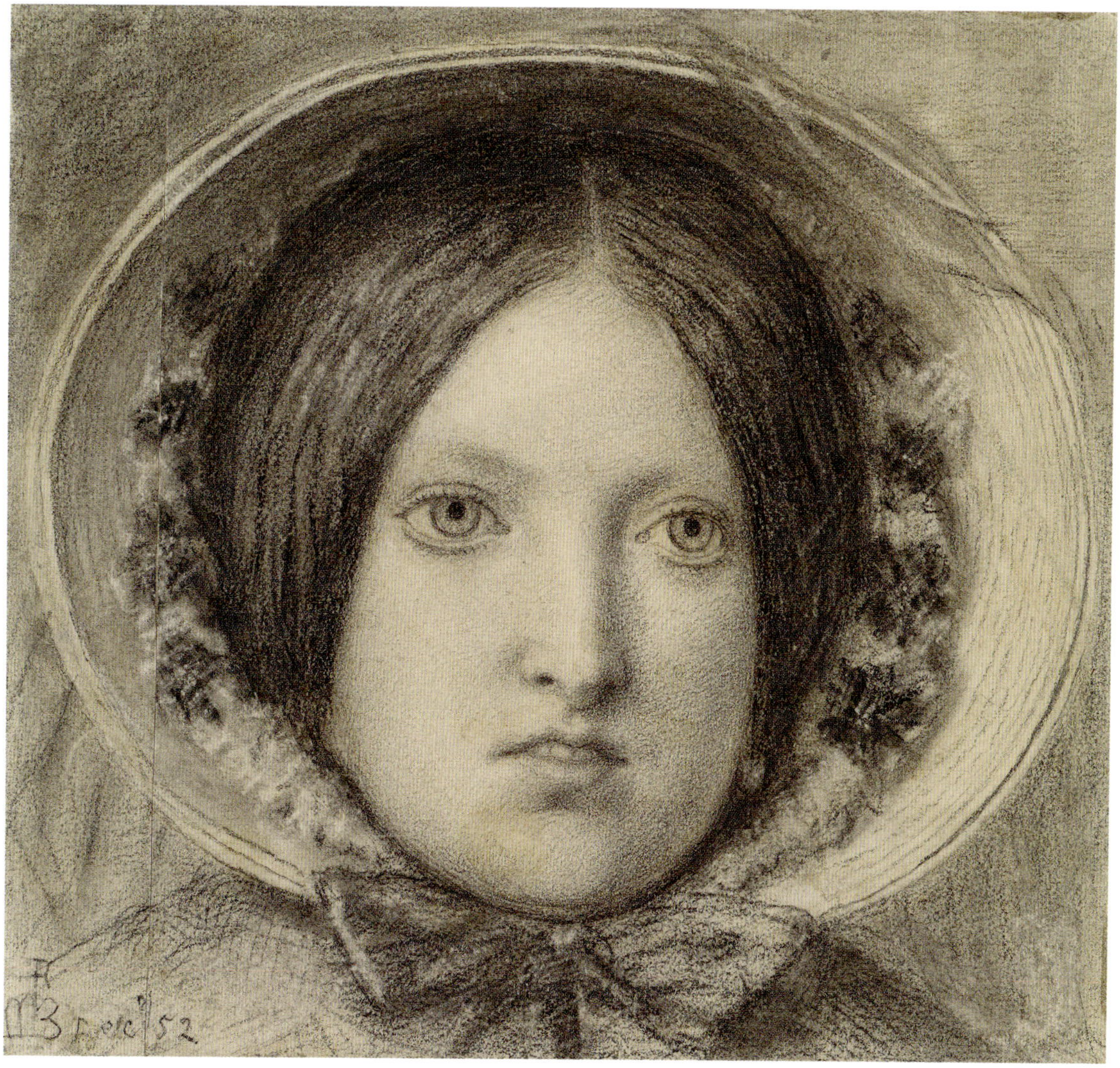

5

EMMA HILL

(Study for 'The Last of England')

(A 61.6)
1852
black chalk and wash, $6\frac{7}{16} \times 7$ (16.4 × 17.7)
signed and dated: *FMB* [monogram] *Decr./52*
Birmingham Museums and Art Gallery

Brown drew this portrait of Emma in December 1852, around the time he was beginning *The Last of England* (cat. 58). She wears a bonnet trimmed with flowers and a bow under her chin. In the painting, instead of the flowers and bow, strands of hair blown across her forehead and a billowing pink ribbon indicate the wind out at sea.

In April 1855 Brown retouched the drawing whilst continuing his work on the painting: 'worked at Emma's head, the drawing I made at Hampstead when I began the picture. Emma would not sit so I worked from feeling.'[7] The head in the painting gave him much trouble before he got it right: her mouth is firmly closed and he painted her to look as if she had been crying. Her expression in the drawing is neither happy nor sad: typically, her mouth is slightly open, revealing her teeth.

Emma's beauty was a constant inspiration to Brown and she modelled for most of the artist's principal paintings of the 1850s. Despite the difficulties of the marriage the couple also experienced great happiness: an idyllic family portrait is included in the landscape painting *Walton-on-the-Naze* (cat. 55), and Emma's distinctive features still appear in works of the '70s and '80s (see cat. 94).

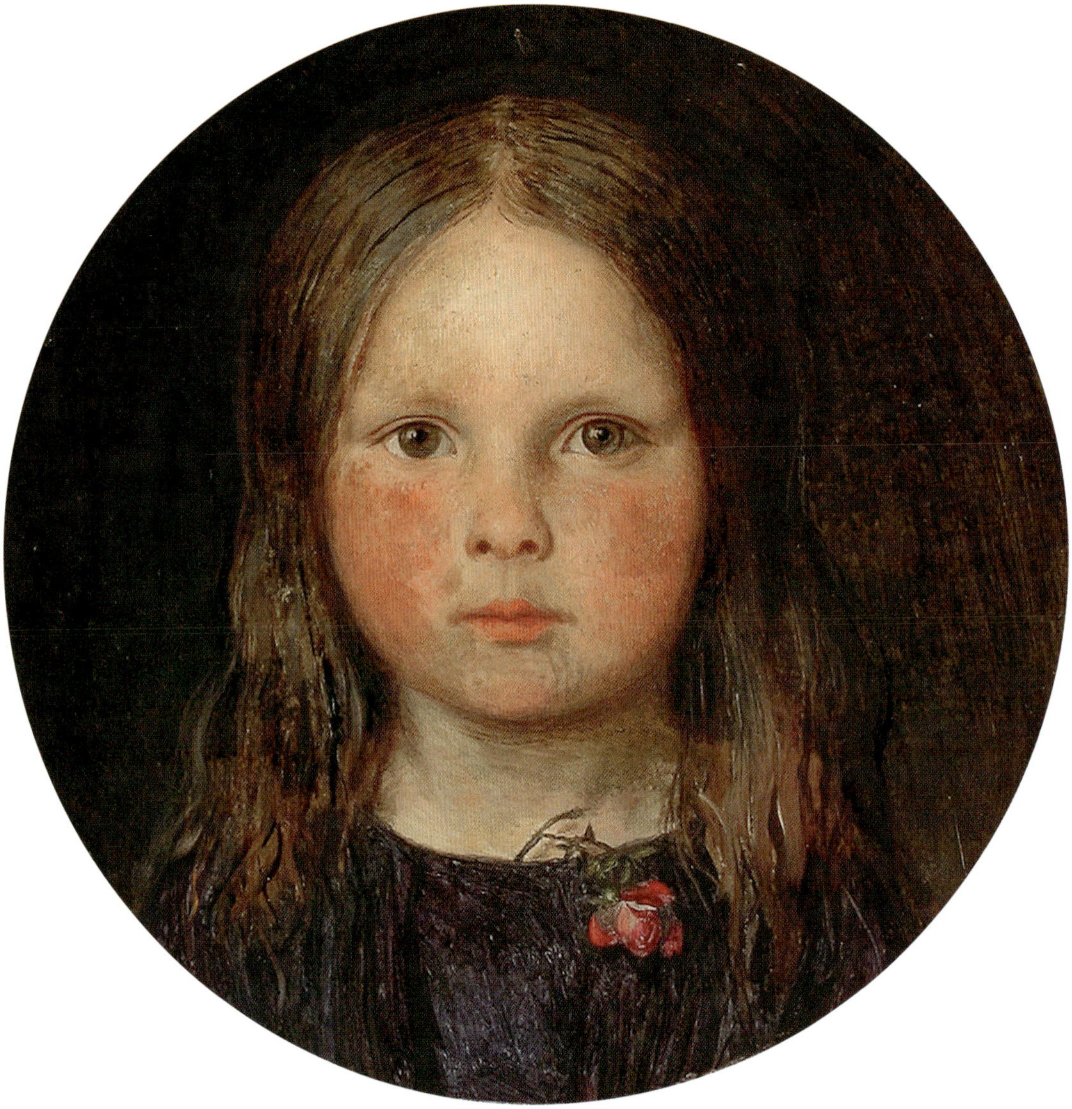

6

6
LUCY MADOX BROWN

(B51)
1849
oil on board, 6¼ diam. (15.8)
Private collection

Lucy, the daughter of Brown's first marriage, was born in Paris on 19 July 1843. On her sixth birthday, shortly before this portrait was painted, Brown wrote in his diary 'My sweet Lucy 6 years old.'[8] Brown painted the portrait at Margate, where he spent two weeks with his daughter around September 1849. Lucy is shown full-face with the characteristic staring directness of the artist's child portraits. She has red cheeks and wears a red rose in her dress; the bright colours and sharp detail are characteristic of the Pre-Raphaelite style.

After Elisabeth died, Lucy was sent to live with Brown's aunt Helen Bromley, who kept a school at Gravesend, but he frequently went to see her there and took her on outings and holidays. Later she was sent to board with Mrs Frances Rossetti, mother of Dante Gabriel, Christina and William Michael, probably to remove her from the domestic troubles caused by her step-mother's drinking bouts. When she was older, Lucy was given painting lessons by her father, and exhibited watercolours in London and at the provincial exhibitions, but gave up painting following her marriage to William Michael Rossetti in 1874.[9] They had five children. In later life, Lucy was a supporter of women's suffrage, and published a biography of Mary Shelley in 1890, but her health was delicate. She died of tuberculosis at San Remo in 1894.

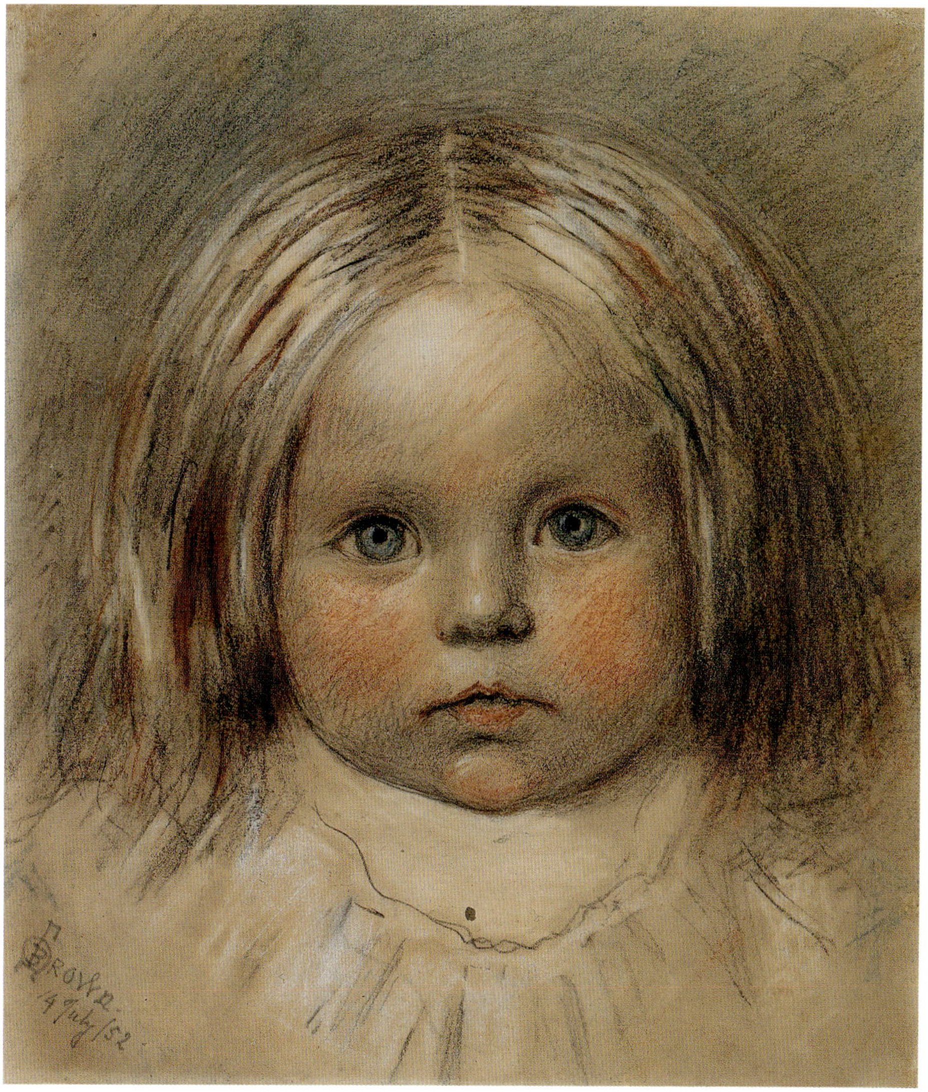

7

7

CATHERINE MADOX BROWN

(B23)
1852
coloured chalks and ink, 7½ × 6½ (19 × 16.5)
signed and dated: *FMBROWN* [initials in monogram]/ 14 July/52
National Museums Liverpool, Walker Art Gallery. Purchased with the assistance of the Art Fund 1984

Catherine, also called by her father Cathy or Katty, was the eldest child of Brown and Emma. She was born on 11 November 1850. The drawing is dated 14 July 1852, when she was twenty months old. In June 1852 Brown moved to Hampstead and Emma went to Dover for the summer;[10] he could have gone to join his wife and child there and made the portrait then.

Catherine had already appeared as the baby in *The pretty baa-lambs* and in *Waiting*, and would later sit for the girl with an apple in *The Last of England* (cats. 49, 56, 58). When she was older, she continued to model (cats. 79, 93) and took up painting, receiving lessons from her father, for whom she worked as studio assistant (see cat. 95; cat.128 is probably an example of her work).[11]

8

OLIVER MADOX BROWN AS A BABY

(B53)
1855
pencil, 6¼ × 5⅝ (15.8 × 14.2)
signed: *FMB* [monogram]
inscribed: *OLIVER MADOX. BROWN. PATER SV DESt JAN 23 1855 AETAS DIE III*
National Museums Liverpool, Walker Art Gallery. Purchased with the assistance of the Art Fund 1984

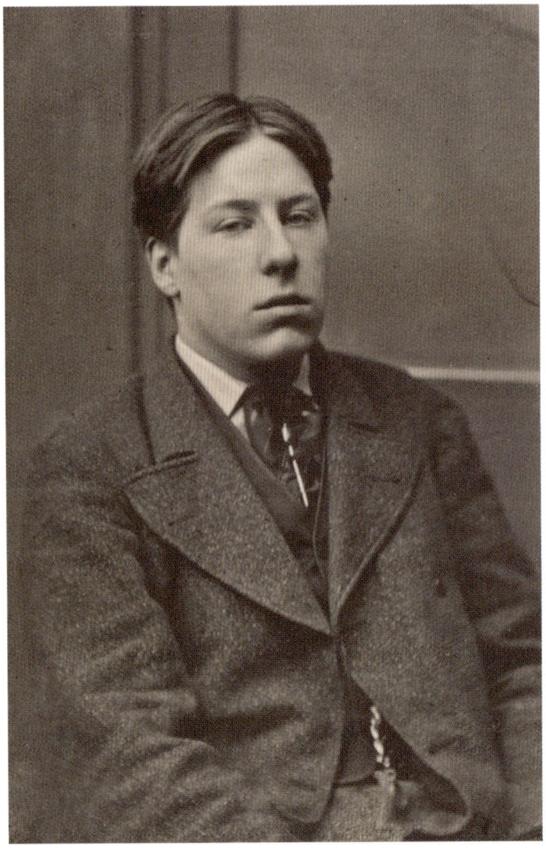

Fig. 47
Oliver Madox Brown aged 16, photograph by Frederick Hollyer, 1871. Royal Photographic Society Collection

Oliver, the second child of Brown and Emma, was just three days old when Brown drew this portrait. On the day his son was born, 20 January 1855, his father wrote in his diary, 'Dearest Emma was delivered of a son, my first. He is very red, a large, nose, eyes & shape of face like a calmuck Tartar, shape of head like a Bosjeman.' The mention of a 'calmuck Tartar' (people from Western Mongolia) probably refers to the new-born baby's eyes as yet not fully open, whilst the 'Bosjeman' were the Bushmen of Southern Africa. These perhaps surprising comparisons testify to the artist's acute powers of observation; for Brown the words were aides-memoire for precise shapes, although in contemporary usage, the terms may have had pejorative associations.

A few days later Brown mentioned this drawing in his diary: 'Tuesday I drew at the boy without his cap & they said I had given him a cold (3 hours). Monday I began it, worked at it with great care but I fear it is not worth anything (8 hours).' The unsentimental realism of this drawing is remarkable, and makes it quite different from the general run of Victorian portraits of infants; but Brown's self-doubt was typical for this period in his life, when many diary entries record his depression at his lack of success. Shortly afterwards he wrote he was 'In a state of great despondency & nervousness all day. An unsuccessful man is a bore to everyone.'[12]

Oliver grew up to be a precocious young man and a talented artist and writer (fig. 47). He exhibited watercolours at the Dudley Gallery and the Royal Academy. At the age of fourteen, he wrote sonnets, much to the surprise of his family who did not realise he even knew what a sonnet was.[13] He published a novel *Gabriel Denver* in 1873. The apple of his father's eye, he died of blood poisoning in 1874, aged only nineteen. Both parents were deeply affected by his death.

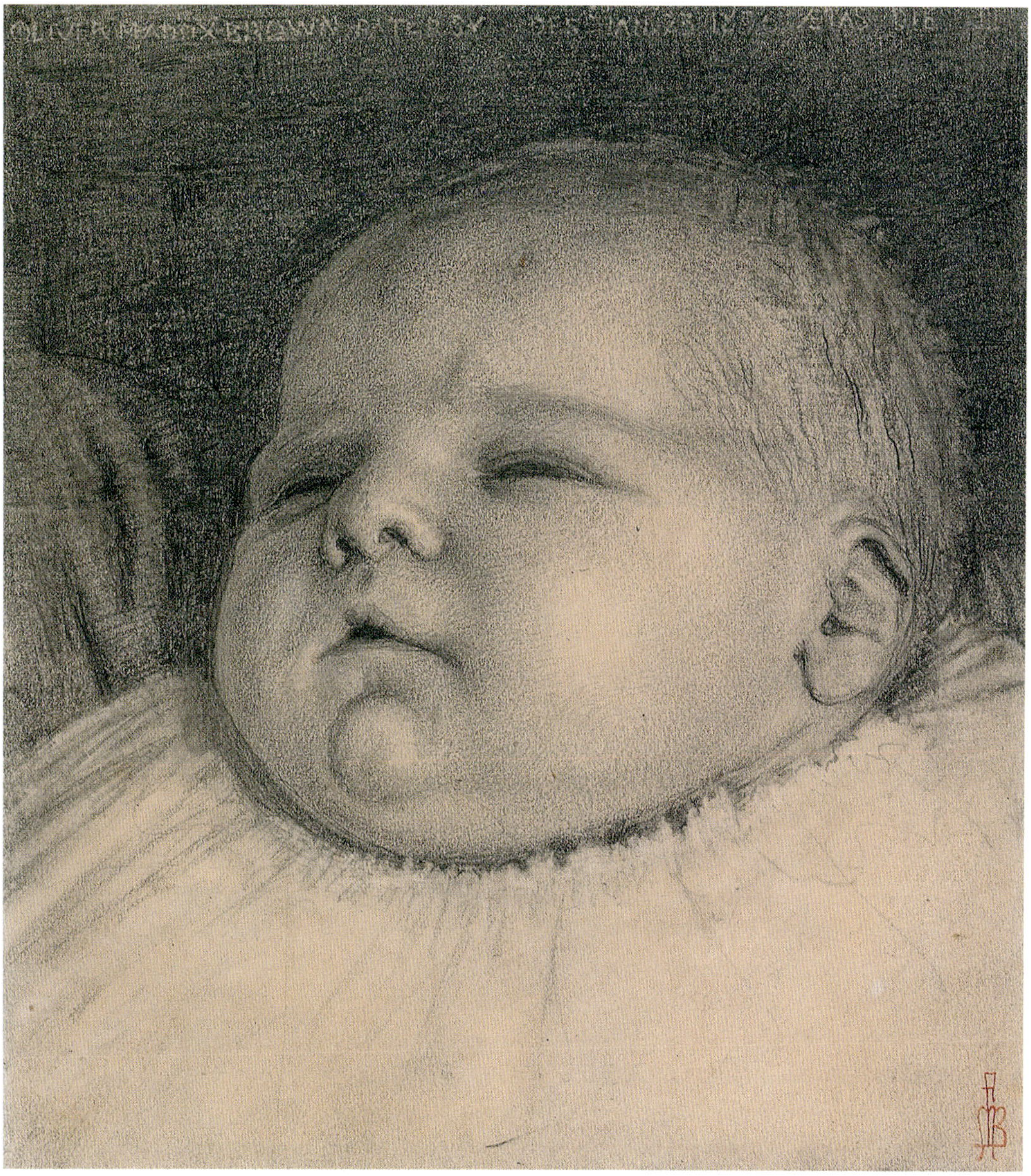

δ

9

ARTHUR MADOX BROWN AS A BABY

(B21)
1856
pencil, 6⅛ × 5½ (15.5 × 14)
signed and dated: *FMB* [monogram] *Sep 26 /56*
inscribed top left: *ARTHUR GABRIEL MADOX BROWN AETAS DIES X*
National Museums Liverpool, Walker Art Gallery. Purchased with the assistance of the Art Fund 1984

Arthur Gabriel, the artist's second son by his wife Emma, was born on 16 September 1856. Brown drew this portrait of Arthur at ten days old to match the drawing of Oliver. Arthur was also drawn at ten weeks for the baby in '*Take Your Son, Sir!*' and he appears as the baby in *Work* (cats. 57, 61). But when he was only ten months old, on 21 July 1857, one week after his baptism, he died of tubercular meningitis. Brown was so hard up at the time that he had to ask his patron Thomas Plint to pay for the funeral. Not long after the baby's death, the family suffered another tragedy when Emma had a miscarriage.[14]

1 The relationships are fully explored in Thirlwell 2008.
2 Hueffer 1896, p. 39.
3 W.M. Rossetti 1895, I, p. 108.
4 Information from Anthea Jarvis.
5 *Diary*, pp. 56, 57–58, 65–66.
6 W.M. Rossetti 1895, I, p. 137.
7 *Diary*, p. 132.
8 *Diary*, p. 66.
9 For examples of her paintings see Marsh and Nunn 1997, pp. 126–29.
10 *Diary*, p. 78.
11 For further examples of her painting see Marsh and Nunn 1997, pp. 130–31.
12 *Diary*, pp. 117–19.
13 DNB, article by Stanley Weintraub.
14 *Diary*, pp. 198–99.

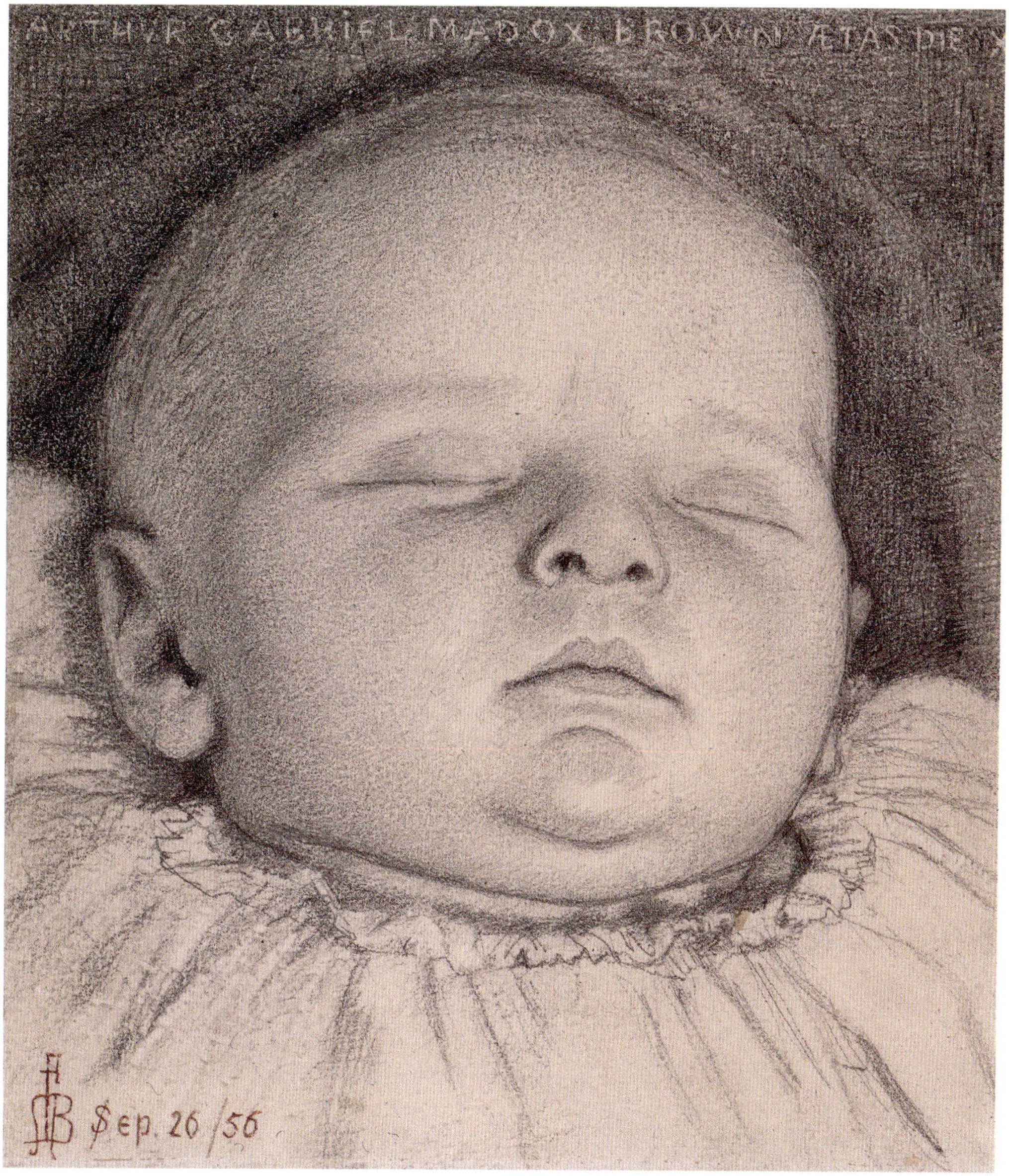

9

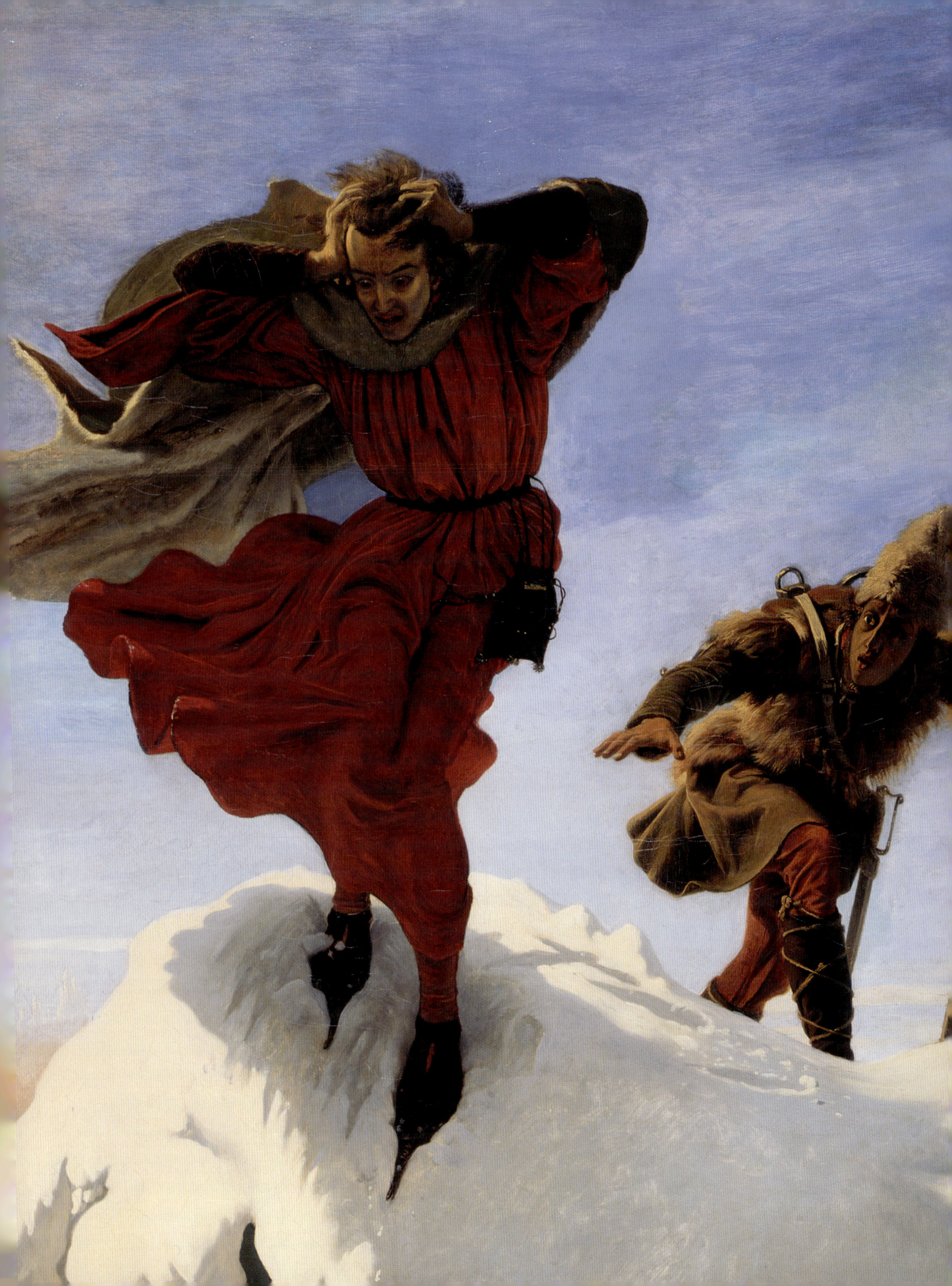

THE EARLY PERIOD

Brown showed an early aptitude for art, and at the age of thirteen was sent to Bruges where he became the private pupil of Albert Gregorius a former pupil of the French painter Jacques-Louis David. Gregorius was Director of the Bruges Academy of Painting, and once Brown was old enough he was enrolled as a student at the Academy. After one year in Bruges, Brown transferred to the Ghent Academy under another pupil of David, Pieter van Hanselaer. No work by Brown can be securely attributed to his time in Bruges, but in Ghent he painted portraits and historical subjects. Finally, in 1838, at seventeen, he began to study at the Antwerp Academy, one of the leading art schools in Europe, modelled on the French Academie des Beaux-Arts. The Professor of Painting (who in 1839 became the director) was Baron Gustav Wappers, the founder of the romantic Belgian school of history painting, and painter of large dramatic figure compositions.

Brown's Belgian training was more rigorous than anything available in Britain. It was grounded in a lengthy and thorough study of drawing, and its aim was to train artists in the making of history paintings, multi-figured compositions on themes from myth, literature and history. They were then regarded as the ultimate test of the painter's art. The creation of a history painting was a long-drawn out process involving detailed research into accurate costume and settings, and the making of numerous preparatory drawings. Students were taught how to group figures to create movement, how to distribute lights and darks to emphasize the important parts of a composition, and how to use gesture and expression to tell a story. These skills stayed with Brown, even after he had rejected the academic style. Brown's earliest history paintings, now lost, were exhibited in Brussels, Ghent, Antwerp and London.

Following his marriage in 1841, Brown and his wife moved to Paris. Here Brown studied independently; he learned from the Old Masters in the Louvre, and was also able to see the works of modern painters such as Delaroche and Delacroix. He exhibited one work at the Paris Salon in 1842, *The Execution of Mary Stuart*, but his submission for the following year, *Parisina*, was rejected. Both paintings are now lost but related works survive (cats. 13, 38) showing that Brown's style at this time was dark and melodramatic, with exaggerated facial expressions. His drawings were equally expressive as can be seen in the *King Lear* series (cats. 17–22). Brown's choice of subjects showed an enthusiasm for Shakespeare and Byron. This was in tune with the current French craze for English history, literature and drama. Although the 'anglomanie' did not last, Brown stuck to his passion for British history and literature throughout his life.

In 1844, Brown entered the competitions for the murals in the new Houses of Parliament (cats. 23–25). Attracted by the possibilities of work in London, he and his wife moved there the same year.

Fig. 48
Detail of cat. 14, Manfred on the Jungfrau

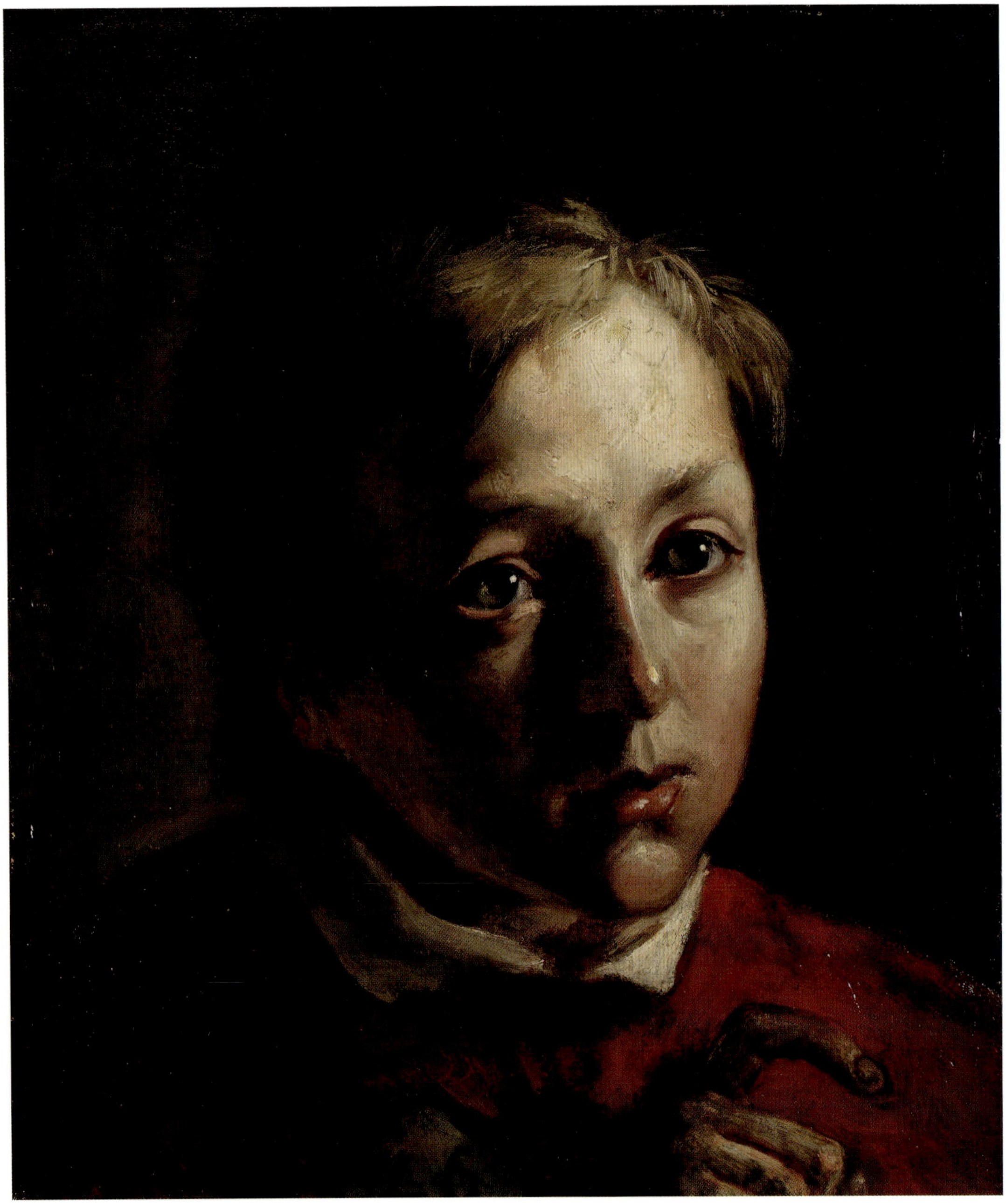

10

10
BOYS HEAD

(A2)
1836/37
oil on canvas, 14 × 13½ (35.5 × 34.3)
Birmingham Museums and Art Gallery

This was painted during the time Brown was studying at the Ghent Academy of Fine Arts. The strong modelling and the broad application of paint is typical of what survives of Brown's early work. The pointing finger, somewhat badly drawn, suggests that the picture could be connected with Brown's earliest recorded work, now lost, entitled *Showing the Way*, painted at Ghent in 1836. The boy is wearing some kind of a badge; its meaning is not known, but it could be part of the uniform of a page or messenger boy.[1]

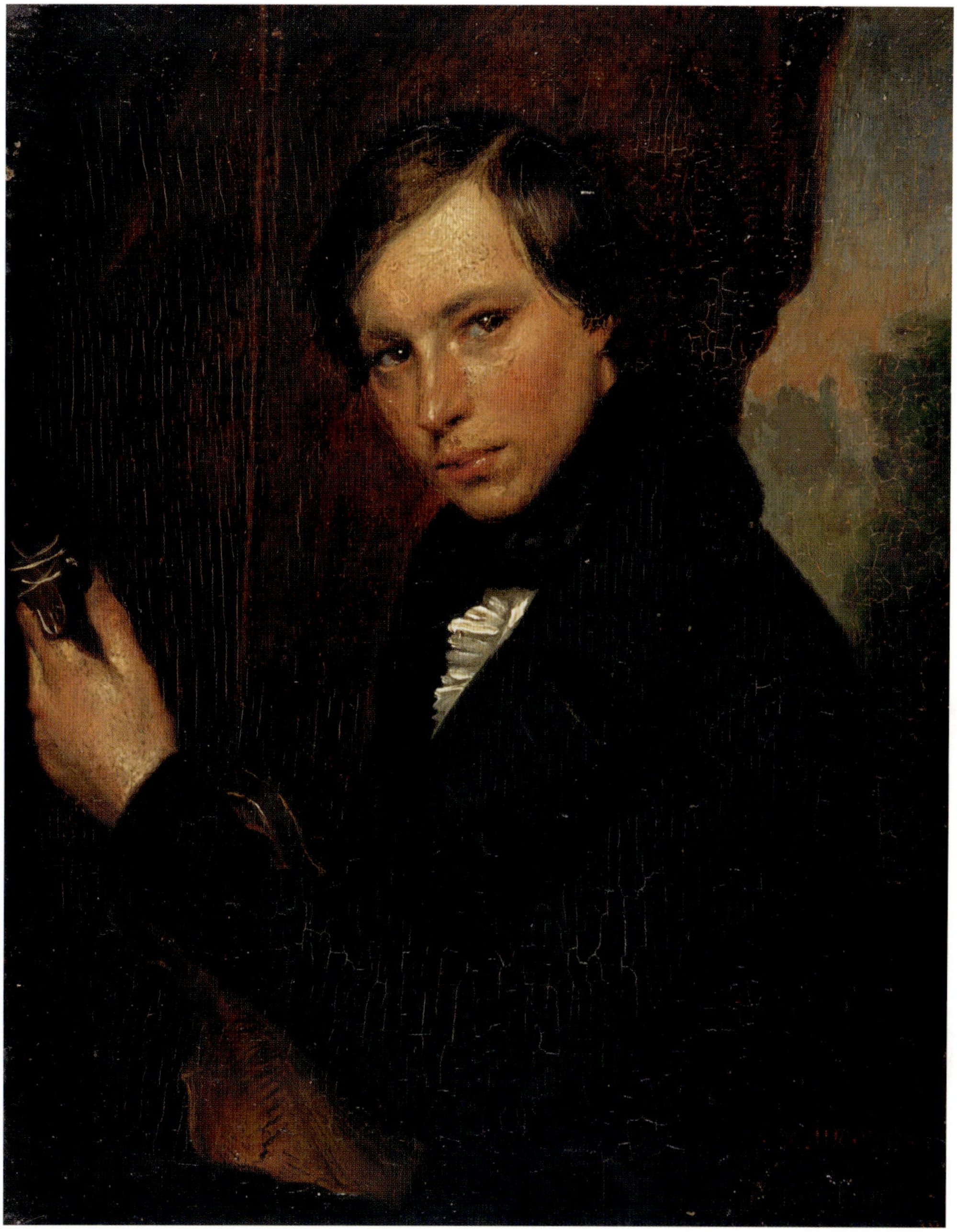

11

11

F.H.S. PENDLETON

(B83)
1837
oil on panel, 6⅝ × 5¼ (16.9 × 13.3)
signed: *F.M.Brown / à son ami*...(illegible)
Manchester City Galleries

The young man holding a violin was a friend of Brown's at Ghent, Frederick Henry Snow Pendleton (1818–88). He taught Brown to play the violin; Brown was interested in music throughout his life. Pendleton later became a clergyman and was still corresponding with Brown in the 1880s.

A label on the back written by Brown in 1876 states that he painted this portrait in 1837 when he was sixteen. Though conventional in style, it shows remarkable accomplishment for such a young artist.

12

HEAD OF A GIRL

(A15)
around 1840
oil on canvas, 20 ¼ × 13 ¾ (51.5 × 35)
signed: *F.M. Brown*
Tate. Purchased 1935

This study may have been painted in Antwerp or Paris, and its exact date cannot be established. The paint has been applied with breadth and confidence so that it tells from a distance. The side lighting, the luminous highlights and the passages of reflected light suggest that the girl may have posed by a window. Already at this stage it seems Brown was experimenting with natural light, disliking the conventional studio light of contemporary academic painting. The identity of the model, who wears a gold-coloured Spanish comb in her hair and a yellow choker, matching her yellow dress, is not known. The study may be related to *The Execution of Mary Stuart* (cat. 13) as it resembles the profile of the Queen, although facing the opposite way.

12

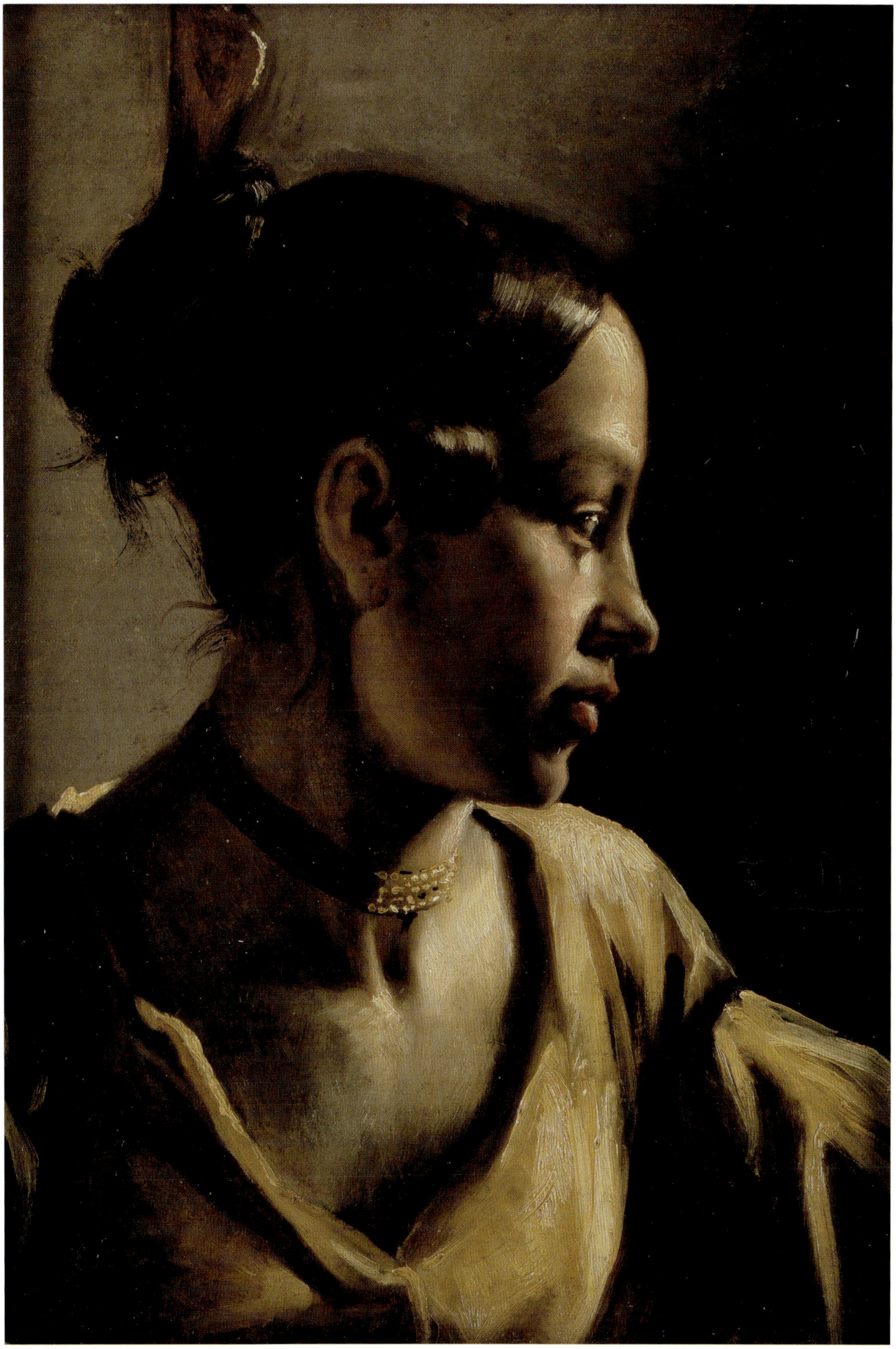

13
THE EXECUTION OF MARY STUART

(A23.1)
1840/42
oil on panel, 30 ¾ × 27 ⅜ (78.2 × 69.5)
signed: *FMB*
The Whitworth Art Gallery, The University of Manchester

Mary Queen of Scots, born Mary Stuart, was executed for treason at Fotheringhay Castle on 8 February 1587 because of her involvement in plots to assassinate Queen Elizabeth I. Brown showed her as described in John Lingard's *History of England* (1847). Mary had been refused permission for her own chaplain to be present and was accompanied on the scaffold by the protestant Dean of Lincoln, who declared she would be damned unless she renounced her Catholic faith. Mary puts her finger to her lips to silence the sobbing of her attendants, one of whom faints into the arms of a companion. A study for the head of the maid who has fainted was painted from Brown's first wife, Elisabeth (Ashmolean Museum, Oxford).[2]

This is a small version of, or possibly a preparatory study for, Brown's first large historical painting, now lost, which was begun in Antwerp in 1840 and finished in Paris in 1841; the following year it was shown at the Paris Salon. One of the Parisian critics described it as more remarkable for its size than its merit and noted that it looked foreign.[3] Brown's daughter later described it as an attempt to reproduce the effect of Velázquez, 'although at the time of commencement, all he knew of Velázquez was from the descriptions of his master, the Baron Wappers.'[4] The weird faces and exaggerated proportions also show the influence of Henry Fuseli, the Anglo-Swiss artist admired by Brown (fig. 51, p. 98).

For his Paris debut, Brown did not adopt the style taught at the French *ateliers*, later writing of his aversion for its 'cold pedantic drawing and heavy opaque colour'.[5] But in depicting a subject from British history, he was in line with French taste: Delaroche had painted several scenes from British history including *The Execution of Lady Jane Grey*, exhibited in Paris in 1834 (National Gallery, London).

Once he had moved back to London, Brown showed the large painting in an exhibition at the Pantheon. There it was admired by the young Dante Gabriel Rossetti who wrote to Brown in March 1848 asking if he would take him on as a pupil, saying 'As for the *Mary Queen of Scots*, if ever I do anything in the art, it will certainly be attributable in a great degree to the constant study of that work.'[6]

13

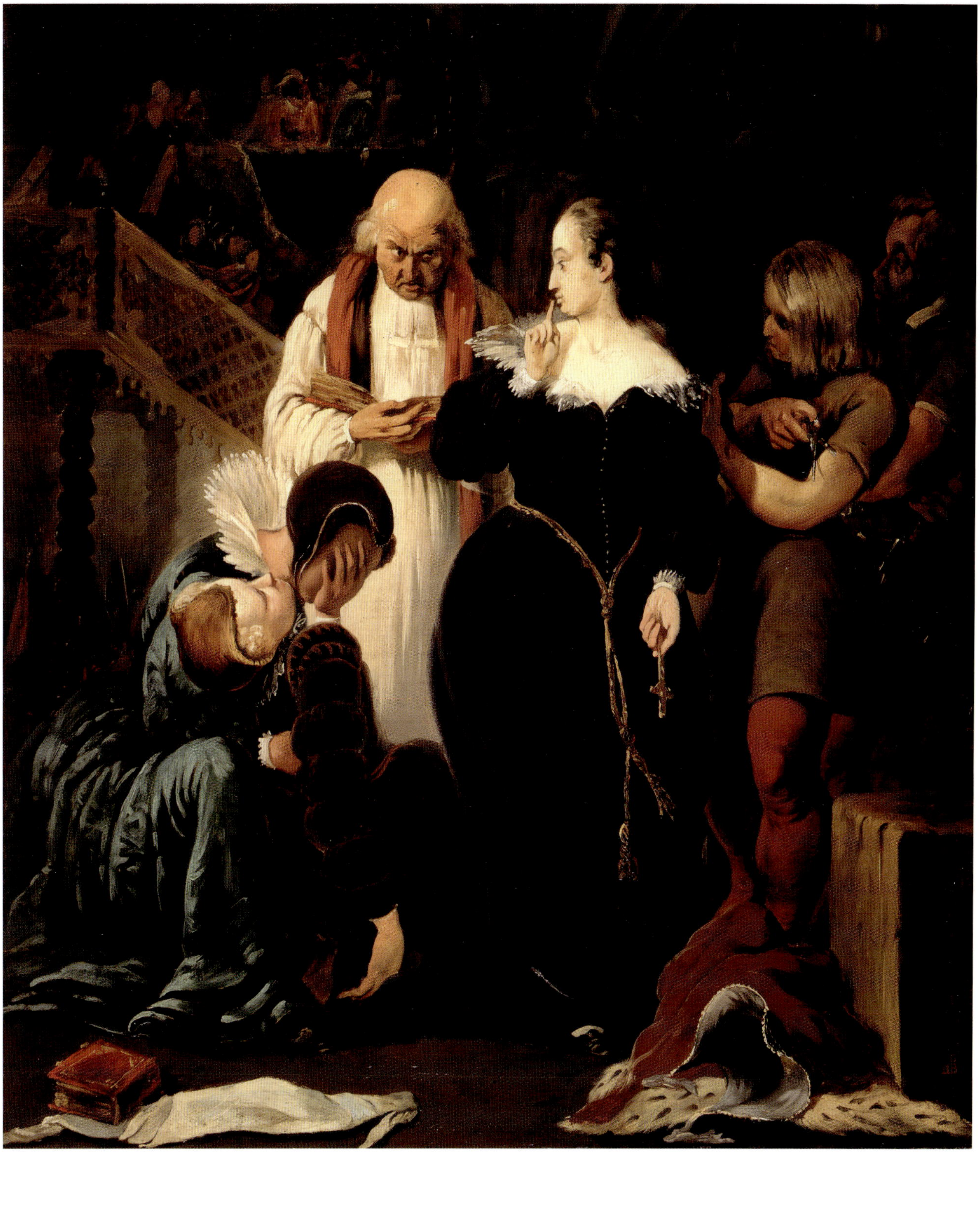

14

MANFRED ON THE JUNGFRAU

(A24)
1841, 1861
oil on canvas
signed: *Ford Madox Brown*
55⅙ × 45¼ (140.2 × 115)
Manchester City Galleries

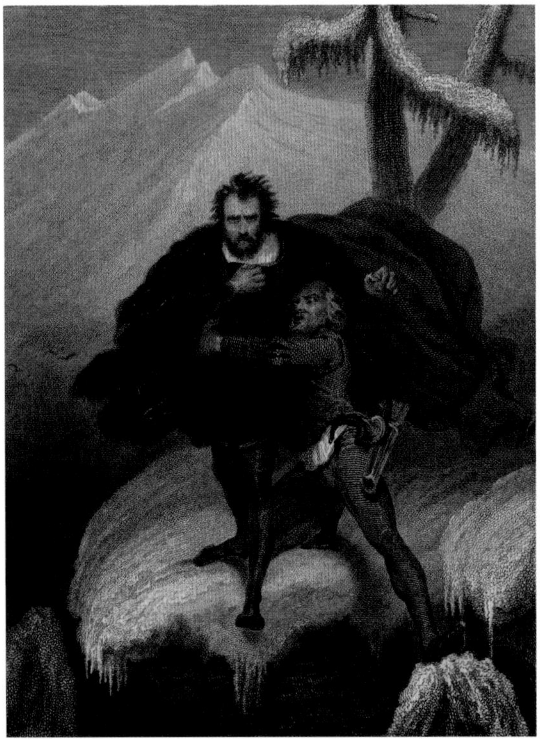

Fig. 49
Tony Johannot (engraved by Koenig), Manfred, *from* Oeuvres de Lord Byron, *1831, Bibliothèque nationale de France, Paris*

Manfred, the eponymous hero of Byron's dramatic poem, published in 1817, is an archetypal Byronic hero, an outsider haunted by secret guilt and longing for death. Brown's painting depicts the moment of crisis in Act I, Scene 2, when Manfred, torn by mental and spiritual conflict, stands on the brink of a precipice, and is tempted to throw himself over. At the last moment, a chamois hunter appears:

> Chamois Hunter: Friend! have a care,
> Your next step may be fatal! – for the love
> Of him who made you, stand not on that brink!
>
> Manfred (*not hearing him*):
> Such would have been for me a fitting tomb;
> My bones had then been quiet in their depth;
> They had not then been strewn upon the rocks
> For the wind's pastime – as thus – thus they shall be –
> In this one plunge!
>
> *The chamois hunter clutches him in the act of springing off.*

Brown designed the composition in Antwerp in 1840 and painted it in Paris in 1841. But its appearance today is quite different from that of 1841, because twenty years later Brown retouched it extensively. The poses of the two figures, and the shape of the snowy peak remain from the original composition, but the colour scheme was 'quite obliterated.'[7] The painting originally had what he described as 'a first, though not very recognisable attempt, at an out-door effect of light'. Because Brown repainted it in a much brighter key, it is not possible to reconstruct its original appearance. The painting is now a hybrid, combining the tense, theatrical poses, melodramatic faces and flying draperies of Belgian and French Romantic history painting, with a daylight effect in the sky painted with the brightness of the Pre-Raphaelite style. The disjunction was acknowledged by Brown: 'The work is intended for consideration merely by the human and dramatic side, glaciers not having formed part of my scheme of study in those days.'[8] By 1865, when Brown wrote this, Pre-Raphaelite painters had, under the influence of Ruskin, learned to depict mountains, rock formations and glaciers with a geological accuracy unheard of in the 1840s.

Brown's visualisation of Byron's hero and the snowy mound on which he stands is similar to Tony Johannot's illustration of *Manfred* in a French translation of Byron's works by Amédée Pichot first published in 1822–25 and reissued in 1831 (fig. 49).[9] Byronic subjects were popular in France and Belgium: in 1839 Brown painted a *Giaour's Confession*, now lost, a subject also previously painted by Delacroix, Ary Scheffer and Wappers.[10]

14

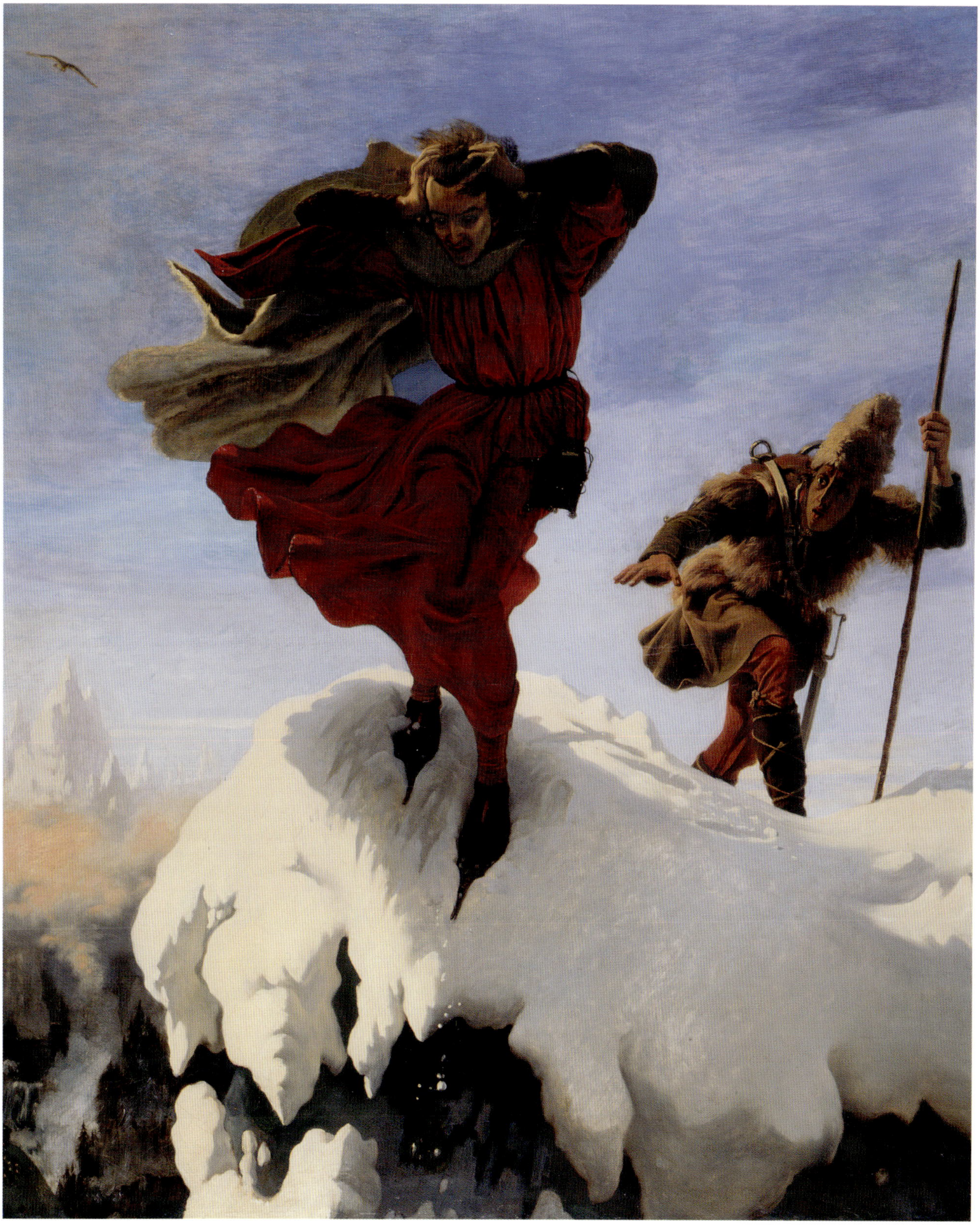

15

THE PRISONER OF CHILLON

(A28)
1843
oil on canvas
20 15/16 × 25 9/16 (53.2 × 64.9)
Manchester City Galleries

The painting was inspired by Byron's poem *The Prisoner of Chillon* (1816), based on the legend of François de Bonivard, a sixteenth-century Geneva patriot who was imprisoned for six years in the castle of Chillon, on Lake Leman. Byron described how Bonivard and his two brothers were each chained to a column; Bonivard was forced to watch helplessly as his brothers died. The painting shows him watching the death of the second brother:

> I saw, and could not hold his head,
> Nor reach his dying hand – nor dead, –
> Though hard I strove, but strove in vain
> To rend and gnash my bonds in twain.

Brown painted it in Paris in 1843. He may have known the painting of the same subject by Delacroix of 1834 which also shows Bonivard straining to reach his dying brother (Louvre, Paris). The depiction of the dark interior, lit by what Byron described as a shaft of 'pale and livid light,' may have been influenced by Brown's study of Rembrandt in the Louvre. Brown heightened the characterisation of the brothers, going beyond Byron's text. The youngest, in the centre, described as 'beautiful as day', is shown as an effeminate fop, and the second, on the left, 'form'd to combat with his kind; Strong in frame', has a muscular torso based on Michelangelo's *The Dying Slave* (Louvre), but also derived from Fuseli whose flickering light effects and mannered gestures was an important element in Brown's style at this period (fig. 51, p. 98).

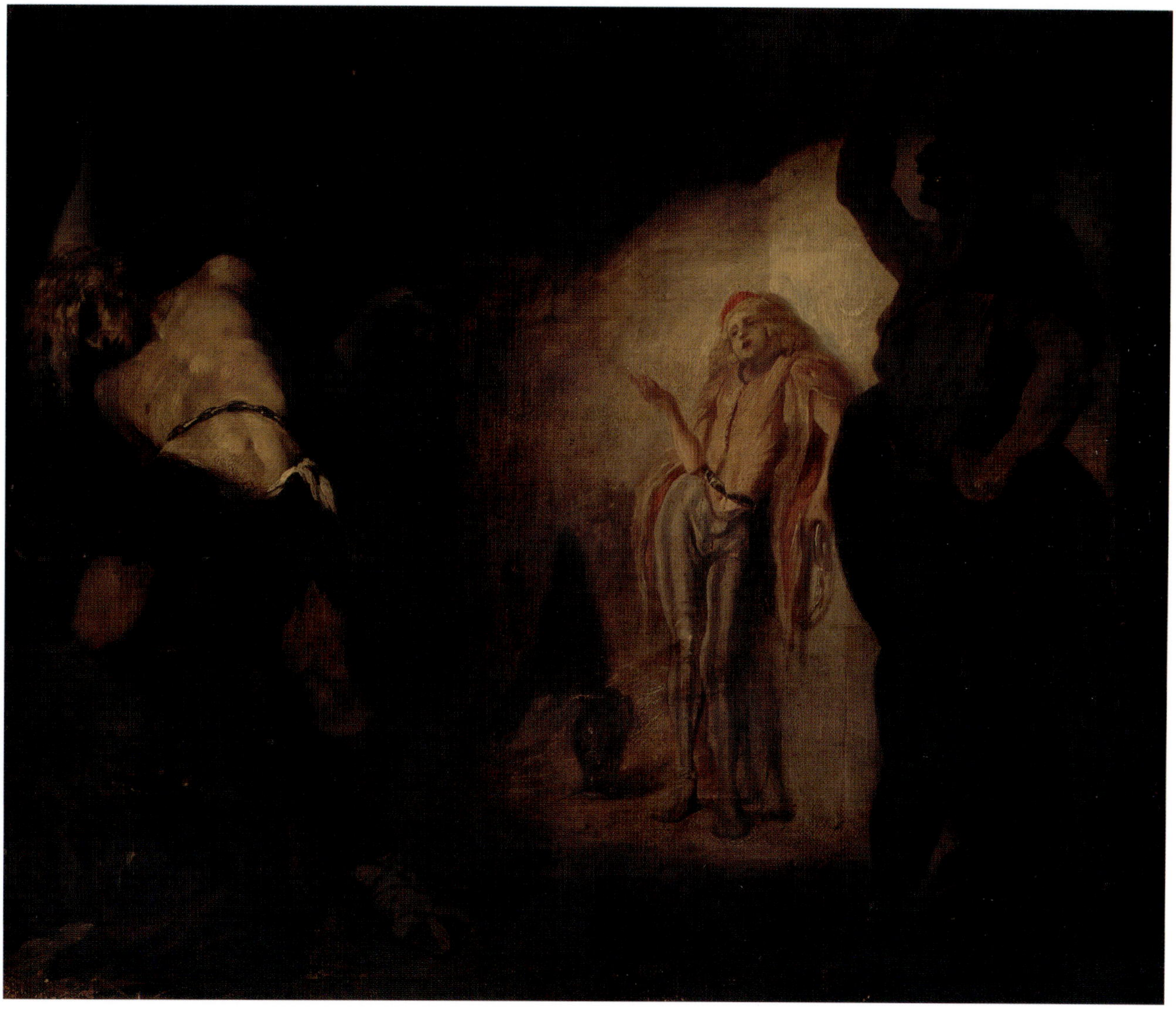

15

16

DR. PRIMROSE AND HIS DAUGHTERS

(A26)
early 1840s
oil on canvas
28⁹⁄₁₆ × 23⅛ (72.6 × 58.7)
Manchester City Galleries

Dr. Primrose and his daughters shows a garden where an old man sits surrounded by his attentive family while a servant brings refreshments. It is supposed to be a scene from *The Vicar of Wakefield*, the popular novel of 1776 by Oliver Goldsmith, although the identification dates from after Brown's death. The painting does not correspond exactly to any scene in the novel, but may be a conflation of different parts. At the beginning of the book, Goldsmith's Dr. Primrose loses his wealth and moves to a simple thatched cottage; after the move, he reproves his wife and daughters for the extravagant finery of their dress, 'their trains bundled up in a heap behind and rustling with every motion' and another passage describes the family taking refuge in simple pleasures, such as tea in the garden at the end of the day.[11] Brown's Dr. Primrose is shown raising his eyes to heaven and could be preaching the virtues of simplicity to his family. The dress of the kneeling daughter has a train like the one in the text. But the opulent furniture looks more like the time before the family lost their money: Dr. Primrose is seated on an ermine rug in a grandiose throne-like chair on castors, placed on a carpet, and in the garden is a large stone lion fountain, an unlikely ornament in the cottage garden described by Goldsmith.

Brown's admiration for Hogarth may have been the inspiration for the broad, coarse brushwork: he may also have taken his cue from Hogarth to turn Goldsmith's gentle irony into mockery of Dr. Primrose's virtuous simplicity. A similar sense of caricature is seen in the drawings Brown made in Paris in 1842 illustrating another eighteenth-century English novel, Sterne's *A Sentimental Journey* (Birmingham Museums and Art Gallery).[12] At this period Brown was still experimenting with different styles, and the resemblance of Dr. Primrose's garden to a French rococo landscape may indicate an additional source in French prints or illustrations.

16

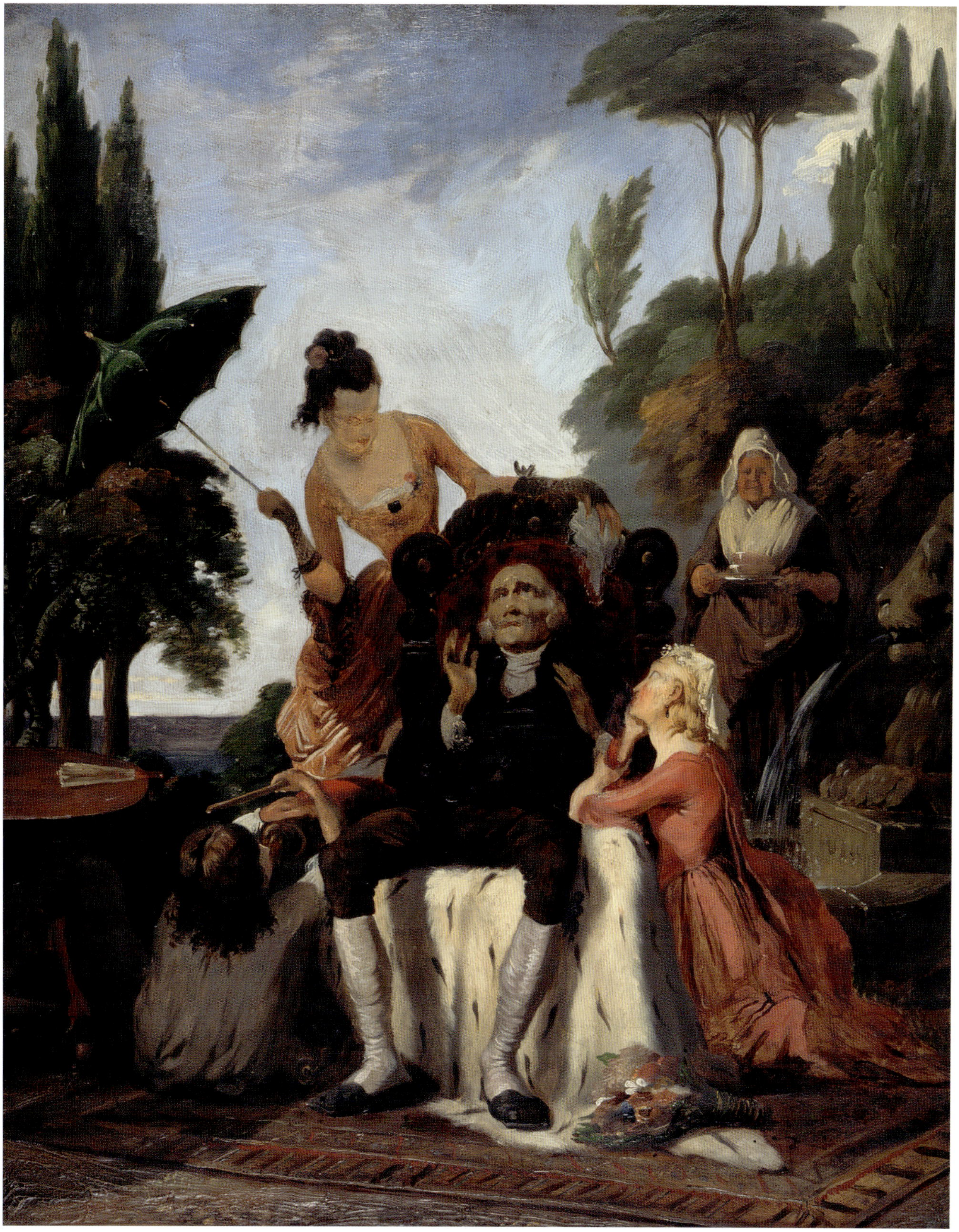

In Paris Brown made a set of drawings of episodes from *King Lear*. Sixteen were shown in the artist's 1865 exhibition and are now in the Whitworth Art Gallery, Manchester and an additional four sheets belong to Birmingham Museums and Art Galleries. Six from the first group are shown here. Brown regarded them as 'rude first ideas for more finished designs'[13] which he never got round to completing. The drawings, aptly described by William Michael Rossetti as 'heaving with energy',[14] are deliberately primitive; their rough and nervous lines contradict all that Brown had been taught in the Belgian academies about draughtsmanship, and he admitted that some people thought the drawings 'offensively unfinished or ill-finished'.[15]

The drawings are the earliest evidence of Brown's passion for Shakespeare and especially for *King Lear*, to which the artist returned at intervals throughout his career. The cult of Shakespeare was strong in Paris from the late 1820s, popularised through theatrical performance, paintings and prints. Delacroix made a set of lithographs of episodes from *Hamlet* (1843–44), almost certainly known to Brown, and he also knew the outline engravings to Shakespeare by the German printmaker Moritz Retzsch which were widely circulated throughout Europe in the 1830s and '40s. These also depicted the plays in episodic form. Retzsch's engravings of *King Lear* appeared in 1838 (fig. 50). In addition to specific borrowings from Retzsch, Brown followed two general features of his work, the staging of some scenes in symmetrical frontally-viewed stage-like spaces, and the restriction to line. But Brown's freely drawn strokes of the pen are much more expressive than the mechanical precision of Retzsch's engraved outlines; whereas Retzsch gave all his figures the same passionless elegance, Brown summmed up the essence of each character, the domineering Goneril and Regan, the ineffectual Lear and the mocking Fool. Brown probably also knew Fuseli's Lear subjects, many of which were available in printed form: for example, *Lear banishing Cordelia* (fig. 51), engraved for Boydell, has a similar symmetrical arrangement to some of Brown's drawings.

In 1892 the set of sixteen drawings was bought by Sir Henry Irving, while Brown was working on designs for Irving's production of *King Lear* at the Lyceum, which opened in November of that year. Brown provided set designs and costumes for three scenes in the first and second acts (fig. 20, p.00). Irving also admired *Cordelia's Portion* (cat. 79), and had an engraving of it in his dressing room.

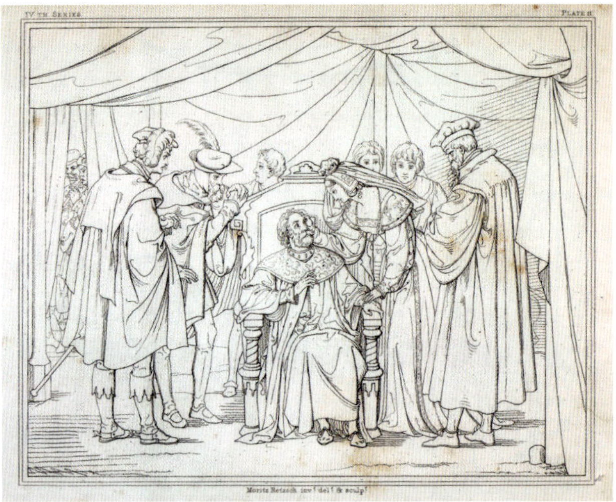

Fig. 50
Moritz Retzsch, King Lear, Act IV, scene 7, *1838. Private collection*

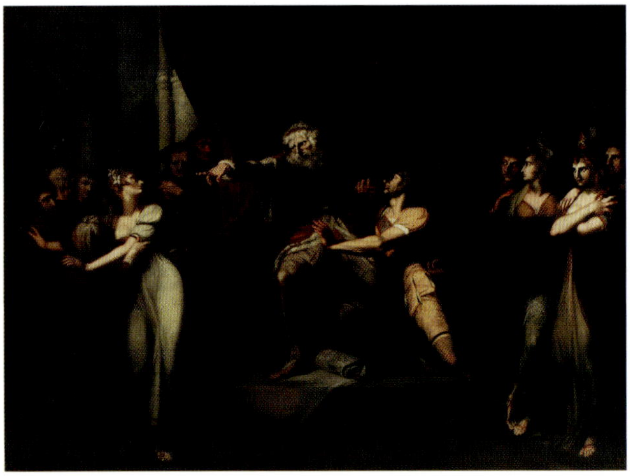

Fig. 51
Henry Fuseli, King Lear banishing Cordelia, *c.1784/90. Art Gallery of Ontario, Toronto*

17

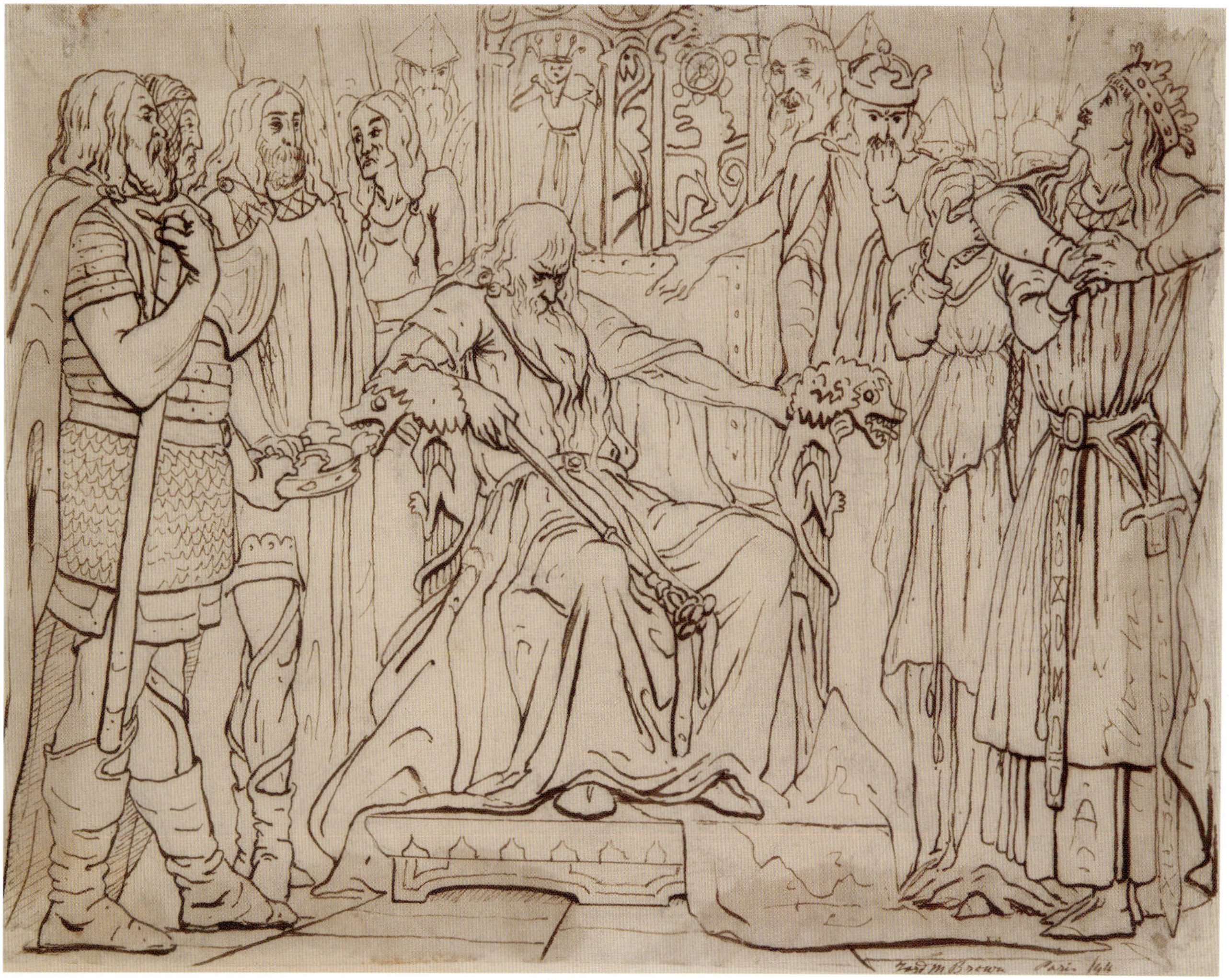

17

HERE CORDELIA, DISINHERITED, IS CHOSEN IN MARRIAGE BY THE KING OF FRANCE.

(C14)
1843/44
pen and ink over pencil, 8½ × 11 (21.6 × 28)
signed and dated: *Ford M Brown Paris /44*
The Whitworth Art Gallery, The University of Manchester

From Act I, scene I. Brown's full title continues *Here Cordelia, disinherited, is chosen in marriage by the King of France. The Duke of Burgundy, who would not take her dowerless, is biting his nails in displeasure. Regan and Goneril sneeringly watch her. With them are their two husbands.*

The design of Lear's throne in this drawing and the next, with its deliberately crude figures and animal and bird heads, is a remarkable example of Brown's primitivism, and was perhaps loosely based on Romanesque ornament.

Brown reused this composition as the basis for *Cordelia's Portion* in the 1860s (cat. 79).

18

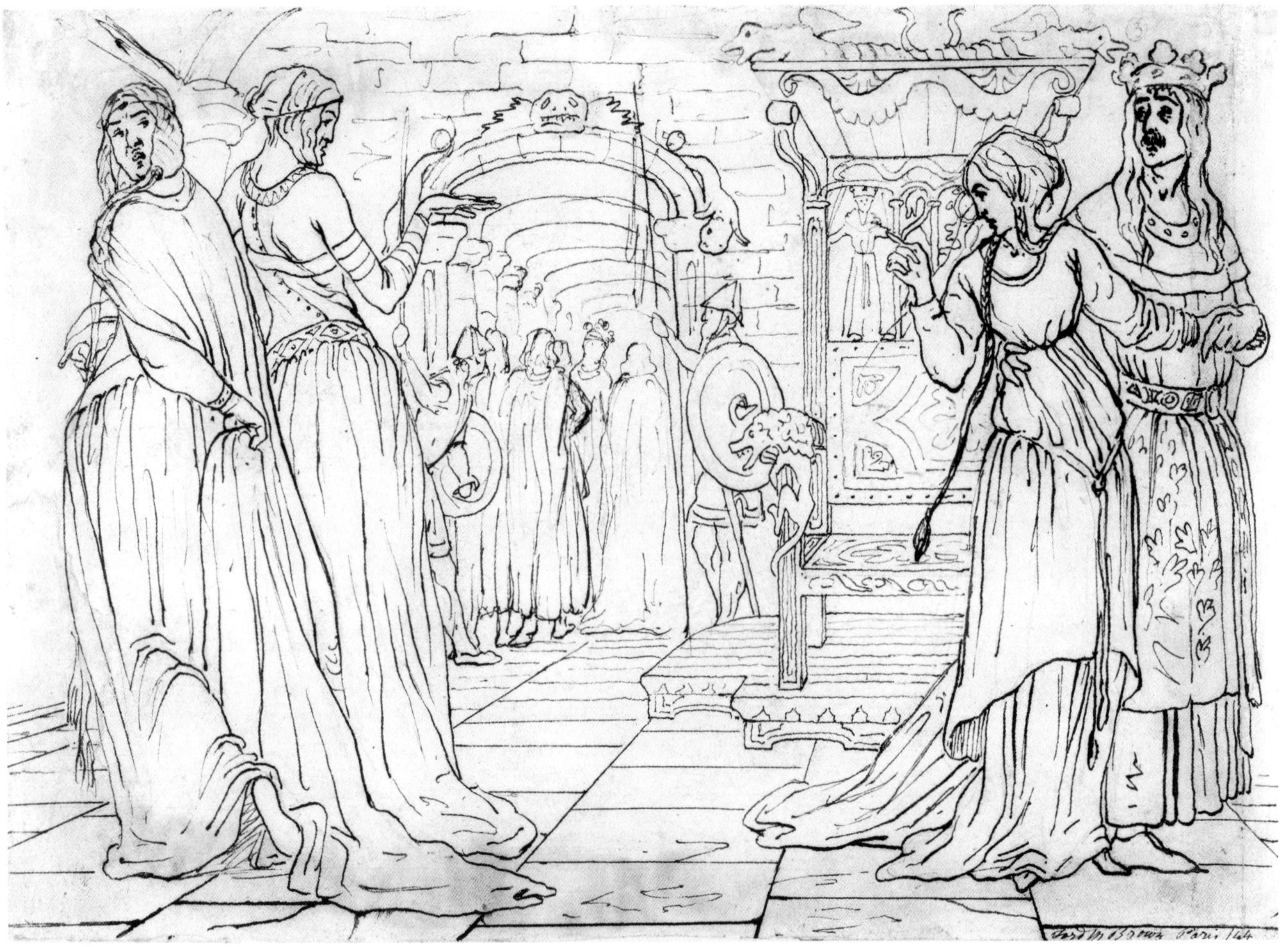

18

THE PARTING OF CORDELIA AND HER SISTERS

(C15)
1843/44
pen and ink over pencil, $8\frac{1}{16} \times 11\frac{1}{2}$ (20.5 × 29.2)
signed and dated: *Ford M Brown Paris /44*
The Whitworth Art Gallery, The University of Manchester

Also from Act I, scene I, showing Goneril and Regan on the left, and Cordelia and the King of France on the right: after Lear has given the disinherited Cordelia to the King of France in marriage, Cordelia says farewell to her sisters. Her pointing finger seems to express her words about them 'I know you what you are'. This scene was chosen by the Pre-Raphaelite Brotherhood for the frontispiece of the Brotherhood's magazine *The Germ*. Brown's etching, which he regarded as a failure, appeared in the third issue, dated March 1850 to accompany a poem about Cordelia written by William Michael Rossetti.

19

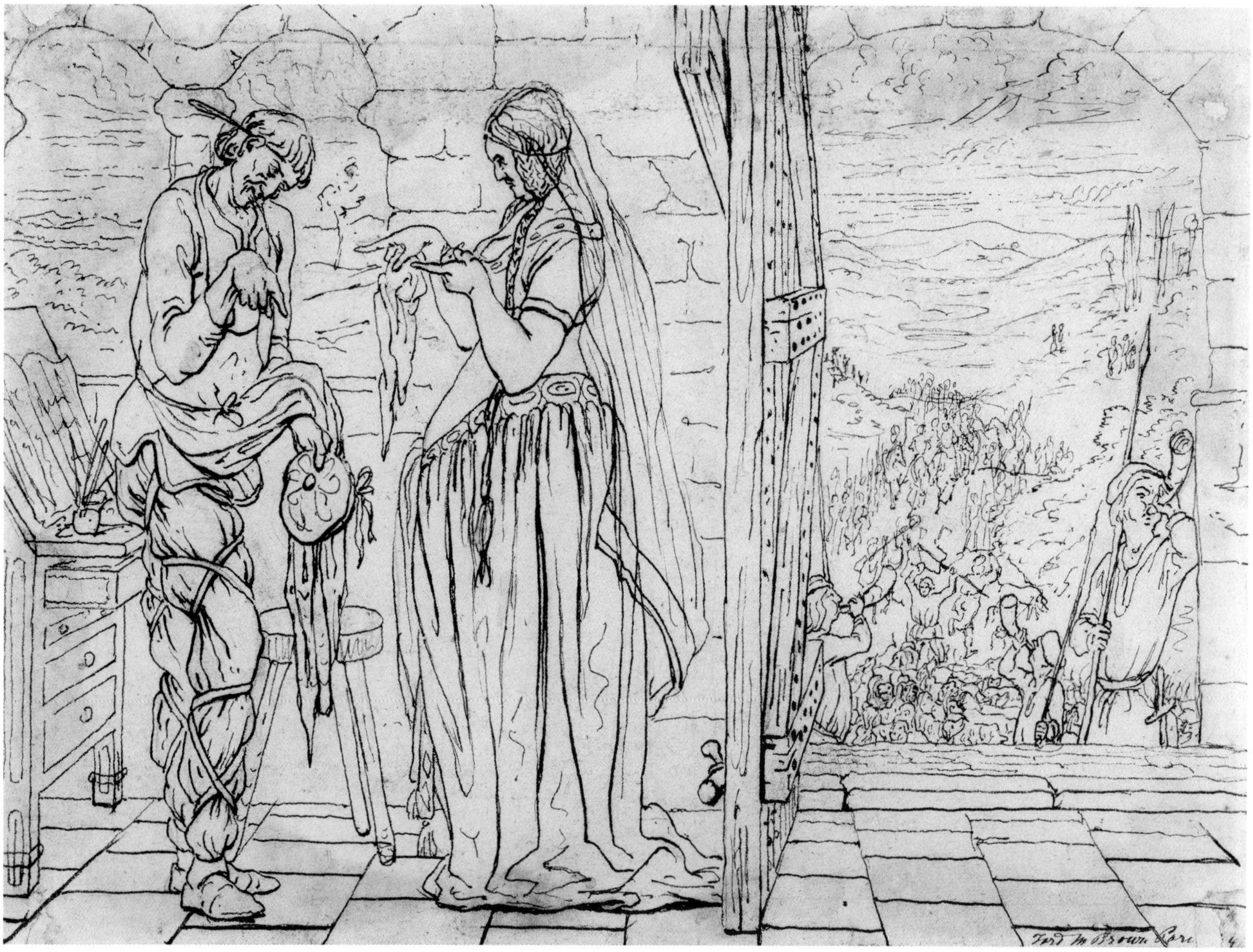

19

KING LEAR, WHO HAS KEPT NOTHING FOR HIMSELF BUT A RETINUE OF 100 KNIGHTS...

(C17)
1843/44
pen and ink over pencil, 8⅛ × 11⅛ (20.6 × 28.2)
signed and dated: *Ford M Brown Pari* [...]*4*
The Whitworth Art Gallery, The University of Manchester

From Act I, scene 3. Brown's full title runs: *King Lear, who has kept nothing for himself but a retinue of 100 knights, has stipulated to live month and month about with either of his two remaining daughters. Goneril, in the absence of her father at the chase, instigates her steward to be less respectful to him.*
The composition is boldly divided into two by the foreshortened vertical of the door, with Goneril and the steward behind it, and the one hundred rowdy knights returning from the chase seen through the doorway. A similar contrast between full size figures in the foreground, and a crowd of tiny figures stretching into the distance, was much later reused by Brown in the mural *The Romans building a Fort at Mancenion* (cat. 116) at Manchester Town Hall.

The Saxon cross-banding of the steward's leggings is similar to the costume of King Harold in *The Body of Harold*, which Brown was painting at approximately the same time (cat. 23).

20

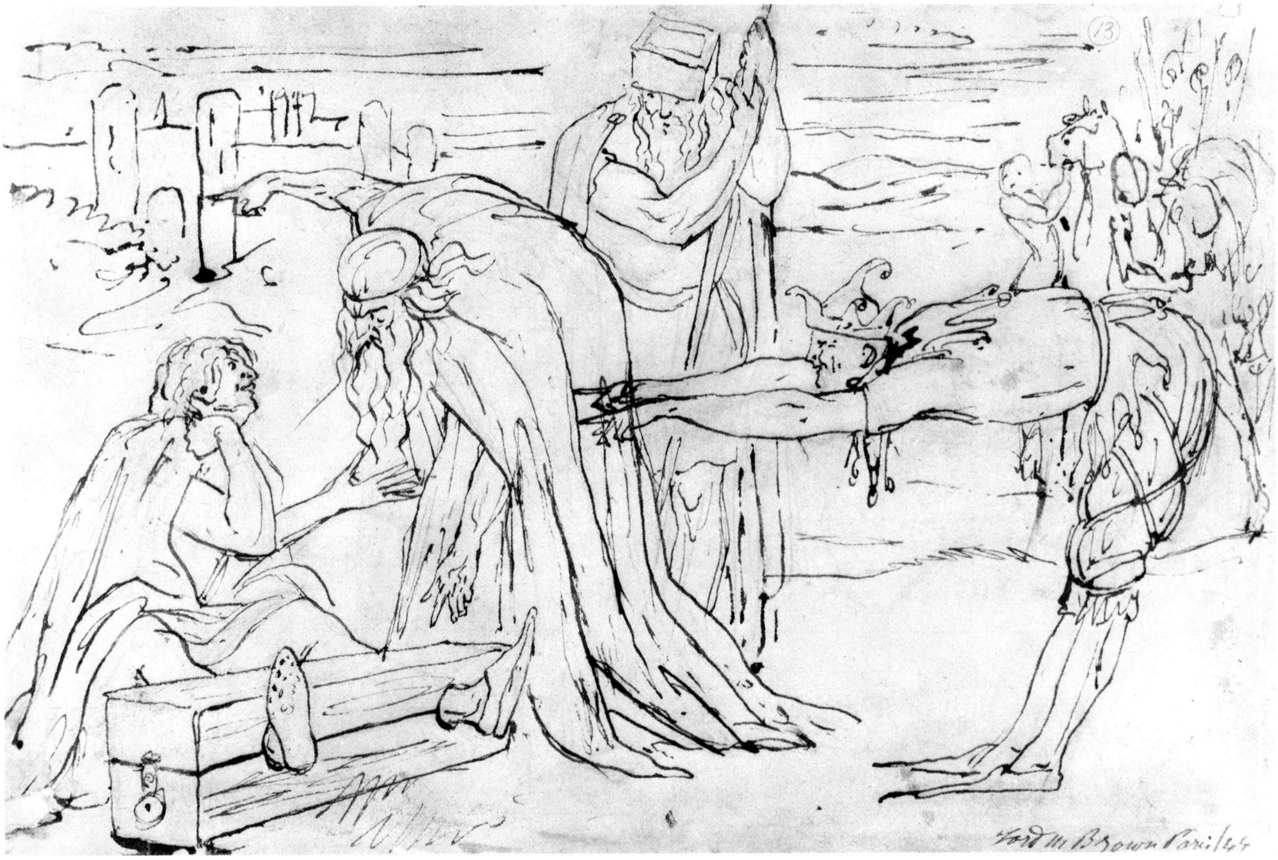

20

KING LEAR WILL NOT BELIEVE THAT HIS OWN DAUGHTER REGAN WOULD HAVE HIS MESSENGER, KENT, PLACED IN THE STOCKS

(C25)
1843/44
pen and ink over pencil, 6⅛ × 9¼ (15.5 × 23.5)
signed and dated: *Ford M Brown Paris /44*
The Whitworth Art Gallery, The University of Manchester

From Act 2, scene 4. The simple but emphatic pose of the jester mocking Kent in the stocks is typical of Brown's expressive use of gesture.

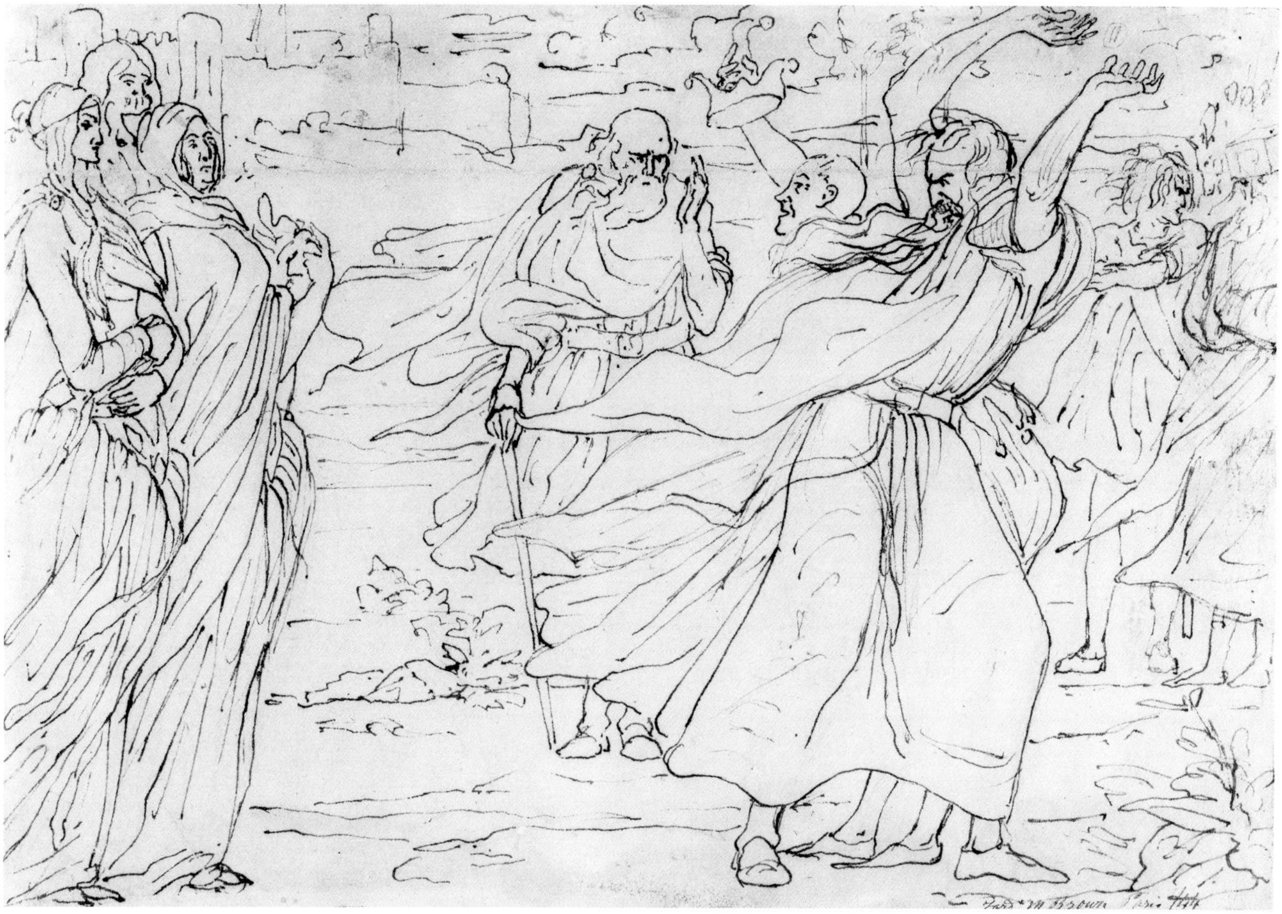

21

KING LEAR PERCEIVING THAT GONERIL AND REGAN ARE BOTH AGREED AS TO THEIR INTENTIONS, CURSES THEM...

(C27)
1843/44
pen and ink over pencil, 7 11/16 × 11 (19.5 × 27.9)
signed and dated: *Ford M Brown Paris /44*
The Whitworth Art Gallery, The University of Manchester

From Act 2, scene 4. The full title runs: *King Lear perceiving that Goneril and Regan are both agreed as to their intentions, curses them, and goes off in the rising storm, shelterless.*

The rising storm is eloquently evoked by the draperies blowing in the wind, whilst Lear utters the curse on his daughters:

> No, you unnatural hags,
> I will have such revenges on you both,
> That all the world shall – I will do such things, –
> What they are, yet I know not: but they shall be
> The terrors of the earth.

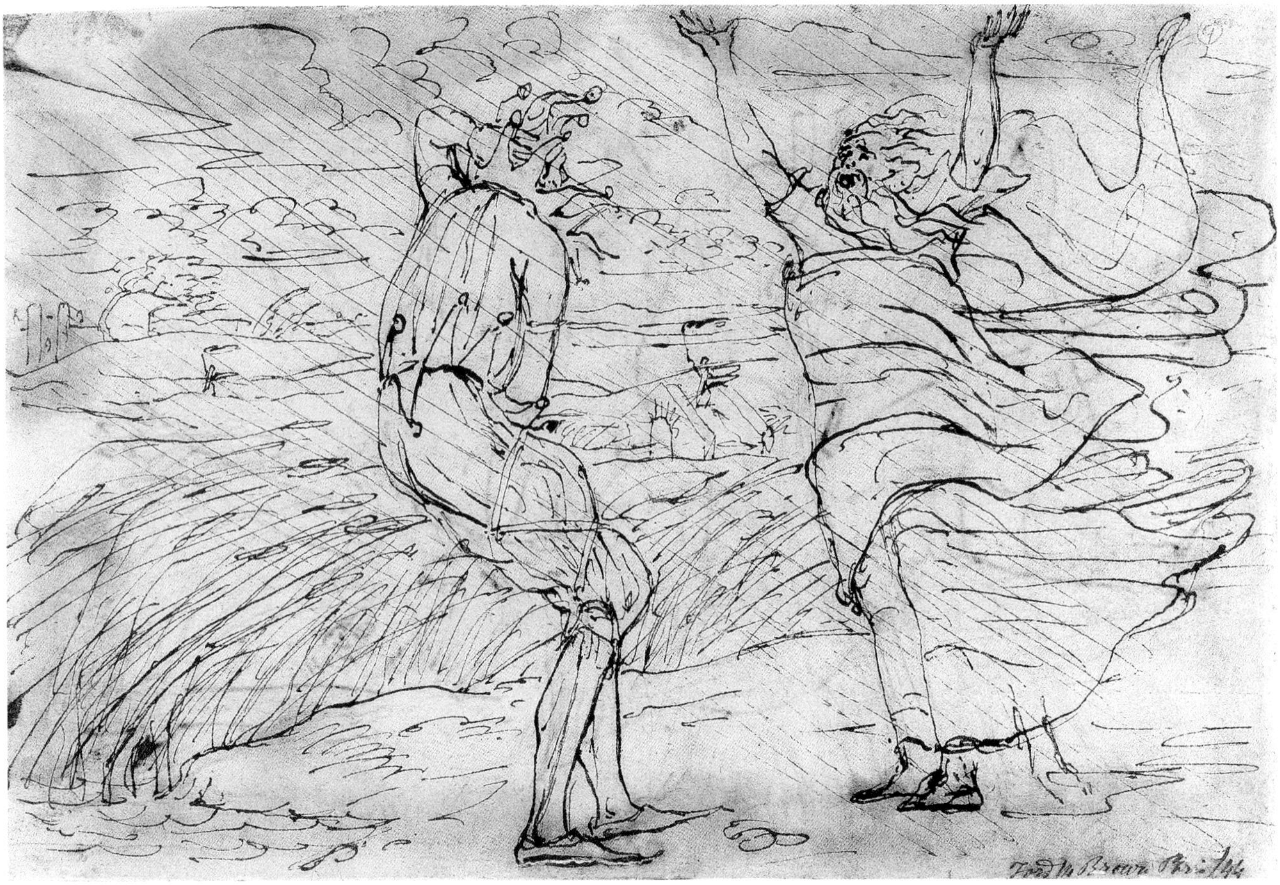

22

22

KING LEAR WITH HIS FOOL IN THE STORM

(C28)
1843/44
pen and ink over pencil, 6⅛ × 9¼ (15.6 × 23.6)
signed and dated: *Ford M Brown Paris /44*
The Whitworth Art Gallery, The University of Manchester

This is one of the most powerful drawings of the series, showing one of the climactic moments in the play. With simple effectiveness, Brown's ink lines conjure up the wind and rain of Lear's speech at the opening of Act 3, scene 2:

> Blow, wind, and crack your cheeks! rage! Blow!
> You cataracts and hurricanes spout
> Till you have drenched our steeples, drown'd the cocks!

COMPETITION ENTRIES

In the early 1840s a Royal Commission headed by Prince Albert recommended that the newly built Houses of Parliament should be decorated with mural paintings depicting British history, literature and tradition. A series of competitions was held to find artists to paint the murals, and three successive exhibitions of the entries were held at Westminster Hall, London, between 1843 and 1845. The competitions attracted a great deal of interest as state sponsorship of the fine arts was rare, and Brown was among the many entrants. His training in Belgium had equipped him better than many British-trained artists to paint large figure compositions. The exhibitions proved very popular with the public, although the general artistic standard was not high. Brown did not gain a commission, but his entries attracted a few favourable notices, and a commendation from the veteran history painter Benjamin Robert Haydon. Brown also entered a separate competition for an altarpiece at St. James's Church, Bermondsey but also without success.

Brown entered the second and third competitions with the subjects shown here. Both have a similar political subtext, depicting the oppression of the weak by the powerful and privileged. Similar themes were to reappear frequently in Brown's work in different guises. In the 1844 exhibition, Brown also showed a large cartoon of a scene from Milton's *Paradise Lost*, depicting a fearful Adam and Eve, seated at the foot of the tree of knowledge in the Garden of Eden with a mighty wind blowing. This was evidently an ambitious composition with echoes of the mysticism of Blake, but it has not survived.

The competition entries changed the direction of Brown's work and gave it greater focus: they provided him with his first opportunity to design public art on a large scale, an ambition eventually fulfilled in Manchester at the end of his career. Although Brown started work on his entries in Paris, the competitions also led to his decision to move to England with his wife in 1844.

23
THE BODY OF HAROLD BROUGHT BEFORE WILLIAM THE CONQUEROR (WILLELMUS CONQUISTATOR)

(A30.2)
1844, 1861
oil with wax encaustic
$41\frac{5}{16} \times 48\frac{7}{16}$ (105 × 123.1)
signed and dated: *F.MADOX BROWN 1844–61*
Manchester City Galleries

Showing the aftermath of the Battle of Hastings in 1066, Brown's painting illustrates lines from David Hume's *History of England* (first published 1754–62): 'After the battle, the body of Harold was found and brought to William the Conqueror' – this was the title originally given in the Westminster Hall Exhibition. Brown set his scene in front of a real landscape, with Beachy Head in the distance, and at a specific time of day: lit by the late afternoon sun, the heavy body of the dead king Harold is hauled by three warriors before the victorious William.

The painting shows the result of Brown's Belgian training in composing powerful figure groups, designed to be effective on a large scale. But he also included idiosyncratic details of his own invention, to demonstrate the 'excessive and exuberant joy'[16] of the victorious Normans: one of William's attendants seizes the puny hand of a camp-boy and contrasts it with Harold's mighty fist, still grasping a broken battle-axe. On the right a surly monk is dressing the wounds of a Norman soldier who, in a contorted posture, strains to see the dead king; on the left, a soldier bites another who is stabbing him in the back. 'The violence and spluttering convulsions in the faces of the figures are preserved from being excessively funny by being excessively disgusting' wrote one critic.[17]

William is shown with large bones hanging round his neck. These were supposed to be the relics of saints over which William had forced Harold to swear to assist him in obtaining the English crown. Holman Hunt, who in general admired the painting, criticized Brown for misunderstanding his source for this detail (the French historian Augustin Thierry): William had gone into battle with a reliquary, not with large bones dangling in front of him, which would have been a 'formidable encumbrance both to riding and fighting.'[18]

Although the subject might seem an unusual one, at the time it was not. The competition organisers requested subjects from British history or from the works of Spenser, Shakespeare or Milton; several entrants to the 1843 and 1844 competitions submitted episodes from the story of Harold, and other Saxon themes such as the conversion of the Saxon King Ethelbert, and the Witangemot (Saxon parliament) were also popular. Brown indicated his political sympathies by placing Harold's head in the centre of the composition, with his body in sunlight, while William, although in a dominant position at the top, is in shadow. This reflects the view of contemporary historians, including Thierry and also Macaulay, that native Saxon freedom had been crushed by the Norman yoke.[19]

Brown consulted the Bayeux tapestry for information about costumes and armour, but finding that it showed the Saxons dressed identically to the Normans, decided that it was better to distinguish Harold from the Normans by putting him in Saxon dress. He cited the examples of Delacroix in France and David Scott in England, who emphasized dramatic truth over archaeological exactitude of setting and costume. Elements of Brown's composition derive from Delacroix's *The Crusaders entering Constantinople* (Louvre, Paris) exhibited at the Paris Salon 1841 and also Raphael's *Entombment* (Borghese Gallery, Rome).

Brown sent in this work for the second murals competition, and it was shown with the rest of the entries in Westminster Hall in 1844. The competition organisers were aware that British artists had little experience of working on a large scale, or of mural technique, and therefore asked the artists to send in cartoons (preparatory drawings) between 10 and 14 feet high with life-size figures, together with a specimen of fresco or other technique suitable for murals. Brown's painting was sent in as an example of wax encaustic, a medium popular for murals in France and Germany at this period. But when on view in the exhibition, the painting must have been overshadowed by the enormous size of his black and white cartoon of the same subject, which still survives (Southwark Art Collection). Brown later retouched his wax encaustic picture in oils, when selling it to the Newcastle patron James Leathart in 1861 (cat. 89). As with *Manfred on the Jungfrau* (cat. 14) the colour scheme is probably brighter than it was originally. At the same time, the painting was retitled *Willelmus Conquistator*, changing the focus from the defeated Harold to the victorious William.

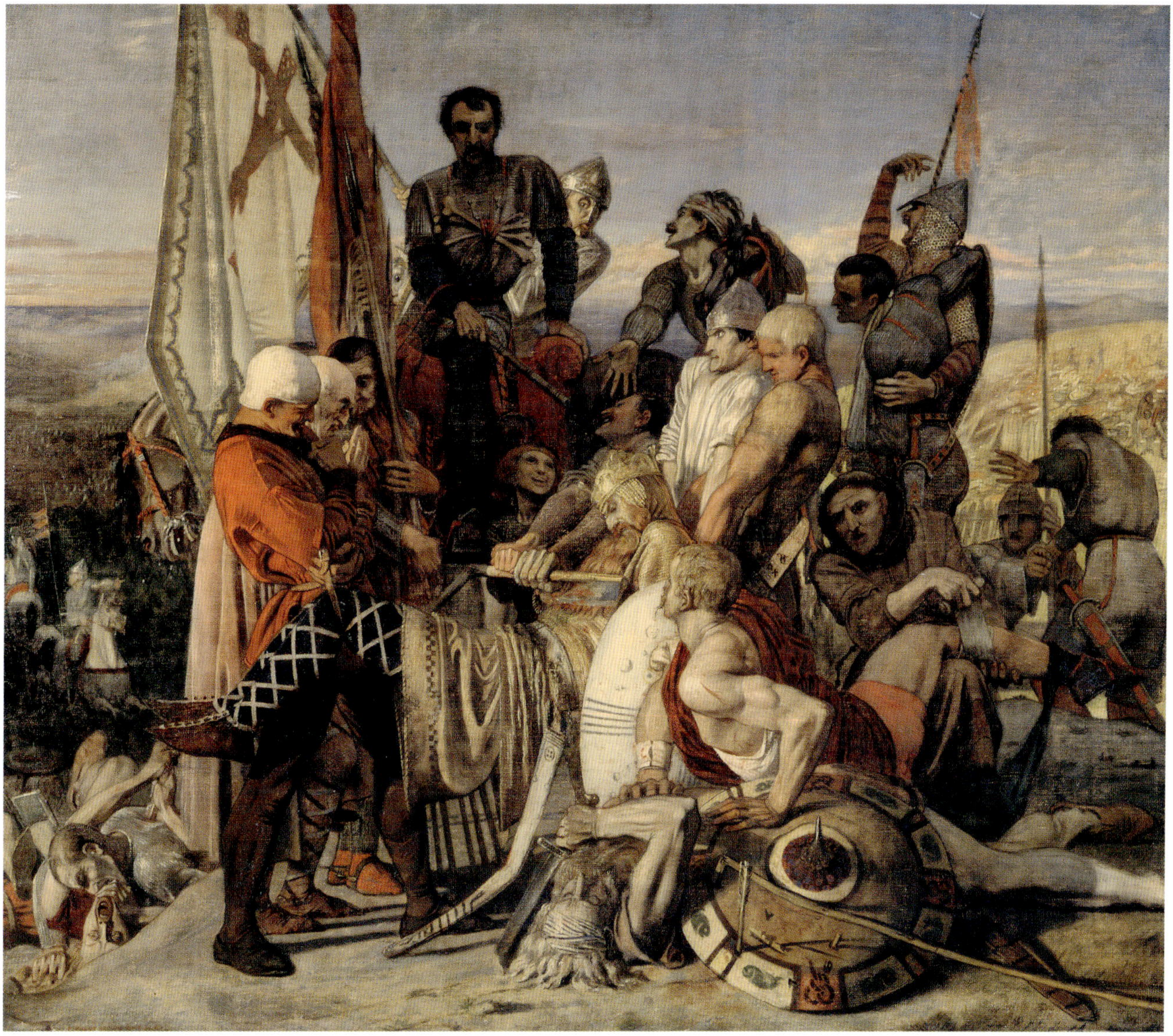

23

24

STUDY FOR 'SPIRIT OF JUSTICE'

(A31.2)
1844–45
pencil, watercolour and bodycolour, 29 13/16 × 20 3/8 (75.7 × 51.7)
Manchester City Galleries

25

FRAGMENT OF CARTOON FOR 'SPIRIT OF JUSTICE'

(A31a)
1844–45
chalk on paper mounted on canvas, 30 3/8 × 20 (77.2 × 50.7)
size of cartoon formerly 192 x 111 (488 x 282)
Manchester City Galleries

For the third and last of the murals competitions, held in 1845, artists were required to design 'personifications of abstract representations of Religion, Justice and the Spirit of Chivalry'. Brown submitted a full size cartoon, of which this is one of several surviving fragments; a coloured sketch, also shown here; and a detail. Brown's three works were included in the 1845 exhibition at Westminster Hall, and he was accorded the compliment of having an outline of his design printed in the catalogue, but he was not awarded a commission or a prize. According to the catalogue:

> The five figures at the top are personifications of Justice, with, on her right, Mercy and Erudition, and on her left, Truth and Wisdom.
>
> The two groups on the foreground are indicative of power and weakness. An unbefriended Widow is seen to appeal to Justice against the oppression of a perverse and powerful Baron, who is assisted by an hired adviser, and supported by the wealth of his father, although not countenanced by his approbation. The Widow is attended by her helpless parents.
>
> The throne of Justice is surrounded by an allegorical representation of the House of Lords, consisting of Lords Spiritual, Temporal, and Barons armed for the maintenance of Justice.[20]

The fragment of the cartoon shows the head of the Lord Temporal on the extreme right. A preparatory drawing for the corresponding Lord Temporal on the extreme left is cat. 40. The conflict between the Baron and the Widow expresses Brown's sympathy for the underdog and his dislike of privilege, exemplified in the evil face of the baron's hired adviser.

Although the confrontation between the two main figures is expressed through strong lines and powerful gestures, as in *The Body of Harold*, this is a different type of design, new for the artist, and more suited to the 'abstract representation' demanded by the competition, than a realistic scene. The Gothic arch, the symmetrical layout, the shallow space and the rows of people in tiers one above the other all emphasize design in the flat over depth. This type of composition was associated with German art, particularly with the mural paintings executed in Munich by the Nazarene school. Brown may have become acquainted with these principles of design through his friend the painter William Cave Thomas, who had studied in Munich. A similar tiered layout is evident in the winning design, by Daniel Maclise, whose fresco of *The Spirit of Justice* in the House of Lords was completed in 1849 (fig. 52).

Brown's cartoon was well received by some of the critics, and

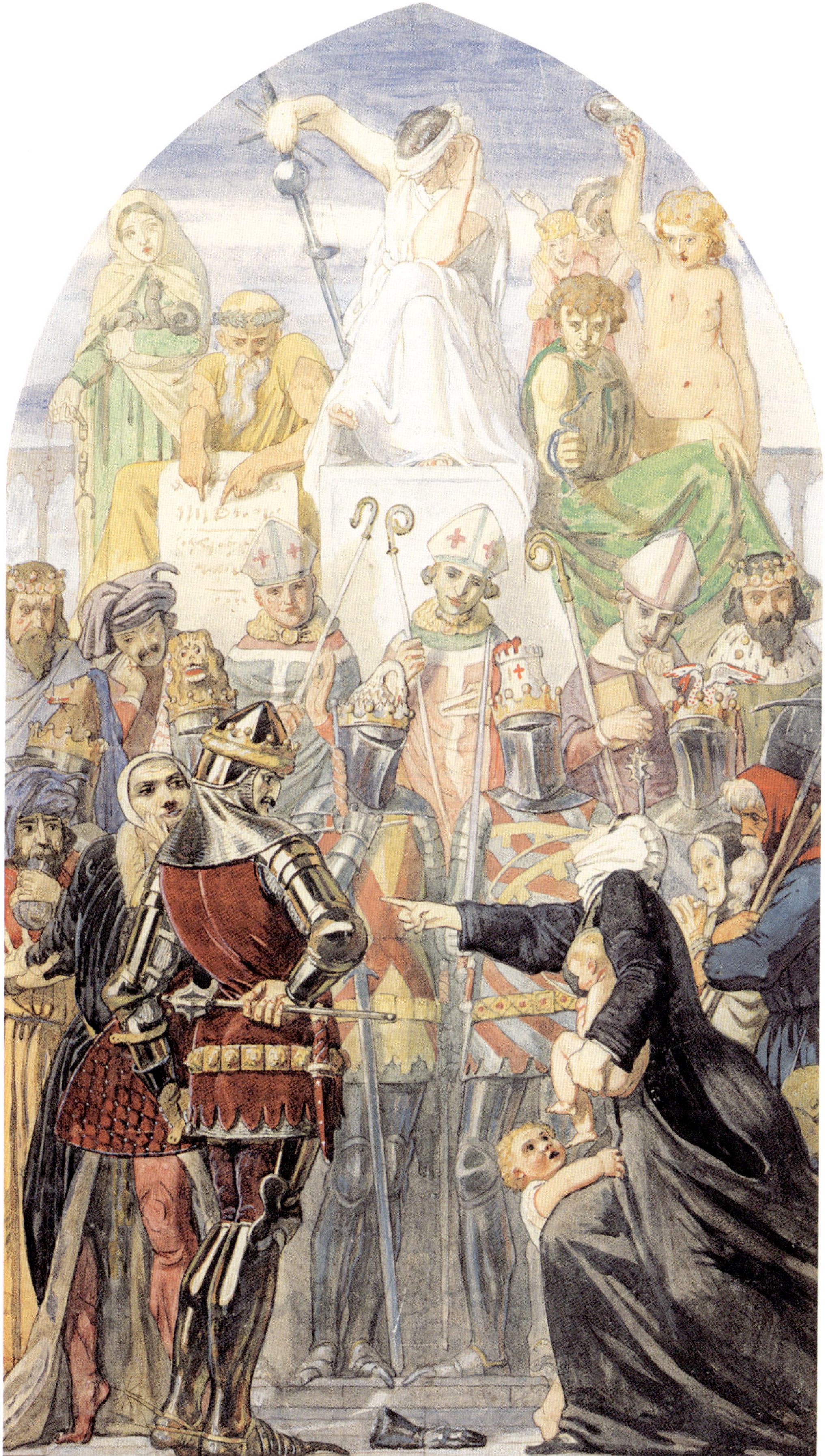

24

perhaps more significantly was admired by artists. The painter Benjamin Robert Haydon, long an advocate of state-supported mural paintings in public buildings, was deeply disappointed at the failure of his own cartoons to win him a commission; nevertheless he wrote in his diary, 'The only bit of fresco fit to look at is by Ford Madox Brown. It is a figure of "Justice", and exquisite as far as that figure goes.'[21] Holman Hunt felt that the four symmetrically arranged armed knights 'their faces covered by large tilting-helms inclined alternately to the right and left', distracted attention from the scene in the foreground; despite this 'Gothic quaintness' he still thought that the work had 'the counterbalancing merit of grace and vitality.'[22] Meanwhile the young Rossetti admired Brown's design so much that he cut out the illustration from the catalogue and hung it in his room.[23]

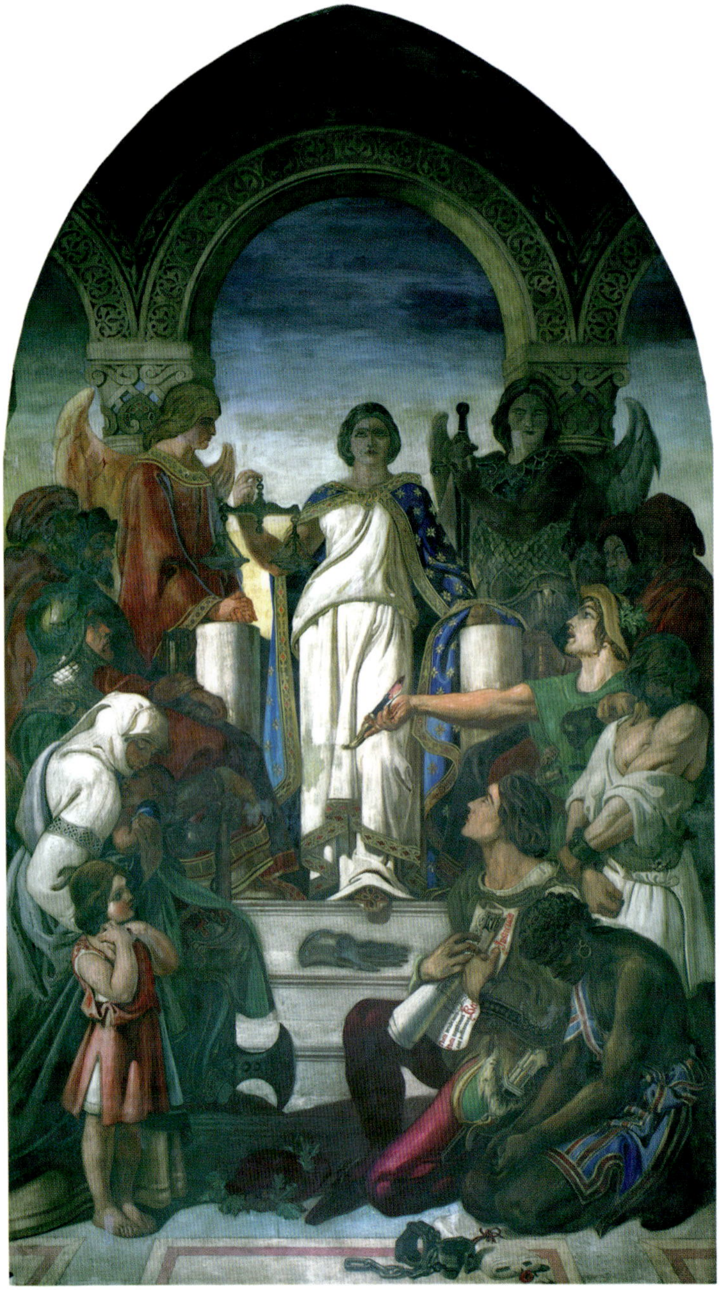

Fig. 52
Daniel Maclise, The Spirit of Justice, *1847/49. Palace of Westminster Collection, London*

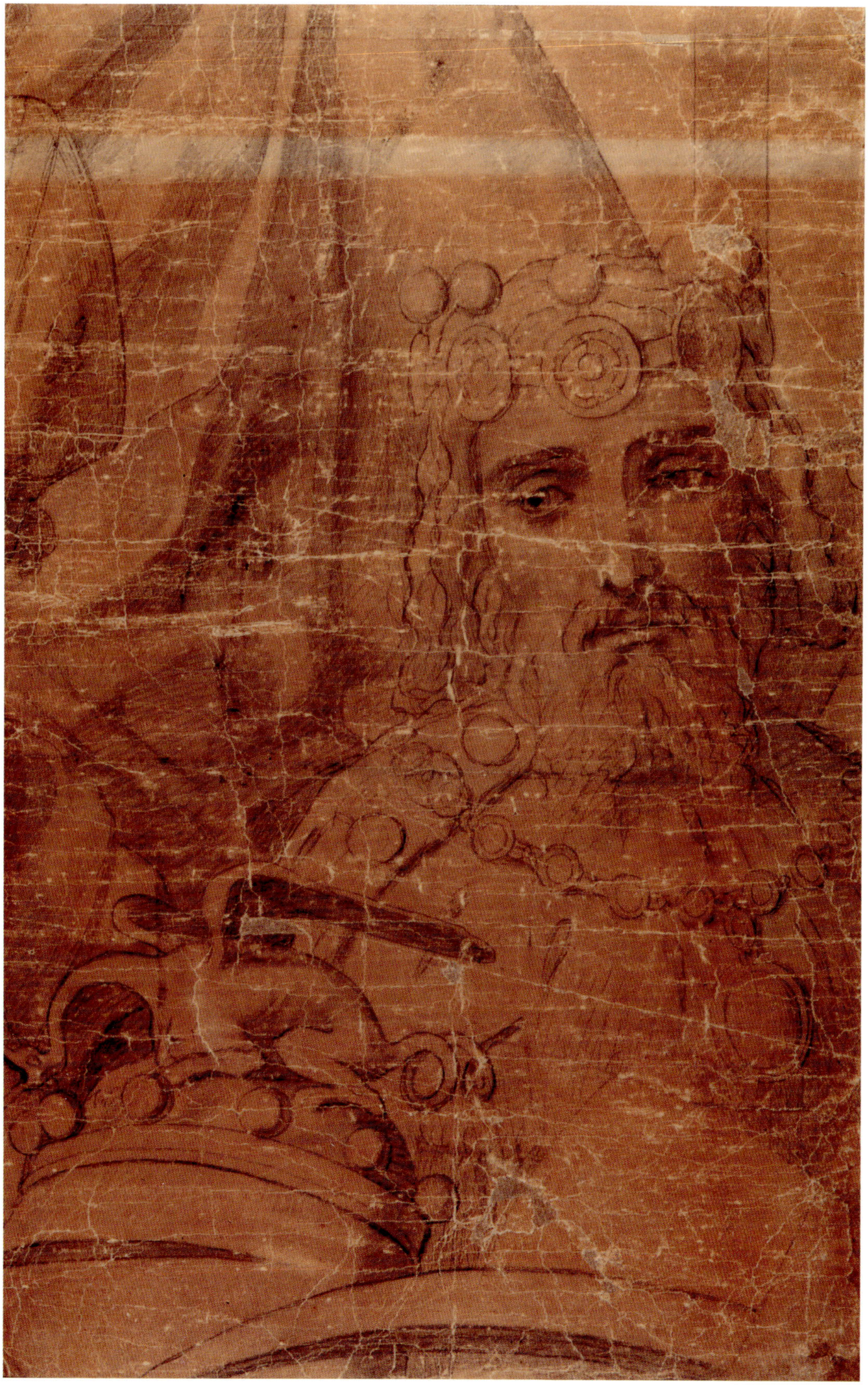

25

26
THE ASCENSION

(A37)
1844
oil on canvas, 36½ × 17½ (92.7 × 44.5)
The Forbes Collection, New York

The Ascension was Christ's last appearance to the apostles, forty days after his Resurrection. He was standing with them on the Mount of Olives when 'he was lifted up and a cloud removed him from their sight.' (Acts I, 9–12). In medieval representations of the event, Christ was often shown disappearing into the cloud, with only his feet visible. Brown perhaps recalled this iconography in showing Christ's legs still visible on earth as he rose through dark cloud to a brilliantly lit heaven. The two flying figures on either side of Christ may represent the two men in white who according to the Bible told the apostles that Jesus would come again the same way that they saw him go.

Brown filled his scene with agitated movement: the mourners gesture wildly, the angels fly in and out, bodies twist in circular motion and heads and arms are tilted backwards and forwards. The pointing figures of the apostles recall Raphael's *Transfiguration* (Vatican Museum) whilst the angels derive from the flying figures seen in the work of Flaxman and Fuseli. A complex lighting effect and a strong vertical movement enhance the emotional and spiritual impact of the painting: the lower part is illuminated by a pool of light from above, but with a darkening landscape beyond, lit by a narrow band of sunset sky glowing on the horizon. The eye is led by upwards gestures to the heavens, where Christ and the angels are lit by a supernatural radiance.

The painting was Brown's entry in the competition for the altarpiece for St. James's Church, Bermondsey. It was advertised in September and October 1844, and artists were invited to send in finished sketches 36 x 17 inches for an altarpiece to be 23 x 11 feet. The competition was won by John Wood, whose painting, more conventionally Raphaelesque than Brown's proposal, is still in the church.

1 Hueffer 1896, p. 432 calls it 'Head of Page.'
2 Bennett 2010, 1, p. 17, A23.3.
3 Rosenthal 1914, p. 101, citing *L'Artiste* 1842.
4 L.M. Rossetti 1890, p. 290.
5 Brown 1865, no. 37.
6 D.G. Rossetti *Correspondence*, 1, p. 58.
7 Brown 1865, no. 42.
8 Brown 1865, no. 42.
9 Meisel 1988, p. 581.
10 The Delacroix is in the Art Institute of Chicago; the Scheffer is in the Musée de la vie romantique, Paris, and the Wappers in the Musée des Beaux-Arts de Pau.
11 Oliver Goldsmith, *The Vicar of Wakefield*, London 1883, chapter 4, p. 26; chapter 5, p. 28.
12 Bennett 2010, 2, pp. 433–34, C10-11.
13 Brown 1865, nos. 52–66.
14 W.M. Rossetti 1865, p. 606.
15 Brown 1865, nos. 52–66.
16 Brown 1865, no. 28.
17 *New Monthly Magazine* cited by Bennett 2010, 1., p. 27.
18 Hunt 1905, 1, p. 120.
19 Wright 2007.
20 Exhibition of 1845, no. 98 from Hunt 1846.
21 Haydon 1926, 2, p. 790.
22 Hunt 1905, 1, p. 121.
23 D.G. Rossetti *Correspondence*, 1, p. 58.

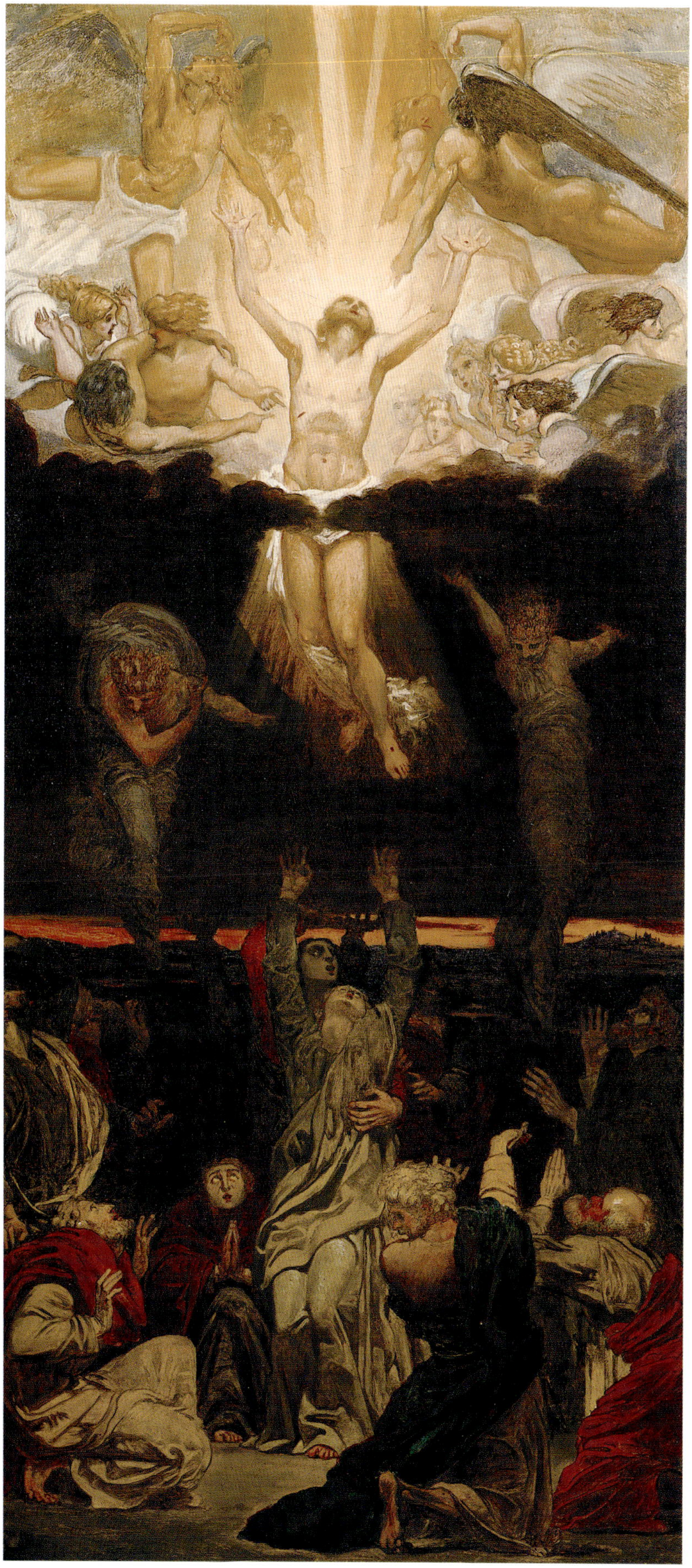

26

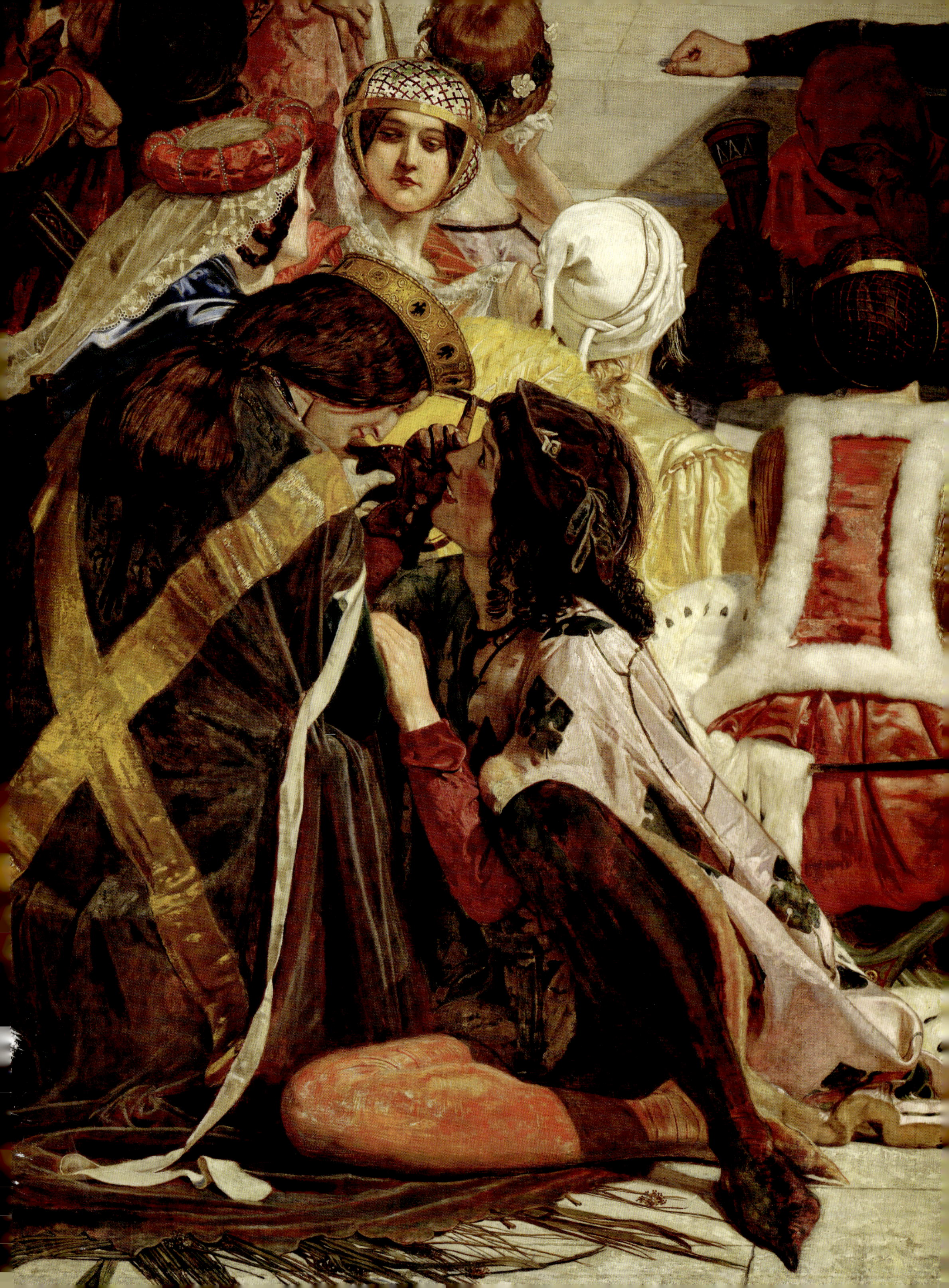

THE CHANGE OF DIRECTION

In 1845–46 Brown, with his wife and young daughter, spent seven months in Rome. The experience gave his art 'an entirely new direction of thought and feeling'[1] but the personal circumstances of the journey were distressing. By the summer of 1845, Elisabeth was suffering from consumption and was advised to go to a warmer climate. In August 1845 the Browns set off from London for Italy. They travelled via Basel where the Holbeins made a deep impression; in Milan they admired the works of Leonardo da Vinci and his assistant Luini, and in Florence the frescoes of Giotto, Masaccio, Filippino Lippi and Fra Angelico. On the way to Rome they saw works by Raphael and Perugino, and at Rome, Brown visited the German Nazarene painters Friedrich Overbeck and Peter Cornelius as well as seeing the works of Raphael, Michelangelo and Titian.[2]

In Rome Brown conceived what was to be his first great work, *Geoffrey Chaucer reading the 'Legend of Custance' to Edward III and his Court*, an English subject, yet set 'amid air and sunshine'[3] like the work of the Italian painters. But because of Elisabeth's worsening health, in May 1846 they left Rome, reaching Paris on 5 June, where she died. The paintings made by Brown in the few years after his return show a change in style. Dark colours, deep shadows and dramatic pools of light were abandoned and replaced by bright colour, even lighting, symmetry and balance. Instead of melodramatic action, the narrative was conveyed by natural-looking poses and gestures, and realistic facial expressions. Brown's first experiments with open-air lighting and with Italianate subjects date from this period, anticipating the foundation of the Pre-Raphaelite Brotherhood. Brown's work struck a chord with the young Rossetti who introduced himself to Brown in March 1848, and briefly became his pupil. In turn Rossetti introduced the older artist to Hunt and Millais and the others who in the autumn formed the Pre-Raphaelite Brotherhood. Although Brown never became a member, his style developed in parallel with their emerging mutual interests.

Fig. 53
Detail of cat. 34, Geoffrey Chaucer reading the 'Legend of Custance' to Edward III and his Court. *Art Gallery of New South Wales, Sydney*

27

THE SERAPH'S WATCH (A REMINISCENCE OF THE EARLY MASTERS)

(A43.1)
1847
oil on panel, 19¾ × 13¾ (50.2 × 35)
Private collection

A seraph and a cherub in heaven contemplate symbols of Christ's suffering on earth, the scourge used at his Flagellation and the crown of thorns placed on his head at the Crucifixion. Seraphs and cherubs were considered to be the highest order of angels. In medieval and early Renaissance art they were represented as heads enfolded by wings: Brown departed from tradition in showing the seraph as a half-length winged child, although he depicted the cherub in the more usual way.

Brown painted a first version of *The Seraph's Watch* immediately after he returned from Italy in 1846. It probably had an autobiographical meaning, referring to the death of his first wife Elisabeth on their way back from Rome (she had been a practising Christian). Brown sent the painting to Rome as a gift to a Dr Richard Deakin, a surgeon who may have attended Elisabeth in her last illness. The first version is now lost, but very soon afterwards Brown made this duplicate version. It was exhibited in London at the British Institution, with the title *A Reminiscence of the Early Masters*. Unlike other paintings begun in Rome or shortly after his return, this one was not retouched later and so is the most immediate expression of the artist's experience of Italian painting during his Italian sojourn. He could have seen many similar angelic figures, as they occur frequently in early Renaissance art, and indeed in Nazarene painting; there is a strong resemblance with winged figures in Veit's frescoes at the Casino Massimo, Rome (fig. 54). However, Brown did not copy his source literally but assimilated it, creating his own new style. The natural-looking children's faces, the clear bright colours, and the simplicity and purity of feeling are utterly different from Brown's previous work.

On the seraph's robe is a complex design of interlinked circles with jewels, with a cross at the centre, while the theme of linked circles is repeated in the fine gold haloes. The design of the five main circles within a fifth is known as a quincunx, a medieval pattern of hermetic meaning, sometimes taken to represent the four evangelists and Christ. Brown could have come across the quincunx in manuscript illumination or in Cosmati work (tiled pavements) found in Rome and elsewhere (including Westminster Abbey), but exactly why he used it here is not known. The colour of the interlinked circles – gold, violet, green, orange, red and blue – may also have had symbolic significance.

The young Rossetti saw the painting on exhibition at the British Institution, and he wrote of his admiration for it in his letter to Brown when asking for lessons. Brown set him to make a copy of it, and until Brown's painting recently came to light, its appearance was known only through Rossetti's copy, which was never finished.[4]

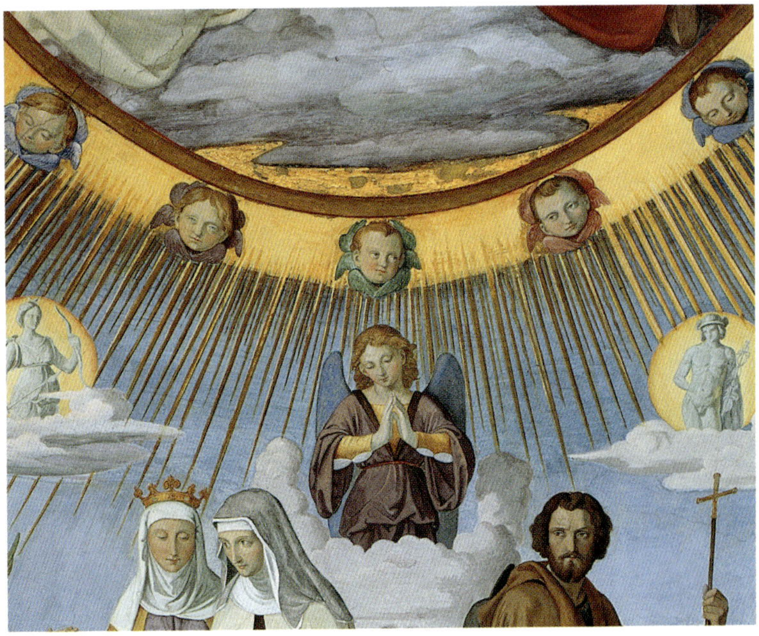

Fig. 54
Philipp Veit, detail of The Heavens of the Blessed and the Empyrean, *ceiling fresco in the Dante Room, 1818/24. Casino Massimo, Rome*

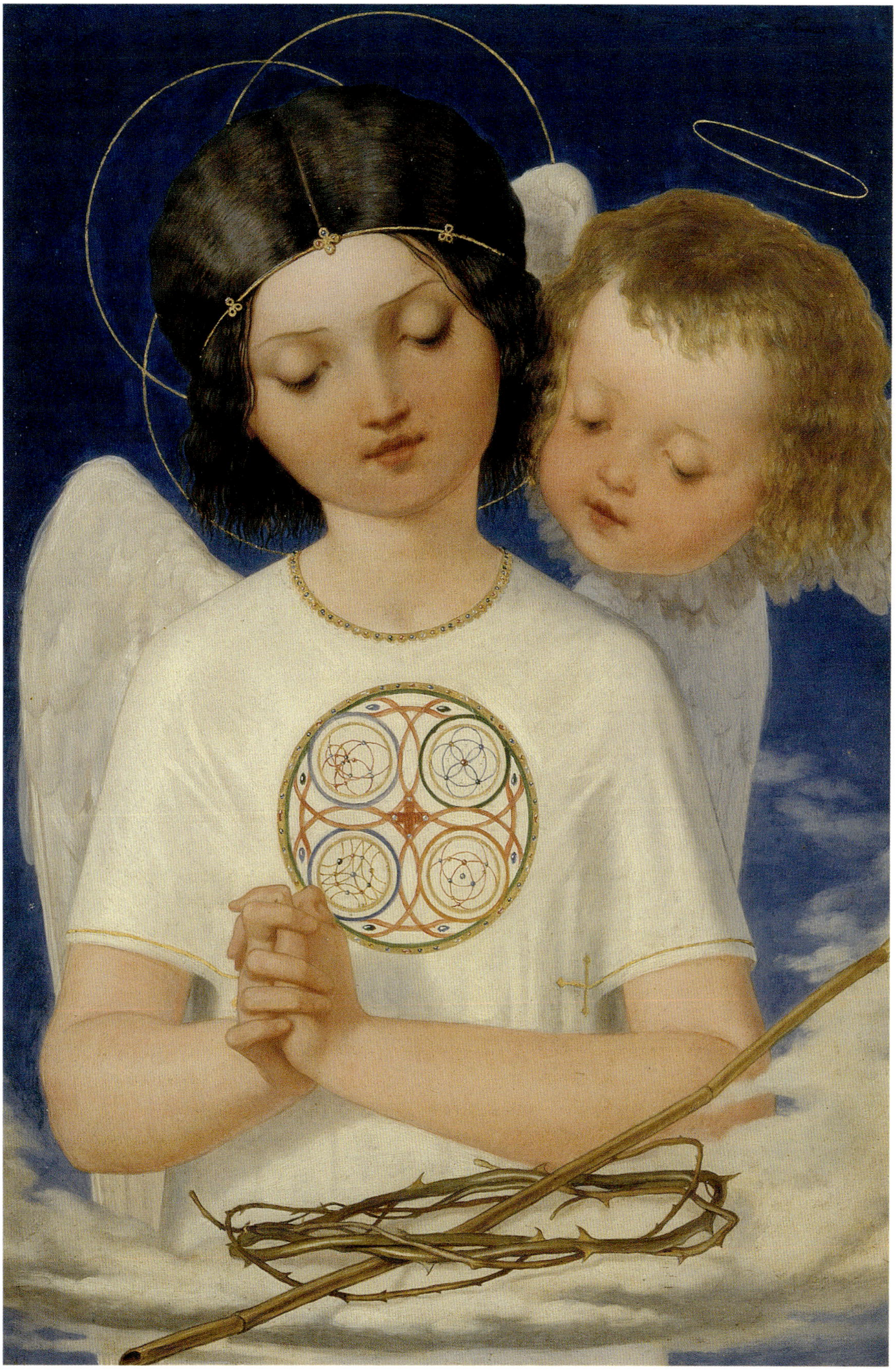

28

OURE LADYE OF SATURDAY NIGHT (OURE LADYE OF GOOD CHILDREN)

(A44)
1847, 1852/53, 1854, 1861
pastel and watercolour over black chalk, with gold paint
30⅝ × 23¼ (77.8 × 59)
signed and dated: *F.MADOX BROWN 1847–61*
Tate. Presented by Alfred A. de Pass 1910

A modern, anglicised interpretation of an Italian Virgin and Child, showing Mary washing the baby Jesus who sits on a towel on his mother's lap. The title *Oure Ladye of Saturday Night* refers to the modern English custom of bathing children once a week. An angel holds out a bowl of water and a matching jug stands below; another angel holds a little girl on her lap saying her prayers, and through the archway on the left in the far distance are figures representing the Flight into Egypt. This was the first of Brown's several paintings on the theme of motherhood. The girl saying her prayers might be based on his daughter Lucy.

Brown later wrote of the painting as 'little more than the pouring out of the emotions and remembrances still vibrating within me of Italian art.'[5] In Italy he would have seen many paintings of the Virgin with the baby Jesus attended by angels, and features such as the patterned cloth of honour hanging behind Mary and the canopy above her were frequent motifs in early Renaissance altarpieces. Brown also sought out early Italian art in Britain, visiting the collection at Christ Church, Oxford, for example, in 1847, where he could have seen Italian paintings of this period with similar features (fig. 55).[6] But in *Oure Ladye of Good Children* Brown depicted the Virgin in the act of washing the Child, a rarely seen iconography in Italian art, although a basin of water, sometimes with a jug and a towel, is an occasional feature of fifteenth-century Flemish paintings of the Virgin and Child in a domestic setting (fig. 65, p. 178). Brown did not record having seen such a painting, and his combination of the theme of bath night with an altarpiece format sounds like one of his typically idiosyncratic ideas; but it could conceivably have come from a memory of a Flemish painting seen during his student days in Belgium.

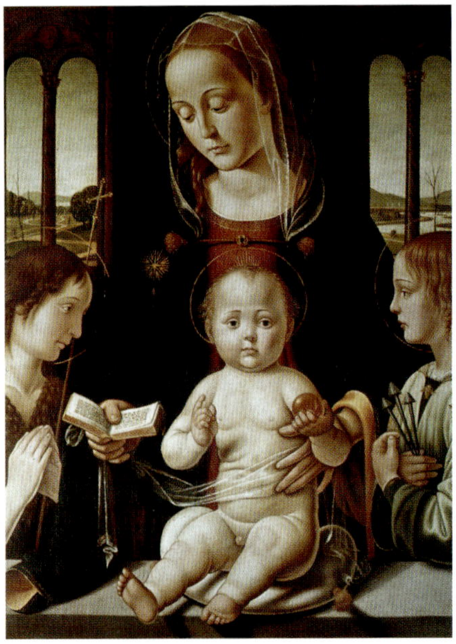

Fig. 55 Attributed to G.B. Utili or Biaggio d'Antonio da Firenze (formerly attributed to Filippo Lippi), Virgin and Child with Saint John and an Angel. *Christ Church Picture Gallery, Oxford*

Oure Ladye is not a simple imitation of fifteenth-century art, nor is it in the revivalist 'Early Christian' style of the Nazarenes or their chief British follower William Dyce. Although the figures are in archaic Italianate dress, and their haloes are similar to those in *The Seraph's Watch*, the faces are more like portraits than idealized Italianate types, and Brown gave the picture some very English features. The Madonna is homely-looking, taken from an English model (a drawing is in Birmingham)[7] and Jesus has blonde curls and pink cheeks; the artist wrote that 'the children are modern English, they are washed, powdered, combed and bedgowned, and taught to say prayers like English Protestant babes.'[8] Further aspects which differentiate the painting from Italian art are the particularised lighting effect of just after sunset, and the slightly off-centre placing of the Madonna's throne.

Oure Ladye of Saturday Night was originally drawn in black and white chalk. Brown submitted it to the Royal Academy in 1847, but it was rejected. It may have been shown elsewhere, because Rossetti mentioned having seen it in his letter of March 1848, when he asked Brown to give him lessons. Brown worked on the picture again intermittently in the early 1850s and it was later sent to the Pre-Raphaelite exhibition in America in 1857–58, where it was damaged. In 1861 Brown transformed its appearance by adding colour for the collector Thomas Plint.

The frame is later still, dating from 1862, when the picture was acquired by James Leathart. The reeded outer moulding, and the broad gilt flat or inner frame decorated with roundels, are typical of Brown's frames of the 1860s; but the Gothic arched opening, a feature of Brown's very earliest Nazarene-influenced frames, and the angel motif within the roundels, were probably chosen for their appropriateness for the subject. They recall the frame of Duccio's *Rucellai Madonna* (Santa Maria Novella, Florence) which Brown could have seen.[9]

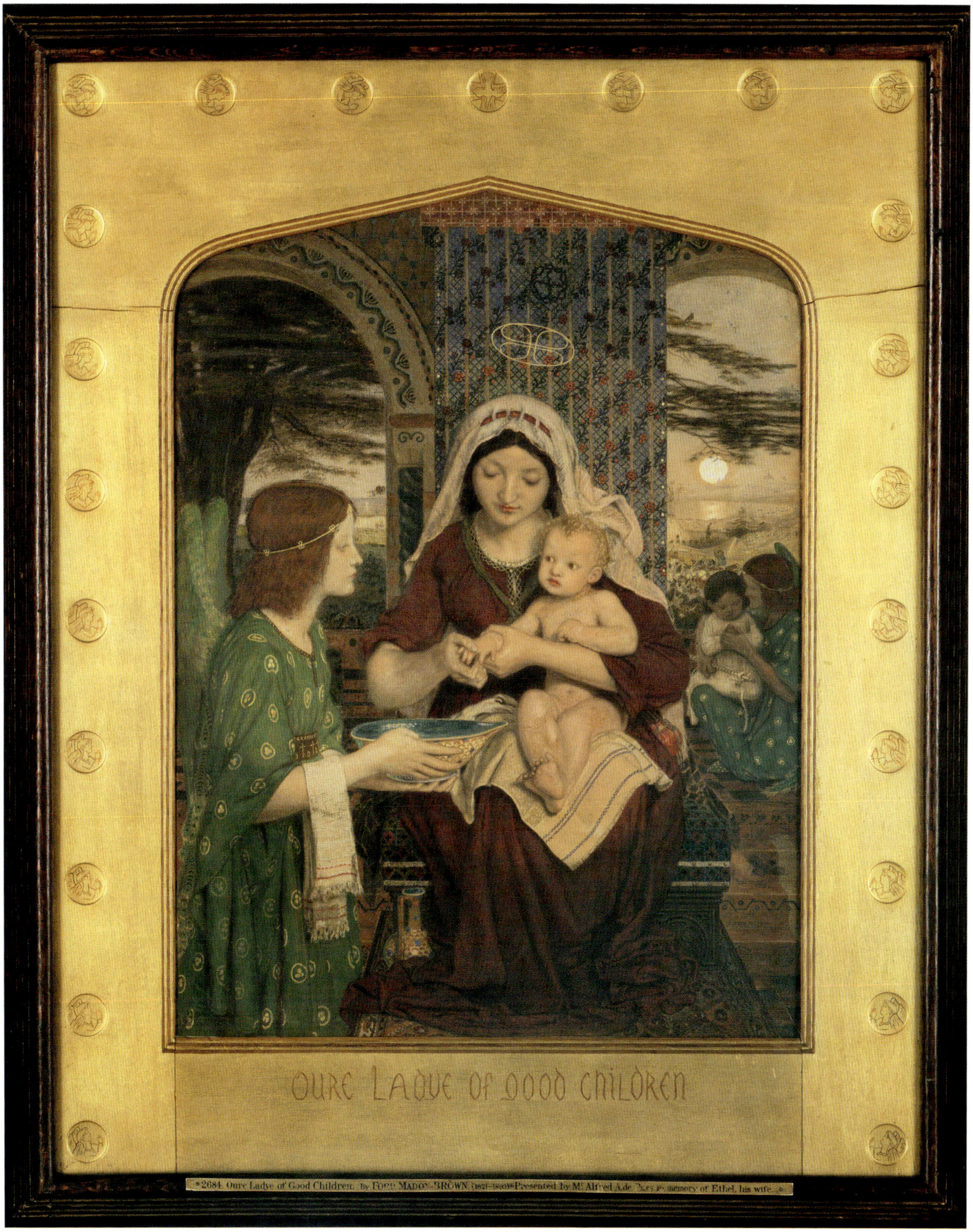
OURE LADYE OF GOOD CHILDREN
2684. Oure Ladye of Good Children. By FORD MADOX BROWN

29
JAMES BAMFORD (A HOLBEIN OF THE 19TH CENTURY)

(B4)
1846
oil on canvas, 30 × 25 (76 × 63.5)
signed: *FORD MADOX BROWN*
Private collection

James Bamford (1794–1862), a London silk manufacturer, commissioned this portrait in 1846. He was a relation of Brown's first wife Elisabeth. In the difficult time immediately after Elisabeth's death, Brown occasionally stayed at Bamford's home at 6 Milk Street. Bamford's wife, Elisabeth's aunt, had died in 1841, leaving him with eight children to bring up, the youngest being only seven in 1846. This may have created a bond with Brown, whose wife's death also left him with a young child. Brown painted two versions of which this is probably the original, and was paid five guineas for each of them.

Bamford stares out of the picture, his thin lips tightly closed, with an uncomfortable expression on his face after reading the letter which he holds before him. The letter has a prominent red seal and postmarks, but they do not give any clues to its contents. Behind Bamford on the left is an inkwell placed on top of a leather-bound atlas. This could perhaps indicate foreign business links, or it may refer to his son Edward, an Ensign in the East India Company's infantry in Madras, whose portrait Brown had painted the previous year.[10] On the right is a metal candlestick supported by a stag, with a red candle stub, the burnt-out candle perhaps a symbol of blighted hope.

Brown submitted this portrait to the Royal Academy in 1847 but it was rejected. Maybe this was because the stark, confrontational expression was not in accord with the more urbane style of the typical Academic portrait. Brown left no record of his own reaction to the rejection, but writing in his 1865 exhibition catalogue he emphasized the importance of the portrait in his development as a painter:

> It is the first evidence of an entirely new direction of thought and feeling on my part … it looks as if painted by another hand, that of a beginner … To those who value facile completeness and handling, above painstaking research into nature the change must appear inexplicable and provoking.... Wishing to substitute simple imitation for *scenic effectiveness*, and purity of natural colour for scholastic depth of tone, I found no better way of doing so than to paint what I called a *Holbein of the 19th century*. I might, perhaps, have done so more effectively, but *stepping backwards* is stumbling work at best.[11]

The comparison with Holbein is evidence of the strong impression made upon Brown by seeing the Holbeins in the Basel Museum on his way to Italy in 1845.

29

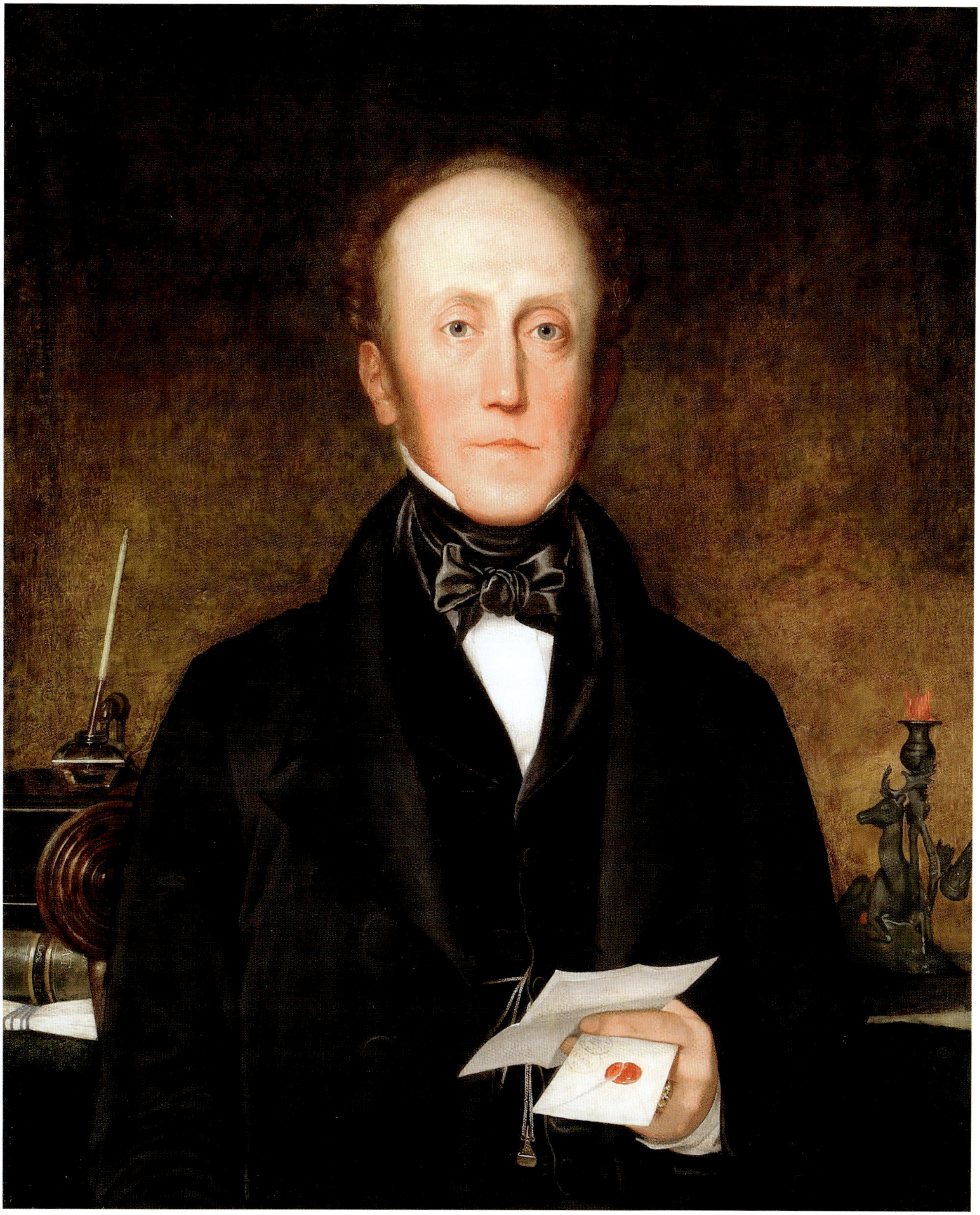

30

MILLIE SMITH

(B103)
1846
oil on paper, laid down on panel, 9 × 6⅞ (22.8 × 17.5)
signed and dated: *F. Madox Brown 1846*
National Museums Liverpool, Walker Art Gallery

Millie's full name was Amelia Smith, and she was the daughter of a grocer, the landlord of the house in Southend where Brown stayed with his small daughter Lucy on his return to England after his first wife's death. Millie and Lucy had played together, and Brown was remembered in Millie's family as having made a great fuss of her. Like *The Seraph's Watch* (cat. 27), this is one of the few paintings made immediately after Brown's Italian trip that has survived without retouching. In contrast to *The Seraph's Watch*, Brown eliminated any direct reference to Italian art in Millie's portrait. But the simple frontal pose, the lack of deep shadows and the delicate painting of the flowers are evidence of the cleansing effect on his style of seeing the work of Holbein and the Italian painters.

At around the same time, Brown also made a double portrait of Millie, this time with her eyes lowered; he painted two sensitive studies of her, each from a different angle (Manchester City Galleries).[12] The stark, full-face stare of the single portrait results in a concentrated and unsentimental image of childhood unprecedented in Victorian art.

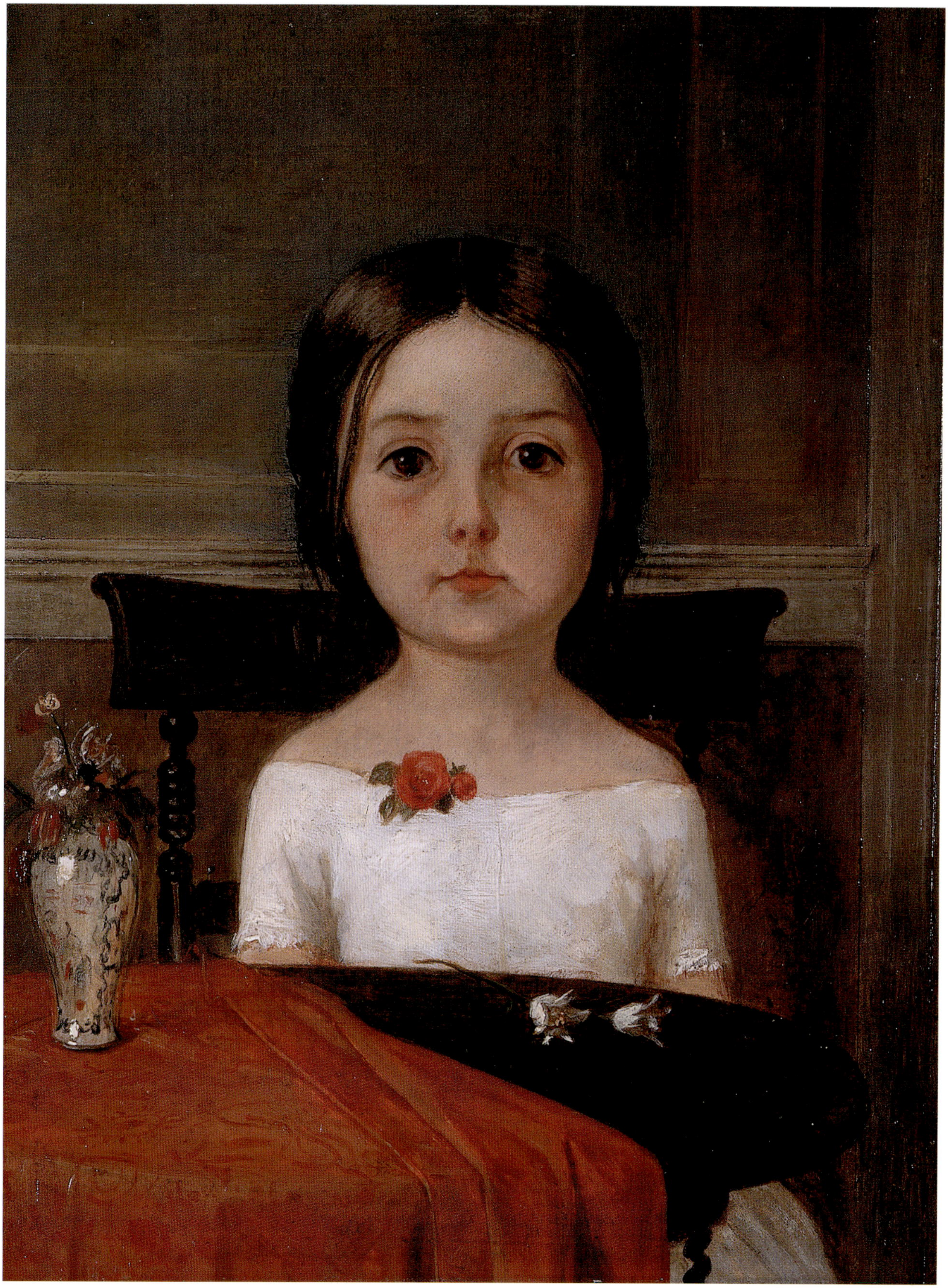
30

31

THE YOUNG MOTHER

(A50.1)
1848–49
oil on board
8 × 5⅞ (20.3 × 15)
Wightwick Manor, The Mander Collection (National Trust)

The Young Mother is a tender and intimate scene of a young woman suckling her child, with a little dog looking up eagerly on the right. It is a genre painting, an ordinary incident from daily life, but set in an eighteenth-century interior with the model in period dress.

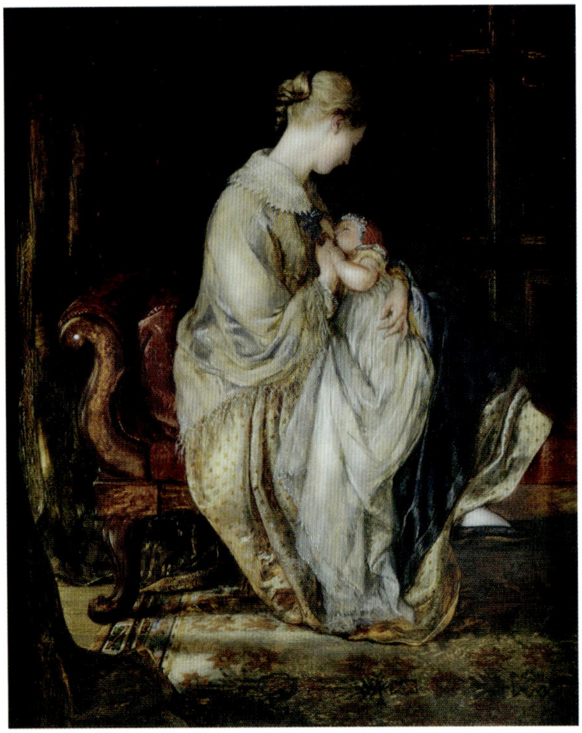

Fig. 56
Charles West Cope, The Young Mother, *1845. Victoria and Albert Museum*

This is the sketch for a more highly finished painting, now lost, entitled *The Infant's Repast*, which was probably not much larger in size as it was described as a 'cabinet picture.'[13] The models were a Mrs. Ashley, a professional model, and her own baby (cat. 44), and Brown also hired a King Charles spaniel for the dog. He borrowed an eighteenth-century green petticoat from his artist friend Charles Lucy, and bought an oak door which he scraped and varnished for the panelling in the painting. Brown recorded in his diary his painstaking progress on the clothing, the stripes of the dress, the Utrecht velvet sofa, the flower in the woman's hair and other details: the *Art Journal* wrote of the larger version that it was 'finished with all the exquisite nicety of an elaborate miniature.'[14] It was shown in London in 1849 at the Free Exhibition, where Rossetti showed his first Pre-Raphaelite work *The Girlhood of Mary Virgin* (fig. 7, p. 17). At the exhibition it was accompanied by the following poem, probably written by Brown himself.

Soft are the throbbing of the mother's breast,
 When pours the stream to meet the eager pressure
Of the child's gums! See it, with nose close pressed
 On milk-white heap, how toils its chin for pleasure?
See how, in strife with sleep, it drops its treasure,
 Then starting, drinks again with jealous fears.
Drink, little baby! Drink thine heart's own measure;
 While other wants are few to wake thy tears,
Lo! Many a bitter draught thou'lt drink through coming years.

This sketch seems to be very close to the larger version, and is remarkably like Charles Cope's *The Young Mother* (fig. 56), exhibited at the Royal Academy a few years before in 1846, although Cope's mother is in modern dress. Cope's picture was bought by the Yorkshire collector John Sheepshanks and this may have led Brown to produce a similar subject. It may also explain why Brown temporarily abandoned the pale, daylit colours of his Italianate works and went back to a more saleable, conservative style, with the mother placed in a shadowy interior picked out by a pool of light. The plan worked, for he sold both versions: *The Infant's Repast* to John Gibbons, a collector of genre paintings, and *The Young Mother* to a Bristol collector, who however only paid £5 for it, half of what Brown was asking.

Whatever the artist's intention when painting it in the late 1840s, by 1865 he wrote teasingly (of the larger version): 'With the single remark that "doggy is jealous," this little picture, I think, needs no explanation.'[15]

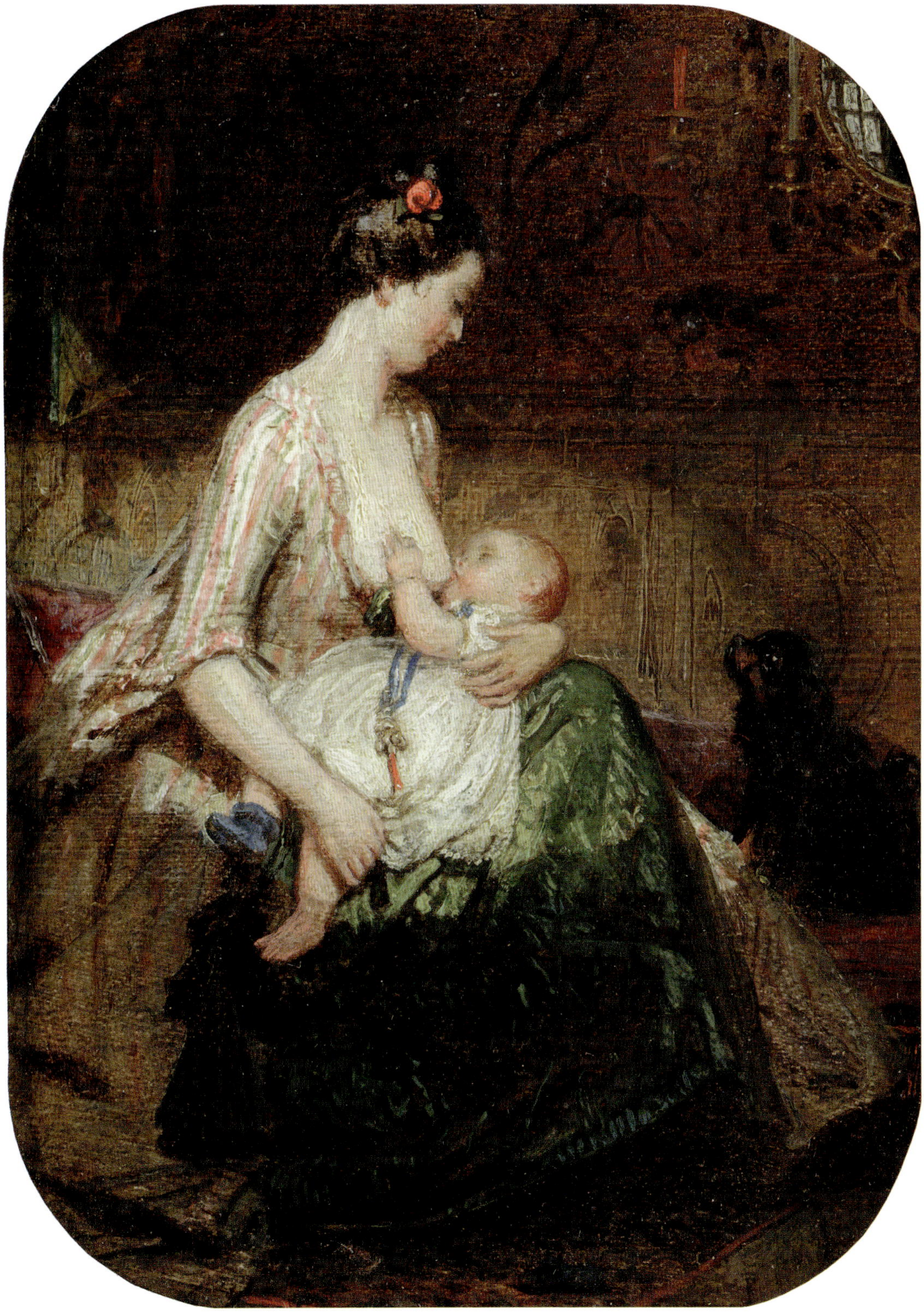

31

PAINTINGS ON THE ORIGINS OF ENGLISH LITERATURE

A passionate reader, Brown between 1845 and 1851 was preoccupied with the theme of early English literature, probably suggested to him by the 1844 murals competition, which had asked for subjects from Spenser, Shakespeare or Milton. Before his journey to Italy he already had the idea of a tribute to Geoffrey Chaucer, whom he admired as the first poet to write in the vernacular English language; and in Rome he planned an elaborate triptych on 'the Origin of our native tongue',[16] representing Chaucer with other poets and prose writers. Finding that there would not be room for both, he decided to concentrate on the poets, and designed a triptych with Chaucer reading to Edward III and his court in the centre, and figures of later poets in the wings. In Rome he started the oil sketch for the triptych (cat. 32) and also began to paint it on a large scale. He brought back the three large canvases with him on his return to London in 1846, and continued to work on them, but because of their size and complexity, and because of his highly detailed style, the work took far longer than he had anticipated.

Realising he could not complete the triptych for exhibition in 1848, he put it aside and in November 1847 turned to the related subject of John Wycliffe, one of the prose writers who was to have been included in his first idea. After completing the Wycliffe painting (cat. 33), Brown returned to the large triptych he had planned, but eventually abandoned the wings, and finished off the central panel depicting Chaucer as an independent picture. It was his largest, most ambitious and most detailed painting so far, and it was not completed until 1851, when it was exhibited at the Royal Academy (see cat. 34).

The whole project, from its first conception to the exhibition at the Academy, took six years. It had a dual significance for Brown: besides expressing his passion for English poetry, it was also closely associated with painful memories of his wife. She had been with him when he first started work on the oil sketch in Rome, where they had gone for the sake of her health and she had died during the return journey: 'never can I forget that *she* gave it her disqualified approbation, prophecied that it would ensure me ultimate success, regretted that she would never live to see it, and *ardered* me to complete it after her death'.[17]

It was whilst working on the large triptych in September 1847 that Brown began to write the diary from which the above words are taken. He kept it up in detail, with a few interruptions, until February 1858, when he stopped, and he resumed it from 1865 to 1868, but with much shorter entries. Besides recording his progress on this and other paintings often in great detail, Brown's diary describes in engagingly misspelt, often highly expressive prose, his relationships with friends, family, models and fellow-artists, and records with frankness and spontaneity his varying moods, worries and ailments; but also at times his intense enjoyment of his work.

32
THE SEEDS AND FRUITS OF ENGLISH POETRY

(A40.1)
1845–51, (1853)
oil on canvas, 13 3/8 × 18 1/8 (34 × 46)
signed and dated: *FORD MADOX BROWN DESt. [I]N ROMA. 1845 / COROLAVIT IN HAMPSTEAD. 1853*
Ashmolean Museum, Oxford. Presented by Mrs W.F.R. Weldon 1920

This is Brown's oil sketch for his projected triptych, 'a love offering to my favorite poets, to my never-faithless Burns, Byron, Spencer & Shakespear.'[18] The central part shows Chaucer reading to

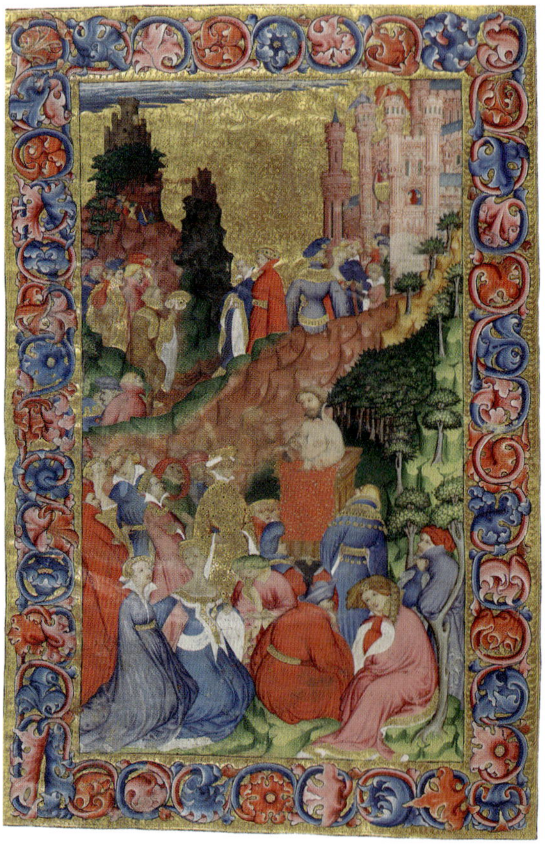

Fig. 57
Frontispiece to Chaucer's Troilus and Criseyde, *English early fifteenth century. Corpus Christi College, Cambridge (MS.61 fol.1)*

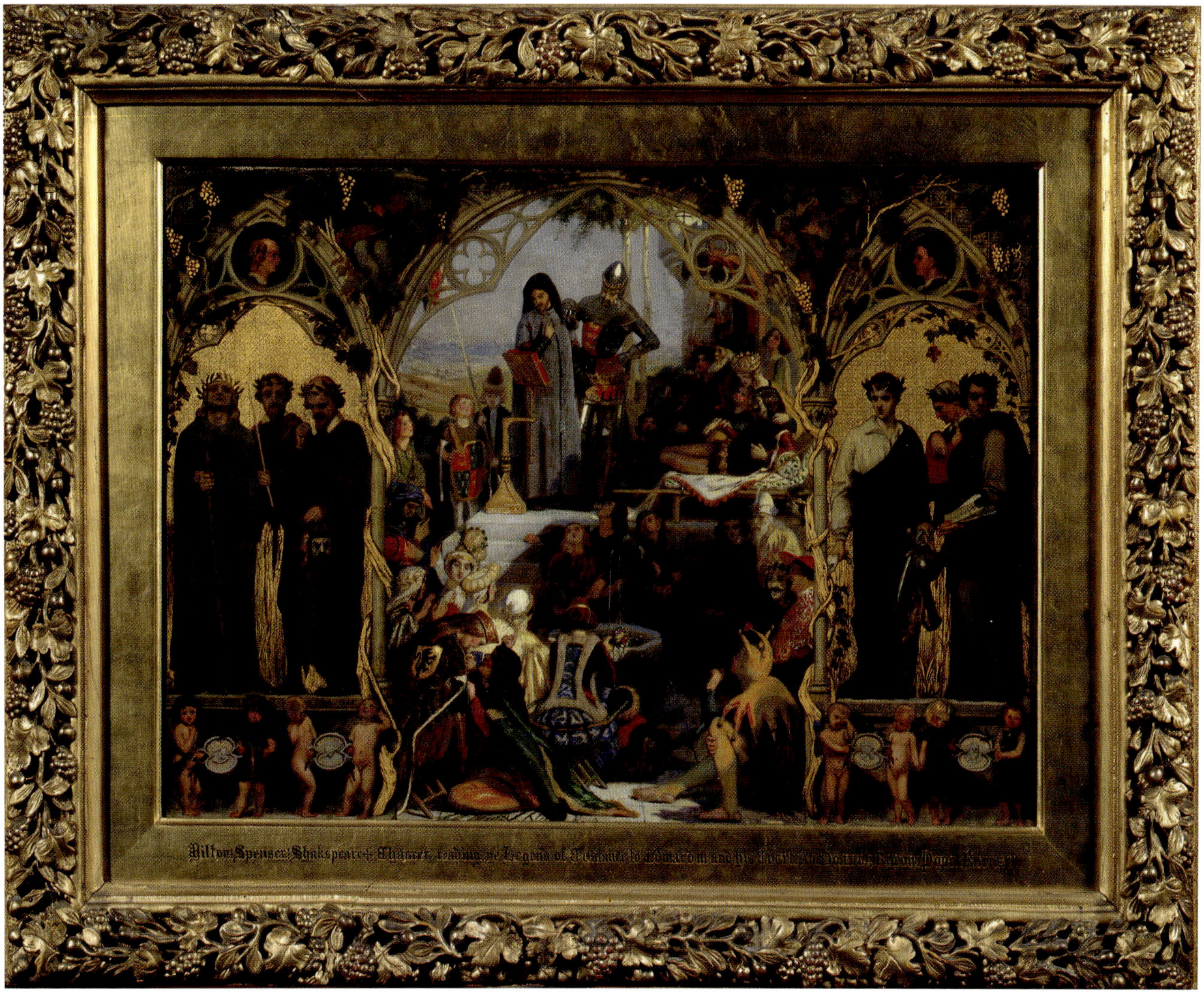

32

Edward III and his court, with Chaucer's patron John of Gaunt standing next to him (in the large oil painting Brown moved John of Gaunt to one side, to place greater emphasis on Chaucer), while Brown's other admired poets are in the wings. It was begun in Rome in 1845.

In the left-hand wing, beneath a Gothic arch with a roundel of Goldsmith, stand Milton, Spenser and Shakespeare; the right-hand wing shows Byron, Pope and Burns beneath a roundel of Thomson. In the upper spandrels of the arches between the three panels are a sleeping poet with a lyre, left, and a poet with a broken harp, right; these two figures were intended to 'symbolize the overthrow, through Chaucer, of the Saxon Bard and the Norman Troubadour.'[19] Below are putti carrying cartouches with the names of more recent poets, on the left Campbell, Moore, Shelley and Keats and on the right Chatterton, Kirke White, Coleridge and Wordsworth. On a visit to Brown's studio, Rossetti attacked Brown's representation of modern poets, saying that Shelley and Keats should have been shown full-length instead of Pope and Burns, and criticizing the inclusion of the now forgotten Kirke White (1785–1806) as 'ridiculous.'[20] This probably contributed to Brown's decision to jettison the wings, which he later explained in his 1865 exhibition catalogue: 'On my coming to England I soon found that the illustrious in poetry were not all among the dead, and to avoid what must either have remained incomplete, or have appeared pretentious criticism, I gave up the idea indicated in the side compartments.'[21] In the light of his growing interest in a more realistic style, he may also have disliked the contrast between the emblematic conception of the wings, and the naturalism of the centre.

The triptych was inspired by an account of the origins of the

English language written by Sir James Mackintosh in his history of England, published in Lardner's *Cyclopedia* (1830). On reading the passage about Chaucer, Brown 'saw visions of Chaucer reading his poems to knights & Ladyes fair, to the king & court amid air & sun shine.'[22] He may here have been influenced by an early fifteenth-century illuminated frontispiece to a manuscript of Chaucer at Corpus Christi College, Cambridge (fig. 57); although there is no proof that he saw it, or a reproduction of it, there is a distinct resemblance between the illumination and Brown's central scene. Many other artistic influences were assimilated in *The Seeds and Fruits*: including Flemish and Italian altarpieces for the layout and framework of the triptych; Italian Renaissance frescoes, particularly Raphael for the standing poets and putti; German book illustrations which inspired the rustic vines twining round the elaborate Gothic arches of the painted frame; and the Germanic mural style of Maclise for the centre part with its tiered arrangement of figures (fig. 52, p. 110). Brown himself cited Maclise's cartoon of *Chivalry* which he saw at the Westminster exhibition of 1845,[23] and whilst in Rome he may well have seen *The Triumph of Religion in the Arts* by the Nazarene painter Friedrich Overbeck (Städel Museum, Frankfurt), with its symmetrical crowd of figures grouped round a fountain. The fountain may also refer to the van Eycks' Ghent Altarpiece which Brown would have known from his student days.

The frame is one of the earliest designed by Brown, with foliage and bunches of grapes echoing the painted vines within the picture, and the names of the poets represented inscribed in Gothic lettering along the lower gilt flat. This the only example amongst Brown's frames of such richly three-dimensional naturalistic ornament, but it is firmly contained within straight lines, and separated from the painted area by a generous gilt flat, foreshadowing the even broader flats of his later frames.

33

THE FIRST TRANSLATION OF THE BIBLE INTO ENGLISH: WYCLIFFE READING HIS TRANSLATION OF THE NEW TESTAMENT TO HIS PROTECTOR, JOHN OF GAUNT, DUKE OF LANCASTER, IN THE PRESENCE OF CHAUCER AND GOWER, HIS RETAINERS

(A48)
1847–48, 1859–61
oil on canvas, 40 × 60½ (119.5 × 153.5)
signed: *F.MADOX BROWN*
Bradford Museums and Galleries (Cartwright Hall Art Gallery)

John Wycliffe, the fourteenth-century theologian and religious reformer, was long credited with the first translation of the Bible from Latin to English although he is now thought to have instigated the translation to be carried out by his associates rather than translated it personally. He stands in the centre of the painting, reading from the New Testament, silhouetted against a clear sunlit sky. Behind him on the lectern is a Bible placed upside-down, one of Brown's comic flourishes. Listening in admiration on the right are Wycliffe's patron and protector, John of Gaunt, Duke of Lancaster with his wife and daughter. The Duke's taut, attentive posture, turning his head towards Wycliffe and leaning slightly out of the picture in the opposite direction, creates a tension that contrasts with the simpler, more relaxed poses of the standing figures. The child has fallen asleep, a typically Brownian touch that brings the elevated subject down to human level.

On the left, a step down from the nobility stand Wycliffe's contemporaries, the writers Geoffrey Chaucer and his friend John Gower, with pageboys carrying books including Chaucer's *Troilus and Criseyde* and Gower's *Confessio Amantis*, both of them written in English. Chaucer and Gower are richly dressed, unlike the barefooted and austerely clad Wycliffe. The scene takes place on a raised platform looking over the tiny details of a distant landscape, perhaps a reminiscence of the backgrounds of Flemish paintings. Let into the gold flat of the frame on either side of the Gothic arch are roundels of symbolic figures: on the left is a monk with his face in shadow, holding a crucifix and a book locked shut by a chain, representing Catholicism, and on the right, a girl with her face in the light, holding an open book and a lily, for Protestantism. These figures are surrounded by fictive Gothic tracery, part of a painted frame which was enclosed in a real outer frame, now lost; this type of framing was characteristic of the Nazarenes. When the original outer frame was removed, it was replaced with a broader frame, concealing the tracery and changing the shape of the opening.

The First Translation of the Bible into English is like a secular altarpiece: it recalls early Italian and also Nazarene painting in its delicate colours, clear overall light without dark shadows, and symmetrical composition. This was recognised when the painting was shown in the Free Exhibition in London in 1848; amongst several favourable notices, the *Art Union* wrote that Brown's painting was 'in the manner of fresco, with a marked feeling for the style of the early Florentine School' and praised it as 'the most entirely successful production we have ever seen in this manner of Art. The aspirations of the old schools are inimitably rivalled and, we confidently say, surpassed'.[24] 'Surpassed', because this was not mere revivalism; Brown combined the archaic style with his own, and introduced a nationalistic theme, celebrating the Protestant

33

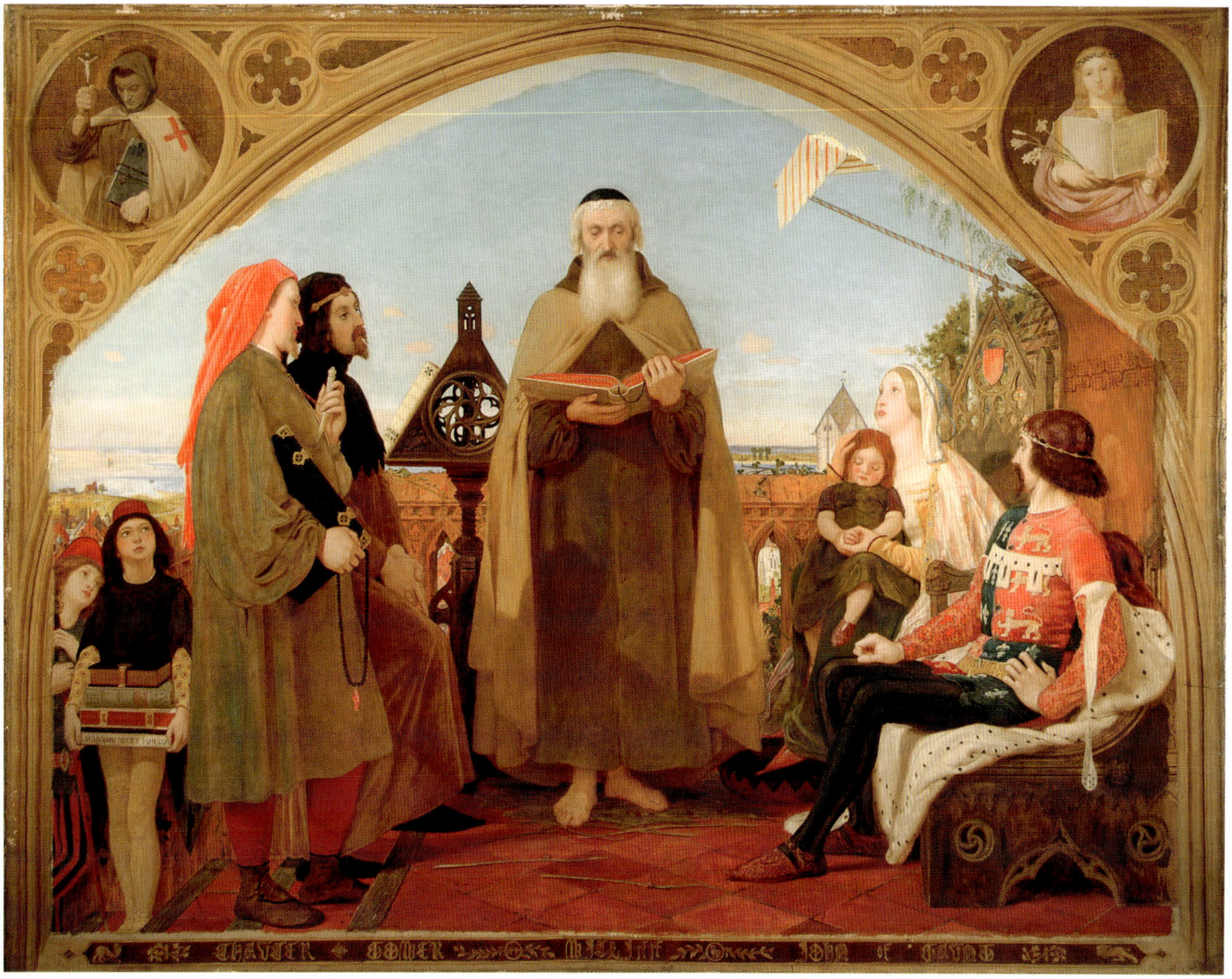

reformation, and honouring the flowering of English prose in the fourteenth century, just as the projected triptych *Seeds and Fruits* was to have paid tribute to poetry.

The details of costume, furnishings and dress were all carefully researched from books on medieval history, furniture and ornament; portraits were consulted for the historical personages, and ermine was hired for John of Gaunt's cloak. Most of the figures were painted from professional models, but the sleeping child was based on studies of Lucy, the artist's daughter, and for the Duchess, drawings were made from James Bamford's daughter Elizabeth (see cat. 29) as well as from a professional model Mrs. Ashley (cat. 44).

To obtain a sunlit effect, Brown used a white undercoat, not yet left wet, but all the same anticipating the technique of wet white under-painting adopted by the Pre-Raphaelites: 'nothing like a good coating of White to get a bright and sunny colour' wrote the artist in his diary.[25] Even so, the fresco-like effect observed in 1848 by the *Art Union* must have looked old-fashioned by 1859, when the picture was bought by the Leeds collector Thomas Plint. At his request, Brown retouched it to make it look more like his more recent works: he brightened the sky, reddened the floor tiles and changed the landscape, introducing the distant tower, based on Sompting church. At the same time the painting was reframed, concealing the Gothic tracery. The result was to make the painting warmer and more brilliant than it had been originally; underneath the new frame, a band of the original cool blue of the sky has been preserved. This and the painted tracery can be seen from the illustration, which shows the painting without its frame.

34

GEOFFREY CHAUCER READING THE 'LEGEND OF CUSTANCE' TO EDWARD III AND HIS COURT

(A40.8)
1850, 1864–65, 1867–68
oil on canvas, 48½ × 39 (123.2 × 99)
signed and dated: *F. MADOX BROWN – 68*
Tate. Purchased 1906

This is a replica of the much larger painting now in the Art Gallery of New South Wales, Sydney, which measures 145⅞ x 116⅜ inches (370.5 x 295.5 cm) and was begun in 1847 and completed in 1851. The replica was begun in 1850 for Brown by Thomas Seddon, who was then working in Brown's studio. It was left unfinished, but around 1864–65 Brown took it up again, and another assistant, possibly Albert Goodwin, at that time a pupil of Brown, worked on it before Brown finished it off. Brown made some small changes in detail and colour in the replica, but the general composition is the same. However, the overall effect of looking at the original is very different, because of its enormous size and its smoother finish. The spectator has to look up into the painting, giving the sensation of being enveloped within the dazzling and colourful crowd (fig. 58).

A development of the central part of *The Seeds and Fruits of English Poetry* (cat. 32), it shows Chaucer reading to Edward III and his court at the Palace of Sheen on the forty-fifth birthday of Edward's son, the Black Prince, in 1375, the year before his death. To the right is the King, seated on a canopied throne, surrounded by the royal family, and below is an array of richly dressed courtiers, some gazing at the poet in rapt attention, others flirting, talking or gesturing to each other. The effect of the tiered arrangement, the heads tilted and foreshortened at different angles, the variety of facial expressions, the lively hand movements, the brightly coloured clothes and the natural-looking distribution of sunlight and shadow is to create an impression of a crowd in constant movement.

The figures can be identified as follows: to the right of Chaucer is John of Gaunt, standing; the King's mistress Alice Perrers, holding a fan, is seated next to Edward III, in a red robe, sitting on the throne with a tall canopy; just behind him is Johanna, Princess of Wales known as the Fair Maid of Kent, and her husband Edward Prince of Wales, the 'Black Prince,' shown in his last illness, seated with a red blanket over his legs; with them are their son the future Richard II and daughter; behind are Princess Margaret and the Princess Royal; half way down on the same side is a cardinal, the papal Nuncio, looking at the Countess of Warwick and pointing to the court Fool in blue, with cap and bells; in the bottom-right corner, the historian Sir John Froissart, wearing a yellow cap, is writing, his head turned towards the poet Gower who is speaking to him. To the left of Chaucer and just behind him is John of Gaunt's son, the future Henry IV, with his father's shield; on the

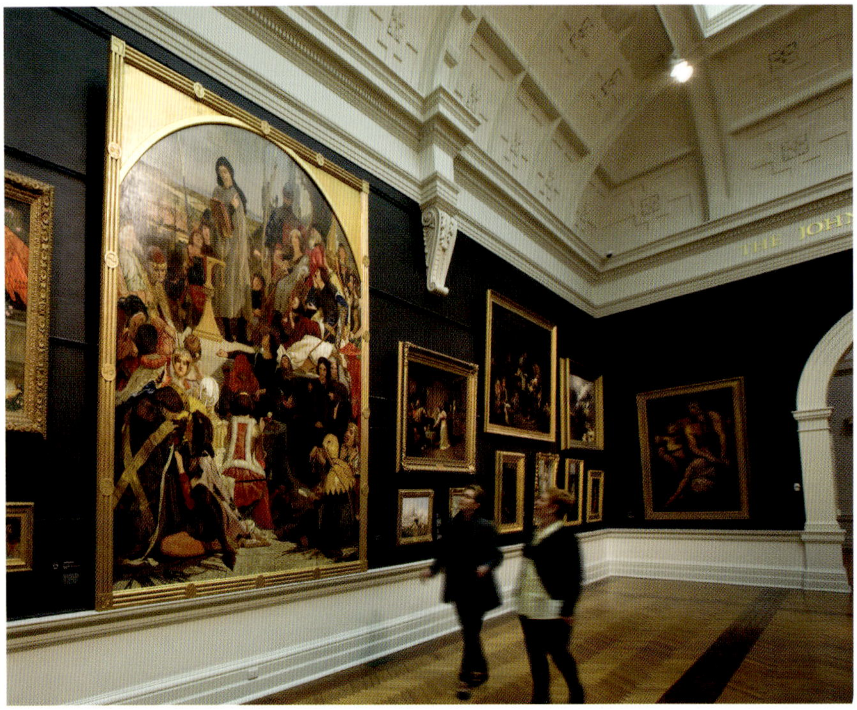

Fig. 58
First version of Ford Madox Brown, Geoffrey Chaucer reading the 'Legend of Custance' to Edward III and his court, *1847–51, hanging in the Art Gallery of New South Wales, Sydney*

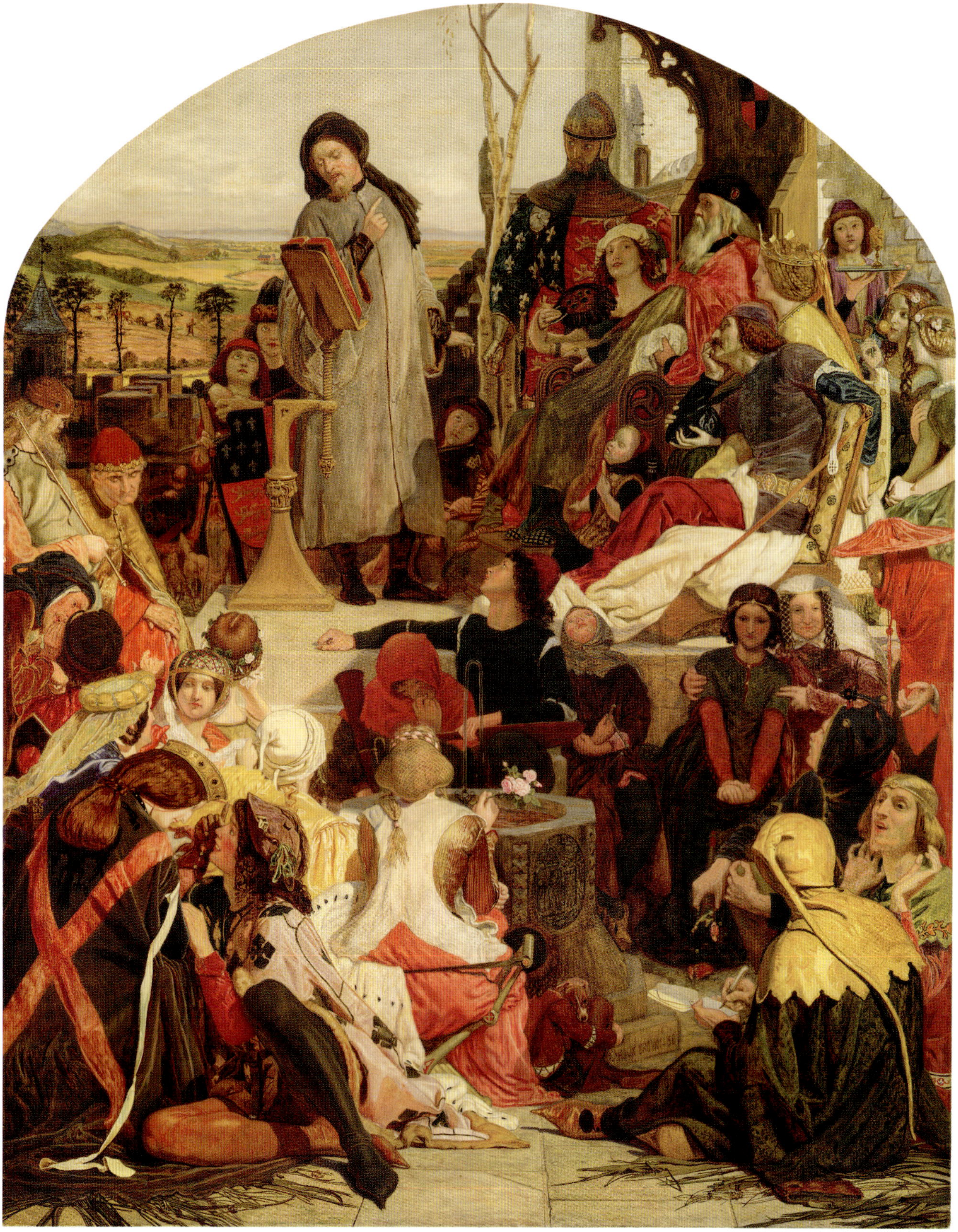

34

left are the grand Chamberlain Robert de Vere, in pale green, with staff, and Edward III's marshal the Earl of Pembroke, in red and gold; below them is Chaucer's wife Philippa, the Picard, in a blue robe, her face partially turned away from the spectator to speak to her sister Catherine Roet, who later married John of Gaunt; in the bottom-left corner Thomas of Woodstock, patron of Gower and fifth son of Edward III is speaking to his future wife Lady Bohun. In the centre, behind the fountain, his face looking up towards Chaucer, is a Provençal troubadour with his minstrels, recalling the troubadour in the *Seeds and Fruits* symbolizing the overthrow of French poetry by English. The fountain in the centre and the sower scattering seed with the ploughmen in the landscape are symbolic of Chaucer's role at the beginning of English poetry.

Brown shows us the historical scene taking place in daylight. 'This picture is the first in which I endeavoured to carry out the notion, long before conceived, of treating the light and shade absolutely, as it exists at any one moment, instead of approximately, or in generalised style. Sunlight not too bright, such as it is pleasant to sit in out of doors, is here depicted.'[26] *The First Translation of the Bible into English*, completed in 1848 (cat. 33) is also set out of doors in sunlight, but Brown took the effect further in the *Chaucer*, which he begun before *The First Translation* but completed after it, in 1851.

Brown's original vision for *Chaucer* was a scene set 'amid air & sunshine' but because of its size and elaboration, it was physically impossible for Brown to paint the whole of *Chaucer* out of doors in natural light. But between the completion of *The First Translation of the Bible into English* and that of *Chaucer*, Brown's younger artist friends had formed the Pre-Raphaelite Brotherhood. Their developing interest in 'truth to nature' perhaps led Brown to intensify his efforts to reproduce specific light conditions in the *Chaucer*: the diary for June and July 1849 records him placing models in the sun to paint them, and arranging fresh blinds in his studio 'to admit the sun if necessary.'[27] Also in accordance with Pre-Raphaelite ideas, he made more use of friends and family to sit for him: Emma sat for Philippa, the Picard and for the Fair Maid of Kent, Lucy for her daughter, his friend the surgeon John Marshall for the Jester, William Michael Rossetti for the troubadour and most appropriately the would-be poet Dante Gabriel Rossetti, whom he had met in March 1848, for Chaucer himself. But he also continued to use professional models: Maitland for the Black Prince and Gower, and Julia Wild for Catherine Roet.

Brown also depicted a real landscape in the background, based on an oil sketch of Shorn Ridgway, Kent, painted on the spot (cat. 48). But there were limits to his naturalism. In the large painting he reversed the view of Shorn Ridgway, and the arched format and the figures piled up in a shallow space still showed the influence of the formalized, Germanic style of the Westminster murals. Holman Hunt later criticised this 'architectonic' construction, writing, 'Impressed as I felt by his work as the product of individual genius, I found nothing indicative of a child-like reversion from existing schools to Nature herself.'[28] This seems somewhat unfair in view of the intense realism with which Brown handled the individual figures.

35
STUDY FOR SIR JOHN FROISSART

(A40.4)
1847
oil on millboard, 24 × 18 5/16 (60.9 × 46.6)
Manchester City Galleries

This is a study for the man in a yellow hood, seated in the bottom right corner of the Chaucer painting, representing the French historian Jean Froissart. He is shown with his back to the spectator, writing on his tablets and engaged in conversation with Gower. Froissart may have met Chaucer in 1368 on a journey to Italy under the patronage of Edward III's Queen, Philippa of Hainault; he is known to have been present at the English royal court on several occasions, and the exploits of the Black Prince feature in the first book of his Chronicles.[29] But his presence at court in 1375 is entirely conjectural, as indeed is the case for many of the other historical figures gathered together by the artist in his imagination for the painting.

Brown's diary for October and November 1847 described his work on this study, typical of the painstaking preparations made before transferring even the smallest details on to the large canvas. He went out in search of old materials, bought some yellow brocade, and had a workwoman make up a 'yellow brocade hood'. He then arranged the hood on a lay figure and painted it for a few hours each day over the course of several days. He also mentioned the other costume details on the right hand side of the study: the sleeve of the woman in white cap, above Thomas of Woodstock, and the Fair Maid of Kent's cape, also made of yellow brocade.[30]

Besides making this and several other oil studies of draperies and heads, Brown made a large number of drawings for the painting. These include tracings made from costume books such as Camille Bonnard's *Costumes Historiques* (1829–30), which was used by several of the Pre-Raphaelites as a source for period dress. One of Brown's tracings (Birmingham Museums and Art Gallery) is a figure of Cimabue wearing a hood with a long 'liripipe' similar to that worn by Froissart.

35

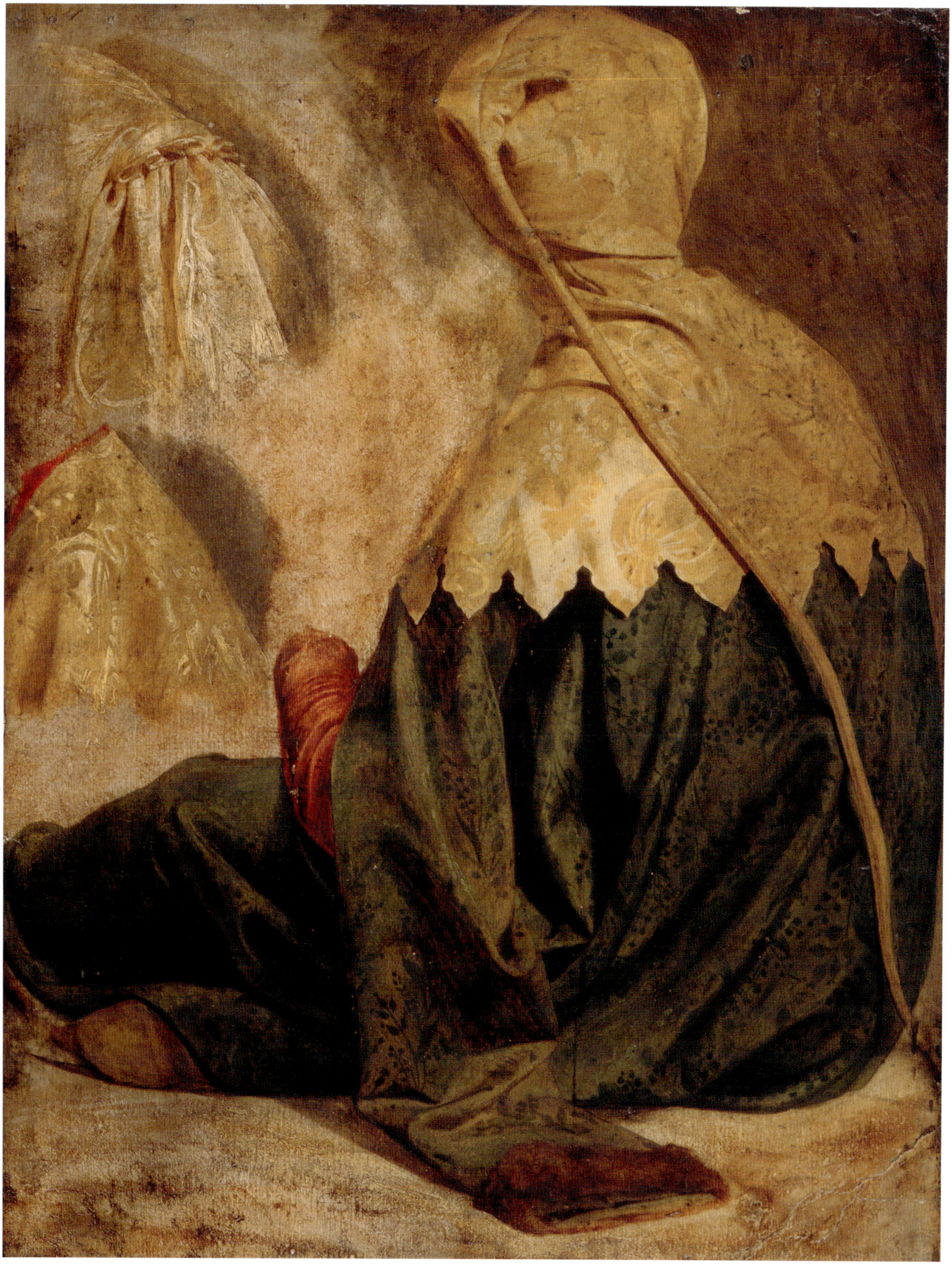

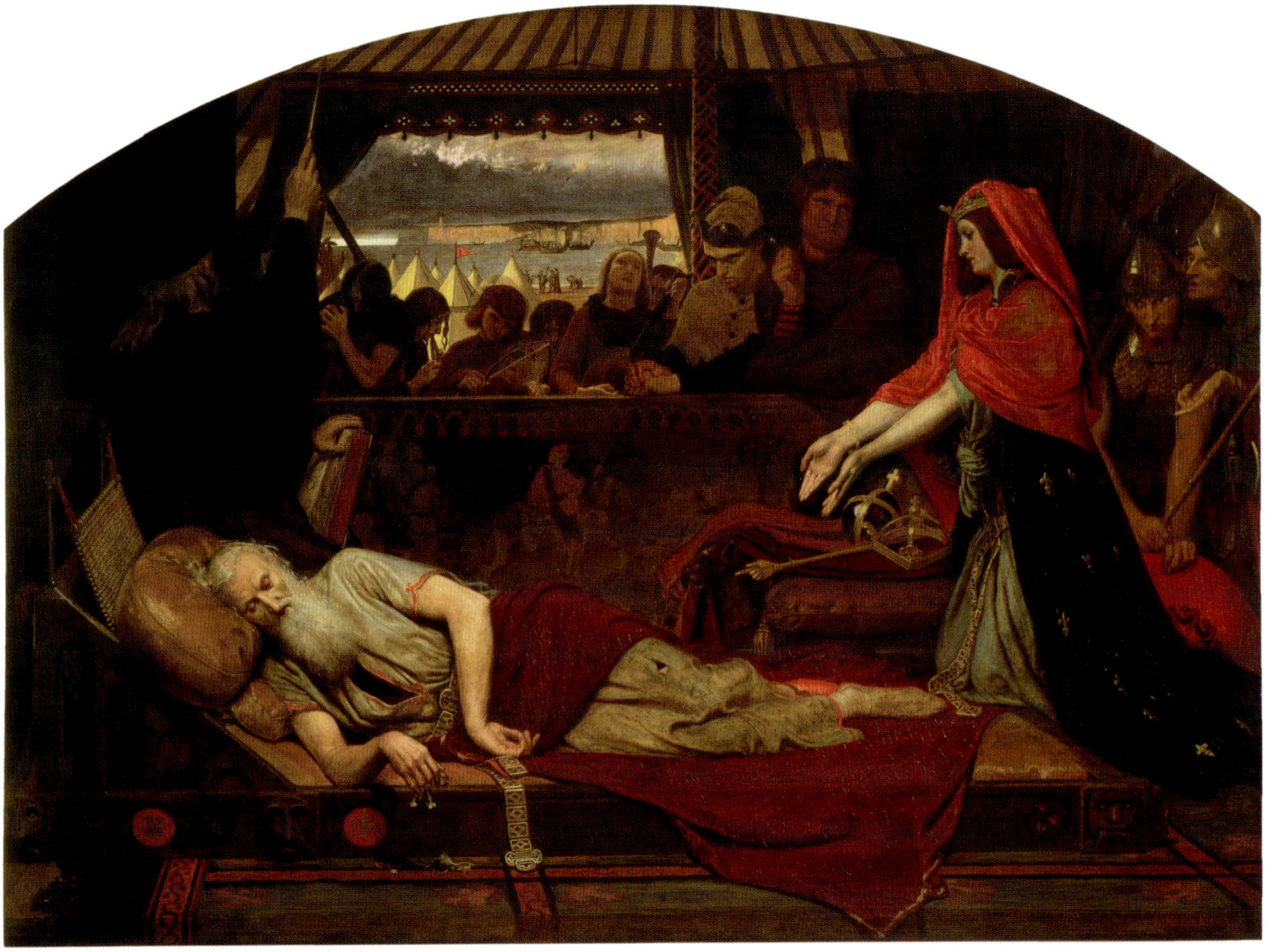

36

36

KING LEAR (CORDELIA AT THE BEDSIDE OF LEAR)

(A51)
1848–49, 1853–54, (1862–63)
oil on canvas, 29 × 39 (71.1 × 99.1)
signed: *F. Madox Brown*
Tate. Purchased 1916

Lear's disinherited daughter Cordelia, now Queen of France, stands before her father, her hands held out before her in a gesture of pity and love, as she tries to reawaken him from exhausted sleep and from madness. Through the window of her tent is a view of the encampment at Dover. The doctor, on the left, represented by Brown as a magician, raises his arm calling for the musicians in the centre to play louder. To the right is the fool with Kent in disguise, and two of Cordelia's soldiers look on from behind her.

The painting closely follows Shakespeare's text from Act 4, scene 7 of *King Lear*, and extracts from Cordelia's speech are written on the frame:

> Had you not been their father, these white flakes
> Had challenged pity of them. Was this a face
> To be opposed against the warring winds?
> To stand against the deep dread-bolted thunder?
> … Mine enemy's dog,
> Though he had bit me, should have stood that night
> Against my fire; and wast thou fain, poor father,
> To hovel thee with swine, and rogues forlorn,
> In short and musty straw?

In May 1848, Brown had seen William Charles Macready's famous production of *King Lear* in which the celebrated actor took the leading role.[31] The production was based on a restored text, and evoked strong emotional reaction in audiences. It emphasized the primitive, barbarous aspect of Lear's Britain; the actors wore ancient Celtic dress, and Macready was the first to play the part of Lear with a beard. In a similar spirit, Brown chose for his painting not Romano-British or medieval costume, but 'the costume prevalent in Europe about the sixth century, when paganism was still rife, and deeds were at their darkest' to emphasize what he called 'the savage and remote' element in the play.[32] The primitivism of the settings for the Lear drawings made in Paris (cats. 17-22) may indicate that Brown already then knew of the Macready production, which had first been performed in 1838. For the screen in the painting, Brown copied a scene of horsemen riding with hawk and hound from the Bayeux tapestry, which he acknowledged was an anachronism.

Brown began the painting in late 1848 and continued it in the early part of 1849. The composition is a development of one of the Lear subjects sketched in Paris (Birmingham Museums and Art Gallery).[33] The painting is darker in tone than most of his work at this period, apart from the view of the camp through the window. But the main figures are carefully painted, with close attention to detail, such as the flowers and grasses in the king's hair, his torn robe and muddy feet.

The artist used a number of his favourite professional models including Maitland for Lear, also using for Lear's head a cast borrowed from Rossetti and a drawing of Coulton, another model who had also sat for Wyckliffe.[34] Rossetti sat for the Fool, and Cordelia was at first taken from Mrs Ashley, who had also previously modelled for the artist (cats. 31, 44), but during the early stages of designing the painting Brown first met Emma (see cat. 4); she appears as Cordelia in the finished work.

It was shown in the Free Exhibition in London in 1849, and in 1852 it was one of a group of English paintings shown in Antwerp, where it was admired by the Belgian King. At both these exhibitions it was praised for its originality, and in Belgium it was singled out for its 'possession of the feeling and inspiration of a former epoch.'[35] Brown worked on it again in 1853–54, and in 1857 it was sent to the Pre-Raphaelite Exhibition in America, where it was damaged. It was eventually sold to Plint, but he sold it on to Leathart, for whom Brown retouched various details in 1862–63. He softened Cordelia's veil, altered the pattern of the carpet, toned down various colours and improved Cordelia's face: 'I think it is a more tearful kind of pity now' – 'by adding a line to the chin, taking somewhat from the smile of the mouth & somewhat elevating a point of the eyebrow I think I have diminished the somewhat too girlish quality of the face.'[36]

1 *Brown* 1865, no. 36.
2 Hueffer 1896, p. 41; L.M. Rossetti 1890, p. 291.
3 *Diary*, p. 2.
4 London 1984, p. 59, cat. 11.
5 *Brown* 1865, no. 3.
6 Bendiner 1998, p. 17, fig. 104.
7 Bennett 2010 1, p. 89, A44.13.
8 *Brown* 1865, no. 3.
9 Bennett 2, p. 565 (section F by Lynn Roberts); I am indebted to this source for information on Brown's frames.
10 Bennett 2010, 2, p.p. 369-70, B3.
11 *Brown* 1865, no. 36.
12 Bennett 2010, 2, pp. 421-2, B104.
13 W.M. Rossetti 1851, pp. 19–20; Bennett 2010, 1, p. 107, A50.
14 1849, p. 105.
15 *Brown* 1865, no. 6.
16 *Diary*, p. 1.
17 *Diary*, pp. 2–4.
18 *Diary*, p. 2.
19 Brown 1865, no. 1.
20 Hunt 1905, 1, p. 126.
21 Brown 1865, no. 1.
22 *Diary*, pp. 1–2.
23 *Diary*, p. 1.
24 *Art Union* May 1848, p. 144.
25 *Diary*, p. 35.
26 Brown 1865, no. 1.
27 *Diary*, pp. 64–65.
28 Hunt 1905, 1, p. 125.
29 DNB article of Froissart by Michael Jones.
30 *Diary*, pp. 12–14.
31 Seen by Brown 2 May 1848, *Diary*, p. 40.
32 Brown 1865, no. 7.
33 Bennett 2010 2, p. 440, C31.
34 *Diary*, p. 57.
35 *Art Journal* 1 October 1852, p. 329.
36 UBC, FMB to James Leathart 20, 27 January 1863.

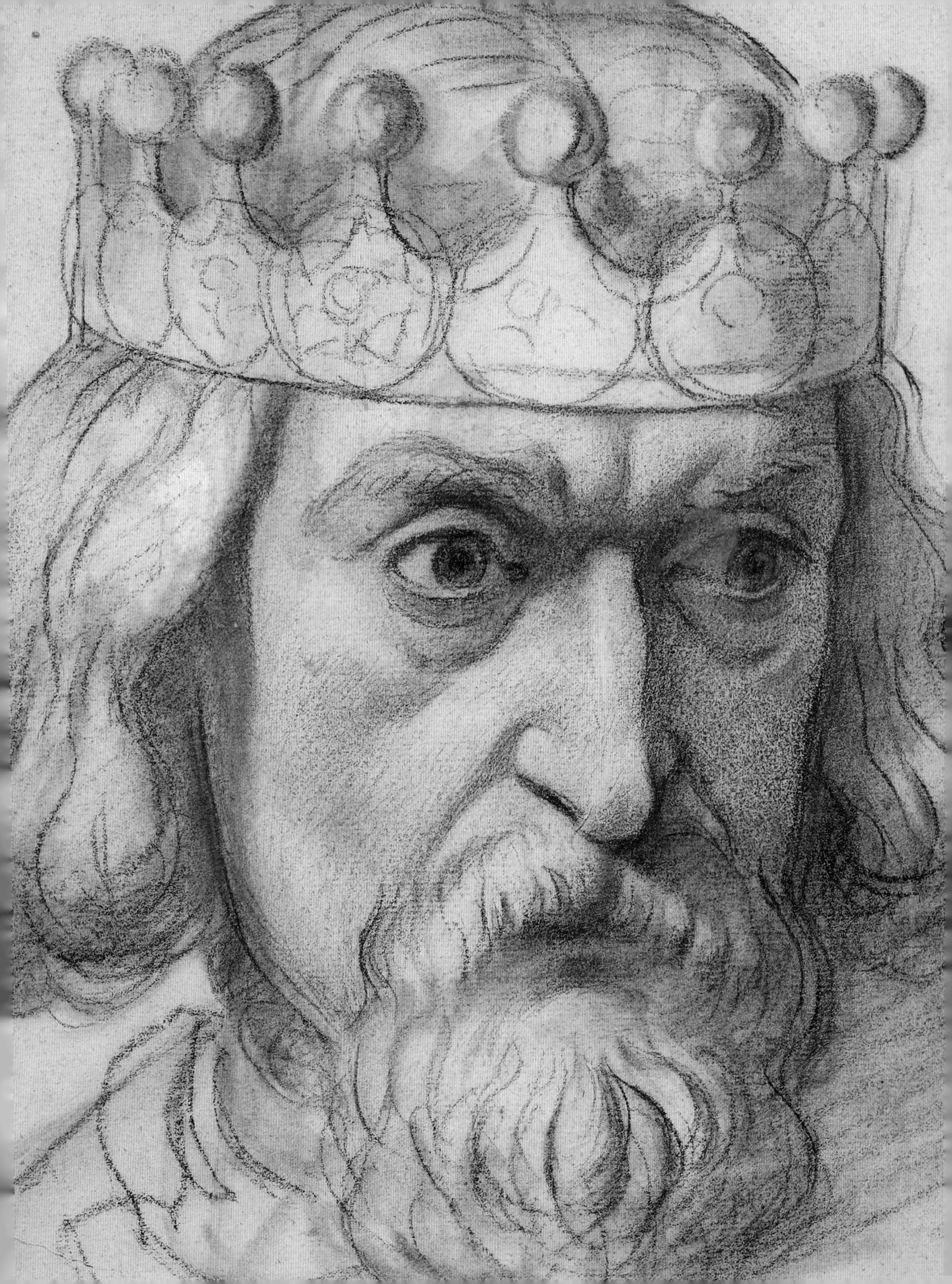

THE DRAUGHTSMAN

Drawing played a fundamental role in Brown's training. Before being allowed to paint, students had to make drawings from plaster casts, and learn the ideal proportions of the human figure and face. It was only when these rules had been learned that they were permitted to study from live models. When preparing to paint a complex figure composition, students would be taught to make a series of drawings – rough sketches of preliminary ideas and groupings of figures; detailed drawings from the life for each figure, first nude, then clothed; and studies of smaller parts such as hands, heads, feet, draperies and accessories. The students would then put all their ideas together into a compositional drawing, and a colour sketch. These would be followed by a detailed full-size preparatory drawing (known as a cartoon), which was then transferred to the canvas for painting.

Brown's drawings survive in large numbers for his earlier works, especially for his more elaborate paintings – over forty drawings for *Chaucer* (cat. 34) and over thirty for *Spirit of Justice* (cat. 24) for example, with smaller quantities for less complicated compositions. But during the 1850s, with the advent of the Pre-Raphaelite style, Brown made far fewer drawings for his figure compositions, and none at all for the landscapes, which were painted directly onto the canvas in front of the view, in accordance with Ruskinian ideas of 'truth to nature'.

A few of Brown's finest drawings have been selected for this section to demonstrate his mastery of the medium. Although none of them were intended to be finished works of art, they can variously be admired for their energy, intensity, clarity and delicacy.

Fig. 59
Detail of cat. 40, Study for Lord Temporal in 'Spirit of Justice'

37

SKETCH OF A MAN PAINTING

(C9)
1839
pencil and Chinese white, $11\frac{13}{16} \times 9\frac{3}{8}$ (30 × 23.8)
signed and dated: *FMB Antwerp/1839*
Tate. Purchased 1919

This drawing of an artist painting, palette in one hand and brush in the other, probably shows one of Brown's fellow-students at the Antwerp Academy. The drawing is quick and spontaneous in style, and although the thumb is out of proportion, Brown has captured the man's concentration as he places a brush-stroke on his canvas.

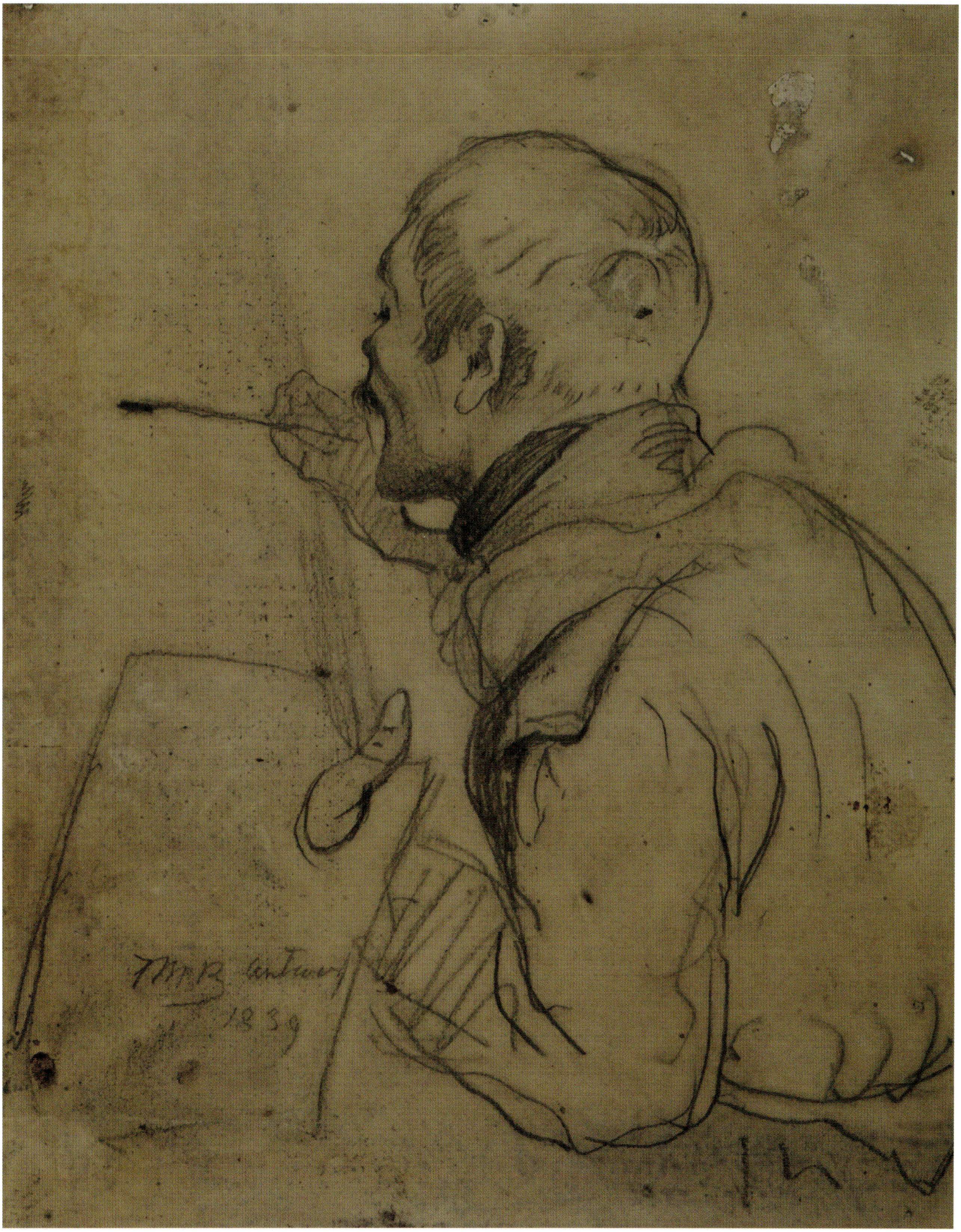

38
HEAD OF AZO (STUDY FOR 'PARISINA')

(A27.2)
1842
black chalk with ink wash, 17 × 12¼ (43.2 × 31)
signed and dated: *FMB /42 Paris*
Birmingham Museums and Art Gallery

This demonic-looking head is a study for a large painting of 1842, *Parisina* (also called *Parisina's Sleep*), in the dramatic style of Brown's Paris years. It was inspired by Byron's poem of the same name, about the illicit love of Parisina, wife of Azo, Duke of Ferrara, for Azo's natural son Hugo. The painting, set in a dark chamber lit by lamplight, depicted the moment when Azo woke to hear his wife murmuring her lover's name in her sleep, and was tempted to murder her. Azo's horrified expression, with distorted eyes and goatee beard, seems to be modelled on the satanic features of Mephistopheles in Delacroix's series of lithographs to Goethe's *Faust*, published in 1828.

Brown sent in the painting to the Paris Salon in 1843 but it was rejected as the subject was thought to be improper. It was certainly an unusual choice for a painting, although consistent with Brown's admiration for Byron. The painting was then shown in London at the British Institution in 1845, and again in 1865. It has now disappeared but it is possible to reconstruct the appearance of the central group from three surviving drawings (Birmingham Museums and Art Gallery): this one, a drawing of the head of the sleeping Parisina and another showing the two figures together (fig. 60).[1]

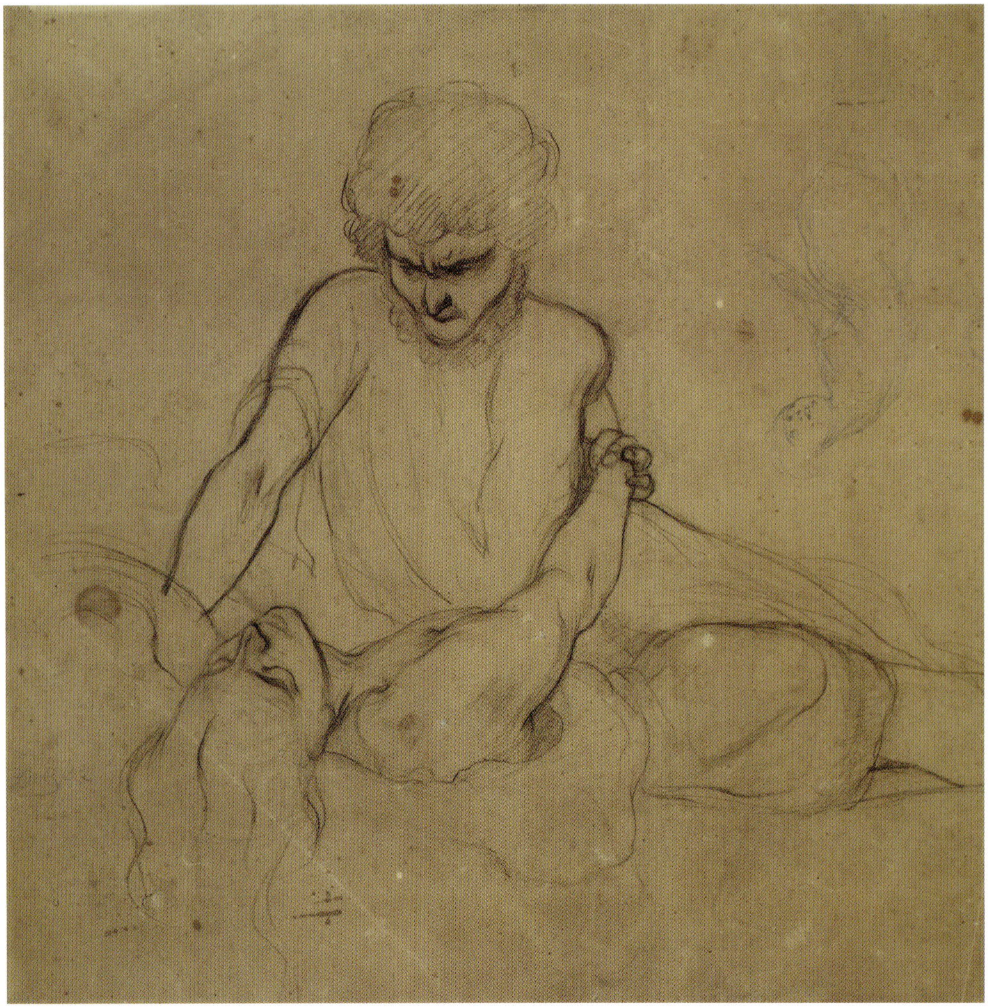

Fig. 60
Ford Madox Brown,
Study for 'Parisina', *1842.*
Birmingham Museums and Art Gallery

38

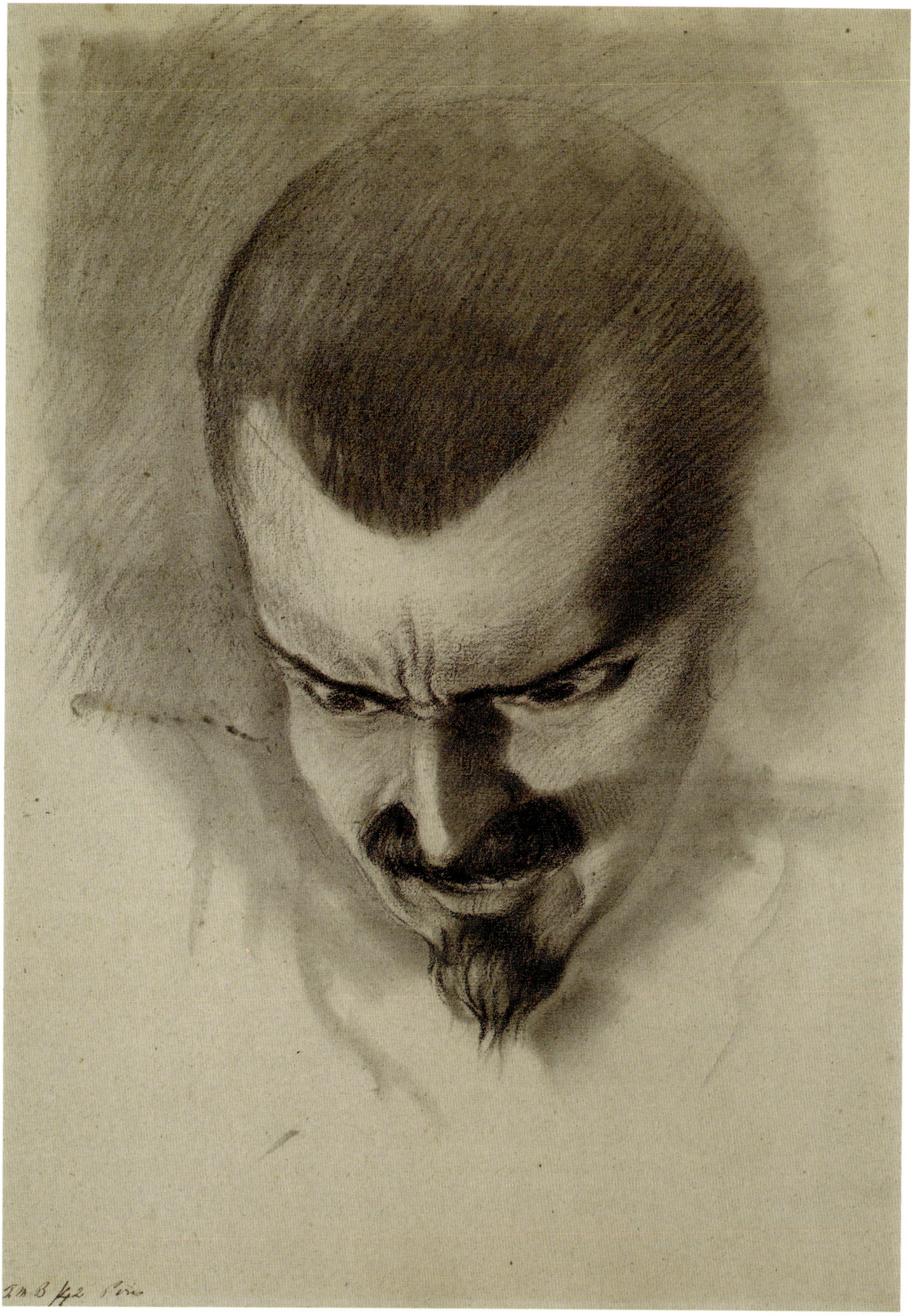

39

DRAPERY STUDY FOR KNEELING APOSTLE IN 'THE ASCENSION'

1844
(A 37.7)
black chalk touched with white, 11⅛ × 8⅝ (28.3 × 22)
signed and dated: *Ford M. Brown /44 (Paris)*
Birmingham Museums and Art Gallery

This is a study for the apostle in red in the bottom right corner of the painting (cat. 26). The style of the drapery-folds and the type of clothing, a toga-like cloak wrapped round the body over a tunic of contrasting colour, comes from a study of Raphael and High Renaissance art in general: there are comparable although less agitated kneeling figures in Raphael's *Transfiguration* (Vatican Museum) and in his tapestry cartoons. But the draperies are so carefully worked out here that in order to make the drawing Brown must have arranged the clothing either on a model or a lay figure. It is the most highly finished of several studies for draped figures that Brown drew for the painting, and the only one with white heightening.

39

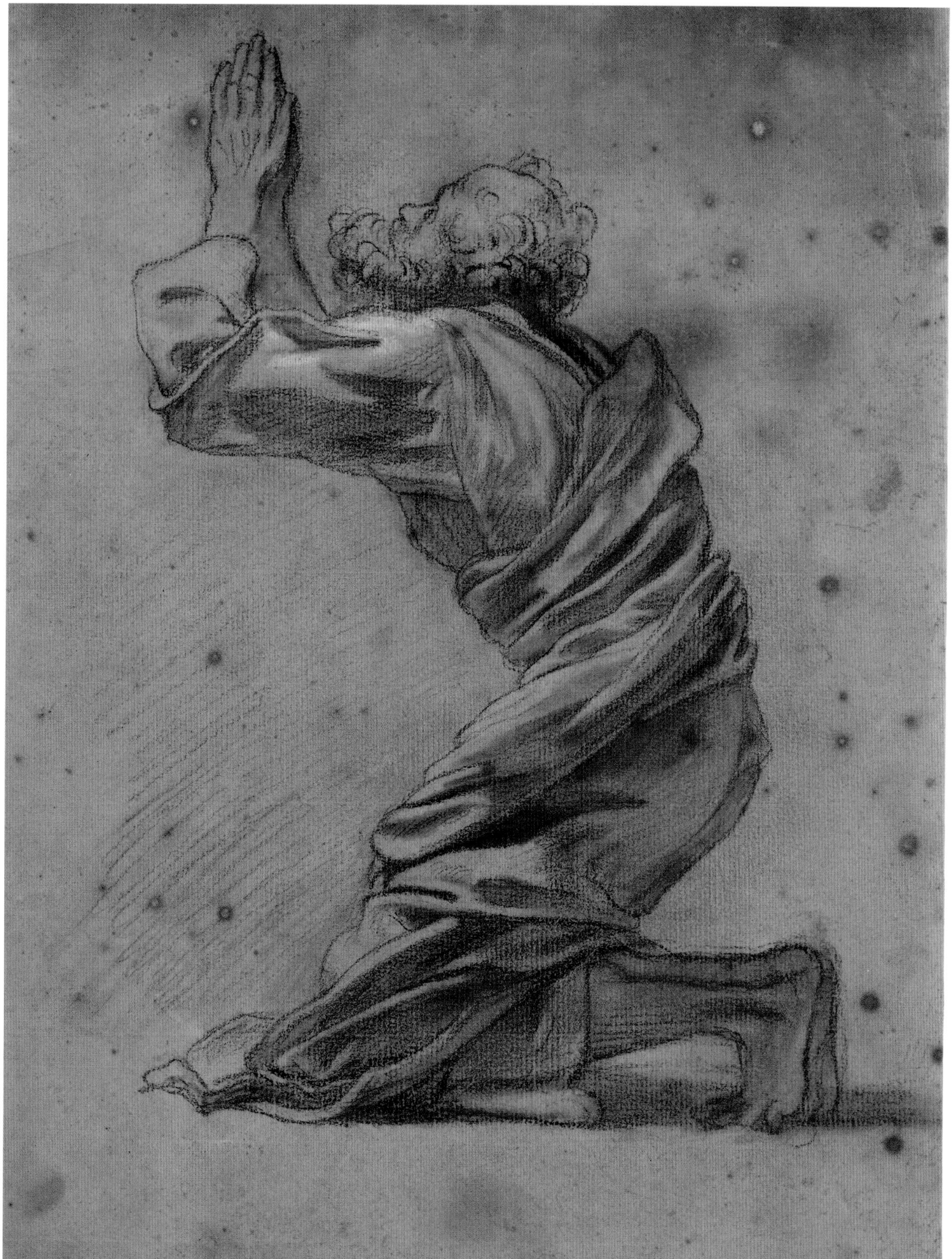

40

STUDY FOR LORD TEMPORAL IN 'SPIRIT OF JUSTICE'

(A31.13)
1844/5
black chalk, 17 15/16 × 12 3/8 (45.5 × 31.5)
Birmingham Museums and Art Gallery

This is a drawing of the head of the Lord Temporal on the left of the middle row of figures in the cartoon of the *Spirit of Justice*, which Brown entered for one of the Westminster murals competitions (cat. 24). The man wears a crown as a sign of his noble rank. It is one of a group of over thirty preparatory drawings for the *Spirit of Justice*, including sketches of figures in medieval costume and armour; drawings of hands, arms, heads and draperies; and figures, both nude and draped. All are at various stages of finish, some very tentative, others more fully worked up, like this one.

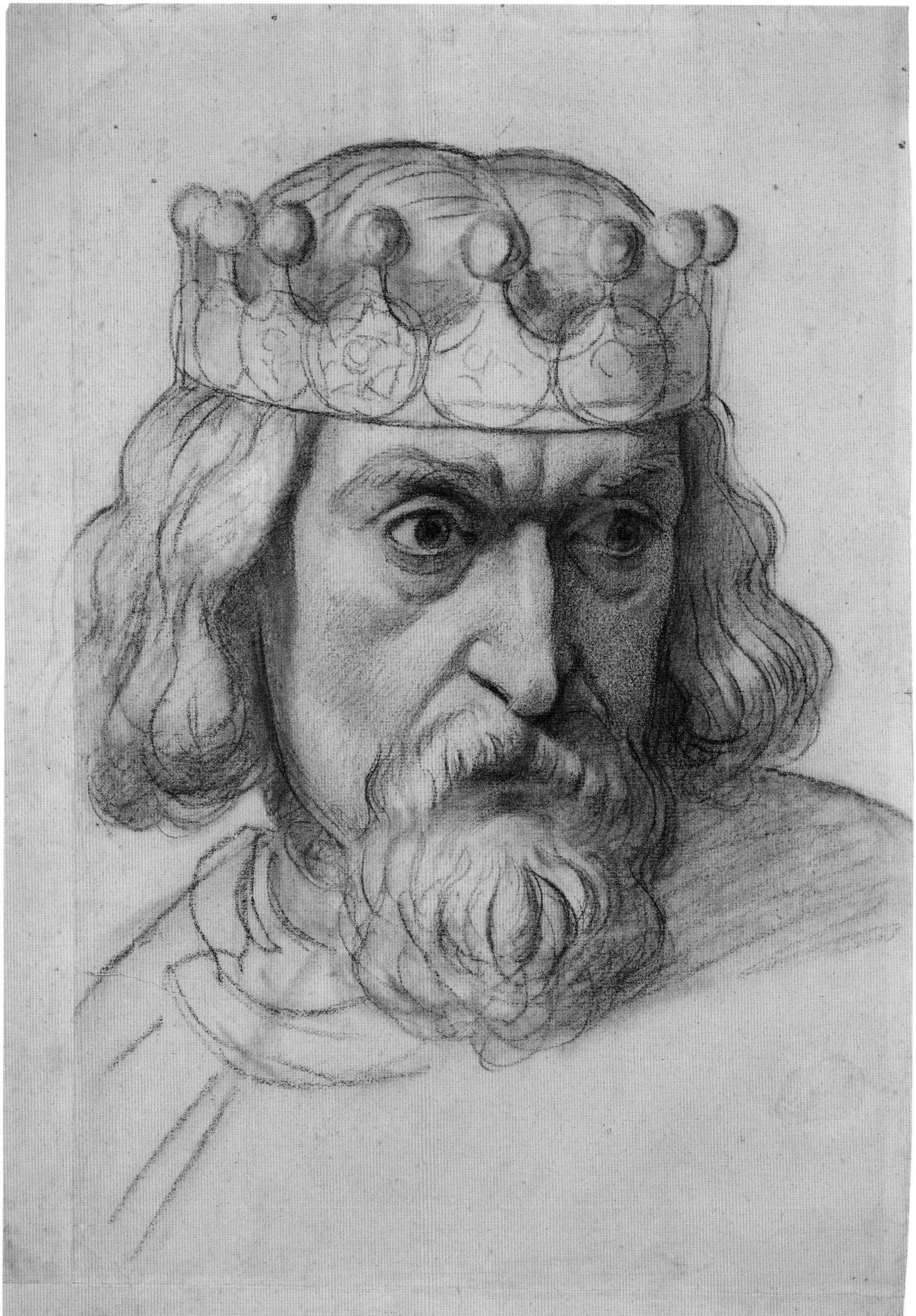

41

LIFE STUDY OF MALE NUDE

(C36)
1847
black chalk, 6¾ × 5⅛ (17.2 × 14.2)
Birmingham Museums and Art Gallery

This is one of a group of four life drawings of male nudes, two of which are signed and dated '*47 London*'. Although Brown must have drawn many nude figures from live models during his training in Belgium, when he came to London he continued to make life drawings of this kind (that is, not posed for specific figures in his paintings) to sharpen his skills. In late 1847 he started to attend life drawing classes at a Drawing Academy started by the Dickinson Brothers at 18½ Maddox Street. Classes were held four evenings a week from 7 to 10 pm for a fee of half a guinea a month. The drawing master was the painter Charles Lucy, a friend of Brown's, and another artist friend William Cave Thomas also attended. It is likely that Brown made this drawing at the Dickinsons' Drawing Academy.

Attendance at such sessions must have helped Brown with his figure compositions. While working on *The First Translation of the Bible into English* (cat. 33) he wrote in his diary, 'found that I was making my figures of Chaucer & Gower to short, quite took me aback. Went & began a drawing at Dickinsons walked home with Lucy, came back bought a bottle of Wiskey to drown care with (8 hours work).' Two days later Cave Thomas 'brought me an outline of the proportions according to Vitruvius', probably based on Leonardo da Vinci's famous drawing of Vitruvian man. On 18 January Brown recorded 'work an hour at lessening Chaucer's legs, had tea & went to Dickingsons academy. Came back worked from ¼ past 10 til ½ past 11 at lessening the head & hands of Gower'.[2]

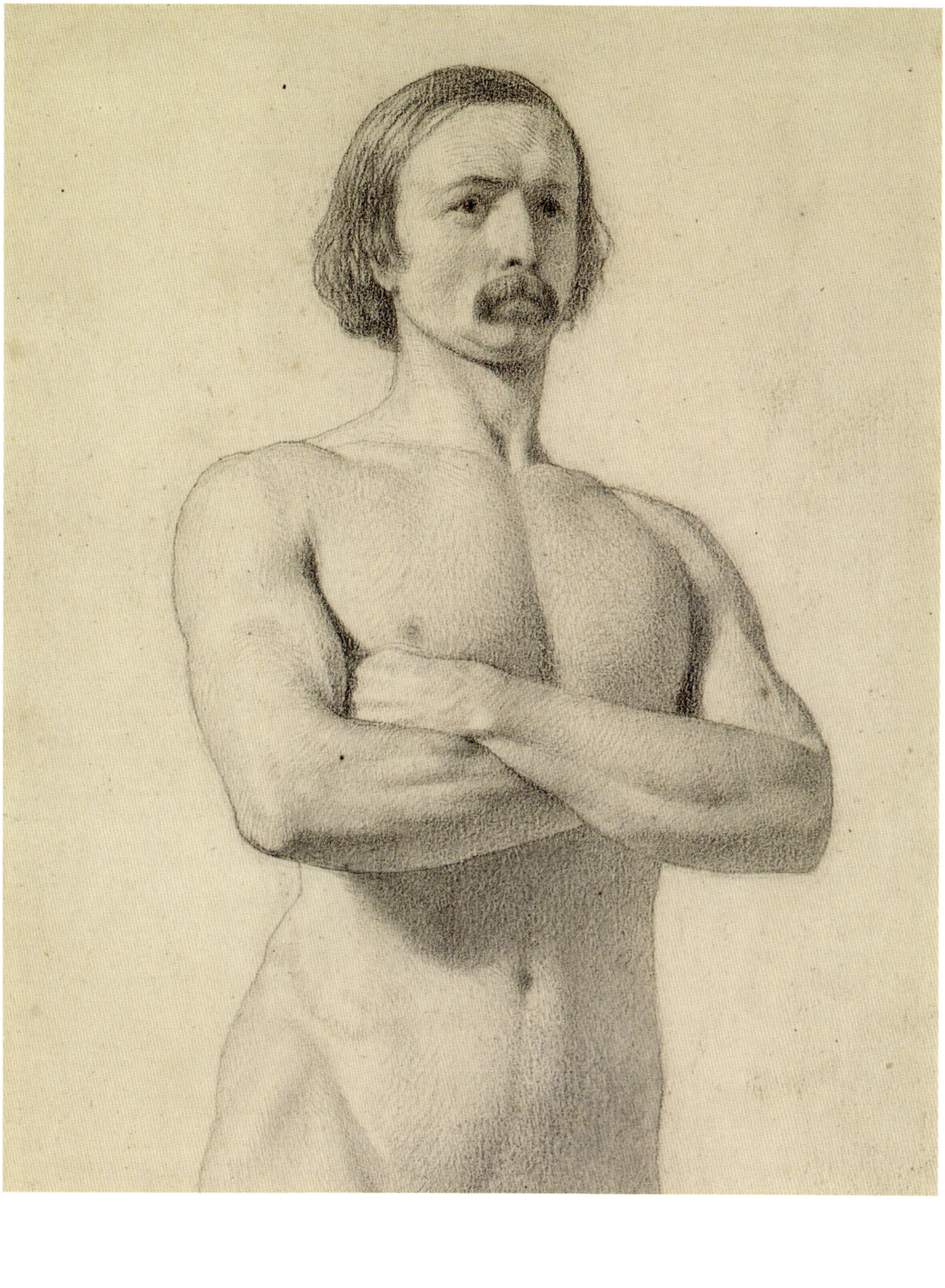

41

42

STUDY OF MAN WITH HOOD AND LIRIPIPE FOR 'CHAUCER'

(A40.24)
1847
black chalk, 8 3/16 × 6 11/16 (20.9 × 17)
Signed and dated: *Ford M Brown London /47*
Birmingham Museums and Art Gallery

This is a study for the man half way up the extreme left edge of *Geoffrey Chaucer reading the 'Legend of Custance' to Edward III and his Court* (see cat. 34). The drawing shows Brown's draughtsmanship at its most clear, elegant and economical. The purpose of the drawing is to study the unusual headgear: the man wears a hood with a long tail called a 'liripipe' similar to the one worn by Froissart (cat. 35) but here the tail is wrapped round the head rather than hanging down the back. Brown took the detail from an illustration of the head of the Count of Flanders in J.R. Planché's book *A Complete History of the Dress of the Inhabitants of the British Isles*, first published in 1834. Brown's diary records that he made the liripipe himself before doing the drawing, which was made on 25 and 26 September 1847.[3]

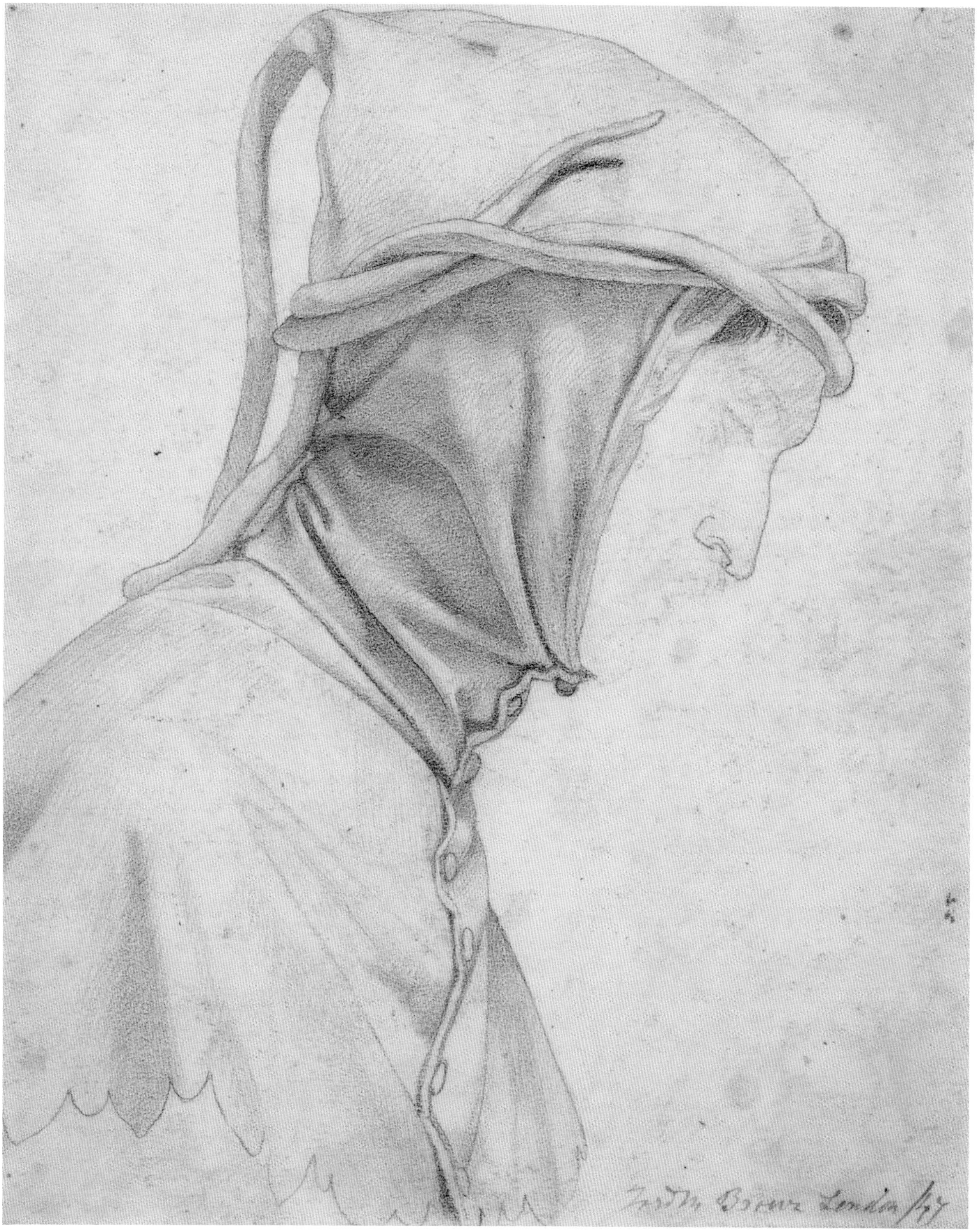

42

43

DANIEL CASEY

(B59.2)
1848
black chalk, 9 ⅞ × 6 ⅞ (25 × 17.5)
Signed and dated: *Ford M. Brown London /48*
Birmingham Museums and Art Gallery

This striking full-face head recalls the portraits of James Bamford and Millie Smith (cats. 29, 30). The drawing has always been supposed to portray Brown's friend the Irish artist Daniel Casey (1817–85), a fellow student at Antwerp. Casey settled in Paris, where Brown visited him in 1848 and painted a portrait of him in oils. The oil portrait is lost and no photograph of Casey can be traced, so that the identification cannot be proved. This is one of two drawings of the same man; the second, also at Birmingham, shows him in three-quarters view. Both are inscribed '*London*'. This may mean that the drawings were finished off in London, but there is a possibility that the sitter is not Casey at all.

Mary Bennett has suggested that the sitter could be a model named Mendoza.[4] 'Mendoes' is mentioned several times in Brown's diary and there is some similarity between the three-quarters view head mentioned above, and the head of Shakespeare in the left-hand wing of *The Seeds and Fruits of English Poetry* (cat. 32).[5] The full-face drawing does not appear to relate to any surviving painting.

43

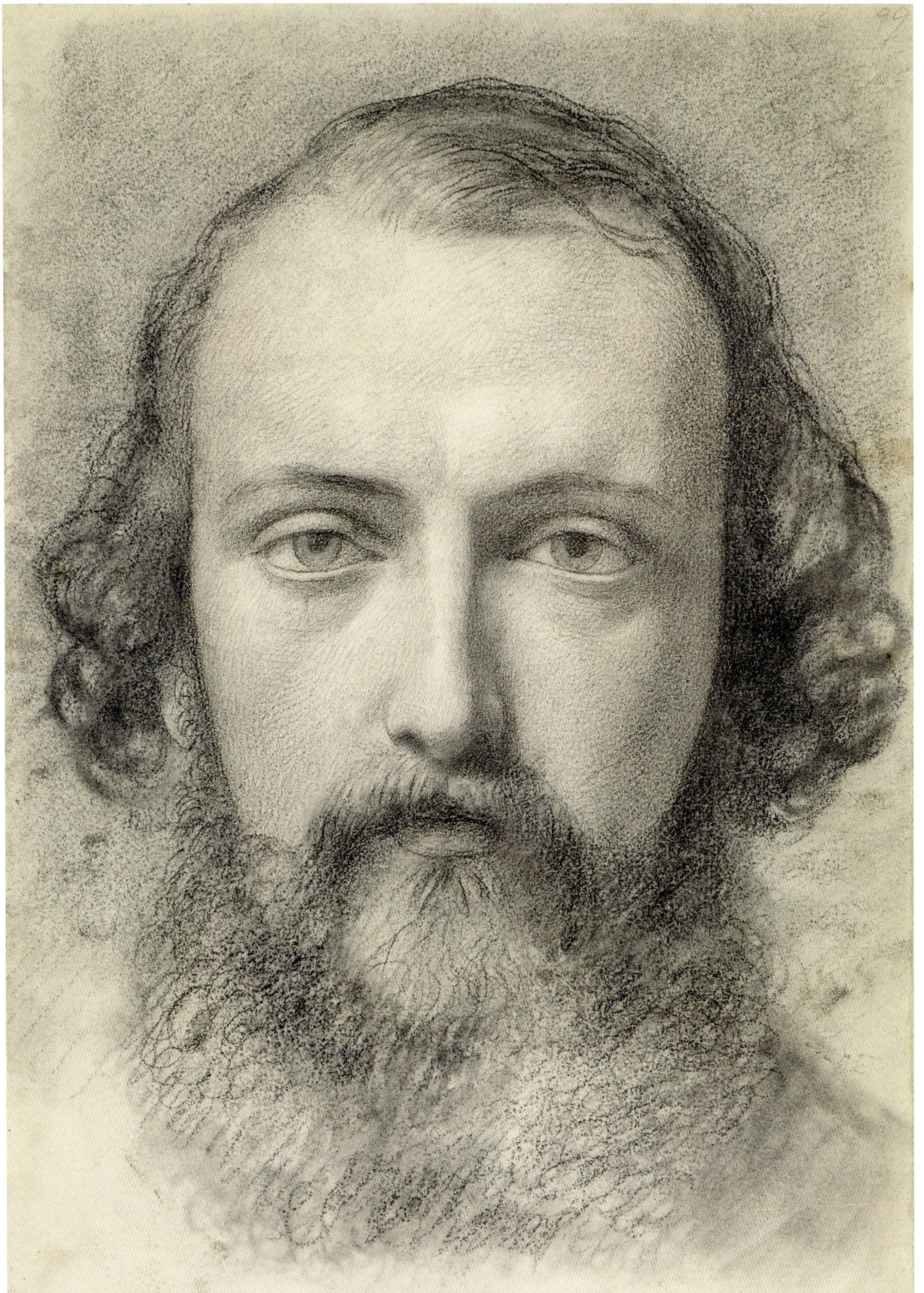

44

SHEET OF STUDIES FOR 'THE INFANT'S REPAST'

(A50.3)
1848
black chalk, 9 7/8 × 6 13/16 (25.1 × 17.3)
Signed and dated: *Ford M Brown London /48*
Birmingham Museums and Art Gallery

These studies for the painting *The Infant's Repast* (see cat. 31) were drawn from a professional model Mrs Ashley and her baby in October and November 1848: 'drew a study of childs head sucking, for little picture' and a few days later 'worked 4 hours from Mrs Ashley & child, made drawing of the Legs & arm etc.'[6] The model's hair in the drawing is drawn back simply, without the elaborate arrangement with a flower seen in the painting, and the artist has concentrated on the heads of the woman and the baby, drawing the rest of her upper body only in outline. This gives the drawing both clarity and intimacy.

The diary gives some intriguing information about Brown's relationship with this model. She first appeared in his diary as 'Miss Ashley' on 26 January 1848 when he was at work on *The First Translation of the Bible* (cat. 33): 'Miss Ashley came at 11 stopped till four let the fire out 3 times & talked all day, will never do'. She sat again several times in February and March, modelling for the head and neck of John of Gaunt's wife, and also made Brown 'some beautiful Castor oil pomatum' for which he paid her threepence (22 February). By 13 October, when Brown sent for her again, she must have had the baby, for Brown referred to her as 'Mrs. Ashley & child' and he began a sketch of them 'for a little picture of a mother and child'.[7]

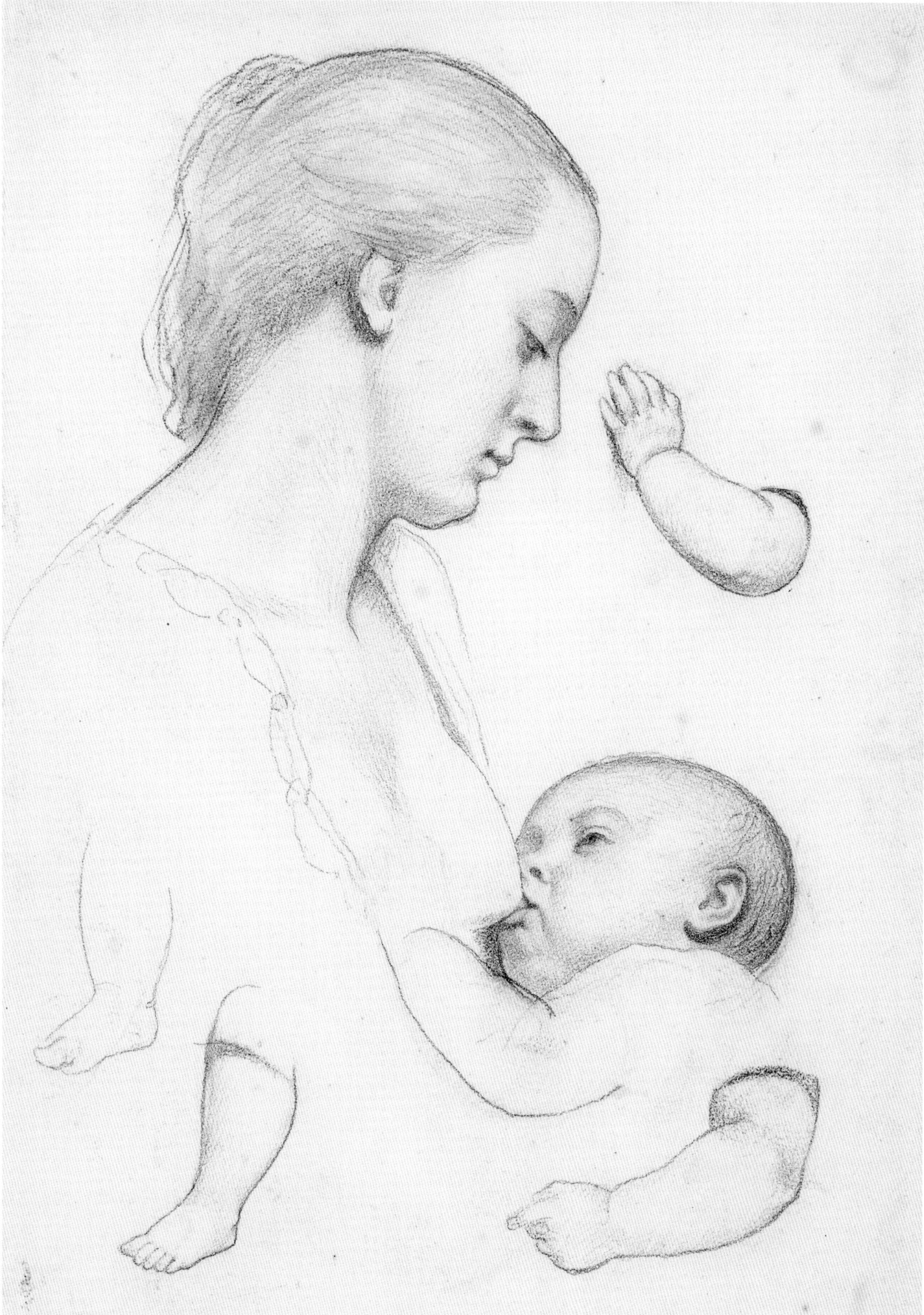
Ford M Brown London /48

45
STUDY OF A CORPSE FOR 'THE PRISONER OF CHILLON'

(C44.3)
1856
pencil, 6½ × 11 (16.5 × 28)
signed: *FMB. University Hospital/ Study for prisoner of/ Chillon/ from Corpse FMB*
Birmingham Museums and Art Gallery

'Out shopping, then to University hospital to ask John Marshall about a dead boddy. He got the one that will just do. It was in the vaults under the disecting room. When I saw it first, what with the dim light, the brown & parchment like appearance of it & the shaven head, I took it for a wooden imulation of the thing. Often as I have seen horrors I really did not remember how hideous the shell of a poor creature may remain when the substance contained is fled. Yet we both in our joy at the obtainment of what we sought declared it to be lovely & a splendid corps. Marshall evidently loves a thing of the kind.' Brown sought out the corpse for his illustration to Byron's *The Prisoner of Chillon*. The next day, 14 March 1856, Brown went back and drew the corpse for four hours, writing that he 'Got on quite merrily' and finished it sooner than expected.[8]

Brown's friend Marshall was an assistant surgeon at University College Hospital. It is typical of Brown's thoroughness that he took the trouble to draw a real corpse even for a small book illustration. Brown's finished drawing, engraved by the Dalziel Brothers, was published in 1857 (cat. 80).

1 Bennett 2020, I, pp. 22–23, A27. 1–3.
2 *Diary*, p. 25.
3 *Diary*, p. 7.
4 Bennett 2010, I, p. 397.
5 *Diary*, p. 43.
6 *Diary*, p. 49.
7 *Diary*, pp. 27, 31, 35, 48.
8 *Diary*, p. 167.

45

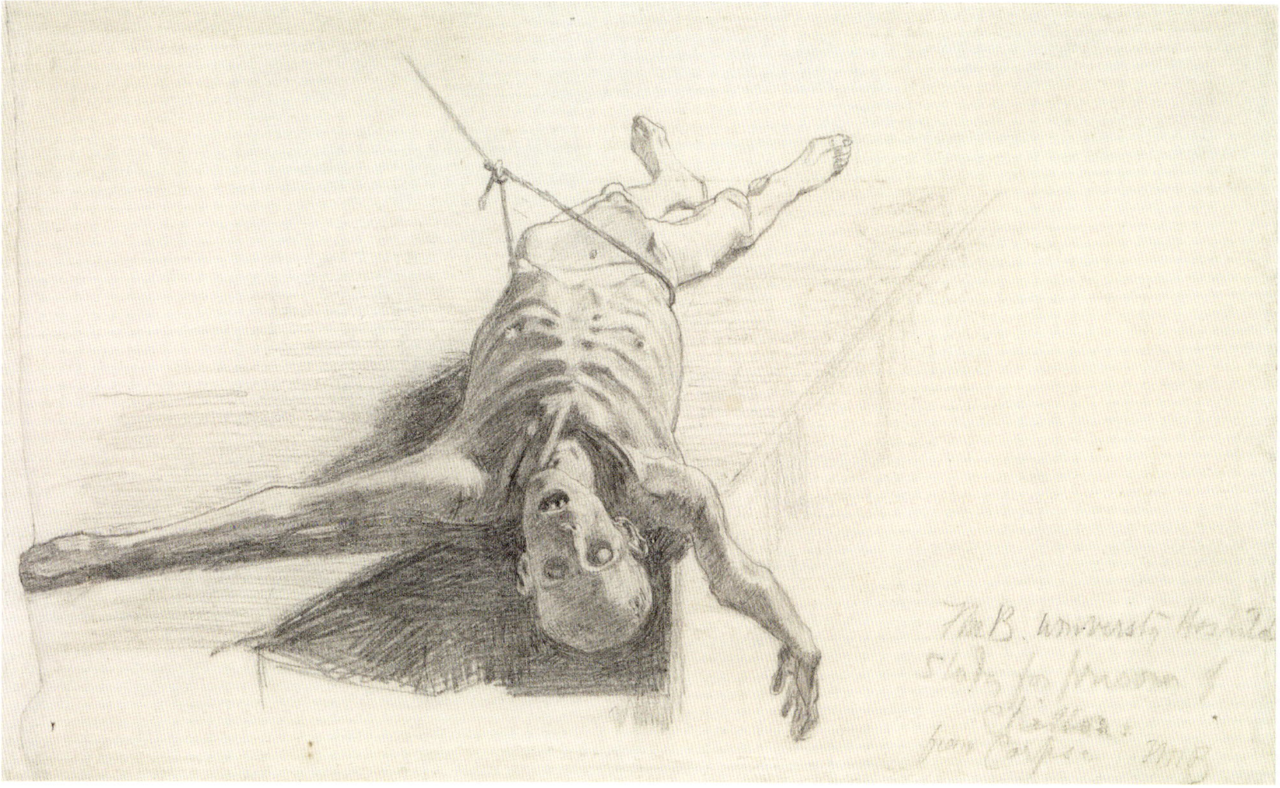

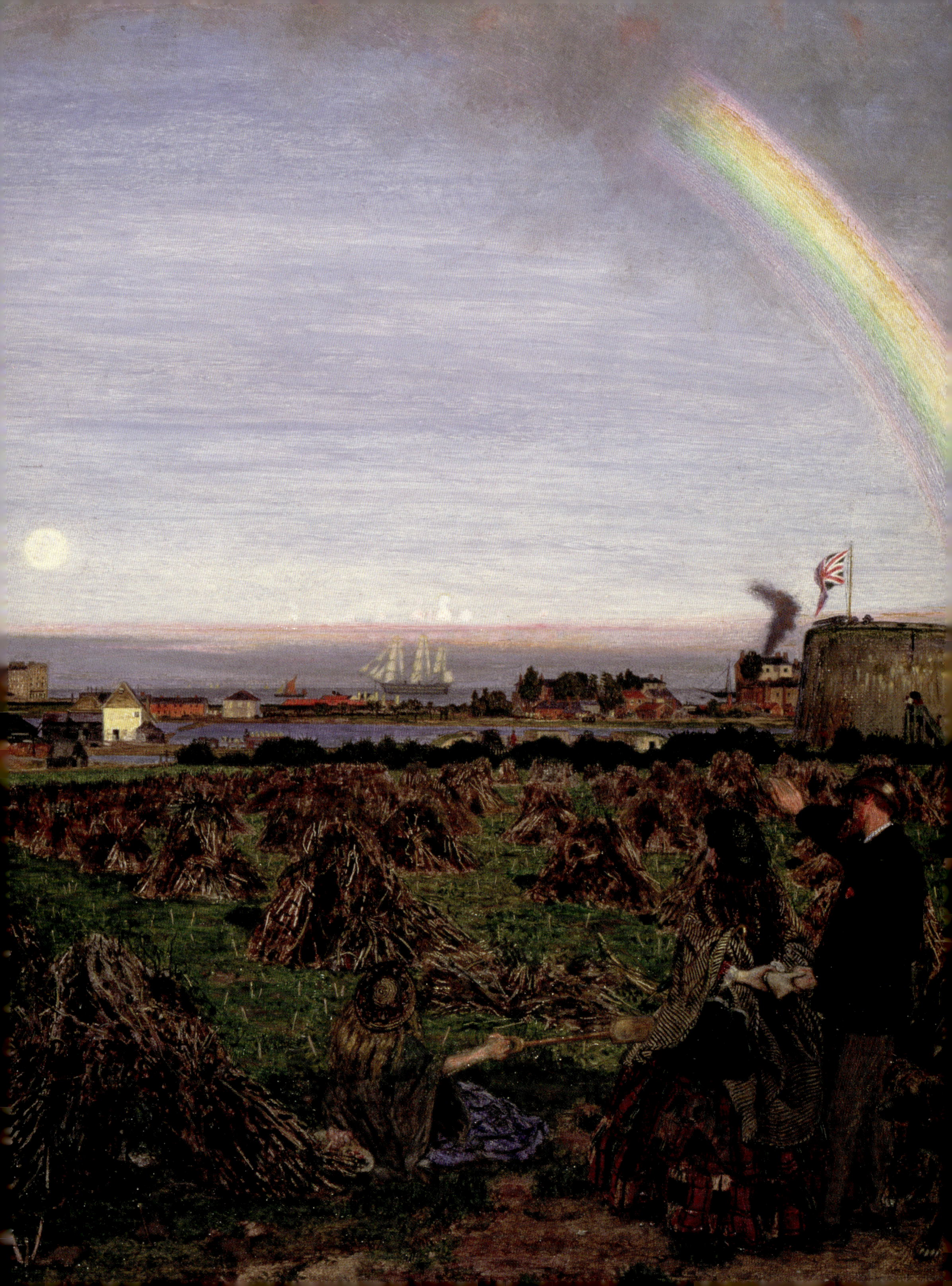

THE LANDSCAPE PAINTER

Brown's first landscapes were in the backgrounds of historical paintings such as *Manfred on the Jungfrau* and *Chaucer* (cats. 14, 34), in which he tried to imitate the effect of outdoor light even though most of the painting was done in his studio. The turning point in his exploration of natural light effects came with *The pretty baa-lambs* (cat. 49). Previously Brown had made landscape sketches outdoors and then copied them into the background of studio compositions; the Pre-Raphaelites had painted larger landscapes out of doors, but left blank areas for the figures which were added later in the studio. Here for the first time Brown sat in the open air and painted the figures and the landscape together, to get a more unified and naturalistic effect. Brown set most of his major subject pictures of the 1850s in the open air, whether they were in historical or modern dress, and explored a wide range of light conditions.

Brown had begun to paint independent landscapes in the late 1840s after his return from Italy. Then, in the 1850s, whilst living in Hampstead and Finchley on the fringes of a still largely rural area north of London, he painted a group of small landscapes of great originality. In these modest, unassuming paintings, he explored different times of day, different seasons, and different types of scenery without recourse to the artificial tricks of previous landscape painters, such as aerial perspective or trees placed deliberately to frame a view. He also experimented with oval and circular shapes, as a way of escaping from the conventional rectangular 'window' format. Just as original as these small works was the larger *An English Autumn Afternoon* (cat. 50), a landscape with figures in modern dress, which brought the grandeur of a history painting to an ordinary, workaday scene.

Although Brown rejected previous landscape conventions, he did not settle into a new, formulaic style. His landscapes lack the sharp precision of some Pre-Raphaelite examples, although they were carefully observed and in some parts minutely painted. They were all different, and each one caused him great trouble in trying to copy the effects he observed in nature: in his diary he repeatedly recorded how he had been struck by a beautiful scene or effect of light, but then struggled to recapture it in paint. Because of the time he took to paint even a small detail, he found it difficult to cope with the ever-changing light and colours of nature. Nevertheless, his landscapes are amongst his greatest achievements.

Fig. 61
Detail of cat. 55, Walton-on-the-Naze

46
SOUTHEND

(A42)
1846, 1858, (1861)
oil on paper, diameter 11½ (29)
signed: *F MADOX BROWN – SOUTHEND*
Private collection

This is Brown's first ever landscape painting, begun in 1846 (the year after his return from Rome), but originally it looked different because he retouched it extensively in 1858 in accordance with his brighter, more detailed Pre-Raphaelite style. However the retouching was not done from memory: Brown returned to Southend, as he explained in a letter to Holman Hunt. 'I brought my wife here last Tuesday for a little change after her illness & with the double purpose of trying to finish a sketch begun here long ago ... Of the sketch I begin to fear I shall make nothing good.'[1] He also wrote to his daughter Lucy, who had been with him on the first visit to Southend, that 'The scenery has not altered, but the trees have grown fatter & the hedge bank higher which makes a great change, however I shall be able to make something of it.'[2] Brown finished it when back home in London, and carried out additional slight retouching in 1861.

The areas reworked in 1858 include the view of houses and boats on the right, and the trees and hedges, repainted to show the growth described in the letter to Lucy. The cow and red-coated figure with pony and trap, possibly a postman, were also added in 1858: there is also a postman in the background to *Work* (cat. 61). Later still, in his 1865 exhibition catalogue, Brown commented that 'The Nore light-ship and the Isle of Sheppy are seen in the distance. Southend is here represented as it was before the invasion of gas and railroad.'[3]

The row of poplar trees on the left is also seen in slightly different forms in the backgrounds of *The First Translation of the Bible into English*, *Chaucer* and *The pretty baa-lambs* (cats. 33, 34, 49). This suggests that Brown may have used *Southend* to help paint these works.

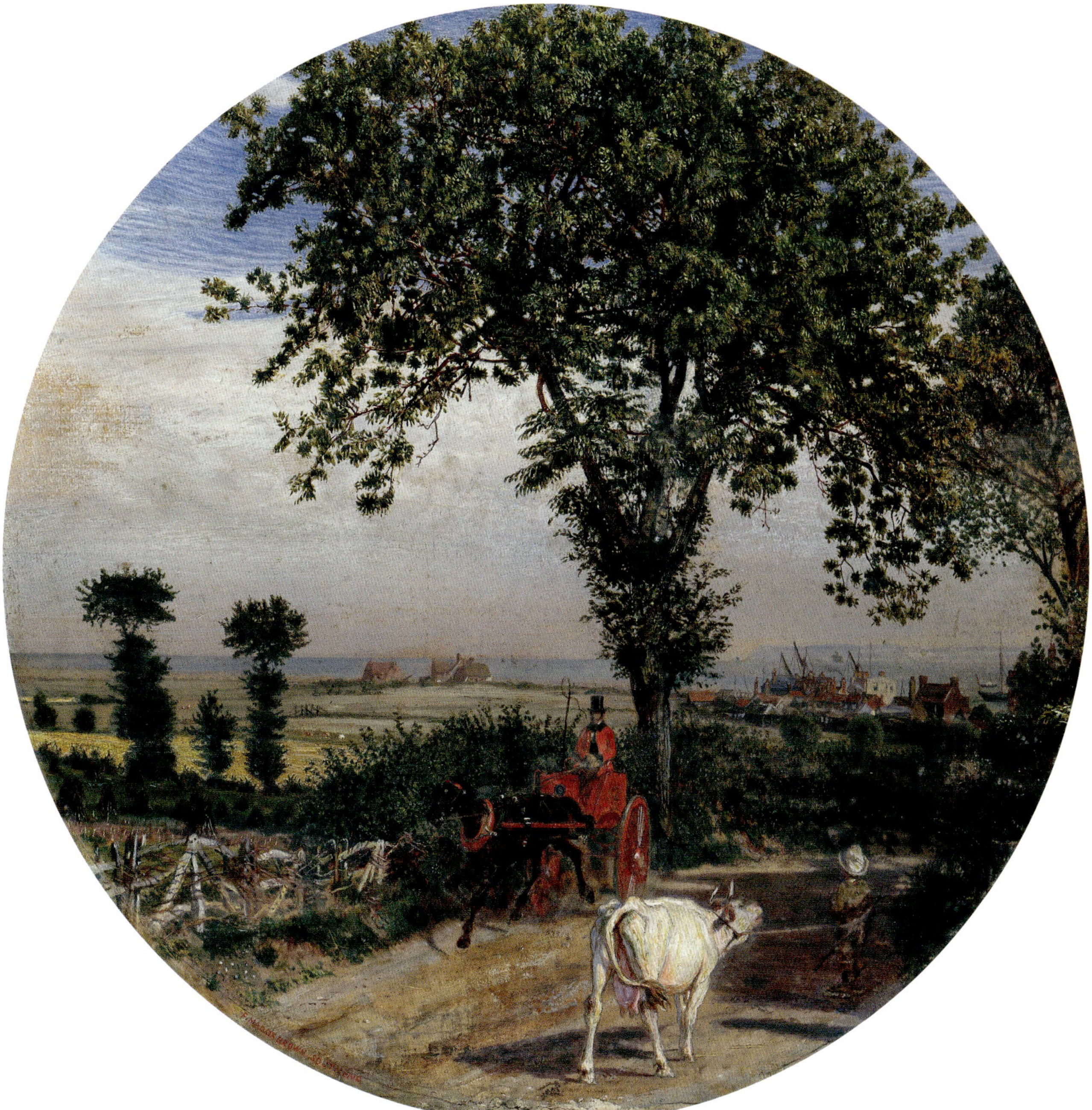

46

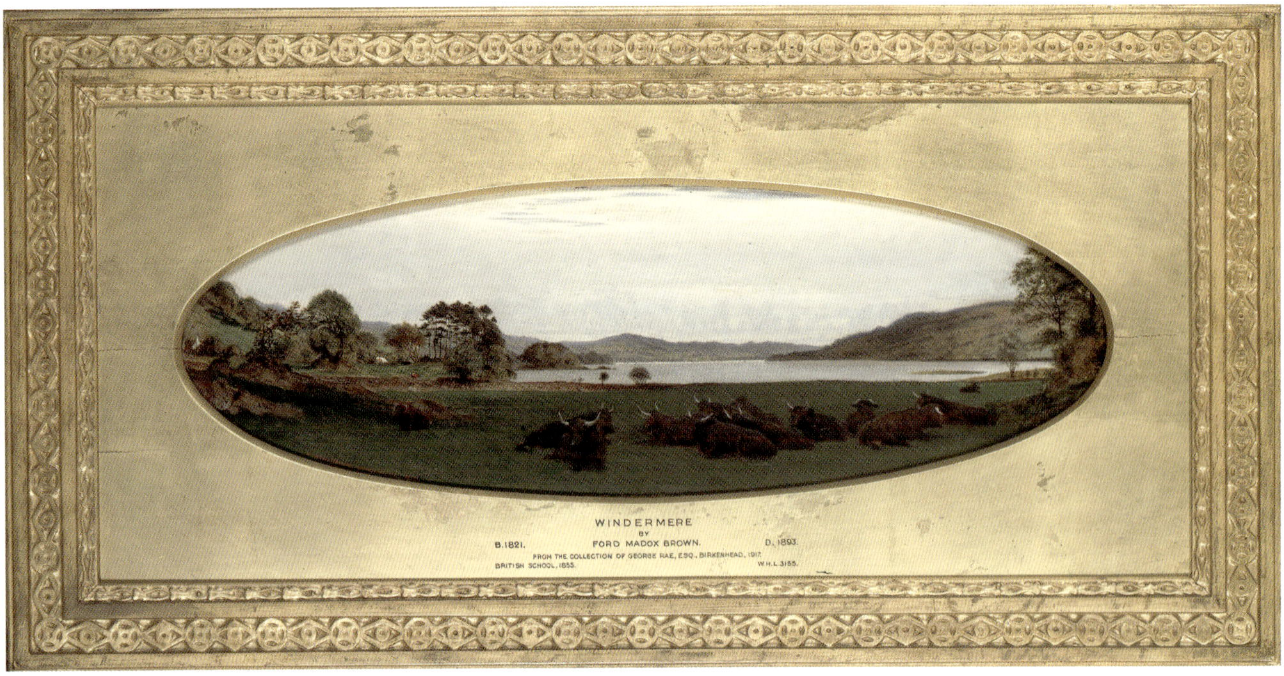

47

WINDERMERE

(A49)
1848, 1854–55
oil on canvas, 6 ⅞ × 19 ⅜ (17.5 × 49.2)
signed and dated: F. MADOX BROWN WINDERMERE 1855
National Museums Liverpool, Lady Lever Art Gallery

In September 1848 Brown went on a short walking tour of the Lake District with his friend the artist Charles Lucy and on 25 September he wrote in his diary: 'Begun painting a veiw of Wendermere, worked 6 days at about 4 hours a day. Last day in the rain under an umbrella.'[4] The view was taken from the north end of the Lake, near Waterhead, below the Roman fort, looking south-east with Bowness and Brant Fell in the distance. Brown later worked on the painting in his studio, and used it as a sketch for a more finished version (destroyed in the Second World War) but in 1854 he took up the sketch again and repainted part of it. He also cut down the original canvas, altering the proportions, and reframed it, making it look very different from before.

Its original appearance is known from a lithograph he made in 1853–54, showing the view dominated by a tall sky with an arc of storm clouds sweeping across it.[5] As first painted, *Windermere* was rectangular in shape, with a lower horizon and a larger amount of sky, and there was a prominent clump of trees on a mound on the right. Altogether this was typical of the 'picturesque' type of landscape paintings of the early nineteenth century, a distant view with vertical elements on either side acting as framing devices. By cutting down the canvas at the top and right, Brown eliminated the dominance of the sky and the vertical accent of the clump of trees; he also repainted the sky to remove the movement of the clouds, although the sky is still overcast. The point of these changes was to make the picture less artificial, and more natural-looking, an effect enhanced by the stretched-out oval shape that Brown had just used in *An English Autumn Afternoon* (cat. 50); in both pictures it seems to make the viewer feel part of the scene, rather than a detached spectator looking through a window.

In the new frame, the oval opening has been cut out of a gilt flat, edged with a narrow band of small designs of fishes, and surrounded by an outer frame decorated with a pattern of alternating circles and lozenges. Brown used the same type of frame in the mid-1850s for two other works, the landscape, *Southend* and the portrait of William Michael Rossetti (cats. 46, 88).

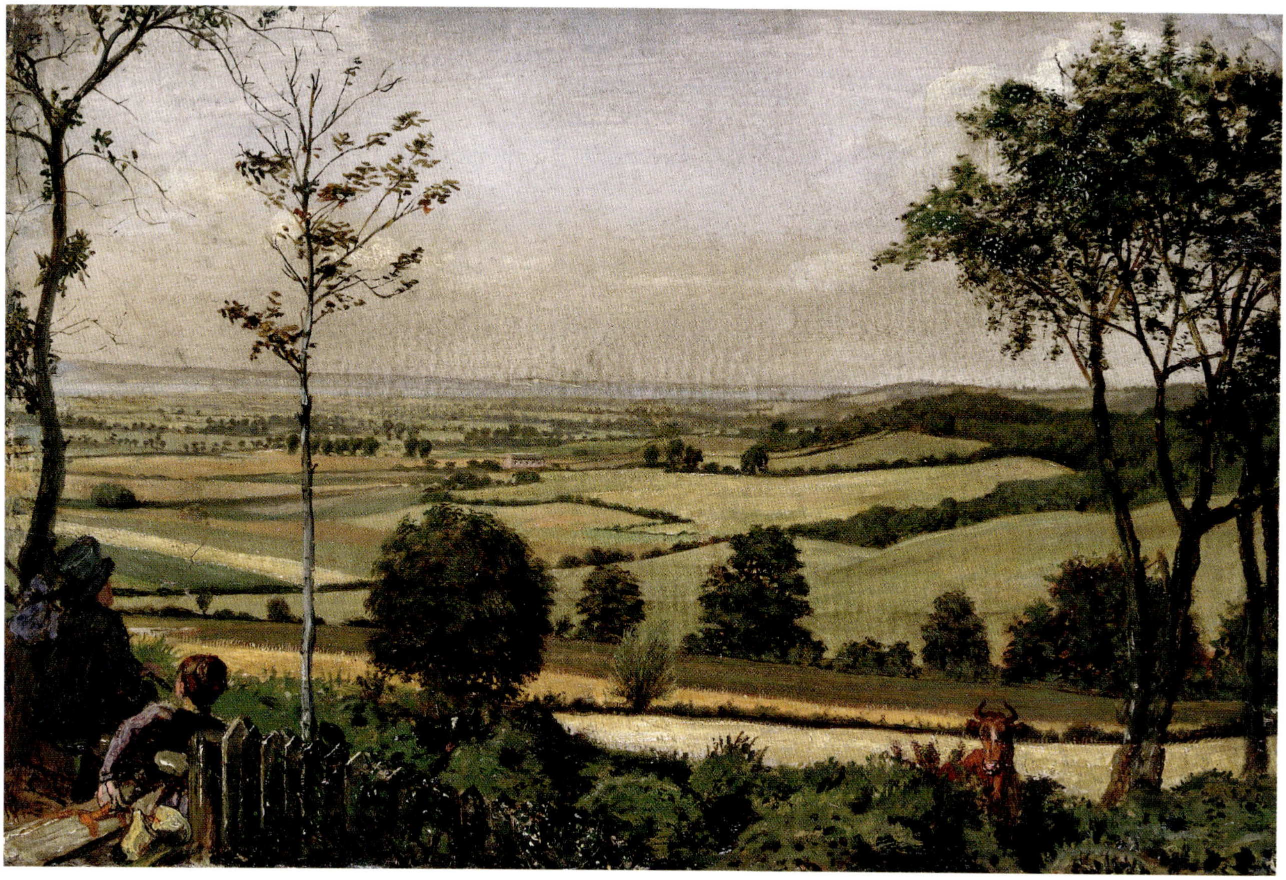

48

48

VIEW FROM SHORN RIDGWAY, KENT

(A40.6)
1849, 1850–51, (1873)
oil on paper, mounted on board, 8¼ × 12³⁄₁₆ (21 × 31)
signed and dated on verso: *F.M.B. 49–73*
Amgueddfa Cymru – National Museum Wales. Given by Sylvia Crawshay, 1990

This picture was made as a preparatory study for *Geoffrey Chaucer reading the 'Legend of Custance' to Edward III and his Court* (cat. 34). In keeping with his aim to make the imaginary historical subject more natural looking, Brown decided to include a real landscape in the background. In July 1849 he went to the village of Shorne Ridgway, near Gravesend, where he 'found some fine scenery overlooking the Thames & Essex.'[6] He painted this view of fields and clumps of horse chestnut trees with the Thames in the distance, finishing it off a little later in his London studio. He retouched it in 1873, which is probably when he added the foreground with the two figures in the left-hand corner and the cow on the right.

Edward III's Palace of Sheen, the location of *Chaucer*, overlooked the Thames, but it was at Richmond, much further west. Brown went to Kent instead, probably because he knew the area; it was close to Gravesend, where his daughter Lucy was brought up by his aunt after the death of Brown's first wife. He may also have had in mind the association of the Kent landscape with Chaucer through the Canterbury pilgrims. When Brown added the landscape to *Chaucer* he did not stick literally to what he had seen. He reversed it and enlarged the fields in the foreground in order to include the medieval sower and ploughman; the latter led to his changing the season from summer to spring. This was perhaps to evoke Chaucer's 'Aprille' and the idea of Chaucer as the springtime of English poetry.[7]

49

THE PRETTY BAA-LAMBS

(A55)
1851, 1852, 1853, 1859
oil on panel, 24 × 30 (61 × 76.2)
signed: *F.MADOX BROWN 1851–59*
Birmingham Museums and Art Gallery

Brown began this painting in the summer of 1851 in the garden of his house in Stockwell, on the edge of Clapham Common in south London; he had the sheep brought from the common to his house every morning in a truck, and took his canvas to the common to paint the grass. The models were his future wife Emma and their daughter Cathy, but he also used a lay figure. In 1852 he reworked Emma's head and later, in 1859, he extended the landscape with a detailed view of the Thames estuary, not visible from Clapham (the small version in the Ashmolean Museum, Oxford shows Brown's original design before the addition)[8]. So, despite the naturalistic appearance of the painting, the landscape was not a literal copy of nature but combined features taken from different places.

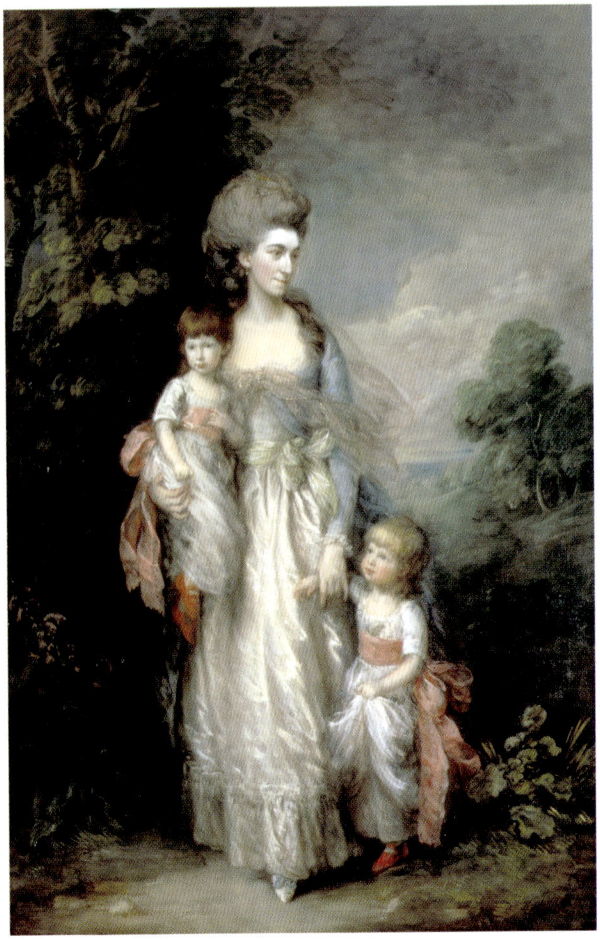

Fig. 62
Thomas Gainsborough, Mrs. Elizabeth Moody with her sons, *1779–85. Dulwich Picture Gallery, London*

Although *The pretty baa-lambs* is not a 'pure' landscape painting, as figures feature prominently in the foreground, the picture is of crucial importance in the development of the Pre-Raphaelite landscape, because both figures and background were painted in the open air. 'The baa lamb picture was painted almost entirely in sunlight which twice gave me a fever while painting.'[9] During that summer and autumn, Millais and Hunt were also painting landscapes with figures, *Ophelia* (Tate) and *The Hireling Shepherd* (Manchester City Galleries): they painted the landscape parts in the open air, but they added the figures later in the controlled lighting conditions of their studios. Brown was the first to paint both landscape and figures together, achieving a convincingly unified atmospheric effect; the first to set his figures against a dominant blue sky; and the first to use coloured shadows, such as the blue shadows cast by the blades of brilliant green grass on the patches of earth and the blue shaded areas on the fleece of the lambs. Brown's effect of dazzlingly bright sunshine with coloured shadows anticipates the *plein-air* landscapes of the Impressionists, in particular Monet who, also painted his wife-to-be in their garden in his *Women in the Garden*, 1866–67 (Museé d'Orsay, Paris).[10]

On the other hand, *The pretty baa-lambs* also shows that Brown was influenced by the innovations of the younger artists. In May 1851 he had noted that the paintings of Millais and Hunt shown at the Royal Academy 'kill everything in the exhibition for brilliancy'[11] and as a result he painted *The pretty baa-lambs* on a white ground, using 'Roberson's undrying copal (Flake White).'[12] This was probably not the wet white ground technique proper, which he did not use until later in the year (see cat. 75).

Brown's subject of a woman showing her baby the lambs was highly idiosyncratic and it caused puzzlement and abuse when the painting was first shown in public, at the Royal Academy in 1852; a critic described it as 'a facetious experiment upon public intelligence.'[13] The baby language of the title was objected to: 'a fantastic and puerile production … an effort worthy of the nursery;'[14] and because it was recognized as a Pre-Raphaelite work at a time when Pre-Raphaelitism was still unfamiliar and controversial, there was an expectation that there might be some hidden allegorical or religious meaning. Brown's own work included several mother and child pictures, some of which carried strong suggestions of the Madonna and Child (for example, cat. 28); and in Holman Hunt's contemporaneous *The Hireling Shepherd* and *Our English Coasts* (Tate) sheep were used for their

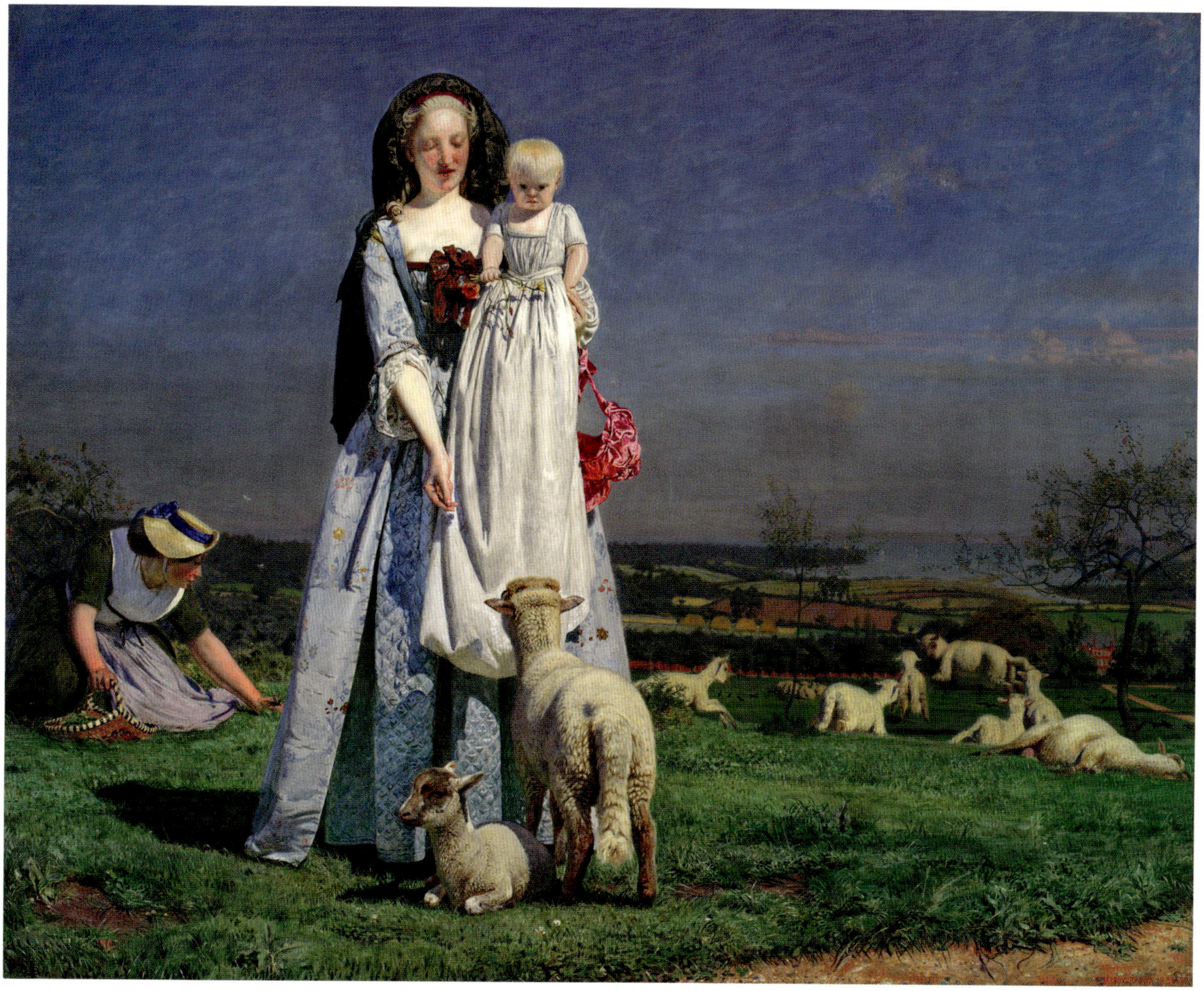

49

symbolic association with the flock of Christ. But Brown later denied that the painting had a meaning beyond 'the obvious one, that is – a lady, a baby, two lambs, a servant maid and some grass … This picture was painted out in the sunlight; the only intention being to render that effect as well as my powers in a first attempt of this kind would allow.'[15]

Brown's choice of eighteenth-century dress for his most realistic picture to date is also difficult to explain, although he had used it before (cats. 16, 31). Like Hunt in *The Hireling Shepherd*, Brown may have intended to demonstrate how different his style was from the artificiality of rococo pastoral scenes: the mother, bolt upright, her cheeks flushed with heat, defies conventional canons of beauty. He may perhaps have had in mind as his starting point Gainsborough's portrait of *Mrs. Elizabeth Moody with her sons* (fig. 62), a landscape with a standing female figure holding up a baby. He could have seen it at the Dulwich Picture Gallery, not far from his home in Stockwell.

50

AN ENGLISH AUTUMN AFTERNOON, HAMPSTEAD – SCENERY IN 1853

(A60)
1852, 1853–54, 1855, (1856, 1861)
oil on canvas, 28¼ × 53 (71.7 × 134.6)
signed: *F. Madox Brown*
Birmingham Museums and Art Gallery

Brown described *An English Autumn Afternoon* as 'a literal transcript of the scenery round London, as looked at from Hampstead … The time is 3 PM, when late in October the shadows already lie long, and the sun's rays (coming from behind us in this work) are preternaturally glowing, as in rivalry of the foliage.'[16] It was the artist's largest and most ambitious landscape, painted from the first floor window of his lodgings in Hampstead, and looking across back gardens over the Heath towards Highgate. He painted it directly onto the canvas, without preparatory drawings. Brown started it in the summer of 1852, but because the colours of the foliage changed as he worked, it became an autumnal view; he then had to stop painting because the room was required by his landlady. He resumed work on the painting again in the autumn of 1853, having waited for the colours to change back to autumn again. This meant he had to go back to Hampstead from Finchley, where he had moved in August. He finished it in 1854, although he worked on it again prior to exhibiting it in 1855, and retouched it again later.

In the portrait that he called 'a *Holbein of the 19th century*' (cat. 29), Brown had sought to 'substitute simple imitation for *scenic effectiveness*, and purity of natural colour for scholastic depths of tone'.[17] Here he seems to be doing the same thing for landscape. 'Simple imitation' – the 'literal transcript' of a precise time and place in specific atmospheric conditions replaces 'scenic effectiveness' – the Claudean repertory of landscape conventions. Rejecting these conventions, the view has a high horizon and a relatively small area of sky, and the colour is as strong in the foreground as in the distance; instead of a single focal point or area in the middle distance, the eye is drawn to two features unusually near the front, the red-tiled roof and the dovecote, and beyond these is a horizontal band of foliage stretching across the canvas from one side to the other, unrelieved by repoussoirs or framing devices.[18] The use of the wide oval, a shape equivalent to human binocular vision, makes the scene seem more natural and less arranged than the customary view through a rectangular 'window'; but Brown used one traditional artistic device, the raised plateau on which he placed the two figures looking over the scene with their backs to us. This was a motif used by artists from van Eyck onwards to lead the eye into a view and to bridge the transition between foreground and distance; the man gesticulates with his stick across the scene.

In aiming at 'simple imitation', Brown seems to have followed Ruskin's advice, 'rejecting nothing, selecting nothing, scorning nothing.'[19] But the critic objected to the painting, asking Brown 'What made you take such a very ugly subject, it was a pitty for there was some *nice* painting in it'; to which Brown replied contemptuously, 'Because it lay out of a back window.'[20] For Ruskin, a landscape had to have scenic beauty or historical associations, whereas Brown's view celebrated the ordinary: an unpretentious mixture of back gardens, sheds and orchards with glimpses of everyday activities such as fruit picking and feeding chickens, and humdrum details such as the blue smoke from the bonfire or the pigeon-house stained with bird droppings. This is neither urban, suburban nor rural; it is an interstitial landscape on the fringes of residential areas, and not previously considered as fit material for the landscape painter – an entirely new, modern manifestation of landscape.

The painting should also be seen against the background of the contemporary democratisation of leisure. The 1840s and '50s saw a broadening of access to landscape, through the public parks movement in Britain and in France the opening-up of the Bois de Boulogne. At the time Brown was painting *An English Autumn Afternoon* the East Heath, seen in the middle distance, was threatened with the building of villas by its aristocratic landowner,

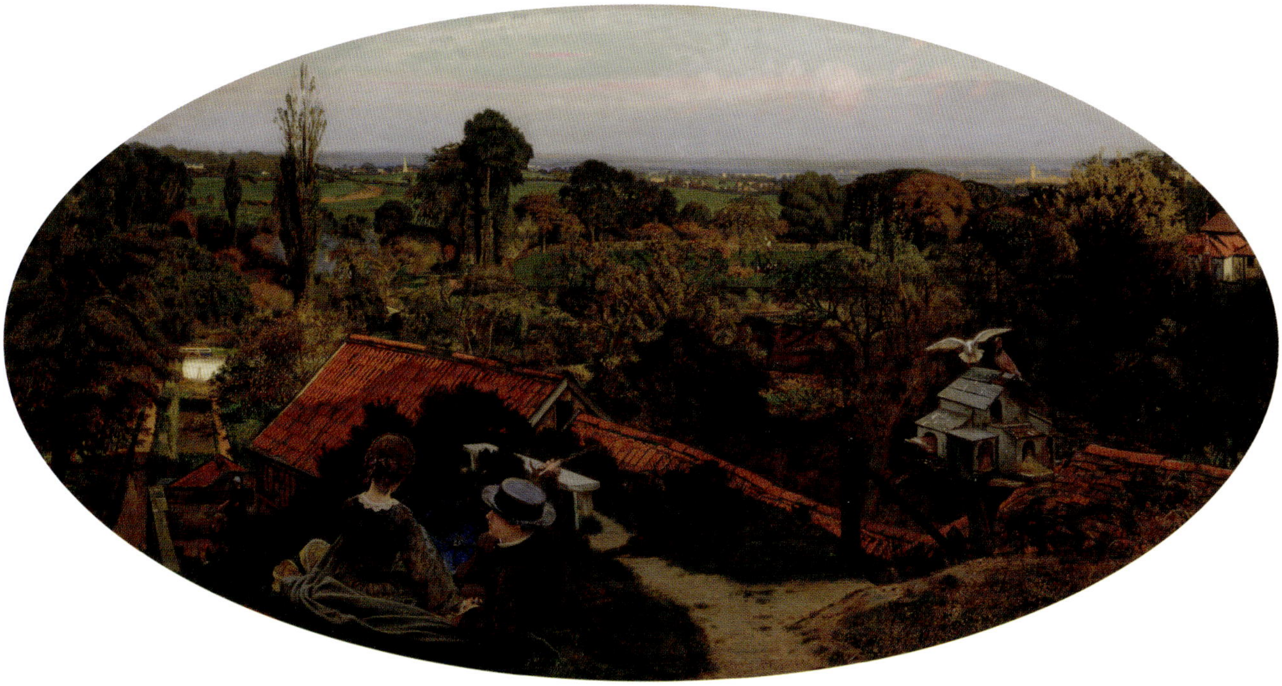

50

indeed the sandy path in the distance on the left was to be the central avenue of the new estate.[21] This caused a popular outcry and there was public debate as to whether the Heath should be for the privileged few, or open to all. The dress of the two people in Brown's picture indicates an ordinary middle-class couple at leisure, and by including them in the foreground looking over the view, Brown made clear his belief in public access, for the view appears as if laid out for their pleasure, like an eighteenth-century prospect painting. Brown was himself familiar with the landscape and would have taken his own pleasure in it for he often walked across the Heath to visit Emma in Hendon.

Brown included himself with Emma as onlookers in one of his landscapes (cat. 55), but despite the personal associations of the Hampstead landscape, the figures here are not portraits. They appear to be a couple, an interpretation supported by the inclusion of doves on the right: Brown could have known Tennyson's poem *The Gardener's Daughter* (1842) comparing young lovers seated on a mound to 'doves about a dovecote.'[22] But Brown, writing ten years after completing the painting, denied that the pair were lovers: 'The figures are peculiarly English – they are hardly lovers – more boy and girl, neighbours and friends.'[23] Whoever they are, they are ordinary people out with their dog and they are freely enjoying their leisure time in the autumn sunshine. Although the picture is usually known as *An English Autumn Afternoon* it was originally exhibited with the extended title *An English Autumn Afternoon, Hampstead – Scenery in 1853*. By designating it as a view of a particular place and at the same time, a typically English scene, Brown gave this most specific landscape painting a generalized meaning, turning it into a contemporary history painting about leisure and landscape, a modern English middle-class pastoral.[24]

51

A STUDY ON THE BRENT AT HENDON

(A64)
1854, 1855
oil on millboard mounted on panel, 8¼ × 10⅜ (21 × 26.4)
signed and dated: *F.MADOX BROWN. Hendon /54*
Tate. Presented by F. Hindley Smith 1920

The view shows the river Brent at Hendon, in North London. Brown was attracted to the spot by the busy patterns made by roots, foliage and dappled sunlight. On first going there, in September 1854, he described it in his diary using typically vivid and idiosyncratic language as 'a mere brooklet running in most dainty sinuosity under overshadowing oaks and all manner of leafgrass. Many beauties & hard to chuse amongst'.[25] The effect of an enclosed, secret place was enhanced by Brown's choice of oval format, giving the impression of spying through a telescope. Emma is hardly visible, seated with a book under the tree on the left and almost absorbed into the scene: 'once embowered in the wooded hollows of its banks the visitor might imagine himself a hundred miles away.'[26] This remark was written almost ten years after painting the picture, but it probably reflects the solace taken by Brown and Emma in nature as an escape from their personal difficulties; when Brown painted *A Study on the Brent at Hendon* in 1854 Emma was pregnant, they had very little money and London was in the midst of a cholera epidemic.

The diary entry quoted above continued with Brown's analysis of the difficulties presented by this subject: 'nature that at first sight appears so lovely is on consideration almost always incomplete, moreover there is no painting intertangled foliage without lossing half its beauties. If imitated exactly it can only be done as seen from one eye & quite flat & confused therefore.' But Brown resolved to paint the view, returning regularly to the scene to continue work on it. Once, after rain, he 'found the weight of the water quite displaced the different branches from their normal possition, making confusion.' Nevertheless he persevered, altering the figure of Emma to make it 'more sentimental' and eventually recording that the picture 'begins to look bravely & beautiful color but still requires all my energy & attention to master the difficulties attending a style of work I have not been bred to.'[27]

The painting is one of three small landscapes painted whilst Brown was living at Finchley (the others being cats. 52 and 53). They were intended as potboilers for quick sale, but they took longer than expected to finish, and sold for very modest prices: Brown received only £10 for *A Study on the Brent at Hendon* when he sold it to the dealer D.T. White in July 1855.

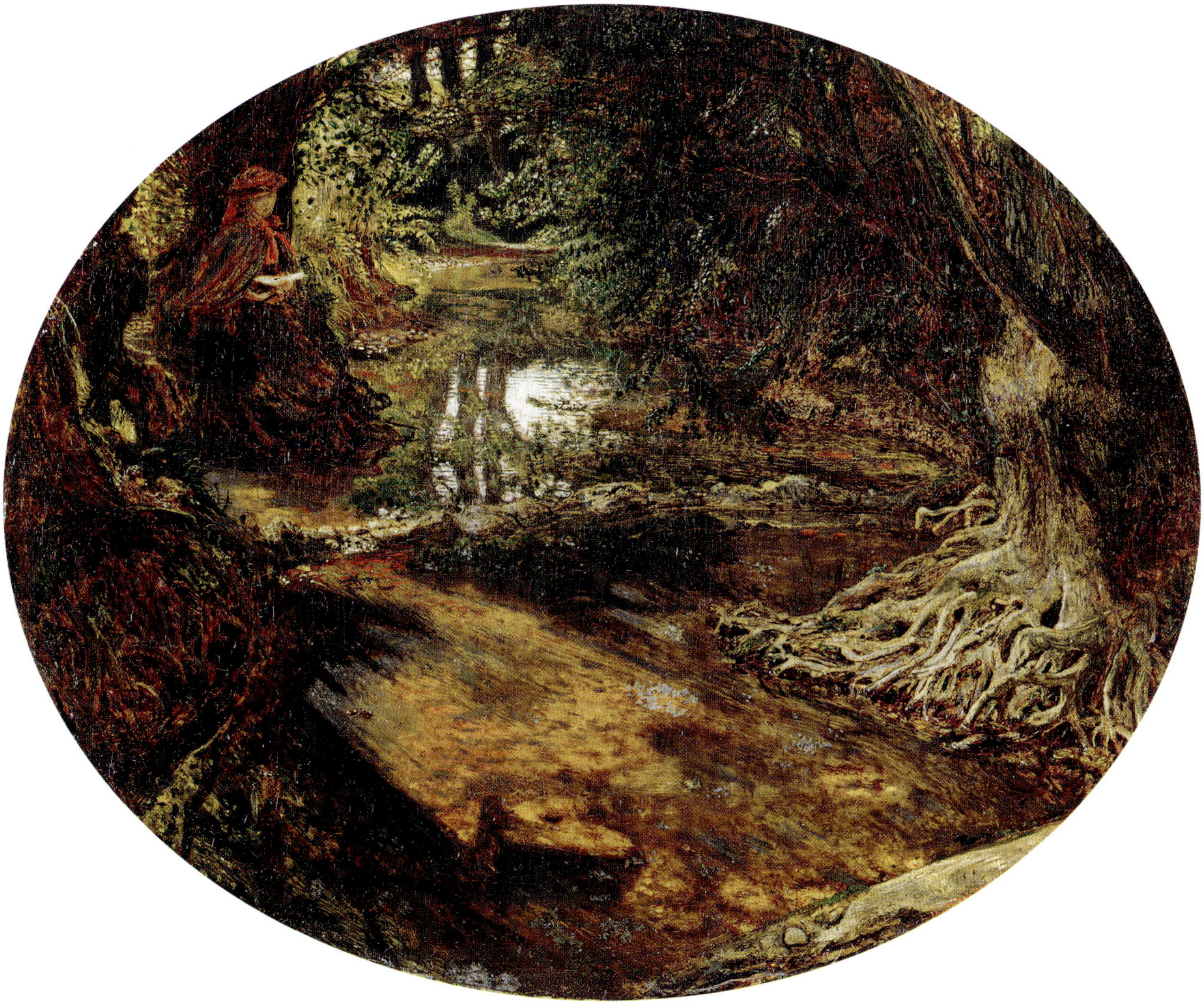

51

52
CARRYING CORN

(A65)
1854
oil on panel, 7¾ × 10⅞ (19.7 × 27.6)
signed and dated: *F.Madox Brown. Finchley /54*
Tate. Purchased 1934

Like the previous item, *Carrying Corn* was painted whilst Brown was living at Finchley in 1854. In late August, he and Emma took temporary refuge from their worries by making an excursion to St. Albans 'in the most lovely weather. Emma in a state of boyant enjoyment … one field of turnips against the afternoon sky did surprise us into exclamation with its wonderful emerald tints.'[28] This must have remained in his mind, for a few weeks later, after painting at the Brent at Hendon in the morning, he found another field of turnips and on 4 September began to paint it: 'out to a field to laying the outline of a small landscape, found it of surpassing loveliness, Corn shocks in long perspective, farm, hayricks, & steeple seen between them, foreground of turnips, blue sky & afternoon sun. By the time I had drawn in the outline they had carted half my wheat, by to day all I had drawn in was gone.'

Brown returned to the field over twenty times in the next few weeks, each session lasting about two or three hours, and recorded in his diary his difficulties and frustrations: he was rained off, he had 'sun shine when I did not want it, cold & wind when it went'; he worried that 'these little landscapes take up too much time to be proffitable'; he had problems with the 'small screen of trees', and with the turnips, which came out the wrong colour: 'I don't know if it would be possible to paint them well, they change from day to day'; eventually on 13 October he wrote: 'Afterwards to the field for the last time thank heaven, I am sick of it. I have now only to work at home at it to put it a little in harmony.'[29] After finishing it off he submitted it to the Royal Academy for the Summer Exhibition of 1855, but it was rejected and eventually sold to the dealer D.T. White for only £12.

In contrast with the dark and enclosed view of the Brent, *Carrying Corn* is an open landscape filled with light and air. It is composed in bands of contrasting colour, ranging from the shaded area of the turnip field in the foreground, the same field turned to vibrant green by the afternoon sun, and the dazzling yellow of the harvest scene, set off by the brightly lit red roofs and the dull green of the trees on the horizon; above is an expansive sky with low pink clouds, a high moon and a flock of birds. There is no concession to picturesque conventions, framing devices or aerial perspective, and the human activities, the woman gathering turnips and the harvesters with their wagon, are not picked out in detail, but take their natural places in the distance. Despite the lack of sharp detail seen in other Pre-Raphaelite landscapes, Brown's touch is delicate and contributes to the overall feeling of naturalism and clarity.

52

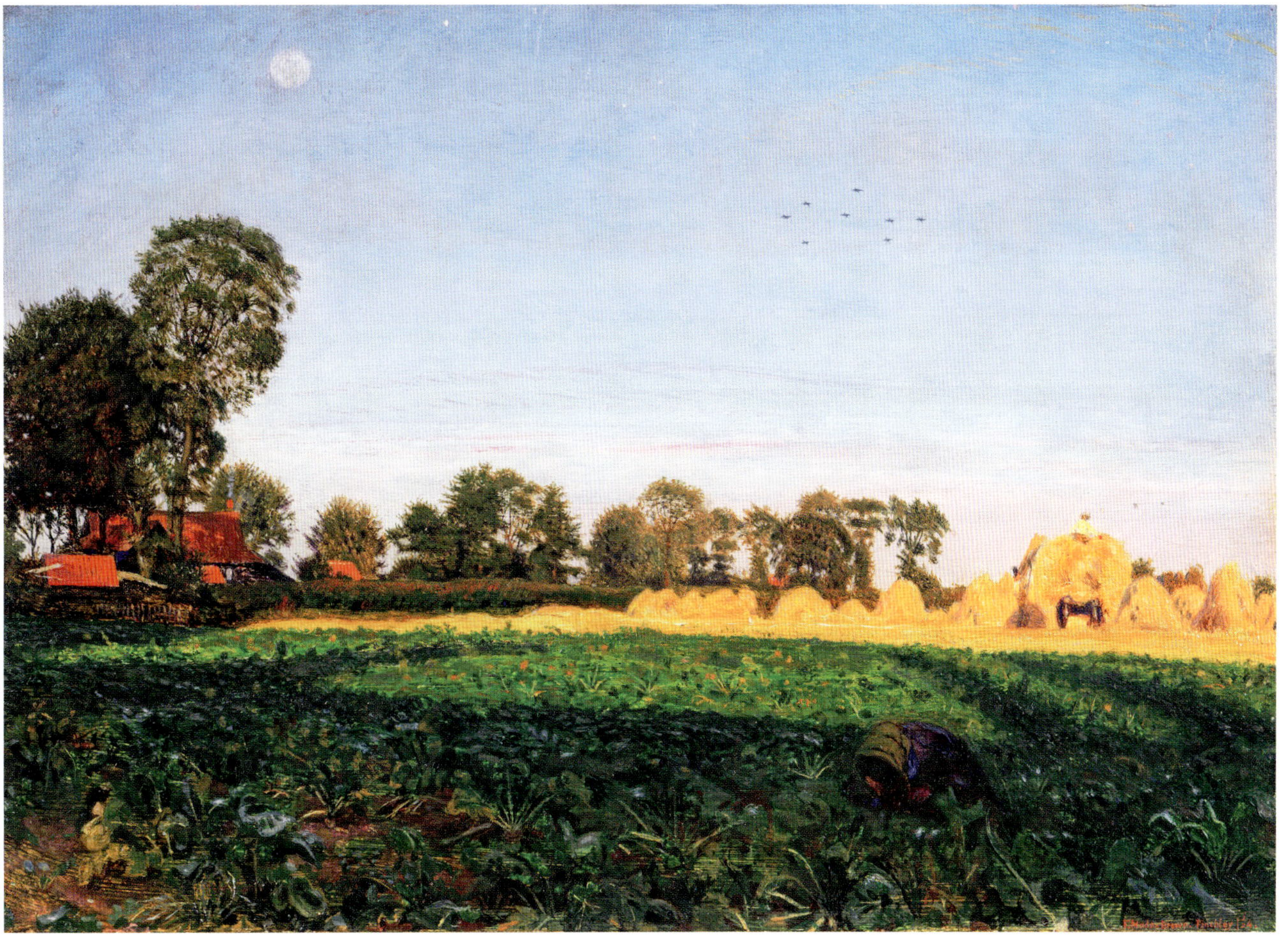

53
THE HAYFIELD

(A66)
1855
oil on panel 9 7/16 × 13 1/16 (24 × 33.2)
signed and dated: *F.MADOX BROWN. HENDON 1855*
Tate. Purchased 1974

This 'moon piece' as Brown called it in his diary is the third of the artist's small landscapes of 1854–55. As well as showing a different light effect, it differs from the others in the amount of human activity depicted: it shows the night-time labour of haymakers on the Tenterden estate near Hendon. They are supervised by the farmer on horseback on the left, with little children riding on the hay wagon, and in the bottom-left corner is the artist himself. He is at rest, while the others work, and he reclines against a pile of hay, still holding his palette, with his umbrella behind him and his paint-box on the grass. Brown here painted a rural counterpart to the scene of urban labour depicted contemporaneously in *Work* (cat. 61). In his first designs for that picture, the artist was shown as a detached onlooker (cats. 63, 64); in *The Hayfield*, the artist looks up at the moon, whose light gives the painting its special quality.

On 21st July 1855, in one of the most lyrical passages in Brown's diary, he wrote of his frustration at being unable to capture nature's transient colours, a theme that had also preoccupied him whilst painting the previous two items:

> What wonderful effects I have seen this eveng in the hay fields, the warmth of the uncut grass, the greeny greyness of the unmade hay in furrows or tufts, with lovely violet shadows & long shades of the trees thrown athwart all & melting away one tint into another imperceptibly, & one moment more & cloud passes & all the magic is gone. Begin tomorrow morning all is changed, the hay & the reepers are gone most likely, the sun too, or if not it is in the opposite quarter & all that was lovelyest is all that is tamest now...[30]

The Hayfield seems to be Brown's attempt to recapture the intensity of his first vision; his struggle to do so can be followed from his diary entries. A few days later he 'saw in twilight what appeared a very lovely bit of scenery with the full moon behind it just risen. Determined to paint it.' Returning the next day, however, he found it 'looking dreadfully prosaic.'[31] Although in the first diary entry quoted above, Brown had written of wanting to find 'little subjects that will paint off at once', *The Hayfield* took even longer than the others. Brown estimated the total time variously as 100 or 120 hours; he painted at it on the spot in the evenings between July and October 1855. In September he found the sky had cracked due to the zinc white under-painting, presumably because in his haste to capture the colour, he had not prepared the ground properly, and he had to repaint it. He continued to work on the painting after his move to Kentish Town in late September, entailing walks of fourteen miles there-and-back to Hendon, once staying two nights at an inn in Finchley and on another occasion permitting himself the extravagance of a cab.[32] During December he worked on the foreground, first going to Cumberland Market to sketch a hay-cart, and then, working in his studio, he painted the farmer, the carthorses, the artist with his equipment, and the children. He also reworked the landscape, scraping it down first; he painted the moon 'from nature', 'went carefully over all the part I painted in at Hendon from nature' and later darkened the hayfield in response to criticism by Lowes Dickinson.[33]

Brown attributed the 'unusual beauty of colour' to rain, which had delayed the stacking of the second crop of hay, heightening the green of the grass and making the hay look pink under the glow of twilight.[34] Brown's picture dealer D.T. White disliked the painting and 'said the hay was pink & he had never seen such.'[35] But in August 1856, Brown sold it to William Morris, still an Oxford undergraduate, whom Rossetti had brought to Brown's studio, and the following year Morris lent it to the Manchester Art Treasures Exhibition. Here it was seen by a young lawyer, Vernon Lushington, who wrote appreciatively to Brown, 'The Hayfield is one of the loveliest summer pictures I have ever seen. Looking at it, I feel as if I were that very artist under the haycock, my legs moving with the pleasure under me like boughs in a breeze, & my hand up to my forehead, shading me from the bright West, that I might look with full eyes upon the happy scene.'[36]

The frame is one of Brown's favourite patterns, with a broad gilt oak flat surrounded by a gilt moulding of bay leaves and berries. The same type of frame was used for *Carrying Corn* (cat. 52). While the earlier gilt flats were covered in gesso and given a burnished gilt finish, in these frames the gold leaf has been applied directly on to the wood (over a layer of size) allowing the wood grain to show. This was one of the most startling innovations of Brown and Rossetti, who used it frequently. Here the corners of the flat are mitred but sometimes mitres were replaced by vertical butt joints.

53

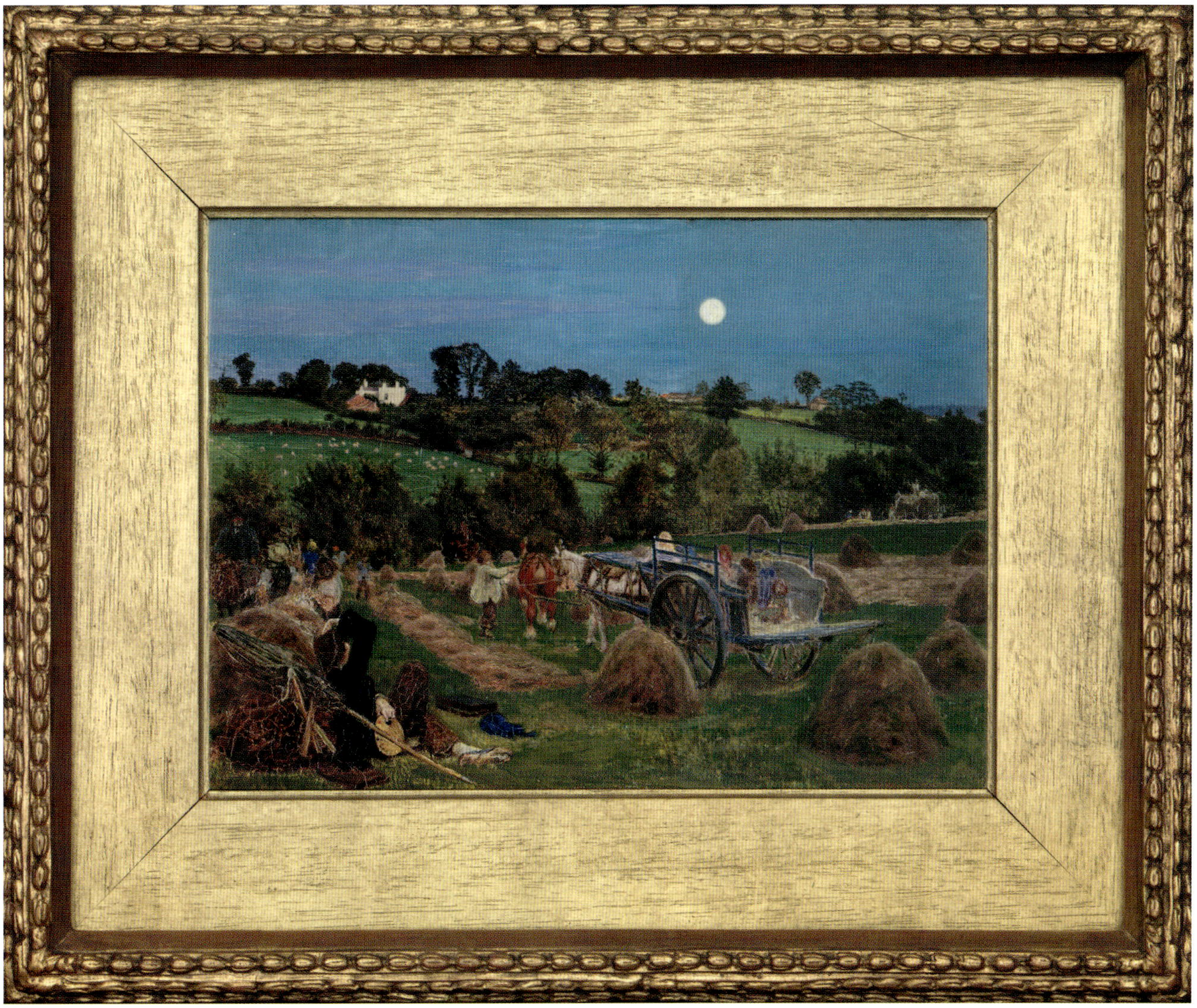

54
OUT OF TOWN

(A70)
1843, 1858
oil on paper, mounted on canvas, 9 1/8 × 5 11/16 (23.2 × 14.4)
signed in monogram and dated: *FMB – 58*
Manchester City Galleries

Brown mixed gentle humour with naturalism in this small painting of a mother and baby, with a little child trying to prevent a turkey from pecking at a bunch of grapes. He began it in 1843 in Paris as a picture of his first wife Elisabeth holding their baby daughter Lucy, but he never took it beyond the stage of a sketch. He took it up again in 1858, giving the woman a purple dress and straw hat characteristic of the latter date, and painting the landscape with the delicate touch and bright colour of his Pre-Raphaelite style. Although the title suggests that the picture shows a rural excursion, the view was that from the Brown's house at 13 (now 56) Fortess Terrace, Kentish Town, then a leafy suburb. A view of Hampstead is seen in the background; a more extensive view from a similar viewpoint is seen in the watercolour *Hampstead – a Sketch from Nature* (fig. 63).[37]

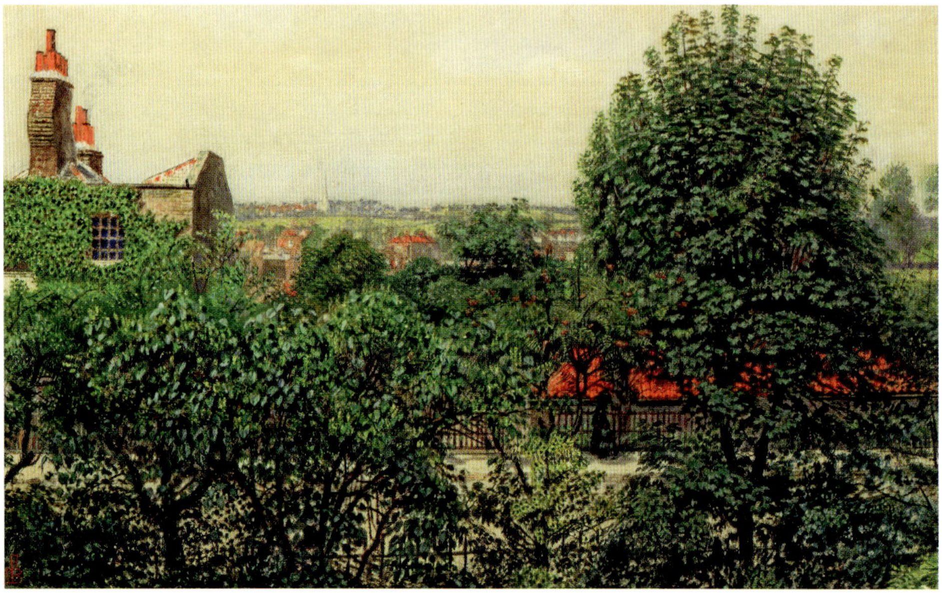

Fig. 63
Ford Madox Brown, Hampstead – A Sketch from Nature, *1857. Delaware Art Museum, Wilmington, Samuel and Mary R. Bancroft Memorial*

54

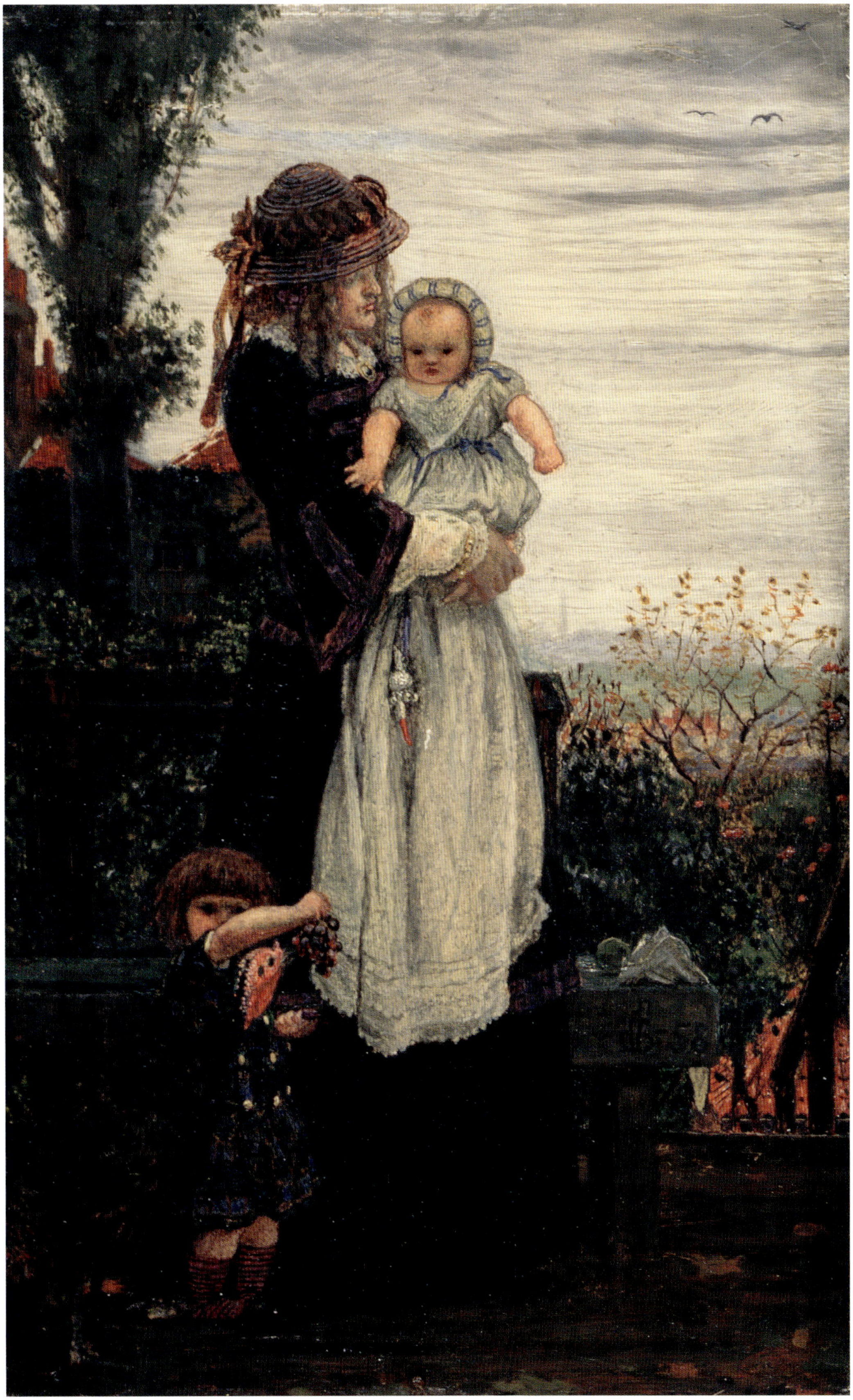

55
WALTON-ON-THE-NAZE

(A72)
1859-60
oil on canvas, 12½ × 16½ (31.7 × 42)
signed and dated: *F.Madox Brown 1860*
Birmingham Museums and Art Gallery

This view of the small Essex coastal town of Walton-on-the-Naze looks towards the sea across fields stacked with wheat-sheaves. In the distance on the right is a loaded hay-cart, with field-workers nearby. The Union Jack flying from the Martello tower, built for coastal defence in 1810–12, and the sailing ship in the distance, a man-of-war, show that the fear of a French invasion was still current at the time Brown was painting. The town is on the left, partially concealed by the Martello Tower, but in the centre of the view, beyond and to the left of the white building, is a block of new development, showing the expansion of the town. In the early-nineteenth century, Walton developed into a holiday resort and during the Victorian period it became a popular destination with Londoners, who could reach it by steamship. Brown stayed there in late August and September 1859 with Emma and Catherine: the idyllic character of the painting suggests it is a recollection of a happy holiday, although the view, seen with Brown's comprehensive eye, mixes leisure with work, and the rural with the urban.

Brown worked at the painting on the spot during his stay and finished it off the following year. As in *The Hayfield* (cat. 53) he included himself in one corner, but this time with his wife and daughter. Emma is fashionably dressed in a tartan crinoline and striped shawl, and touchingly holds Brown's hand. Catherine sits on the ground nearby, holding out a wooden spade. Behind Brown is the family dog. 'The lady and little girl, by their let-down hair, have been bathing – the gentleman descants learnedly on the beauty of the scene' wrote Brown with humorous self-mockery.[38] He depicted everything minutely whether near to the eye (like the field mice in the bottom left corner), or distant – the haycart, the boats, the windmill and the other buildings. The clear warm afternoon light, the risen moon, the rainbow arching over the expanse of sky and the mirage-like reflection of the ship's sails in the clouds, give the scene a dreamlike serenity.

1 Huntington, FMB to Holman Hunt, nd (from 2 West Cottages, Southend).
2 UBC, FMB to Lucy Madox Brown, nd (from 2 West Cottages, Southend).
3 Brown 1865, no. 23.
4 *Diary*, p. 46.
5 Bennett 2010, 2, p. 540, D6.
6 *Diary*, p. 65.
7 Newman and Watkinson 1991, p. 51.
8 Bennett 2010, 1, p. 124, A55.1.
9 *Diary*, p. 76.
10 Staley 2004, p. 68.
11 Hueffer 1896 p. 77. The paintings were *The Woodman's Daughter, The Return of the Dove to the Ark* and *Mariana* by Millais; and *Valentine Rescuing Sylvia* by Hunt.
12 *Diary*, p. 76; Townsend, Ridge and Hackney 2004, p. 131.
13 *Art Journal* 1 June 1852, p. 175.
14 *Illustrated London News* 2 June 1852, p. 407.
15 Brown 1865, no. 11.
16 Brown 1865, no. 13.
17 Brown 1865, no. 36.
18 Staley 2001, pp. 41–42.
19 Ruskin 3, pp. 623–24.
20 *Diary*, p. 144. See also essay by Angela Thirlwell.
21 Bryant 1997, p. 42; Wright 1997, pp. 188–89. The land was owned by Sir Thomas Maryon Wilson.
22 Daniels 2004, p. 26.
23 Brown 1865, no. 13.
24 Treuherz 2007, p. 244–45.
25 *Diary*, p. 88.
26 Brown 1865, no. 18.
27 *Diary*, p. 93.
28 *Diary*, p. 84.
29 *Diary*, pp. 90, 93, 96, 102.
30 *Diary*, p. 145.
31 *Diary*, pp. 145–46.
32 *Diary*, pp. 155–56.
33 *Diary*, pp. 159–60.
34 Brown 1865, no. 19.
35 *Diary*, p. 162.
36 V&A, Vernon Lushington to FMB, 16 August 1857 (date on envelope).
37 Bennett 2010, 1, p. 189, A.69.
38 Brown 1865, no. 27.

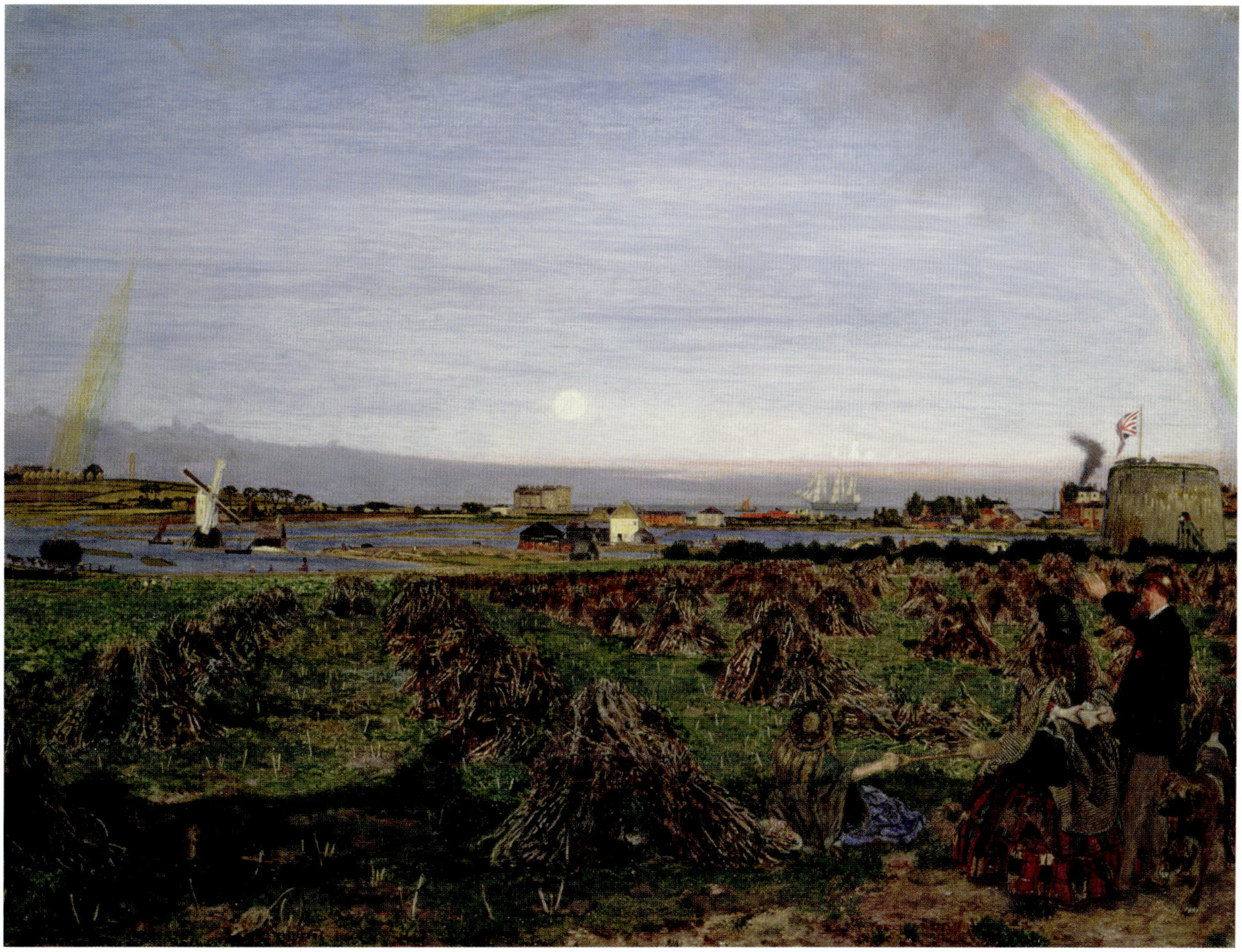

55

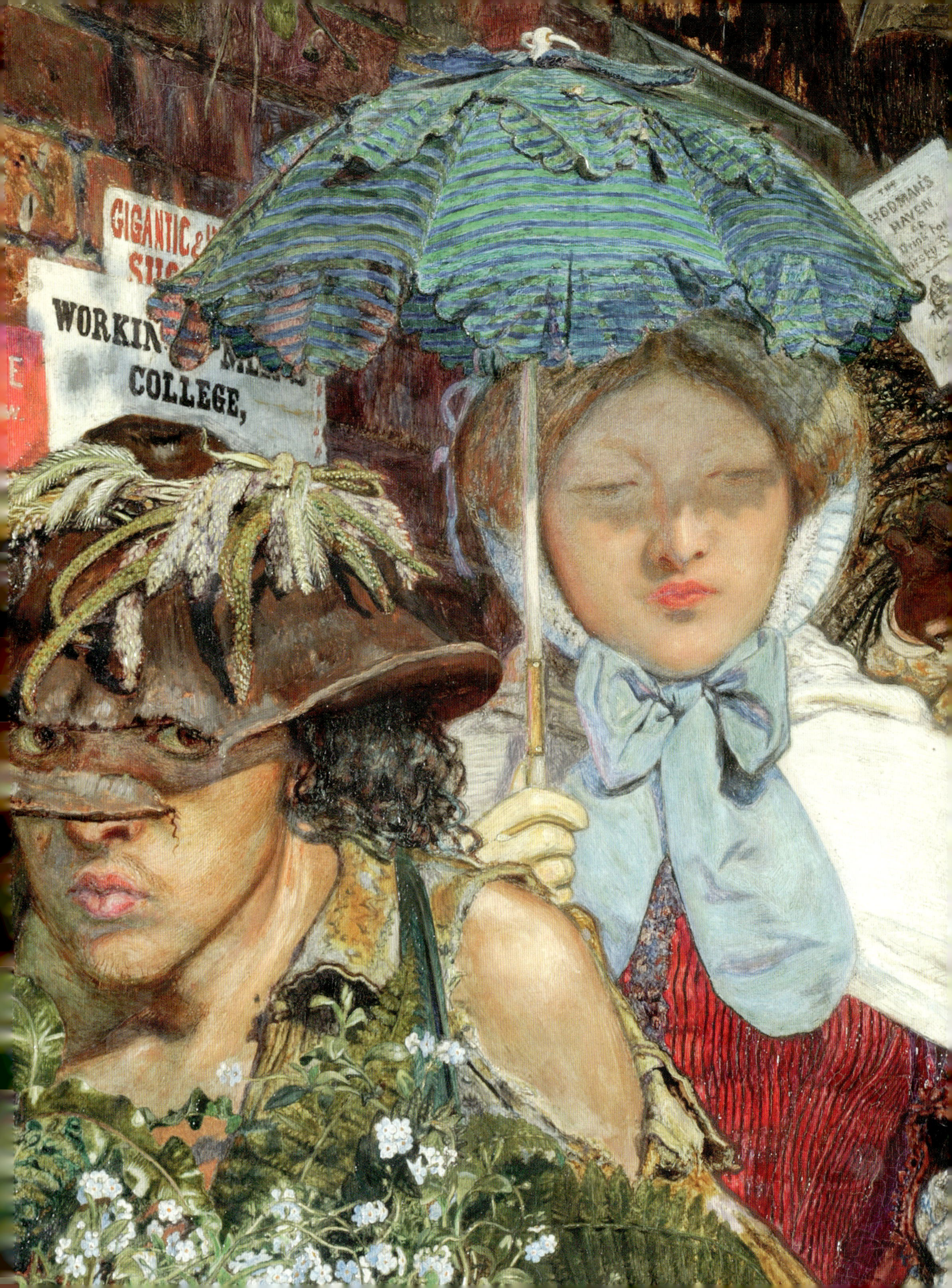
GIGANTIC &
WORKIN
COLLEGE,
HAVEN

THE PAINTER OF MODERN LIFE

Brown's historical subjects such as *Spirit of Justice* conveyed messages of contemporary relevance, but it was only after his involvement with the Pre-Raphaelite Brotherhood that he painted truly modern subjects. Brown's earliest modern-life subject, *Waiting* (cat. 56), was an intimate domestic scene, begun in 1851. The following year, whilst living in Hampstead, a period when he described himself as 'most of the time intensely miserable very hard up & a little mad,'[1] he had the first ideas for three paintings dealing more broadly with contemporary issues. These were eventually realised as his modern landscape *An English Autumn Afternoon*, his emigration picture *The Last of England*, and his panorama of modern society *Work* (cats. 50, 58, 61). Each of them was painted over a period of several years, contemporaneously with other pictures.

Brown was much influenced by the social and political ideas of Thomas Carlyle, but his chief artistic weapons in making his modern subjects vivid and convincing were his penetrating eye, which rejected artifice and convention, his exploration of natural and artificial light, and his relentless pursuit of accurate and minute detail. He was also a great admirer of William Hogarth's satires of contemporary mores, although Brown toned down the coarseness and cruelty of Hogarth to suit the tastes of the Victorians. Brown also put his personal experience into his art: his love for Emma and the children, and his moods of delight and despair.

Fig. 64
Detail of cat. 61, Work

56
WAITING: AN ENGLISH FIRESIDE OF 1854–55

(A58)
1851–52, 1854–55
oil on panel, 12 × 8 (30.5 × 20.3)
signed and dated: *F.Madox Brown /55*
National Museums Liverpool, Walker Art Gallery. Purchased with the aid of grants from the National Heritage Memorial Fund, the V&A Purchase Fund, the Pilgrim Trust and the Friends of Merseyside Museums and Art Galleries 1985

This is Brown's first modern subject. He began it in the winter of 1851–52 as a domestic scene showing Emma sewing by the fireside with baby Catherine sleeping on her lap in their house at Stockwell. But between December 1854 and February 1855 he spent a considerable time reworking the picture. By this time Britain had become involved in the Crimean War and in the autumn of 1854 the newspapers were full of the battles of Balaclava and Inkerman and the lengthening siege of Sebastapol. Brown added a miniature painting of a soldier and a pile of letters on the table at the left, turning what had been a straightforward domestic scene into a topical one: 'an officers wife thinking of him at Sevastapol.'[2] A larger version of the painting (private collection) was left unchanged.[3]

All the accoutrements of the simply-furnished, middle-class interior are painted with affectionate fidelity, the patterned tablecloth, the wicker basket or cot under the table, the Turkey carpet, the fender and fire-irons, the corner of the gilt frame and the spray of flowers on the mantelpiece. With the letters and portrait on the table is a tiny reel of cotton, and the objects on the cupboard include a white dish, a piece of Parian ware, 'The Bride's Inkstand', perhaps a wedding present (Brown and Emma had married in April 1853), and an allusion to the theme of married bliss. Emma's dark gown is set off with a red scarf, a brooch and a white lace collar, and her wedding ring is visible on her left hand, holding the sewing.

The composition is one of great intimacy, viewed from above and close-up in steep perspective, implying the spectator's presence within the space: in the bottom right-hand corner we look down on the seat of a chair, with the poker leaning on it, in a tangle of discarded child's clothing. The lighting effect is particularly original, combining the light of an oil lamp from one side with firelight from the other: the fire, unseen, creates glowing pink reflections on the marble and on the child's gown, whilst the rest of the picture is seen in the cooler lamplight which casts a large shadow of Emma onto the wall and cupboard. There is no prettification: Emma's teeth catch the light and the baby, her cheeks flushed in the heat, lies in an awkward position, precariously balanced on her mother's lap.

Detail, realism, composition and lighting combine to create a painting remarkable for its intensity of feeling, celebrating motherhood and the intimacy of home. Devoid of any explicit religious reference, it is Brown's modern, secular equivalent to the Italian paintings of the Virgin and Child that had made such a strong impression on him. But the iconography of *Waiting* has a Flemish rather than an Italian precedent, in a small number of paintings associated with the Master of Flémalle (Robert Campin). One of these (fig. 65) depicts, like *Waiting*, a mother in intimate domestic surroundings, seated by the fireside with the child sprawled on her lap, and with a table and fire-irons nearby. There is no record that Brown knew this painting, but he could have seen similar ones during his time in Belgium.[4] Whether he did so or not, *Waiting* appears entirely natural and realistic, not a piece of revivalism but a scene of modern domestic life.

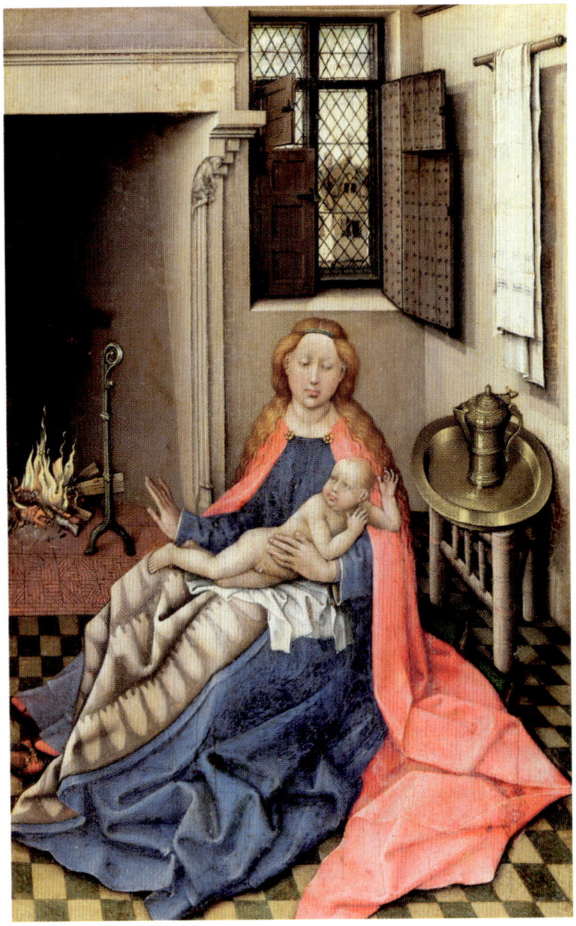

Fig. 65
Workshop of the Master of Flémalle, Madonna and Child by the Fireside. *State Hermitage Museum, St. Petersburg*

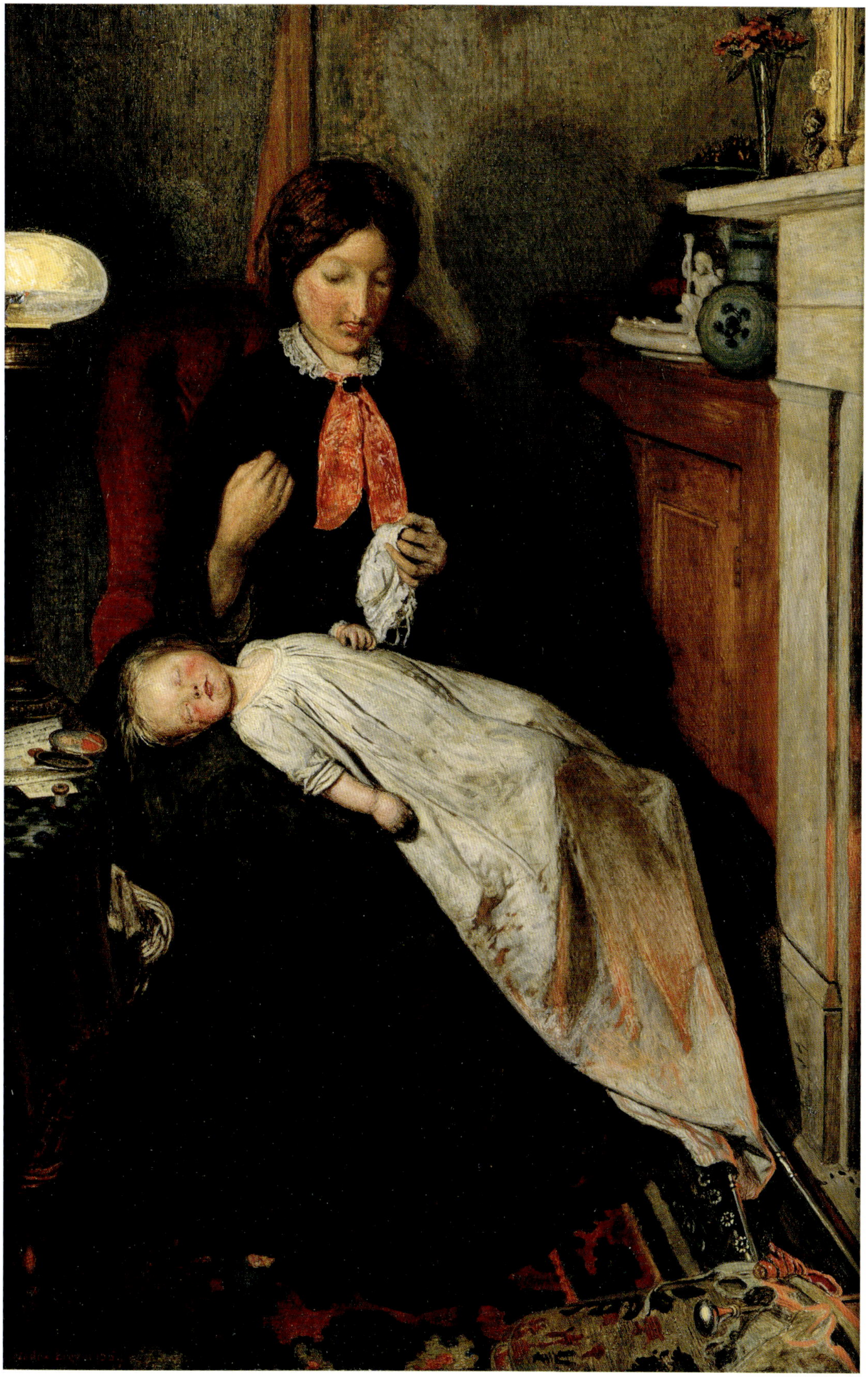

56

57
'TAKE YOUR SON, SIR'

(A68)
1851–52, 1856–57, 1860
oil on canvas, 28 ³/₈ × 15 (72 × 38)
signed: *F.M. Brown / Take your Son Sir*
Tate. Presented by Miss Emily Sargent and Mrs Ormond in memory of their brother, John S. Sargent 1929

'Take your Son, Sir' shows a woman presenting a baby to a man who can be seen reflected in a convex mirror behind the woman's head. The painting has been interpreted in two opposing ways, as showing a proud wife and mother presenting the new baby to its father, or as an unmarried mother, a 'fallen woman', accusingly handing over an illegitimate baby to the reluctant father.

Brown never clarified its meaning, but the title *'Take your Son, Sir'* is his own: it is written on the canvas in his writing. He started the painting in the winter of 1851 when he described it as 'a study from Emma with the head back laughing'.[5] At this time it showed only Emma's head and the upper half of her body.[6] About five years later, around November 1856, he took it up again, and had the canvas enlarged in order to make room to show Emma holding their newly born baby son Arthur. He painted in the baby, but was still unhappy with the picture, and had it enlarged again at the bottom and sides. It was still in hand in 1860 according to Brown's account book, where it was listed under its title, although Brown later referred to it as 'the first-born'.[7] But he never finished it and it was never exhibited during his lifetime.

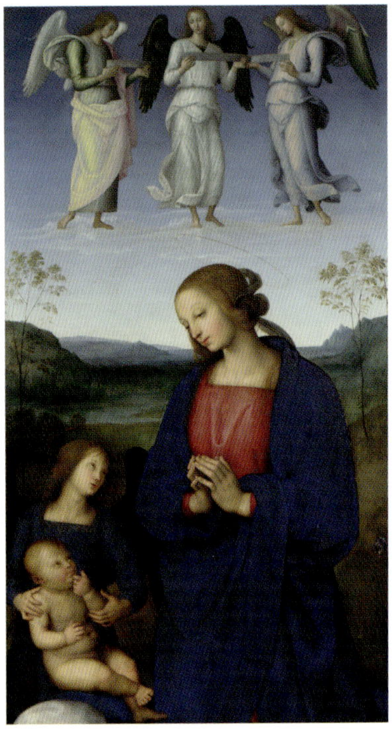

Fig. 66
Pietro Perugino, Virgin and Child with an Angel, *c.1496/1500. National Gallery, London*

It seems unlikely that Brown would cast his wife in the role of a fallen woman, or his son as an unwanted child (it should be remembered that Catherine was born before the Browns were married); the attitude of the father, holding out his hands, seems to be one of welcome rather than refusal (the father's hairstyle vaguely resembles that of Brown himself, although the face is an exaggerated caricature). The mirror directly behind Emma's head appears as a halo, sanctifying the mother with her child. These observations support the idea that the painting is about happy parenthood and indeed it was described as such for example in 1911, when it was shown in Manchester: 'The happy father, coming forward with outstretched arms, is seen reflected in the circular mirror on the wall.'[8] But the grimacing faces of the mother and the father do not immediately suggest joy.

The most remarkable feature of the painting is the confrontational attitude of the mother, placed centrally and thrusting the baby forward in a way that boldly invades the space of the spectator. The picture is also extended backwards by the convex mirror reflecting the part of the room behind the spectator, a device Brown took from the Arnolfini portrait by Jan van Eyck in the National Gallery, London. Brown visited the National Gallery on 1 September 1856[9] when he admired a newly acquired Perugino, a Madonna with a naked child (fig. 66) whose posture probably influenced Brown's representation of Arthur, particularly the position of the baby's feet. Brown did not mention the van Eyck in his diary, but the painting was much admired by the Pre-Raphaelites, several of whom also borrowed the motif of the convex mirror.

The second interpretation, that the painting represents a woman with an illegitimate baby, was first made in the late 1960s at a time when historians were writing about Victorian double standards and rediscovering the 'fallen woman' pictures by Hunt and Rossetti.[10] There is nothing in Brown's writings to support this reading; the grimacing faces and bold composition do not prove anything as they were frequent features in his work. Other subjects by Brown do not help resolve the issue. When he started the picture he was also painting *Waiting* (cat. 56), an unambiguously positive view of motherhood; but by the time he took up *'Take your Son, Sir'* again, he was working on *Stages of Cruelty* (cat. 60), a Hogarthian modern moral subject critical of human behaviour. The fact that Brown never finished *'Take your Son, Sir'* suggests that he was unhappy with it, and unable to resolve it. Nevertheless, it is more likely that it was a failed attempt to convey joy in parenthood than a picture about illegitimacy or immorality.

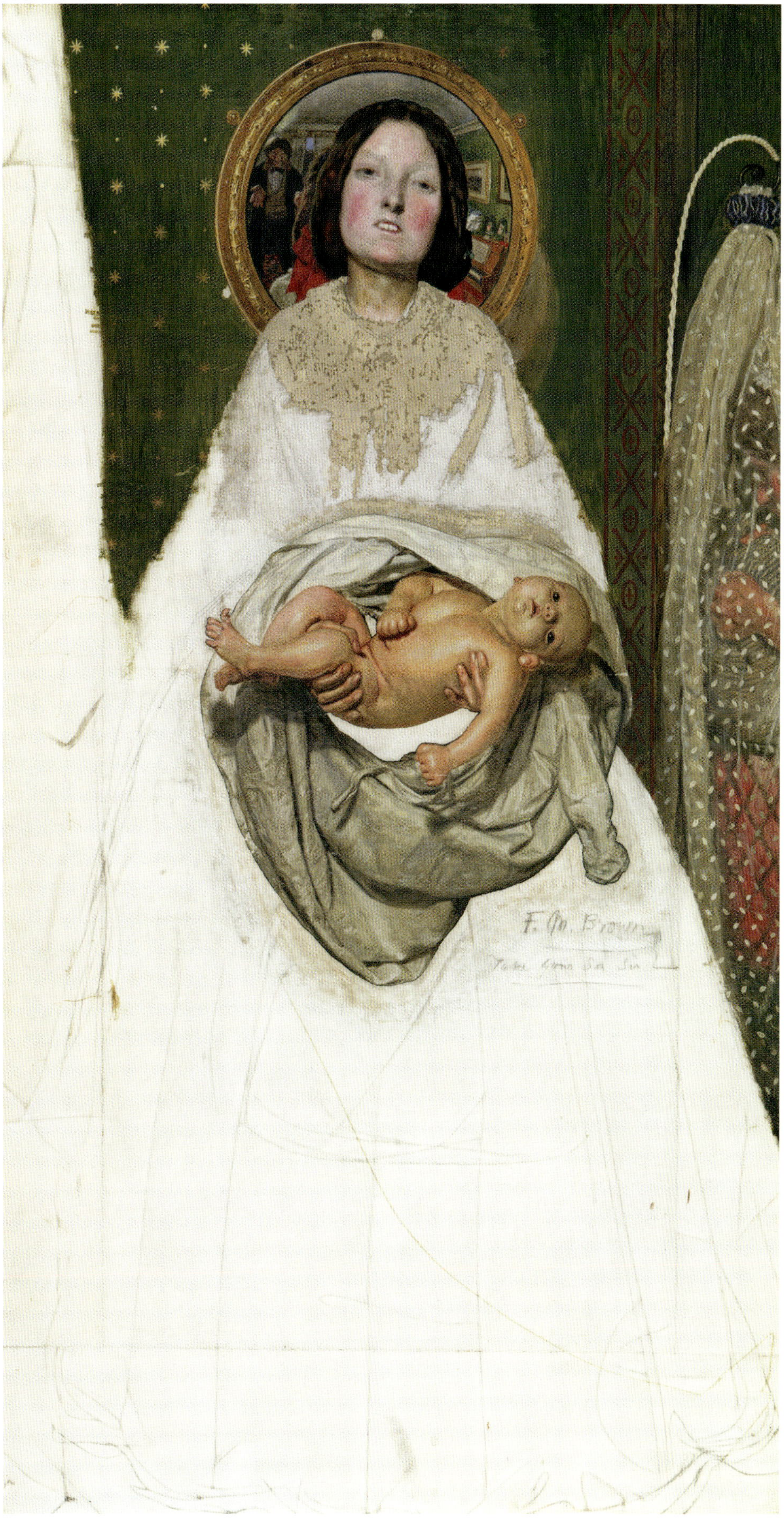
F. M. Brown

58
THE LAST OF ENGLAND

(A61)
1852–55
oil on panel, diameter 32½ × 29½ (82.5 × 75)
signed and dated: *F. MADOX BROWN 1855*
Birmingham Museums and Art Gallery

59
FIRST SKETCH FOR 'THE LAST OF ENGLAND'

(A61.1)
1852–55
oil on panel, 7¾ × 6⅞ (19.7 × 17.5)
signed and dated: *Brown 55*
Private collection

In *The Last of England* Brown took as his subject the great emigration movement of the mid-nineteenth-century. During the century after 1820, about ten million people left Great Britain for the colonies and for America, mostly driven by poverty to seek their fortunes in a new country; the movement was at its height during the years between 1847 and 1854, because of the Irish potato famine in 1846 and the gold discoveries in California and Australia.[11]

Brown's painting depicts a couple seated in the stern of an emigrant ship bound for Australia, looking back at the receding English coast. The scene is realised in extraordinary detail. A grey wintry light fills the scene, with the swell of a dull green sea in the background. The man wears a thick greatcoat, the woman a woollen shawl, with her knees under a tarpaulin, the textures almost tangible. The ribbons of her bonnet flap in the wind, strands of hair blow across her forehead, and the pair, muffled up against the cold, huddle together under an umbrella dotted with droplets of sea-spray.

The two main figures sit side by side, staring straight ahead, not looking at each other, but their shapes interlock and the woman's ribbon blows across his body. They are also linked by a third figure, almost invisible, a baby wrapped up in the woman's shawl. She holds the baby's tiny fingers in one hand, and with the other, daintily gloved, she clasps the much larger hand of the man. He in turn holds the baby's foot, clad in a red bootee. Within the circular shape of the painting, the family forms its own circle, united by the clasped hands and outlined by the umbrella, the tarpaulin, and the right arm and shoulder of the man.

Behind them is a jumble of rowdy fellow-passengers, identified by Brown in his 1865 exhibition catalogue: a pair of drunken reprobates, one of them shaking his fist and cursing the land of his birth; the mother of one of them, seen from behind, scolding them with raised hands; a man with a pipe (only his hat and the pipe can be seen); a woman in a straw bonnet (one eye disconcertingly visible behind the male emigrant's face), her arm round a kneeling red-haired boy dressed in green corduroy and a white scarf; and a girl with an apple, holding on to the scarf. These last were described by Brown as 'an honest family of the green-grocer kind, father (mother *lost*), eldest daughter and younger children'.[12]

Right at the back, a cook's assistant (Brown called him a cabin boy), indifferent to the emotions of the emigrants, is taking vegetables from a boat: his blue-striped shirt is the authentic sailor's dress of the period. On this boat, a small gig or jolly boat used for ferrying people ashore from an anchorage, can be seen the name of the ship, 'Eldorado'. In Brown's preparatory drawing (Birmingham Museums and Art Gallery),[13] the words 'White Horse Line of Australia' were written on the boat, but Brown changed this to 'Eldorado', the mythical kingdom of gold, presumably to suggest the futility of the emigrants' dreams of the riches to be found in the Australian goldfields. (A ship called *Eldorado* sailed in the Liverpool Black Ball Line to Australia in 1854).[14]

Brown was not the only Victorian painter to take emigration as a subject, but his picture lacks the sentimentality often associated with scenes of departing emigrants, and was unusually sensitive to the nuances of social class and gender, as most Victorian emigration scenes featured only the lower classes:

> I have, therefore, in order to present the parting scene in its fullest tragic development, singled out a couple from the middle classes, high enough, through education and refinement, to appreciate all they are now giving up, and yet depressed enough in means, to have to put up with the discomforts and humiliations incident to a vessel "all one class." The husband broods bitterly over blighted hopes and severance from all he has been striving for. The young wife's grief is of a less cantankerous sort, probably confined to the sorrow of parting with a few friends of early years. The circle of her love moves with her.[15]

As indicated in Brown's words, the two main figures are differentiated in character. The man's face is shadowed by a wide-awake hat, worn low over the forehead: a type of headgear associated more with bohemians and intellectuals than the top hat of the reprobate or the straw boater of his drunken companion. The woman's bonnet and ribbon encircle her face without shading

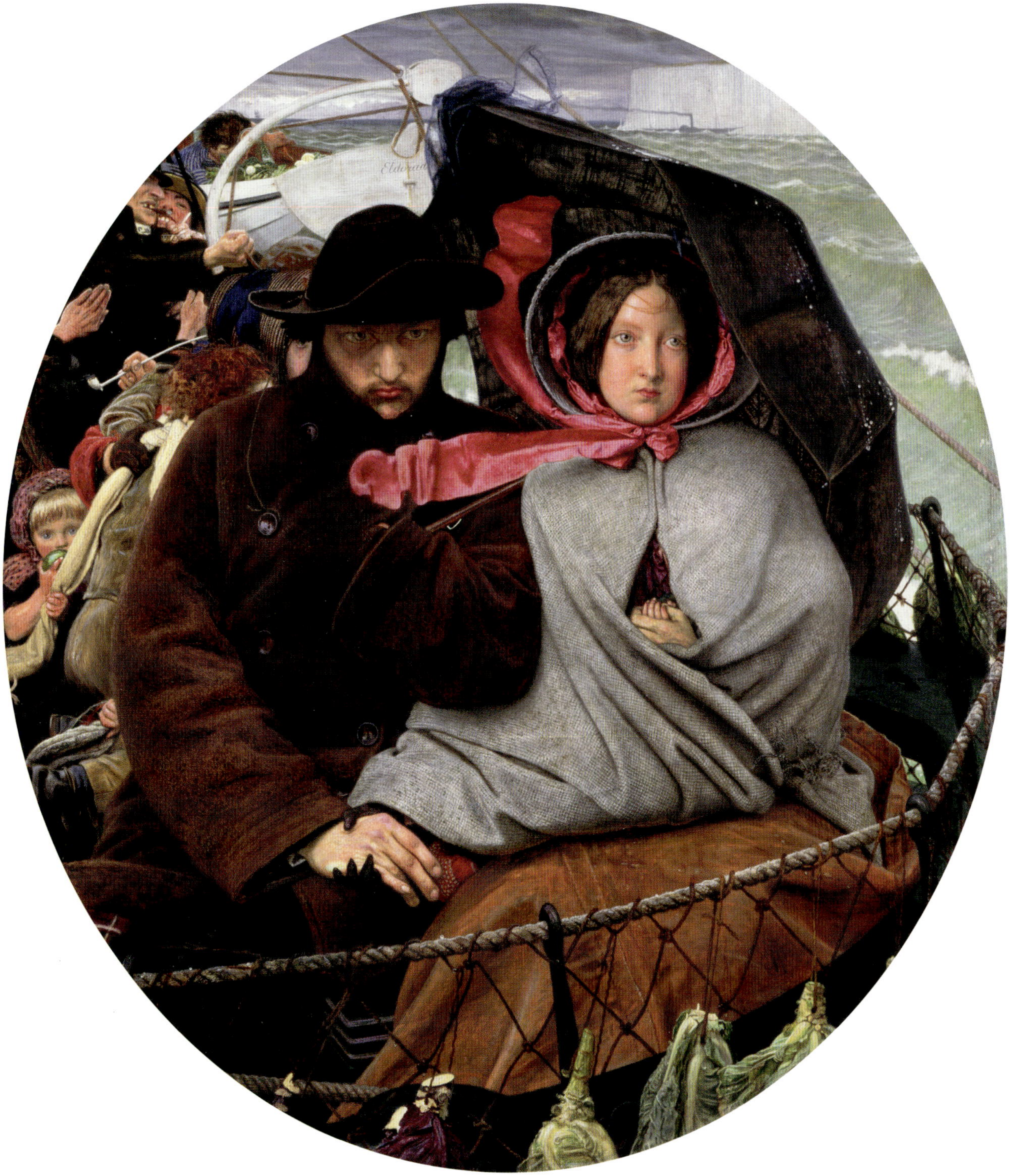

58

it: 'her face, indeed, is the chief charm of the picture' wrote the poet Coventry Patmore.[16] The man's expression mingles bitterness with grim determination; she is tearful but looks sad rather than bitter, resigned to what awaits her. One in shade, the other in light; perhaps Brown intended him to be overburdened by the past, whilst she looks forward to the future: 'Through rainbow-tears she sees a sunnier gleam' wrote Brown in the sonnet composed for the 1865 exhibition catalogue. Although the title of the painting suggests they are looking at the receding view of England, their eyes are unfocused; they seem to be looking inside themselves.

The faces of the couple are portraits of the artist himself, and his wife Emma. Although not strictly autobiographical, the painting reflects Brown's inner feelings: his dark expression sums up all the disappointment and self-doubt evident in his diary at this period. He conceived the painting at the end of 1852, at a time when his fortunes were at a particularly low ebb. A few months before, in July, the Pre-Raphaelite sculptor Thomas Woolner had left for Australia to seek his fortune with two other artists of the circle, Edward Bateman and Bernard Smith. Holman Hunt, Dante Gabriel Rossetti and his brother William had seen them off and Brown may have been there too, although this is not certain. Throughout the period when Brown was struggling with the details of the picture, as well as trying to complete his small landscapes (cats. 51–53), he was often racked with despair and recorded in his diary thoughts of emigrating himself, though to India not Australia.[17]

In preparation for the painting, Brown made a small coloured sketch in oils (cat. 59) and the drawing already referred to, both begun November 1852, besides a drawing of Emma's head (cat. 5). At this period Brown was living alone in Hampstead, often in a depressed state. The coloured sketch has an overall darker appearance than the finished painting – the woman is shown wrapped in blue, green and black tartan, even more complicated to paint than the pale grey shawl eventually adopted, and the tarpaulin on her knees is black, both of which make her stand out less. The faces are paler than in the finished work, and the woman wears gloves on both hands. There are also fewer figures in the background, with only one reprobate, no boy with vegetables and no little girl. Although parts of the sketch are thinly painted, some details, including the faces and hands are highly finished: Brown worked on the sketch again in spring and summer 1855, when the large painting was well under way although not yet complete.

Brown seems to have started on the full-size canvas early in 1853, working for about six weeks 'Emma coming to sit to me in the most inhuman weather from Highgate … The madder ribbons of the bonnet took me 4 weeks to paint.'[18] He then put the painting aside, realising he would not be able to complete it in time to submit it to the RA Summer Exhibition, working on it for a month in late 1853 or early 1854. His most intensive period of work on it was between September 1854 and September 1855, when he was now living with Emma in Finchley. The zinc white ground that he had originally applied caused the paint to crack, so that he had to scrape it off and repaint the man's head and coat. He decided to change the blue and green tartan shawl seen in the oil sketch, to a plain 'shepherd plaid shawl … This is a serious affair which has caused me much perplexity.' The decision to simplify the pattern of the shawl was taken on 20 September 1854.[19] Even so, subsequent diary entries record many hours spent on the shawl, and on other details laboriously painted and repainted, often out of doors in the cold: heads, hands, items of clothing, cabbages, drops of water, netting and rope, the last two items bought from a chandlers in Limehouse. He used his children as models: the baby's hand was Oliver's (born 20 January 1855), the woman's gloved hand was Lucy's, holding that of her nurse, and Cathy posed for the girl with the apple. 'All the red headed boys in Finchley' came to the studio for Brown to paint the curly hair of the boy whose face is invisible behind the man's shoulder.[20] A local washerwoman was found for the reprobate's mother, and other sitters included a 'poor wretch with a nose I thought would do for my scoundrel'.[21]

A point of crisis was reached on 31 August 1855 when personal and artistic difficulties combined, causing nervous illness and acute self-doubt, but suddenly on 2 September 'fortune seemed to favour me. It has been intensely cold, no sun, no rain – high wind, but this seemed the sweetest weather possible, for it was the weather for my picture & made my hand look blue with the cold as I require it in the work'. Two days later was 'My last day at the picture Thank God' and the next day he sold it to White, the art dealer, for £150, £50 less than he had asked.[22] White had also bought the little oil sketch, and he sold both to the prominent collector, B.G. Windus, who around this time also acquired *The First Translation of the Bible* (cat. 33). The following April, Brown recorded in his diary that he had an interview with Windus at White's, where it was decided not to send the painting to the Royal Academy, presumably because of Brown's previous experiences there, when pictures had been rejected or badly hung. However the painting was shown in Liverpool in 1856 and at the Russell Place exhibition in London, a semi-private exhibition for members of the Pre-Raphaelite circle, and again at the London International of 1862. It was praised in the press on all three occasions, but Brown was disappointed that it was never engraved.[23]

Brown had taken immense trouble to depict the scene accurately: he would have had ample opportunity to study emigrant ships whilst visiting his daughter Lucy in Gravesend, the point of departure for many bound for Australia, including Woolner. The ship in the painting appears to be passing the white chalk cliffs in

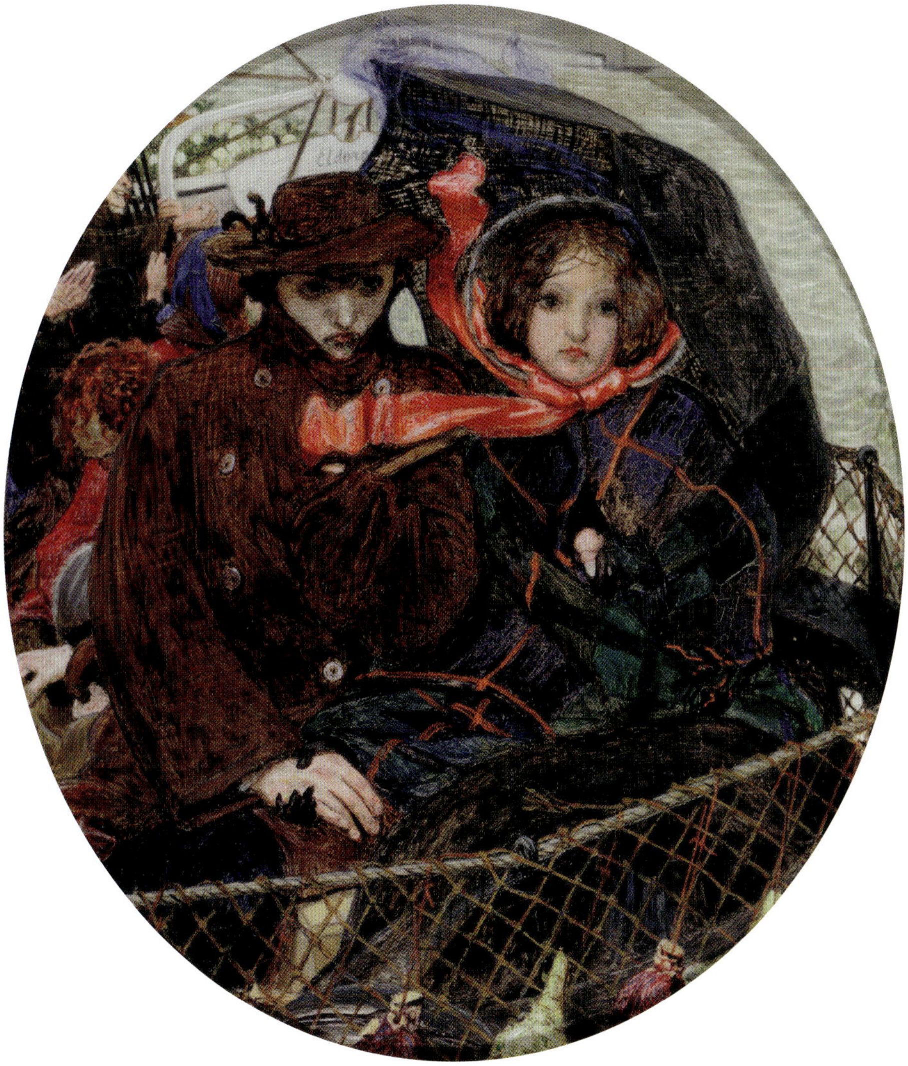

59

the Dover-Folkestone area, sailing in the main channel which is quite close inshore because of offshore sand banks. The paddle steamer depicted in the background heading back towards England also argues for such a location. Its smoke and the direction of the waves (which are right angles to the wind) show that the wind is coming roughly from the north-east. The sea is the characteristic greenish shade of the Channel found in these shallow waters.[24]

Writing in the catalogue to his 1865 exhibition, Brown felt it necessary to explain the amount of detail in the painting. It was required, he wrote, because of his chosen light effect, 'the peculiar look of *light all round*, which objects have on a dull day at sea'; and also 'as bringing the pathos of the subject more home to the beholder.' But he also made a third point: 'Absolutely without regard to the art of any period or country, I have tried to render this scene as it would appear.' Although Brown's painting makes references to previous art, they have been assimilated so that the scene appears completely natural. The round shape, not a true circle but a slightly elongated oval, must have been inspired by the Renaissance tondo format, associated with religious paintings and sculptures, but here also suggests a view through a telescope as well as a the circle of the family's love. Emma's bonnet carries a distant echo of a halo, but the central characters are entirely believable as a modern couple.

Behind them, their fellow passengers are condensed into a boldly foreshortened space, as if caught by a telephoto lens: Brown wittily challenges us to discover their identities from a confusion of overlapping details, gesturing hands and partially concealed faces. And who but Brown would lead us into such a tragic scene with a row of cabbages? Hanging on the netted railing, they 'indicate to the practised eye a long sea voyage'.[25] It was typical of him that such objects, almost laughable in their ordinariness, frame a painting of universal appeal.

60
STAGES OF CRUELTY

(A67)
1856, 1857–60, 1890
oil on canvas, 28 7/8 × 23 9/16 (73.3 × 59.5)
signed with monogram: *FMB – 56 – 90*
Manchester City Galleries

A woman is ignoring the pleas of a lovesick man; her heartlessness is paralleled in the girl's behaviour towards her dog, which she is hitting with a spray of flowers. Brown took the title *Stages of Cruelty* from a series of prints by William Hogarth showing cruelty to animals in children turning into criminal behaviour in adults: Brown's painting was intended as a modern morality, a Victorian version of Hogarth's biting social critique (fig. 67).

Brown had the first idea for the painting on 19 June 1856: 'in the garden a young lady seated on the wall working [ie sewing] under a lilac tree & a youths head just visible on the far side, to be called "Stolen pleasures are sweet".'[26] It was modelled on the paintings of pairs of lovers by Millais, with their detailed backgrounds of tangled foliage and brick walls; the immediate inspiration was *April Love* by Millais's follower Arthur Hughes (Tate), which Brown had admired the previous summer. But at some point Brown must have decided to change the bittersweet emotions of Hughes's lovers into something more disturbing, even misogynistic: the face of Brown's woman is locked in a mask-like grimace as she looks on amused at the cruelty of the girl, and completely indifferent to the desperate entreaties of her suitor.

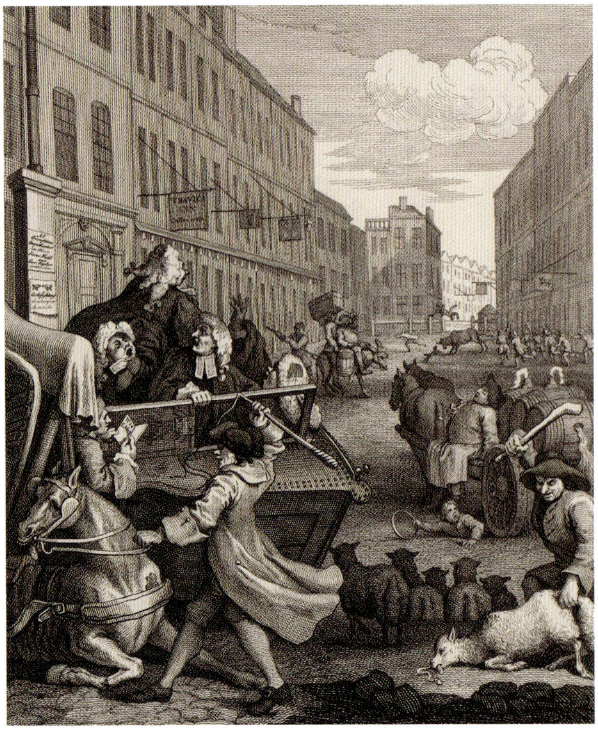

Fig. 67
William Hogarth, The Second Stage of Cruelty, *1751. The British Museum, London*

The red flower which the girl is aiming at the dog, a bloodhound, is love-lies-a-bleeding, which Brown must have chosen to underline the moral, although he presumably chose lilac for the background because there was a lilac in his garden (he was then living at Fortess Terrace, Highgate). Victorian books about the language of flowers often give multiple alternative meanings,[27] but love-lies-a bleeding was commonly used to indicate 'hopelessness' or 'hopeless not heartless'; morning glory, which climbs up the balustrade can mean 'love in vain'. Although Brown did not include any lilac flowers, only the leaves, lilac flowers signify 'first emotion of love'. The geranium in the posy pinned to the woman's bodice means either 'deceit' or 'preference'.

The lilac leaves gave the artist tremendous trouble; he took over one month to complete them (24 June – 27 July 1856), often painting at them for seven or eight hours in one day. He shaded them with a tent in the garden to prevent them looking flat and colourless in the sun, and had to rearrange them 'pinning on fresh ones where they are blighted & placing the branches where they are pressed to one side by the heat.'[28] The figures were begun from the artist Thomas Seddon and his wife, but after they proved to be unreliable sitters, he used a lay figure, also painting from himself and Lucy in a mirror, and later from others. He worked on the painting again in 1857 in the hope of making a sale, and it was still in hand in 1860, but did not sell it until 1890, when it was bought by Henry Boddington of Manchester. Just before this, Brown retouched the painting of the girl, using as the model his grand-daughter Juliet, whose mother had sat for the girl over thirty years before.

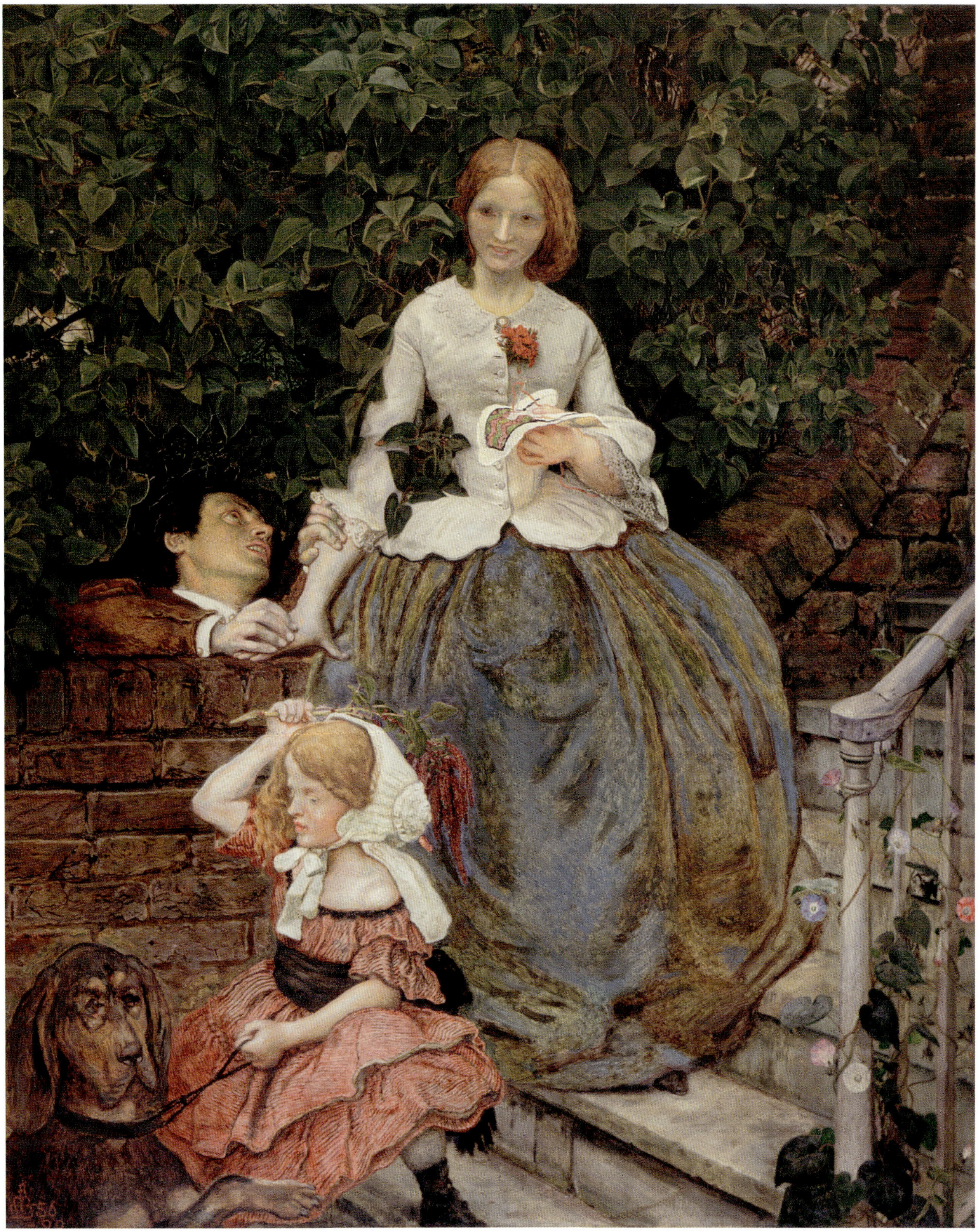

WORK

Work is Brown's largest and most elaborate modern life subject. He began it in 1852 but it occupied him intermittently until 1863, during which time he also painted many other pictures, but this was the most ambitious of them all; he regarded it as 'the work of my life.'[29] On one level it is a vivid street scene, representing the ceaseless bustle and movement of the ever-expanding Victorian city, crowded with convincingly individual characters from different walks of life. That in itself makes the picture unusual in the Victorian period, when many artists regarded modern dress as ugly, and when, if they represented workers at all, they would usually be agricultural labourers or peasants, living in an idealised rustic world.

But *Work* is also an allegory about the place of work in society. Brown deliberately chose his characters to represent different types, bringing them together to make contrasts: work and idleness, poverty and wealth, physical work and mental work. He showed the rich who do not need to work and the unemployed who cannot find work; he showed manual workers, street traders, voluntary do-gooders and intellectuals who provide the ideas that influence society. The intellectuals, called by Brown 'brainworkers', are the two men looking on from the right, portraits of real people, the polemical writer Thomas Carlyle and the Christian Socialist clergyman Frederick Denison Maurice. They are the key to the ideas embodied in *Work*, although many other currents in Victorian life are present in the multifarious details crammed into the painting.

An allegory might imply a fixed meaning, but Brown's painting is deliberately complex and cannot be reduced to one simple explanation. It is a 'real allegory' in the sense used by Courbet (fig. 6, p. 15), in which the ideas are represented not by artificial symbols but by convincing-looking objects and people whose demeanour implies thoughts, behaviour and histories beyond the single moment shown in a static painting. Brown enriched his painting with jokes and puzzles, and embedded texts into it, posters, notices, and the quotations on the frame. He also wrote a sonnet for it, and a long description, enlarging on the characters of the different people and speculating about their thoughts. The sonnet and description were written in 1865 and so represent the artist's mature thoughts about a painting that was started in 1852, and reached its final form over a long period of development.

In visual terms, so much is going on in the picture that at first sight it appears confusing. Although the composition is structured, it breaks many of the rules of academic painting that Brown had been taught in his youth. There is no aerial perspective, and no clear centre, so that the eye jumps restlessly from one part to another, not knowing where to settle. Everything is painted in minute detail and equally sharp focus whether in the foreground or background, creating a crowded image of clashing colours, sudden juxtapositions and fragmented encounters, very different from the concentrated clarity of Brown's other modern-life paintings. This confusion itself expresses the experience of modern urban life, with its constantly distracting movement and noise.

61

WORK

(A59)
1852, 1855, 1856–63, (1865)
oil on canvas, 53 15/16 × 77 11/16 (137 × 197.3)
signed and dated: *F. MADOX BROWN 1852-/65*
Manchester City Galleries

The central idea behind Brown's epic painting is the gospel of work put forward by Thomas Carlyle in his book *Past and Present*, the taller of the two 'brainworkers' depicted by Brown on the left of the painting (fig. 68). In *Past and Present* Carlyle wrote that 'All work, even cotton-spinning is noble' ' … there is a perennial nobleness, and even sacredness in Work … in Idleness alone is there perpetual despair.'[30] For Carlyle work was the basis of a just society; he believed that it was a form of prayer and a means of salvation for all classes. The second brainworker, standing next to Carlyle, is the preacher, social reformer and educationalist Revd. Frederick Denison Maurice (fig. 69). He seems to stand for practical social improvement, as opposed to the theoretical writings of Carlyle. Maurice was leader of the Christian Socialist

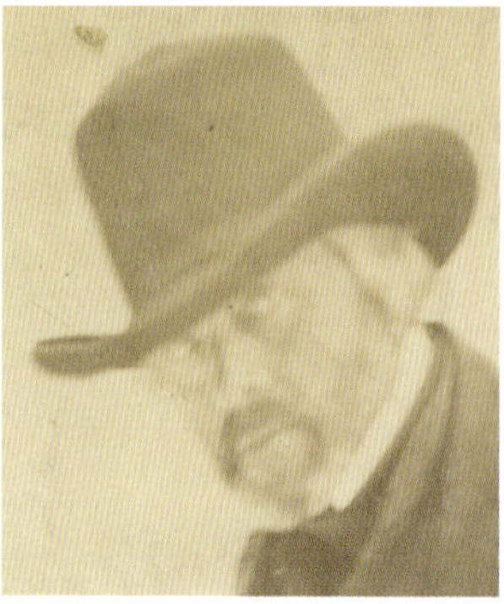

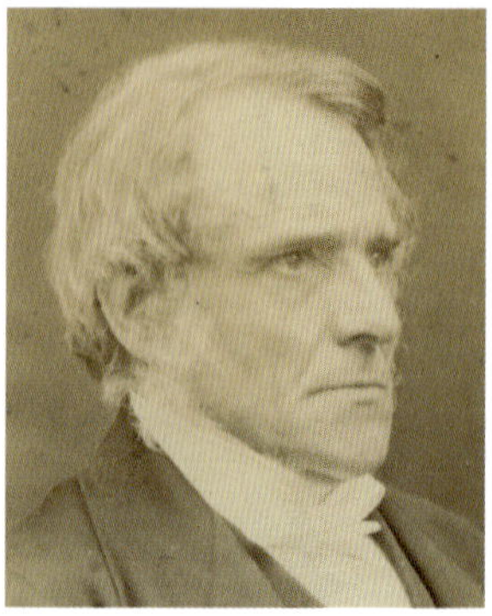

Fig. 68 (above left)
Detail of cat. 74, Photograph of Thomas Carlyle
Fig. 69 (above right)
Frederick Denison Maurice, photograph by William Jeffrey, 1860s.
National Portrait Gallery, London

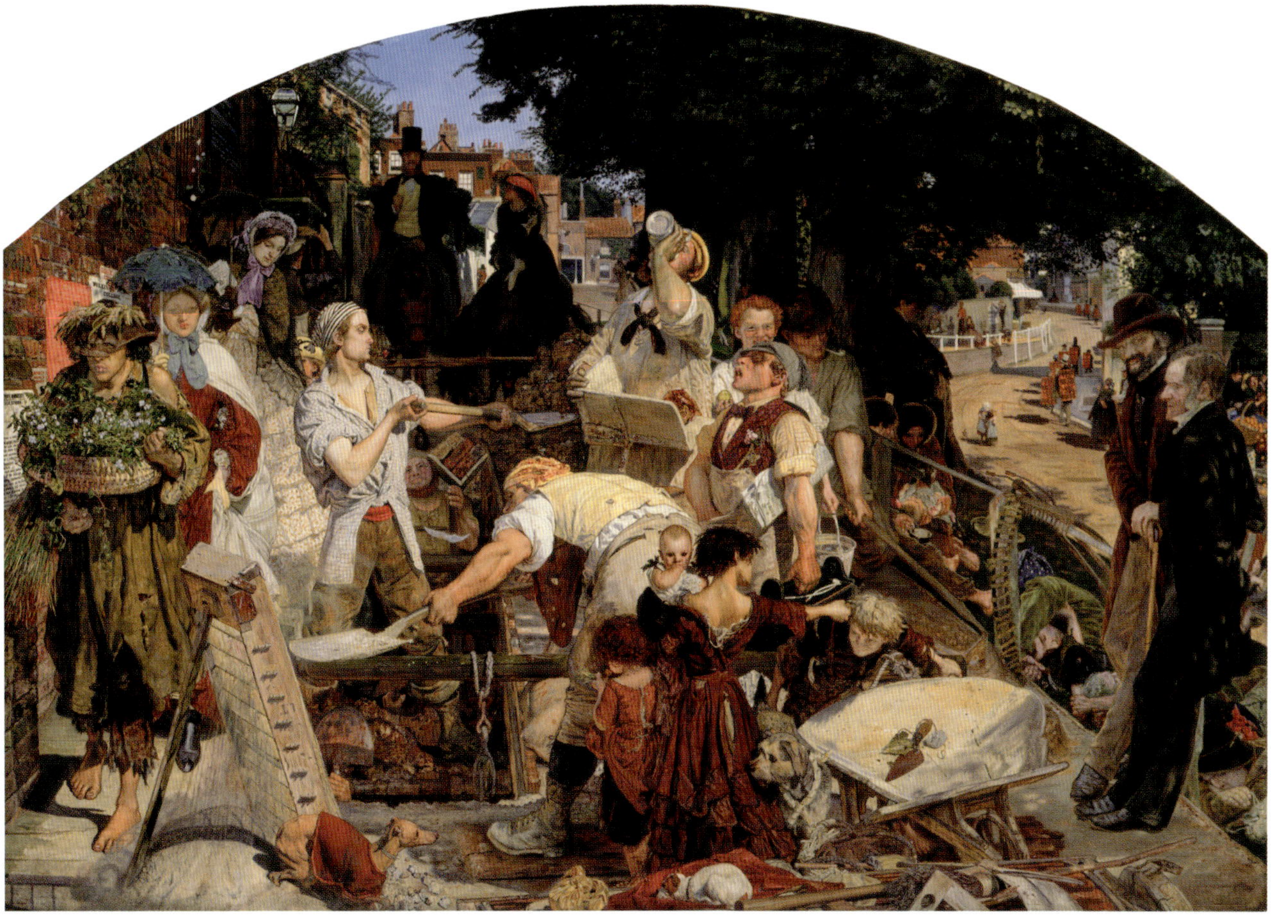

61

party and an example of his practical work was his role in the foundation of the Working Men's College in London, where Brown taught an evening class in drawing for two years. Brown painted into his picture a poster for the college, pasted on to the wall on the left.

Although Brown had long admired both men, they were not included in his first idea for the painting. But present from the start was the central position of the manual workers and the poor children. In the summer of 1852 he saw a group of navvies digging a trench in Heath Street, Hampstead, and this gave him the idea for the painting. For Brown the navvies were 'the outward and visible type of Work' (this and all quotations in this entry come from Brown's description of *Work* in the catalogue to his one-man exhibition of 1865, unless otherwise indicated).[31] In contrast, the poor children show the ill-effects of the lack of work; unemployment is also represented in the picture on the right, in the people under the tree and on the bank. Brown perhaps had in mind an attempt to create a modern equivalent to Hogarth's series of prints *Industry and Idleness*.

Brown carefully differentiated the navvies in age and physique. To the left is the young navvy 'in the pride of manly health and beauty' whom Brown described as the hero of the painting; in the centre is 'the strong fully developed navvy who does his work and loves his beer', drinking from a tankard. Next, 'the selfish old bachelor navvy, stout of limb and perhaps a trifle tough in those regions where compassion is said to reside' is presumably the man in the trench carrying a hod full of bricks; and at the front of the group, bent over with his back to us and shovelling earth through a sieve, is the navvy whose 'strong animal nature' has been tamed by his having been taught to work when young. Further right is an apprentice boy with red hair (often associated with the Irish) carrying a bucket of water, presumably for mixing cement, and an apple.[32] Beside him stands another Irishman, 'Paddy with his larry and his pipe in his mouth'; he is mixing up cement with his 'larry', a long-handled hoe. The young navvy stands on a platform over the trench, shovelling earth that has been excavated by two men working below; they are unseen apart from their hands holding spades.

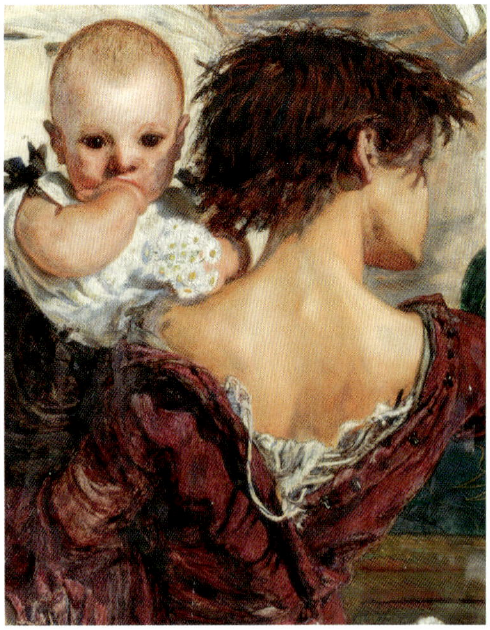

Fig. 70 *Detail of cat. 61, Work, The ragged girl with the baby*

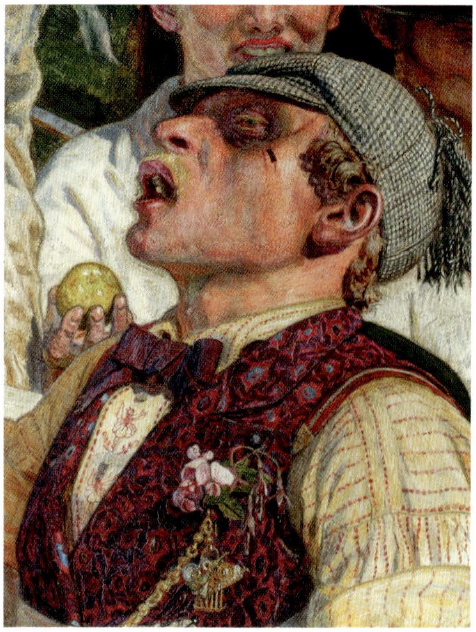

Fig. 71 *Detail of cat. 61, Work, The beer seller*

The navvies Brown had seen in Heath Street were excavating for a water main, part of a scheme to bring a supply of fresh water to the area. Health and sanitary improvement were key issues for social reformers and philanthropists in the campaign to improve conditions for the working class, known as 'the Great Unwashed'. Hygiene was regarded as a moral and religious problem as well as a practical one: Brown had already associated cleanliness and godliness in *Oure Ladye of Saturday Night* (cat. 28). Fresh water was vital in the fight against poor housing and disease. There were several cholera outbreaks in the 1840s and '50s and Brown himself contributed to a church collection for 'the poor Cholera parentless brats' in October 1854.[33]

In the foreground of the picture Brown included 'just such a group of ragged dirty brats as anywhere get in the way and make a noise … That they are motherless, the baby's black ribbons and their extreme dilapidation indicate' (fig. 70). The black ribbons indicate mourning for the mother's death; as for the children's absent father, Brown wrote that 'I have no doubt he drinks and will be sentenced in the police-court for neglecting them.' Without parents, the eldest girl has to look after her siblings and 'she has become a premature scold', pulling her brother's hair. The brats represent the association between dirt, disease, unemployment and anti-social behaviour. Even so, like the navvies, they look fairly clean, and not at all like 'the Great Unwashed', although the girl is 'fearfully untidy', wearing a dress that is too big for her 'evidently the compassionate gift of some grown-up person'.

A tiny detail in the background on the right, two girls carrying jugs, illustrates the lack of fresh water: before the provision of a water supply, people had to walk sometimes long distances to a pump or standpipe, stand in a queue for the water, and carry it home.

Reformers hoped that the free supply of fresh water would encourage temperance and sobriety: water from a standpipe had to be paid for, whereas beer was often cheaper and much more readily available. Drink is prominent in the painting: the navvy drinking beer is positioned in the centre at the apex of the group of workers, and next to him is a pot-boy or beer seller (fig. 71), recognisable from his green beer tray. Brown describes him as 'stunted with gin in his childhood', recalling Hogarth's prints of *Beer Street* and *Gin Lane* about the evil effects of gin, as opposed to the benefits of drinking beer; from his black eye he looks as though he has been in a brawl. By the Victorian period, the campaign against gin had become a fight against all alcohol. One of the well-dressed ladies on the left is carrying a bundle of leaflets or 'tracts', advocating temperance, and entitled 'The Hodman's Haven, or Drink For Thirsty Souls' (fig. 72). She has just thrown one down into the trench towards the man with the hod, but he takes no notice of it.

The tract distributor is part of Brown's group of 'the rich, who have no need to work – not at least for bread … The pastry-cook's tray the symbol of superfluity, accompanies these.' This is the green tray carried by the man behind the tract distributor. Brown speculated in his commentary that the lady with the tracts might also make a charitable contribution to the Boy's Home in the Euston Road, advertised on a poster on the wall beside her (this was another charity with which Brown was associated through the

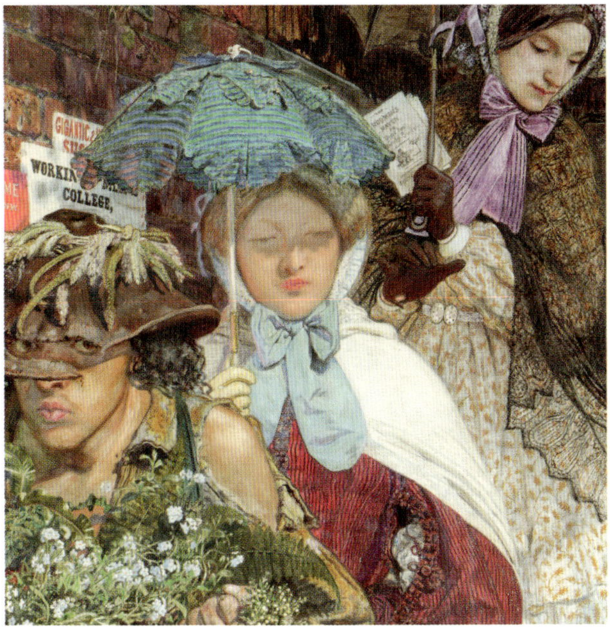

Fig. 72 (left) *Detail of cat. 61,* Work, *The chickweed seller and the rich ladies*

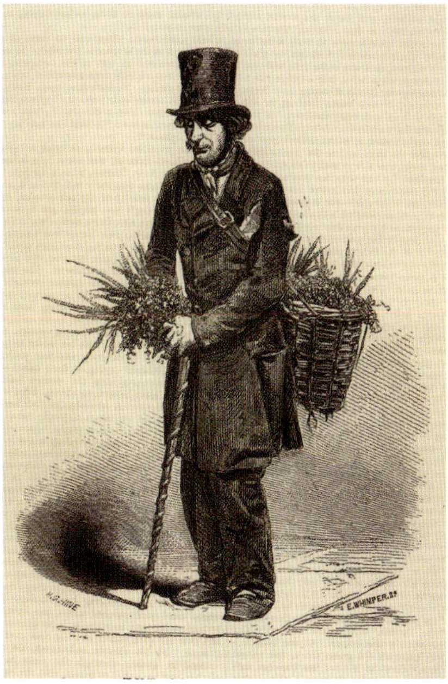

Fig. 73 (right) The Groundsel Man, *from a daguerreotype by Richard Beard (engraved by H.G. Hine and E.Whimper), illustration in Henry Mayhew,* London Labour and the London Poor, *1861*

philanthropist William Gillum, one of Brown's patrons). In front of her is a younger lady 'whose only business in life as yet is to dress and look beautiful for our benefit', looking down after her 'scarlet-coated hound,'[34] which is wandering off the pavement towards the mongrel dog belonging to the ragged children. The rich and poor dogs regard each other with uncomprehending curiosity, while a third dog, the little bull-terrier of the navvies, looks on.

In the background of the picture are two further people representing wealth, a man on horseback and his daughter. He is 'very rich, probably a Colonel in the army, with a seat in Parliament, and fifteen thousand a year … he is not an overdressed man of the tailor's dummy sort'. He wears a sober black top hat and a discreet yellow waistcoat (fig. 74). Throughout the painting, Brown used clothing as an indicator of character and social position, a theme that Carlyle wrote about in *Sartor Resartus*. From the garish waistcoat and the ballerina embroidered on the shirt front of the beer seller ('in all matters of taste, as vulgar as Birmingham can make him look in the 19th century'), to the soft felt hat of the literary and artistic classes worn by Carlyle himself, people can be read by what they are wearing.

One piece of headgear needs further explanation, the battered hat worn by the ragged man on the left, who carries a basket of wild plants (fig. 72). He is a chickweed seller, sometimes colloquially known as a Botany Ben.[35] Henry Mayhew in his survey of street life, *London Labour and the London Poor*, described a similar street seller, the groundsel man, who collected wild plants at various places including Highgate, selling bunches as fodder for singing birds (fig. 73). According to Mayhew, street sellers like this were vagrants, little more than beggars.[36] Brown's chickweed seller is wearing a type of hat known as a 'billy-cock' or 'wide-awake'. Brown recorded in his diary that he went out to buy a 'dirty old wide awake off the head of a man I met'.[37] On top of the hat are ears of grain and straw: this was used as an indicator of madness (for example by Hogarth in his Bedlam scene in *The Rake's Progress*).[38] Brown described the chickweed seller variously as a 'Pariah', as a 'ragged wretch who has never been taught to work' and as 'harmless'. He has a demented, furtive look, peering through the broken brim of his hat, a frightening sight to respectable middle-class people.

The proximity of the mad chickweed seller to the lady whose sole business is to look beautiful, as well as the dogs looking at each other, suggests not just a contrast between rich and poor, but a lack of communication. Brown expanded on this theme in his commentary. He speculated on the thoughts of the man with the hod, that 'ladies might be benefited by receiving tracts containing navvies' ideas!' And as for the Member of Parliament (who was modelled by Brown's artist-friend Robert Braithwaite Martineau), Brown wrote: 'he looks to me an honest, true-hearted gentleman … and could he only be got to hear what the two sages in the corner have to say, I have no doubt he would be easily won over. But the road is blocked, and the daughter says we must go back, papa, round the other way.'

These are not just 'literary' ideas added in the commentary. On the contrary, they are built into the painting by visual means, in its composition and lighting, combining naturalism with symbolic meaning. The manual workers occupy the centre between the

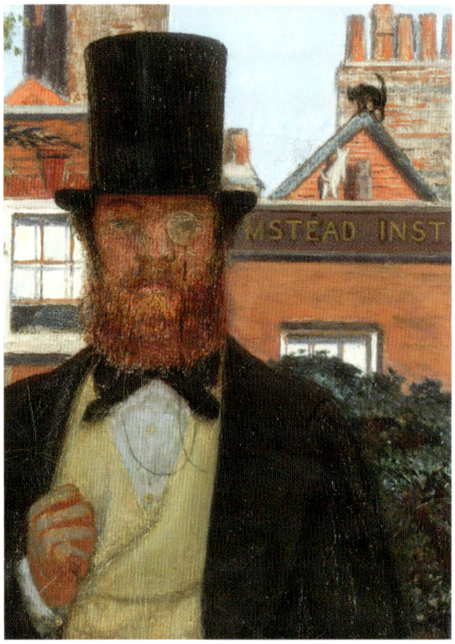

Fig. 74 (left) Detail of cat. 61, Work, *the Member of Parliament, with the cats on the roof*

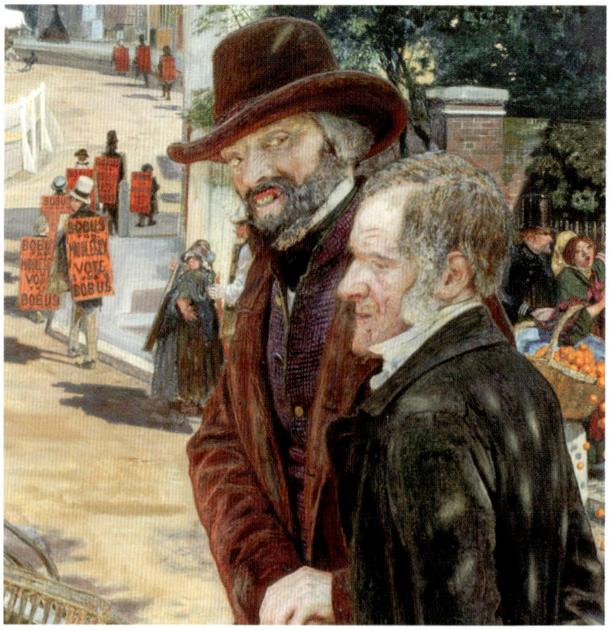

Fig. 75 (right) Detail of cat. 61, Work, *Carlyle and Maurice, with the orange seller and the sandwich board men*

wealthy classes at the rear and left, the poor in the foreground and the intellectuals on the right. The central position of the workers blocks any potential communication between the Member of Parliament and the intellectuals, or between the intellectuals and the rich, well-meaning ladies. The Member of Parliament is right at the top of the composition, above all the figures, as befits the ruling class, but he is in shadow (similar to the position of William the Conqueror in cat. 23). Whereas the rich are in various degrees of shade, the workers and the poor children, the chief objects of the artist's sympathies, are brightly lit by the 'hot July sunlight' that Brown regarded as 'peculiarly fitted to display *work* in all its severity'.

On the extreme left, behind Maurice is a tiny scene of a policeman aggressively pushing a girl selling oranges, an illegal street trader (fig. 75). According to Mayhew most sellers of oranges were women and children, many of them Irish. Brown may well have seen the anonymous cartoon published in the middle-class humorous magazine *Punch* showing a policeman moving on an orange girl, while ignoring 'the real street obstructions' of the cartoon's caption, the obtrusive portable advertisements (fig. 76).[39] In the street behind the orange seller, Brown put a procession of men carrying similar advertisements on sandwich boards. Carrying sandwich boards was usually a job done by tramps and vagrants. Their placards carry election slogans: 'Bobus for Middlesex. Vote for Bobus'. Bobus Higgins was a fictional character from Carlyle's *Past and Present*, a wealthy sausage-maker, embodying the values opposed to the gospel of work: capitalism, the pursuit of wealth for its own sake, nouveau-riche worship of money and fame. A poster on the wall at the left of the painting reads 'Money!! Money!! Money!!', a slogan used by Carlyle in his attack on materialism in *Past and Present*. Another poster being put up on the wall above the white railings, shows that Bobus won the election, whilst 'Thackeray' received only three votes. The novelist and art critic William Makepeace Thackeray actually stood as an independent in the 1857 election but lost. Brown had seen a real election in progress in the summer of 1852, which had provoked public outrage for corruption, bribery and intimidation.[40] His lack of faith in authority and government is expressed in these vignettes.

Besides the red-haired apprentice and the 'Paddy' already mentioned, there are several more Irish people in the painting, including the man standing under the tree, 'a stoic from the Emerald Island' (fig. 77) and 'a young shoeless Irishman, with his wife, feeding their first-born with cold pap.' By 1851 there were many people of Irish origin living in London, who had come because of the Great Famine in the mid-1840s. Brown was more than usually aware of the distress in Ireland because his late wife's brother Richard Bromley, a civil servant in the Admiralty, had been sent there to assist in the relief. Brown had written a sonnet about the famine, and recorded in his diary that he painted the Irish characters from real people that he found in the streets. The other people lying on the bank below the railings are migrant rural labourers in search of harvest work, the scythe, bound up with a rope, a clue to their occupation.

In the background to *Work* Brown included a variety of incidents, some barely visible. Many of these details are witty and playful, included purely for fun. Behind the white railings at the

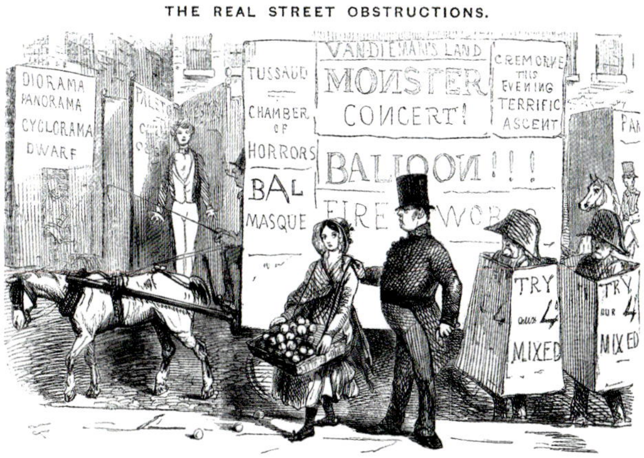

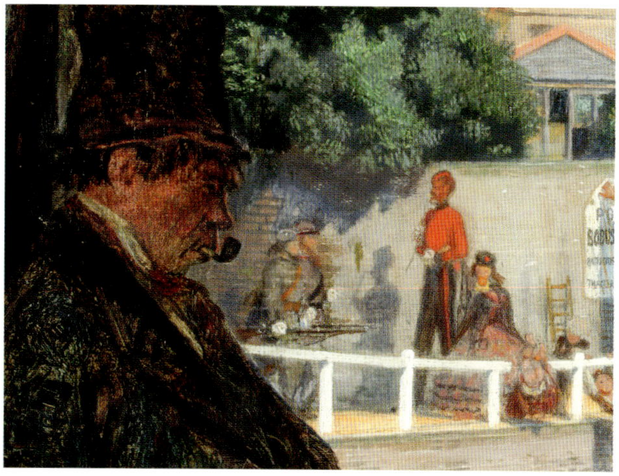

Fig. 76 (above) The real street obstructions, *cartoon from* Punch, *1850*
Fig. 77 (above right) Detail of cat. 61, Work, *The stoic from the Emerald Island, with background figures*

right is an improbably tall soldier accompanied by a short woman (fig. 77); children play on the railings, one of them turning over and exposing a naked bottom; nearby is a greengrocer's shop, and a coach and horses which is just coming into view round the corner. In the centre between the beer drinker and the MP's daughter is a man putting up posters; between the MP and the daughter is a postman in uniform delivering a letter; above him cats crawl on the roof of the 'Flamstead Institute of Arts' (fig. 74) where 'Professor Snoox is about to repeat his lecture on the habits of the domestic cat': this was a Pre-Raphaelite in-joke referring to Professor Athanasius Snoox, an imaginary character invented by Rossetti.[41] There are also many flowers in the painting: the navvy has a flower in his mouth (perhaps a rose for beauty), the pot-boy has a fuchsia in his button-hole,[42] the orphan baby carries common-or-garden daisies, and the chickweed seller's basket contains groundsel, ferns and forget-me-not. Sometimes Brown tells us the symbolic meaning of objects he includes, such as the pastry-cook's tray, sometimes not: is the sieve used by the navvies just a sieve, or is it a metaphor for discriminating and judging moral worth, as described by Carlyle in *Past and Present*?[43]

Brown also made words an integral part of his picture: the posters, signs and sandwich-boards, the pastry-cook's name 'R.Puff,' on the delivery tray and the masthead of 'The Times' on the newspaper tucked under the beer-seller's arm. Like the partially-obscured figures of the labourers sleeping on the shaded bank, some of the words are fragmentary, such as those on the torn bills advertising a house to let and offering a reward for a stolen dog. Brown also wrote a sonnet for the painting (reprinted below) which was included in the 1865 exhibition catalogue with his description, while more words literally surround the painting: written on the frame are stern Biblical quotations on the moral necessity and the egalitarianism of labour:

'I must work while it is day, for the night cometh when no man can work' (John 9:4)

'Neither did we eat any man's bread for nought; but wrought with labour and travail night and day' (II Thessalonians 3:8)

'Seest thou a man diligent in his business? He shall stand before Kings' (Proverbs 22:29)

'In the sweat of thy face shalt thou eat bread' (Genesis 3:19)

Sonnet

WORK! Which beads the brow, and tans the flesh,
Of lusty manhood, casting out its devils!
By whose weird art, transmuting poor men's evils,
Their bed seems down, their one dish ever fresh.
Ah me! For lack of it what ills in leash,
Hold us. It's want the pale mechanic levels
To workhouse depths, while Master Spendthrift revels.
For want of work, the fiends him soon immesh!

Ah! beauteous tripping dame with bell-like skirts,
Intent on the small scarlet-coated hound,
Are ragged wayside babes not lovesome too?
Untrained, their state reflects on thy deserts,
Or they grow noisome beggars to abound,
Or dreaded midnight robbers, breaking through.

F.M.B. – Feb., 1865.

The painting and its commentary present a 'maze of references and cross references.'[44] Work is a composite, an interplay of text and image which asks to be explored and enjoyed. It is without doubt one of the most important works of art of the Victorian age.

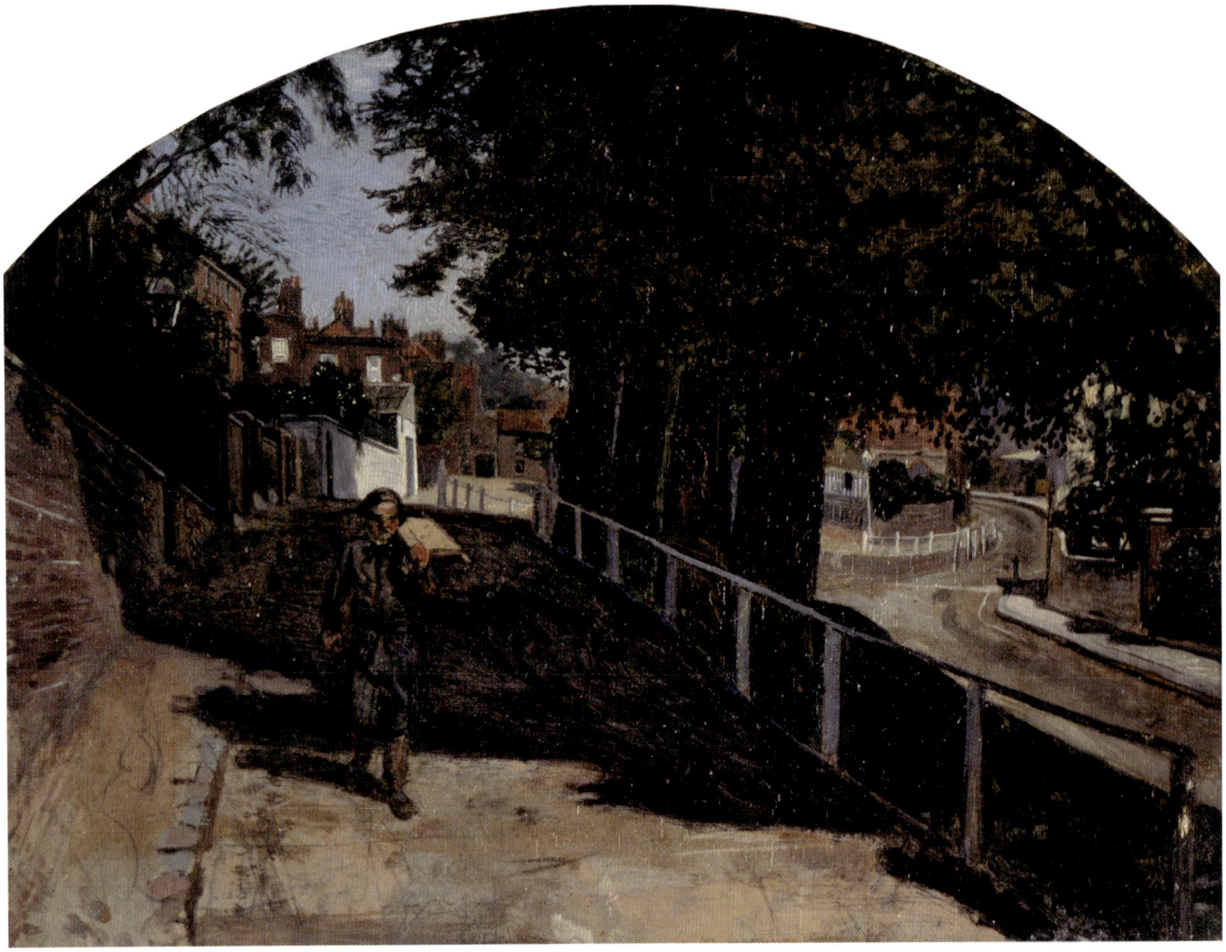

62

62

THE MOUNT AND HEATH STREET, HAMPSTEAD (THE BUTCHER BOY)

(A59.1)
1852, 1855–56
oil over pencil on canvas, 9 × 12⅛ (22.8 × 30.8)
Manchester City Galleries

63

ROUGH SKETCH FOR 'WORK'

(A59.4)
1852/1855 (?)
pencil, 10 15/16 × 15⅝ (27.8 × 39.7)
inscribed on separate piece of paper: *First rough sketch for "Work" Hampstead /56*
Manchester City Galleries

64

STUDY OF 'WORK'

(A59.2)
probably 1864
watercolour and pencil, 7¾ × 11 (19.7 × 28)
signed with monogram: *FMB*
Manchester City Galleries

Brown began *Work* in around June of 1852 with a pen and ink design, now lost. At about the same time, he painted the small oil sketch of Heath Street as a study for the background. The raised portion of the street at the front, where the navvies were digging in the picture, is called The Mount, and Heath Street itself is below it on the right. The view is very much the same today (fig. 78). The oil sketch was painted on the spot, but later finished off with the addition of the butcher's boy carrying his tray, added between December 1855 and February 1856 when Brown gave the picture to Thomas Woolner.

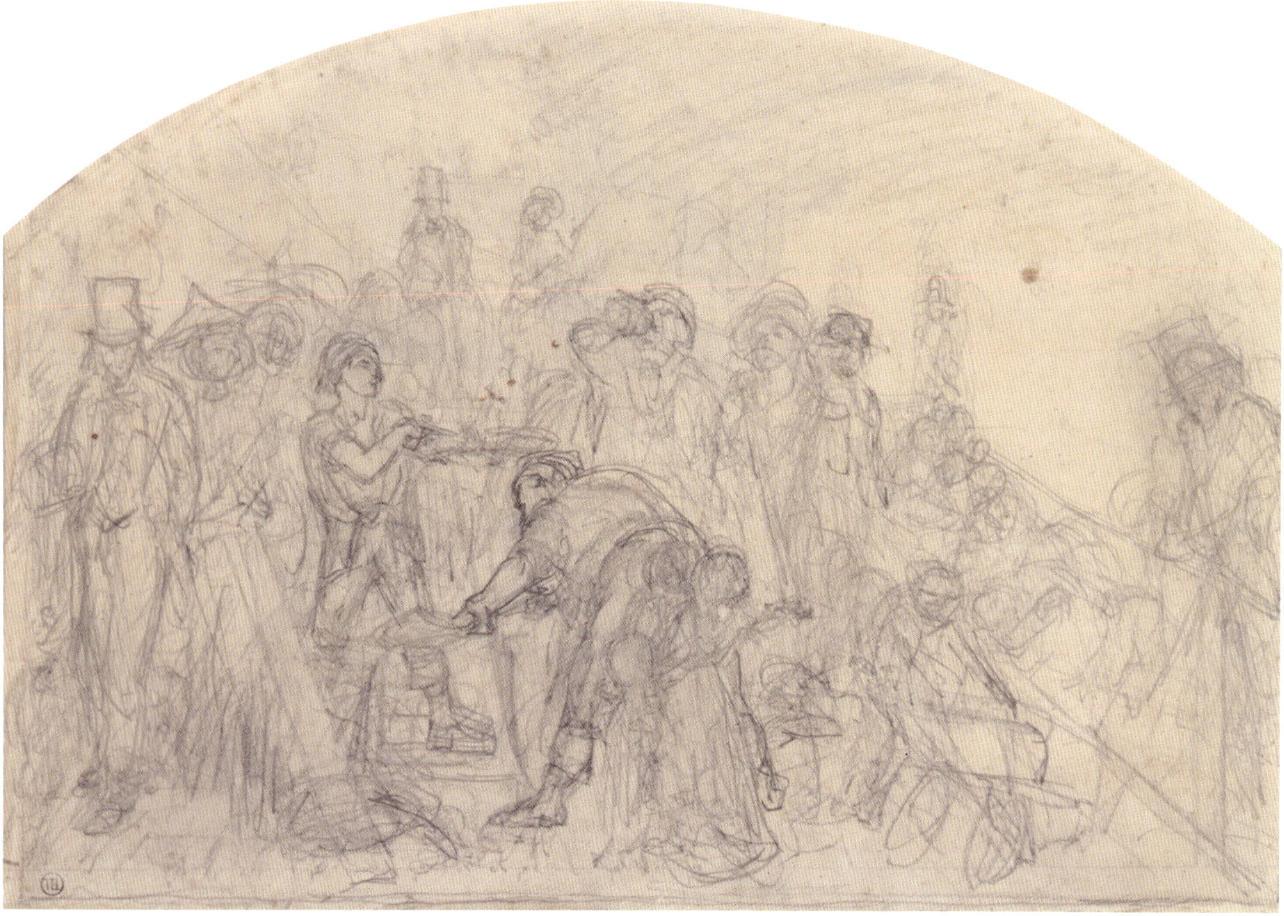

63

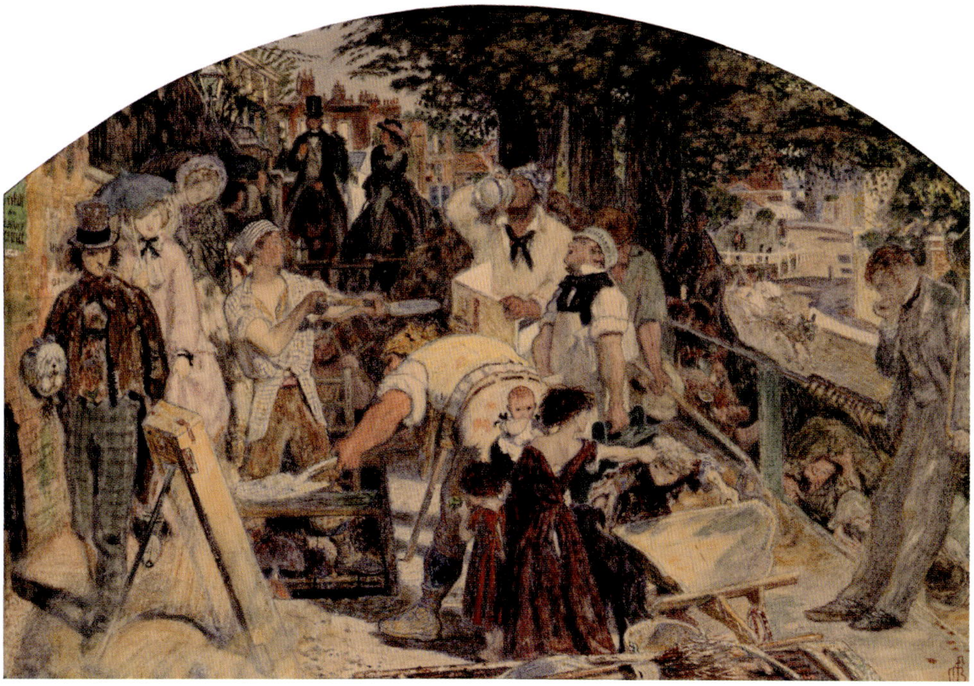

64

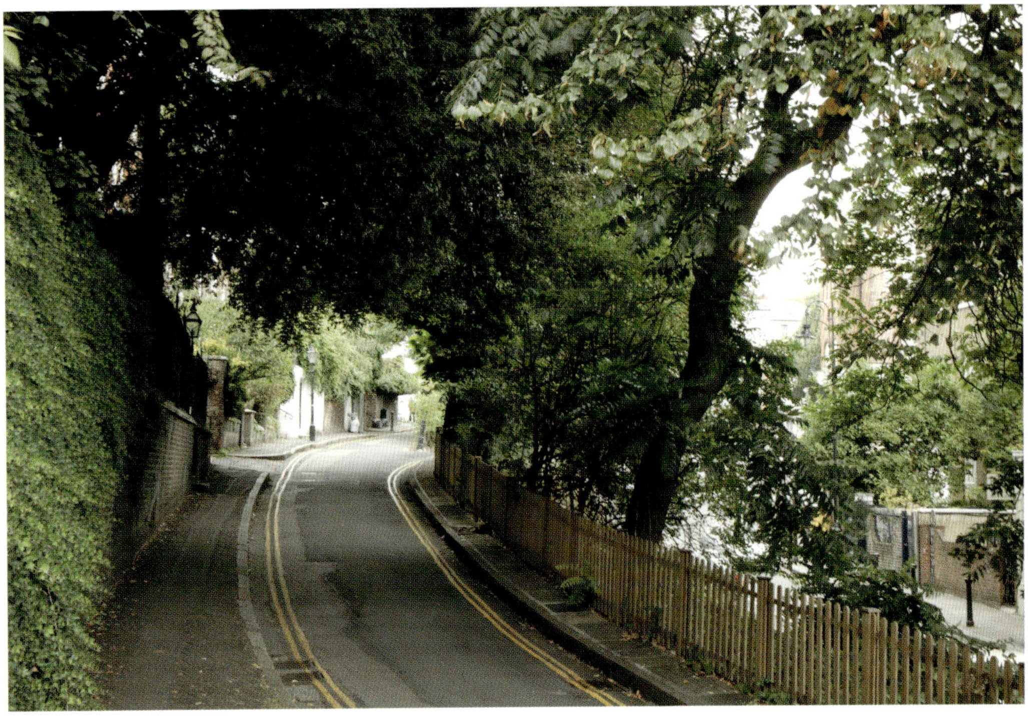

Fig. 78 (left)
Heath Street, Hampstead, from The Mount

Fig. 79 (below)
Ford Madox Brown, Sketch showing the artist painting 'Work' on his barrow, *1852, from letter to Lowes Dickinson. Princeton University Library*

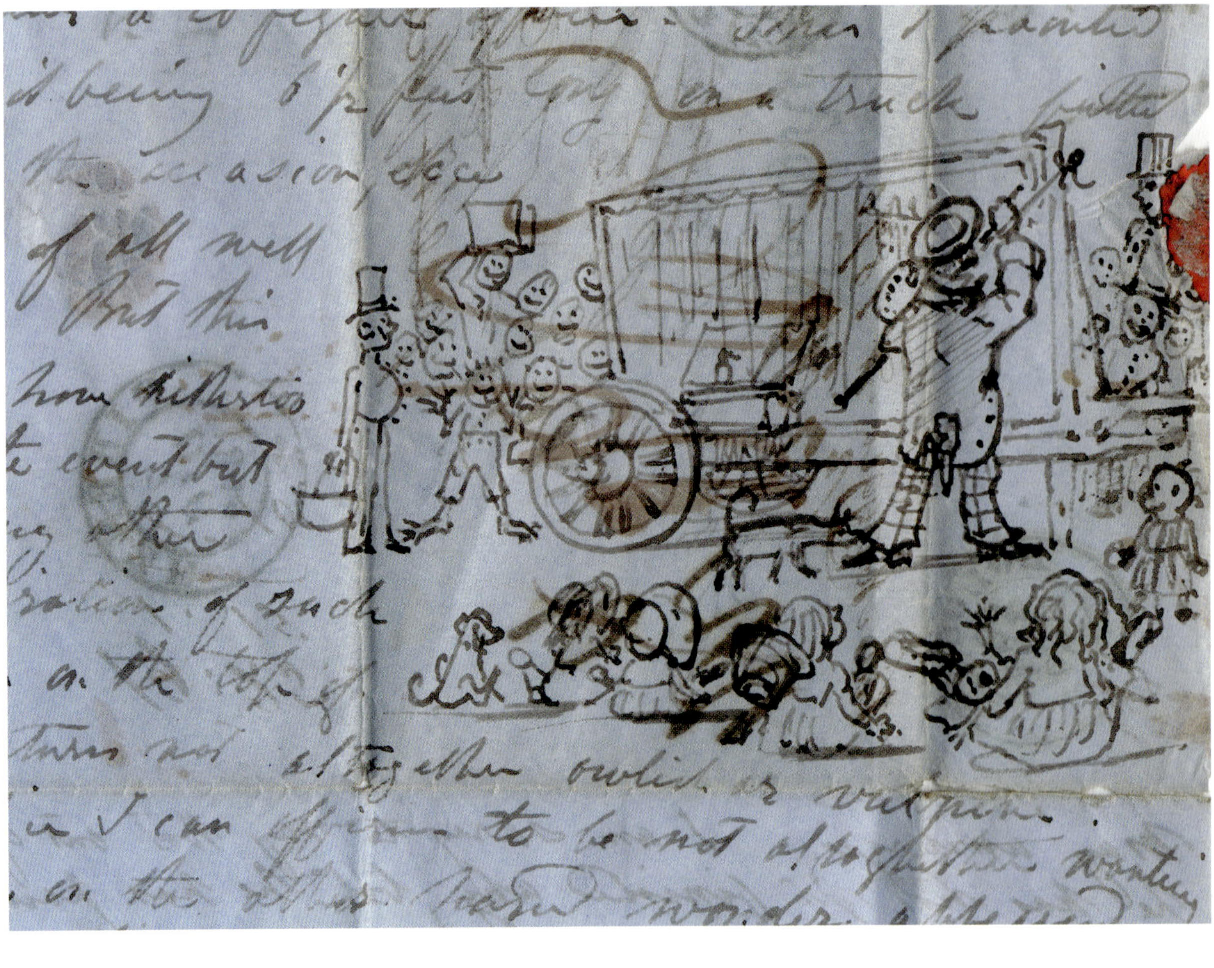

Also in the summer of 1852, Brown obtained a large canvas and took it to Heath Street to paint the background on the spot, in accordance with Pre-Raphaelite practice of working directly from nature. To do this he had to go to a great deal of trouble, mounting the canvas on a costermonger's barrow, which he fitted with curtains on hinged rods probably to protect the painting from the sun. He worked away in the street in June and July of 1852, 'much to the astonishment of all well-regulated people,' as well as of the local children who can be seen in the sketch Brown drew in a letter (fig. 79). In the same letter he described the painting as 'a twenty figure affair',[45] showing that the idea for the painting had already taken shape (probably in the lost pen and ink drawing), even though the large canvas had only the background painted into it.

Back in his studio, Brown put aside the large canvas for other pictures. He did not resume work on the project until January 1855. Between then and April 1855, he concentrated on making designs for the figures, leaving the large canvas as it was. During this period a new note entered his diary, as he took refuge from his financial and other worries in the world he was creating: 'Whenever I set to at designing it I feel in the most ethereal & extatic state possible. I do not hurry with it because it is such enjoyment.' 'Evening 4 ½ I worked at the navvies – the pot boy a triumph, the mortarman perfection & the ragged child upsetting the barrow and getting cuffed, all creations – & the whole becoming more and more exciting.' '... all day at the designe of "Work". This is now to me a species of intoxication. When I drew in the poor little vixen girl pulling her brothers hair I quite growled with delight.'[46]

The rough pencil sketch and the watercolour show that Brown's first idea was different from the finished painting. The dates of these are not known; the drawing may relate to the lost ink drawing of 1852, or it could have been done in 1855 when Brown was working on the figures. The watercolour almost certainly dates from 1864, but it is a coloured version of the first design, representing his earlier ideas and showing that the main changes were to the figures on either side. Standing on the left is a man whose shabby but modish clothes identify him as a 'gent'. With his check trousers and top hat, the gent, was an urban type much mocked in cartoons by John Leech and others.[47] Brown's gent holds a white dog under one arm. This identifies him as a street dog-seller, as described by Mayhew. Brown eventually changed him into the chickweed seller, but a torn poster on the left in the finished oil still offers a reward for a stolen dog.[48] On the right, in the place occupied by the brainworkers in the final painting, is a man with bowed head possibly smoking a cigar or cigarette, and holding his stick up with his top hat on it. This was a self-portrait of the artist himself, contemplating the scene as also depicted in some of Brown's landscapes (cats. 53, 55). There are also other differences from the finished oil in these studies: in the drawing, the background is very sketchy and Brown has not yet put in the boy delivering pastries, the temperance tracts, the dogs, the election procession, or the coach and horses. In the watercolour, the pastrycook's boy and the mongrel dog have been added, and a dog cart is dashing down the street at the right.

The changes to the figures at the sides came about as a result of the intervention of Thomas Plint, the Leeds evangelist and Pre-Raphaelite collector. In November 1856, 'Mr. Plint called, inveigled here by Gabriel Rossetti'[49] and later wrote confirming that he wished to commission the painting, but requested that Brown 'put 2 more figures in, one a young lady as a tracts or bible distributor, & the other to give more fully the idea of the *head & heart work* of the *male* sex'. Commendably, Plint was concerned that Brown should only make the additions '*consistently* with *your own concept* of the subject.'[50] In further correspondence Plint asked Brown to increase the number of figures: 'cannot you introduce *both*, Carlyle & *Kingsley*, & change one of the four *fashionable* young ladies into a *quiet, earnest, holy* looking one, with a book or two & *tracts*. I want *this* put in for I am much interested in *this* work *myself*, & know others who are.'[51] Charles Kingsley, future author of *The Water Babies*, and a campaigner for sanitary reform, was, like Maurice, a founder member of the Christian Socialists, and would have been an appropriate choice. It is not clear why in the end Maurice was decided on; perhaps Kingsley was not willing to sit, or maybe Maurice was Brown's preference. At any rate, Plint's intervention made the religious and moral aspects of the painting more explicit

Such requests for changes were not unusual at this period. Brown's Newcastle patron James Leathart (see cat. 89) commissioned him to paint a reduced version of *Work* incorporating his wife's portrait as one of the fashionable ladies (Birmingham Museums and Art Gallery)[52] and Holman Hunt repainted the face of the woman in *The Awakening Conscience* (Tate) at the request of his patron Thomas Fairbairn, who found her expression too painful.[53] Plint's support gave Brown the financial means to continue work on the painting. But Plint died unexpectedly in 1861, and his executors repudiated the commission, which was then taken over by the dealer Ernest Gambart. Brown completed *Work* in August 1863. But Gambart's plan to have *Work* engraved and to exhibit the painting in London fell through, and eventually Brown organised an exhibition of his own in 1865 with *Work* as the centrepiece.

65

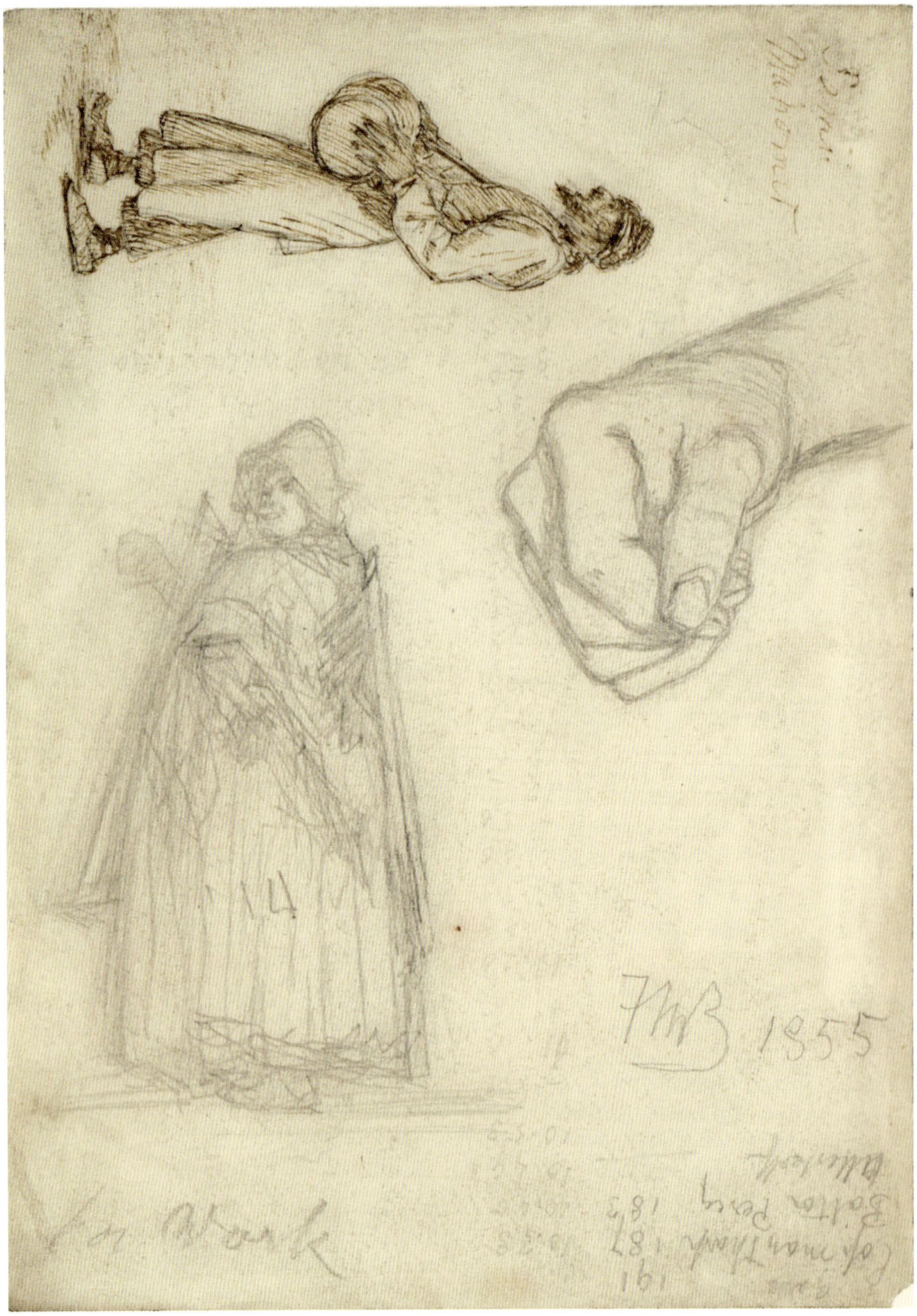

65
SHEET OF STUDIES FOR 'WORK'

(A59.15)
probably late 1850s
pencil and ink, 4⅞ × 6⅞ (12.4 × 17.5)
signed and dated (possibly at a later date): *FMB 1855*
Tate. Presented by Edmund Houghton 1898

The study on the left is for the old woman in the background who has volunteered to carry one of the sandwich boards for the election. On the right of the sheet is a study of the right hand of the chickweed seller. The drawing at the top is for a drummer in oriental costume, and may be the 'hindoo nigger' included in a list of characters (not all of them used in the final painting) written by Brown on the top left of the canvas, in an area now concealed by the arch of the frame.

66

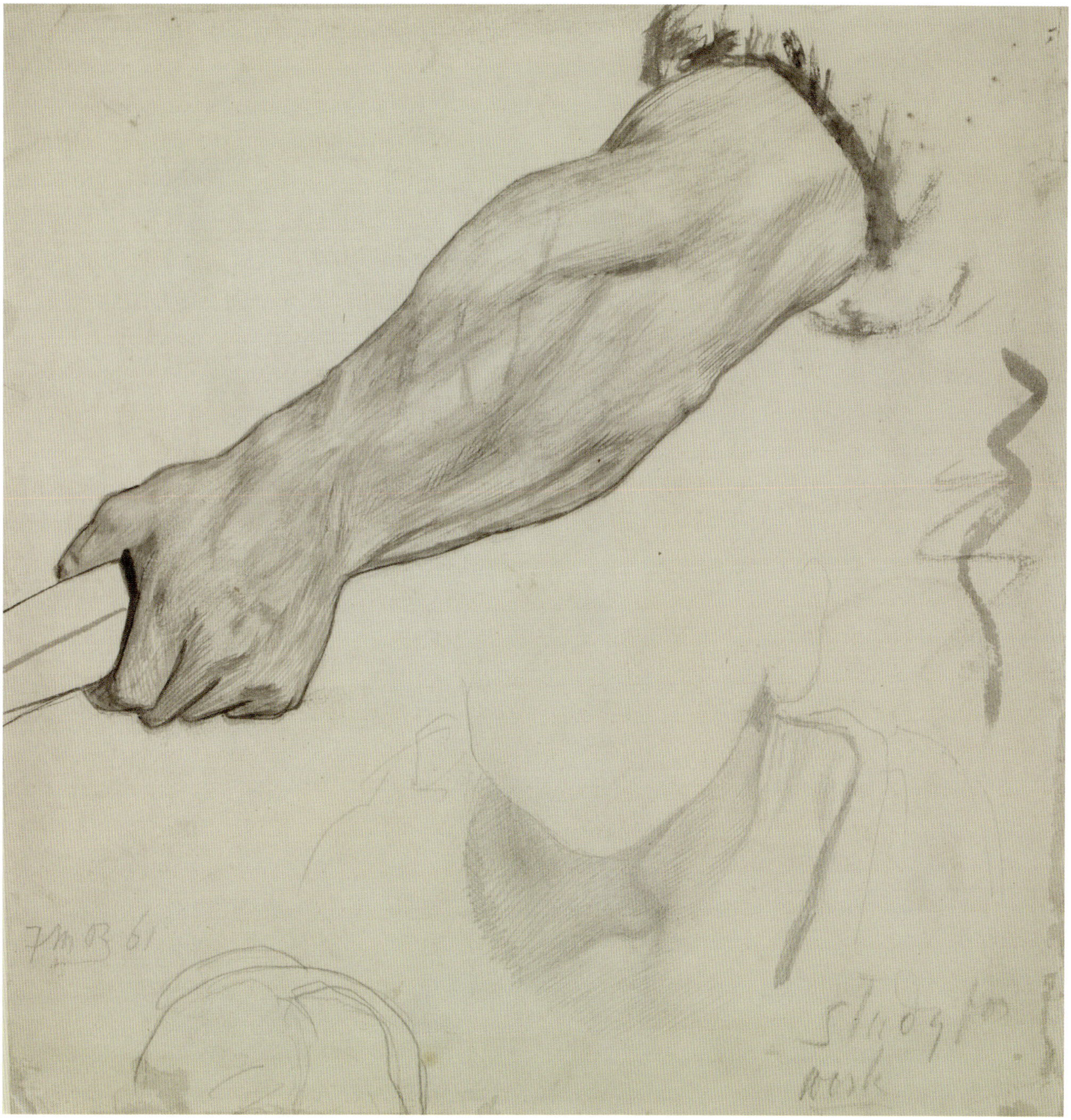

66

STUDY OF THE NAVVY'S ARM

(A59.16)
probably late 1850s
pencil and wash, 9¼ × 9 (23.5 × 22.9)
signed and dated (possibly at a later date): *FMB 61*
The British Museum, London

This is a study of the powerfully built arm of the navvy shovelling earth through the sieve. It must be a life study and was probably drawn from one of the people that Brown found in the streets and asked to pose for him: in 1857 he drew 'the man with the hod, chiefly in the open air from a navvy I had met in the streets.'[54] Below is a sketch for the chin and neck of the chickweed seller.

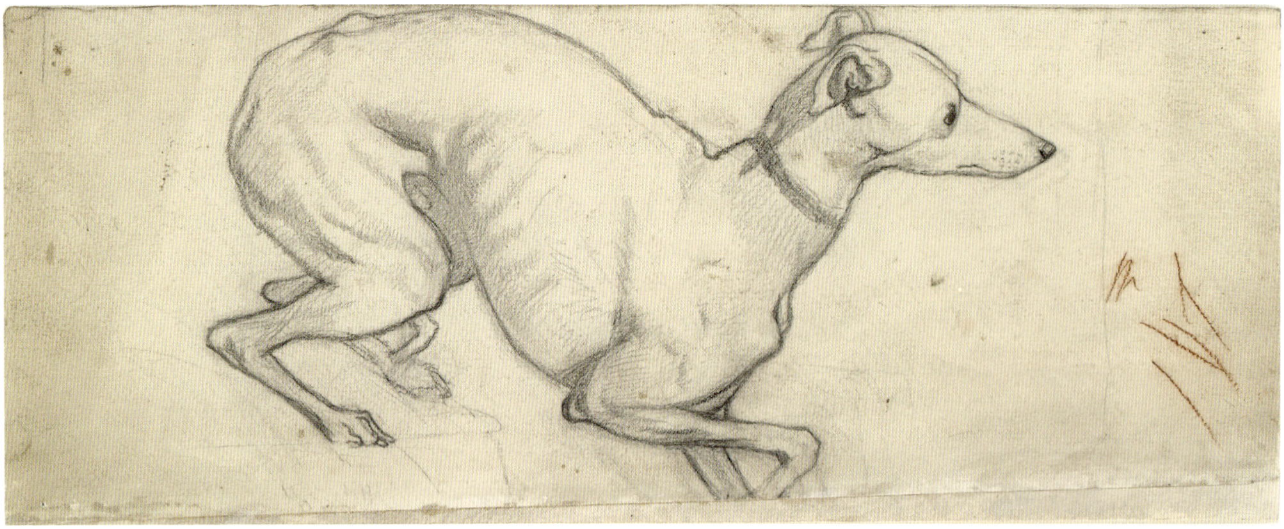

67

67
CARTOON FOR THE GREYHOUND

(A59.14)
probably late 1850s
pencil, 5⅞ × 15⅜ (15 × 39)
Ashmolean Museum, Oxford. Presented anonymously in memory of James Bannantyne Stewart Robertson 1966

68
CARTOON FOR THE BULL-TERRIER PUP

(A59.12)
probably late 1850s
pencil, 5 × 7 (12.7 × 17.8)
signed and dated (possibly at a later date): *FMB/55 / Bull Dog*
Manchester City Galleries

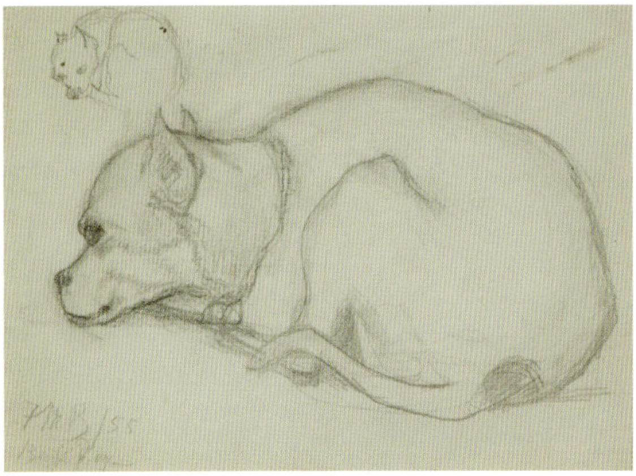

68

69
CARTOON FOR THE MONGREL

(A59.13)
probably late 1850s
pencil, 9 × 5½ (22.8 × 14)
signed bottom left (possibly at a later date): *FMB/64*
Manchester City Galleries

The dogs in the painting reflect the class and character of their owners (in addition to the three dogs in these studies, there is a black spaniel in front of the woman on horseback at the rear). The greyhound belongs to the younger of the rich ladies, and in the painting wears a red jacket, equivalent to the fashionable clothes of its mistress. The bull-terrier pup echoes the character of 'the selfish old bachelor navvy' and 'instinctively distrusts outlandish-looking dogs in red jackets.' The mongrel belongs to the poor children and 'is evidently of the same outcast sort as themselves … he frequently fights, as by his torn ear you may know … rugged democrat as he is, he is gentle with them, only he hates minions of aristocracy in red jackets.' Could Brown be thinking of himself in this canine character sketch?

The cartoon for the greyhound is outlined on reverse in red chalk for transfer to the canvas. Brown refers to painting one of the dogs into the canvas in 1857,[55] but the exact dates of the drawings are not known.

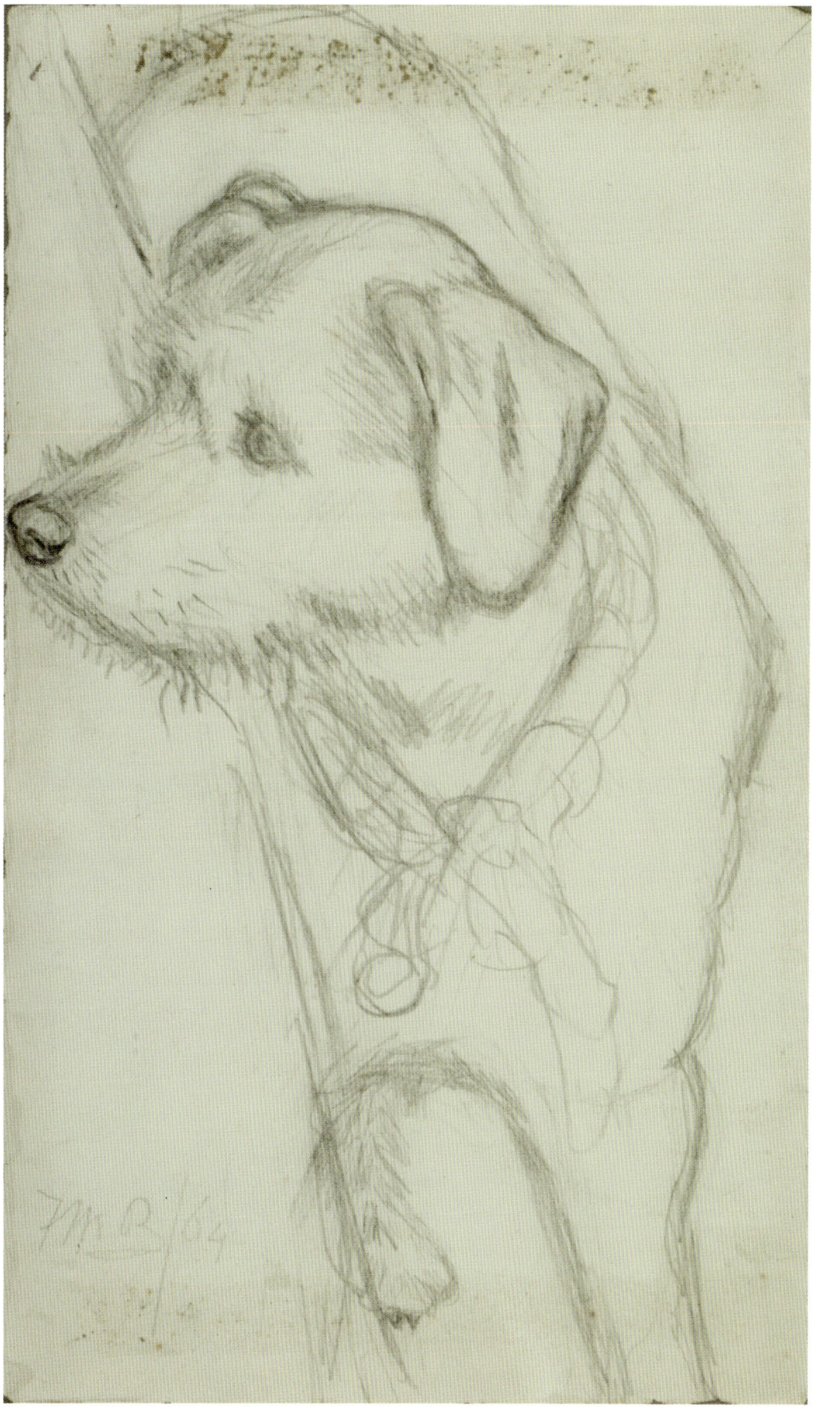

69

70

CARTOON FOR THE NAVVY DRINKING BEER

(A59. 9)
probably late 1850s
black chalk, 15½ × 9½ (39.3 × 24.1)
Manchester City Galleries

This cut-out drawing is the same size as the figure in the painting. The lines are drawn both on the front and on the back, where they are thicker to enable Brown to transfer the outline on to the canvas. There is a similar cut-out for the same figure in the Ashmolean Museum, but apart from this no others exist, although Brown may have made more for other people in the painting. His diary refers to arranging 'the chief navvy tossing off the beer' in January 1855 but none of the figures were transferred to the canvas until early in 1857 when Brown wrote he was 'drawing in the figures in pencil without nature.'[56] Brown recorded that the man with the hod was drawn from a real workman and not a professional model, and the same might be the case here, although Brown may have also had in mind a similar figure in Hogarth's *Beer Street* (fig. 80).

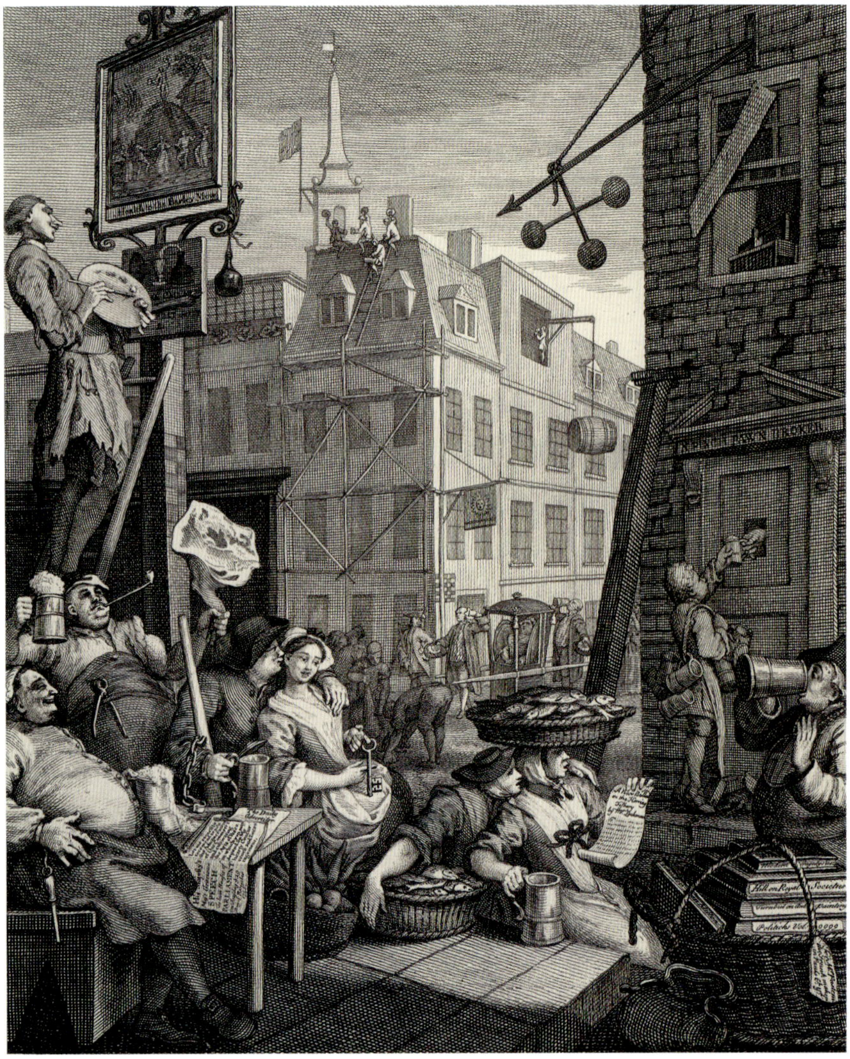

Fig. 80
William Hogarth, Beer Street, *1751.*
The British Museum, London

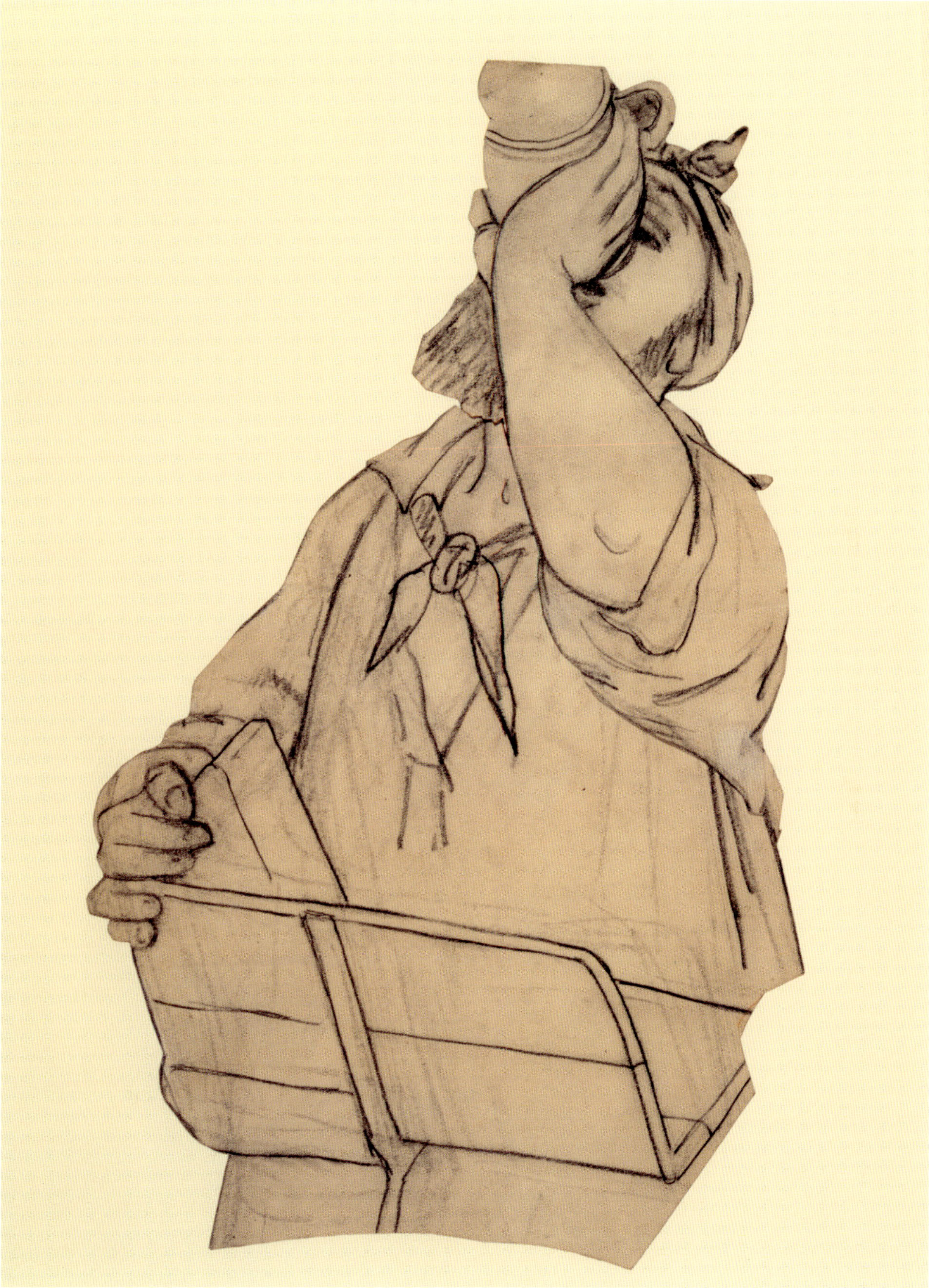

70

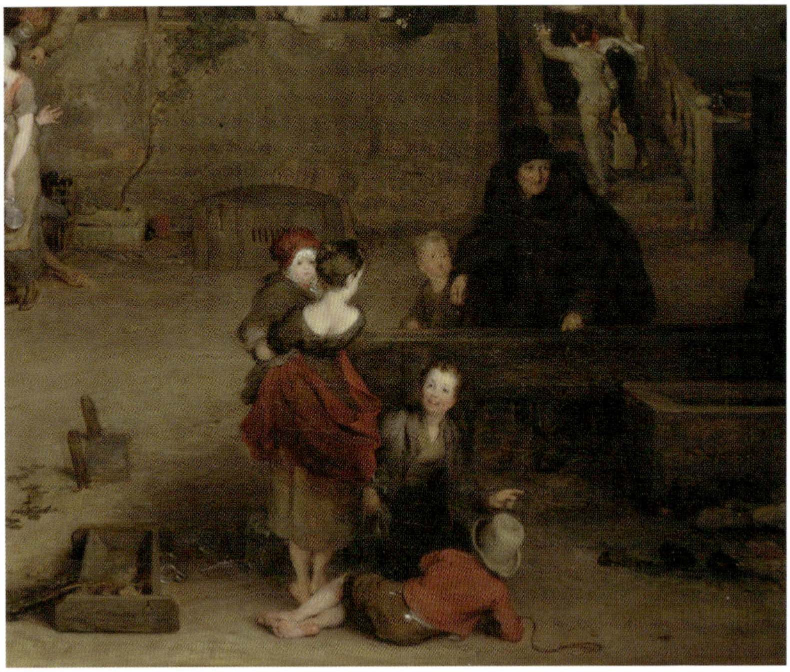

Fig. 81
David Wilkie, detail of The Village Festival, *1809–11. Tate*

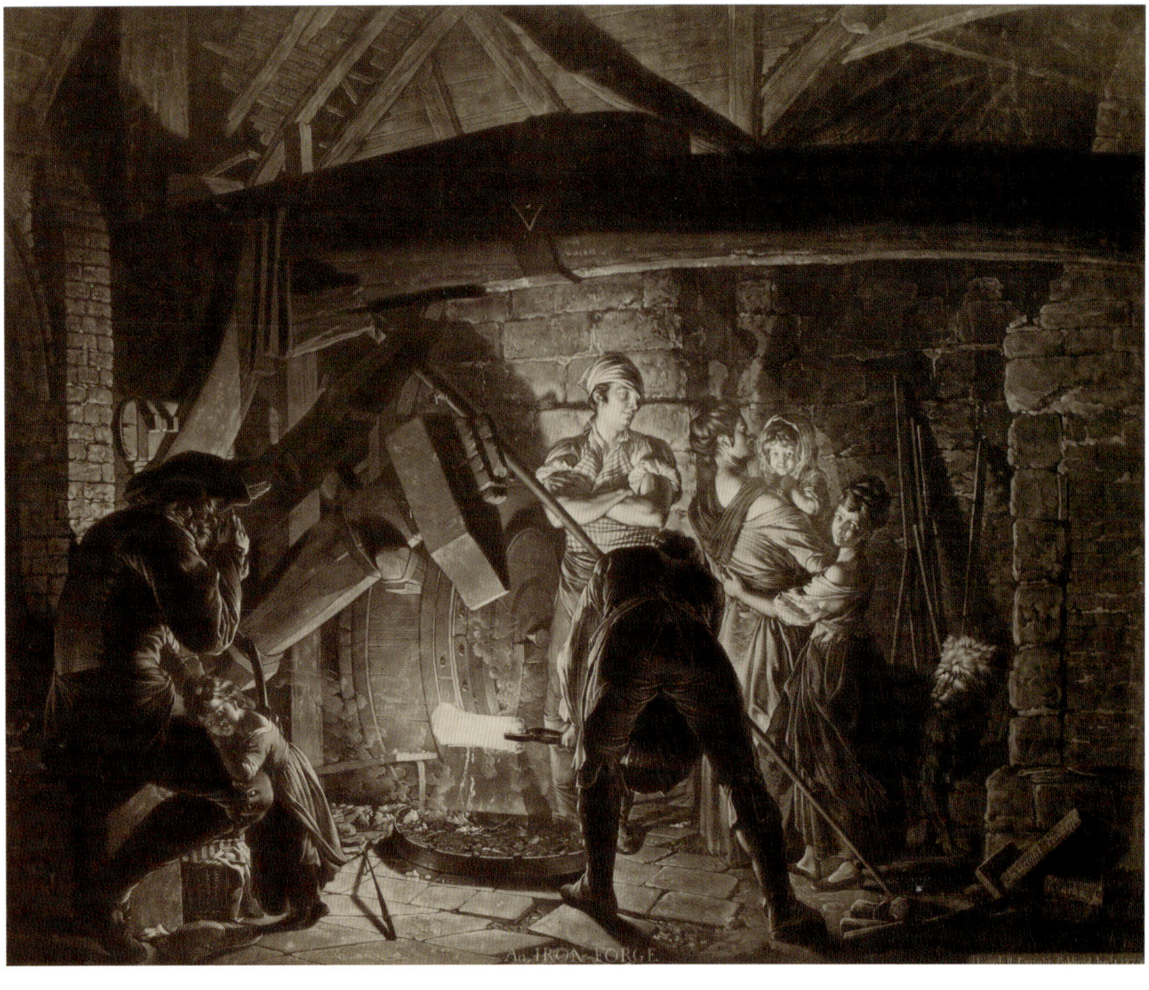

Fig. 82
Joseph Wright of Derby (engraved by Richard Earlom), An Iron Forge, *1773. The British Museum, London*

71

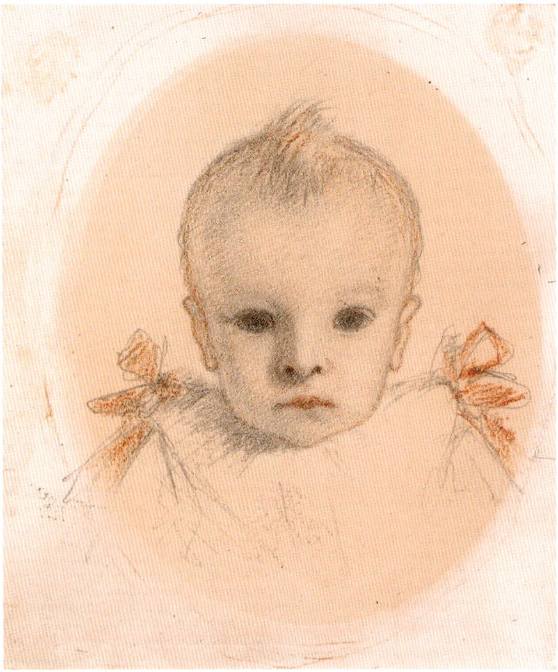

72

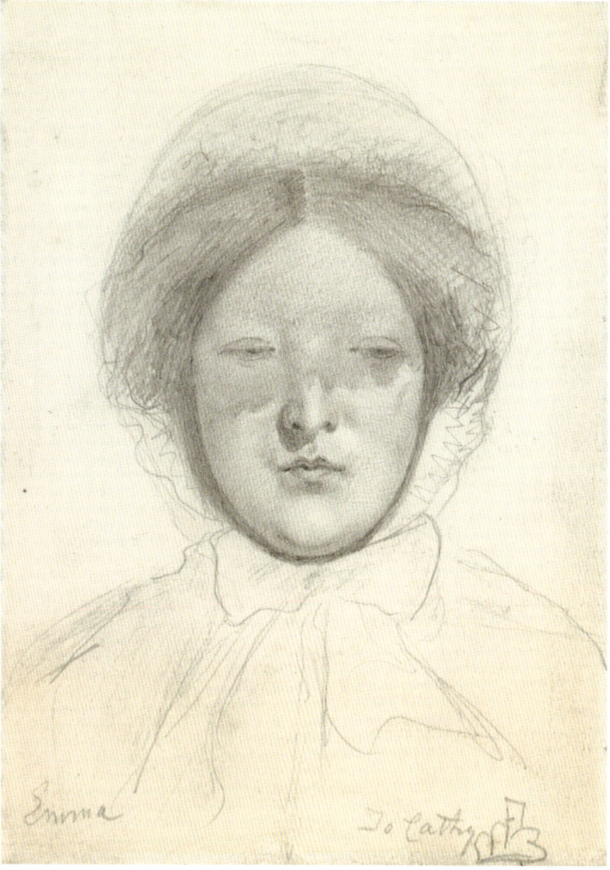

71

STUDY FOR THE BABY

(A59.7)
1857
coloured chalks, $4\frac{3}{4} \times 3\frac{7}{8}$ (12×9.8)
National Museums Liverpool, Walker Art Gallery. Purchased with the assistance of the Art Fund 1984

Brown's son Arthur, who died in July 1857 aged only ten months (see cat. 9), was portrayed as one of the poor children. Brown's description of *Work* calls him: 'the sunburned baby which looks wonderfully solemn and intellectual' and 'has even been put into poor mourning for mother'. The red ribbons on this drawing have been changed to black in the painting. Brown's diary recalled how he 'drew in poor little Arthur's head for the baby and began painting it the day he was taken ill & had to rub out what I had done.'[57]

The pose of the ragged girl seen from behind with the baby in her arms may be derived from the similar group of children in the foreground to David Wilkie's *The Village Festival* (Tate, but at that time in the National Gallery, fig. 81). There is also a similar figure group in Joseph Wright of Derby's *An Iron Forge* (Broadlands collection) which Brown could have known from the engraving by Richard Earlom (fig. 82). Brown could well have turned to this because, like *Work*, it is a scene showing manual labour; indeed, Wright's iron-founder, with his hair tied up in a kerchief may have provided the inspiration for Brown's hero navvy.

72

STUDY FOR THE LADY WITH THE PARASOL

(A59.11)
probably late 1850s
pencil, $6\frac{7}{8} \times 4\frac{7}{8}$ (17.5×12.5)
signed in monogram: *FMB* (also inscribed probably at a later date: *Emma / To Cathy*)
National Museums Liverpool, Walker Art Gallery. Purchased with the assistance of the Art Fund 1984

Emma was the model for the 'beauteous tripping dame with bell-like skirts, Intent on the small scarlet-coated hound,' as she was described in Brown's sonnet. Her eyes look down towards the dog and her face is partially shaded by her parasol; Brown took care to observe the exact outline of the shadow cast on to Emma's face by the frilly edge of the parasol. Plint, who had complained of the Pre-Raphaelites' tendency to paint 'ugly female faces' wrote to Brown, 'I am sure you will get two or three pretty models for the young ladies in my picture, and don't have red hair please!!'[58]

73

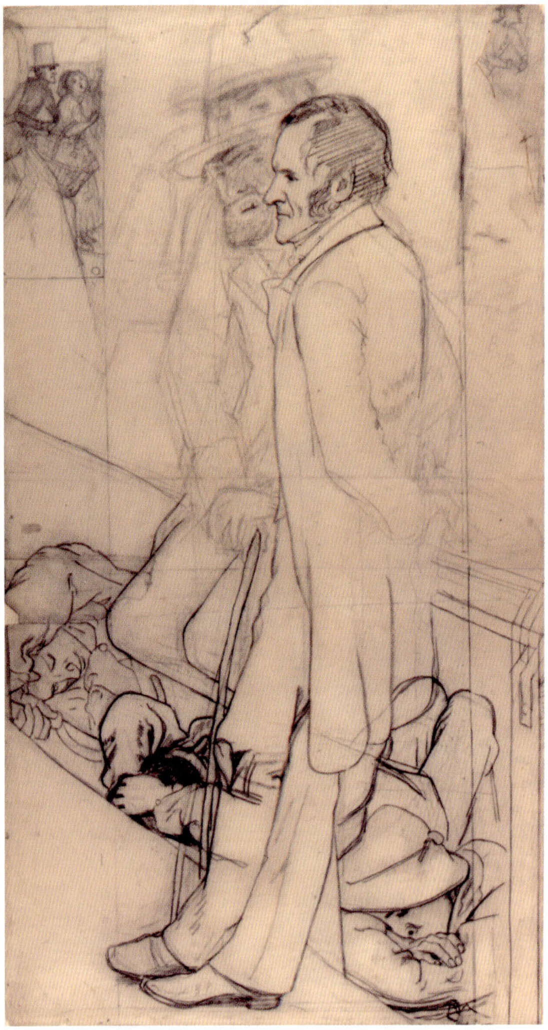

74

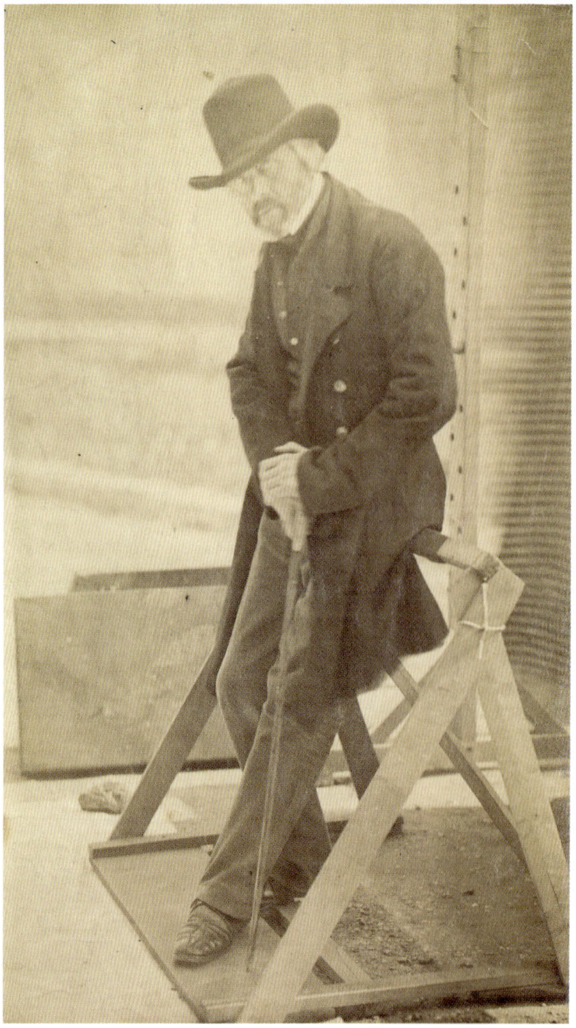

73

CARTOON FOR FREDERICK MAURICE AND THOMAS CARLYLE

(A59. 10)
1858
pencil, 32 11/16 × 17 13/16 (83 × 45.3)
Manchester City Galleries

74

PHOTOGRAPH OF THOMAS CARLYLE

photograph by Thomson, commissioned by Brown
1859
albumen print, 12 5/16 × 7¼ (31.2 × 18.5)
Birmingham Museums and Art Gallery

The portraits of Carlyle and Maurice gave Brown some difficulties. On 27 January 1858 he recorded spending 'all last week in trying to compose Carlyle & Maurice'. A few days later, Maurice gave Brown short sittings, posed against a wooden rail made by the artist, but after he had drawn him into the painting he found 'it looks rediculously stumpy & the head enormous. I must either falsify it or make the head bigger' and so went out 'to see about a photographer for Maurice.'[59]

These difficulties are reflected in the cartoon. Although it shows the two brainworkers the same size as in the painting, there are some differences. In the drawing, Carlyle is sitting on the railing with both his knees bent and his head is on a level with Maurice's, but Brown partly erased Carlyle's head and sketched it again higher up: in the finished painting, Carlyle is standing and is taller than Maurice. In the drawing Maurice leans back on the railing holding a book behind him, as in the painting. The drawing also shows the sleeping harvesters, although without the scythe wrapped in rope seen in the painting. Also in the drawing, top left, is a sketch of the policeman and the orange seller.

No photograph of Maurice posing for *Work* can be traced but the photograph of Carlyle leaning on a wooden railing is a rare survival, showing how a photograph could be used in a like manner to a preparatory drawing, a practice probably more widespread among Victorian painters than is now apparent. Carlyle had at first refused to sit and be drawn by Brown, because he was too busy, but he eventually agreed to have his photograph taken. In the meantime, Brown had drawn both men onto the canvas: Carlyle was portrayed with his mouth open, in the act of speaking to Maurice. The painting was seen by the artist G.P. Boyce in Brown's studio in December 1858, and was also seen by Holman Hunt who described Carlyle's expression as a 'horrid grimace.'[60] Brown then arranged for Carlyle to be photographed on 12 May 1859 at Mr Thomson's Photographic Establishment in South Kensington.[61] This probably refers to Charles Thurston Thomson of 7 Gordon Terrace, Kensington, the official photographer to the South Kensington Museum. In the photograph Carlyle's hands are in a different position from the painting, and he has his mouth shut, but Brown kept to the open-mouthed portrait in the final painting, and the likeness was approved by Rossetti who wrote 'Your new Carlyle is a vast improvement.'[62]

In the exhibition catalogue, Brown did not name the two brainworkers who 'seeming to be idle, work and are the cause of well-ordained work in others,' but even if contemporaries did not recognize them in the painting, he included clues to their identities in his commentary. He compared one to a 'Sage' (Carlyle was known as 'the Sage of Chelsea'), and mentioned his 'wild sallies and cynical thrusts'; the other was described as 'a clergyman ... a gentleman without pride, much in communion with the working classes ... Scholar, author, philosopher and teacher too in his way, but not above practical efforts, if even for a small result, in good.'

1 *Diary*, p. 78.
2 *Diary*, p. 114.
3 Bennett 2010, I, p. 135–36, A58.1.
4 A number of variants of the Leningrad composition are listed in Loewinson-Lessing and Nicouline 1965, pp. 16–17. I am grateful to Dr. Lorne Campbell for help with this.
5 *Diary*, p. 78.
6 Townsend, Ridge & Hackney 2004, p. 155.
7 NML, FMB to George Rae 26 December 1863.
8 Manchester Art Gallery, *Ford Madox Brown and the Pre-Raphaelites*, 1911, no. 93.
9 *Diary*, p. 186.
10 Plumb 1969, p. 30.
11 *Encyclopedia Britannica* 14th edition 1929, 15, 469.
12 Brown 1865, no, 14.
13 Bennett 2010, I, p. 174, A61.5.
14 Stammers 1978, p. 451. Woolner travelled by steamer to Plymouth where he transferred to a sailing ship bound for Australia, but it was more usual to set sail for Australia out of Gravesend. I am also grateful to Michael Stammers for his identification of various features in the painting.
15 Brown 1865, no, 14.
16 Patmore 1857.
17 *Diary*, pp. 151, 153.
18 *Diary*, p. 80.
19 *Diary*, p. 93.
20 *Diary*, p. 127.
21 *Diary*, pp. 138–39.
22 *Diary*, pp. 152–53.
23 Bennett 2010, I, p. 167.
24 I am grateful to Michael Stammers for this information.
25 Brown 1865, no. 14.
26 *Diary*, p. 178.
27 Curtis 1992, p. 630.
28 *Diary*, pp. 178, 183.
29 NML, FMB to George Rae, undated, probably May 1864.
30 Carlyle 1843, pp. 190, 223.
31 Brown 1865.
32 Curtis 1992, p. 630, n. 46 discusses and convincingly rejects the idea that the boy carries a bar of soap.
33 *Diary*, p. 96.
34 Sonnet for *Work*, printed in *Exhibition* 1865 and reprinted here.
35 Curtis 1992, pp. 632–35.
36 Walker 2006, p. 73.
37 *Diary*, p. 196, 17 March 1857.
38 Curtis 1992, p. 632.
39 *Punch* 19, 1850, p. 30.
40 Walker 2006, pp. 75–76.
41 Hueffer 1896, p. 196.
42 Brown planted fuchsia on the grave of his first wife, *Diary*, p. 18.
43 Arscott 1979, cited by Walker 2006, p. 65.
44 Hueffer 1896, p. 415.
45 Princeton, FMB to Lowes Dickinson, 17 October 1852.
46 *Diary*, pp. 113, 114, 135.
47 Cowling p. 120.
48 Curtis 1992 pp. 633–35 speculates on who stole the dog.
49 *Diary*, p. 192.
50 V&A, Thomas Plint to FMB, 17 November 1856.
51 V&A, Thomas Plint to FMB, 24 November 1856. Plint's reference to four ladies is probably a mistake.
52 Bennett 2010, I, pp. 150–51, A59.3.
53 Bronkhurst 2006, I, p. 168.
54 *Diary*, p. 199–200.
55 *Diary*, p. 198.
56 *Diary*, pp. 113, 194.
57 *Diary*, p. 198.
58 Hueffer 1896, pp. 165–66.
59 *Diary*, pp. 200–1.
60 Boyce 1980, p. 25; Hueffer 1896, p. 164 (4 May 1859).
61 Carlyle 2007, pp. 88–91.
62 D.G. Rossetti, *Correspondence*, 2, p. 259 (22 June 1859).

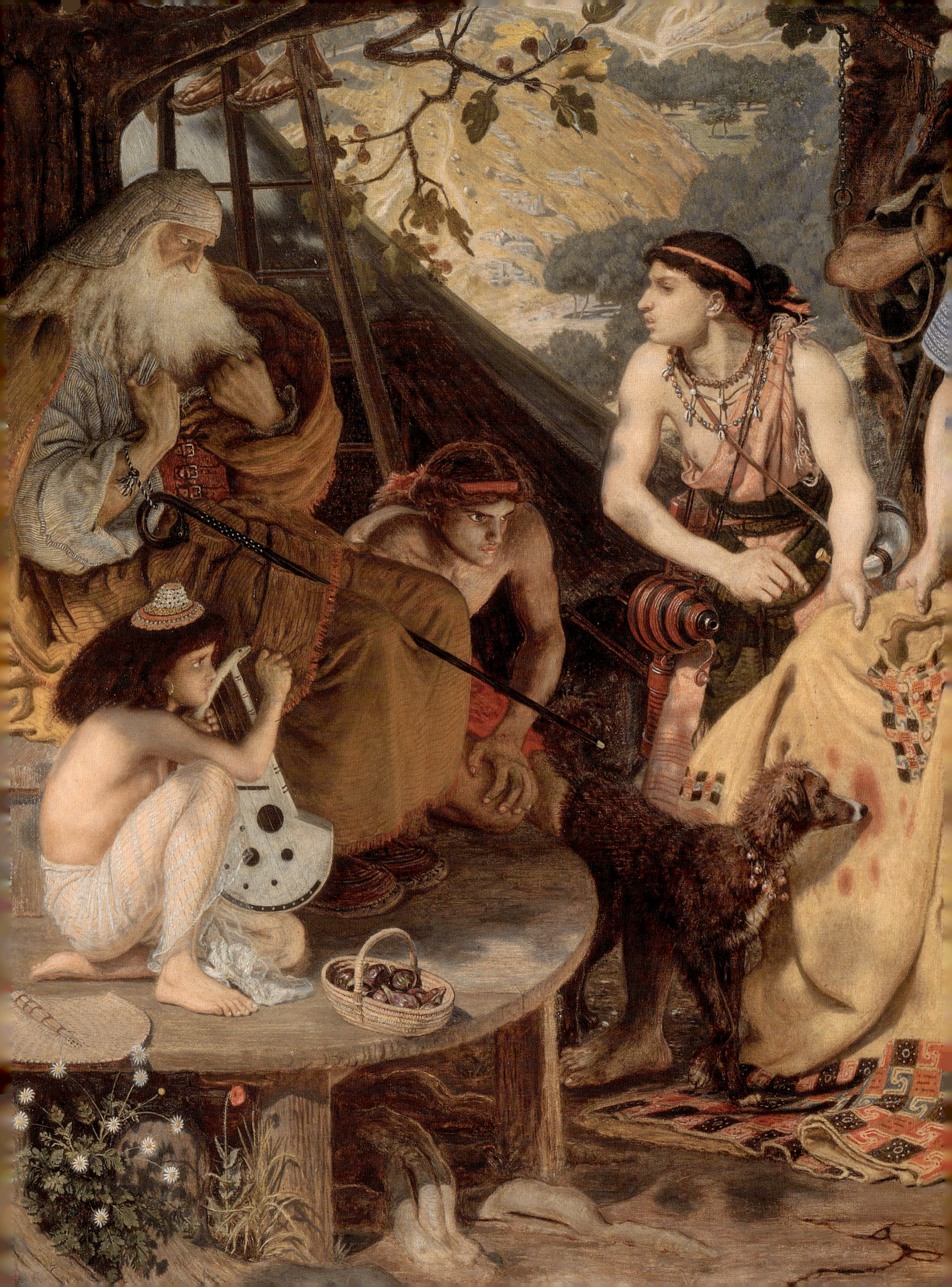

THE STORYTELLER

Brown's ability to tell a story in a picture was an element of continuity that ran through the stylistic changes from his early romantic manner, through Pre-Raphaelite sharpness and brightness to his late style of flowing lines and muted colours. In narrative painting he could combine the skills of the history painter with his love of literature; he could convey a dramatic situation, portray character and milieu, and suggest in a single image events that might have happened before and after the moment depicted. This facility for storytelling can be seen in his modern subjects as well as the paintings and drawings in historical settings.

Brown was an avid reader and at various times in his career he depicted scenes from his favourite authors Byron and Shakespeare. *King Lear* held a special fascination for him, and he returned to it at different times in his career. The writings of Thomas Carlyle were also a crucial source of inspiration. Carlyle's *Lectures on Heroes* included Shakespeare in the section on 'The Hero as Poet', and put forward 'The Hero as Man of Letters' as a modern equivalent of the divinities, prophets and priests of the past: Brown depicted Carlyle himself as such a hero in *Work*. Another of Carlyle's heroes, Oliver Cromwell, became the subject of one of Brown's most powerful late paintings (cat. 87).

Christ was conspicuously absent from Carlyle's *Lectures on Heroes*. Although Brown was in youth and early manhood a conventional member of the Church of England, by the time of his death he had become an agnostic and was buried with a secular rite. Nevertheless, he painted a number of religious subjects. His early religious paintings came from his experience of Italian and Flemish art and were more about archaism than devotion. Most of his later religious subjects did not originate in his own ideas, but were the result of commissions from others; the majority were stained glass designs for William Morris but Brown also contributed to an illustrated Bible. However, his most important and original religious painting, *Jesus washing Peter's Feet* (cat. 75), was his own conception; it depicts Christ as a hero in society, emphasizing his humility rather than his divinity. This painting, and his depiction of Wycliffe reading the Bible (cat. 33), suggest that Brown admired the Bible for its moral and literary content and not as a source of religious doctrine.

In this section works are grouped by source, with religious subjects first, followed by Shakespeare, Byron and subjects from other authors.

Fig. 83
Detail of cat. 76, The Coat of Many Colours

75

JESUS WASHING PETER'S FEET

(A57)
1851–52, 1854, 1856, (1857, 1858)
oil on canvas, 45¾ × 52¼ (116.2 × 132.7)
signed and dated: *F. Madox Brown 1852–/56*
Tate. Presented by subscribers 1893

The message of this subject, chosen by Brown from the New Testament, is the lesson of humility given by Jesus after the Last Supper. 'He riseth from supper, and laid aside his garments; and took a towel and girded himself. After that he poureth water into a basin, and began to wash the disciples' feet, and to wipe them with a towel wherewith he was girded. For I have given you an example, that ye should do as I have done unto you' (John, 13:4–5, 15).

Brown concentrates attention on the washing of the feet, right in the centre of the picture. The principal figures of Jesus and Peter have been pushed towards the front, filling the canvas from top to bottom, with the apostles placed much further back. Jesus kneels below the platform on which the table is standing, his upper body highlighted against the white tablecloth. He bends his head forward in self-abasement as he wipes Peter's feet with a cloth. Peter also bows his head in 'intense veneration.'[1] The heads of Jesus and Peter, the lines of their limbs and the gazes of the apostles lead the eye to the centre of the painting, the point where Jesus grasps Peter's foot. The other apostles look on with expressions varying from concentration to disbelief. Only two are identifiable, the young St. John looking eagerly from the right, and the red-haired Judas on the left, tying his sandal after his feet have been washed, his money in a purse on the table. The apostles wear richly coloured draperies, but only Peter's sash, of vaguely Middle Eastern design, suggests the Biblical period. The green water jar and copper bowl give an impression of an earlier time, but the blue and white pots on the table strike an odd note: this may be a deliberate anachronism to suggest timelessness.[2]

The apostles are portraits, although the identity of some of the models is disputed. Those recognisable are F.G. Stephens as Jesus, William Michael Rossetti as the second apostle from the left, the poet and translator C.B. Cayley (fig. 109, p. 297) as the blonde man in the centre and next, on the right, D.G. Rossetti. St. John may be a portrait of Walter Deverell.

The painting gave Brown much trouble. In November 1851 he visited the farm in Ewell, where Millais and Hunt were painting the backgrounds to *Ophelia* (Tate) and *The Hireling Shepherd* (Manchester City Galleries). There he saw them using the new technique of painting on a wet white ground to make flesh and other colours look more vivid, and Millais explained the process to him, although Hunt had wanted to keep it a secret.[3] Brown enthusiastically adopted it for *Jesus washing Peter's Feet*. He began the work in his studio in late 1851 but had to finish it in a great rush in the spring of 1852, as he had left only ten days to paint the heads in time to submit it for the Royal Academy Summer Exhibition. He recorded in his diary his frustration when the method went wrong: 'This picture was painted in four months, the flesh painted on *wet white* at Millais' lying instigation, Roberson's Medium, which I think dangerous like Millais's advice.'[4] Roberson's medium was a type of varnish, commonly used by artists in the nineteenth century. It made paint easy to handle, prevented dripping or flowing, and gave an attractive glowing quality to the pigment; according to Hunt, the flesh in Brown's painting looked streaky because the colours had not blended with the wet white, and some of the paint had not had time to dry.[5]

When the painting was first exhibited, at the Royal Academy of 1852 it showed Jesus wearing only a towel around his waist, and his torso and legs were naked. This was Brown's interpretation of the text quoted above: Jesus 'laid aside his garments; and took a towel and girded himself'. But the critics found the semi-naked Christ undignified, and the flesh colours livid and purple. The academicians also took exception to it, hanging it high, and

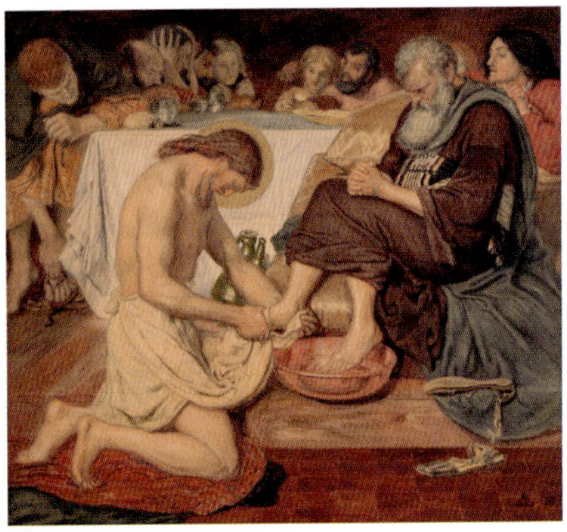

Fig. 84
Ford Madox Brown, Jesus washing Peter's Feet, *watercolour version 1876. Manchester City Galleries*

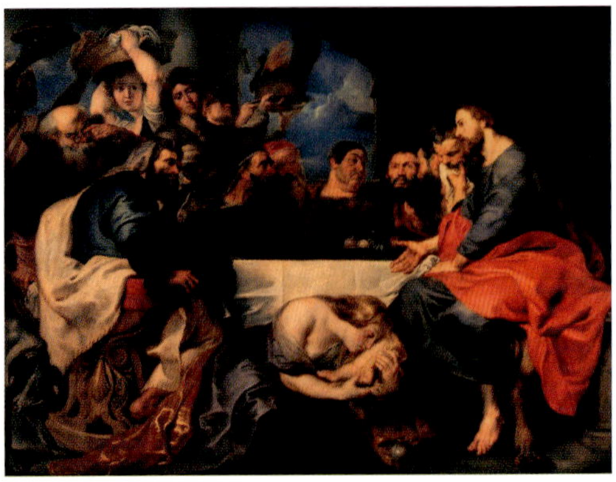

Fig. 85
Peter Paul Rubens, Feast in the House of Simon the Pharisee, *1618/20. State Hermitage Museum, St. Petersburg*

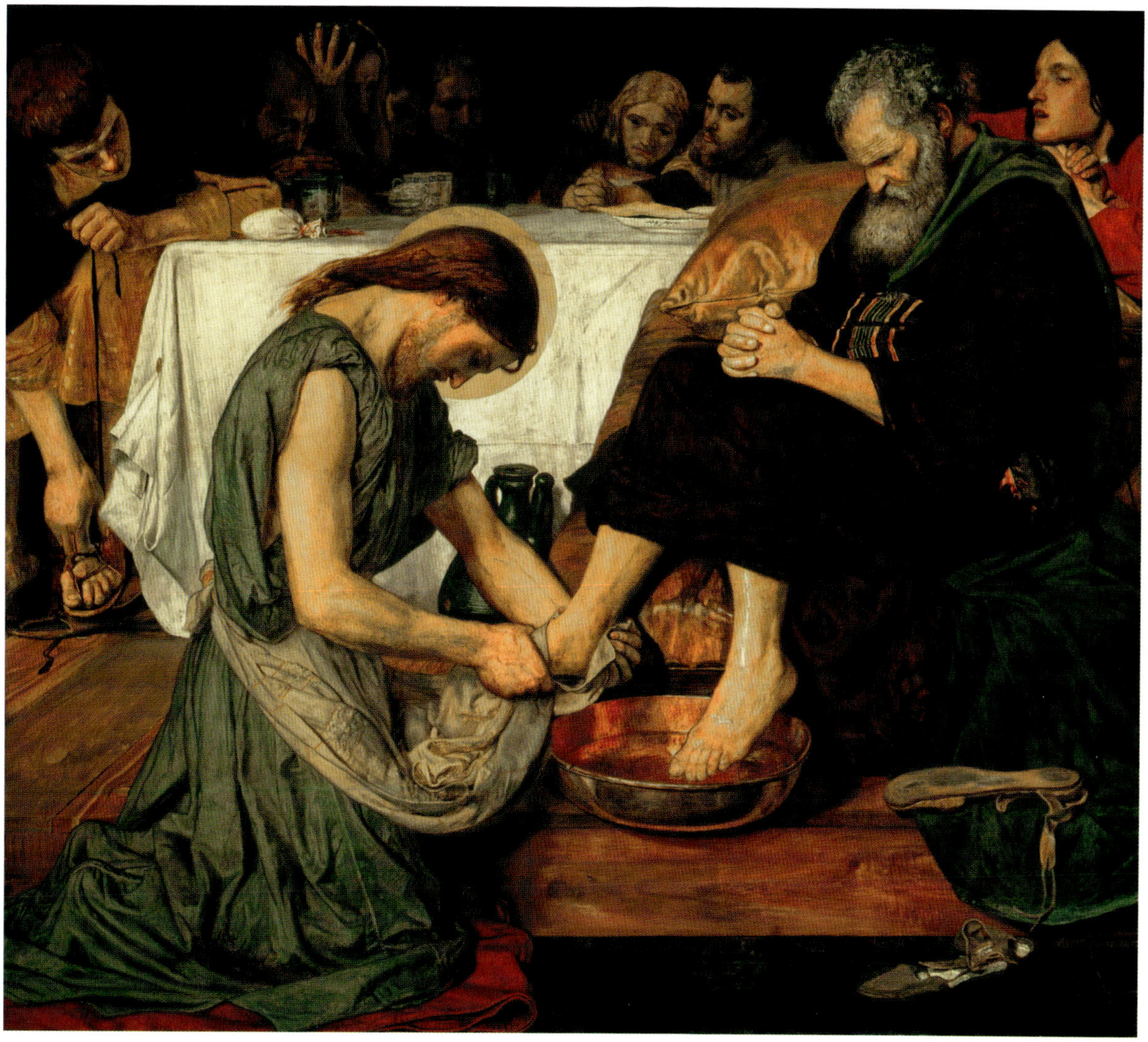

75

Brown refused to accept their apologies. Dissatisfied with his creation, Brown reworked it in December 1854 and again in the summer of 1856, when he added clothes to Christ's upper body and cut out his legs, inserting new canvas on which he painted the draperies now covering the legs. This caused fresh difficulties, still apparent in the unrealistically short legs under the robe, and in the uncertain placing of Christ's body relative to that of Peter. Nevertheless, when sent to the Liverpool Academy exhibition of 1856 it won the main prize of £50, and the following year after being shown in the Manchester Art Treasures exhibition, it was bought by Plint. Brown later made two watercolour versions of which one (fig. 84) shows Christ's body naked as originally intended.[6]

In *Jesus washing Peter's Feet*, Brown attempted to recreate an Old Master painting for the nineteenth century. He combined the monumental figures, rich colour and solemnity of a Titian or Tintoretto with a modern realism, although less dense with detail than the modern-life subjects. Brown may have used as his starting point a painting by Rubens, *Feast in the House of Simon the Pharisee* (fig. 85) which was engraved in the *Art Journal* for 1851. But he transformed his sources with a modern egalitarian message of his own: the subject, reversing the roles of master and servant, and emphasizing the sanctity of menial labour, complements that of *Work*, begun at about the same time. Jesus is shown with a halo, the clothing is generalised as in Old Master paintings, and despite the relatively small size of the canvas, Brown gave the figures an appearance of breadth and grandeur, so much so that Vernon Lushington felt that 'the picture seemed scarcely tall enough; I was afraid the apostles might bump their heads against the ceiling, if they rose suddenly to their full height.' But Lushington also felt that 'The simplicity & religious feeling in it reminds of the early Italian painters.'[7]

76
THE COAT OF MANY COLOURS

(A83)
1864-66, (1869)
oil on canvas, 42½ × 40⅝ (108 × 103.2)
signed and dated: *F.MADOX BROWN /66*
National Museums Liverpool, Walker Art Gallery. Presented by Eleanor Coltart 1904

Joseph's coat of many colours was a gift from his father Jacob, who treated him as his favourite. Joseph's envious brothers sold him to a company of merchants. The brothers kept the coat, dipped it in goat's blood, and showed it to their father saying that Joseph had been killed by wild animals. The subject comes from the book of Genesis in the Old Testament (37:32).

Brown depicted the brothers showing the bloodstained coat to Jacob, who is seated under a fig tree, rending his garments. Behind him kneels his youngest son Benjamin 'with darkling countenance', gazing suspiciously at the coat. In the centre is Levi, pointing to the coat with a deceitful expression. Behind him are Issachar, in shadow, described by Brown as 'the fool', sucking his shepherd's crook; next is 'the leonine Judah' watching his father's reaction intently and 'the cruel Simeon' who 'looks at his father guiltily and already prepared to bluster.'[8] The Bible does not characterise the brothers, so that to create a believable drama, Brown created personalities for them; Brown's suggestion of enmity between Benjamin and the others was based on the fact that they were his half-brothers, Jacob's sons by Leah, whereas the mother of Benjamin and Joseph was Rachel.

The painting stemmed from the commission from the Dalziel brothers for wood-engravings to be published in an illustrated Bible. Brown was asked to contribute in November 1863, and was sent a list of subjects to choose from, including this one. The Nazarenes had painted a series of frescoes of the story of Joseph at the Casa Bartholdy, Rome (1816–17) and Brown may have chosen the subject with them in mind; Cornelius's painting of a later episode in the story, showing Joseph recognised by his brothers in Egypt (Berlin, Nationalgalerie), includes a striking group of the brothers with sinister faces. Not long after undertaking the commission for Dalziel, Brown offered to paint the subject in oils for George Rae, who accepted in March 1864. The painting was completed in April 1866 and was retouched in 1869 to make Simeon look more oriental and to throw the landscape background a little further away from the figures. The illustration was not published until 1881.

Very different from the generalised treatment of *Jesus washing Peter's Feet*, this painting tells its story through detail and characterisation. It should be seen in the context of Holman Hunt's reinvention of Biblical subjects, involving the use of supposedly authentic backgrounds and accessories, although, unlike Hunt, Brown did not travel to the Holy Land. He copied the landscape in the background to *The Coat of Many Colours* from a watercolour by his friend Thomas Seddon, *The Well of Enrogel*, painted in Palestine in 1854 (fig. 86). For the textiles and other accessories Brown used the collections in the British Museum, and consulted books about the Assyrians and the Egyptians; he also visited the London Zoo to study a camel. The girl with the musical

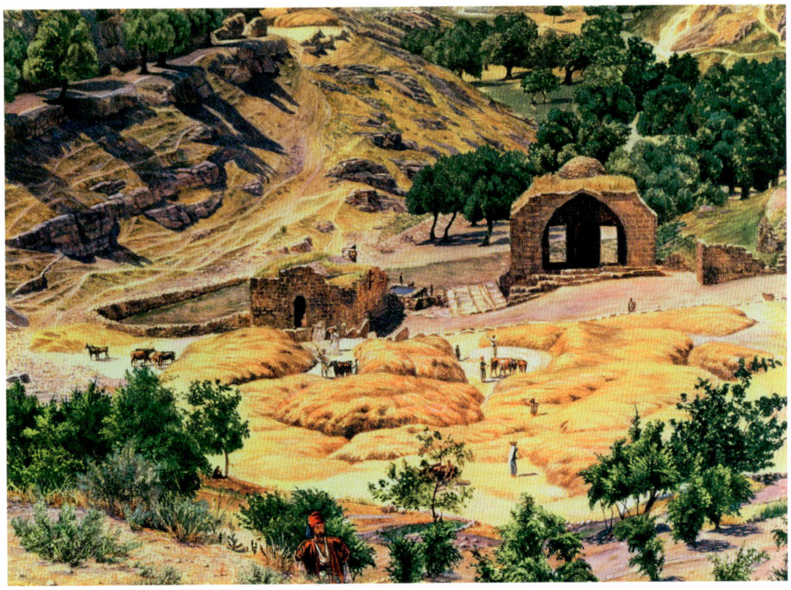

Fig. 86
Thomas Seddon, The Well of Enrogel, *1854. Harris Museum and Art Gallery, Preston*

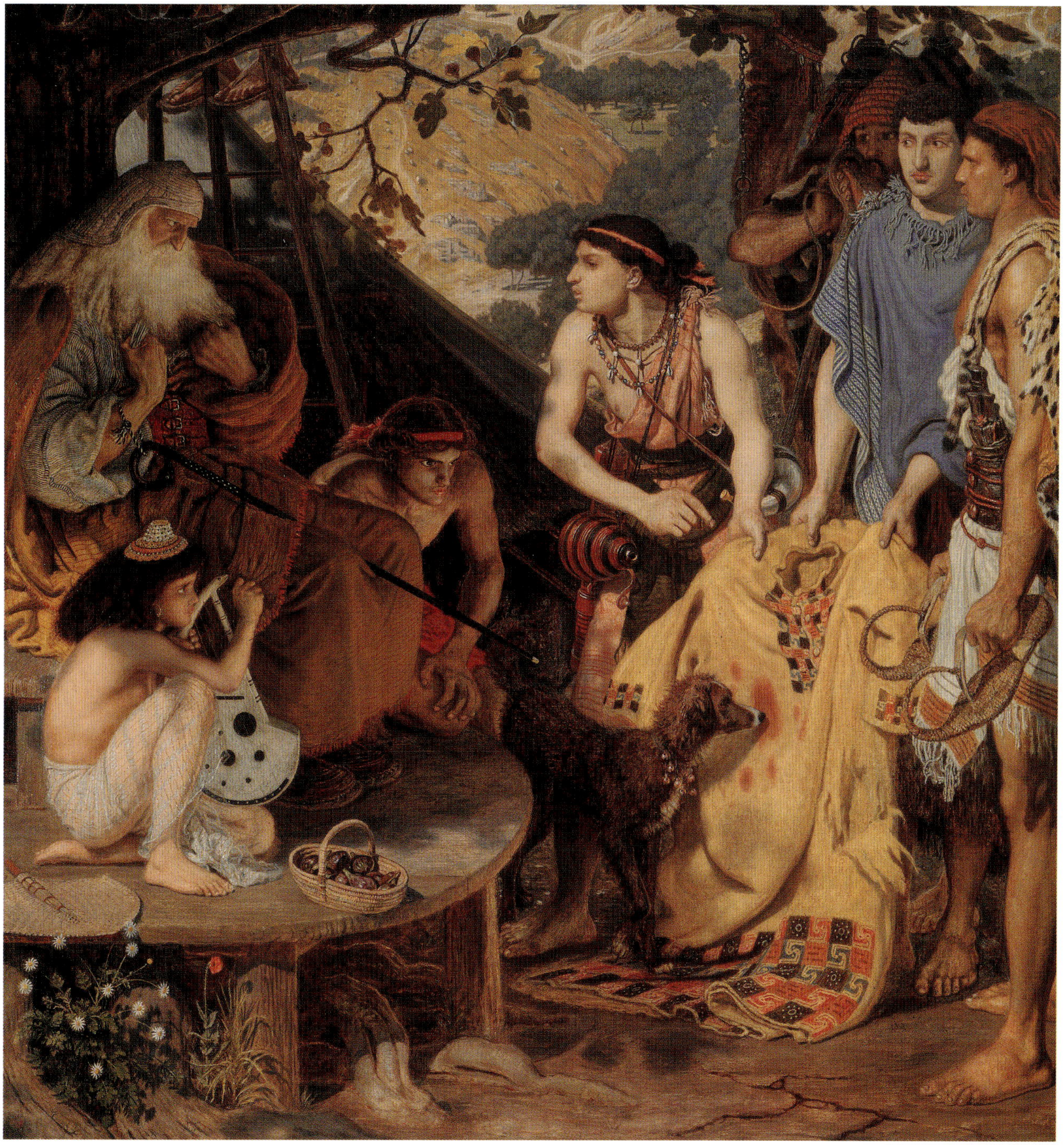

76

instrument, described by Brown as Jacob's grand-child, was perhaps suggested by Simeon Solomon's scenes depicting Biblical musicians, also dependent on ancient sources.[9]

The ladder behind Jacob is a reference to Jacob's dream of the ladder of angels going up to heaven. Typically, Brown poked fun at this by including at the top of the ladder a pair of sandalled feet, their owner otherwise invisible. This and the 'the ultra-grotesque action of the dog, who sniffs the blood-fouled coat of Joseph'[10] were found objectionable by one critic who thought them unsuitable for a sacred subject. Yet the critic missed the point of the dog; sensing that the blood was an animal's and not a man's, it showed that the brothers had deceived their father.[11]

77
ELIJAH AND THE WIDOW'S SON

(A82.2)
1868, (1869)
watercolour and bodycolour, 37 × 24⅛ (94 × 61.2)
signed in monogram and dated: F Madox Brown 68
Victoria and Albert Museum

The prophet Elijah restored to life the widow's son, who had fallen ill and was thought to be dead. Brown showed the prophet carrying the boy down from the upper chamber to his thankful mother, illustrating the passage 'And Elijah said, See thy son liveth. And the woman said to Elijah, Now by this I know that thou art a man of God, and that the word of the Lord in thy mouth is truth' (I Kings 17: 23–24). As if speaking these words, the widow kneels at the foot of the staircase 'in an ecstasy of passionate thankfulness.'[12]

As in the case of *The Coat of Many Colours* (cat. 76), many of the details were researched from ancient sources so as to represent the Biblical period accurately, but Brown also chose details for their symbolic meaning. At the top of the painting is a bottle, set into the wall to attract nesting swallows: the shadow of the returning bird signifies the return of the soul to the body.[13] To show that the boy had only just come to life, Brown depicted him still bound up in his grave-clothes, studied from ancient Egyptian sources. The Hebrew writing around the doorway is from the Shemah, the prayer which the Jews were commanded to write on their doorposts (Deuteronomy 6:4–9). Through the doorway is a glimpse of a kitchen with a barrel and other vessels; this refers to the preceding passage in Kings, in which the widow's handful of meal in a barrel provided meals for herself and the prophet. Similarly, the oil lamp in the upper room represents the cruse of oil that did not fail. Brown included other homely details such as the string of garlic and the hen with its chick riding curiously on its back, a detail taken from the Luttrell psalter (fig. 30, p. 41). The identity of the model for the widow is not recorded, but she may have been Fanny Eaton, a mixed-race model used by several artists of the Pre-Raphaelite circle for Eastern characters.[14]

Like *The Coat of Many Colours*, this painting is based on one of the illustrations made by Brown for Dalziel's Bible, commissioned in 1863 although not published until 1881. Brown made several versions in oil and watercolour.[15] This one is the most impressive, a tour de force of watercolour technique, in which Brown skilfully depicted the patterns and textures of the Middle Eastern textiles and the brilliant colours in the hot sunshine, which he described as an effect of 'vertical sunlight'.[16] It was painted between September and November 1868 for Frederick Craven, and retouched the following year at Craven's request.

Craven lent it to the autumn exhibition of the Royal Manchester Institution in 1869. When the annual Heywood prize for the best picture was awarded to a view of the Piazza Navona at Rome by the genre and landscape painter Keeley Hallswelle, a furious controversy arose in the local press. Shields and others including Sidney Colvin complained that Brown's painting, 'the finest picture in the exhibition'[17] should have won the prize, arguing that the prizewinning painter's aim was 'a low one whereas Madox Brown's is of the highest.'[18]

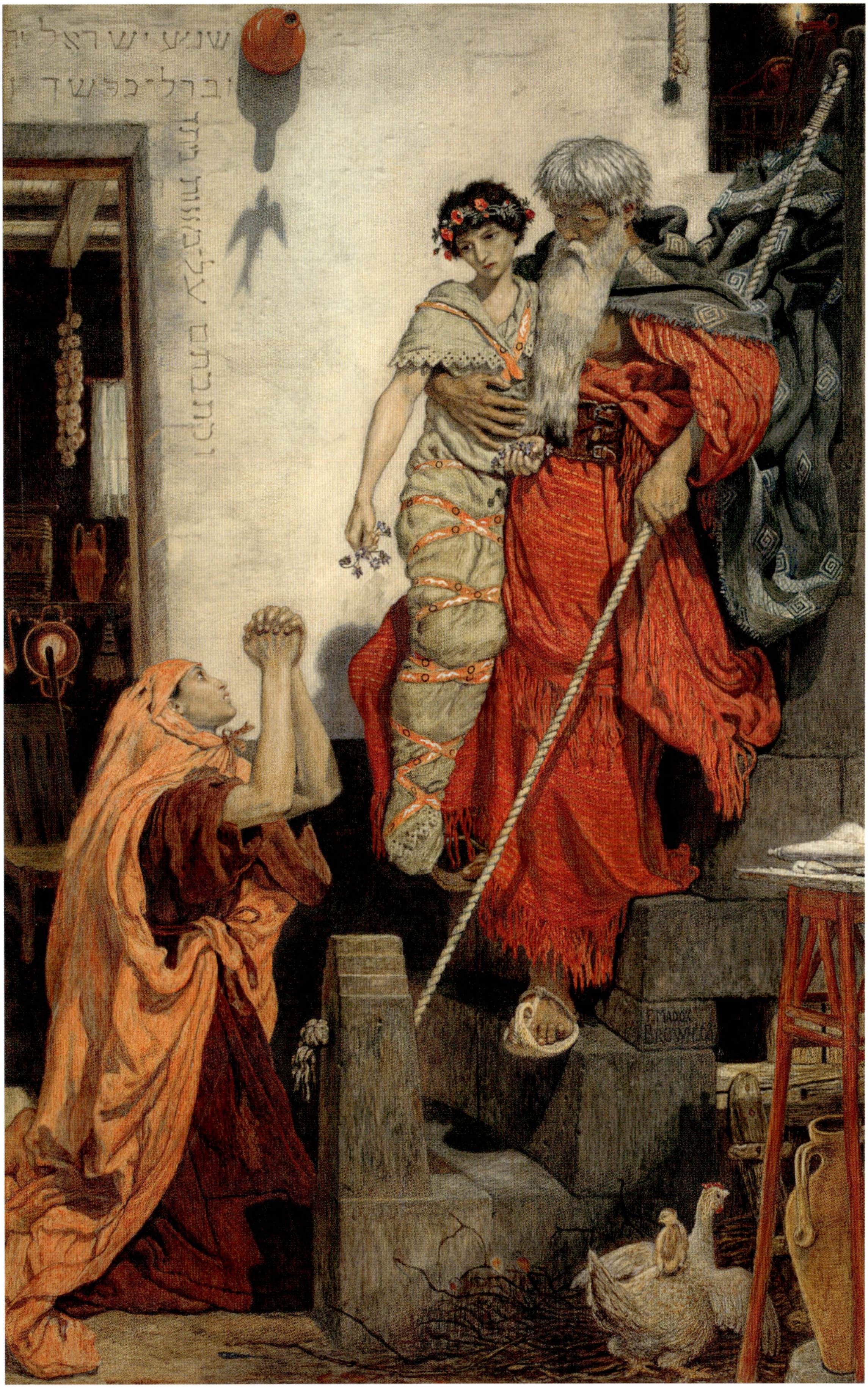
F MADOX
BROWN

78
THE ENTOMBMENT

(A88)
1866–69
watercolour with gold paint, 21½ × 24 (54.6 × 60.9)
signed in monogram and dated: *FMB 69*
Private collection

The dead Christ is carried into the tomb by Nicodemus (his head already inside the entrance) and St. John, leaning forward; the curved shapes of Nicodemus's orange cloak and John's green robe create a sense of movement towards the tomb. Behind him stand Joseph of Arimathea, the Virgin Mary (in pale blue) and Mary Altera. Looking on at the left is Mary Magdalen, and at the right two ordinary people witnessing the scene: a woman trying to get a little boy, who is holding a palm, to bow his head. In the background is a landscape showing the three crosses and a field of sheep. A vine grows over the tomb, and Hebrew letters over the entrance translate as 'The House of Life.' In a note explaining the composition Brown wrote that it combined 'something of the archaeological & something of the traditional in its way of treatment … the golden Auriols or Nimbuses are not intended to represent facts but rather the traditional glory which ... attaches to certain of the great personalities in the divine drama … The tomb itself is formed according to the most recently received archaeological views ... The sheep may be accepted as emblematic of the flock deprived of its pastor.'[19]

The style of this watercolour, with its sinuous lines, undulating draperies and overlapping planes of rich colour, is very different from that of the artist's other religious pictures. This may be explained by its origins in a stained glass design of 1865 for part of the east window at St. Olave's church, Gatcombe on the Isle of Wight. Brown used the same design for a wood-engraving in a book of hymns translated from the German, *Lyra Germanica*, published in 1866, and for three paintings (two watercolours and an oil) of which this, the earliest of the three, dates from 1866-69.[20] Brown opened up the shallow space of the original design with the landscape and the figures looking on from the right, not present in the stained-glass. The pallid body of Christ, enfolded in a white shroud, contrasts with the gold haloes and the glowing colours of the other draperies; Brown described the effect to its first owner, James Leathart, as 'exceedingly solemn, deep in tone & free in execution'.[21]

The frame has a broad gilt oak flat, butt-jointed at the corners, and surrounded by a narrow reeded moulding, with square motifs in the corners and roundels along the sides. This is one of the most frequently used frame styles adopted by Brown and also by Rossetti from the early 1860s onwards. Brown used it not only for new works, but also when reframing earlier pictures, sometimes with variations, such as the addition of a bevel to the reeded moulding, and the decoration of the flat with small roundels like those on the surround. The simplicity of this style of frame has the effect of drawing attention to the surface pattern of a painting, and enhancing its formal, abstract qualities.

78

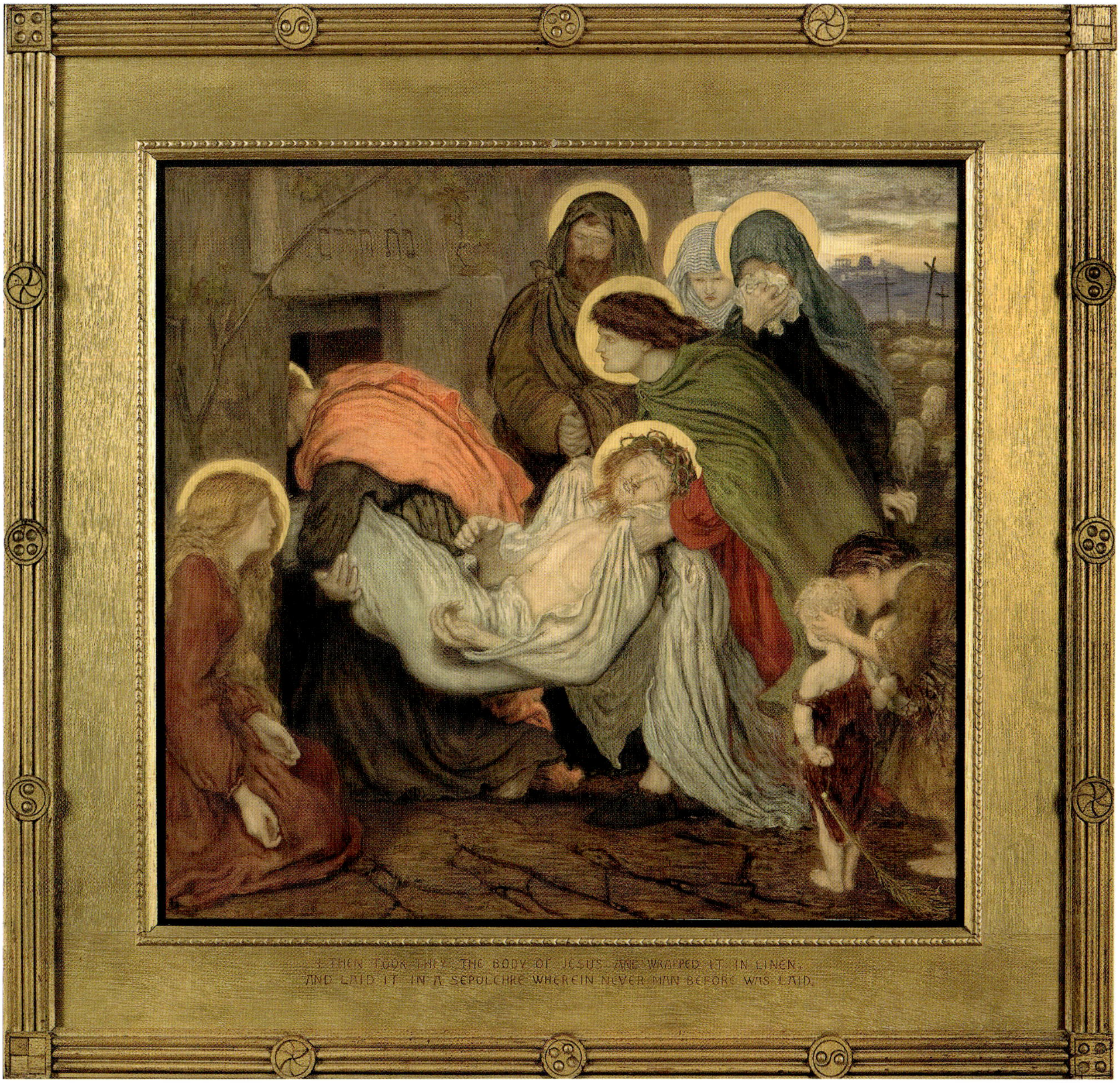
THEN TOOK THEY THE BODY OF JESUS AND WRAPPED IT IN LINEN,
AND LAID IT IN A SEPULCHRE WHEREIN NEVER MAN BEFORE WAS LAID.

79
CORDELIA'S PORTION

(A87)
1865–66, (1867, 1872, 1883)
watercolour, gouache and pastel, 29½ × 42¼ (75 × 107.3)
signed in monogram: *FMB 66–72*
National Museums Liverpool, Lady Lever Art Gallery

Cordelia's Portion shows the opening scene of *King Lear*, after Cordelia has refused her inheritance, and the King of France offers to take her as his Queen. It is a reworking of one of Brown's drawings of 1843–44 (cat. 17), but the nervous line of the Paris period has been replaced by Brown's full-blooded late manner, making great play of the decorative folds of drapery rippling across the surface, and the rich patterning of textiles, jewellery and historical accessories. Brown combined the harmony and beauty of the aesthetic movement with the expressive content of the narrative painter.

He described the characters for F.G. Stephens: on the right of the throne stands the King of France 'youthful and gallant of bearing' about to speak the lines 'Fairest Cordelia, that art most rich being poor'; Cordelia 'stands as though dazed, with eyes ripe for weeping'; to her left is the rejected Duke of Burgundy 'biting his nails in disappointment'. On the other side of the throne 'the two elder sisters & their husbands are represented as all 4 clutching the crown … Just one eye of the fool is visible, directed on Goneril – the poor duke of Gloucester observes what is passing with an air of vacillating concern.' Goneril, on the left, is 'swelling with constitutional pride & scorn, stout, ruddy & red of hair … in gorgeous crimson robes' and Regan is shown with a 'snake-like malignity of smile'.[22] At the heart of the composition is Lear himself, aptly characterised by a critic: 'His head droops as with age, and the cloud of his great white beard covers his breast; but it is the whirlwind of his passion which imparts that withered and half-palsied look, and beneath his beetling eyebrows we discover a vitality of awful intensity. This figure, indeed, is a noble creation'.[23]

Further quirky details characteristic of the artist include the map in the foreground, divided into areas marked with the sisters' names, and torn through Cordelia's inheritance; the tiny figure of the Duke of Kent departing through the doorway in the top left corner; a child's face in profile cut off by the left edge; and a glimpse of a dog, its head above and its paws beneath the table. Some of these inventions attracted the ire of critics, who felt that the artist's 'energy is not accompanied by moderation and good taste,' but on the whole the picture was praised for its thoughtful and expressive qualities and its splendid colour.[24]

Since making the Lear drawings in Paris, Brown had reused one of them, *The Parting of Cordelia and her Sisters*, for an etching in the Pre-Raphaelite magazine *The Germ* in March 1850, but he did not think very highly of it. He later made a small oil sketch of the same subject (private collection), intended as the basis for a finished oil, but no-one commissioned it.[25] He was therefore delighted when in November 1865 the Manchester collector Frederick Craven accepted Brown's proposal to paint him another subject from the Paris series, which he had 'long had in mind to do.'[26] It was intended to be a pendant for Rossetti's *The Return of Tibullus to Delia*, which Craven had commissioned. Brown did not record the names of his models, but the stout figure of Goneril resembles Emma, Cordelia was probably modelled by Catherine, and the bearded man on the left of the throne looks like William Michael Rossetti. There is an element of self-portraiture in the depiction of Lear himself, although Brown seems to have identified more with Cordelia and her proud refusal to flatter, than with the character of Lear.[27]

Brown finished Craven's picture, now titled *Cordelia's Portion*, in November 1866, although Craven, a fussy patron, insisted on alterations being later carried out later. Two further versions in oil were painted, and the monochrome cartoon, originally made as a preliminary study, was later finished off and sold to Charles Rowley of Manchester (cat. 150), this being the occasion of the first contact between the two.[28]

79

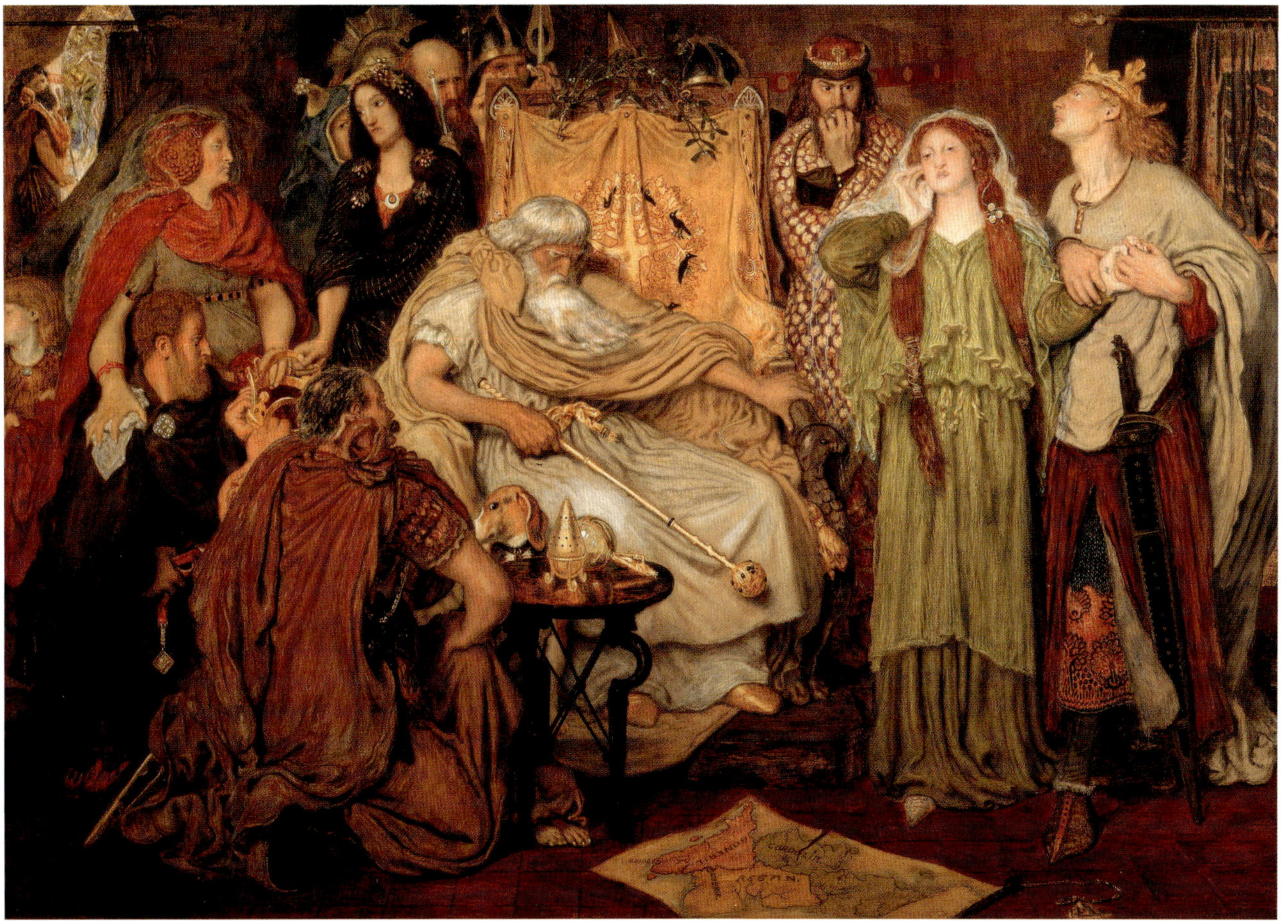

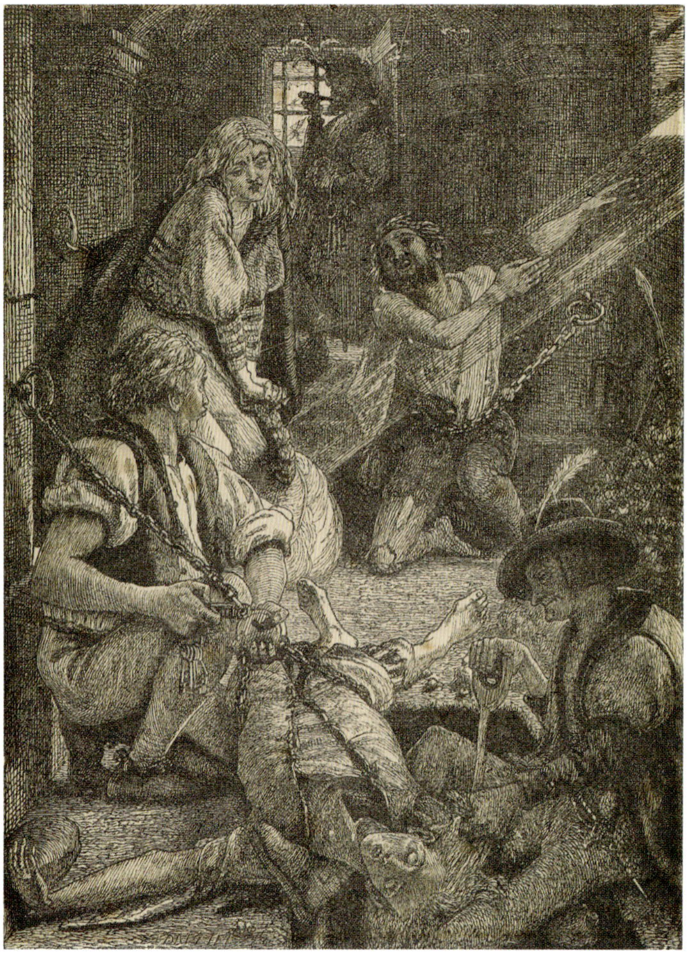

80

80

THE PRISONER OF CHILLON

(D8)
1857
wood-engraving by Dalziel Brothers after design by Brown,
5 × 3¾ (12.5 × 9.5)
printed inscription: *DALZIEL Sc*
Birmingham Museums and Art Gallery

81

STUDY FOR 'THE PRISONER OF CHILLON'

(C44.2)
1856
pencil 5 × 3¾ (12.7 × 9.5) (image)
signed with monogram and dated: *FMB /56*
The British Museum, London

This scene is from Byron's poem *The Prisoner of Chillon* (1816), based on the legend of François de Bonivard. Brown had already painted a small oil inspired by the poem (cat. 15) but this is a different composition, showing the death of one of the three brothers imprisoned in the castle of Chillon, on Lake Geneva. Brown's illustration is based on a close reading of the text.

> He died – and they unlock'd his chain,
> And scoop'd for him a shallow grave
> Even from the cold earth of our cave.

In the foreground, one of the jailors is unlocking the chain of the dead body, whilst on the left is the figure described in Brown's diary as 'the jeering gravedigger' dressed in 'a kind of sleeve' which Brown made up and pinned to a waistcoat.[29]

In the background is another jailor, seen in sinister pose against a window, and in front of him are the two surviving brothers, the narrator on the right, stretching his hands to the sunlight, pleading with the jailors to bury his brother out of doors:

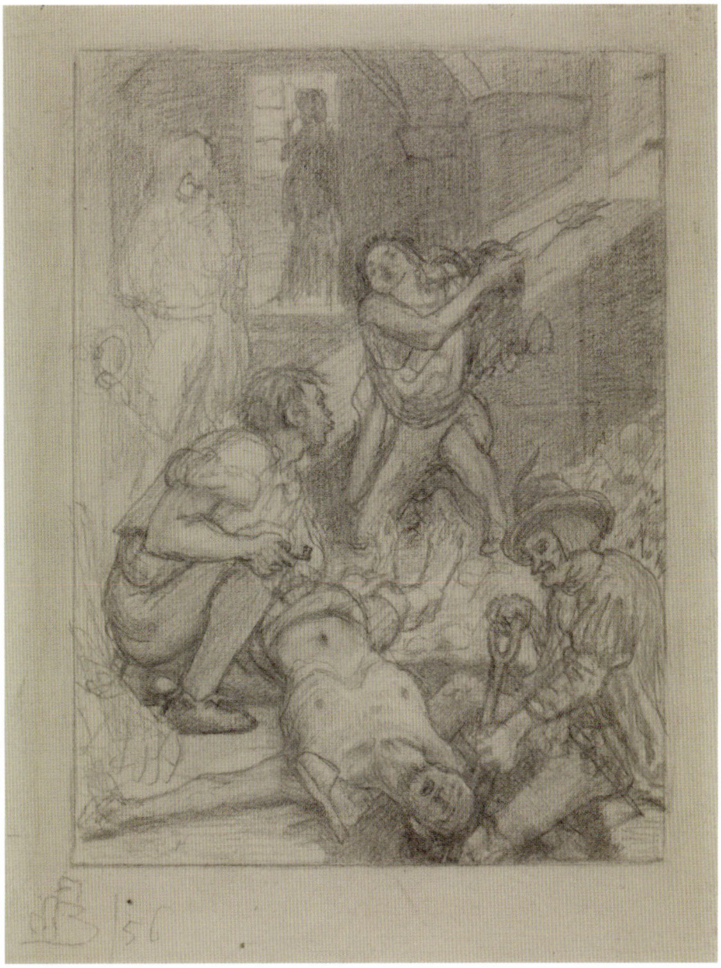

81

I begg'd them, as a boon, to lay
His corse in dust whereon the day
Might shine – it was a foolish thought,
But then within my brain it wrought,
That even in death his freeborn breast
In such a dungeon could not rest.
I might have spared my idle prayer –
They coldly laugh'd – and laid him there.

It was Brown's first commission for a wood-engraving, received from the Dalziel Brothers on 4 March 1856. Lacking in self-confidence with the unfamiliar medium, he examined wood-engravings already made by the Dalziels from illustrations by Millais and John Gilbert, and a few days later tried to make a start. 'In the eveng I designed but could absolutely do nothing. I kept thinking of Gilbert & his great facility,' but the next day 'I began to make something of the Prisoner though, which partly revived my spirits again.'[30] Over the next few weeks Brown made several preparatory drawings, including one of a corpse (cat. 45), and used himself and other models for various details.

The rough pencil sketch (cat. 81), one of two (the other is in Birmingham),[31] is the same size as the engraving, although the pose of the grave-digger on the left, leaning forward, is slightly different from the final work and the chained brother on the left is only roughly sketched in. After the initial studies, Brown made a finished ink drawing, now lost, which he copied on to the wood block. This was sent to the Dalziels to be cut in mid-April; by this time the artist had already spent at least twelve days and four half-days on the commission. The Dalziels requested alterations to a sleeve; Brown then spent more time working on photographs of it, and on 7 July corrected the proof, noting that 'the heads were all execrable.'[32] For all this work he was paid £8, although he was able to make more later by selling the ink drawing, and by painting a replica in watercolour. The illustration was published in 1857 in *Poets of the Nineteenth Century*, an anthology edited by Revd. R.A. Willmott, which also included wood-engravings after Millais, Gilbert and Arthur Hughes.

82

THE CORSAIR

(C134)
1869
chalk, 9¼ × 15⅛ (23.5 × 38.4)
signed in monogram and dated: *FMB 69*
Manchester City Galleries

The drawing illustrates the passage in Byron's poem 'The Corsair (1814) when Conrad, the pirate captain returns from captivity to find his true love Medora dead (Canto 3, stanzas 19–20).'His steps the chamber gain — his eyes behold/ All that his heart believed not — yet foretold!' The flower in Medora's hands and her long hair spread lifelessly about her are both details from the poem.

The drawing is one of six supplied in 1869 by Brown (together with two by his son Oliver) to the publisher Edward Moxon to illustrate *The Poetical Works of Lord Byron* edited by William Michael Rossetti, and published in 1870. The drawings were reproduced in steel-faced etching, and so were made in a soft atmospheric style, unlike the precise lines of drawings made for wood-engraving. Brown later made a version in watercolour (fig. 87).

The other illustrations in the book by Brown are the frontispiece showing *Byron's Dream* (fig. 88, p. 226), *Childe Harold's Pilgrimage*, *Sardanapalus*, *The Two Foscari* and *Don Juan*. Several of these were also turned into paintings.[33]

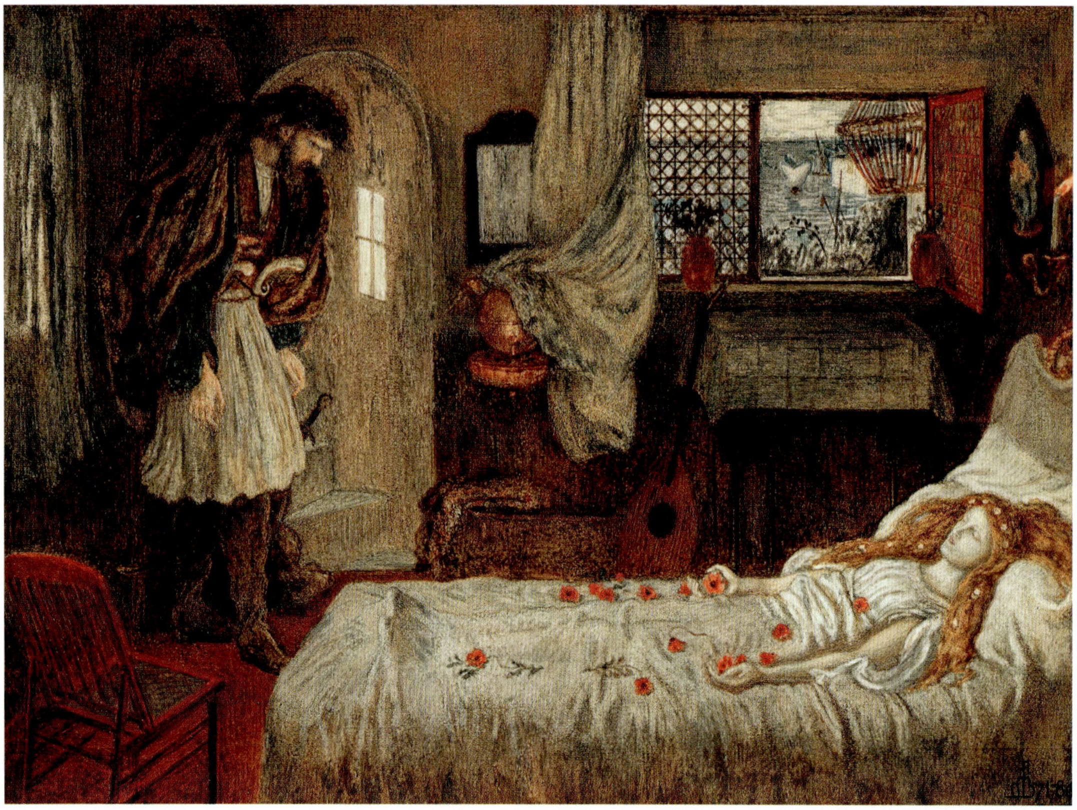

Fig. 87
Ford Madox Brown, The Corsair, *1870–71. Delaware Art Museum, Wilmington, Samuel and Mary R. Bancroft Memorial*

82

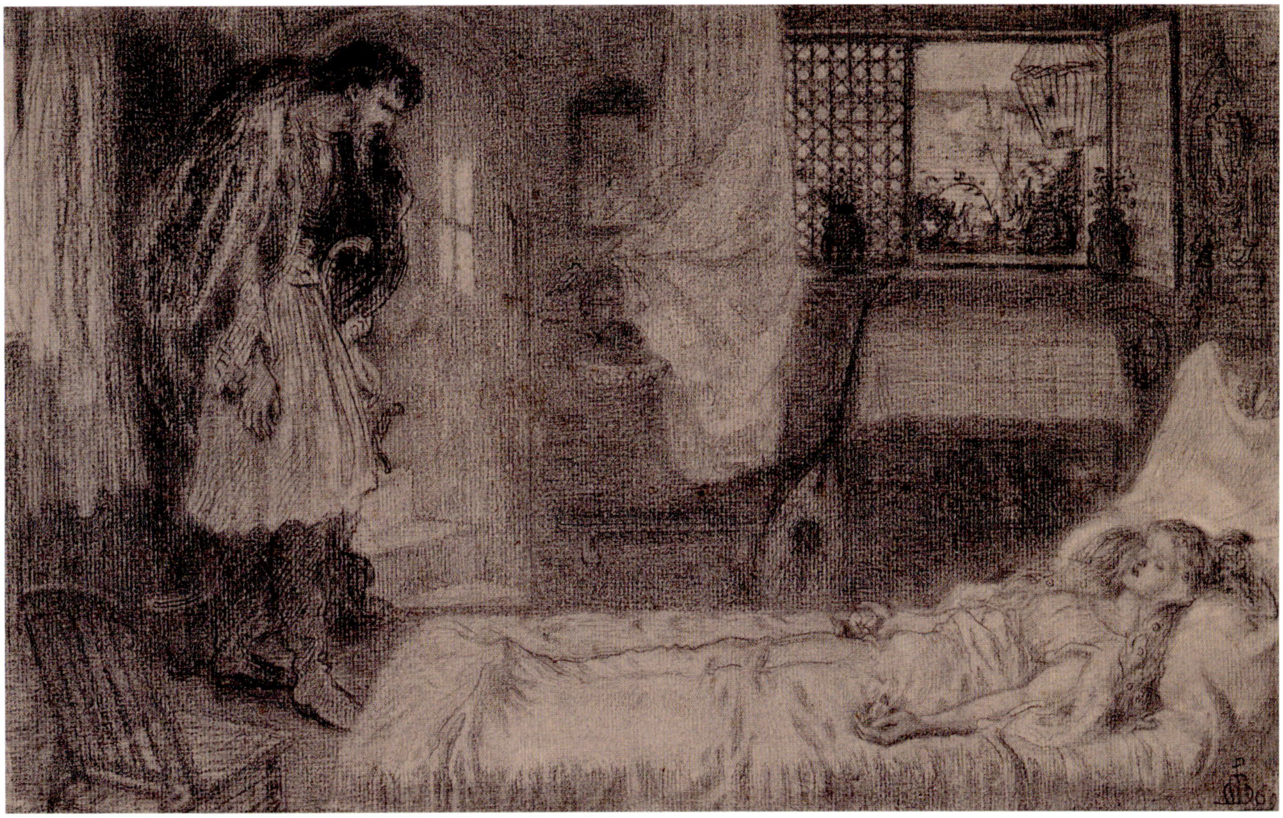

83

DOWN STREAM: LAST YEAR'S FIRST OF MAY

(D23)
1871
wood-engraving, 4¼ × 5⅞ (10.8 × 14.9)
engraved signatures: *Jenkin Sc* bottom right in monogram: *FMB*
Birmingham Museums and Art Gallery

84

DOWN STREAM: THIS YEAR'S FIRST OF JUNE

(D24)
1871
wood-engraving, 1¾ × 4¼ (4.5 × 11)
engraved signature in monogram: *FMB*
Birmingham Museums and Art Gallery

In the early 1870s, Rossetti helped to set up *The Dark Blue*, a monthly magazine containing poetry and articles, although it proved to be short-lived, lasting only from March 1871 to March 1873. In 1871 Brown was asked to illustrate something written by Rossetti for the magazine, and Rossetti sent him a poem he had written in the summer of 1871 at Kelmscott, a story of love and betrayal with a tragic ending. The poem was published with two illustrations by Brown in October 1871. Rossetti was pleased with the result, writing, 'It is like a tenderer kind of Hogarth & seems to me the most successful of your book illustrations,' and judging it even better than *The Traveller*. But he observed that he had intended his 'unheroic hero' to be 'an Oxford swell' whereas 'at first sight the 2 people in the boat both look like rustics.'[34]

Brown's full-page engraving was inspired by the first stanza and shows a man seizing a woman in a passionate embrace.

Between Holmscote and Hurstcote
 The river-reaches wind,
The whispering trees accept the breeze,
 The ripple's cool and kind:
With love low-whispered 'twixt the shores,
 With rippling laughters gay,
With white arms bared to ply the oars
 On last year's first of May.

Brown's second engraving, the tailpiece, is slighter, but shows the tragic outcome of the story, the drowning of the mother with her illegitimate child, seen by moonlight.

Between Holmscote and Hurstcote
 The summer river flows
With doubled flight of moons by night
 And lilies' deep repose:
With lo! Beneath the moon's white stare
 A white face not the moon,
With lilies meshed in tangled hair,
 On this year's first of June.

The larger of the two illustrations is one of Brown's most erotic images: the woman appears to be taken by surprise, perhaps reluctant to accept the man's too ardent advances. Of mature proportions, she closely resembles Emma – that spring, Marie Spartali had married William James Stillman, and the engraving may express Brown's resolve to forget about her and make a fresh start with his wife.

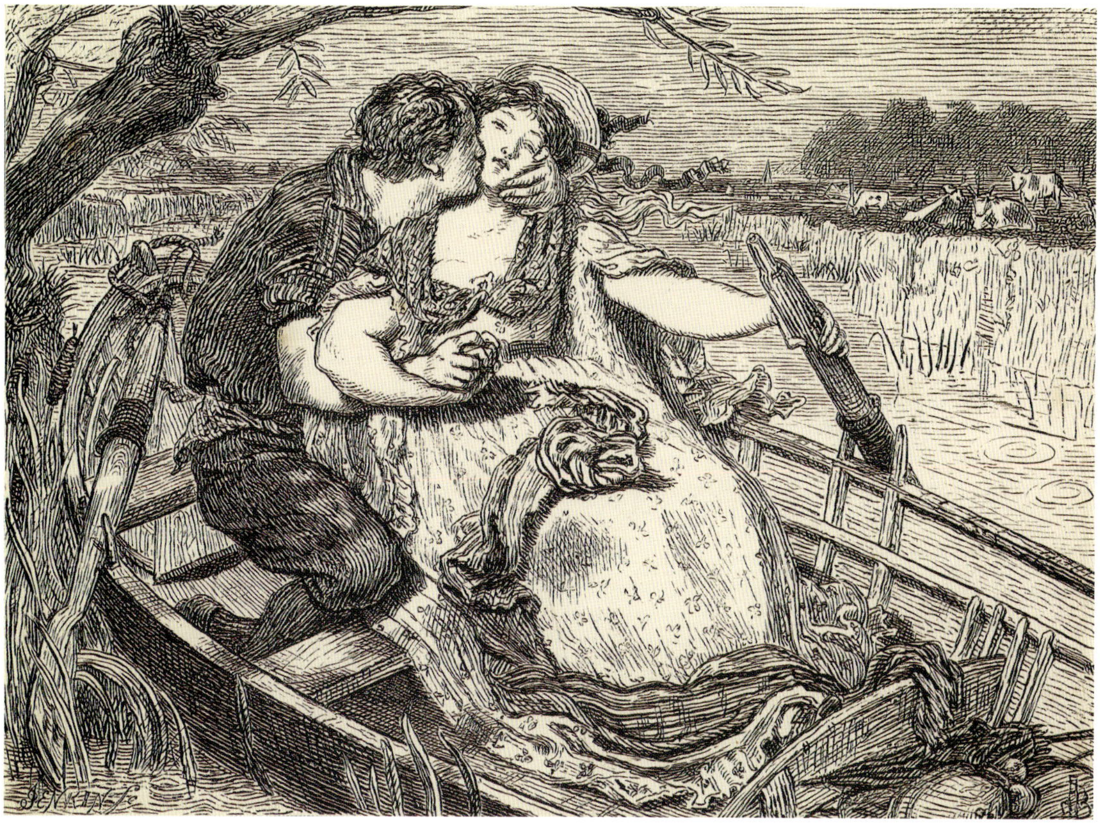

83

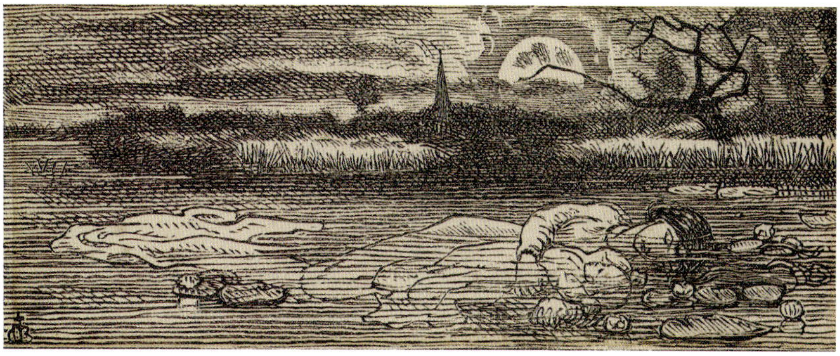

84

85
BYRON'S DREAM

(A95)
1874
oil on canvas
$28\frac{1}{8} \times 29\frac{9}{16}$ (71.5 × 54.8)
signed in monogram and dated: *FMB – 74*
Manchester City Galleries

The painting illustrates a scene from the poem of 1816, *The Dream*, a remembrance of Byron's boyhood passion for his first love, Mary Chaworth, who rejected him:

> ...even now she loved another,
> And on the summit of that hill she stood
> Looking afar if yet her lover's steed
> Kept pace with her expectancy, and flew.

Brown painted Mary as a statuesque beauty towering over the infatuated boy; virtually ignoring him, she eagerly looks out for the approaching figure of Jack Musters, whom she later married. Byron sits awkwardly behind her, his club foot under a rug. With them is Boatswain, Byron's Newfoundland dog; Brown travelled to Byron's ancestral home at Newstead where he made a sketch of Boatswain, presumably stuffed, and also studied the Nottinghamshire landscape for the view in the painting.

Brown's first sketch of this composition was made for the title page of *The Poetical Works of Lord Byron*, published in 1870 (see cat. 82). The sketch dates from 1869, around time that Marie Spartali fell in love with William Stillman, her future husband. The pathetic figure of Byron in thrall to the heartless Mary seems to express Brown's state of mind at his rejection by Marie. In the book, the scene appears, minus the dog, in a circular vignette (fig. 88), surrounded by a view of sea, and in the foreground is a grave on the seashore, overgrown with grass and flowers, and a melancholy verse from *Don Juan* (1819–24):

> The grass upon my grave will grow as long
> And sigh to midnight winds, but not to song.

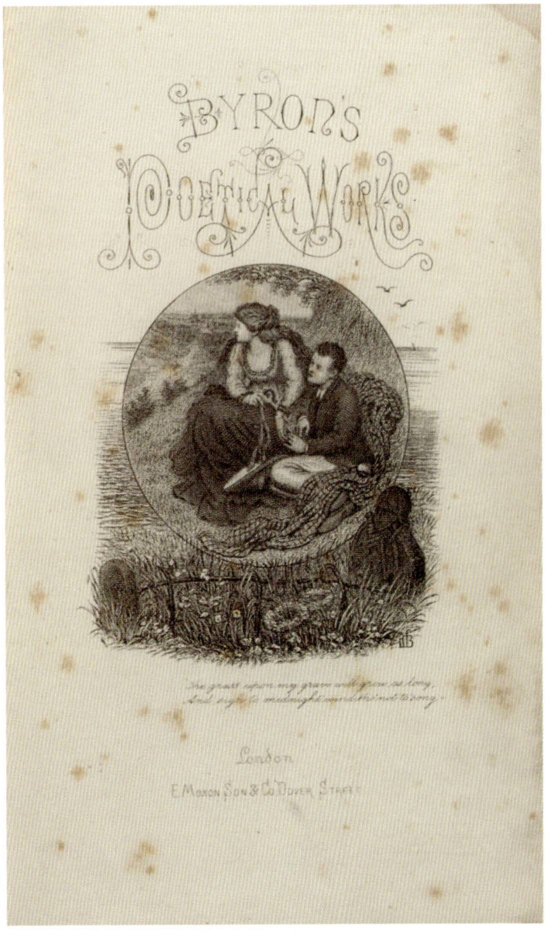

Fig. 88
Title page to Byron's Poetical Works, *1870 with vignette of* Byron's Dream *by Ford Madox Brown. Victoria and Albert Museum*

85

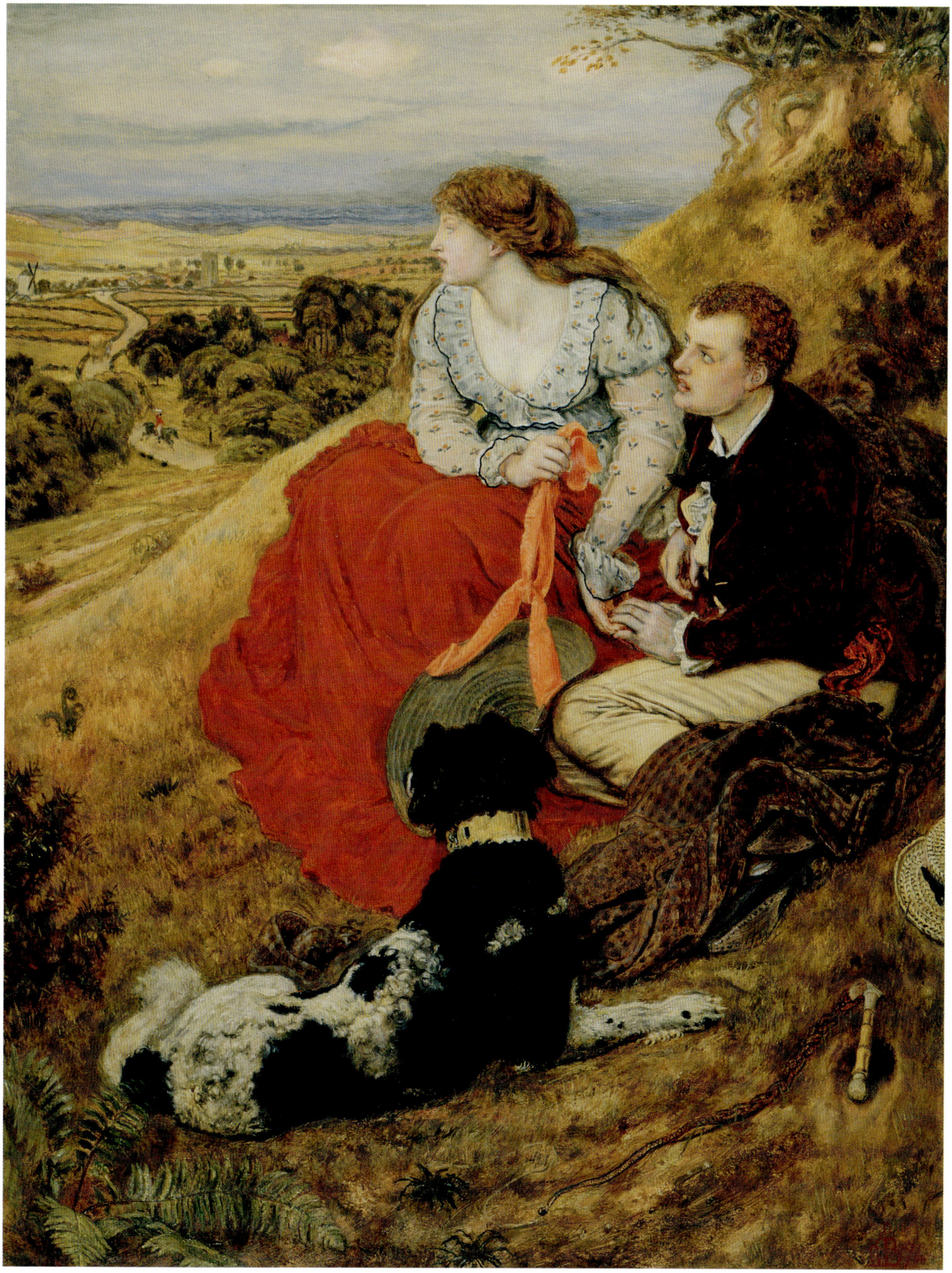

86

THE TRAVELLER

(A90.1)
1868, 1884
oil on panel, 12 7/16 × 19 1/8 (31.6 × 48.6)
signed in monogram and dated: *FMB 84*
Manchester City Galleries

You lonely night-time traveller, scurrying quickly on
While your timorous dog accompanies your course,
When sleep is calling you, when fiery day has gone,
Where do you ride so late on your submissive horse?

Voyageur isolé, qui t'êloignes si vite,
De ton chien inquiete la nuit accompagné,
Après le jour brûlant, quant le repos t'invite,
Où mènes-tu si tard ton cheval rèsignè?

These are the closing lines of a ballad by Victor Hugo, *A Un Passant* (1825), which was the inspiration for Brown's painting.[35] The lonely night-time traveller rides past an inn. Watching him pass is the hostess holding her baby, with her son, dressed in clogs, and her daughter, who has just left her spinning-wheel. On the right is a glimpse of the back wheels of a post-chaise with travelling trunks strapped to it, belonging to the guests who are eating and drinking within, silhouetted in the light of the window. Across the cobbled road are a drinking trough and buckets for the horses: the sign over the door offers food and drink for man and beast ('Nourriture pour Homme & Bête'). The traveller is urging his tired horse round the corner, lured by a will-o-the-wisp lighting up a wayside shrine.

Few of these charming details are present in the poem, which evokes the brigands, witches, demons and illusory visions that beset the traveller: the only elements of the poem retained by Brown apart from the central conceit of the lonely night-time traveller with his dog are the will-o-the-wisp, and the tempting visions of lighted windows promising hospitality. From Hugo's impressionistic hints, Brown created a world of his own, equally evocative but more detailed, with the figures clad in late eighteenth-century dress. The twilit sky, the will-o-the-wisp and the radiance emanating from the inn illuminating the figures and the cobbled road, show that Brown was still interested in exploring different lighting effects.

Brown originally devised the scene for a black and white wood-engraving.[36] In 1867 he had been asked by Joseph Swain, head of the firm of wood-engravers, to suggest a subject for illustration in the magazine *Once a Week*, and put forward Hugo's poem: he had admired Hugo since his time in Paris. The engraving was published on 27 February 1869, although, unusually the poem did not accompany it. Brown repeated the subject in watercolour in 1867, and began this oil version in 1868. It was left unfinished until 1884 when Brown completed it, and he sold it to Henry Boddington three years later.

86

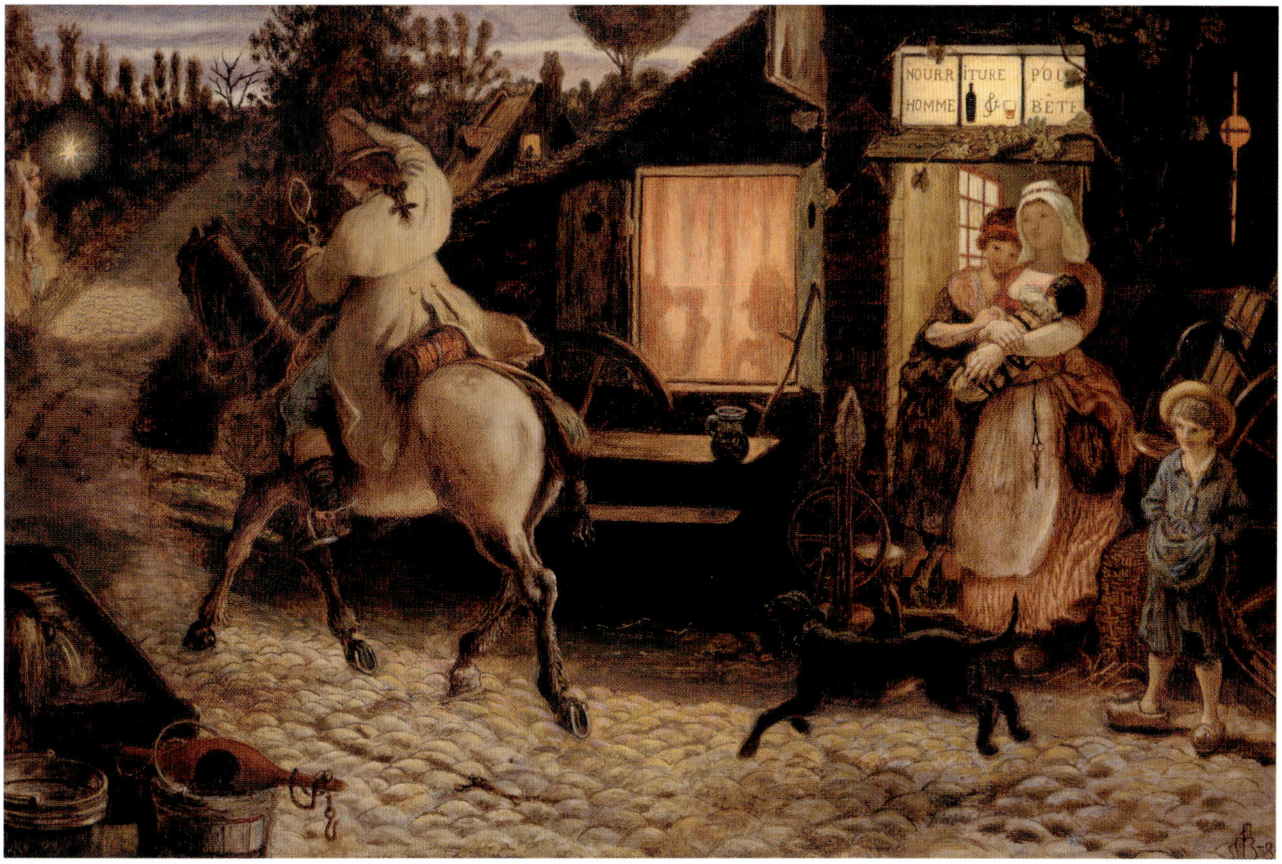

87
CROMWELL ON HIS FARM

(A97)
1873–74
oil on canvas, 56¼ × 41 (143 × 104.3)
signed in monogram and dated: *FMB 74*
National Museums Liverpool, Lady Lever Art Gallery

Cromwell is depicted in a mood of deep religious reflection, oblivious to the noise and activity of the farm all around him. The painting draws on Carlyle, both his vindication of Cromwell's honesty and sincerity against accusations of hypocrisy in *Lectures on Heroes* (1840), and his more detailed *Oliver Cromwell's Letters and Speeches* (1845). The latter includes a description of the period when Cromwell retired from public life and returned to the country, living the life of a 'solid substantial inoffensive Farmer of St. Ives', following Charles I's dismissal of Parliament in 1629: 'Diligent grass farming; mowing, milking, cattle-marketing: add "hypochondria", fits of the blackness of darkness, with glances of the brightness of very Heaven; prayer, religious reading and meditation; household epochs, joys and cares ... Much wider destinies than he anticipated were appointed him on Earth.'[37]

Brown seems to have first read the *Letters and Speeches* whilst living alone at Hampstead in the early 1850s, when he described himself as 'intensely miserable very hard up and a little mad;'[38] he must have identified with Cromwell's isolated and introspective state at this period in his life, and his sense of his own destiny.[39] Brown resolved to paint his hero, and in 1856–57 made a small watercolour *St. Ives A.D. 1636* (Whitworth Art Gallery, Manchester) intended as a sketch for a major oil painting.[40] Brown described the idea behind the sketch, with its very personal conception of Cromwell: 'At this date, 1636, when Cromwell was engaged in cattle farming, the electrical unease of nerves which is felt by nations prior to the bursting of the psychological storm, seems to have produced in him a state of exalted religious fervour mingled with hypochondria.'[41] Much later Brown was to write in a letter 'I have suffered so much myself from imaginary nervousness ... No man ever does any good in the world without passing through the phase some time between the ages of thirty and forty. This is what I have endeavoured to depict in the *Cromwell on his Farm.*'[42]

Brown had to wait until 1873 to paint it. It was commissioned in that year by William Brockbank of Manchester and on its first exhibition in 1874, at the Royal Manchester Institution, the catalogue gave the two quotations also written on the frame. The first comes from Psalm 89, verse 46, in the Book of Common Prayer, which Cromwell holds in the painting, marking the page open with his finger: 'Lord, how long wilt thou hide thyself – forever? And shall thy wrath burn like fire?' The second is an extract from Cromwell's speech to the First Protectorate Parliament, given on 12 September 1654: 'Living neither in any considerable height, nor yet in obscurity ... I did endeavour to discharge the duty of an honest man.'[43]

In June 1856 whilst engaged on the watercolour, Brown visited Huntingdon to explore the landscape and the buildings associated

87

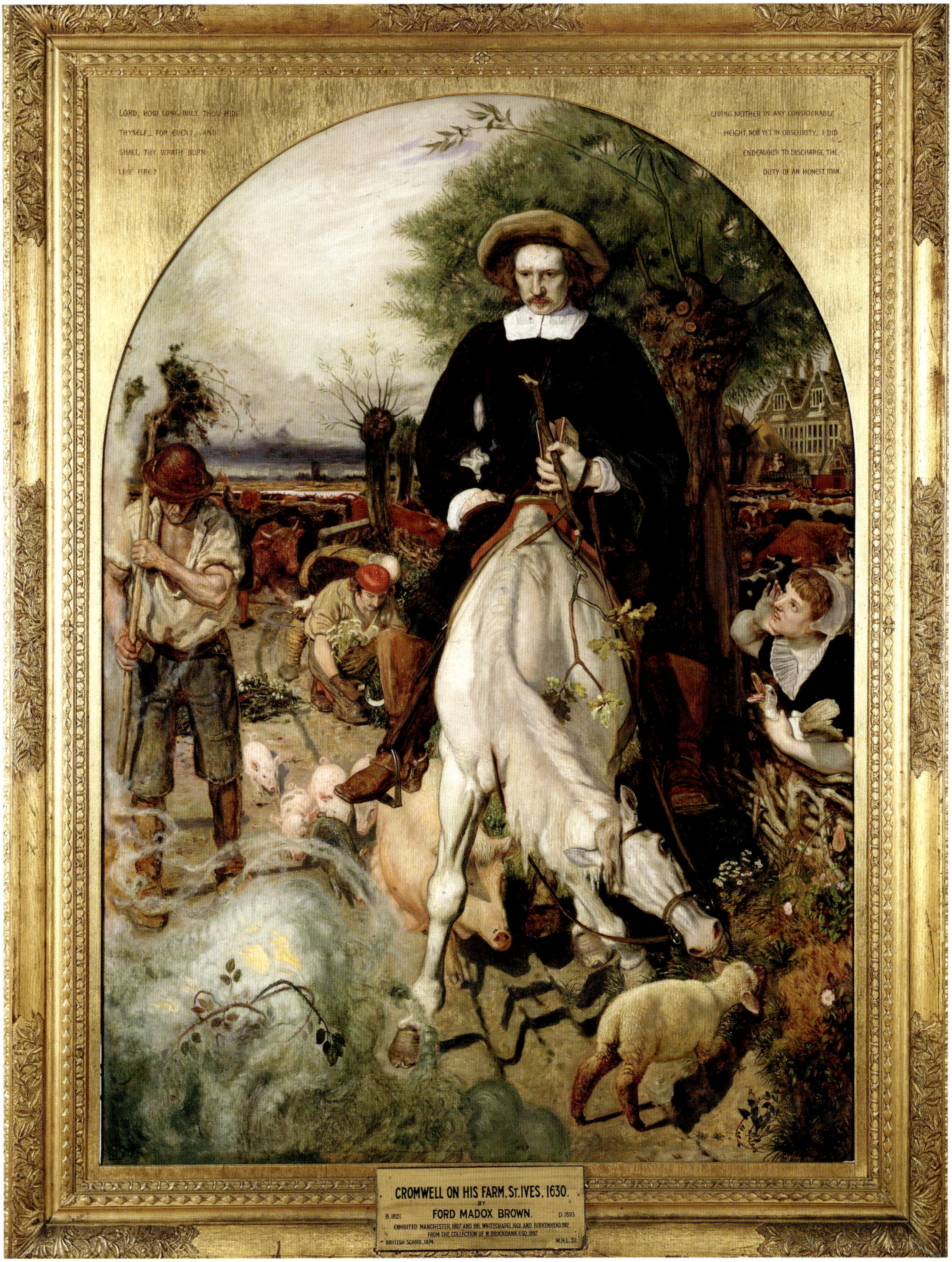
LORD, HOW LONG WILT THOU HIDE
THYSELF _ FOR EVER? AND
SHALL THY WRATH BURN
LIKE FIRE?
LIVING NEITHER IN ANY CONSIDERABLE
HEIGHT, NOR YET IN OBSCURITY, I DID
ENDEAVOUR TO DISCHARGE THE
DUTY OF AN HONEST MAN.
CROMWELL ON HIS FARM, St. IVES, 1630.
BY
FORD MADOX BROWN.
B. 1821.
D. 1893.
EXHIBITED MANCHESTER, 1887 AND 1911, WHITECHAPEL 1901 AND BIRKENHEAD 1912
FROM THE COLLECTION OF W. BROCKBANK, ESQ. 1897
BRITISH SCHOOL. 1874.
W.H.L. 21.

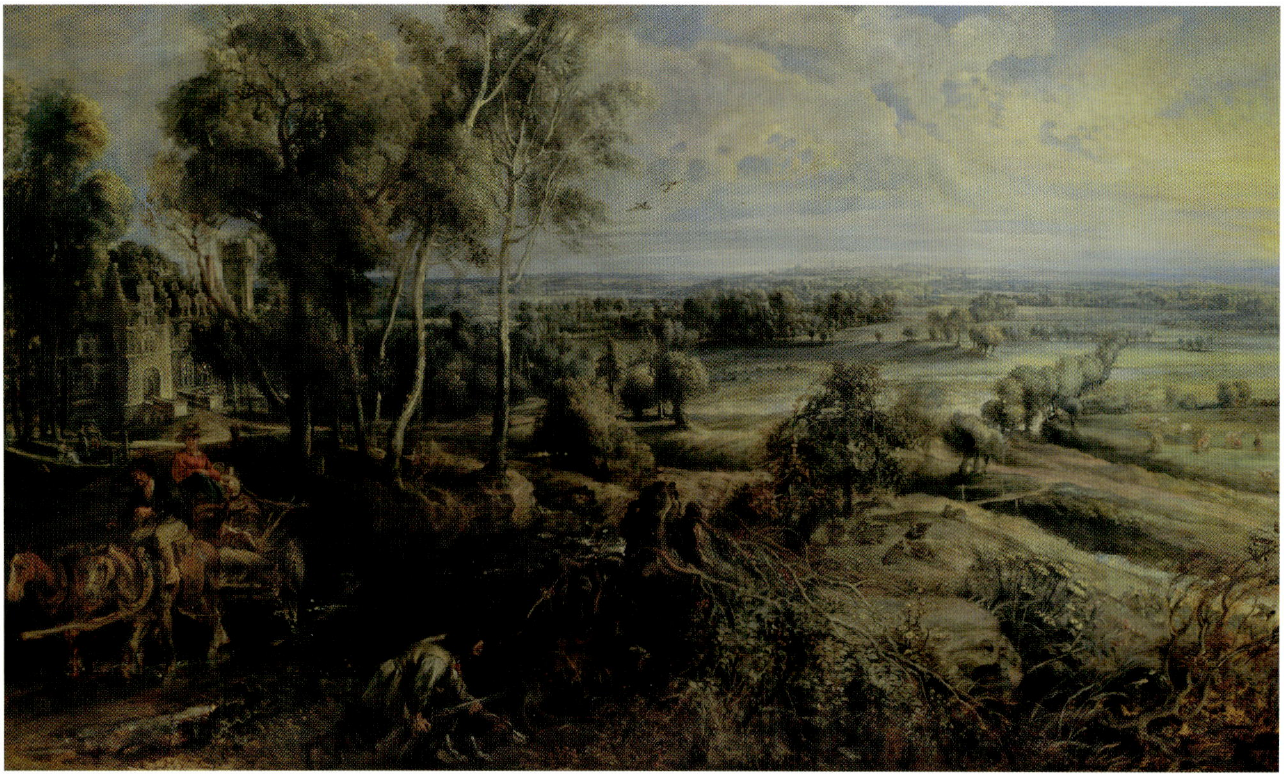

Fig. 89
Peter Paul Rubens, An Autumn Landscape with a View of Het Steen in the early morning, *probably 1636. National Gallery, London*

with Cromwell, which Carlyle described in the book. Brown was disappointed to find that Slepe Hall, where, according to Carlyle, Cromwell rented his farm, had been demolished and that 'Carlyle speaks much of the Willow & alder but in reallity, but for a good many of the first, the scenery is much like any other although more level than usual in England.'[44] The tower of Huntington church is seen in the distance across fields bordered with pollarded willows, with the Ouse in the background. St. Ives is out of view to the right. Dog roses, camomile and mallow are amongst the plants depicted.

Brown shows Cromwell riding home, his wife and child in the distance watching from outside the hall on the right; there is an echo of Rubens's *A view of Het Steen in the early morning* (fig. 89) in the representation of the manor house in the landscape. Cromwell's clothing is sober, and his serious demeanour is contrasted with the homely activity of the farm animals – the quacking duck held by the maidservant calling him to dinner, the horse distracted by the lamb nibbling at the grass, and the sow and her squealing piglets rushing between the horse's legs (on his visit to Huntingdon he had encountered two sows and their pigs making a lot of noise). Labourers are clearing the hedges and burning weeds and stubble, but Cromwell's face shows he is looking inwards, oblivious to the world around him. Straight ahead is the bonfire, a symbol of the burning bush from which God spoke to Moses, as well as alluding to the words of the psalm from the prayer book in his hand,'And shall thy wrath burn like fire?' Cromwell's future is symbolised by the oak sapling in his hand, a symbol of his future role as Lord Protector, ruler of England. On his white bands is a drop of blood: Brown did not explain this detail, but it may be a reference to his future role as regicide.

In the watercolour sketch, Cromwell's face was partially shaded by a tall black Puritan hat, but in the painting he followed Rossetti's advice to 'do away with Cromwell's hat, & so give the subject a less quaint and more dignified aspect'.[45] Cromwell wears a slouch beaver hat, so that his face is fully lit and more visible. Brown included the warts on Cromwell's chin and brow evident from his portraits, recalling the apocryphal story that Cromwell asked Lely to paint his portrait with 'all these roughnesses, pimples, warts and everything as you see me.'[46] Although not recorded as a self-portrait, the face of Cromwell bears some resemblance to Brown himself, suggesting the degree of self-identification between the artist and his hero.

The frame is in the so-called Lely style because of its resemblance to an English seventeenth-century pattern, with shaped floral panels set off by plain areas. The style was frequently used by Brown from the 1870s, usually for historical scenes, although a version of it is seen on *Work*. The Lely frames contrast strongly with the original modern patterns also seen on his later paintings.

1 Brown 1865, no. 12.
2 Bennett 2010, 1, p. 216.
3 Hunt 1905, 1, p. 278.
4 *Diary*, p. 76
5 Hunt 1905, 1, p. 319; Townsend, Ridge & Hackney 2004, pp. 143–44.
6 Bennett 2010, 1, pp. 130-32, A57.1 and A57.2.
7 V&A, Vernon Lushington to FMB, 16 August 1857.
8 Brown 1865, no. 69.
9 Cruise 2006, pp. 77, 88.
10 *Athenaeum* 10 November 1866, p. 612.
11 Brown 1865, no. 69.
12 *Saturday Review*, 25 March 1865, p. 345.
13 Brown 1865, no. 33.
14 Cf. Marsh 2005, p. 192.
15 Bennett 2010, 1, pp. 209–213, A82, A82.1–2; 2, p. 471, C95.
16 Brown 1865, no. 33.
17 *The Sphinx* (Manchester), 9 October 1869.
18 *Manchester Examiner and Times*, 6 January 1870.
19 MAG Horsfall, undated description in FMB's writing.
20 Bennett 2010, 1, pp. 233–38, A88.1–2; ; 2, pp. 484–6, C.122–123; p. 542, D.13.
21 UBC, FMB to James Leathart 8 April 1869.
22 Bodleian, FMB to F.G. Stephens Nov/Dec 1866.
23 *The Reader*, 1 December 1866.
24 *Saturday Review* 2 March 1867, pp. 269–70; further reviews reprinted in Bennett 2010, 1, pp. 227–29.
25 *PRB Journal* p. 67; Bennett 2010, 2, pp. 539–40, D4;, 1, p. 178, A63.
26 V&A, FMB to Frederick Craven, 6(?) November 1865.
27 Borowitz 1978, p. 333
28 Bennett 2101, 1, pp. 229–32, A87.1–3.
29 *Diary*, pp. 167–68.
30 MacCullough 2008, p. 33; *Diary* p. 166.
31 Bennett 2010, 2, p. 44, C.44.1.
32 *Diary* , p. 182.
33 Bennett 2010, 1, pp.247–49, A. 91-95; 2, pp. 490–93, C132–37, pp. 543033, D17–22.
34 D.G. Rossetti *Correspondence*, 5, p. 164.
35 Hugo 2004, pp. 6–9.
36 Bennett 2010, 2, p. 543, D.16.
37 Carlyle 1845, pp. 53–54.
38 *Diary*, p. 78.
39 Newman and Watkinson 1991, p. 77.
40 Bennett 2101, 1, pp. 176–77, A62.
41 Brown 1865, no. 20.
42 Hueffer 1896, p. 315.
43 Carlyle 1845, part 8, p. 41.
44 *Diary*, p. 177.
45 D.G. Rossetti, *Correspondence*, 6, p. 113.
46 Walpole 1786, p. 22.

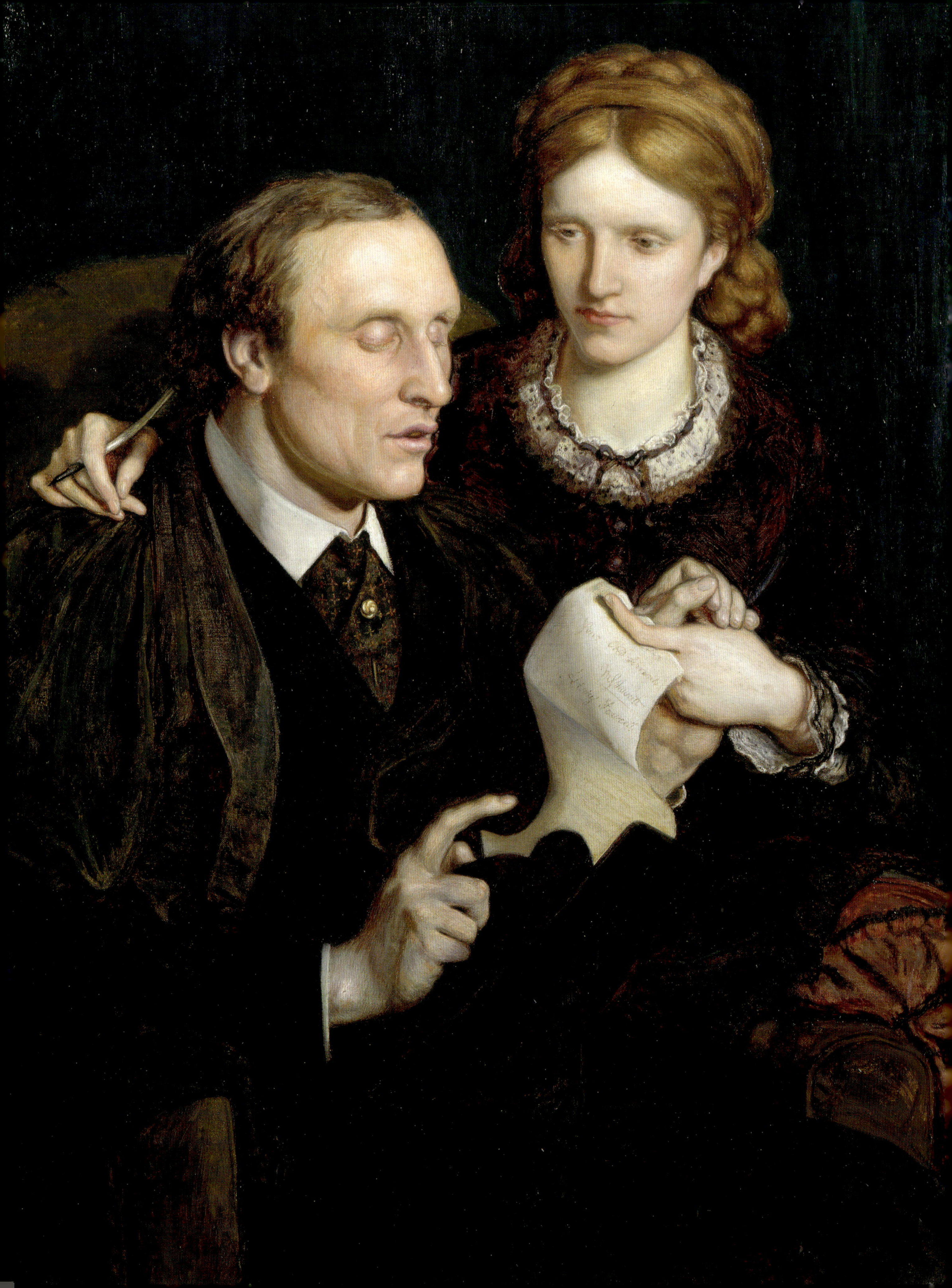

THE PORTRAIT PAINTER

Although Brown took a keen interest in depicting individual faces in his subject paintings, he did not paint many independent portraits, and hardly any of them were commissions. Most of his portraits were of people he wanted to paint, his friends and family. Their likenesses also appear in many of his narrative paintings. Although at first he employed professional models, he also followed the Pre-Raphaelite practice of using friends and relations: his wife Emma, who was an artist's model when they first met, was one of his most frequent sitters. He painted a few commissioned portraits when he was a student, and a few more in the 1870s and 80s, when he was short of funds and would have liked to have received more portrait commissions. But he probably would not have enjoyed having to flatter rich patrons.

Most of Brown's portraits are informal, direct and intimate, many of them drawn in chalk, quicker and more immediate than oils. Apart from his early portraits, Brown did not use the standard formulae of the professional Victorian portraitist; characteristically, he varied the pattern in response to each sitter. *William Michael Rossetti* (cat. 88) is caught in the glare of gaslight; Brown's patron *James Leathart* (cat. 89), the art-loving captain of industry, is shown at home; and the double portrait of *Henry and Millicent Fawcett* (cat. 97) goes beyond portraiture into modern history painting. Brown was also particularly good at portraying children as real people without artificial sweetness or mawkishness.

In the 1860s Brown painted a small number of 'fancy portraits', combining a specific likeness with a more generalised meaning. The best of these, *The English Boy* and *The Irish Girl*, are reunited here for the first time in twenty-five years (cats. 90, 91). They show the influence of Rossetti's half-length paintings of beautiful women but without the eroticism. Precisely observed, direct and vivid in colour, they are amongst Brown's most appealing works.

Fig. 90
Detail of cat. 97, Henry and Millicent Fawcett

88
WILLIAM MICHAEL ROSSETTI

(B96)
1856
oil on panel, 6¾ × 6½ (17 × 16.5)
signed and dated, with both sets of initials in monogram: *To FMLR 1856 FMB*
Wightwick Manor (National Trust)

This sympathetic portrait shows William Michael Rossetti (1829–1919), the younger brother of the painter Dante Gabriel Rossetti, and one of the original members of the Pre-Raphaelite Brotherhood. William was not an artist; he became the chronicler of the brotherhood, writing the PRB Journal between 1849 and 1853, editing its magazine *The Germ*, and later writing books about his brother. William also published a great deal of art criticism, although his main source of income came from working for the Inland Revenue, entering as a clerk in the Excise Office in 1849 and becoming its Assistant Secretary in 1869.

William was twenty-seven when this portrait was painted, and already prematurely bald, but with curly whiskers and a moustache, although not yet the beard seen in later portraits. He had already sat to Brown for the troubadour in *Chaucer* (cat. 34) and for one of the apostles in *Jesus washing Peter's Feet* (cat. 75). William came to Brown's house in Fortess Terrace in February, July and October 1856 to sit for the portrait. Because of William's job, he could only come in the evenings, when Brown had to paint by artificial light, on one occasion working until 2 a.m. William came straight from work and is shown in his office clothes, with a black and white onyx pin on his tie, probably given to him by his father. Brown had already observed the effects of artificial light in *Waiting* (cat.56), which was painted by the light of an oil lamp, but this portrait shows the harsher light of a gas lamp; William described it as 'Done by gaslight' in an inventory of 1908.[1] William's head is painted in close-up, with an alert expression, his brown eyes looking to one side; the brightness of the gaslight, the closeness of the wall with its patterned wallpaper, and the shadow cast by the sitter's head intensify the feeling of intimacy and candour. William described the portrait as 'capital in painting and likeness.'[2]

The initials beside Brown's monogram in the top right-hand corner are those of Frances Mary Lavinia Rossetti, William's mother. In February 1856 she agreed to take in Brown's daughter Lucy as a boarder for private tutoring on favourable terms, and Brown gave the portrait to Mrs. Rossetti in thanks. At the time the portrait was painted, William was art editor of *The Spectator* and was engaged to marry Henrietta Rintoul, daughter of the editor. The engagement was broken off and much later, in 1874, William married Lucy Madox Brown, becoming the artist's son-in-law.

88

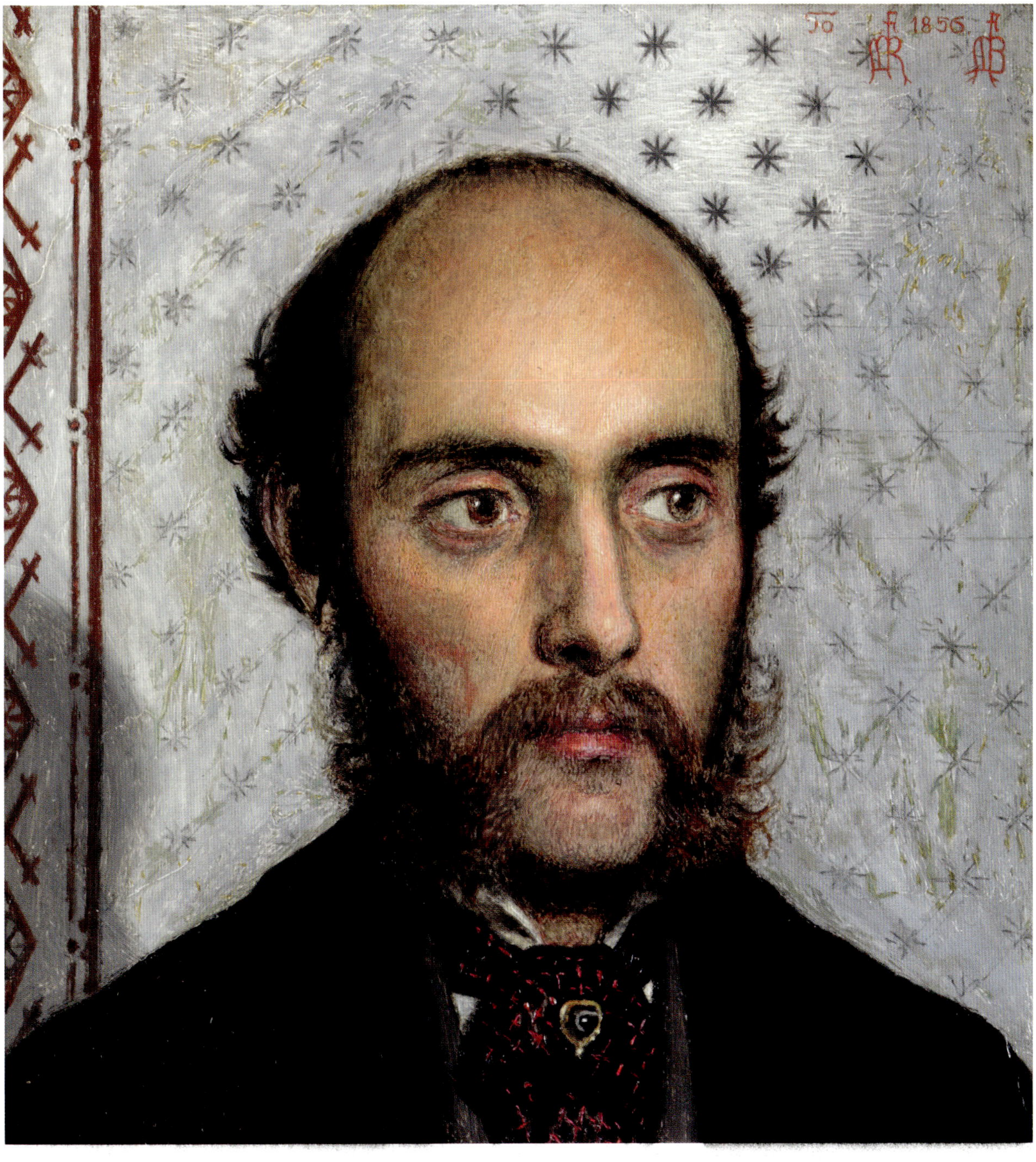

89

JAMES LEATHART

(B76)
1863, 1869
oil on canvas, 13½ × 11 (34.3 × 27.9)
signed: *F. MADOX BROWN*
Leathart Family Collection

James Leathart (1820–95) was a Newcastle-upon-Tyne industrialist, art collector, and one of the chief patrons of the Pre-Raphaelites. He joined the lead manufacturers Locke, Blackett and Co., in 1835, rising to become managing partner in 1851. Leathart met the Pre-Raphaelites through the painter William Bell Scott, Master of the Newcastle School of Art, of which Leathart was Secretary. Scott introduced him to Hunt, Millais, Rossetti, Hughes and Brown and encouraged him to collect their work. Leathart befriended the artists he favoured and invited them to stay at his home in Newcastle. His first purchase from Brown, made in 1859, was *The pretty baa-lambs* (cat. 49).

This portrait was commissioned as a companion picture to the portrait of Leathart's wife Maria, painted by Rossetti in 1862–63 (private collection). On 31 January 1863 Leathart wrote to Brown to say that his wife wanted Brown to paint her husband. Brown wrote back to accept: 'as it is to be one of *the* collections of Great Britain, I think the portrait of the collector as well as his lady's ought to form part of it.'[3] Brown began the portrait on a visit to Newcastle in October 1863, finishing it off in London, and receiving payment on 4 January. In 1869, at Leathart's request, Brown enlarged the painting, changed the hot coppery colour of the curtain to green, and made some adjustments to the likeness.

This is a rare example of a portrait of a Victorian art patron in informal surroundings. Leathart is at home, seated on a red leather armchair, and placed slightly to one side of the canvas, to make room for a view of the lead works at St. Anthony-on-Tyne. The factory was not visible from Leathart's home at 14 Framlington Place, where he and his wife Maria were living when Brown made the portrait, and Brown had to go to the south side of the river to sketch the works from there. The inclusion of the factory indicates the source of Leathart's wealth, and the industrialist's workforce is also represented in the picture, as Brown painted a ferry boat on the river carrying people across to the factory. The rose leaves outside the window were added by Brown in response to Rossetti's opinion that the landscape created an imbalance in the picture.

Despite the small size of the canvas, Leathart comes across as a strong but sympathetic character. Brown has pushed him to the front of the space, so that he is cut off at the sides by the frame, and the arm of the chair projects forwards out of the picture. Leathart's striking blue eyes gaze out from under his domed forehead, with fair hair slightly greying at the temples and bushy side-whiskers. Behind him on an easel is a glimpse of his first commission from the artist, the small replica of *Work* (Birmingham Museums and Art Gallery) which, at Leathart's request, includes a portrait of Maria as the rich lady with the parasol, instead of Emma.[4] The depiction of Leathart at leisure recalls Brown's description of the brainworkers in *Work* who 'seeming to be idle, work, and are the cause of well-ordained work and happiness in others.'[5]

In 1864 the Leatharts moved to a larger house at Bracken Dene, Gateshead. A photograph of the interior around 1895 shows the portrait hanging there as a pendant to the Rossetti of Mrs Leathart.[6]

The frame has a gilt oak flat surrounded by a 'thumbmark' moulding, a triangular section relieved by a snaking pattern of alternating semicircles gouged out in relief. This pattern, one of the most original of Pre-Raphaelite frames, was designed by Rossetti and used frequently by him and occasionally by Brown in the 1860s.

89

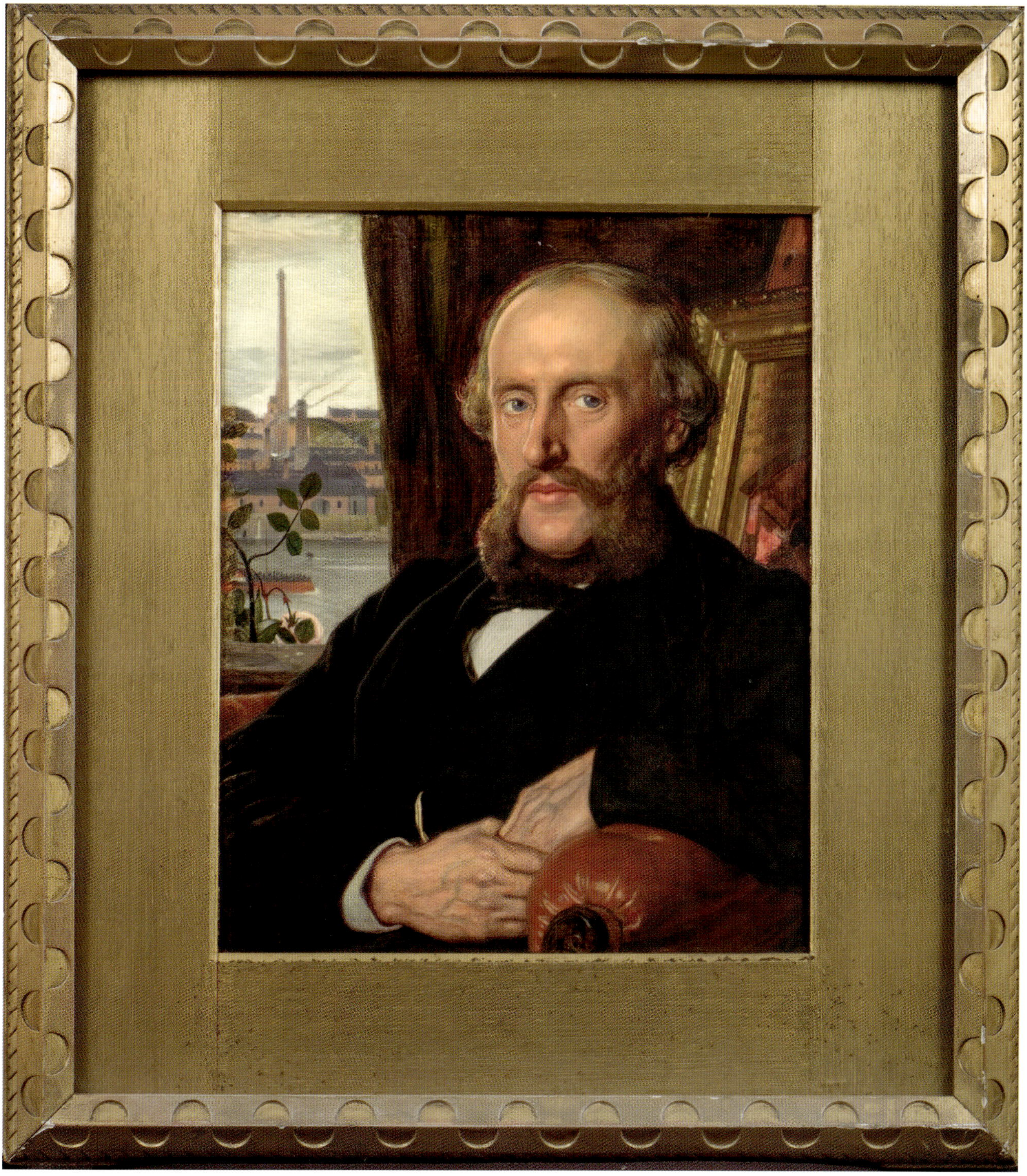

90

THE ENGLISH BOY

(A73)
1860
oil on canvas, 15 9/16 × 13 1/8 (39.6 × 33.3)
signed and dated: *F. MADOX BROWN /60*
Manchester City Galleries

The English Boy is a portrait of the artist's son Oliver, at five years old. He wears a straw hat and a white smock over a red checked dress, and holds a whip and top, a common Victorian child's toy. Centrally placed, his face staring deadpan out of the canvas, the portrayal is disarmingly direct, without a smile or hint of sentimentality. Oliver holds his whip and top like an orb and sceptre, and his straw hat is tilted like a Tudor beret; this is a witty appropriation of Holbein's portrait of *Edward VI as a boy* (National Gallery of Art, Washington). Brown probably knew it through the medium of the engraving by Wenceslas Hollar (fig. 91), which reversed the oil, so that the prince holds the gold regalia in his right hand, corresponding to Oliver's hand with the top. Brown may also have known Reynolds's portrait of *Master Crewe* dressed as a diminutive Henry VIII (private collection).

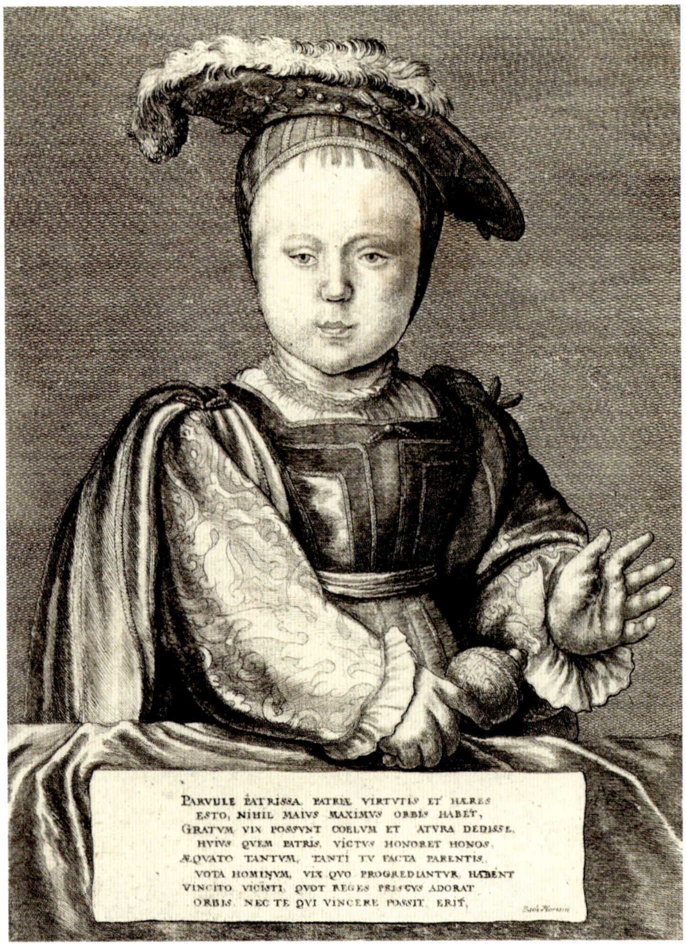

Fig. 91
Wenceslas Hollar after Holbein, Edward VI, *1650. Thomas Fisher Rare Book Library, University of Toronto*

90

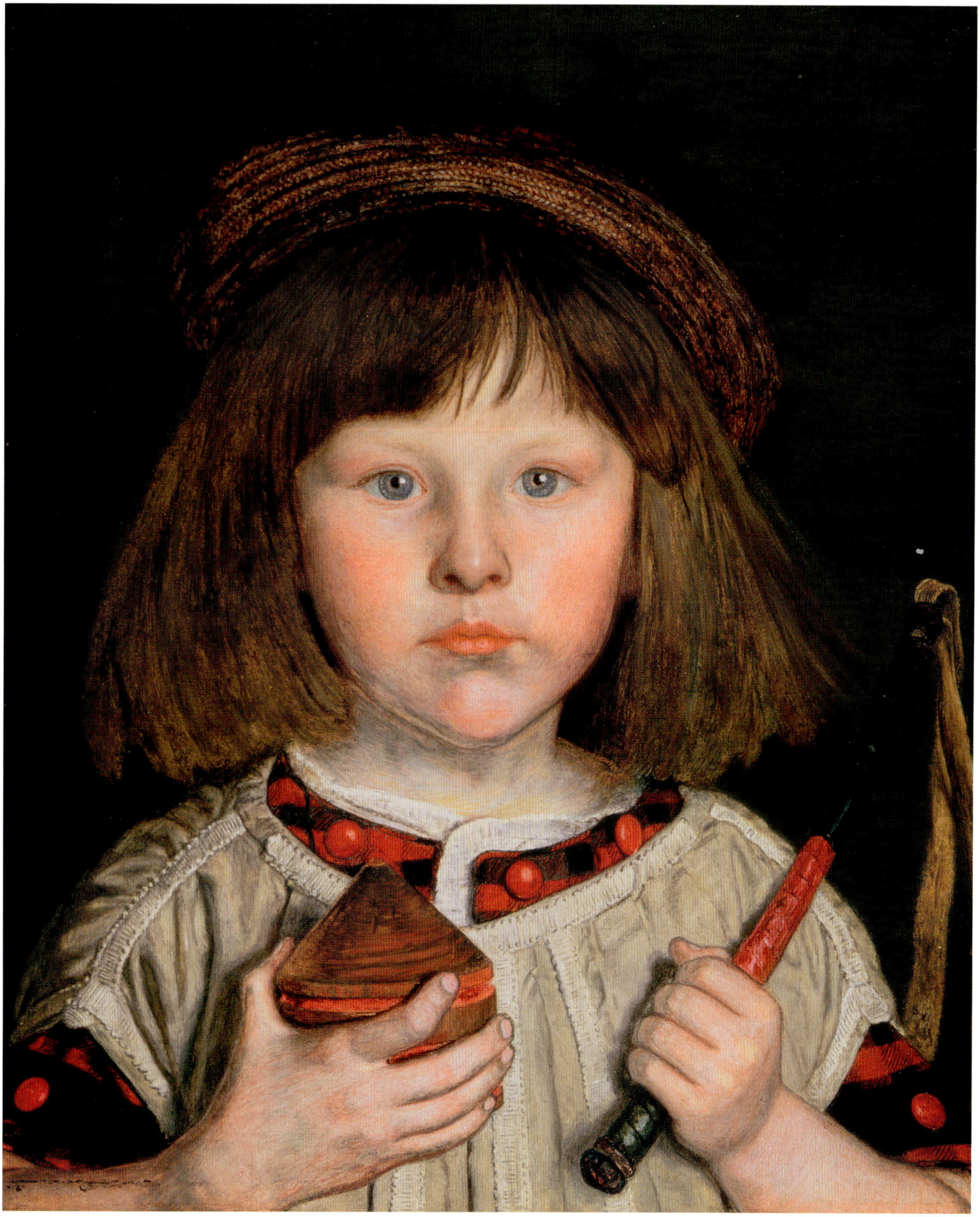

91

THE IRISH GIRL

(A74)
1860
oil on canvas, 11 × 10¾ (28 × 27.5)
signed and dated: *[FORD MADOX] BROWN 1860*
Yale Center for British Art. Paul Mellon Fund

In contrast to Oliver's confident gaze (cat. 90), *The Irish Girl* seems uneasy, tilting her head slightly and looking sideways. She was an orange seller whom Brown came across when searching for Irish models for *Work* (cat. 61). She clutches a Paisley shawl about her shoulders, and holds a cornflower. Although the two works are not the same size, they are companion pictures.

The bust-length format and modest scale show Brown responding to the new type of portrait which Rossetti had started to paint in 1859. In contrast to Rossetti's remote beauties, Brown's children are real individuals, with none of Rossetti's idealisation or languorous eroticism. But the titles imply national and gender stereotypes: the frank gaze of the fair-skinned, blue-eyed English boy and the wary look of the black-haired, brown-eyed Irish girl suggest English reliability and Irish fecklessness.

Brown, showed a new interest in colour harmonies in these paintings, following the example of Rossetti. Oliver's rosy cheeks and lips are echoed in the red of his tartan dress with its bright red buttons, whilst the Irish girl wears a red shawl complementing the colour of her lips. These features answered the preference for small colourful pictures expressed by the Leeds patron T.E. Plint, for whom they were painted in 1860.

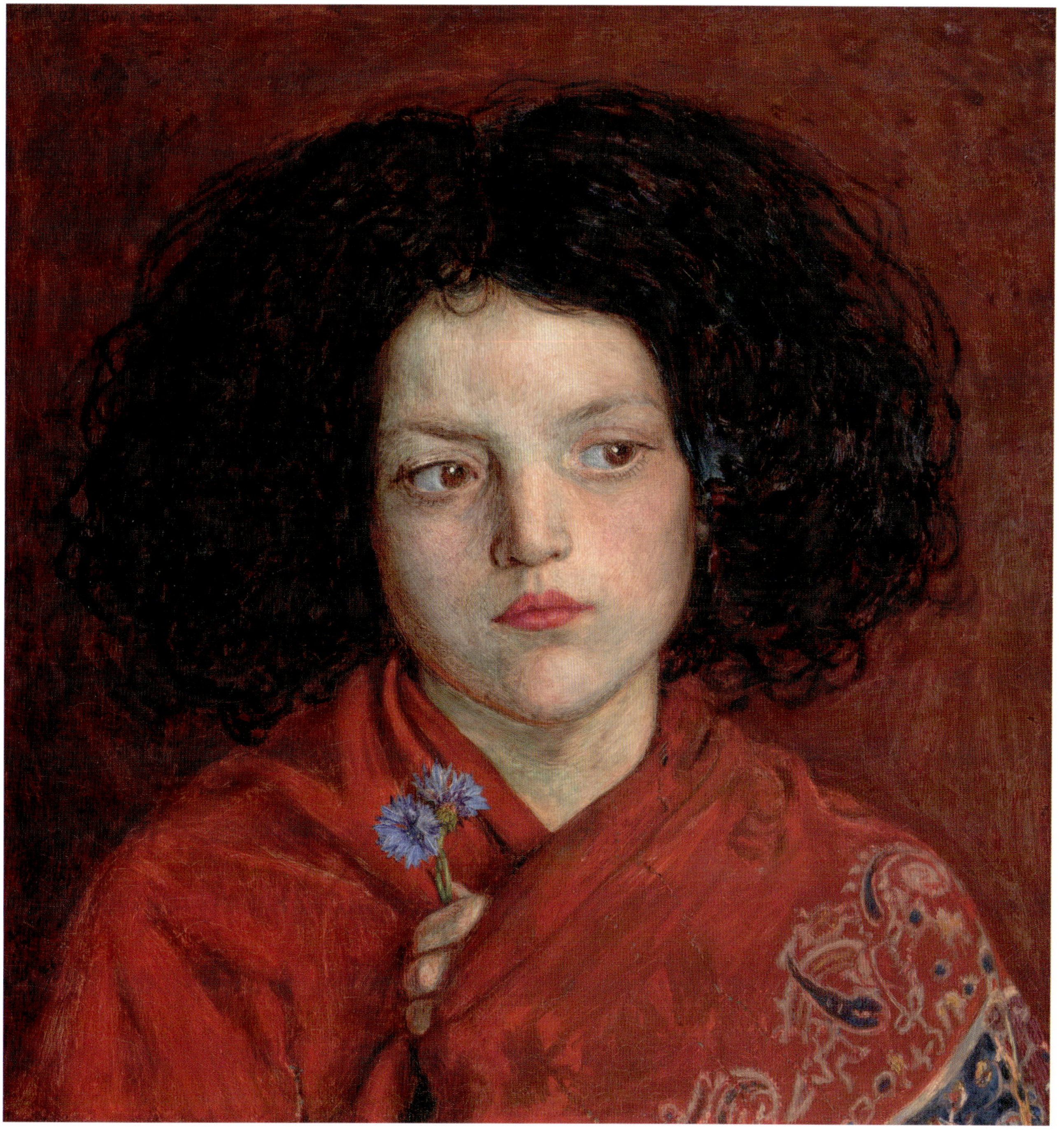

91

92

MAUVAIS SUJET (THE WRITING LESSON)

(A76)
1862
watercolour, 9 3/16 × 8 1/4 (23.4 × 21)
signed in monogram: *FMB //MAUVAIS SUJET*
Tate. Purchased 1917

The title is French for good-for-nothing: Brown described the picture as 'a naughty little girl called Mauvais Sujet.'[7] The picture shows a young girl at a desk with an exercise book and quill pen, suggestively biting at an apple instead of concentrating on her writing lesson; she has scrawled her name, Mary, and a crude drawing of a sailor on the desk, which also has the initials CH scratched onto it. Her dark eyes and hair suggest that she is a gypsy or an Irish girl. Like *The Irish Girl* (cat. 91) the format is taken from Rossetti's bust-length female portraits such as *Bocca Baciata* (Museum of Fine Arts, Boston), which also gives prominence to the mouth and the apple, both expressing sexual temptation. There is a hint of adolescent sexuality in Brown's reluctant pupil, with her artfully disarranged hair and languid expression, her red earring, her red lips provocatively open to disclose pearly teeth, and a black lace tied round her prominent neck. The picture is delicately painted, with a carefully considered colour scheme of greens and pinks, but its tone is uncertain, neither a *femme fatale* nor a modern genre subject.

The picture was given by the artist to a raffle in aid of the Lancashire Relief Fund. This was organised to help the Lancashire cotton workers during the cotton famine, when the blockade of cotton imports from the southern states of America during the Civil War caused immense hardship in the North of England.

92

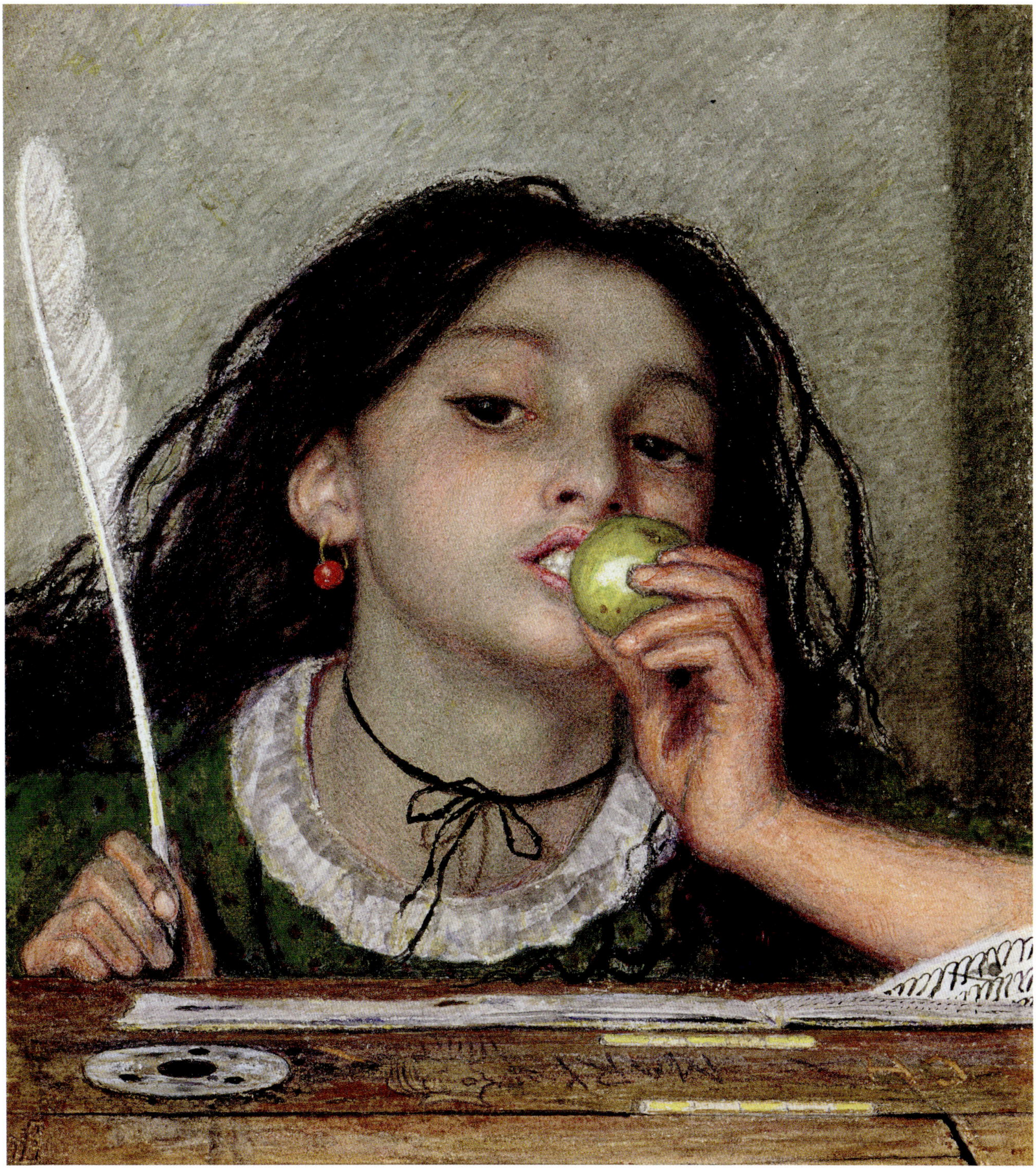

93
THE NOSEGAY

(A84)
1865, (1868)
watercolour, 18 5/8 × 12 11/16 (47.3 × 32.2)
signed in monogram: FMB
Ashmolean Museum, Oxford. Presented by Mrs W.F.R. Weldon 1933

Brown painted *The Nosegay* in the summer of 1865. Though not a straightforward portrait, the watercolour shows the artist's daughter Cathy, then aged twenty-four. She is gathering a bunch of flowers including carnations, pinks, roses and nasturtiums, whilst kneeling by a border planted with a pink climbing rose, convulvulus and a clump of tall lilies. The brick wall and the tangle of leaves and flowers forms the kind of intricate naturalistic background seen in Pre-Raphaelite oil paintings of the 1850s, also harking back to *Stages of Cruelty* (cat. 60). The flowers in the picture are associated with purity, love and beauty, while Cathy's fair hair and pale skin, her white dress and the skipping rope on the path suggest innocence and youth. A cat rubs lazily against her skirts; cats are traditional symbols of female sexuality but despite this and Cathy's low neckline, any eroticism in the picture is very subdued. Brown would hardly have wished to portray his daughter as a *femme fatale* and seems to be aiming primarily at a beautiful picture without a story, in accordance with the changing taste of the 1860s. *The Nosegay*, and *Myosotis* (fig. 27, p. 40), another picture in the same idiom, have something in common with Rossetti's portrayals of beautiful women with flowers. There are very few examples of this type of 'aesthetic' painting in Brown's work. His so-called sensuous style, the new more decorative manner he adopted in the 1860s, usually included a much stronger element of narrative.

Brown referred to *The Nosegay* as a 'pot-boiler.'[8] It was painted for the Manchester collector Frederick Craven, who had bought a watercolour of a praying boy entitled *Devotion* (fig. 92) from William Henry Hunt. Craven had commissioned a companion picture from Hunt, but the artist died before he could paint it. According to Rossetti, Craven had asked for a picture of 'a goldenhaired female'.[9] The commission was transferred to Brown, and apart from this requirement, Craven left him free as to subject and style. While a pretty young woman with flowers and a cat is not exactly an appropriate pendant to a boy kneeling with a rosary, it could have been intended as a contrast between the sacred and the profane or even as a comment on aestheticism as the new religion of beauty.

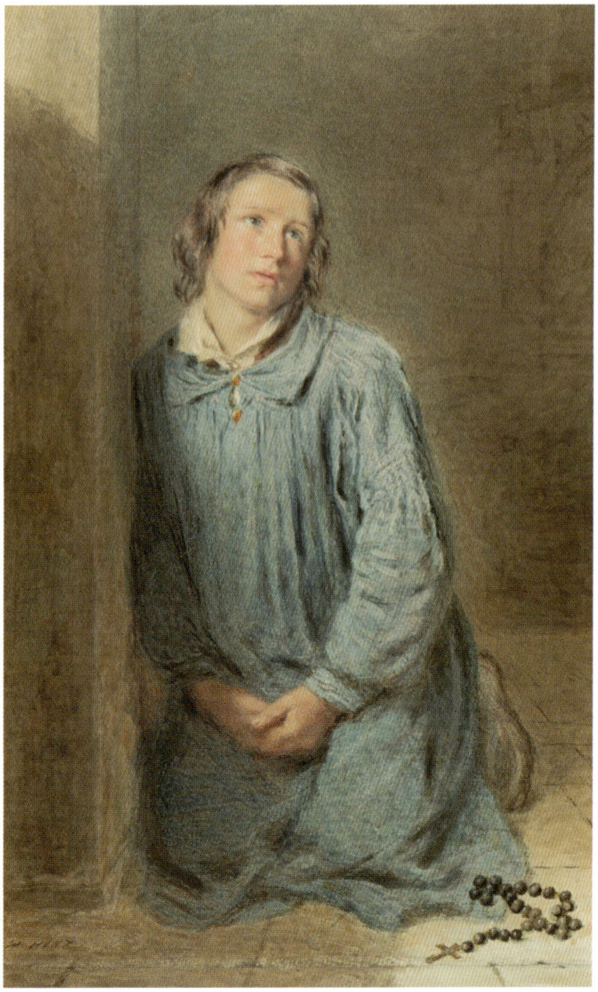

Fig. 92
William Henry Hunt, Devotion, *1836/42. Manchester City Galleries*

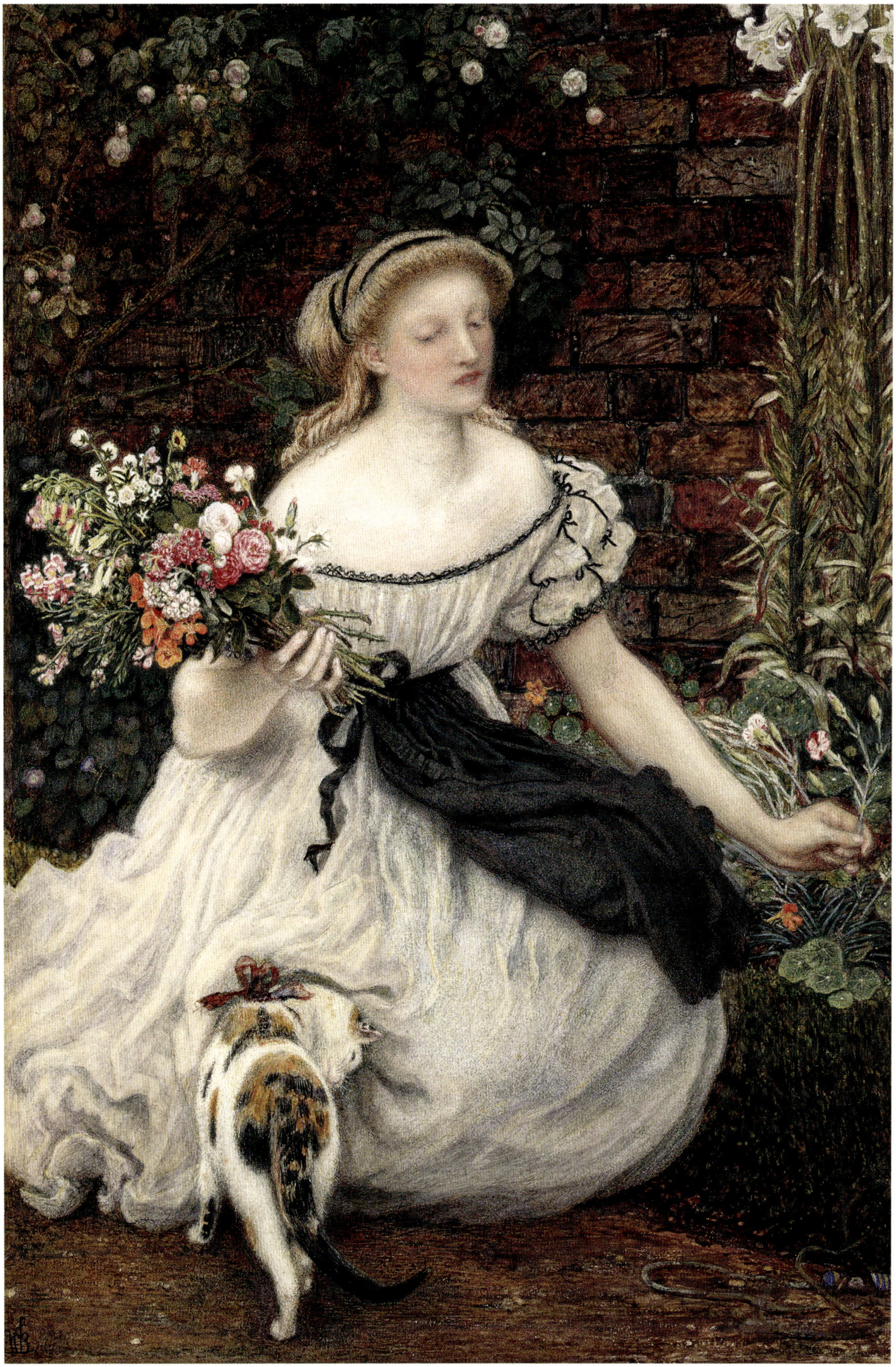

94

THINKING (EMMA MADOX BROWN)

(B42)
1869
coloured chalks, 31½ × 22½ (80 × 57)
Signed in monogram and dated: *FMB 69*
Maidstone Museum & Bentlif Art Gallery

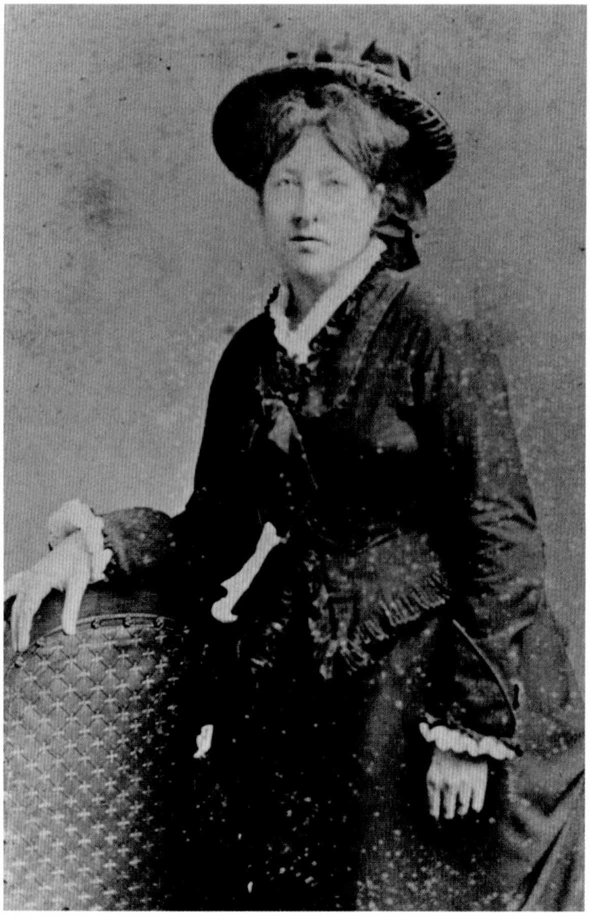

Fig. 93
Emma Madox Brown, photograph by Elliot and Fry, 1874/75. Stow Hill Collection, Parliamentry Archives, London

Photographs of Emma in middle age make her look plain (fig. 93), but she did not lose her looks, and despite the vicissitudes of their marriage, Brown continued to use her as a model. She was probably about forty when Brown drew this affectionate portrait of her. William Michael Rossetti described it as 'the best of her' when he saw it in Brown's studio on 8 July 1869.[10]

The drawing is in the artist's later style, with sweeping draperies, strongly curving lines and muted colours; an orange ribbon in Emma's hair picks up the colour of her dress, to which a spray of red and white flowers is pinned. When, towards the end of his life, Brown was invited to exhibit in Brussels with the Belgian avant-garde society Les XX (The Twenty), this was one of the works chosen. It had been admired by the Belgian art writer Olivier Destrée when he visited Brown's studio. While on exhibition it was described as 'superb' by a Belgian art critic, and another noted its affinity with Rossetti.[11]

Although in the 1860s, Cathy modelled for several paintings of young women (cats. 79, 93) Emma's features continued to appear in Brown's work; she appeared as Juliet in *Romeo and Juliet* in 1867 (fig. 26, p. 40) and Mary Chaworth in *Byron's Dream* in 1874 (cat. 85). In the 1880s she sat for some of the Manchester murals: 'I suppose that I am beginning to look old now' she wrote of her appearance as Queen Philippa of Hainault in the mural of the *Flemish Weavers* painted in 1882 (cat. 122).[12]

94

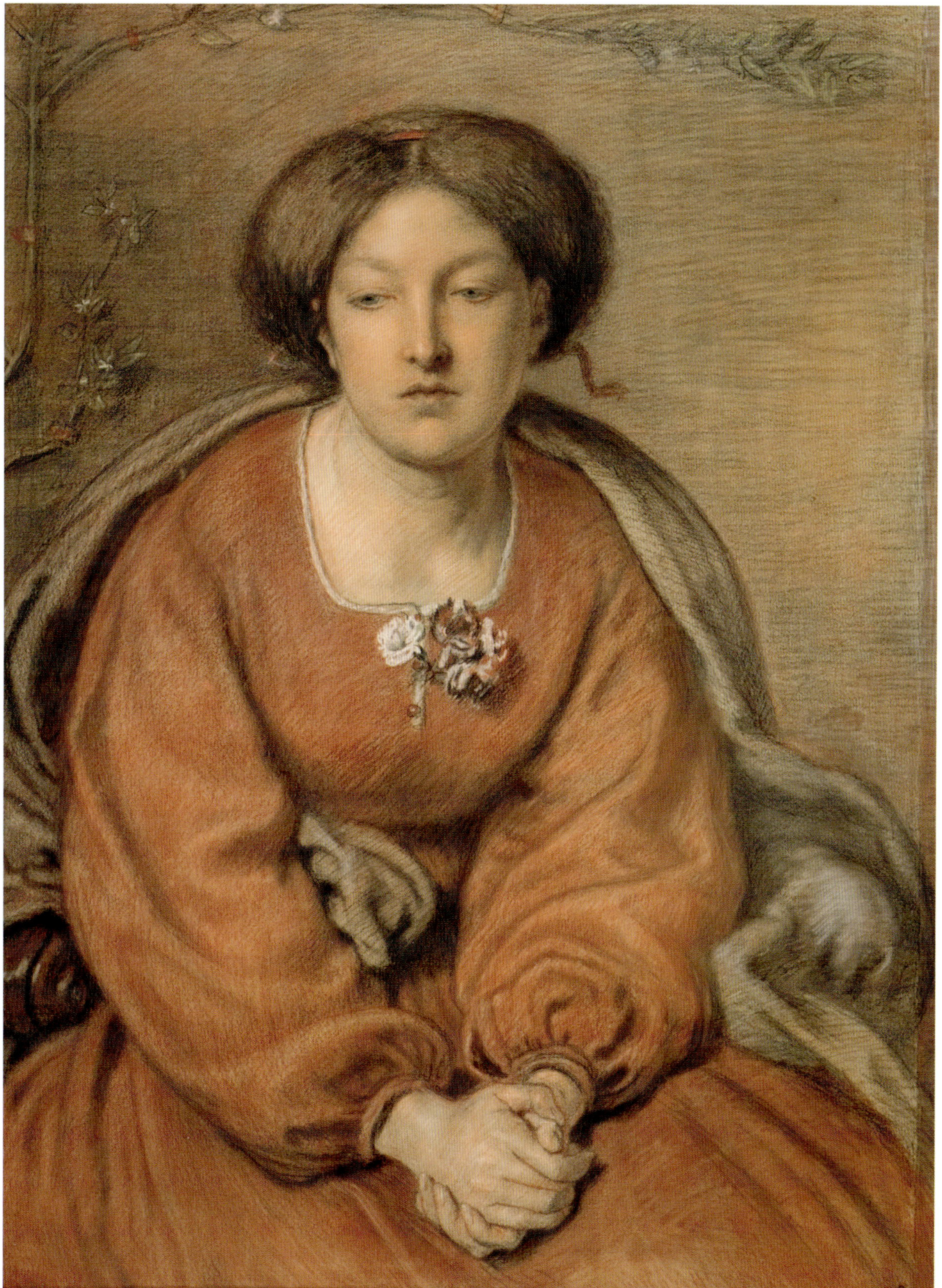

95

CATHERINE MADOX BROWN

(B27)
1872
coloured chalks, 30 × 22 (76 × 56)
Private collection

This unfinished portrait of the Browns' daughter Cathy dates from just before her marriage to the German musicologist and music critic of *The Times*, Franz Hueffer. She is shown with a paint box on her lap to indicate her chosen pursuit. She exhibited in London and the provinces, and continued to paint and to assist her father in his studio after her marriage: she was probably responsible for the replica of the mural *Weights and Measures* (cat. 128).[13]

Her daughter Juliet recalled her appearance: 'My mother was very pretty. She had fair hair and an absolutely straight nose, and a nicely shaped mouth with beautiful even white teeth and her eyes were a bright clear blue.' The memoir continued, 'When she was a girl she had painted some very beautiful pictures ... But she couldn't give much time to painting because there was always some one ill or in trouble, or who wanted taking care of.' For a time, she gave up painting because of the demands of looking after her parents, her husband and her children. 'Sometimes when she was telling me about it her face would look wistful and she'd sigh and say, "It *did* seem a pity!" But then she'd correct herself immediately afterwards and say she thought perhaps she had been happier taking care of other people than painting pictures.'[14]

Juliet was the youngest of Cathy's three children. The eldest, Ford Madox Hueffer, published a biography of his grandfather Ford Madox Brown in 1896.[15] Hueffer, who anglicised his surname in 1919, is better known as the novelist Ford Madox Ford.

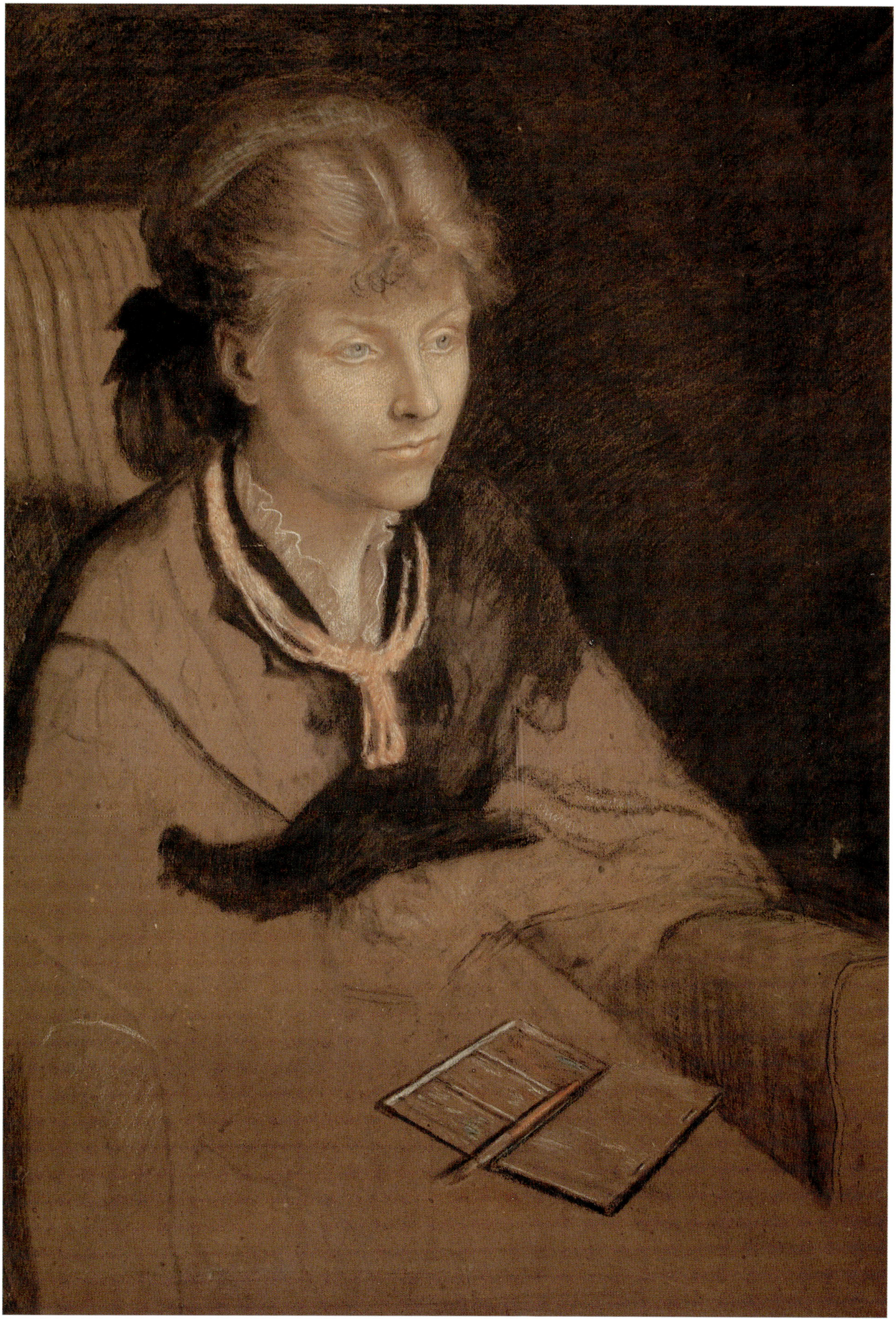

96

IZA HARDY

(B69)
1872
pastel and coloured chalks, 30 3/8 × 21 7/8 (77.1 × 5.6)
inscribed: *IZA HARDY* and signed in monogram: */FMB 72*
Birmingham Museums and Art Gallery

Iza Hardy (1850–1922) was a novelist and short-story writer, the daughter of Sir Thomas Duffus Hardy (1804–78), Deputy Keeper of the Public Record Office and his second wife Mary Anne, Lady Hardy, a novelist and travel writer. The Hardys were close friends of the Browns, especially of Brown's daughter Lucy. In the portrait Iza has an abstracted gaze, and seems slightly ill at ease, with restless hands. The portrait shows Brown's fondness for orange colour harmonies seen in other chalk portraits of this period.
It never belonged to the sitter, as it was in the sale organised by Brown's executors after his death, so it was likely that Brown drew it for himself rather than at Iza's request.

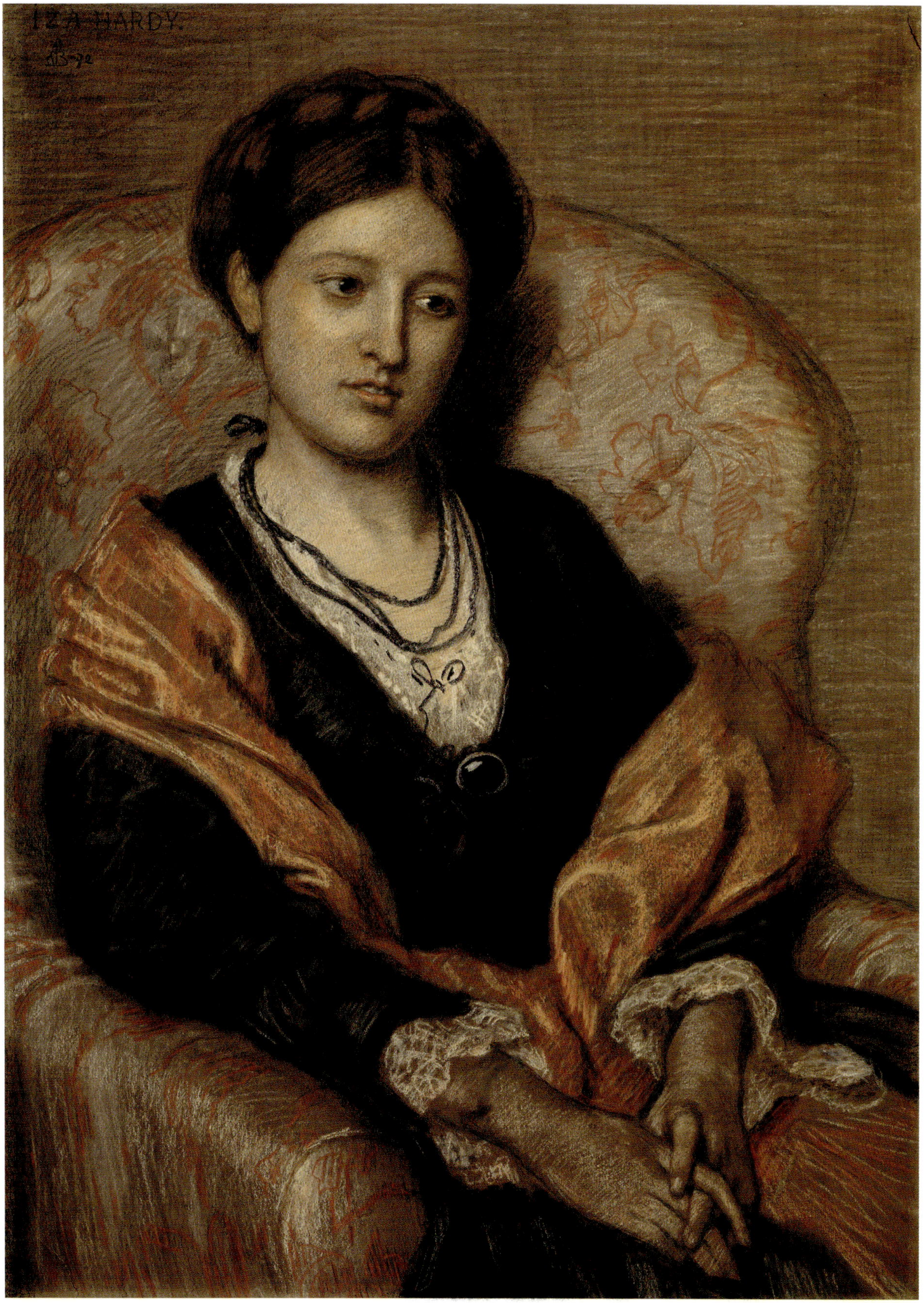
IZA HARDY.

97
HENRY AND MILLICENT FAWCETT

(B65)
1874
oil on canvas, 42¾ × 33 (108.5 × 84)
inscribed: *HENRY FAWCETT Esq. M.P. & Mrs. FAWCETT* and signed in monogram: *FMB 72*
National Portrait Gallery, London. Bequeathed by Sir Charles Wentworth Dilke, 2nd Bt, 1911

The portrait depicts a famous radical Liberal couple, Henry Fawcett (1833–84) and his wife Millicent Garrett Fawcett (1847–1929). Henry's career at the bar was cut short in 1858 when he was blinded in a shooting accident, but he became a Liberal MP and in 1863 he published a *Manual of Political Economy* which led to his election to the Chair of Political Economy at Cambridge in that year. Brown's portrait shows him in academic dress, with his tasselled mortarboard on his lap. He was involved in the passing of the Reform Bill of 1867, campaigned to improve the position of women in employment, and later became Postmaster General.

In 1867 he married Millicent Garrett, who shared his intellectual and political interests, and acted as his secretary and guide. In 1872, the year of the portrait, they jointly published a book of *Essays and Lectures on Social and Political Subjects* but she also developed a career as a writer and speaker in her own right, publishing works on political economy, and biographies including a life of Queen Victoria. Her most important work was as the leader of the constitutional movement for women's suffrage, joining the first women's suffrage committee in 1867. In 1897 she became president of the influential National Union of Women's Suffrage Societies, although she did not support the violent tactics of the militant suffragettes.

The painting was commissioned by their friend, the radical politician Sir Charles Wentworth Dilke. Brown probably received the commission through Frederick George Stephens, a member of the original Pre-Raphaelite Brotherhood, and a supporter of Brown. Stephens was the art critic of the *Athenaeum*, which was owned by Dilke. It was Brown who suggested a three-quarter length double portrait rather than the heads on their own: 'My idea of painting Fawcett & his wife seems to me the most interesting, a group might be made of them full of character & pathos.'[16] Brown shows Mrs. Fawcett seated on the arm of her husband's chair while he speaks to her about the letter which she is holding in one hand; a pen in the other suggests he has just dictated it to her. The letter is inscribed: *Your Obt. Servants/ M G Fawcett/ Henry Fawcett*. Although she usually published under her own name as Millicent Garrett Fawcett, as a public figure she was always styled Mrs Henry Fawcett.[17] This is reflected in the portrait, where she is shown as supporter to her husband; but the partnership was very close and they were intellectual equals.

Brown has transformed what might have been a simple portrait into a moving and tender representation of a relationship. The artist's friend Frederic Shields believed that Brown had elevated it 'to the rank of an historical picture.'[18] Brown's portrait supports Lawrence Goldman's assessment of Henry Fawcett that 'for his contemporaries, it was the triumph over handicap of the first blind man who, it was believed, had ever been elected to parliament, which was Fawcett's greatest achievement. His life was understood to exemplify virtues like courage, fortitude, and optimism, and was presented as an inspiration for others.'[19]

1 UBC Angeli-Dennis Collection 18–4. I am grateful to Angela Thirlwell for giving me this reference.
2 Peattie 1990, p. 57.
3 UBC, FMB to James Leathart 8 February 1863.
4 Bennett 2101, I, pp. 150–51, A59.3.
5 Brown 1865, no. 30.
6 Newcastle 1989, repr. p.6.
7 V&A, FMB to Leathart, nd [Christmas 1862].
8 NML, FMB to George Rae, 5 October 1865.
9 D.G. Rossetti, *Correspondence*, 3, p. 304.
10 W.M. Rossetti 1903, p. 402.
11 Laughton 1967, pp. 375–76, 379; Bennet 2010, I, p. 386.
12 V&A, FMB to Catherine Hueffer 2 April 1882.
13 For examples of her original compositions see Marsh and Nunn 1997, pp. 129–31.
14 Soskice 1921, pp. 202, 204.
15 Hueffer 1896.
16 BL Dilke Papers, FMB to F.G. Stephens 21 January 1872.
17 DNB, article by Jane Howarth.
18 Shields 1874, pp. 49–50.
19 DNB, article by Lawrence Goldman.

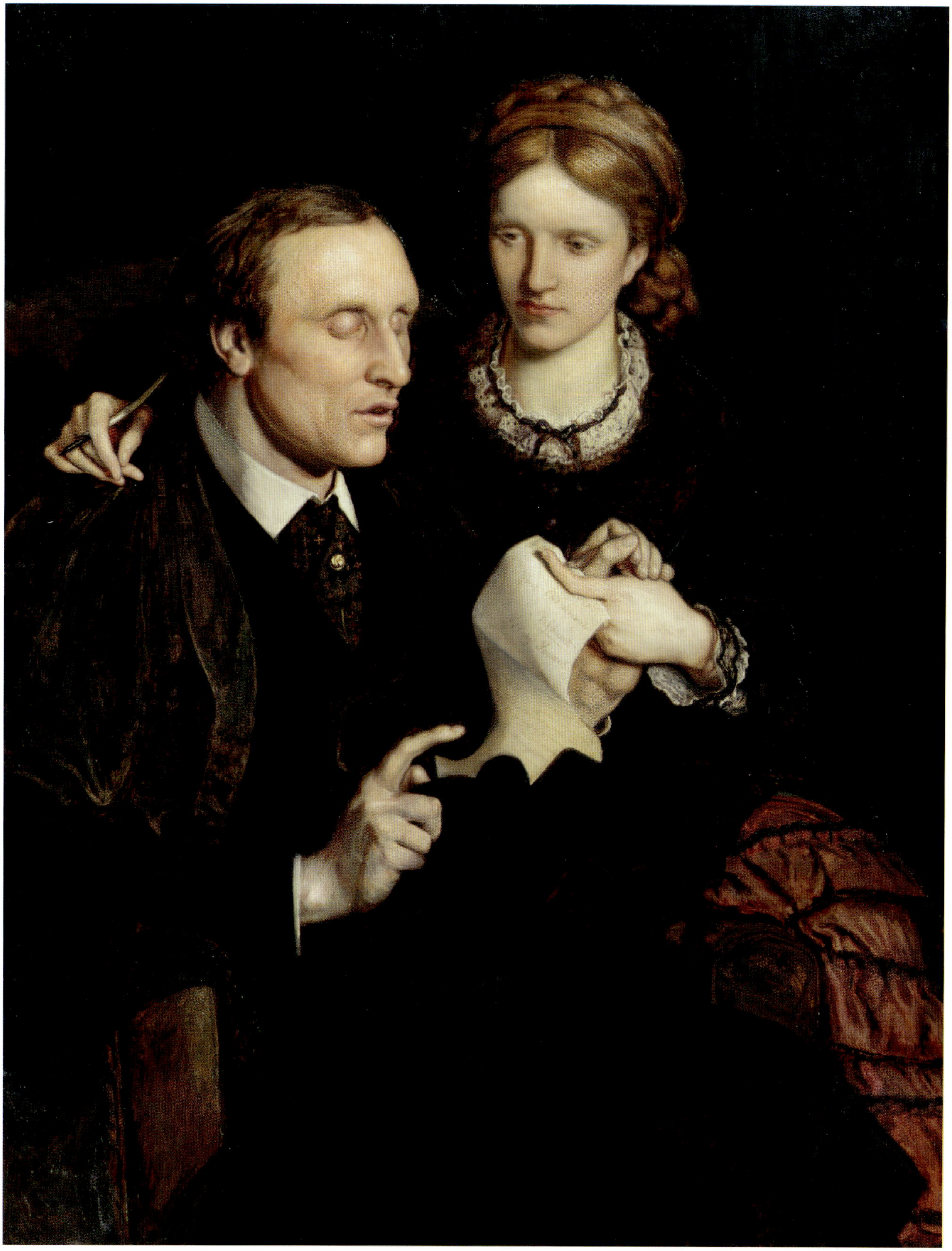

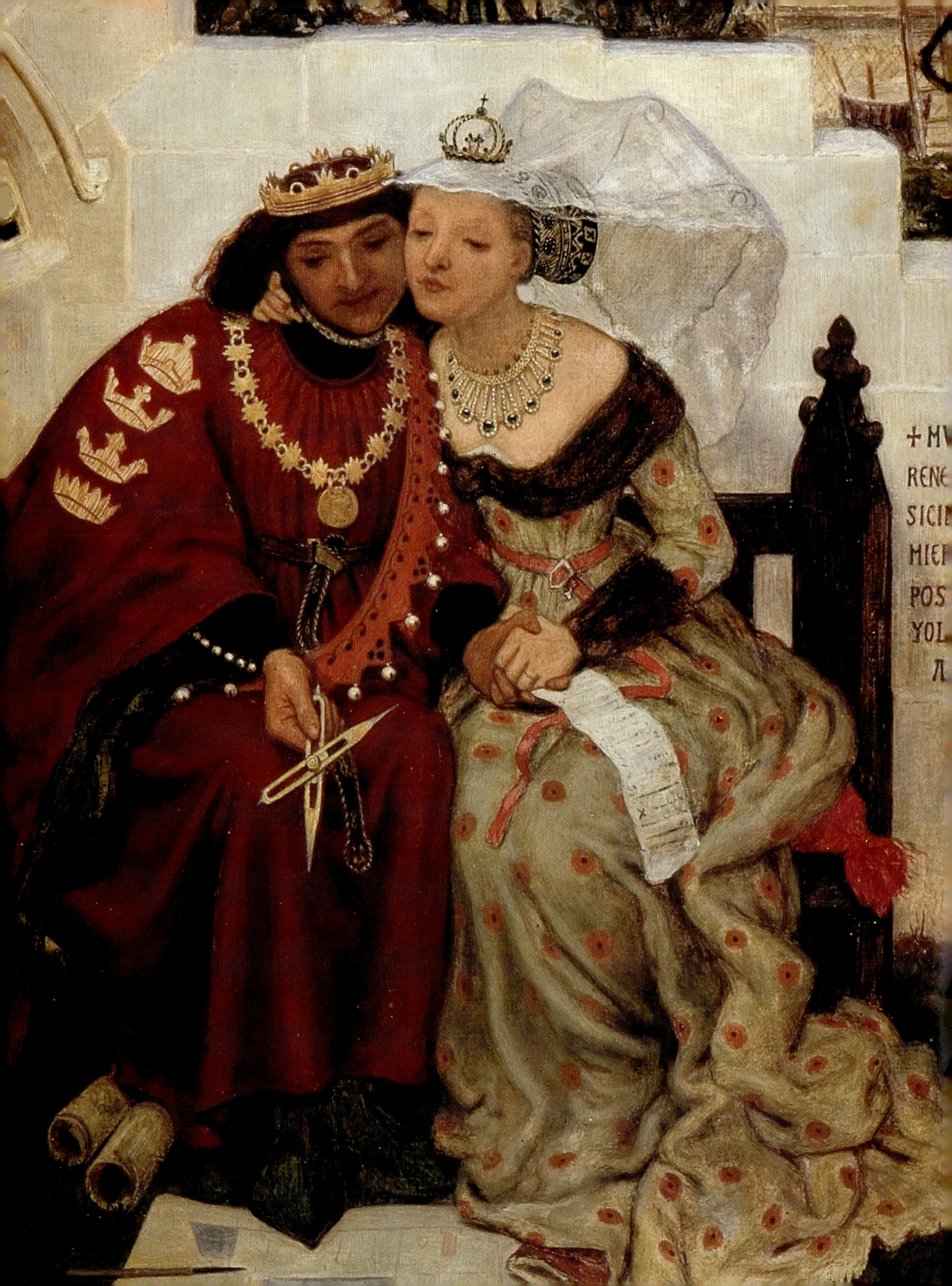
+ MV
RENE
SICI
MIEI
POS
YOL
A

THE DESIGNER

Brown was not just a fine artist, but also a designer. He was one of the original partners in Morris, Marshall, Faulkner & Co, founded in 1861; he designed many types of object for the firm including textiles and wallpapers that can no longer be identified, but his principal contribution was the design of stained glass windows.

Between 1861 and 1874, when the firm was reconstituted as Morris & Company, and Brown ceased to be a partner, he produced about 115 designs for windows, a total only exceeded by that of Burne-Jones, the firm's principal glass designer. Their designs were made in the form of black and white cartoons. These were then handed over to Morris and Philip Webb, who were responsible for coordinating the designs of the different artists into complete windows, as well as for planning the colours and the architectural arrangements, and for designing the decorative parts of the windows such as foliage patterns. The designs would then be executed in glass and lead by specialised craftsmen. Brown's stained glass designs have a vigour that marks them out from the rest of Morris glass. They possess the 'invention, expression and good dramatic action' that together with fine colour he defined as the essentials of stained glass.[1]

Brown's earliest furniture designs were contemporary with Morris's first experiments in furniture design before the foundation of the firm. Brown was then already knowledgeable about medieval furniture as he had incorporated elaborate Gothic thrones and lecterns into his historical pictures (cats. 33, 34). In contrast, his real furniture was remarkable for its austerity and simplicity, but it was not very commercial, and few examples were made, apart from his rush-seated chair for Morris, which was still in production around 1910.

Brown also designed his own picture frames; he saw the frame as an integral part of the painting, rather than as a decorative addition, and disliked the standard designs available from commercial framers. Brown shared this interest in frame design with the other Pre-Raphaelites, especially with Rossetti. The two often used similar frames, and their individual responsibility for authorship is not always clear.[2]

Brown's ideas on framing were derived from the early Flemish works he saw in Belgium, and from the Nazarenes, who designed their own frames in the Gothic style. These influences can be seen in the original frame, now replaced, for *The First Translation of the Bible into English* (cat. 33) and in the real and painted frames for *The Seeds and Fruits of English Poetry* (cat. 32). From the late 1850s Brown's frames became simpler, and more emphatically rectilinear, some with hardly any decoration, apart from bevels and stepped lines. The richness of colour in a painting was set off by surrounding it with a broad flat of gilt oak, with the wood grain showing through the gold. At the outer edge of the flat was a much narrower outer moulding, typically a simple reeded band, often punctuated with circular and square motifs, or with a 'thumbmark' pattern of alternating semicircles. From the 1870s, Brown also used a historical style of frame, based on a seventeenth-century type associated with the painter Peter Lely. Brown was an early advocate of the equality of the fine and decorative arts, an attitude fundamental to the philosophy of Morris and later to the Arts and Crafts movement. In 1859 he resigned from the Hogarth Club when it rejected the furniture designs he sent in with his paintings to their summer exhibition. He freely translated his designs into different media: just as he made paintings from subjects originally drawn as book illustrations, he also produced paintings from some of his stained glass designs, and made glass cartoons from decorative paintings and tile designs. Later he took part in the early exhibitions of the Arts and Crafts Exhibition Society, whose leading figures, including Mackmurdo and Lethaby, were admirers of his work.

Fig. 94
Detail of cat. 100, King René's Honeymoon

98
THE DEATH OF SIR TRISTRAM

1862
made by Morris, Marshall Faulkner & Co., after design by Brown
stained glass panel, 30½ × 24 (76 × 61)
lettered: *How Sir Tristram & King Mark were made at one again by King Arthur's means & how nevertheless King Mark / slew Sir Tristram by treachery as he sat harping to La Belle Isoude & Isoude died the third day after*
Bradford Museums and Galleries (Cliffe Castle Museum)

The Death of Sir Tristram is an episode from the story of Tristram and Isoude, the tragic tale of doomed love from Malory's *Mort d'Arthur*. Tristram sailed to Cornwall bringing Isoude in marriage to his uncle, King Mark of Cornwall. During the voyage Tristram and Isoude drank a love potion that was intended for Isoude to drink with King Mark, and fell deeply in love. When they arrived, King Mark married Isoude, and Tristram went to Britanny. After many adventures Tristram and Isoude were reunited, but King Mark was jealous of Tristram and killed him (Malory, book 19, chapter 11). Brown depicted the traitorous King Mark brandishing the weapon with which he had killed Tristram from behind, whilst Isoude throws herself in anguish on Tristram's dead body.

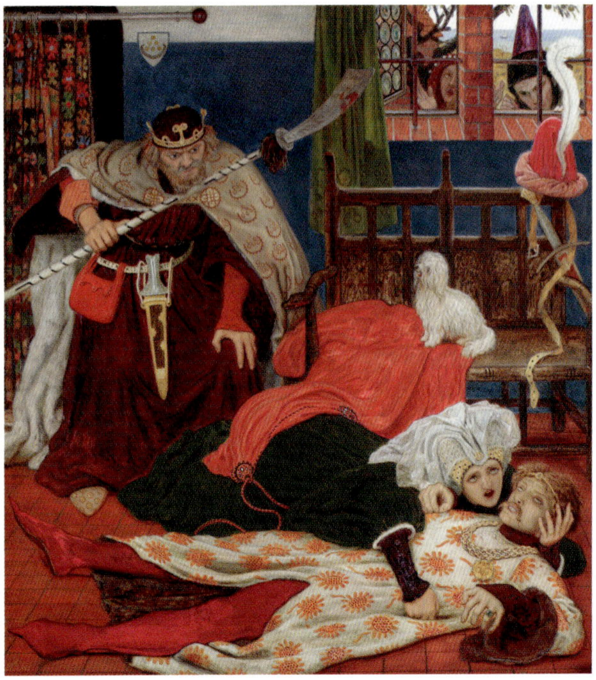

Fig. 95
Ford Madox Brown, The Death of Sir Tristram, *1864. Birmingham Museums and Art Gallery*

The panel comes from a set of thirteen stained-glass windows telling the story of the doomed lovers. They were made by Morris, Marshall, Faulkner & Co. for a Bradford merchant, Walter Dunlop, to go in the entrance hall of his house, Harden Grange, near Bingley, Yorkshire. This was one of the firm's first domestic commissions, and the subjects were shared among several artists: Burne-Jones, Hughes, Prinsep, Rossetti and Morris himself designed the other panels in the series. The commission came about through the agency of the Bradford decorator John Aldam Heaton, a patron of Rossetti, and a neighbour of Dunlop. As this was an early commission, before the Firm was very experienced in glass making, the glass is thinner and less richly coloured than later Morris windows.[3]

The Tristram and Isoude legend was one of Morris's favourite episodes from Malory and it seems to have been his idea to use it for this commission. In Malory's poem the Death of Sir Tristram was only briefly mentioned, but the story was retold by Matthew Arnold in a poem of 1852 and was included in Tennyson's *Idylls of the King* of 1859. It became more widely known when Wagner used it for his opera *Tristan und Isolde*, first produced in 1865.

Brown reused the design in 1864 for an oil painting (fig. 95). In his description of the painting he identified King Mark's weapons as a 'glaive', a blade on a long pole, and an 'anelace', a type of long dagger dangling from his waist. The dog seated on the settle is the 'brachet' by which Tristram was recognised when he returned from exile.[4] The greater realism required for the painting makes for too much distracting detail and the faces of Tristram and Isoude look unconvincing, whereas in the stained glass, the heavy lead lines, flat colours and schematic drawing give the scene a primitive dramatic force.

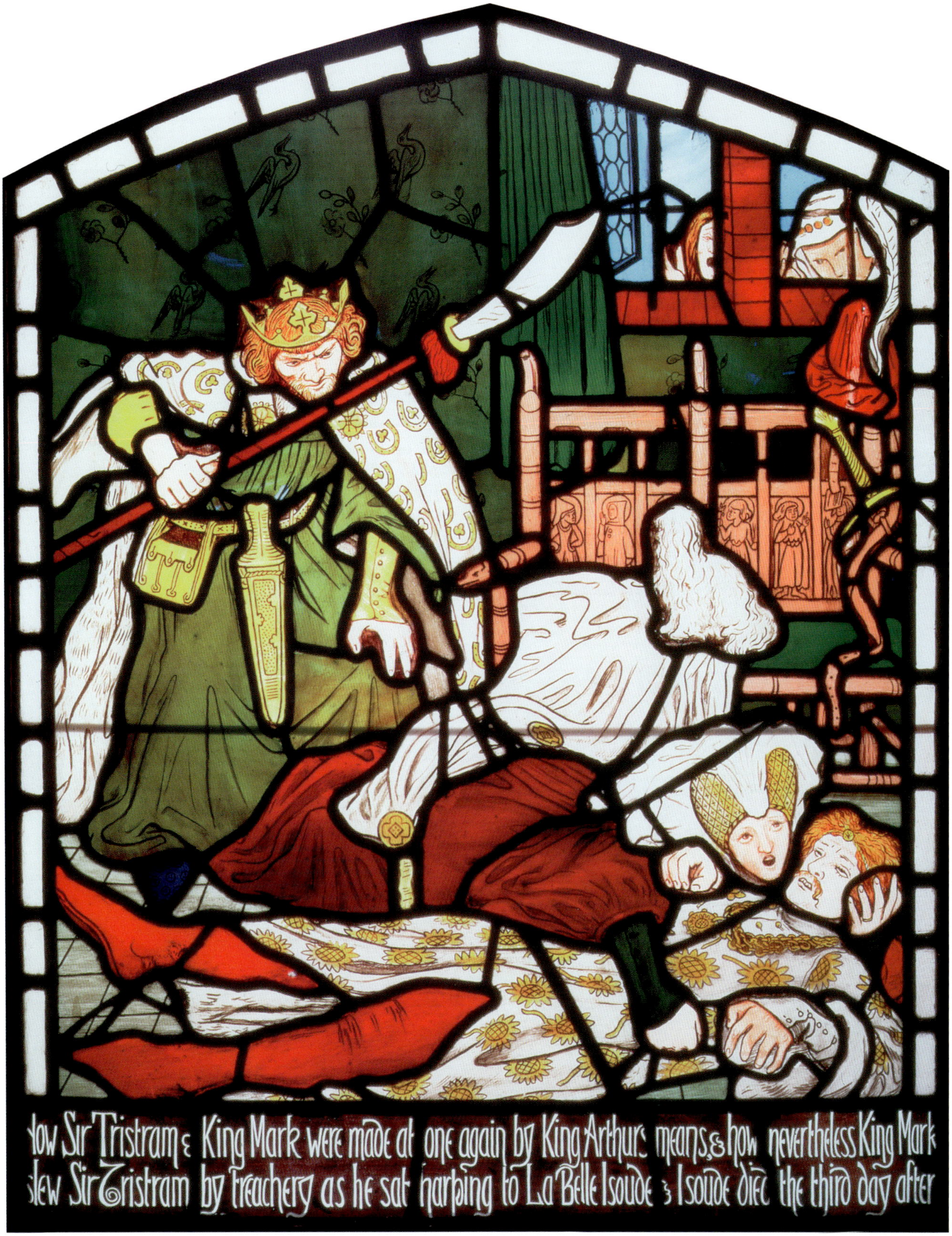
low Sir Tristram & King Mark were made at one again by King Arthurs means & how nevertheless King Mark
slew Sir Tristram by treachery as he sat harping to La Belle Isoude & Isoude died the third day after

98

99

PRUNING (THE WOODCUTTER)

1863
made by Morris, Marshall Faulkner & Co., after design by Brown
stained glass panel, 14 3/8 x 12 3/16 (36.5 x 31)
William Morris Gallery, London Borough of Waltham Forest

The man climbing a tree with a saw, rope and a pruning hook represents March, from a series of the Labours of the Months; in the top right is the corresponding sign of the zodiac, Aries the ram. The stained-glass panel was probably made for a five-light window intended for the drawing room of a house designed by Norman Shaw for Charles Hastings, a Bradford manufacturer and an associate of John Aldam Heaton (see cat. 98). The house was never built.

Brown originally designed this and three other figures representing *Hawking, Sowing and Sheepshearing* for painted tiles. Three of Brown's designs, including this one, feature on the elaborate tiled overmantel made by Morris, Marshall, Faulkner & Co. in 1863 for the fireplace in the Old Hall at Queen's College, Cambridge. The other months were designed by Rossetti, Burne-Jones and Morris.

The Labours of the Months, twelve scenes each showing a seasonal rural activity, often also with the associated sign of the Zodiac, were often represented in medieval art. They were depicted in illuminated manuscripts, especially Books of Hours, and in sculptured decoration in churches. The iconography of the Labours of the Months would have been familiar to Morris and his partners in the Firm from their studies of medieval manuscript illumination.[5]

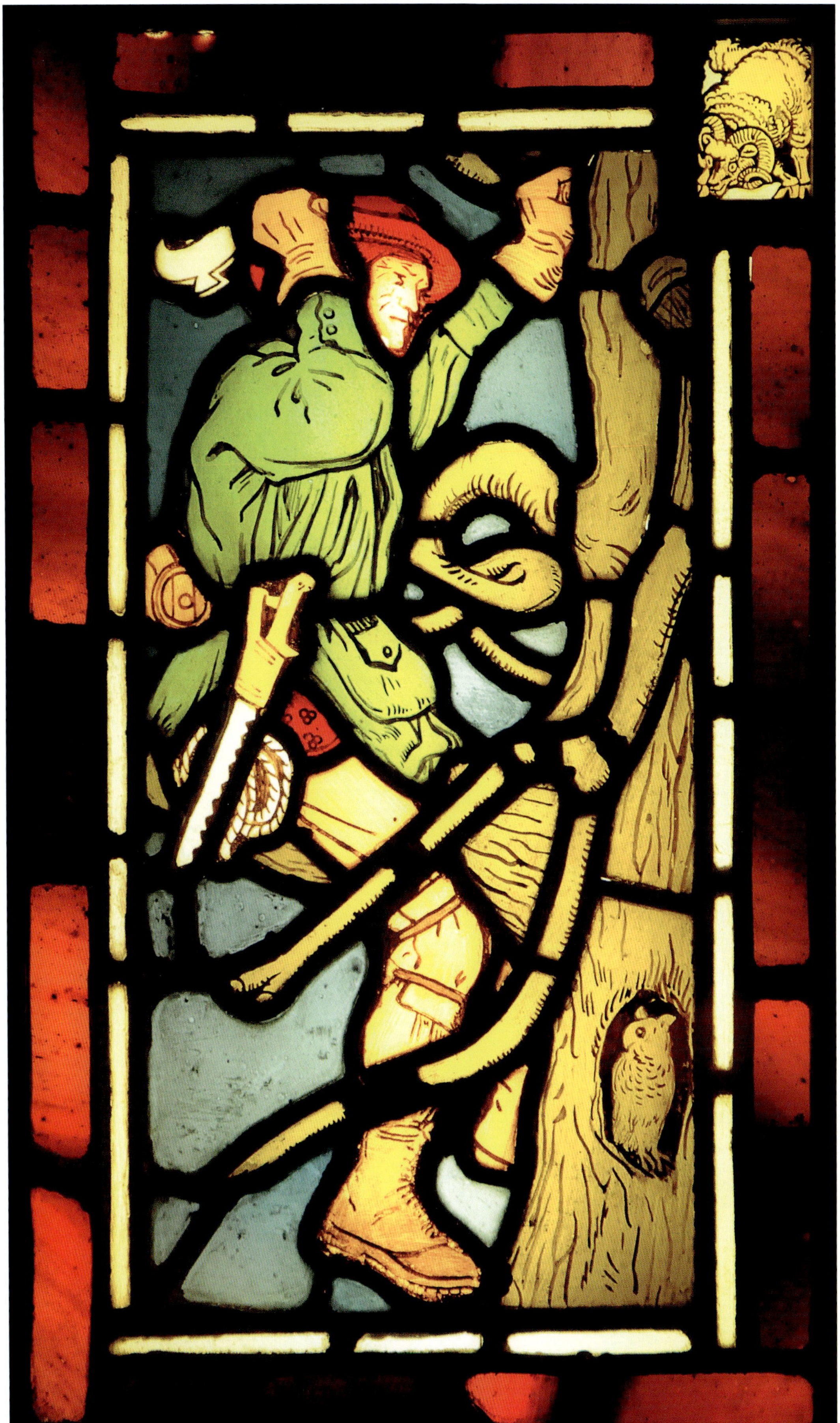

100

KING RENÉ'S HONEYMOON

(A81.1)
1864
oil on panel, 21 3/8 × 13 7/8 (54.3 × 35.2)
signed in monogram and dated: *FMB – 64*
Amgueddfa Cymru – National Museum Wales. James Pyke-Thompson Collection

King René (1409–80), 4th Duke of Anjou and titular King of Naples, Sicily, Cyprus and Jerusalem, was an important patron of the arts. This is an imaginary portrait representing René as a patron of architecture, and was intended to be humorous: 'Of course, as soon as married, he would build a new house, carve it and decorate it himself, and talk nothing but Art all the "Honeymoon" (except indeed love.)' wrote Brown.[6]

King René's Honeymoon was originally conceived not as an independent picture, but as a decorative painting for a piece of furniture, a large desk (fig. 96) designed in 1861 by the architect J.P. Seddon to store his architectural drawings. Seddon commissioned Morris, Marshall, Faulkner & Co. to provide ten painted panels for the desk, and Brown suggested the idea of an imaginary cabinet that the King might have commissioned for his honeymoon, illustrating his love of the arts. The desk was therefore named the *King René's Honeymoon Cabinet*. It has four large painted panels along the front showing René and his Queen engaging in artistic pursuits: Brown's panel showing *Architecture*; *Painting* and *Sculpture* by Burne-Jones; and *Music* by Rossetti.

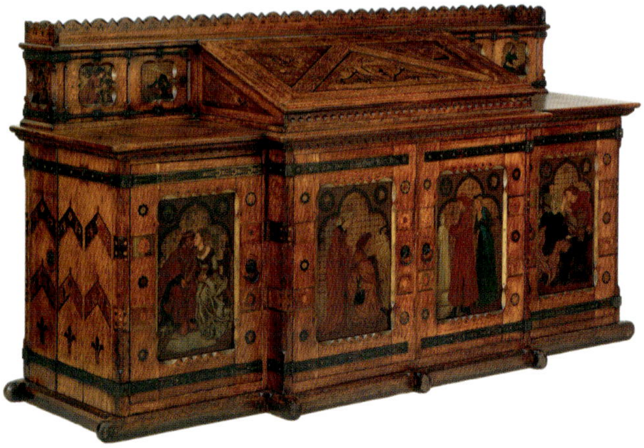

Fig. 96
King René's Honeymoon Cabinet, designed by J.P. Seddon and decorated by various artists including Ford Madox Brown, 1861–62. Victoria and Albert Museum

There are also smaller scenes at the top showing gardening and the decorative arts painted by Rossetti, Prinsep and Burne-Jones. All the panels have diapered backgrounds designed by Morris, whose portrait was included in the panel of *Ironwork*.

In 1864, Brown repeated the design in two watercolours and in this oil painting, which is the same size as the panel on the cabinet itself.[7] The scene, with *Painting, Sculpture* and *Music*, was also executed in stained glass by the Morris firm for the house of the painter Myles Birket Foster at Witley (Victoria & Albert Museum). The humour of the subject appears less forced when used for furniture or glass than in an independent picture.

The painting shows the King and Queen holding hands and cuddling together on a Gothic bench, as they look down at an architectural drawing of their new house spread on the ground. The bench and the house in the drawing look more like the 1850s than the 1450s, and Brown may have intended an in-joke about Morris contemplating the design of Red House. The four gold coronets on René's cloak represent his four titular kingdoms. He points to the drawing with a pair of compasses with intersecting legs known as a reduction compass. A T-square and a pen lie on the drawing. Instead of the decorative background seen on the cabinet, the couple sit in front of a half-built wall with part of a lettered foundation stone, and behind the wall, beyond a screen of trees is a glimpse of further building works, lit by the moon: 'it is twilight when the workmen are gone.'[8] In the scene on the cabinet, in the stained-glass version and in one of the watercolours, the Queen's head is turned towards the king and she is kissing his cheek. Rossetti's panel also showed the couple kissing while the Queen played the organ.

Brown's source for the life of King René was Sir Walter Scott's novel *Anne of Geierstein* (1829). In chapters 29 and 30 the hero went to Provence where he met King René, whom Scott portrayed as a frivolous monarch who enjoyed dancing, music, painting and writing poetry as well as architecture and restoring classical monuments. The idea of a king totally devoted to the arts would have appealed to Morris and his fellow artists. But the novel made no mention of the King's honeymoon, and it must have been Brown's idea to combine the themes of love and art in a collaboration between artists and craftsmen, a demonstration of the equality of the fine and decorative arts.

The frame is a variation on the type with a narrow outer surround relieved with reeding much favoured by the artist. Here the reeded frame has a bevelled edge and an inner fillet, and instead of having roundels on the frame, as in *The Entombment* (cat. 78), the roundels have been cut into the gilt flat.

The painting was sold to the Brighton wine merchant J. Hamilton Trist, the patron of Arthur Hughes.

100

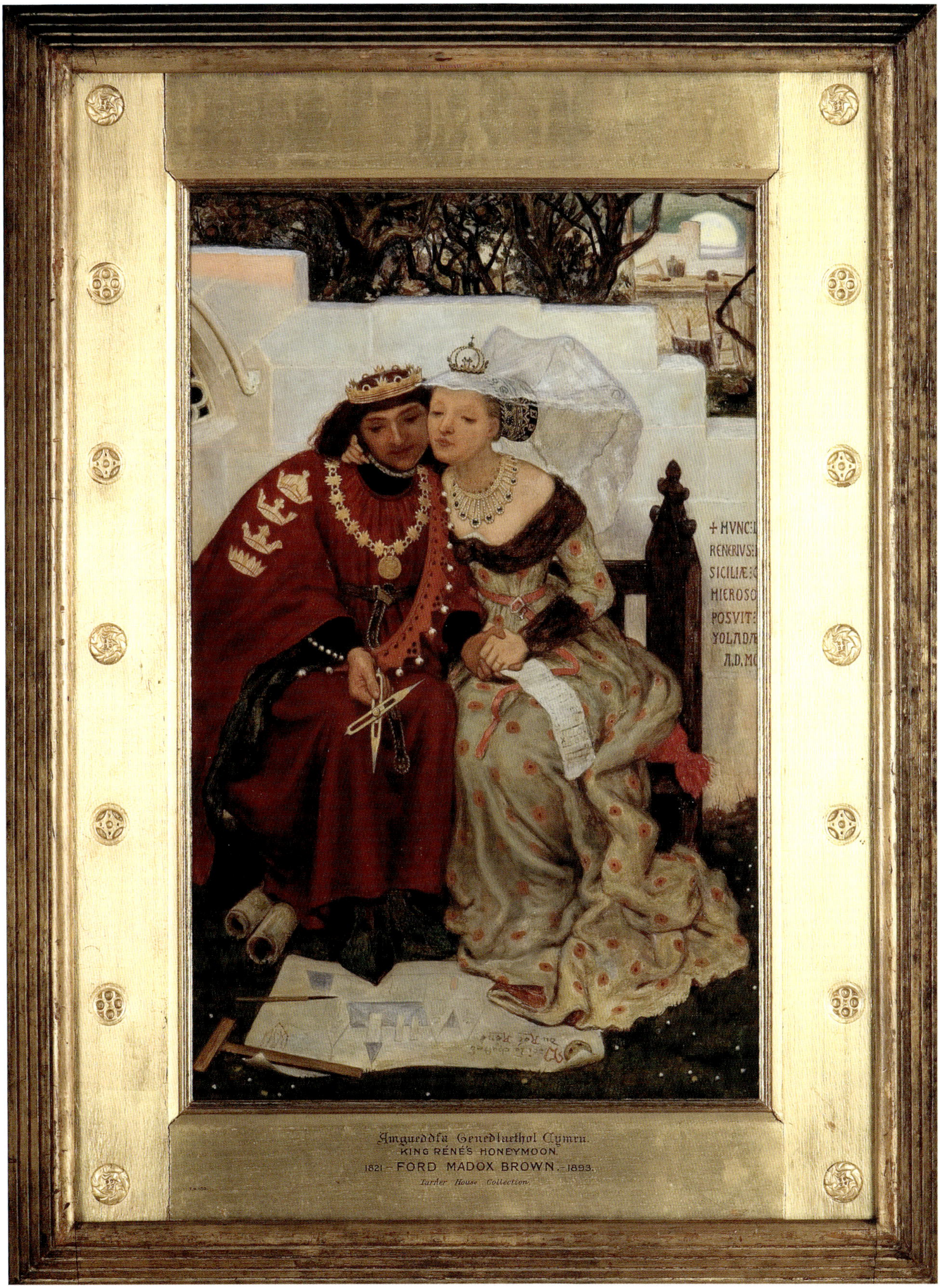
+ HVNC:L
RENERIVS:
SICILIÆ:
HIEROSO
POSVIT:
YOLADÆ
A.D.MC
Amgueddfa Genedlaethol Cymru.
KING RÉNÉ'S HONEYMOON.
1821 - FORD MADOX BROWN. - 1893.
Turner House Collection.

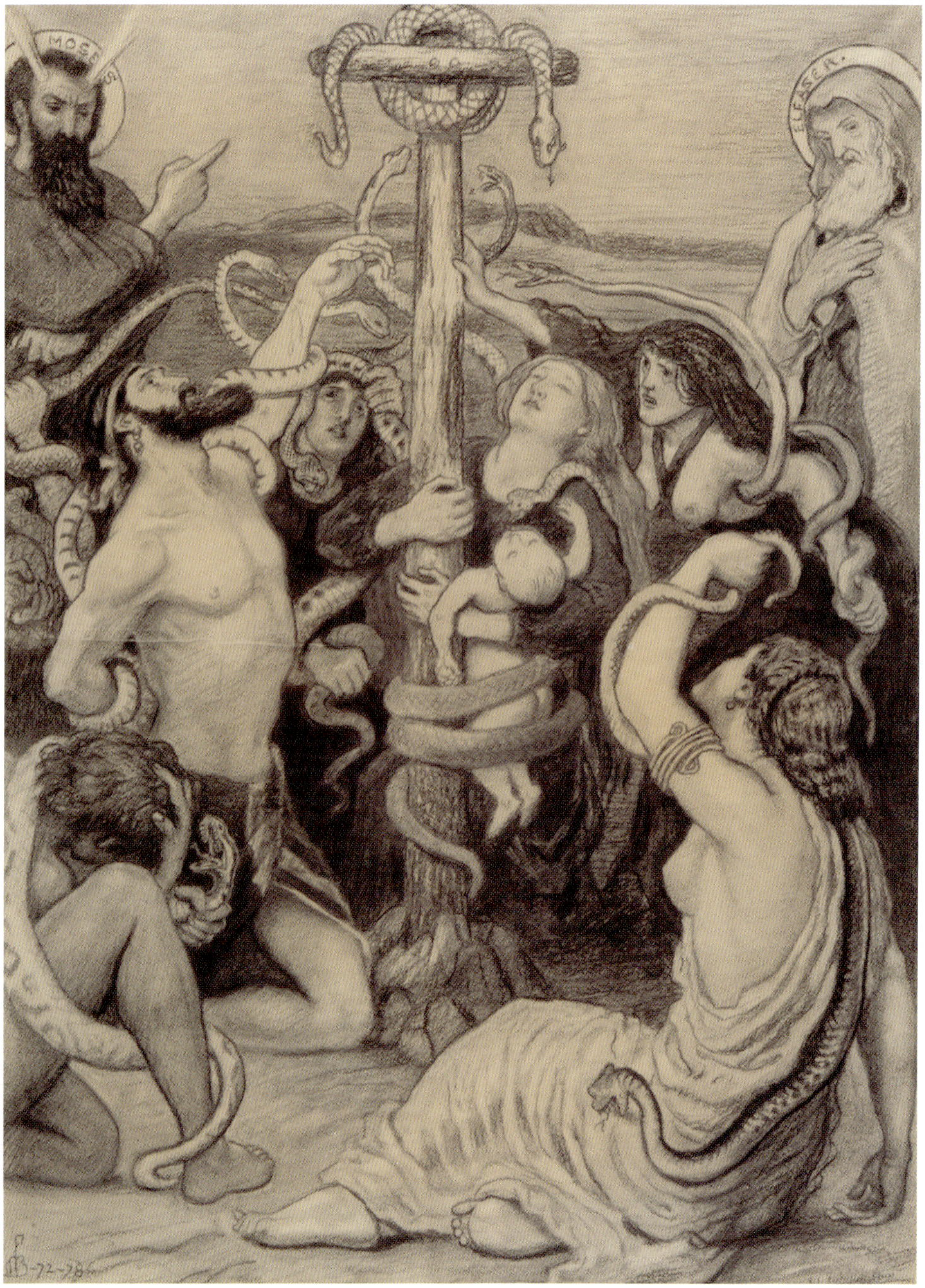

101
THE BRAZEN SERPENT

(C177)
1872, (1878)
cartoon for stained glass, black chalk and wash,
27⅛ × 19⅞ (68.8 × 50.5)
signed in monogram and dated: *FMB – 72 – 78*
Private collection, on loan to Manchester City Galleries

During the time the Israelites were wandering in the desert, God sent a plague of serpents as punishment for their lack of faith. The Israelites repented, and Moses prayed to God for them. 'And the Lord said unto Moses, Make thee a fiery serpent, and set it upon a pole: and it shall come to pass, that every one that is bitten, when he looketh upon it, shall live' (Numbers 21:8). Brown's stained glass design is one of his most vigorous compositions, with the plague of snakes writhing round the bodies of the kneeling Israelites, who raise their eyes towards the Brazen Serpent to be

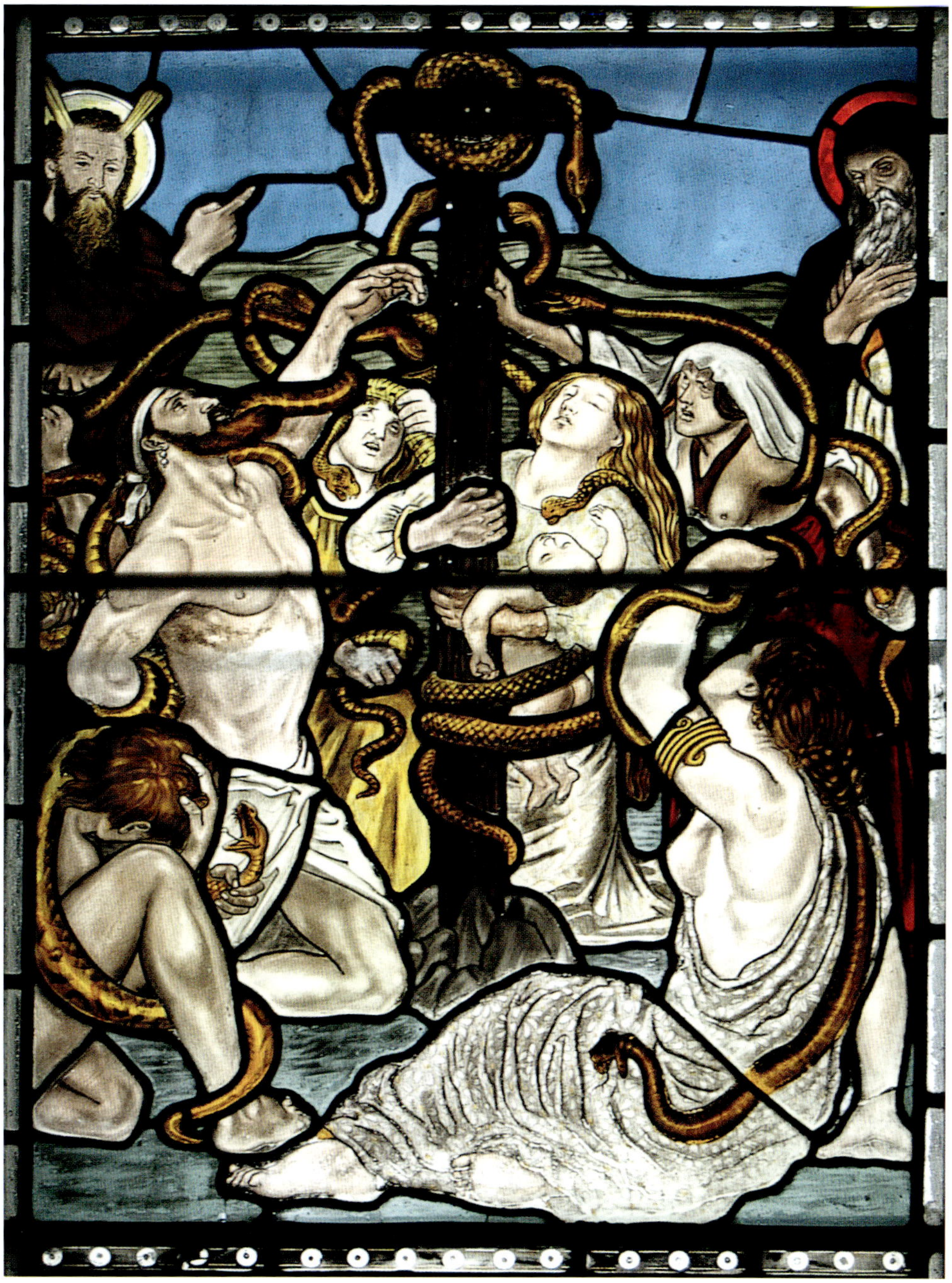

Fig. 97
The Brazen Serpent, *stained-glass window, Holy Cross, Haltwhistle, designed by Ford Madox Brown and made by Morris, Marshall, Faulkner and Co., 1872*

cured of their bites. Moses stands behind at the left pointing to the Serpent and on the left is Eleazer, who took over from his father Aaron as High Priest.

The window was designed in 1872 for the East Window of Holy Cross, Haltwhistle, Northumberland (fig. 97). It forms the lower section of the central lancet, the upper part of which is occupied by a Crucifixion designed by Burne-Jones. The Brazen Serpent was often paired with a scene of Christ on the Cross, and also represented in the shape of a cross, because it was thought to prefigure the Crucifixion. This followed the book of John, in which Jesus said 'And as Moses lifted up the serpent in the wilderness, even so must the Son of man be lifted up' (John 3:14). Brown and Burne-Jones also designed the two flanking lancets. Brown retouched the cartoon in 1878 before sending to Manchester where it was shown at the Horsfall Museum.

102
KING ATHELSTANE GIVES AWAY HIS SISTER

103
ST. EDITHA

104
THE KING OF NORTHUMBRIA

105
THE BISHOP'S NUPTIAL BENEDICTION

(C201-4)
1878, after designs of 1873
cartoons for stained glass, each ink and wash,
41¼ × 16½ (104.8 × 42)
St. Editha inscribed: *FMB 73*
The Whitworth Art Gallery, The University of Manchester

According to medieval tradition, St. Edith was the sister of the Anglo-Saxon King Athelstan, King of England from 924/5 to 939. He gave her in marriage to Sigtrig, the Danish King of Southern Northumbria. The Anglo-Saxon Chronicle records that the marriage took place at Tamworth, the Mercian royal seat, on 20 January 926 although Edith was not mentioned by name. Sigtrig was said to have repudiated the marriage and renounced Christianity but died suddenly in 927. Athelstan then seized Northumbria, bringing the whole of England under one ruler for the first time. Edith returned south, founded the abbey of Polesworth, near Tamworth and became its abbess.[9]

The four figures on the theme of the marriage of St. Edith, were designed in 1873 for one of three Morris windows on the south side of the clerestory at the parish church of St. Editha, Tamworth (fig. 98). Each window has four lights, each containing a single figure, plus a smaller trefoil above. Besides the marriage of St. Edith, the other windows show her as the abbess with her nuns, and with Lord Marmion, who evicted the nuns from Polesworth and was admonished by the saint (Brown depicted her striking him with her crozier). Sigtrig was probably much older than Edith, although Brown portrayed him as a young man.

The twelve designs comprising this scheme formed one of Brown's most elaborate and striking stained glass ensembles, and the one which he regarded as his most important.[10] However, their position high up in the clerestory makes them very difficult to see. Brown's designs, made in 1873, were sold to Charles Rowley and cannot be traced; these drawings are copies made for reproduction in *The British Architect* in 1879.[11] Brown gave them to W.E. Axon, of Manchester, according to whom they were made under the artist's close supervision, finished off by him and approved by him for reproduction.

Brown boldly linked each figure to the next so that a strong sense of movement unites the separate lights, linking the four figures into a single composition: the King, his back to the spectator, stretches his arm towards his sister, giving her in marriage; she offers her hand to Sigtrig who places the ring on her finger; and the Bishop (Ella of Lichfield) holds his hand up to Sigtrig in blessing. Similar flowing draperies and linking gestures run through the other two windows. 'Really I must say they are inconceivable. Every figure (it is a long series) is passing one hand through the stone mullion of the window into the next panel of glass!!' wrote Rossetti, suggesting that the design must have reduced Morris to desperation.[12]

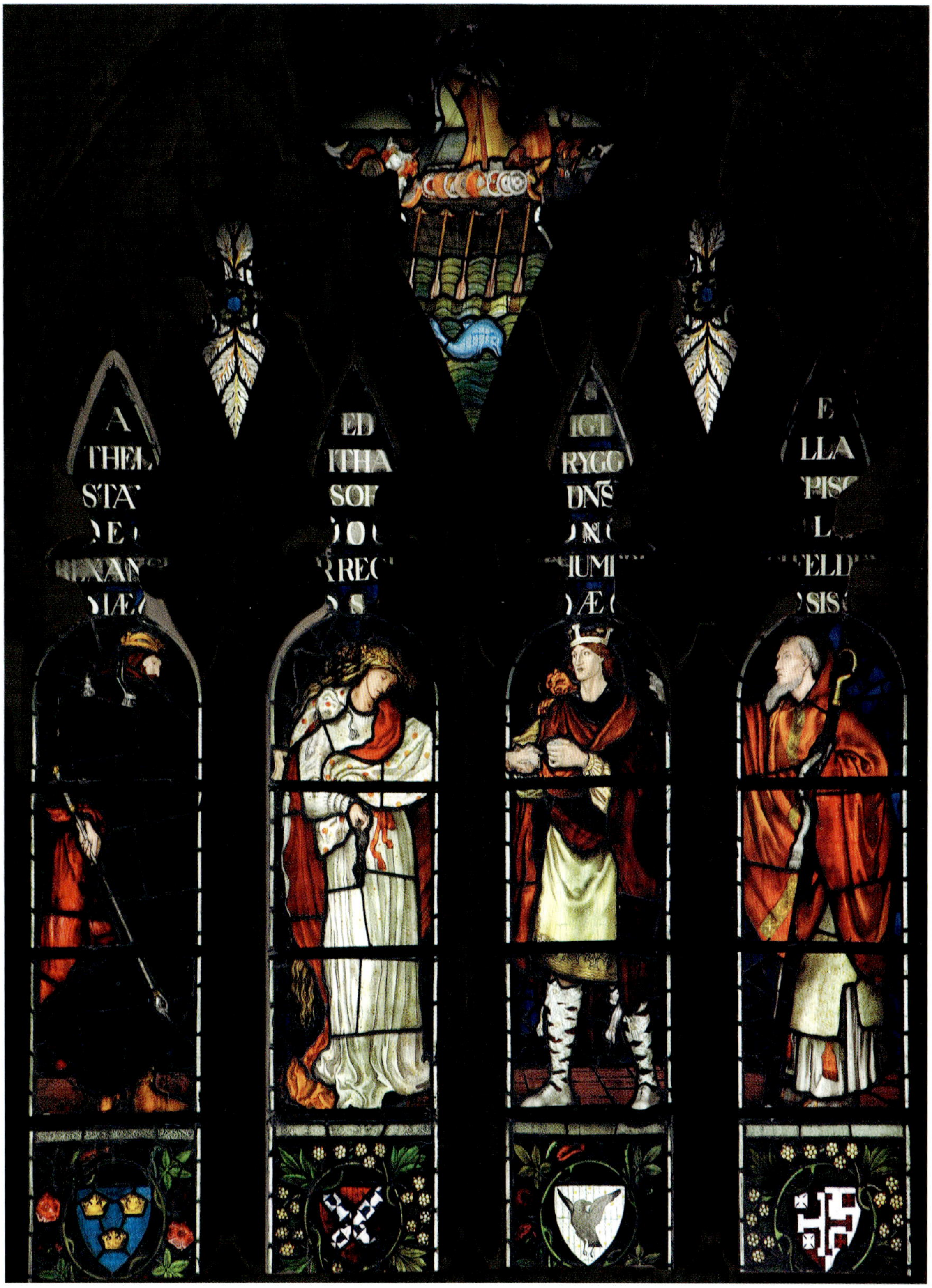

Fig. 98
The Marriage of St. Edith, *stained-glass window, St. Editha, Tamworth, designed by Ford Madox Brown and made by Morris, Marshall, Faulkner and Co., 1873*

102

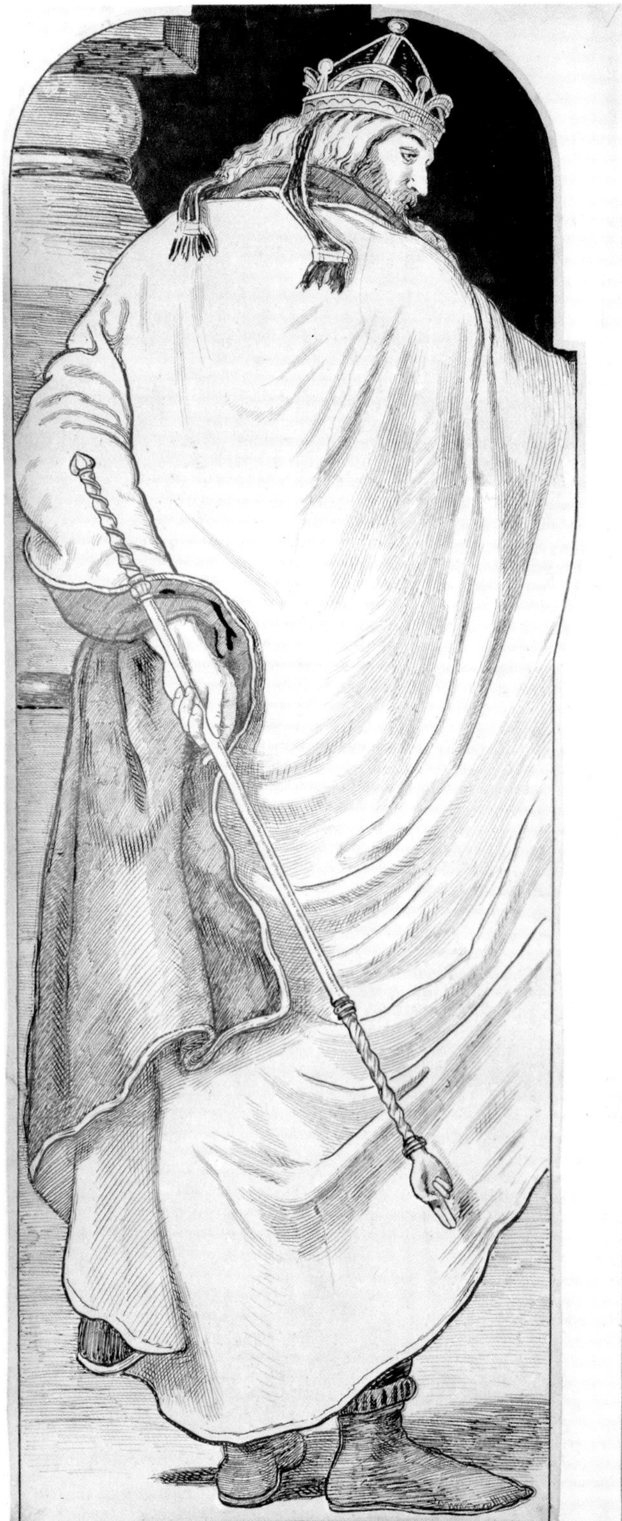
: KING : ATHELSTANE :
GIVES : AWAY : HIS : SISTER

103

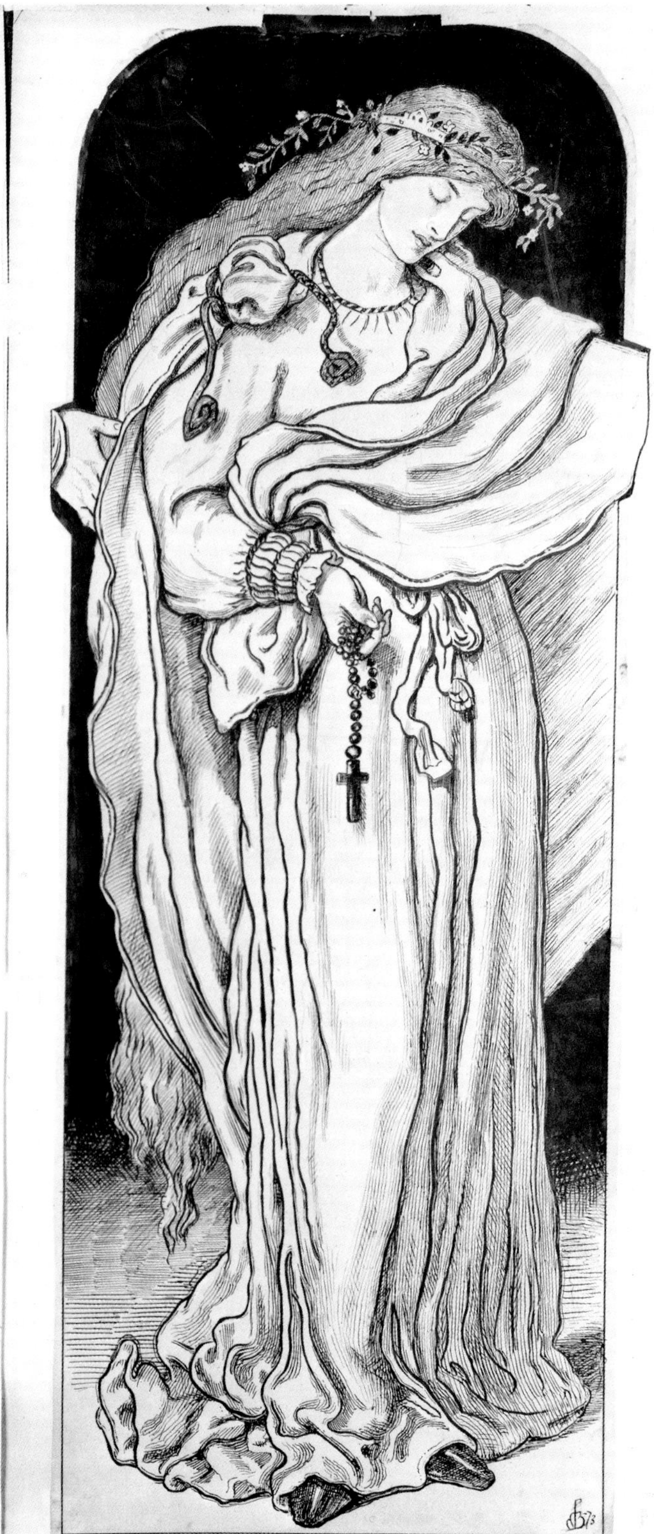
EDITH : WHO : IS : MARRIED
TO : SIGTRIG

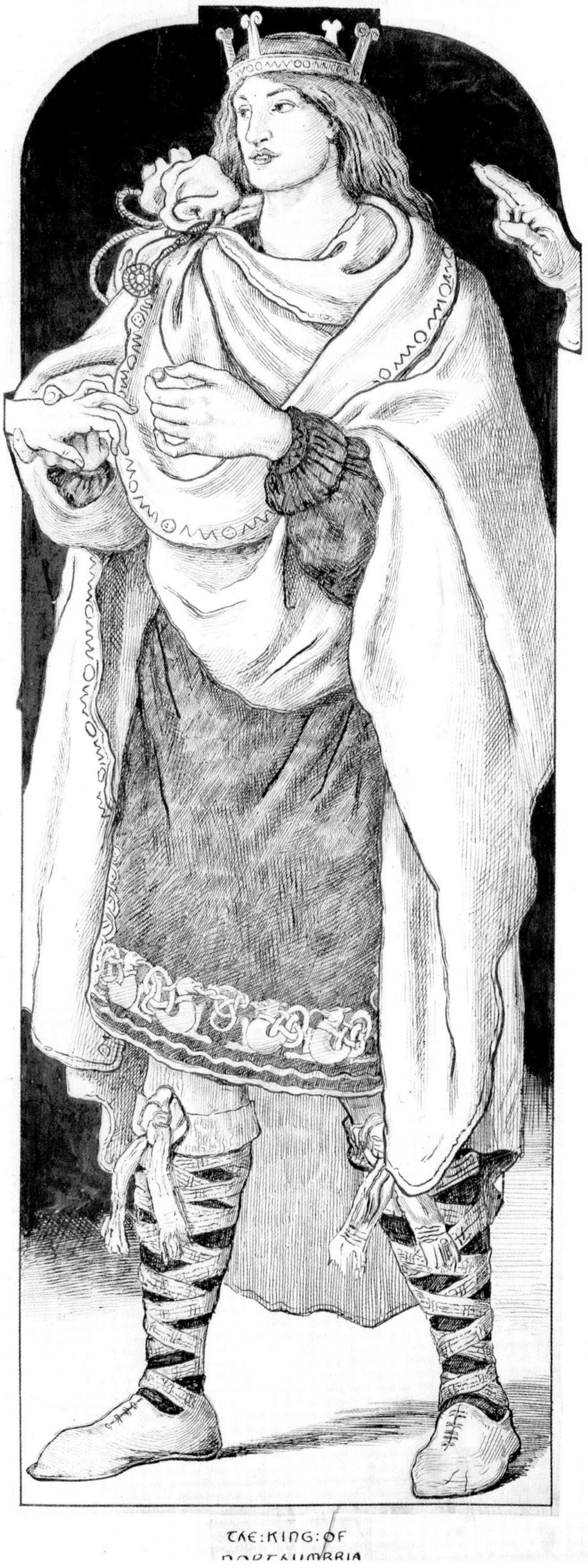
THE:KING:OF
NORTHUMBRIA

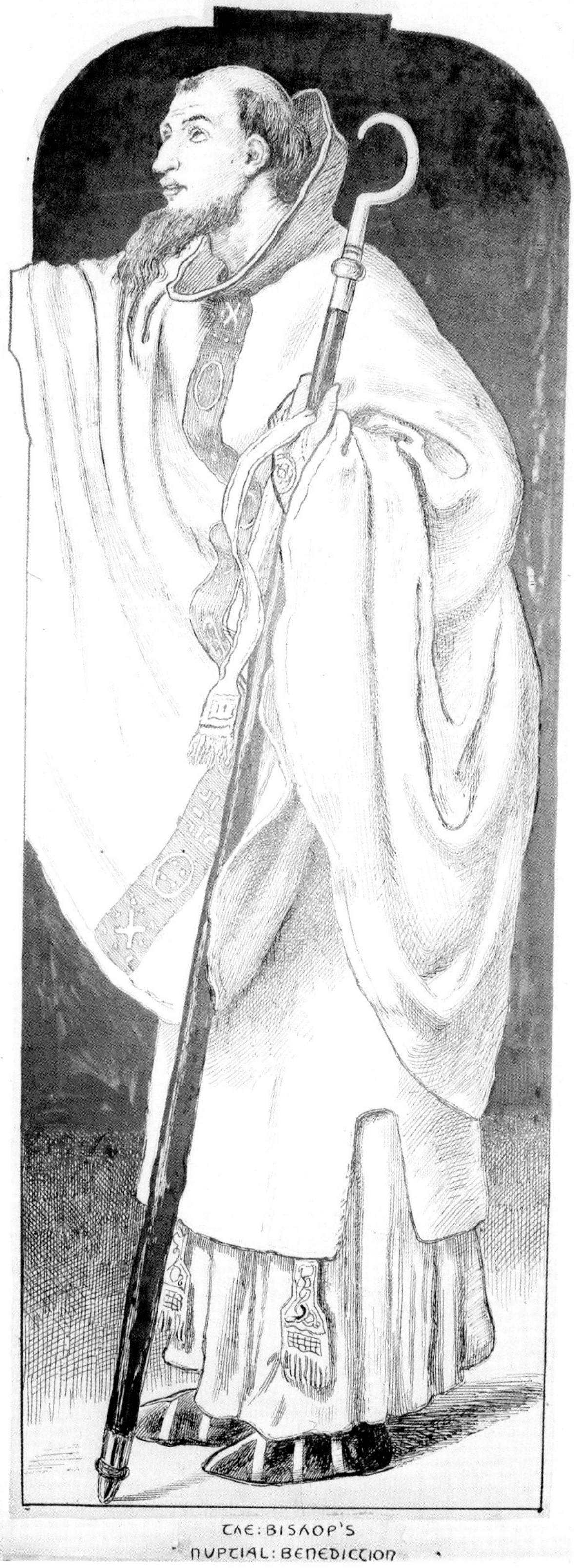
THE:BISHOP'S
NUPTIAL:BENEDICTION

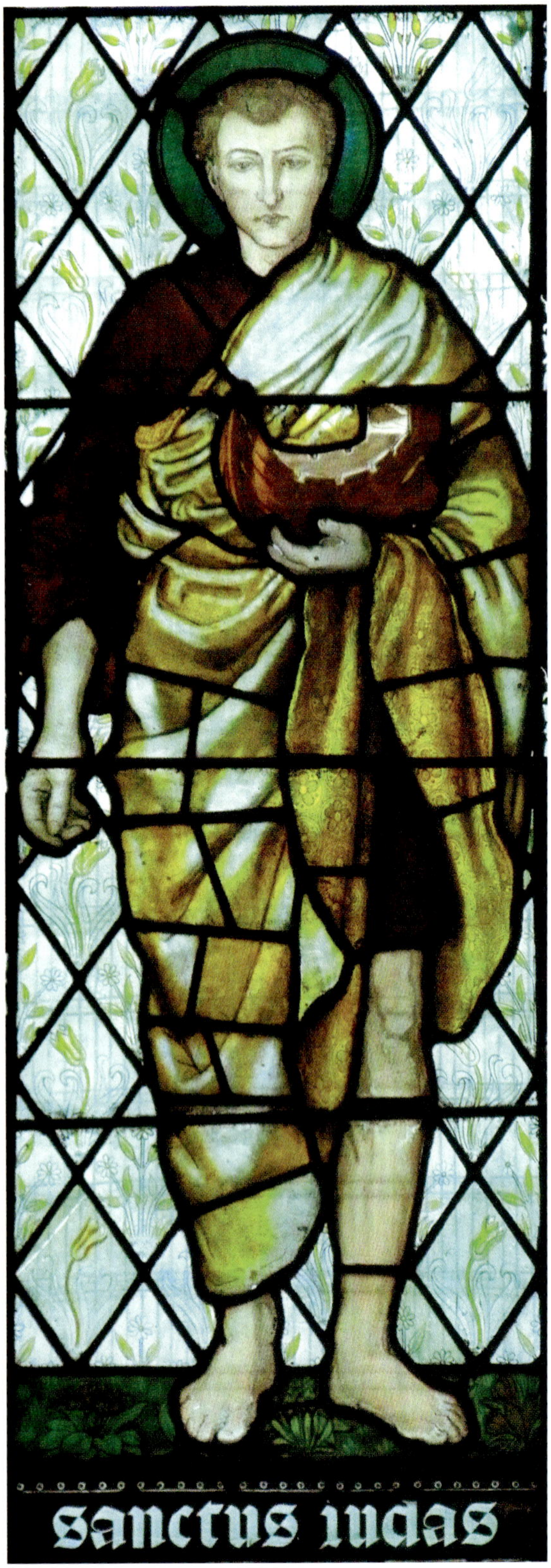

Fig. 99
St. Jude, *stained-glass window, Llandaff Cathedral, designed by Ford Madox Brown and made by Morris, Marshall, Faulkner and Co., 1874*

106

ST. JUDE

(C213)
1874
cartoon for stained glass, black chalk and wash
53 7/8 × 20 3/4 (136.8 × 52.6)
National Museums Liverpool, Walker Art Gallery. Presented to the Walker Art Gallery by Subscribers to the Fund for Purchasing and Presenting Cartoons to Principal Galleries 1894

St. Jude, the patron saint of hopeless causes, is usually represented holding an image of Christ, but Brown here depicted him holding a boat. The figure was designed for a three-light window in the north aisle of Llandaff Cathedral (fig. 99): the central lancet shows *St. Peter*, and the two outer lancets, by Brown, show *St. Simon* on the left, holding a fish, and *St. Jude* on the right, both of them barefoot. Below are three smaller scenes, all designed by Brown on related themes, *Christ raising Peter from the Sea* in the centre, flanked by *The Miraculous Draught of Fishes* on the left, and *The Shipwreck of St. Paul* (cat. 107) on the right, below *St. Jude*. The young saint, with his curly hair and strongly individualised face, is one of the most striking of all of Brown's single figure cartoons, exemplifying the artist's view that in stained glass 'expression and action can be conveyed in a few strokes equally as in the most elaborate art.'[13]

The saint's tunic is shaded grey in the monochrome cartoon, and the robe is depicted as all one colour, but in the finished window, his tunic is dark red, and the robe is in two shades of gold-yellow, plain on the outside with a darker patterned lining. The two shades have been differentiated by numbering parts of the cartoon, 2 for the paler and 3 for the darker yellow. The numbers were probably not written by Brown but added later in the stained glass studio. 'The cartoons for this firm are never coloured,' wrote Brown '– that task devolving on Mr. Morris, the manager, who makes his colour (by selecting glass) out of the very manufacture of the article.'[14]

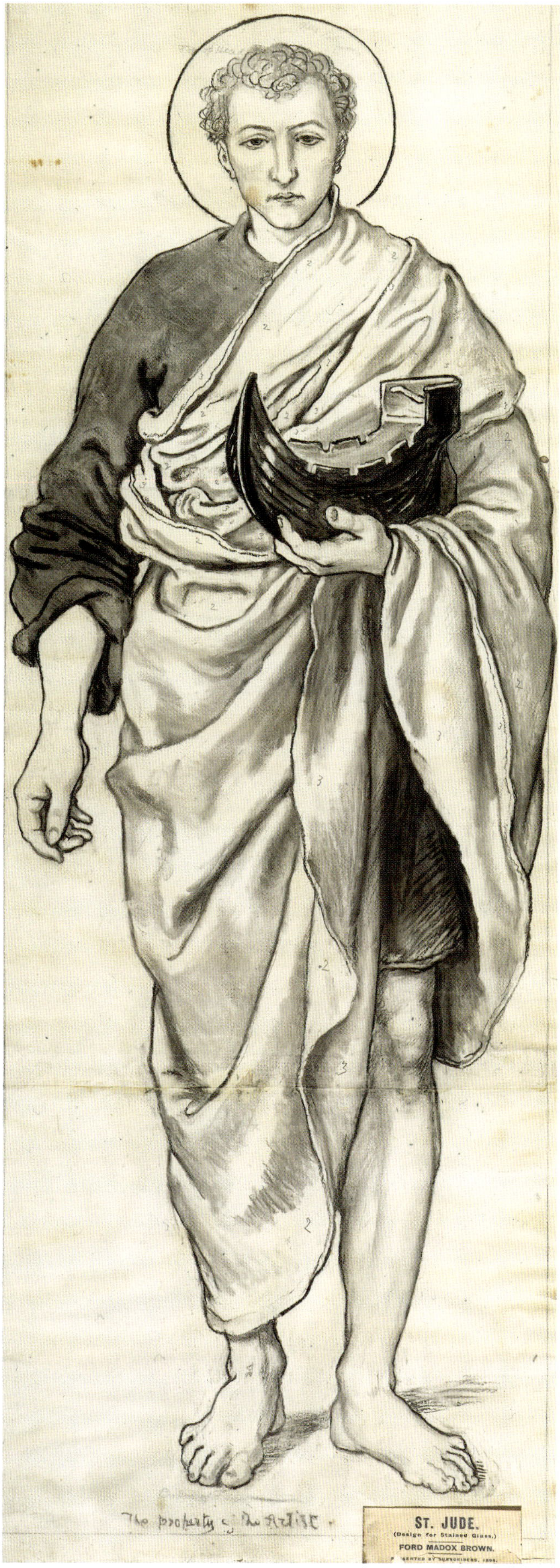
The property of the Artist
ST. JUDE.
(Design for Stained Glass.)
FORD MADOX BROWN.

107
SHIPWRECK OF ST. PAUL

(C215)
1874
cartoon for stained glass, black chalk and wash,
25 × 20 (63.5 × 51)
signed in monogram and dated: *FMB – 74*
Manchester Metropolitan University Special Collections

The captive St. Paul was on a ship bound for Rome, but the vessel was caught in a terrible storm and drifted for fourteen days. Paul had faith in God, and urged the men not to abandon ship but to break their fast and eat; the ship ran aground and at daybreak they found they were on the island of Malta, and escaped safely to land. Brown shows the scene before the storm abated: 'Wherefore I pray to you to take some meat: for this is for your health: for there shall not an hair fall from the head of any of you. And when he had thus spoken, he took bread, and gave thanks to God in presence of them all: and when he had broken it, he began to eat' (Acts 27:34–35). Brown shows Paul handing out bread to a centurion on the right and an oarsman on the left. The saint's face is strongly characterised, seen against the sky riven by lightning, his cloak billowing out extravagantly in the wind.

The window (fig. 100) was designed in 1874 for Llandaff Cathedral, below the figure of St. Jude (cat. 106). The dynamic shape of the cloak dominates the window, realised in a silvery pale blue glass, which stands out against the deep blues of the robe and sky. The halo unusually is in ruby red glass.

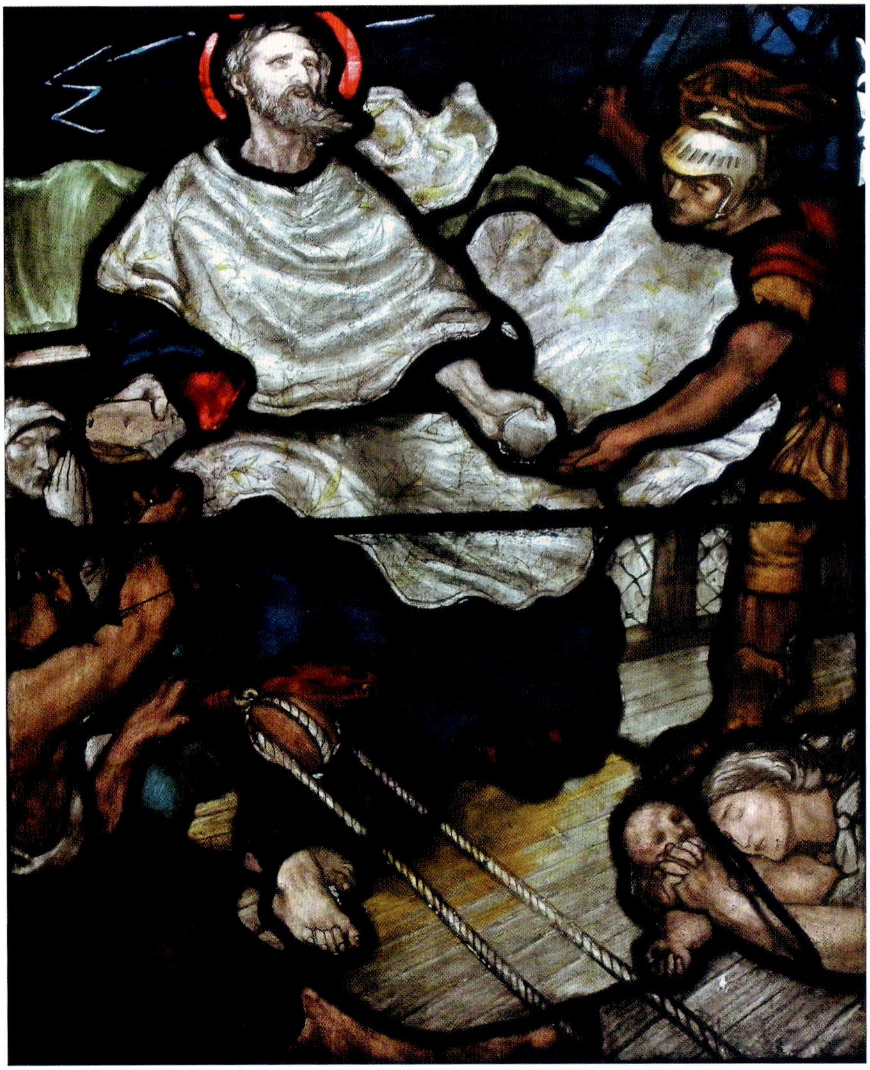

Fig. 100
Shipwreck of St. Paul, *stained-glass window, Llandaff Cathedral, designed by Ford Madox Brown and made by Morris, Marshall, Faulkner and Co., 1874*

107

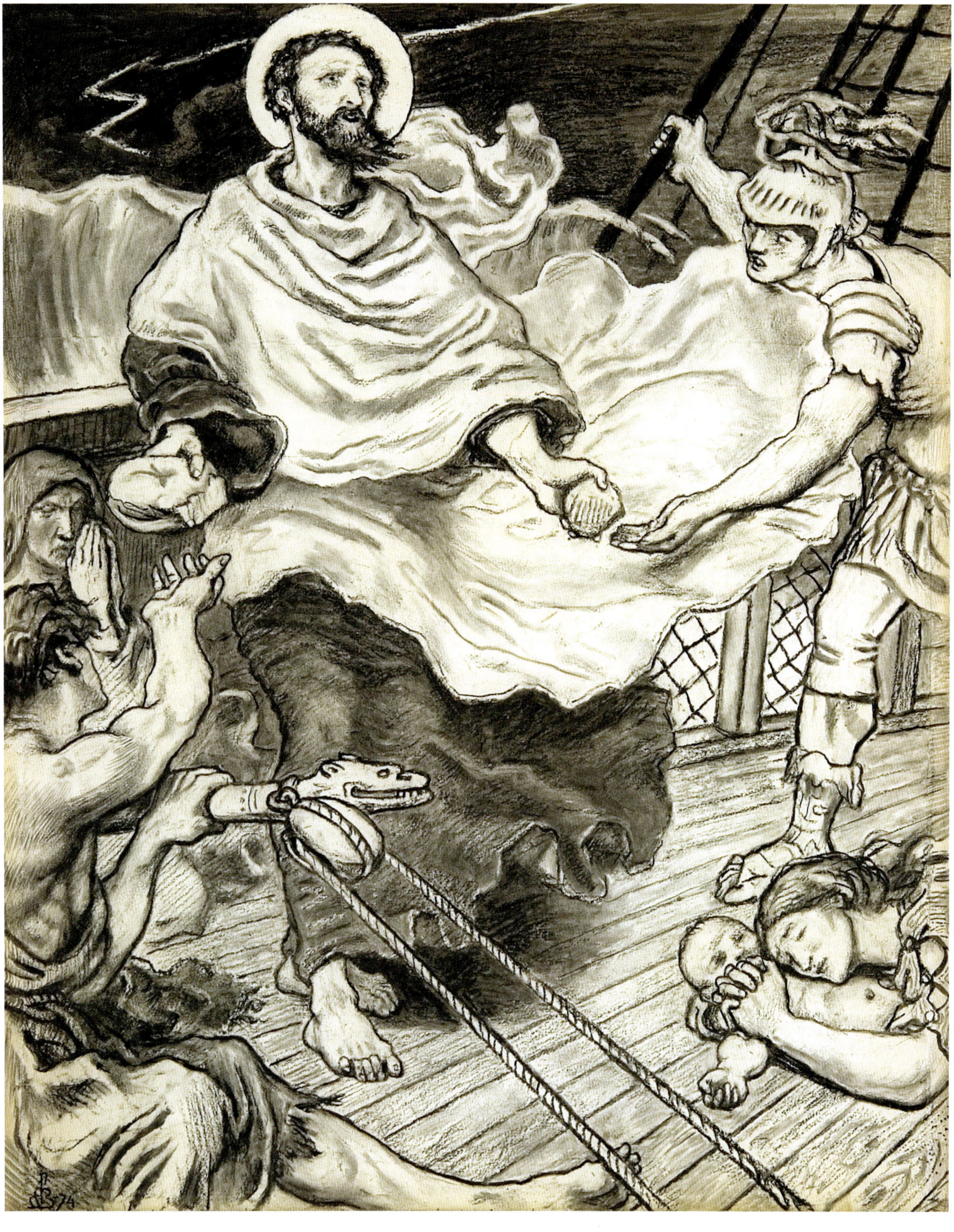

108
ARISTOTLE (PHILOSOPHY)

(C153)
1870, 1878
inscribed: *ARISTOTLE* and signed in monogram and dated:
FMB / 70–78

109
ALFRED THE GREAT (KINGSHIP)

(C221)
1878
inscribed: *KING ALFRED /THE GREAT* AND signed in monogram and dated: *FMB – 78*

110
WILLIAM SHAKESPEARE (DRAMA)

(C225)
1878
inscribed: SHAKESPEARE and signed in monogram and dated:
FMB – 78
each black chalk and wash, 46 × 16½ (117 × 42)
The University of Manchester

These three drawings are part of the set of twelve cartoons of Great Men, produced by Brown in 1878 as a pantheon of heroes of learning and the arts. Six of them had been drawn in 1870 as stained-glass cartoons for the bay window in the Hall at Peterhouse, Cambridge, part of an extensive Morris scheme for the College, including tiles as well as stained glass; the other six were drawn in 1878 for Charles Rowley. The six commissioned by Rowley were never executed in stained glass, indeed the Great Men series was principally intended to promote Brown as a historical painter when he was being considered for the Manchester Town Hall Murals commission. The twelve were published as a set of sepia photographs, although the date of publication is not known. The quality of the figures varies but the best of them demonstrate Brown's powers of expression, as well as the importance for him of heroes, derived from his reading of Carlyle's *Lectures on Heroes* (1840). The series was probably Brown's idea, even though Rowley was the patron.

Aristotle (Philosopy) is perhaps an unexpected figure to be portrayed by Brown, and one of the few subjects from classical antiquity in his work. *Aristotle* was recycled from the Peterhouse windows, which featured figures from the world of learning and so also included *Homer (Poetry)* and *Cicero*

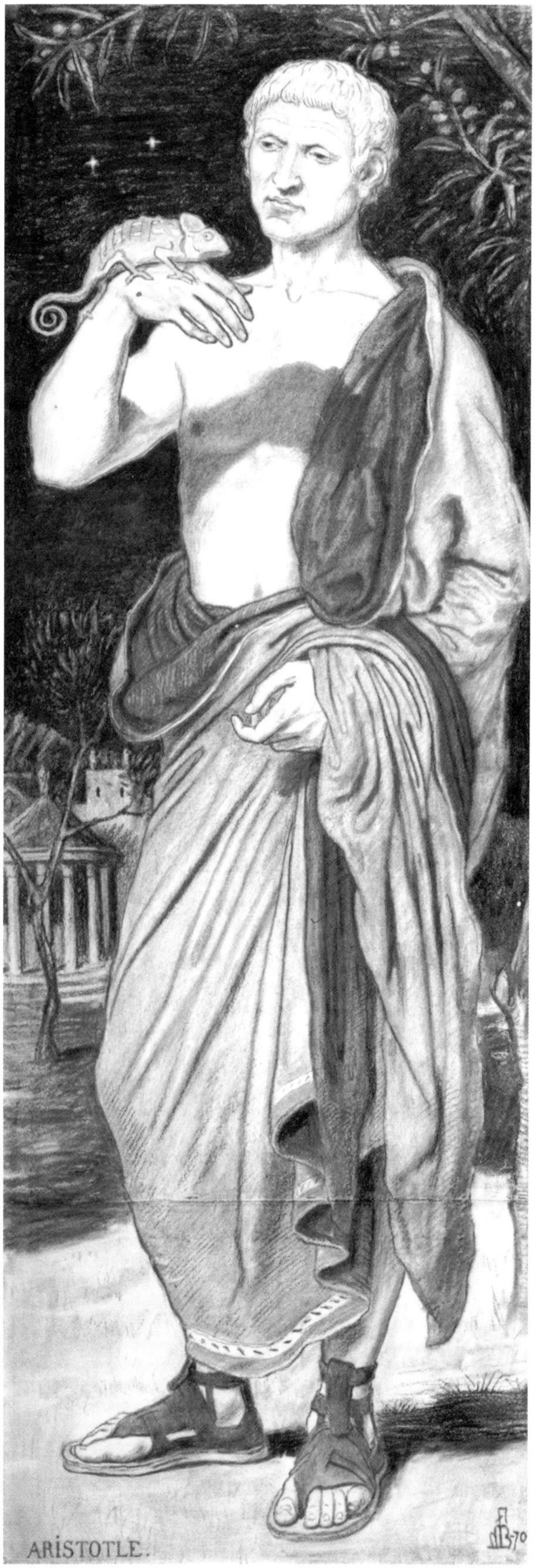

108

109

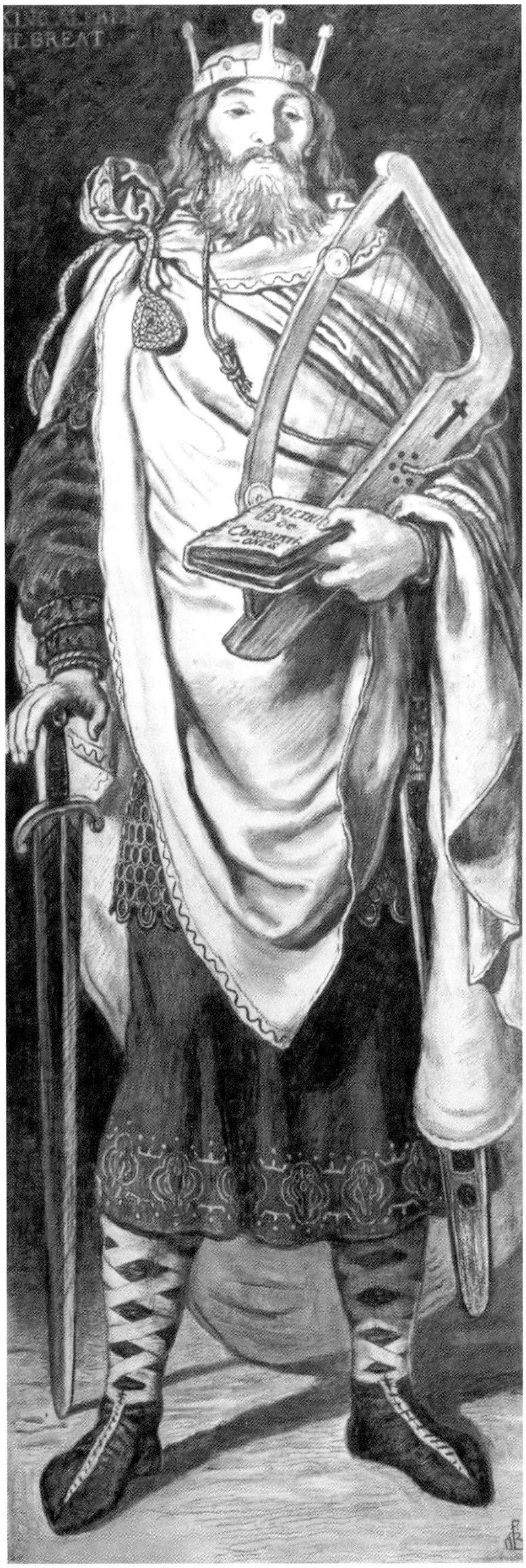

110

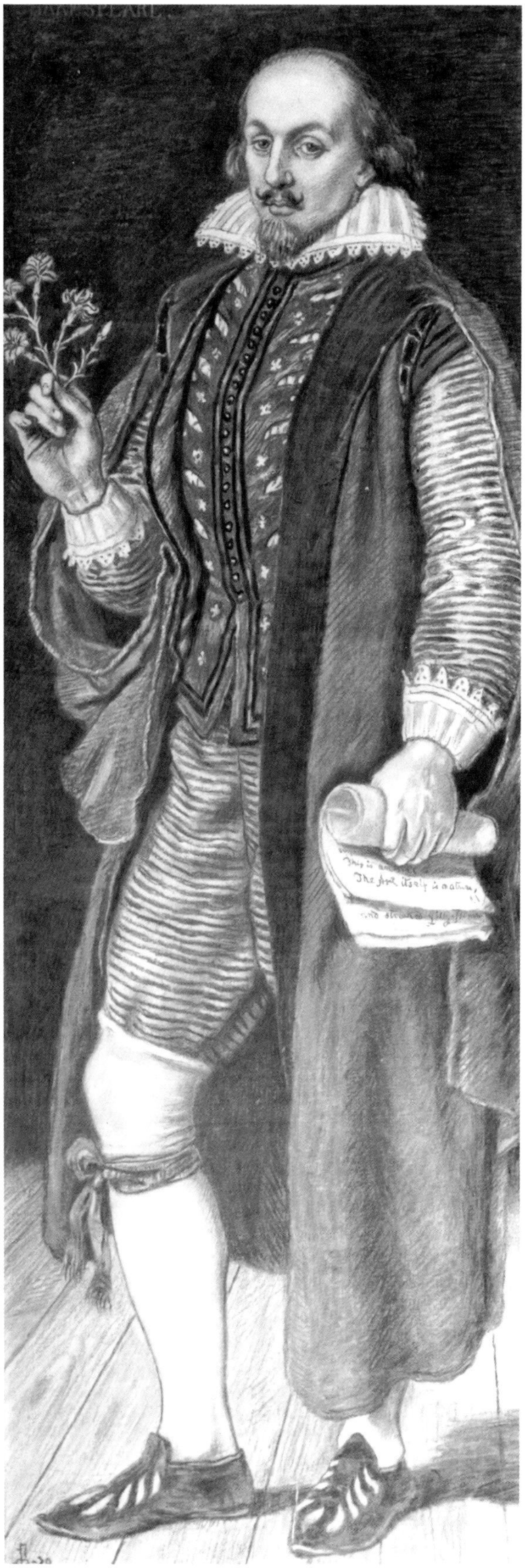

(Oratory). In Brown's portrayal, the Greek philosopher is shown studying a chameleon, which he described in his *Historia Animalium*. It is possible that Brown chose the chameleon because of Aristotle's investigations into change and identity in humans and animals. Behind Aristotle are classical buildings beneath a starry sky. These were added in 1878: the Peterhouse cartoons were originally without illustrative backgrounds, and in the windows the figures were placed against coloured floral designs by William Morris.

More typical for Brown are *Alfred the Great (Kingship)* and *William Shakespeare (Drama)*; both come from the second group, drawn for Rowley. Brown had previously designed a younger Alfred, also with an expressive bearded face, for the stained glass at Cheddleton (1864), as part of a series of Anglo-Saxon rulers appropriate for the dedication of the church to St. Edward the Confessor. In the Great Men version Alfred stands boldly with his legs apart, with 'the crown of a wise and good king, the sword of a valiant, merciful soldier, the harp of a sweet-natured singer and poet, and the book of one of the first writers in the English language.'[15] The book is Boethius's *Consolation of Philosophy*, which Alfred translated into Old English.

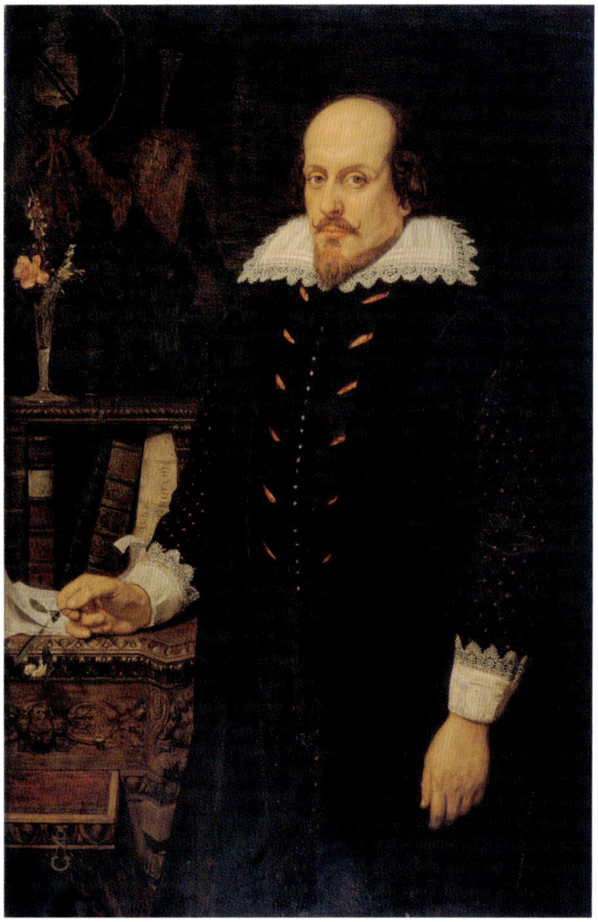

Fig. 101
Ford Madox Brown, William Shakespeare, *1849, Manchester City Galleries*

The cartoon of *Shakespeare*, one of Brown's heroes, is a full-length version of an imaginary oil portrait of Shakespeare that Brown had painted in 1849 (fig. 101), collated from the different known portraits including the bust at Stratford.[16] The flowers and the words on the papers held by Shakespeare in the cartoon come from Act 4, scene 4 of *The Winter's Tale:* Shakespeare holds 'a striped wallflower, as a symbol of his own marvellous compound of nature and art, showing indeed that the art of his great works is nature itself.'[17] This is a reference to Perdita's speech about the 'streak'd gillyvors, Which some call nature's bastards' which prompts Polixenes' response 'This is an art, Which doth mend nature, change it rather, but/ The art itself is nature'.

The whole series comprises *Homer (Poetry), Aristotle (Philosophy), Cicero (Oratory), Francis Bacon (Learning), Isaac Newton (Science)* and *Roger Bacon (Science)* taken from Peterhouse; and *Alfred the Great (Kingship), Joan of Arc (Patriotism), Christopher Columbus (Discovery), Michael Angelo (Workmanship), William Shakespeare (Drama) and Beethoven (Music)* made especially for the Great Men group. Although the series was known as 'Great Men', one is a woman, Joan of Arc; in addition to the twelve, there is one extra cartoon from the Peterhouse series, *Henry Cavendish (Science)* which has no background added and was not included in the published photographs.

111
EGYPTIAN CHAIR

(E2)
1858
stained wood, partly ebonised,
33¼ × 21⅝ × 21½ (84.5 × 55 × 54.5)
Victoria and Albert Museum

Brown designed this chair, one of a pair, after admiring a more elaborate pair of Egyptian-style chairs designed by Holman Hunt and made by J.G. Crace, a leading maker of luxury furniture (Birmingham Museums and Art Gallery). Hunt invited Brown to see his chairs in December 1857 and much later wrote that Brown had 'idolised' the chairs and 'set a carpenter to work to make some

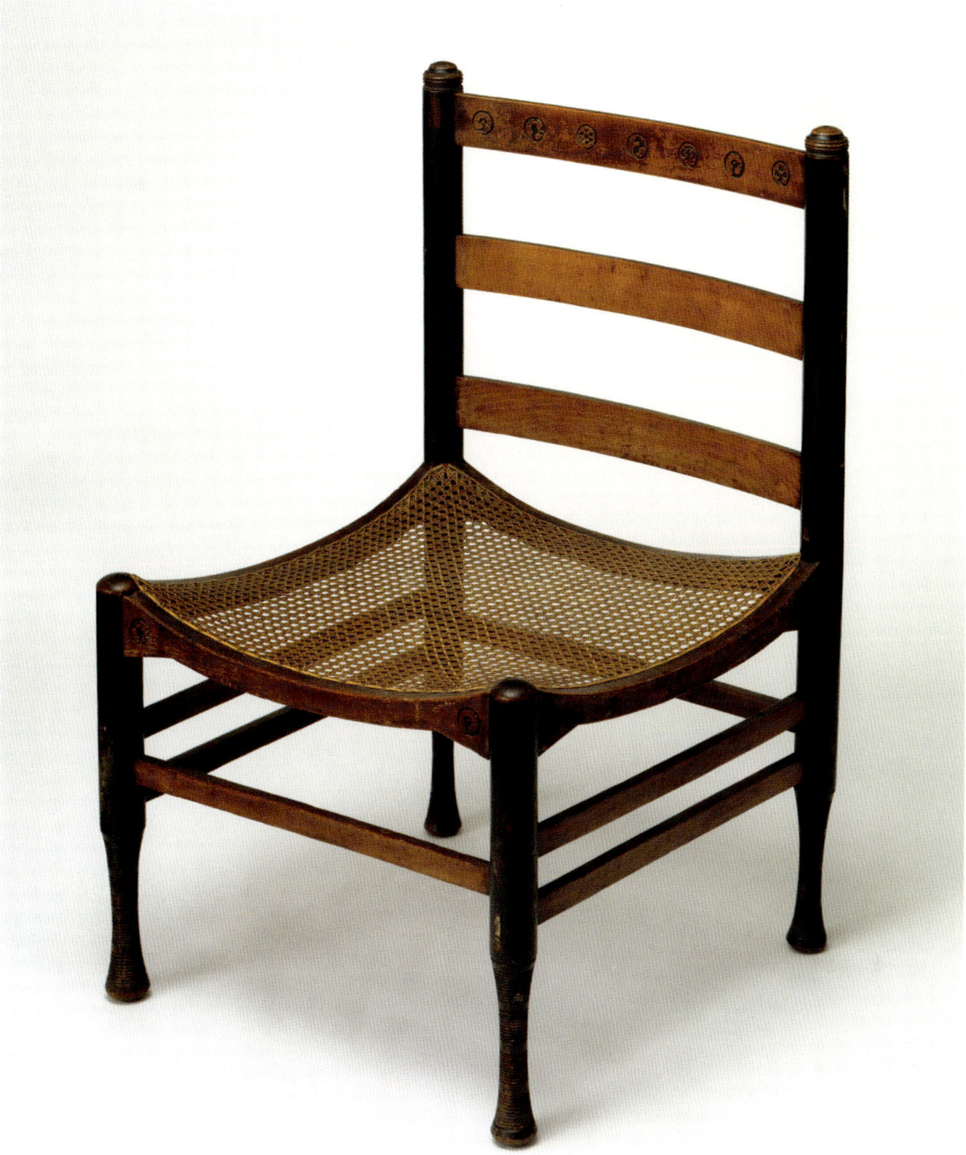

111

of similar proportions.'[18] The design of Hunt's chairs was based on the Thebes stool and other Egyptian furniture in the British Museum.[19] Brown's chair was simpler; a ladder back resembling traditional country chairs replaced Hunt's slender diagonal bars, and instead of Hunt's lotus decoration inlaid with ebony and ivory, Brown had circle designs incised along the back and on the rails supporting the seat. These anticipate the motifs he and Rossetti used on their picture frames in the early 1860s.

In his diary for 17 January 1858 Brown wrote of having finished four designs for chairs.[20] This probably refers to the pair of Egyptian chairs and a pair of simpler country-style ladder-back chairs with rush seats (private collection). Brown's first piece of furniture, a massive oak X-framed table in the medieval style, had been designed not long before, in 1856 or '57. He had one made for his own use and a similar one was made for Hunt by Brown's carpenter, who was less expensive than Crace. Neither appears to have survived.[21]

These early designs were probably the ones that caused Brown's rupture with the Hogarth Club, the private exhibition society that he had taken a leading role in founding in 1858. Brown, an early advocate of the equal status of the fine and decorative arts, submitted furniture designs as well as paintings to the exhibition in 1859. The furniture designs were rejected, and because of this, Brown resigned, although he was later persuaded to rejoin.[22]

112
WASHSTAND
(E8)
green-stained wood, 34⅝ × 36⅝ × 24¾ (88 × 93 × 63)

113
TOWEL-RAIL
(E10)
green-stained wood, 41 × 36⅜ × 28 (106 × 92.5 × 71)

114
DRESSING TABLE
(E11)
green-stained wood, 33⅜ × 48¾ × 24½ (85.5 × 124 × 62)

all designed 1860/62 and made by Morris, Marshall, Faulkner & Co.
Kelmscott Manor Collection. By permission of the Society of Antiquaries of London

These pieces, almost certainly designed by Brown,[23] were probably made for Red House, which the architect Philip Webb designed in 1859 for Morris and his new wife Jane. The couple moved there in 1860 and over the next two years a circle of friends including Rossetti, Burne-Jones and his wife, Charles Faulkner, Webb and Brown collaborated with the Morrises on designing and making textiles, furnishings and decorations. The vernacular style of Brown's furniture is in keeping with other elements of decoration of the house.

The simple and massive designs are similar to very early pieces by William Morris, such as a green-painted circular table (Cheltenham Art Gallery), probably made for Morris's London lodgings in 1856, and inspired by the furniture of the architect G.E. Street, in whose office Morris and Webb had both worked. Brown's designs were made for boarded construction, with mortise, tenon and halving joints, pegs and dowels, and chamfering, and thus could be made by a joiner rather than a cabinet-maker. The pieces made for Red House also include a bed and a double washstand. When Morris left Red House, he must have taken the bedroom suite with him and eventually he took it to Kelmscott (fig. 102). Additionally, Brown had a washstand, a double washstand and two towel rails made for his own use. The range was not put into general production apart from the dressing table, which was advertised in a catalogue of around 1910. These items can best be considered as experiments – their heavy, somewhat ungainly character was neither practical nor marketable. Indeed, the use of green stain, which Brown is thought to have originated, and which was also used on other early furniture produced by the Firm, was discontinued after the appointment of Warrington Taylor as manager in 1865, because marks could not be easily removed from it.

Despite the impracticality of the pieces, an anonymous magazine article of 1898 praised them and the artisan's furniture Brown exhibited in Manchester in 1887 (fig. 38, p. 56) for their 'qualities of simplicity, strength and that certain grave dignity that he most cared for,' adding, 'They were certainly not costly. As far as he himself was concerned, he was socialist enough to consider that what was good enough for an artisan's house was fit for his own.'[24]

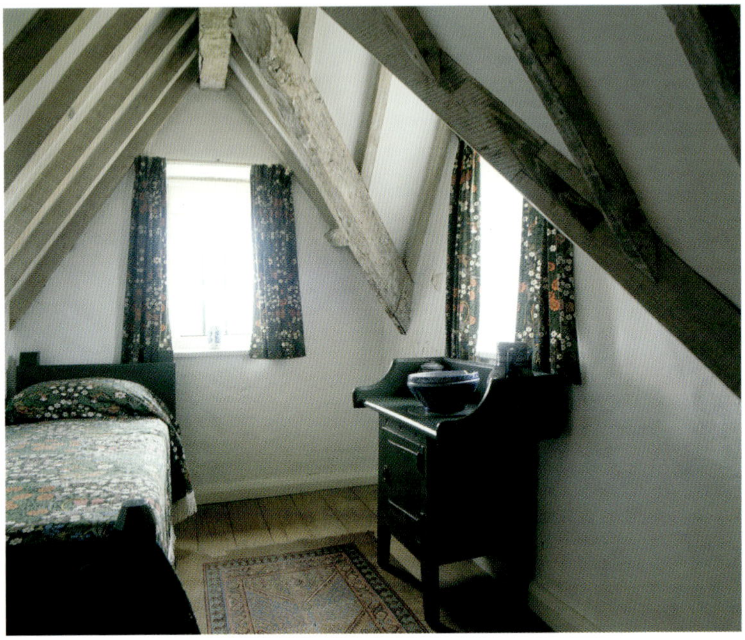

Fig. 102
Interior of Kelmscott Manor showing bed and washstand designed by Ford Madox Brown. Country Life

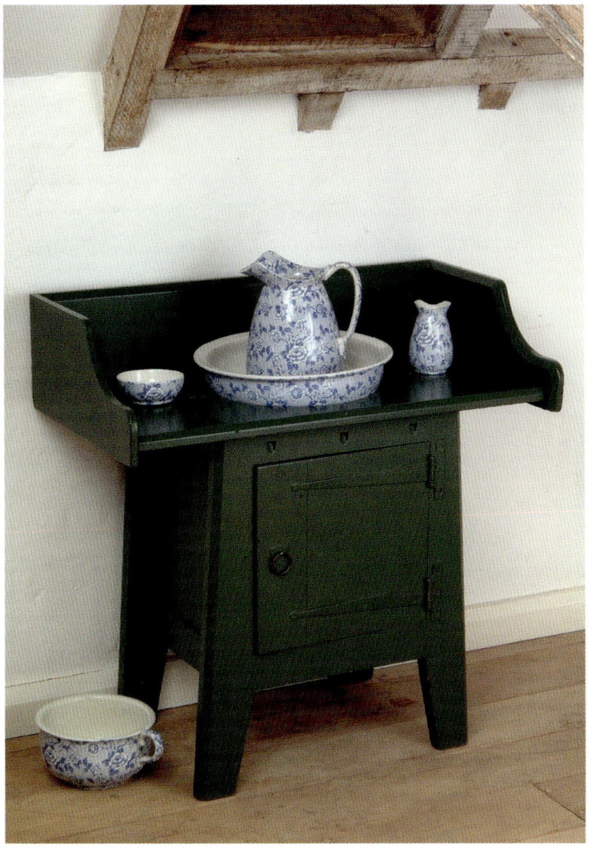

112

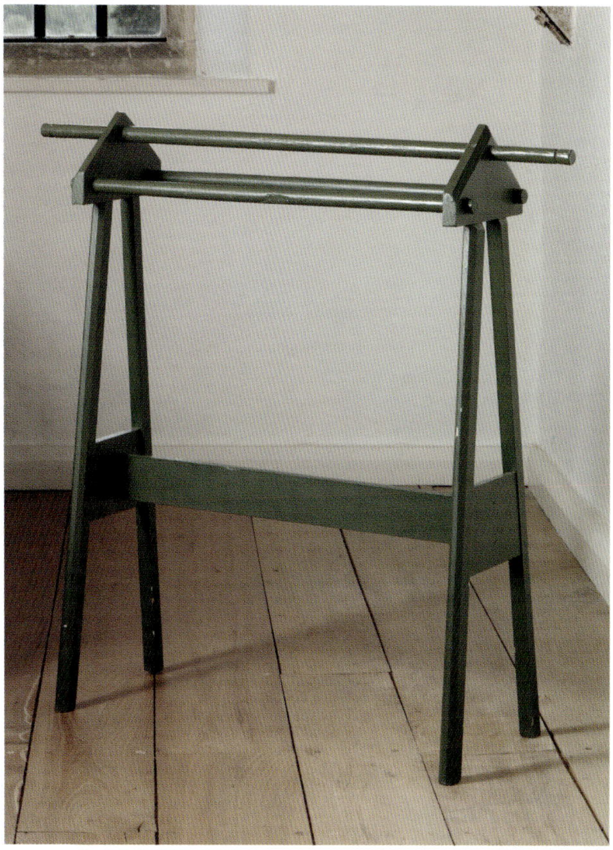

113

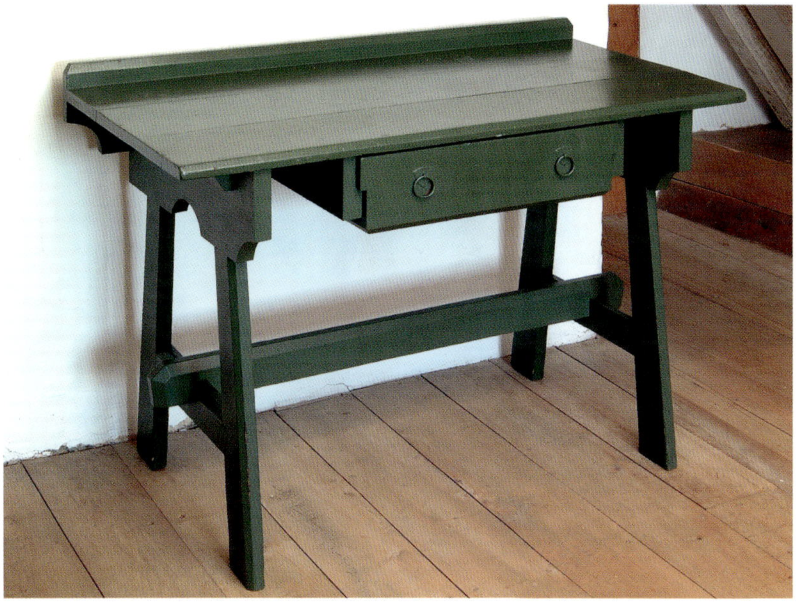

114

115
'SUSSEX' ROUND-SEATED CHAIR

(E13)
ebonised wood with rush seat, 32⅝ × 16½ × 17 (83 × 41.9 × 42)
manufactured by Morris, Marshall, Faulkner & Co., and in production from around 1865
Kelmscott Manor Collection. By permission of the Society of Antiquaries of London

Although the earliest Morris furniture was in a heavy medieval style, the firm soon began to produce lighter ebonised furniture with rush seats, and spindly imitation-bamboo frames. These pieces were known as the 'Sussex' range because their design was adapted from country chairs found in Sussex, probably dating from the Regency period. The earliest chair in the range to be sold by the Firm was the armchair designed by Philip Webb with a square seat and four turned uprights in the back. Another variant with a round seat and curved uprights on the back is thought to have been designed by Rossetti.[25]

The round-seated chair with cross shaped members on the back has traditionally been associated with Brown although there is no documentation for his authorship.[26] The chair seems to have been in production from around 1865, and is illustrated in the Firm's catalogue of c.1910 together with a taller version described as a piano chair.

In 1881 this type of chair, described as a bedroom chair, was recommended for its cheapness and serviceability in a book on house decoration by Robert Edis. Burne-Jones ordered four of them at a cost of £2 in 1878, and they can be seen in a photograph of Georgiana Burne-Jones's sitting room at The Grange, Fulham.[27]

1 Brown 1865, introductory text to section on Cartoons for Stained Glass and Designs for Furniture.
2 See Lynn Roberts, in Bennett 2010, 2, pp. 557–89.
3 Banham and Harris 1984, p. 182.
4 Bennett 2010, 1, p. 204, A80; Brown 1865, no. 32.
5 Treuherz 1984 p. 168.
6 Brown 1865, no. 31.
7 Bennett 2010, 1, pp. 206–9, A81, A81.2.
8 Brown 1865, no. 31.
9 Thacker 2001.
10 Image 1890, pp. 115–16.
11 3 January 1879.
12 D.G. Rossetti, *Correspondence*, 8, p. 243.
13 Brown 1865, introductory text to section on Cartoons for Stained Glass and Designs for Furniture..
14 Brown 1865, p. 27.
15 Ancoats 1880, p. 13 (probably written by Charles Rowley).
16 Bennett 2010, 1, pp. 118–19, A54.
17 Ibid. note 15.
18 Hunt 1905, 2, p. 136.
19 Bronkhurst 2, pp. 287–88.
20 *Diary*, p. 200.
21 Bennett 2010, 2, pp. 550–51, E.1, E1.1, E3.
22 Hueffer 1896, pp. 161–62.
23 Bennett 2010, 2, p. 553; the writer of *Artist* 1898, who evidently knew Brown, stated the designs were his.
24 *Artist* 1898, p. 51.
25 Parry 1996, pp. 160, 168–69, 176.
26 Tait 1900, pp. 61–63 attributes the design to Brown; see also Bennett 2010, 2, p. 554, and Sale 1894, lots 7–9.
27 Parry 1996, pp. 161, 176.

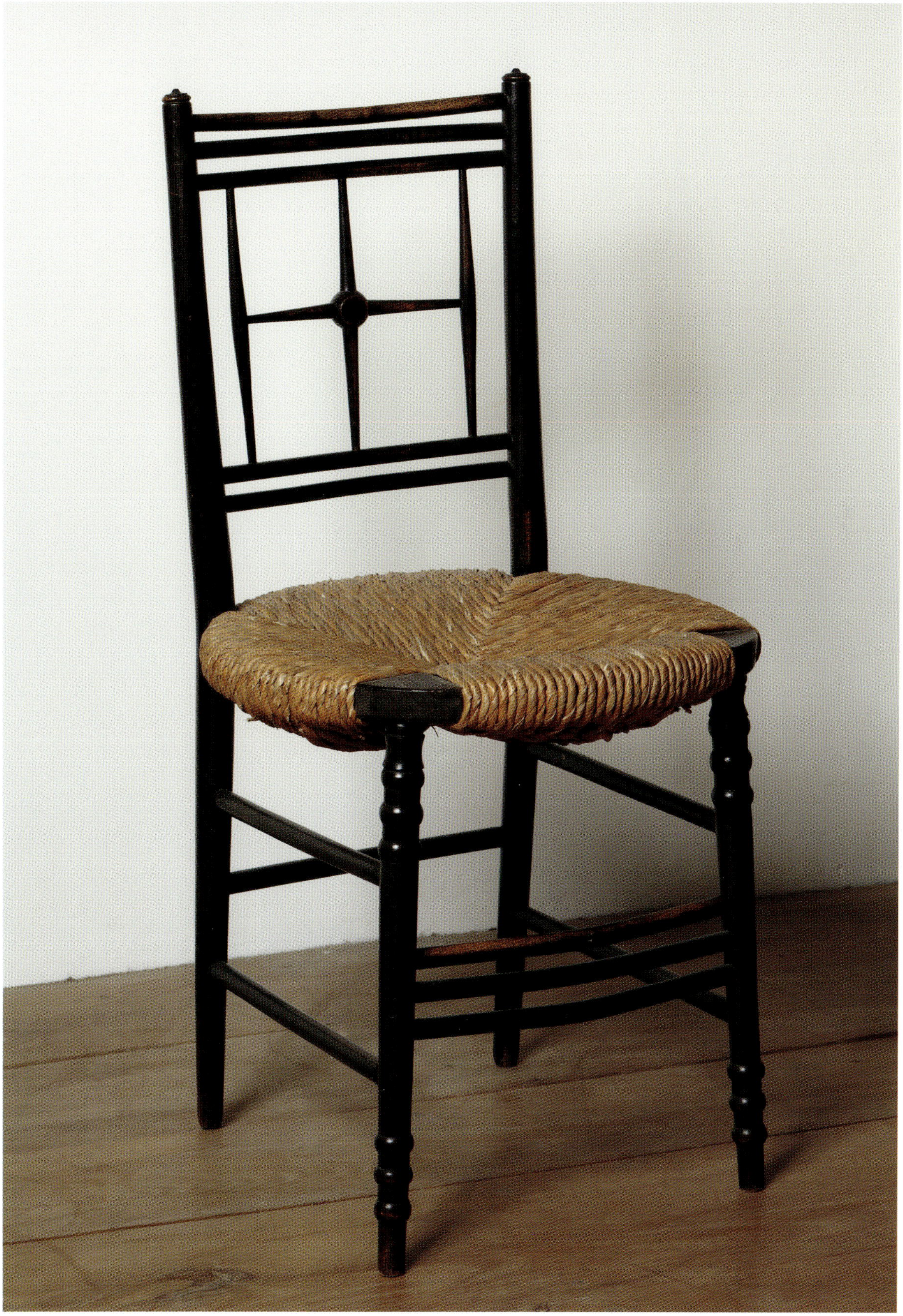

115

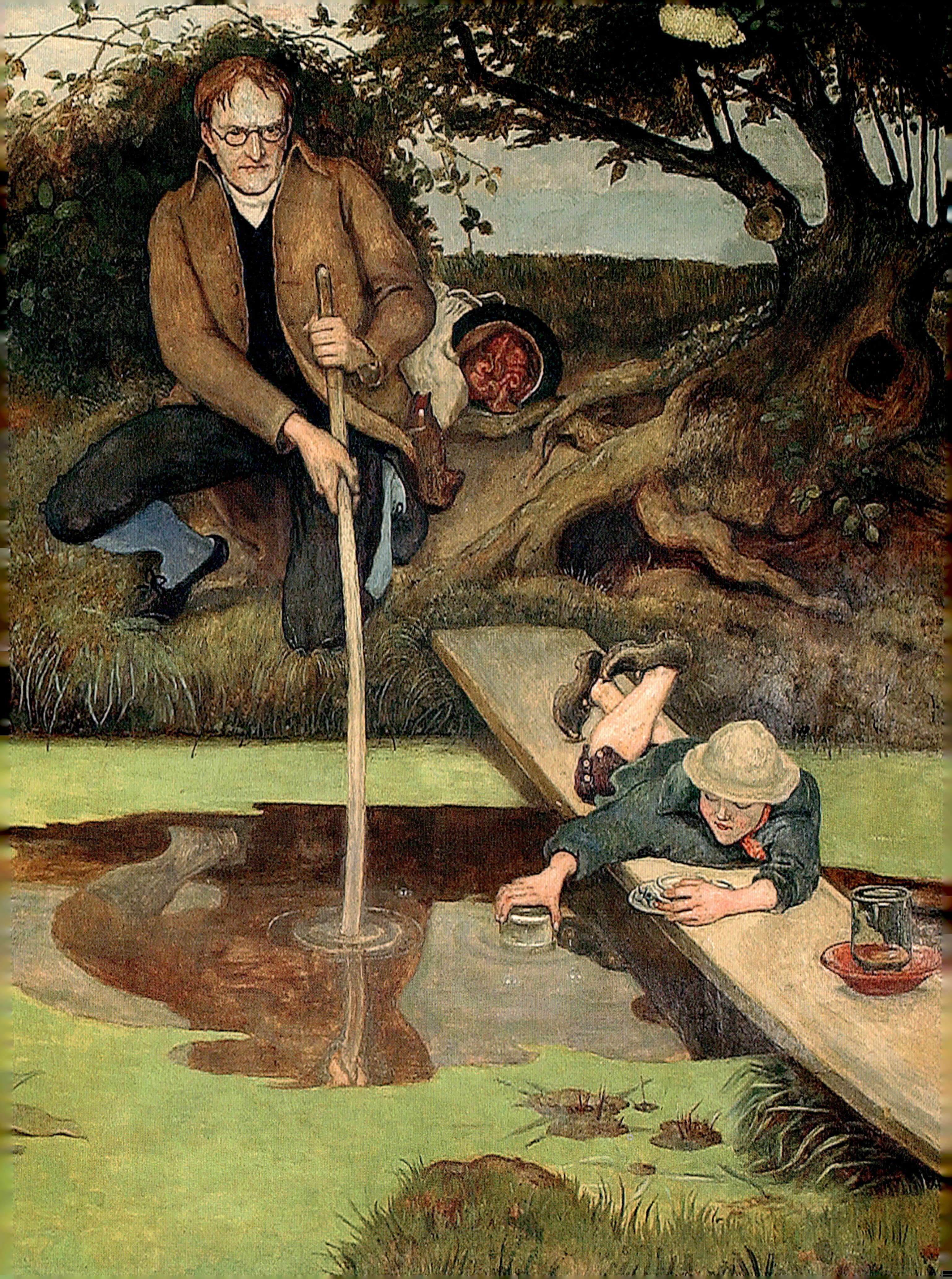

THE MANCHESTER PERIOD

In 1878 Brown was commissioned by the Corporation of Manchester to paint murals of the history of Manchester in the new Town Hall. At first Brown worked on the designs in London, and came up to Manchester for short periods to paint the murals, but the work took far longer than expected. Originally he and the Manchester artist Frederic Shields had been asked to paint six murals each. Shields later withdrew, and it was agreed that Brown should paint all twelve. In August 1881 Brown sold his London house and moved to Manchester, living first in Crumpsall and then in Victoria Park.

The first seven murals were painted directly on to the walls in the Great Hall, using the Gambier Parry process of spirit fresco, more suitable for the damp English climate than true fresco. Seven panels were completed in situ but because of the difficulties of working in the Town Hall during the cold winter of 1885, the last five subjects were painted on canvas in the artist's studio (one in spirit fresco and the rest in oils) and then sent to the Town Hall to be fixed to the wall. As it was no longer necessary for Brown to live in Manchester he returned to London in December 1887. There he continued work on the murals, despite suffering from gout and a minor stroke which affected the quality of his work. He completed the last panel in March 1893, some six months before his death.

When the subjects of the murals were announced, they were criticized as inaccurate by a local antiquarian named William Axon. Some adjustments were made, but Brown felt that 'it was not the province of art to supply documents,'[1] and wrote that the selection of subjects was 'calculated to arouse our sympathies for certain great ideas and beautiful phases of nature.'[2] Each mural seems to stand for a particular idea: Christianity, nonconformism, commercial integrity, the textile industry, philanthropy, education and science. Some of the subjects also portray Manchester as a source of innovation and independent thinking.

Shields and Brown wanted to end with the Peterloo Massacre, to represent the nineteenth century, but this was rejected by the councillors as politically sensitive. The last two scenes show the Bridgewater Canal and John Dalton, representing transport and science. From today's perspective, neither of these adequately represents the powerful forces that shaped nineteenth-century Manchester.

While in Manchester, Brown also provided colossal decorative paintings for the Royal Manchester Jubilee Exhibition of 1887, and took part in social and cultural activities. His social circle is reflected in the portraits of his friends included in the murals. Brown acquired a new patron, the brewer Henry Boddington, who made a large collection of Brown's pictures at his house in Wilmslow. The artist's reputation in the city was sealed when in 1885 the City Art Gallery purchased his masterpiece *Work* (cat. 61).

In the murals, Brown rejected the academic conception of history painting as the idealised representation of noble or heroic acts. He presented history as a conglomeration of seemingly random and humdrum details, expressive faces, visual asides and humorous incidents. These compete for attention with the main figures, sometimes providing a mocking commentary on them, and emphasising the role of ordinary people in history. Brown's motive was to engage the viewer, as he was conscious that the murals were 'for the instruction of the people.'[3]

With their adventurous compositions and rich colour the paintings make a perfect complement to the architecture yet do not dominate it. The murals were Brown's last great achievement, the culmination of his early ambitions to be a mural painter. At the end of his career, Manchester gave him the opportunity he had always wanted.

Fig. 103
Detail of cat. 142, Dalton collecting Marsh-Fire Gas

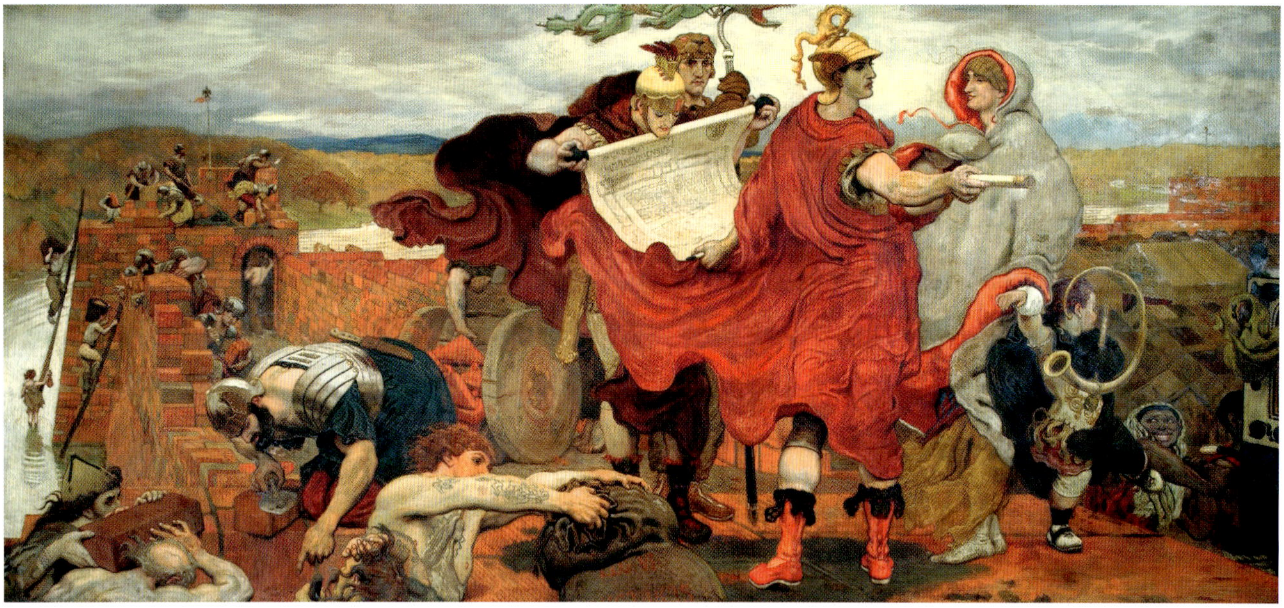

116

MANCHESTER TOWN HALL MURALS

The order follows the historical sequence of the murals as they appear in the Great Hall, not the order in which Brown painted them, which is slightly different.

116
THE ROMANS BUILDING A FORT AT MANCENION, A.D.80

(A 107)
1880
Gambier Parry process of spirit fresco, 57½ × 125¼ (146 × 318)
signed in monogram and dated: *FMB–80*
Mural painting in Manchester Town Hall

117
DESIGN FOR 'THE ROMANS BUILDING A FORT AT MANCENION'A.D.80'

(A107.1)
1879–80, 1890
oil on canvas, 29¼ × 64 (74.4 × 162.6)
signed in monogram and dated: *FMB–79–90*
Aberdeen Art Gallery & Museums Collections

For Brown, the subject embodied the foundation of Manchester as a place which barely existed before the Romans built a fort there. The original intention to depict the Roman governor of Britain, Agricola, had to be abandoned when Axon pointed out that there was no evidence he had ever visited Manchester. So Brown depicted an unnamed Roman general with his wife and their son visiting the fort to inspect the building works, with a centurion showing them a plan. In the background is the river Medlock, and a view of the Peak District, its autumn colours harmonising with the red sandstone and the red cloaks.

Brown devised the composition and much of the detail to show the subjugation of the Mancunians by the foreign conquerors. The Romans are in a dominant position, placed above the Britons. The legionaries are laying the stones, but the heavy work is carried out by the locals. The luxury of Roman life is made clear by the general's wife, robed in fur; her chair is carried by Nubian slaves and her hair is dyed yellow but her eyebrows remain black. Through touches of comedy, Brown also shows that the conquerors' attempt to impose order is disrupted. They are discomfited by the chilly northern climate, and have to peer at the plan of the fort upside down, as they try unsuccessfully to stop it flapping in the wind: the straight lines and symmetry of the plan contrast with the swirling lines of their disorderly cloaks. The general's little boy 'is mischievously aiming a kick at one of his mother's Nubian slave chair-bearers.'[4] The Nubian grins back insubordinately, a Hogarthian touch.[5] The boy holds a bugle: Brown is supposed to have climbed to the top of the Town Hall tower to see the bugle clear of reflections from the gas jets in the

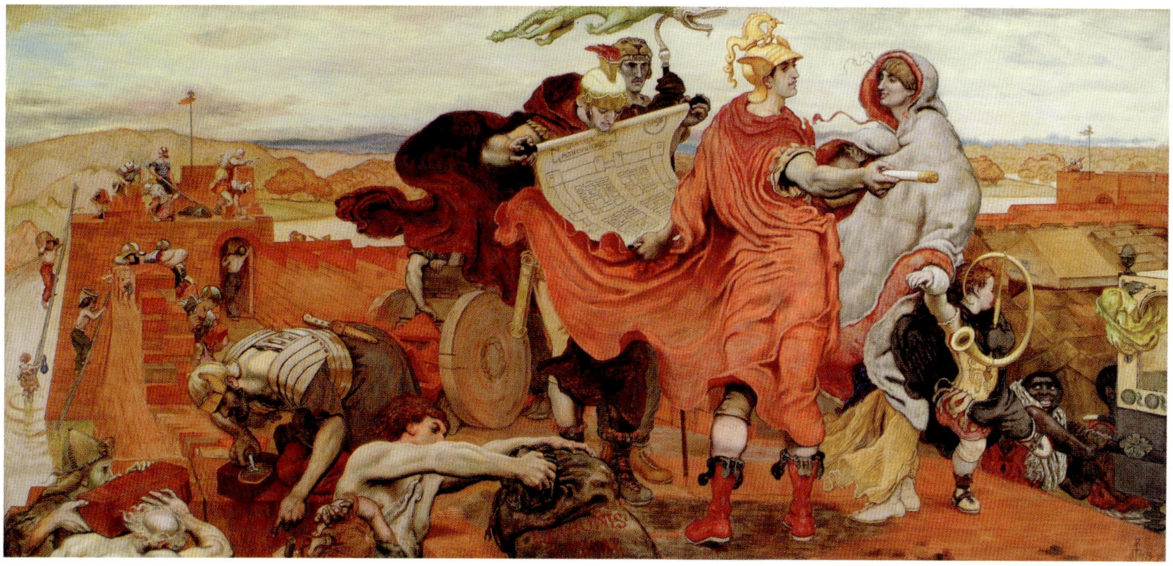

117

Great Hall. William Michael Rossetti sat for one of the soldiers, possibly the helmeted and bearded man with a trowel on the left.

Brown's ant-heroic subtext favours the Mancunians, exemplified by the tattooed labourer lifting a heavy sack of cement, cut off by the bottom edge. Brown has pushed him to the front of the picture space and placed him on the same level as spectators in the Great Hall. Like the young navvy in *Work* (cat. 61), he is the real hero of the painting, and typifies the prominent, sometimes subversive role Brown gave to ordinary people throughout the series.

Brown would certainly have known the mural of *The Roman Wall* at Wallington Hall by the Pre-Raphaelite associate William Bell Scott (fig. 104). This may have suggested the motif of the full-length Roman with the small figures building the wall receding into deep space.

The oil (cat. 117), one quarter the size of the mural, was the artist's original design for the wall-painting. He began the design in monochrome, but added the colour while he was painting the full-size mural. *The Romans building a Fort at Mancenion* was the first in the historical sequence but the second to be painted, taking from April to September 1880.

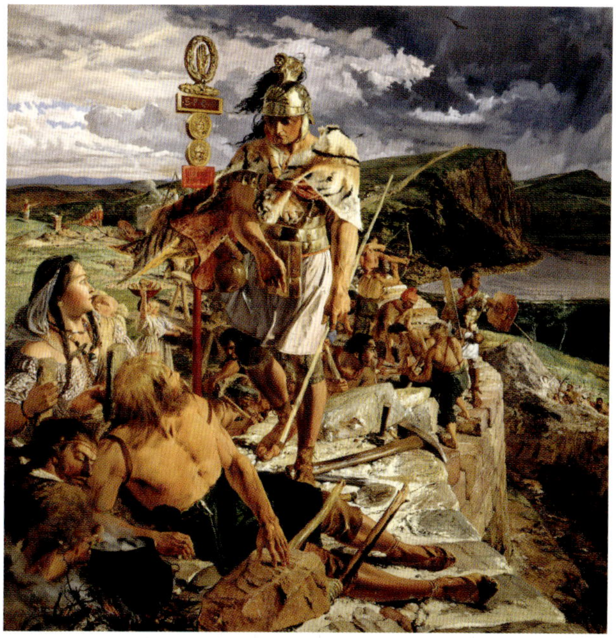

Fig. 104
William Bell Scott, The Building of the Roman Wall, *mural at Wallington Hall, 1856–57. The Trevelyan Collection (National Trust)*

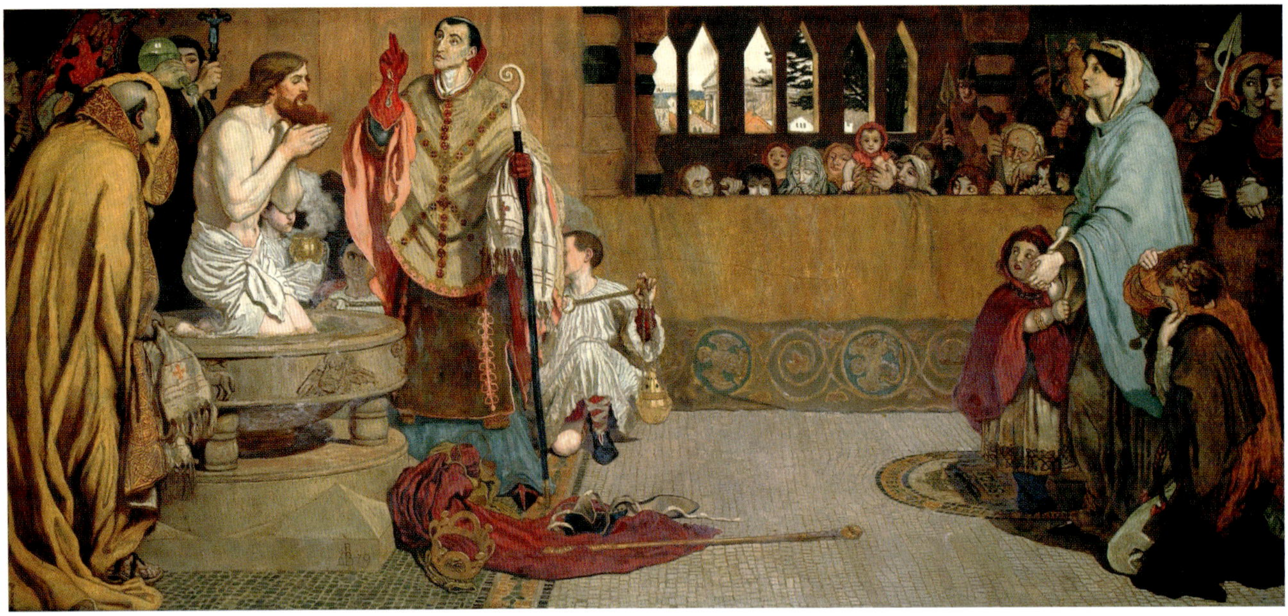
118

118

THE BAPTISM OF EDWIN, A.D.627

(A 106)
1879
Gambier Parry process of spirit fresco, 57½ × 125¼ (146 × 318)
signed in monogram and dated: *FMB–79*
Mural painting in Manchester Town Hall

119

COLOUR SKETCH FOR 'THE BAPTISM OF EDWIN, A.D.627'

(A106.1)
1879
oil on panel, 7 × 15⅝ (17.8 × 39.7)
signed in monogram and dated: *FMB–79*
Tullie House Museum & Art Gallery. Bequeathed by Dr Gordon and Emily Bottomley 1949

This subject shows the introduction of Christianity to Manchester, but as there was no record of any relevant event in Manchester itself, such as the conversion of a pagan chieftain there, Brown had to depict a scene that took place at York, following the account of the Venerable Bede. On the left Edwin, King of Northumbria and Deira (the latter kingdom included Manchester), kneels in the font, as he is baptised by Bishop Paulinus. On the right is his wife, Queen Ethelberga of Kent, a Christian, who persuaded Edwin to adopt her faith. Bede recorded that the ceremony took place in a small wooden church in York. To give continuity with the first mural, Brown depicted the event taking place on a mosaic floor, showing that the church was built on Roman foundations, and a view of Roman York can be seen through the Saxon triangular-headed windows. In contrast with the preceding mural of *The Romans* and *The Expulsion of the Danes*, which follows, the scene is calm and ordered, dominated by horizontal lines. The narrative is clear, but the subsidiary figures such as the crowd of onlookers peering over the barrier, and the acolytes making faces at each other humanize the solemnity of the baptism.

For his depiction of Bishop Paulinus, Brown followed Wordsworth's sonnet *Paulinus*, where the bishop was described as 'of shoulders curved, and stature tall,/ Black hair, vivid eye and meagre cheek,/ His prominent feature like an eagle's beak.' Frank O'Donnell MP for Dungarvan, County Waterford, agreed to model for Edwin but Charles Rowley also sat for him.[6] Lucy Madox Brown was probably the model for the Queen, raising her eyes to heaven, and the little girl with her was probably painted from her daughter Olivia. Amongst the people watching in the background, Brown

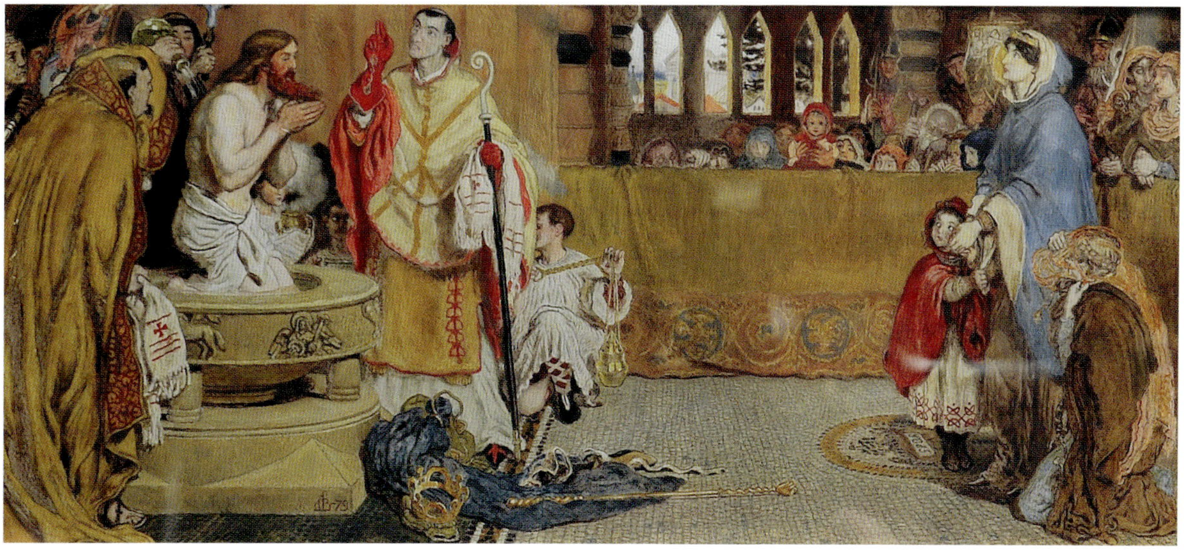

119

included a portrait of Frederic Shields (with white beard, resting his head on his arm on the right; see fig. 34, p. 48) and his own self-portrait (left of the child wearing a red hood).

The kneeling king repeats the figure of St. Oswald from Brown's stained-glass design for *The Baptism of St. Oswald*, 1864 (St. Oswald's Church, Durham),[7] but the ultimate source is William Dyce's mural in the House of Lords, *The Baptism of St. Ethelbert* (fig. 105). This has a similar kneeling figure being baptised, and a row of spectators behind a barrier, but instead of Dyce's orderly row of idealised Raphaelesque types, Brown painted a more realistic looking crowd of people with individualised faces. He had already used a similar arrangement in *King Lear* (cat. 36) with spectators peering over a barrier and a window giving an exterior view at the back. The composition, with its empty centre and horizontal emphasis, is also indebted to another mural by Dyce in the House of Lords, *The Admission of Sir Tristram to the fellowship of the Round Table*, 1848–64.

The small sketch (cat. 119) was made as a study for the colour effect and finished off after completing the mural. The frame was made by Charles Rowley's firm to Brown's design. Brown also made a full scale cartoon for the mural, initially in black and white but coloured later (National Gallery of Victoria, Melbourne).[8] He worked at the mural on the wall from April to July 1879; it was first to be painted although second in the sequence.

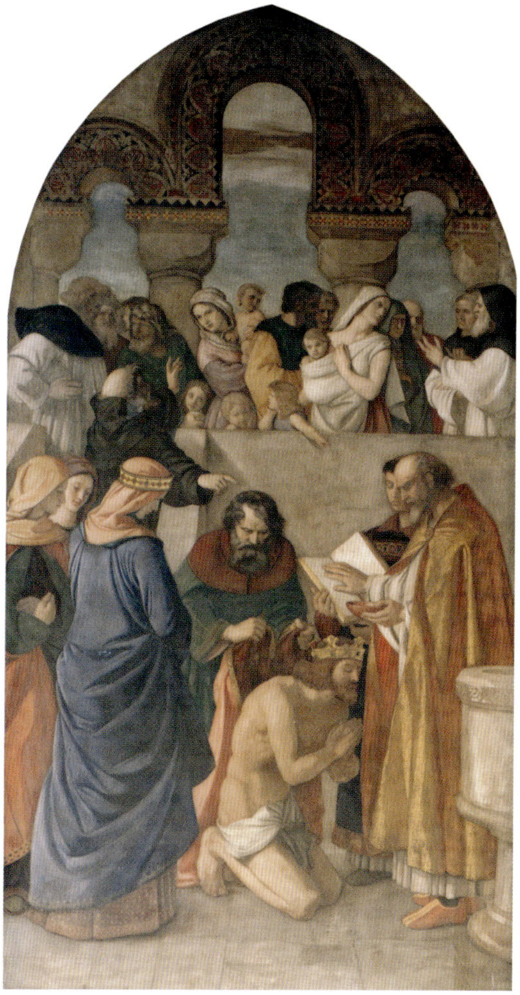

Fig. 105
William Dyce, The Baptism of St. Ethelbert, *1845/47. Palace of Westminster Collection, London*

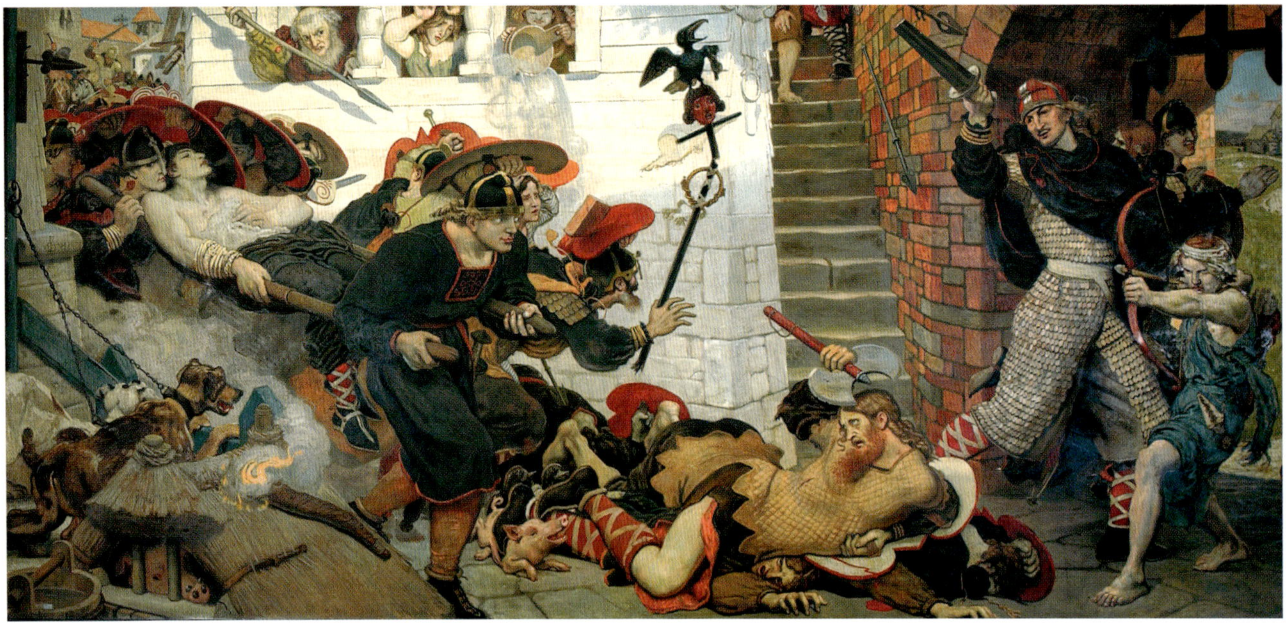

120

120
THE EXPULSION OF THE DANES FROM MANCHESTER, A.D.910

(A 108)
1880–81
Gambier Parry process of spirit fresco, 57½ × 125¼ (146 × 318)
signed in monogram: *FMB–81*
Mural painting in Manchester Town Hall

121
CARTOON FOR 'THE EXPULSION OF THE DANES FROM MANCHESTER, A.D.910'

(A108.2)
1879–80
black chalk, 30 × 64 (76.2 × 162.5)
signed and dated: *F.M.B. 1880*
Victoria and Albert Museum, London

Based on a brief passage in the Anglo-Saxon Chronicle about Edward the Elder sending men to Manchester after the town had been damaged by the Danes, Brown invented a scene showing the Danish invaders driven out of Manchester pursued by the Saxon soldiers. In a confused mêlée of smoke, pigs, dogs and fallen bodies, the Danish invaders carry a young chieftain out on an improvised stretcher, whilst the townspeople fire missiles at the Danes including boiling water and a roof tile, which lands on the head of the standard-bearer. The improvised interventions of the Mancunians, in bright sunlight, are featured more prominently than the activity of Edward the Elder's soldiers, seen in the distance on the left. At the town gate, a young Dane looks back with a gesture of defiance, and a boy fires an arrow; Brown emphasized the extreme youth of the Danish warriors, who were sent out in quest of booty as young as fifteen. Further didactic details include the gold bracelets worn by the wounded chieftain to show the wealth acquired by the Danes from melting down booty; and the polygonal blocks of the pavement, indicating the Roman road. Juxtaposed with the broken standard is a stone figure of Christ, symbolizing the victory of Christianity over heathenism, but Christ's head is cut off at the top, perhaps a veiled allusion to Brown's agnosticism. Christianity is also represented by the churches at the far left and right.

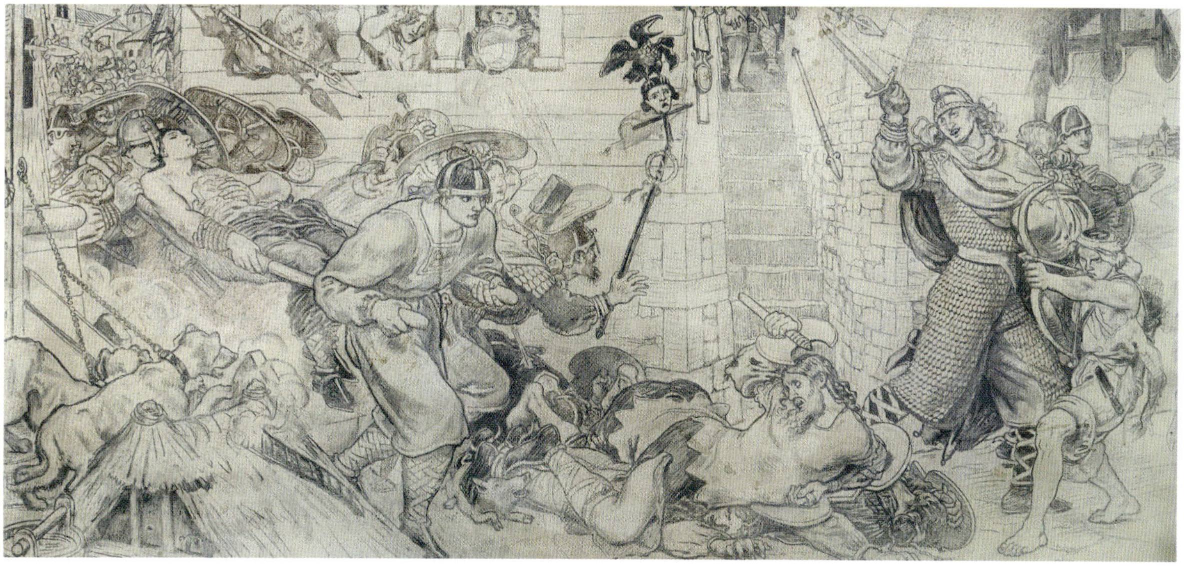

121

The sweeping composition with gesticulating figures recalls the work of Brown's teacher in Antwerp, Baron Gustav Wappers (fig. 3, p. 11), but in place of the heroic action of Wappers' protagonists, Brown's central figures are faintly ridiculous. Brown's composition places the action in a narrow space in the centre, with distant views opened up at the edges. He used variants of this type of composition elsewhere in the series.

Charles Rowley (cat. 150) was the model for the defeated chieftain lying on the ground, and the novelist Hall Caine was used for the stretcher bearer with the prominent eyes (fig. 106).[9] The black chalk version of the composition (cat. 121) is the artist's preliminary cartoon, a quarter the size of the mural. This was the third subject to be painted (September 1880–March 1881).

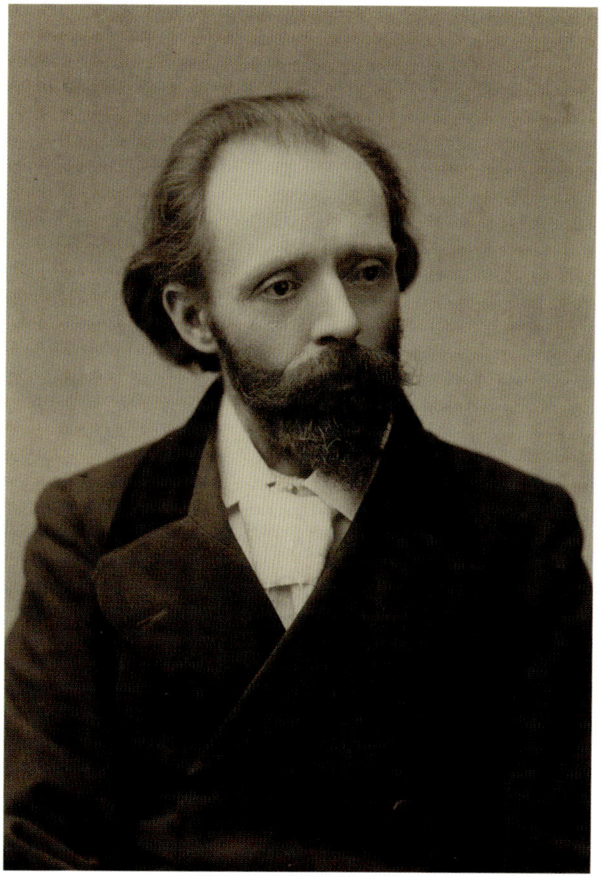

Fig. 106
Sir Hall Caine, photograph by London Stereoscopic Company, c. 1915. National Portrait Gallery, London

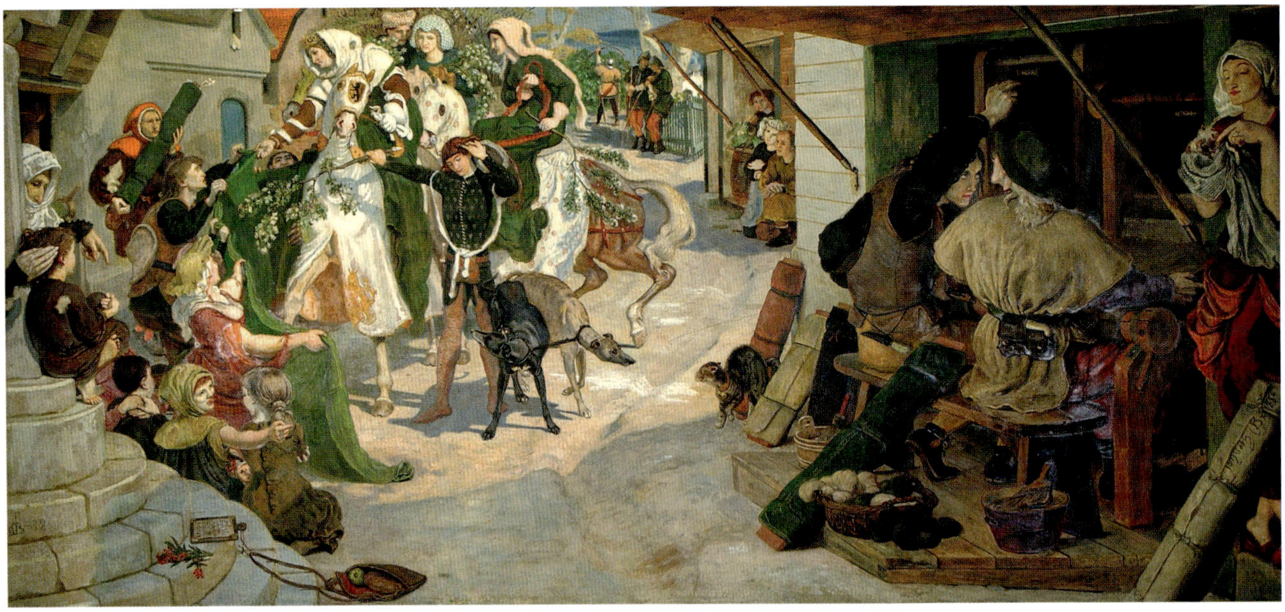

122

122

THE ESTABLISHMENT OF THE FLEMISH WEAVERS IN MANCHESTER, A.D.1363

(A 109)
1881–82
Gambier Parry process of spirit fresco, 57½ × 25¼ (146 × 318)
signed in monogram and dated: *FMB–82*
Mural painting in Manchester Town Hall

123

DESIGN FOR 'THE ESTABLISHMENT OF THE FLEMISH WEAVERS IN MANCHESTER, A.D.1362'

(A109.1)
1881, 1888
tempera on panel, 10⅝ × 22 (27.1 × 55.9)
signed in monogram and dated: *FMB–88*
Manchester City Galleries

124

STUDIES OF A HORSE FOR 'THE ESTABLISHMENT OF THE FLEMISH WEAVERS IN MANCHESTER, A.D.1362'

(A109.2)
1882
inscribed (verso): *F.M.B.*
coloured chalks, 22½ × 25⅝ (57 × 65)
Birmingham Museums and Art Gallery

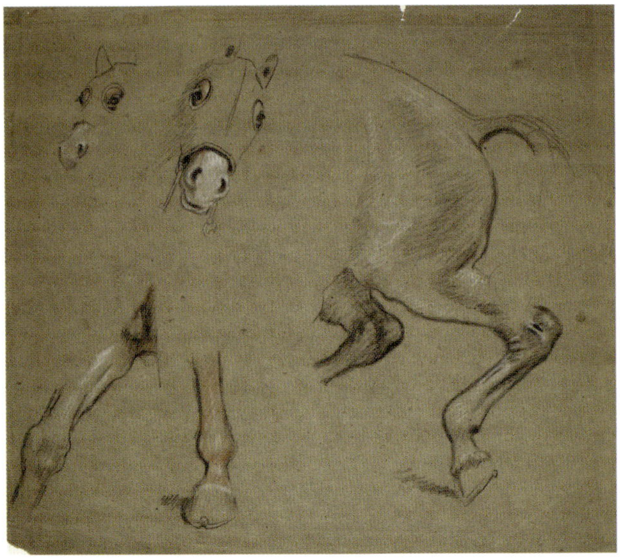

124

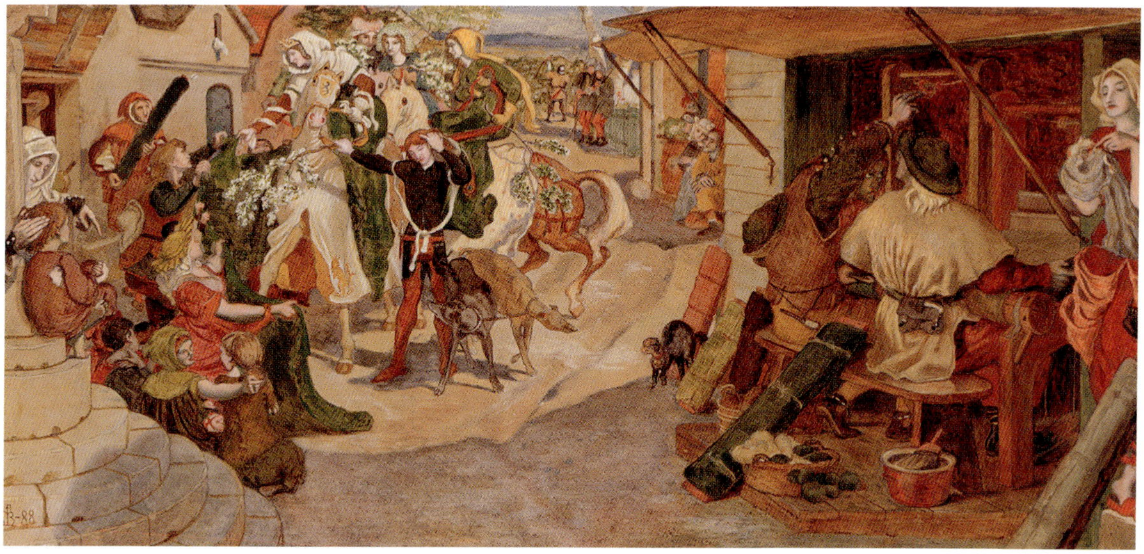

123

Queen Phillipa of Hainault, wife of Edward III was supposed to have settled Flemish weavers from her native country in England, and Brown designed an imaginary scene showing her visiting them in Manchester, which at that period was part of the land held by her son, John of Gaunt, Earl Palatine of Lancashire. Axon had commented that textile production in Manchester predated the Flemings, but did not object to the subject, which was intended to commemorate the origins of Lancashire's supremacy in textile manufactures.

The Queen and her ladies, dressed in Lincoln green, admire the cloth of the same colour held out to her by the Manchester weavers. The time of year is indicated by the spring sunlight and the branches of may-blossom held by the visitors. Brown reversed the social hierarchy, placing the court group in the background, and again giving greater prominence to the ordinary Mancunians, the weavers holding out bolts of cloth and the children with satchel and slate. The Flemings are on the right: the old weaver, seated at the loom, gazing at the Queen, is marked out as a settler as his name 'Jan van Brugge' is written on the bale of cloth in the bottom right corner, also a reference to Brown's admiration for Jan van Eyck.[10] Brown hints at tension between locals and immigrants: one of the Manchester children is pulling her tongue out at the Flemish girl with the kitten standing on the right, her nationality conveyed by her clogs, and the Flemish girl is studiously ignoring the attentions of the apprentice weaver, presumably a Mancunian.

According to Brown this subject had 'been in my head near 30 years.'[11] It repeats his delight in recreating the colourful details of fourteenth-century costume in spring sunlight, as seen in *Chaucer at the Court of Edward III* (cat. 34). Brown cited Chaucer in his description of the mural, in which he wrote of spring as 'still the finest part of the year in Lancashire, at which season Chaucer tells us the English people delighted "to go on Pilgrimages."'[12] Other echoes of Brown's previous work are the attention given to different qualities of light, direct sunlight for the Queen and her group, and reflected sunlight for the weavers under the awning; and the use of animals to parody the human drama, with the sleek court greyhounds sniffing at the hostile Manchester cat, recalling the dogs in *Work* (cat. 61).

Brown did not make a full-size or even a quarter-size cartoon for this mural, but instead made a much smaller design (cat. 123). 'It is not a cartoon this time for I find I can advantageously use living models on the wall itself' the artist wrote to Stephens.[13] Amongst the models he used were Emma for the Queen (see cat. 94); Mrs. Pyne (cat. 148), the wife of his friend the organist, and Miss Brockbank, daughter of one of his patrons, both sat for court ladies.[14] The cat was painted from a drawing supplied by (although not made by) Shields. For the horses, he used a jointed wooden lay figure of a horse, but the sheet of studies, presumably made from real horses, shows the trouble taken to capture their restless pacing movements (cat. 124).

The mural was the fourth to be painted, begun in October 1881 and completed May or June 1882.

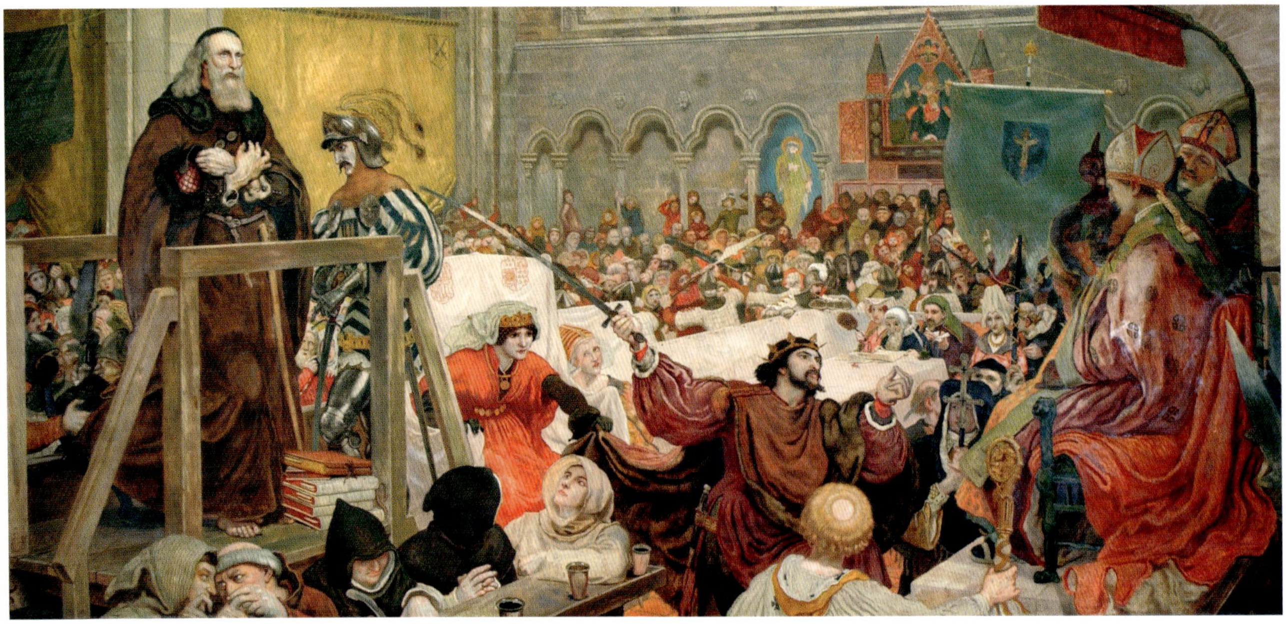
125

125

THE TRIAL OF WYCLIF, A.D.1377

(A 112)
1885–86
Gambier Parry process of spirit fresco, 57½ × 125¼ (146 × 318)
signed in monogram: *FMB–86*
Mural painting in Manchester Town Hall

126

'STUDY FOR THE TRIAL OF WYCLIF, A.D.1377'

(A112.1)
1884-85
oil on canvas, 21 × 43 (53.3 × 109)
Culture and Sport Glasgow on behalf of Glasgow City Council.
Given by the Trustees of the Hamilton Bequest 1929

Brown here represented a real historical event, the trial of Wyclif for heresy in the Lady Chapel of Old St. Paul's Cathedral, London, on 19 February 1377.[15] On the left Wyclif stands in the dock; next to him is the Earl-Marshal Lord Percy. In the centre is John of Gaunt, Wyclif's defender at the trial, making a point with one hand, and with the other brandishing his sword at Wyclif in a grand gesture. Behind Percy is his wife Constance who tries to restrain him. On the right are his judges, William Courtenay, the Bishop of London and Simon Sudbury, Archbishop of Canterbury, who whispers into his ear. In the foreground are the five mendicant friars appointed as Wyclif's counsel, and in the middle distance towards the left, wearing a green hood, is Chaucer, John of Gaunt's protégé, taking notes.

The subject was included to show the beginnings of nonconformism in Lancashire, even though it took place in London. Axon would have preferred the martyrdom of the Manchester born reformer John Bradford (which also took place in London), but Brown was an admirer of Wyclif, whom he had already painted in his role as translator of the Bible in to English (cat. 33). The dramatic and busy quality of the mural is very different from the calm repose of the earlier painting. Brown consulted written sources before painting the picture: the pile of books in front of Wyclif alludes to the words of Percy, who enraged the bishops by asking for a seat for the aged reformer: 'An [sic] you must answer from all these books, Doctor, you will need a soft seat.'[16]

Although Brown consulted historical portraits for guidance, he also used his friends as models. The Archbishop of Canterbury is

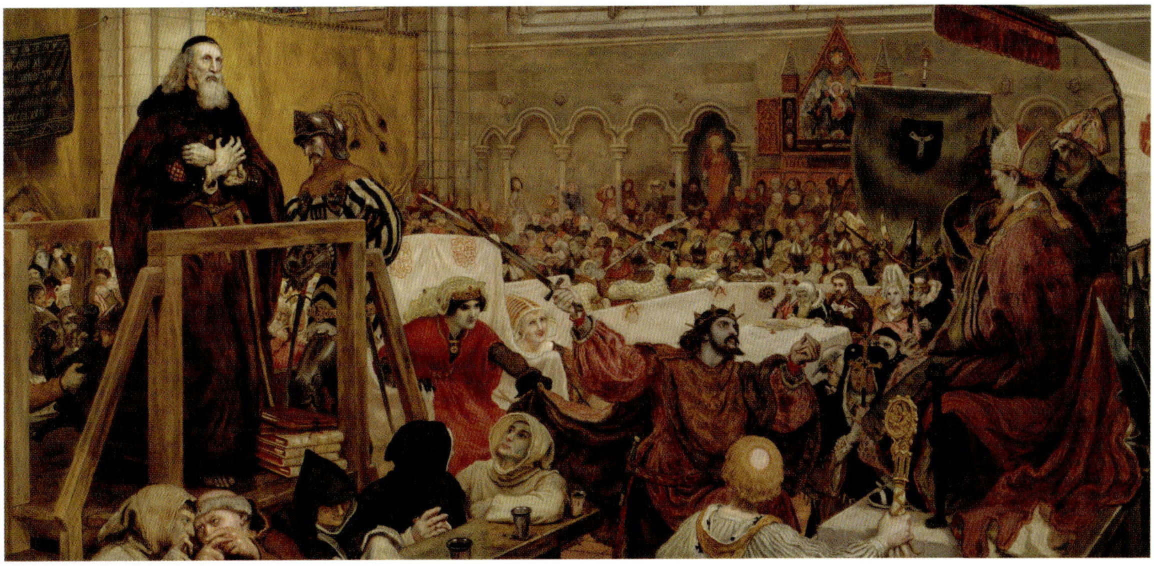
126

a self-portrait, a wry touch. The other models are Frederic Shields for Wyclif (fig. 34, p. 48), Mrs. Boddington for Constance (fig. 107), Brown's pupil Harold Rathbone for John of Gaunt (fig. 108), his old friend Dante Gabriel Rossetti for Chaucer and the Manchester organist Kendrick Pyne for the Bishop of London (fig. 37, p. 54).[17] The figures are richly dressed: Brown was given permission to borrow historic vestments and embroidered textiles from the Art Gallery for use when painting the mural.[18] For the details of Old St. Paul's, he used engraved views but some of the architectural detail is conjectural, and in the altarpiece on the back wall, Brown introduced a satirical joke by showing the Virgin raising her arms in horror at the proceedings.

This is the fifth subject, but the seventh to be painted; at first Brown left the space blank because it was originally assigned to Shields, and in the meantime, rather than draw a cartoon, or small design, he made a preliminary study in oil (cat. 126) 'so as to avoid the difficulties of working from models on the walls, and have the luxury of working in my nice studio.'[19] More highly finished than previous preparatory studies and designs, it occupied him from June 1884 to May 1885. He began to paint the subject on the wall in June 1885 but left it unfinished in the winter because of the severe cold in the Great Hall. He completed it in 1886. It was the last to be done using the Gambier Parry method.

Several years later, in 1892, Brown began a full-size oil replica of *The Trial of Wyclif* (Birmingham Museums and Art Gallery).[20] Towards the end of the previous year, Shields, knowing that Brown was desperately short of money, had persuaded many of his friends to subscribe to a fund to help him. The fund was meant to be a secret but in January 1892, Brown found out about it when a note about it was published in the *Pall Mall Gazette*. Brown was furious, and refused to accept what he regarded as charity, despite his evident need. Eventually he was persuaded to take the money as payment for a work to be presented to the National Gallery as a tribute to his achievements. Brown chose to paint a replica of *The Trial of Wyclif* but sadly, never completed it. After his death, the funds were used to buy *Jesus washing Peter's Feet* (cat. 75), which was presented to the nation in instead.

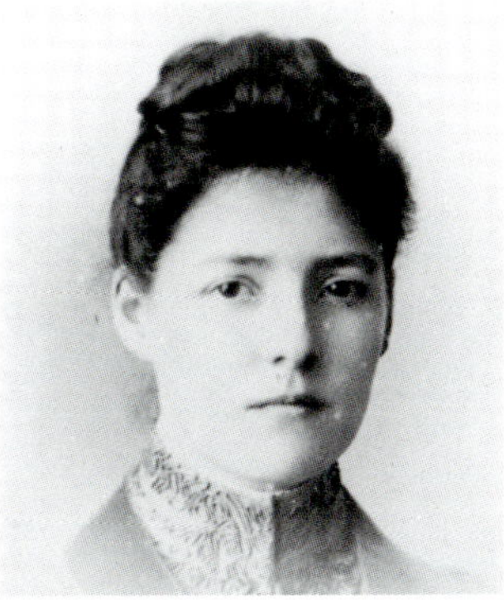

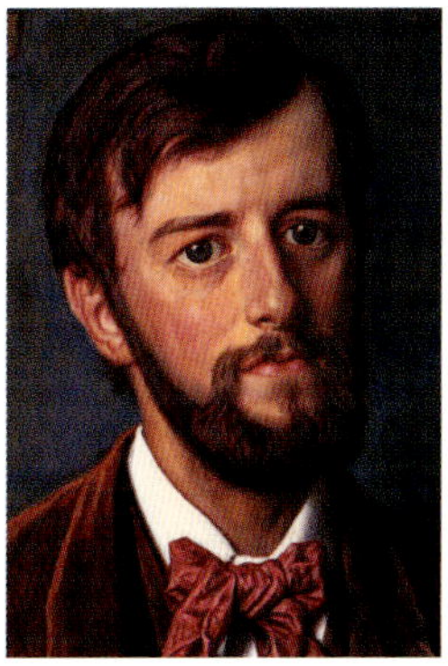

Fig. 107
Mrs Henry Boddington, photograph. Private collection

Fig. 108
William Holman Hunt, Harold Rathbone, *1893. National Museums Liverpool, Walker Art Gallery*

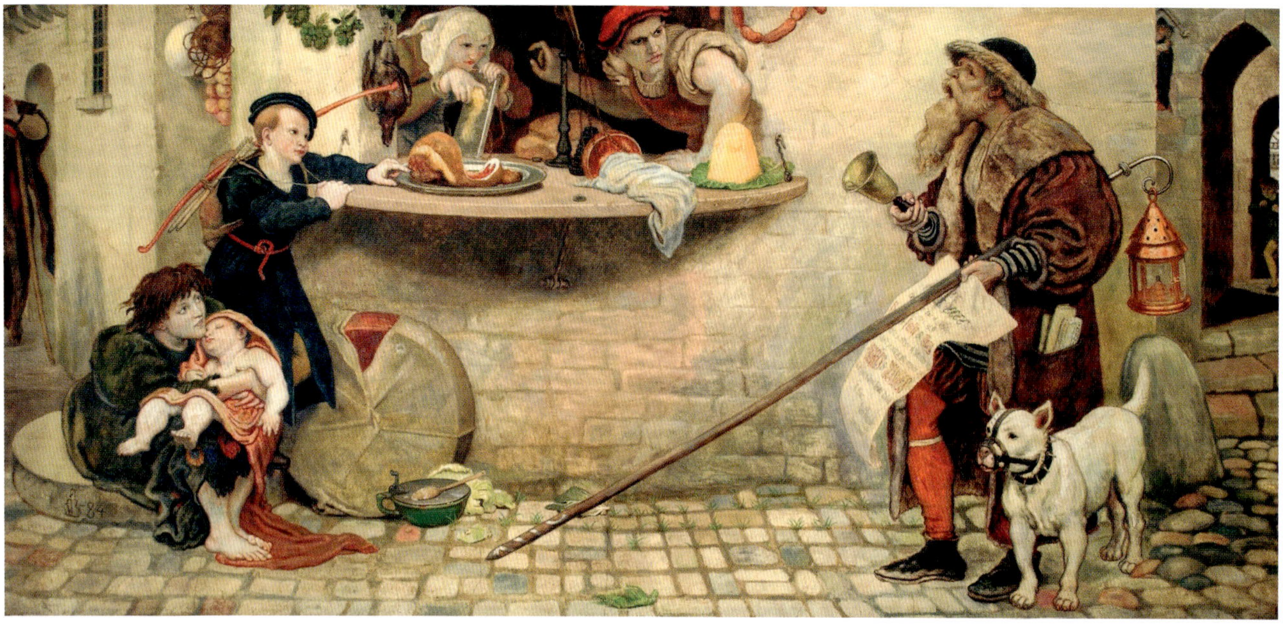
127

127

THE PROCLAMATION REGARDING WEIGHTS AND MEASURES, A.D.1556

(A III)
1883–84
Gambier Parry process of spirit fresco, 57½ × 125¼ (146 × 318)
signed in monogram and dated: *FMB–84*
Mural painting in Manchester Town Hall

128

REPLICA OF 'THE PROCLAMATION REGARDING WEIGHTS AND MEASURES, A.D.1556'

(AIII.1)
1889
Tempera on panel, 10⁵⁄₁₆ × 22⅜ (26.2 × 56.9)
signed in monogram and dated: *FMB Nov 89*
Manchester City Galleries

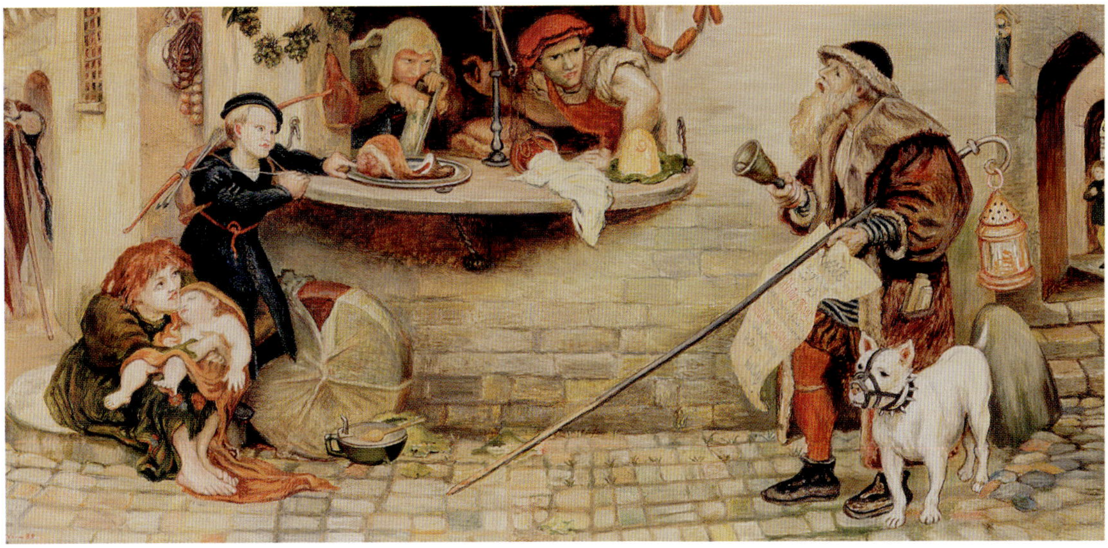
128

A town crier walks the streets ringing a bell announcing a court order requiring the testing of weights and measures. In the food shop the grocer looks indignant whilst his wife removes butter sticking to her scales. On the right their son, a schoolboy in uniform with bow and arrow, fingers a joint of meat and a beggar girl sits with a naked child who looks very well-fed, another Brown joke. From the sides a man on crutches and another boy come to listen.

The subject was chosen to show the foundation of commercial integrity in Manchester, and was based on Brown's reading of the Court Leet records for Manchester, although he made a mistake over the date of the order, changing it from 1566 to 1556. Axon approved the subject although observed that this was not the earliest instance of market regulation. Brown included incidental details of other quaint laws and customs discovered in the course of his researches, such as the bow and arrow carried by the boy, and the requirement to muzzle dogs.

After the drama of Wyclif, the composition is again clear and simple, with a shallow space in the centre opening back into deeper spaces at the edges, as seen in the mural of the Danes. Brown seems to have used Netherlandish and Italian Mannerist sources for the figures: the grocer and his wife derive from paintings of shops and markets by Pieter Aertsen or Joachim Beuckelaer, and the schoolboy recalls figures by Bronzino or Pontormo.

For this painting Brown returned to the practice of drawing a preliminary chalk cartoon (private collection).[21] He began the subject on the wall in July 1883 and finished it in March 1884; it was the sixth mural to be painted. The small painting (cat. 128) is a replica made for sale after completion of the mural; the artist's daughter Catherine is recorded as having worked on a duplicate of *Weights and Measures*, and the uneven quality of this painting, for example the figure of the beggar girl and child, suggests her authorship, although it was then signed by Brown.

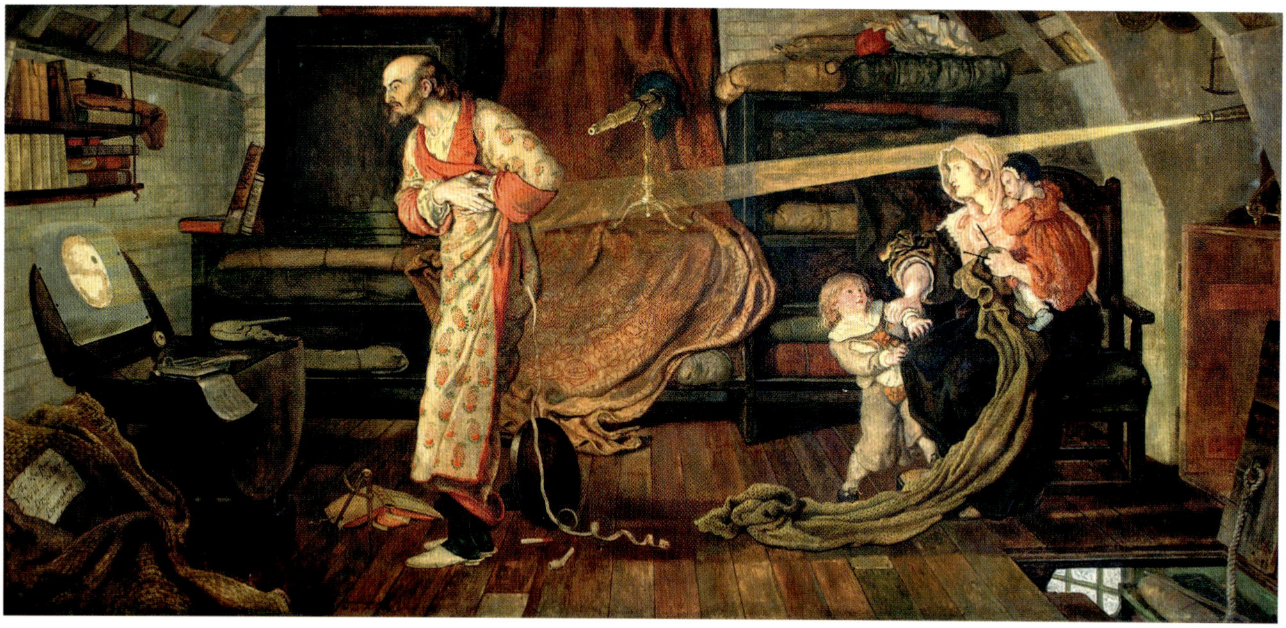

129

129

CRABTREE WATCHING THE TRANSIT OF VENUS, A.D.1639

(A 110)
1882–83
Gambier Parry process of spirit fresco, 57½ × 125¼ (146 × 318)
signed in monogram and dated: *FMB–83*
Mural painting in Manchester Town Hall

130

DESIGN FOR 'CRABTREE WATCHING THE TRANSIT OF VENUS, A.D.1639'

(A110.1)
1881, 1888
tempera on panel, 10⅜ × 22 (26.4 × 55.9)
signed in monogram and dated: *FMB–81–88*
Manchester City Galleries

William Crabtree, a draper from Broughton, Salford, gazes at the shadow of Venus crossing the sun, projected through a telescope across a darkened room onto a paper diagram representing the sun's disk. The astronomer Jeremiah Horrox[22] had discovered an error in Kepler's tables and computed that the transit would take place on 24 November 1639. He asked his friend Crabtree to watch the event to corroborate his own observation. Brown depicted Crabtree as so astonished at the sight that he failed to make any measurements. The subject was included in the murals to represent scientific achievement.

Brown's understanding of the event contained several errors, as it was based on contemporary hagiographic literature: Horrox was erroneously supposed to have been a curate, and Brown thought that Crabtree had been asked to watch because the transit was predicted for a Sunday when Horrox might have been in church. But it is true that Crabtree, who had extensive correspondence with Horrox about astronomical matters, encouraged Horrox to revise Kepler's tables, and that Crabtree's observation confirmed that also made by Horrox.[23]

Axon complained that Crabtree's observation was less significant than the one made by Horrox, but in the end Crabtree was preferred for the mural because Horrox had no connection with Manchester: he was from Liverpool, and was based in Hoole, near Preston, when the transit of Venus took place. The fact that Crabtree was a linen-draper and not a learned man must also have appealed to Brown, who shows him in an attic room above a draper's shop, appealingly cluttered with books, bolts of cloth and scientific instruments. Crabtree wears a patterned silk robe and

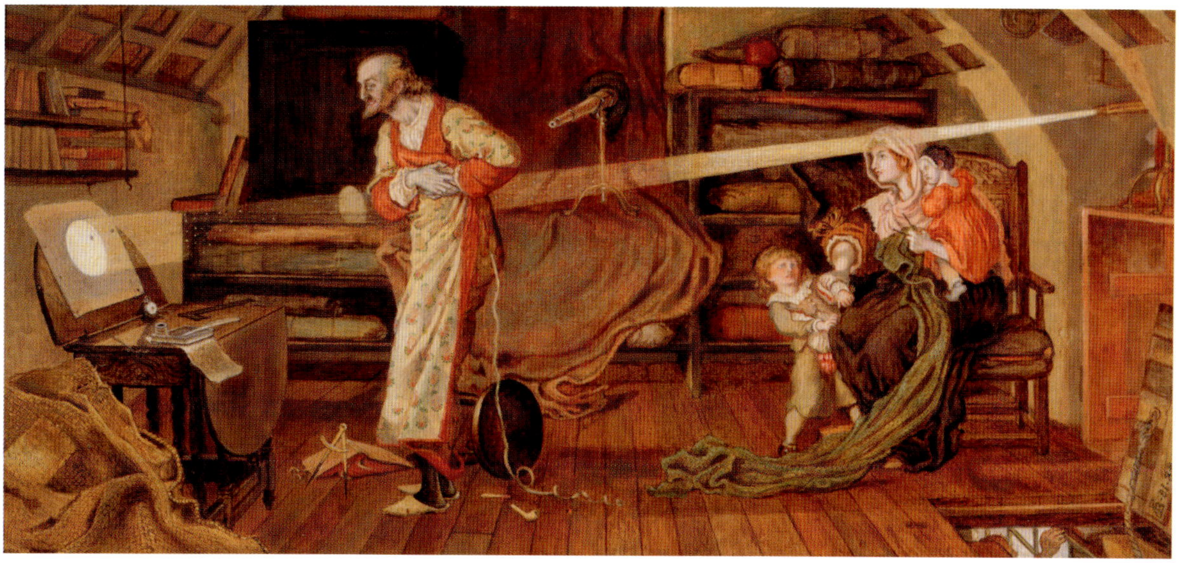

130

clutches at his heart in excitement, as he leaps up, upsetting his stool and dropping his compasses and papers.

In the bottom-right corner is a trapdoor giving a glimpse of a room below, showing that the observation took place on an upper floor, a device taken from an early drawing by Holman Hunt of Lorenzo in his office above a warehouse (Louvre, Paris). The frosty windows of the lower room allude to the time of year. Brown devised an unusual lighting effect for the scene: there are two sources of light, a soft daylight coming from the lower room, and a sharper light emanating from the reflection of the sun on the paper and highlighting the figures. The line of the sunbeam, the gazes of the two principal figures and the sweeping curves of the draperies lead the eye across the picture to the glowing image of the sun with Venus passing across it.

Brown consulted a member of the Royal Astronomical Society for information about the observation and the apparatus used. C.B. Cayley, the translator of Homer, modelled for Crabtree (fig. 109) and Cathy's son Oliver Hueffer for the little boy.[24] Mrs. Crabtree resembles the artist's daughter Lucy and the baby was taken from an old drawing of Oliver Madox Brown.[25] Her pose seems to be derived from sixteenth-century representations of Charity, traditionally shown as a woman nursing two children, or a Virgin and Child with St. John. She is shown knitting to while away the time, a detail that caused some controversy about whether knitting was permitted on a Sunday in the mid-seventeenth century.

The small panel (cat. 130) is the original design for the mural, finished off later to be sold as a replica. The mural, the fifth to be painted, but the sixth in sequence, was started on the wall in June 1882 and completed in May 1883.

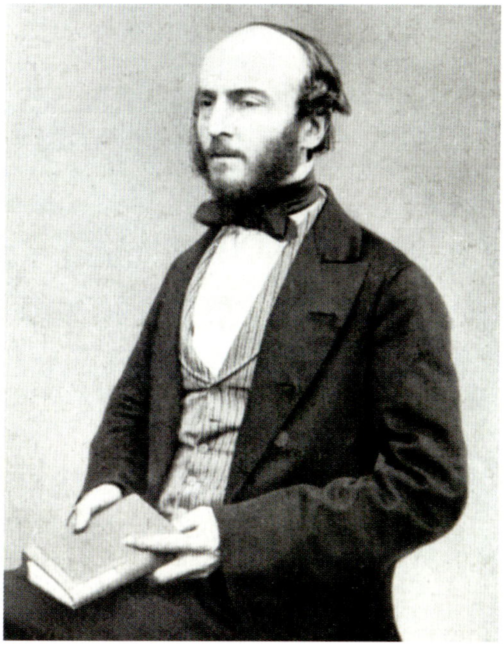

Fig. 109
Charles Cayley, photograph, 1866, from The Family Letters of Christina Rossetti, *ed. W.M. Rossetti, 1908*

131

CHETHAM'S LIFE DREAM, C.A.D.1640

(A 113)
1885–86
oil on canvas, 57½ × 125¼ (146 × 318)
signed in monogram and dated: *FMB–86*
Mural painting in Manchester Town Hall

In his will, Humphrey Chetham, a Manchester cloth merchant and financier, endowed a school for forty poor boys in the college buildings of the old Collegiate Church of St. Mary, later to become Manchester Cathedral. Brown depicted Chetham holding his will, which occupied four sheets of parchment, imagining the realisation of dream: in his mind he has peopled the courtyard with schoolboys. The date given in the title, c. 1640, was conjectural, but ensured that the chronological order of the murals was respected, as the next scene took place in 1642 (the actual date of Chetham's will was 1651).[26] Chetham died in 1653, and the school and the library endowed in his will opened in 1656. Chetham's Hospital School operated until 1969 when it became Chetham's School of Music. The subject represents education and philanthropy. Bishop Hugh Oldham, founder of the Manchester Grammar School, was also considered but as with Crabtree and Horrox, the layman was preferred to the learned.

Brown depicted the courtyard with trees, which was an invention, as there were no trees there; his painting of leafy Platt Lane (cat. 152) was begun as a study for the mural. The stylised treatment of the branches appears to derive from Japanese ornament, then fashionable in artistic circles. Schoolboys play around the central tree: at the foot of the tree two boys read a book, 'Jack the Giant Killer', one boy sits in the tree eating an apple, and another cradles a kitten. On the left, a teacher admonishes a row of boys, and the school cook beckons to the butcher's boy delivering a tray of meat. On the right boys are engaged in a variety of games – leap-frog, wrestling and an early form of cricket. The boys' activities are loosely based on Bruegel's *Children's Games* (Kunsthistorisches Museum, Vienna) which Brown could have known through engravings. The dog may have been inspired by the one in the Arnolfini portrait by Jan van Eyck in the National Gallery or by Dürer (fig. 29, p. 41).

Brown would have been able to visit the school, and could have consulted Whatton's *A History of Chetham Hospital*, 1833, which includes engravings of the buildings and the school uniform. Chetham himself resembles the portrait at the college, showing him wearing a ruff and a cap with an embroidered border, although Harold Rathbone also sat for him. Brown's grandson Oliver was used as a model for one or more of the boys.

Brown made a preparatory cartoon (private collection),[27] and began working on the painting in August 1885, but work was interrupted by an attack of gout in October. This may account for the weak drawing of some of the figures in the finished mural: a general lack of vigour compared with the execution of the earlier scenes may also be connected with the change of medium: this panel, the eighth to be painted, and eighth in sequence, was the first to be painted in oil on canvas in Brown's studio. Brown completed it in February 1886, after which it was brought into the Town Hall and attached to the wall.

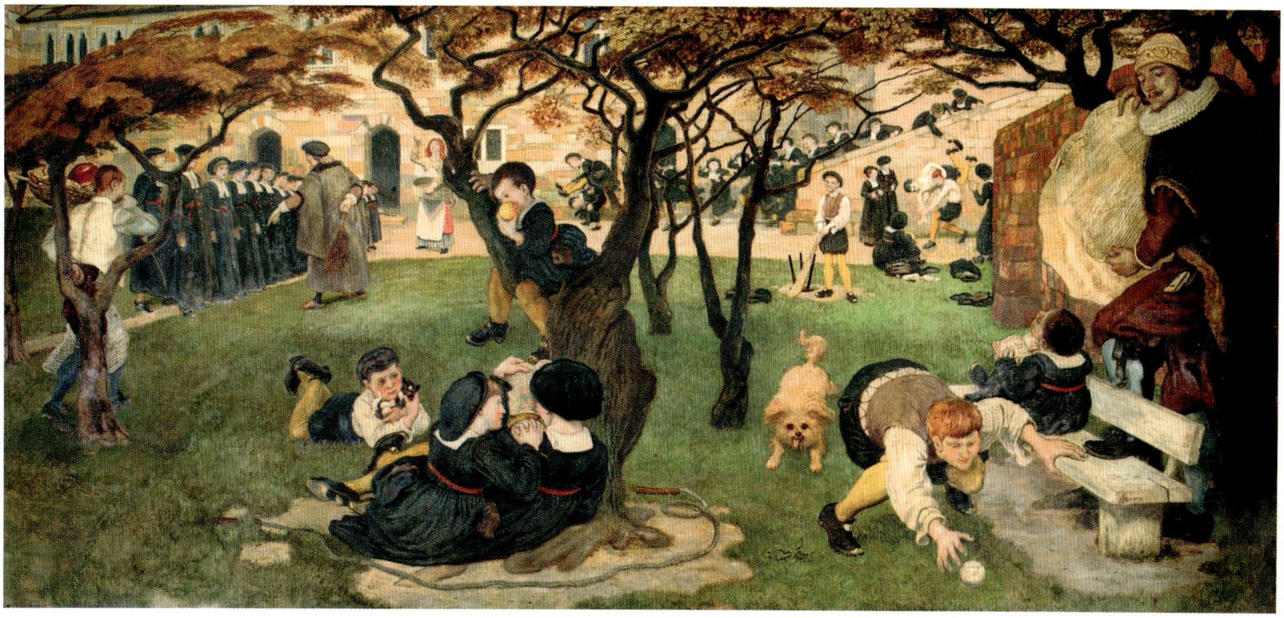

131

132
BRADSHAW'S DEFENCE OF MANCHESTER, A.D.1642

(A 117)
1892–93
oil on canvas, 57½ × 125¼ (146 × 318)
signed in monogram and dated: *FMB–93*
Mural painting in Manchester Town Hall

This subject represents Manchester's role in the Civil War: the town was Parliamentarian, and repelled a Royalist attack. In the background Captain Bradshaw fires his musket at the Royalists from the Manchester end of the Salford Bridge, then the only bridge across the Irwell. Bradshaw, with only forty musketeers, was said to have defeated a Royalist army of between three and four thousand men. The Royalists were led by Lord Strange and Lord Montagu, who is depicted in the foreground fallen from his horse, supported by his men, with dead and wounded soldiers on the bridge.

Although Brown based his painting on research into historical sources, his scene is not strictly accurate. The Salford bridge was defended by a German military engineer, Captain Rosworm, whom Brown eliminated from the story, probably because of his nationality; and Brown seems to have conflated Captain Bradshaw, recorded as fighting at Deansgate, with John Bradshaw, a Manchester lawyer, one of the regicides who signed the death warrant of Charles I in 1649. Brown's changes, whether deliberate or not, boosted the importance of the mural's subject, connecting the defence of what was then a small market town with the national ideological struggle. The subject was perhaps held to pre-figure Manchester's nineteenth-century reputation as a source of radicalism.

Brown used drawings of a bridge sent by Shields, but could also have seen engravings of the medieval bridge over the Irwell, which had been replaced in 1837. Behind Bradshaw is the Collegiate Church (later Manchester Cathedral) but Brown showed only the lower part of the tower as it had been raised in height in 1868. Brown's assistant, Robert Bruce Wallace, pointed out an error in the depiction of the guns, and sent Brown accurate drawings of firearms. Charles Rowley was the model for Lord Montagu.[28]

This was the final mural to be painted, although ninth in sequence in the Great Hall. After making a cartoon (untraced) Brown began the painting in his London studio in April 1892 and it was finished in March 1893. It was sent up to Manchester in April 1893, but a dispute arose between Brown and Manchester Corporation. Because of the criticism of the *Bridgewater Canal* painting the previous year, the Town Hall Committee had passed a resolution that the artist should submit a drawing of *Bradshaw* for approval before commencing the final painting. Brown had refused to do this, and when informed that the corporation would not accept the *Bradshaw* mural or pay for it without inspecting it, he offered it for sale elsewhere. Rowley seems to have intervened, speaking to Joseph Thomson and to Abel Heywood, the Lord Mayor, who had seen the painting informally; eventually the committee accepted it and paid Brown's fee. *Bradshaw* was finally installed in September 1893.

The painting shows considerable signs of the artist's failing powers. During 1892 and '93 Brown had been ill several times, and also suffered from a mild stroke which temporarily deprived him of the use of his painting arm, causing him to paint much of the mural with his left hand. The figure drawing is weak, and Brown seems to have used the gun-smoke behind Bradshaw as a pretext for limiting the number of figures. The flames of the burning thatch and the clouds of smoke, each with a bright explosion at its centre, have decoratively curving shapes, but fail to give a convincing illusion of space or atmosphere, and the treatment of the landscape on the river bank is perfunctory. Nevertheless, the boldly foreshortened composition demonstrates that Brown's powers of invention were still strong right at the end of his life.

132

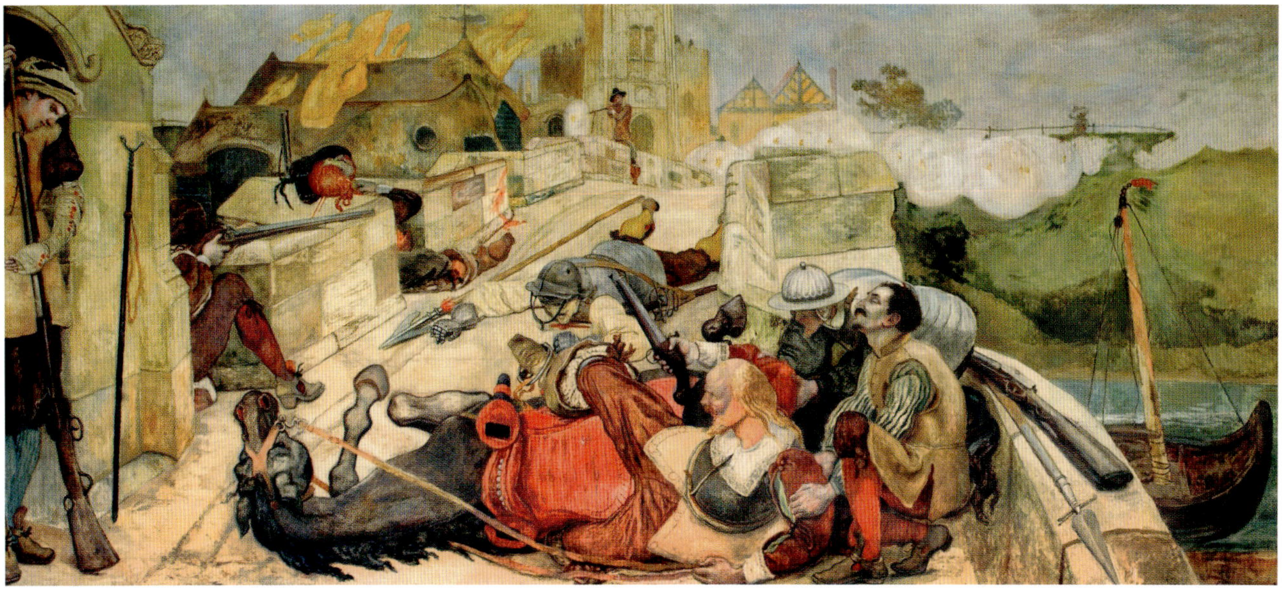

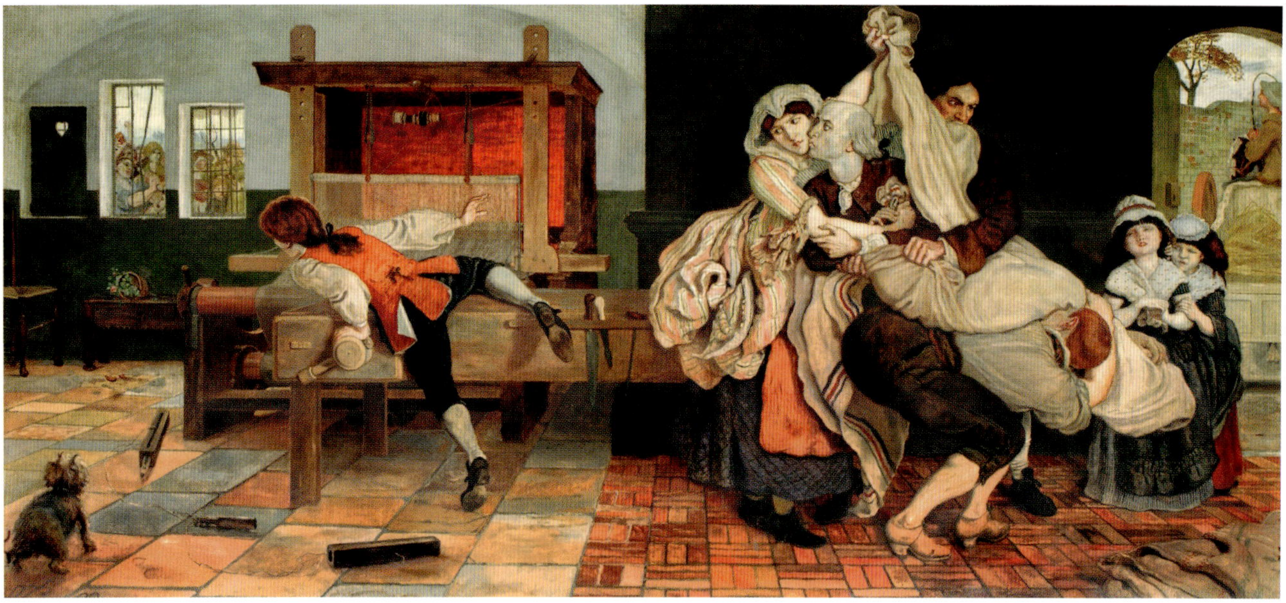

133

133

JOHN KAY, INVENTOR OF THE FLY SHUTTLE, A.D.1753

(A 115)
1888–90
oil on canvas, 57½ × 125¼ (146 × 318)
signed in monogram and dated: *FMB–90*
Mural painting in Manchester Town Hall

134

UNFINISHED CARTOON FOR 'JOHN KAY, INVENTOR OF THE FLY SHUTTLE, A.D.1753'

A115.1)
1888
tempera on panel, 13 15/16 × 31 (35.4 × 78.8)
Manchester City Galleries

135

STUDY OF LOOM FOR 'JOHN KAY, INVENTOR OF THE FLY SHUTTLE, A.D.1753'

(A115.3)
1888/89
pencil, 7 × 10 1/16 (17.8 × 25.5)
Signed: *FMB 89*
Tate. Presented by Edmund Houghton 1898

In 1733 John Kay of Bury patented a new type of lightweight wheeled shuttle, which, with his later improvements, speeded up the weaving process and enabled looms formerly operated by two people to me worked by one; the invention was the first step towards an entirely automatic loom. The fly shuttle threatened the livelihood of weavers, and Brown shows rioters trying to break into Kay's house to smash the machinery. Kay delivers an undignified farewell kiss to his wife, as he is bundled up in a wool sheet and taken out to a cart waiting outside. Kay's two small daughters stand wailing whilst his son Robert, who later developed his father's inventions, leans over a workbench in front of the loom, keeping watch.

Despite Axon's objections that John Kay's house was in Bury, outside Manchester, the subject was included because Brown felt that without Kay's invention 'all the wonders and achievements of steam-weaving would never have been perfected'.[29] However, it was an ambiguous way of introducing the industrial revolution to the

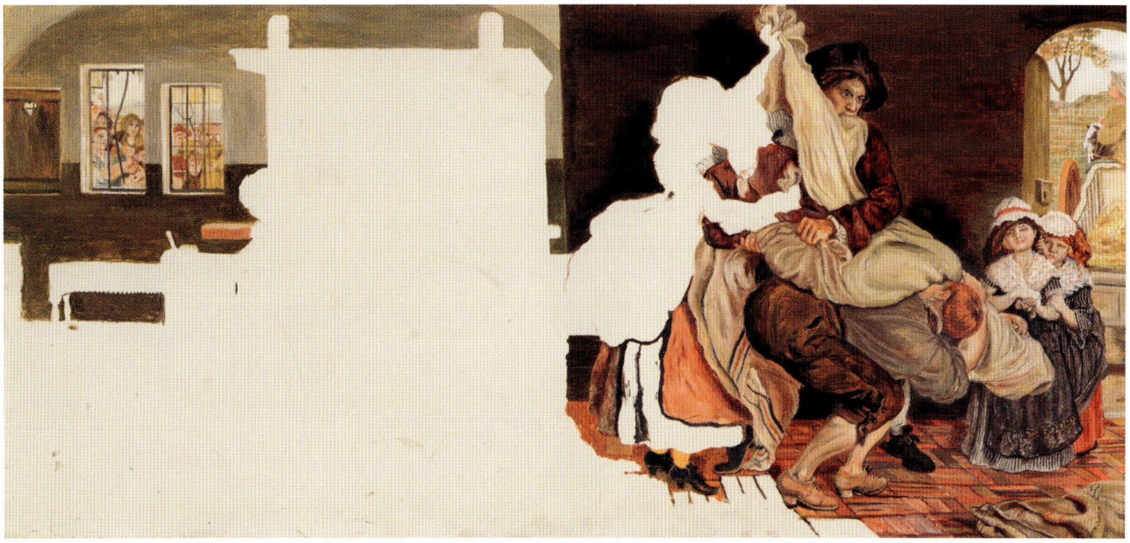

134

story being told by the murals. The scene conveys the importance of invention and mechanisation, but the independence of the ordinary working man, a theme dear to Brown, expressed itself here in Luddite conservatism. This and the comically grotesque presentation of Kay undermine the idea of Manchester as progressive.

Although machine breaking by rioters occurred in various parts of the country, this incident, supposedly from 1753, never took place; in 1747, Kay emigrated to France, where he continued his work. 'Tradition tells us that his wife saved him from their fury by having him hurried away in a wool sheet,'[30] wrote Brown, but according to modern scholarship, the story was one of the various myths that arose in the mid-nineteenth century when Kay began to be seen as 'the archetype of the heroic inventor who failed to profit from his own invention.'[31] Brown may well have identified himself with this interpretation of Kay.

Brown made an initial study for the composition, but it no longer survives; the unfinished reduced version (cat. 134) seems to have also been used as a cartoon. Brown also made a pencil study of a loom, with a sketchy figure operating it (cat. 135), although the study shows the loom from an oblique angle; in the mural the loom is seen head-on, its lines, together with those of the interior, forming a rectilinear framework, contrasting with the wriggling curves of the main figures. Comic touches include another little dog looking on, a smashed flower pot knocked from the windowsill by the mob, and the grotesque faces of Kay, his wife and the man holding the sheet in his teeth.

The pose of Kay appears to be adapted from the traditional scheme for the descent from the cross, with Kay in the position of Christ, and his wife as the Virgin. The figure bent over to carry the body derives from a type such as the *Deposition* by Pontormo (Sta. Felicita, Florence), whilst Robert Kay's pose is taken from the Marcantonio Raimondi engraving after Raphael's *Bathers*. The models for Mrs Kay and her children were Mrs Henry Boddington and their children Henry, Olive and Gladys.[32]

This was the tenth mural to be painted as well as the tenth in sequence in the Great Hall. It was begun in oil on canvas in October 1888. Despite an attack of gout in the winter of 1889 which held up his work, Brown completed it by April 1890.

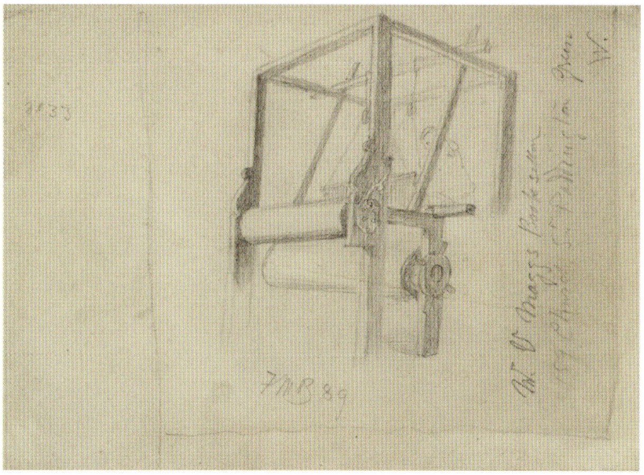

135

136

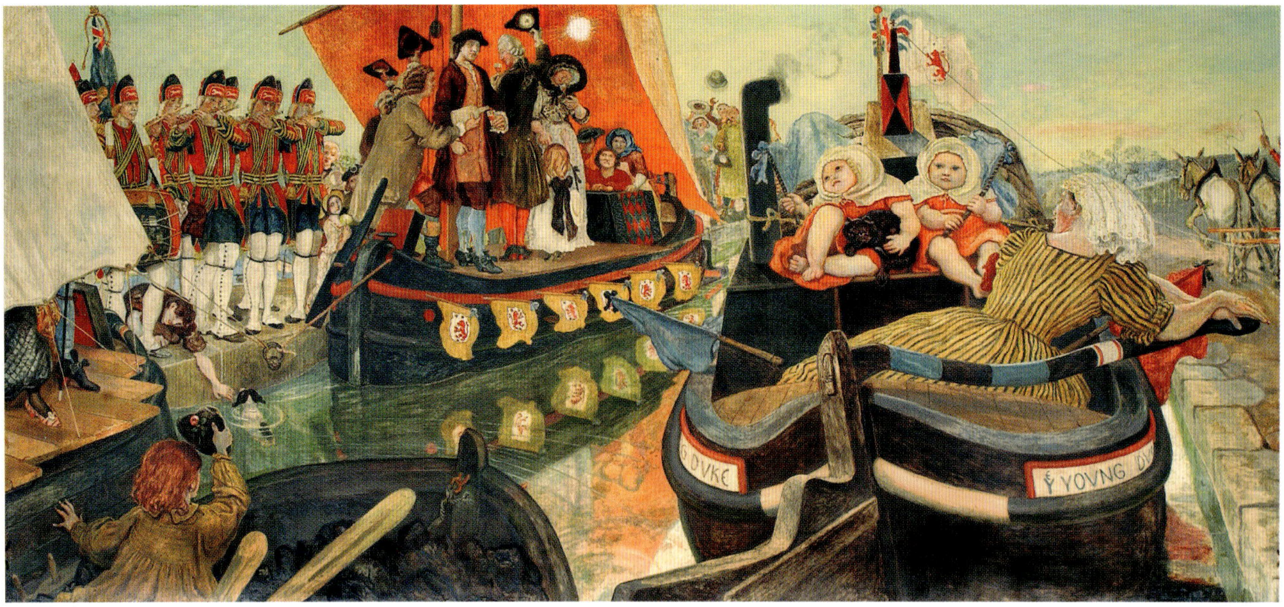

136

THE OPENING OF THE BRIDGEWATER CANAL A.D.1761

(A 116)
1891–92
oil on canvas, 57½ × 125¼ (146 × 318)
signed in monogram and dated: *FMB–92*
Mural painting in Manchester Town Hall

STUDIES FOR THE OPENING OF THE BRIDGEWATER CANAL A.D.,1761
by Brown's assistant, Robert Bruce Wallace (1845/46–93)

137

TOWPATH OF THE BRIDGEWATER CANAL WITH FIGURES

(A116.4)
1890
black chalk, 3¾ × $6\tfrac{13}{16}$ (9.5 × 17.3)

138

TOWPATH OF THE BRIDGEWATER CANAL WITH EVENING EFFECT

(A116.6)
1890
black chalk, 4½ × 7 (11.4 × 17.8)

139

SECTION OF THE BRIDGEWATER CANAL AT BARTON ACQUEDUCT

(A116.2)
1890
pen and ink, $4\tfrac{7}{16}$ × $6\tfrac{15}{16}$ (11.3 × 17.6)

140

A BARGE ON THE BRIDGEWATER CANAL

(A116.3)
1890
pencil and chalk, 3¼ × 6¾ (9.5 × 17.2)
dated: Apl./90

141

THE HARBOUR, BRIDGEWATER CANAL WITH BARGE

(A116.5)
1890
pen and ink and pencil, $4\tfrac{7}{16}$ × $6\tfrac{7}{8}$ (11.3 × 17.5)
inscribed: *The Harbour/April 1890*
All lent by Tate. Presented by Edmund Houghton 1898

Brown depicted the opening ceremony of the Bridgewater canal on 17 July 1761, with the first coal barge setting forth on the canal, drawn by two mules and steered by the powerfully built bargee's wife, accompanied by her twin babies. Further back, in the centre of the painting is another barge, decorated with flags of the Duke of Bridgewater's coat of arms. The Duke stands in the centre in red whilst his canal engineer James Brindley pours him a drink. To the Duke's right are the Earl and Countess of Stamford with a child stretching her arms up for a drink, and the bargee and his wife. On the edge of the canal, left, a band plays fife and drum, and in the foreground a boy sits in a third barge, waving his hat at the Duke.

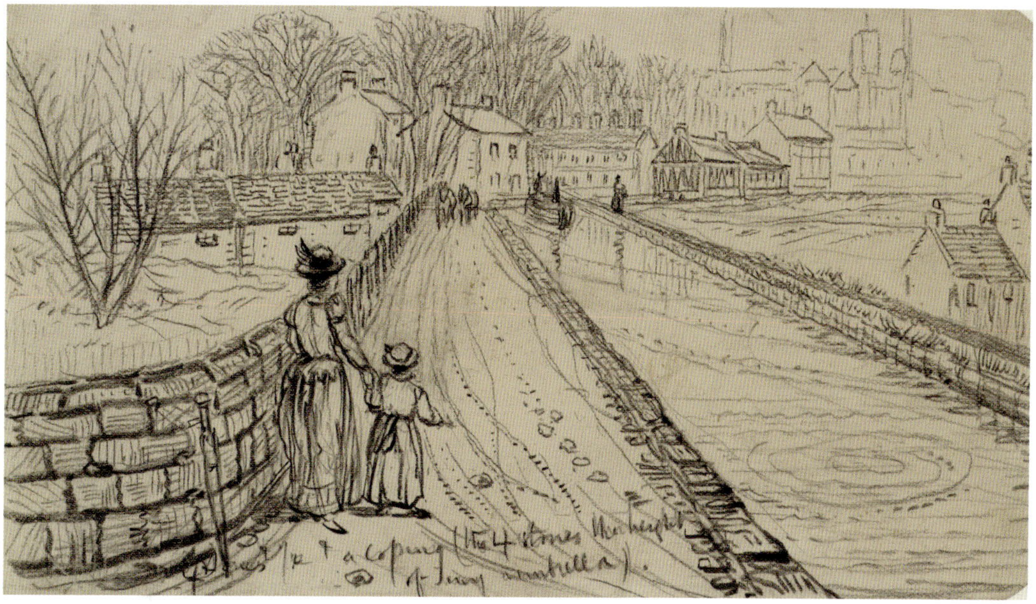

137

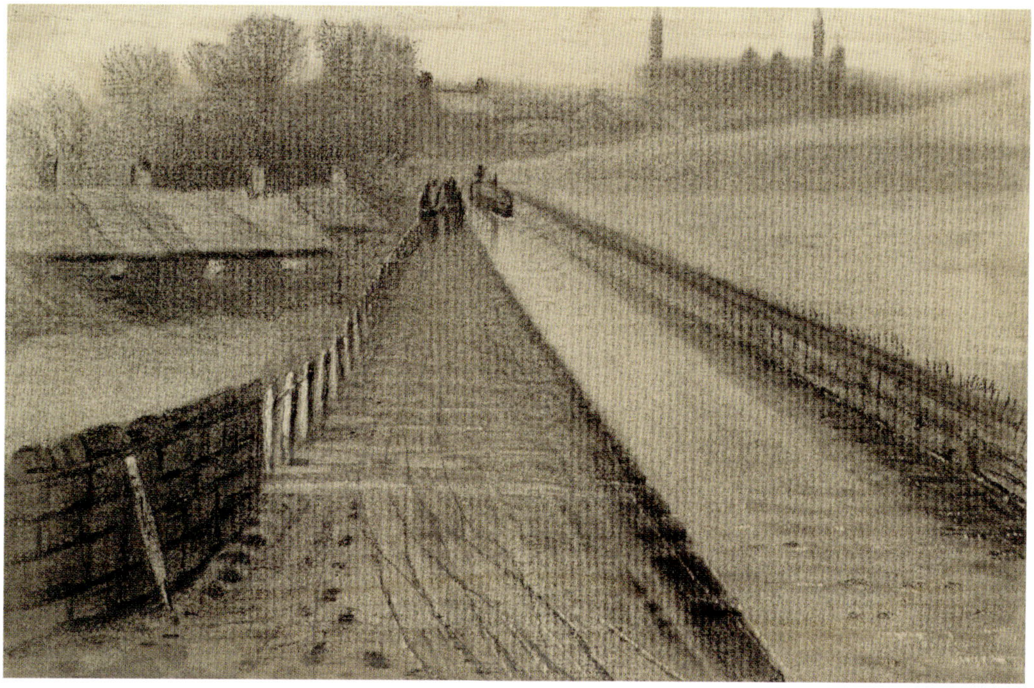

138

The scene combines the industrial revolution, transport and invention; it was not in the original list of subjects but was selected after the rejection of Peterloo. Brown showed coal transport, the raison d'être of the canal, prominently in the foreground, but the general effect of the painting is one of gaiety and colour, making the most of the uniforms, the flags and the eighteenth-century dresses; the scene is lit by warm yellow sunlight without strong shadows. Brown filled out the formal events with humour, with hats being thrown into the air, the glimpse of dainty shoes under the awning on the left, the boy trying to rescue his dog from the water, and the twin babies with a cat. Brown's description added a few didactic points: the boy in the coal barge was included because 'the Duke's orders were always to execute the smaller orders first', and Brindley pours the Duke a glass of brandy from his flask to denote that in contrast to the engineer, the Duke was 'not of a convivial turn' and had 'omitted providing refreshments.'[33] It is notable that the aristocratic party is much less prominent than the working class characters, the boy on the coal barge and the bargee's wife with her children.

The scene is the Barton aqueduct, which carries the canal over the river Irwell, although this is not immediately apparent from Brown's painting. The better known view of the aqueduct is from the side, as in the engraving by Pollard published by Aikin in 1795,[34] but Brown chose a view of the canal head-on. This appears to be based on a drawing by Brown's assistant, the Manchester artist, Robert Bruce Wallace, one of a group of five studies of the canal (cat. 137–41), that he must have made at Brown's request, as Brown had by then moved back to London. The studies include information to assist Brown with his painting. One (cat. 137) shows an umbrella leaning on the adjacent wall and is annotated '4 stones & a coping (the 4 stones the height of my umbrella' and another (cat. 139) is a cross section of the canal with estimated dimensions. Two include canal boats (cats. 140 and 141), although the type of narrow boat depicted in the drawings and repeated by Brown, was only introduced after 1777. The twin babies were painted from a single model, found by the artist at a baby show in Camden town; the bargee's wife with them was painted from a Mrs Hall, wife of a cabman who lived in the mews near Brown's home; and Juliet Hueffer, the artist's grand-daughter, posed for the little girl reaching up for a sip of brandy.[35] Brown used historical portraits for the Duke and for Brindley, but Kendrick Pyne (fig. 37, p. 54) is also supposed to have sat for the Duke and the artist William Cave Thomas for Brindley. The wife of the bargee on the Duke's barge resembles Emma.

The artist began the cartoon, now lost, in 1890, and worked on the canvas between April 1891 and March 1892, when it was fixed to the wall in the Great Hall under Brown's supervision. It was the eleventh to be painted and the eleventh in the series. The composition was bold and original, using deep foreshortening, bright colours and a decorative feeling appropriate for the festive

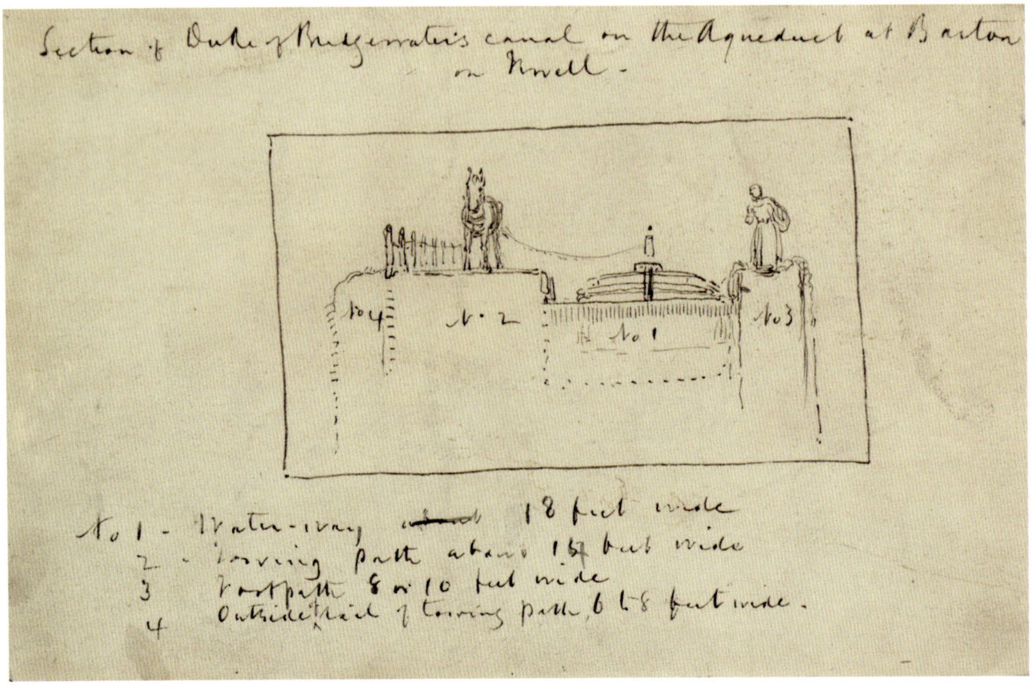

139

subject, but the execution was uneven, especially in some of the larger areas of single colour. The mural provoked a great deal of criticism, the overall yellow cast and the babies coming in for particular opprobrium. One councillor described it as a 'burlesque … one of the most painful things he has seen in the way of art for many a long year,'[36] and the Town Hall Committee passed a resolution asking Brown to submit a drawing for approval before commencing his next and final mural, *Bradshaw's Defence of Manchester*. Brown's supporters rallied to his defence in the extensive newspaper correspondence that followed, *The Builder* calling the Committee's request at this late stage 'a peculiarly unfortunate and ungracious kind of proceeding.'[37]

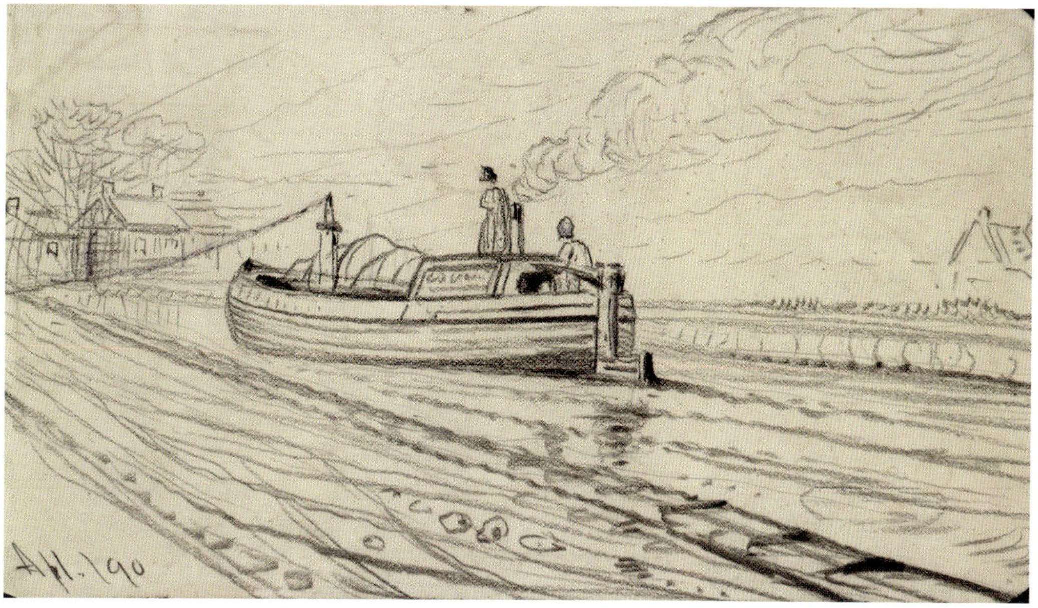

140

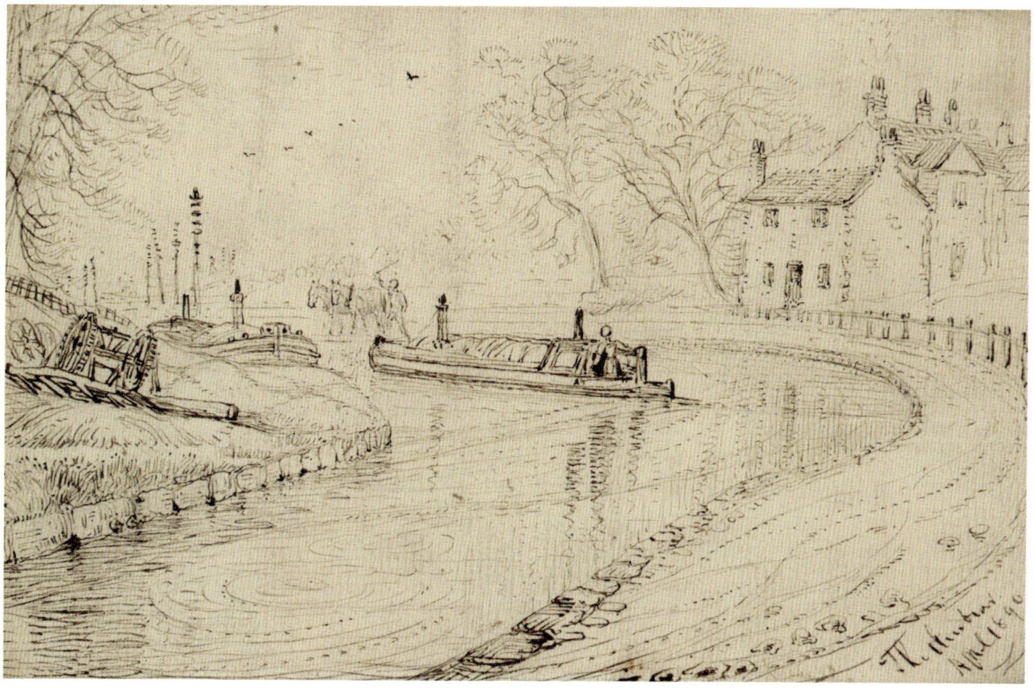

141

142
DALTON COLLECTING MARSH-FIRE GAS

(A 114)
1886–87
Gambier Parry process of spirit fresco on canvas
57½ × 125¼ (146 × 318)
signed in monogram and dated: *FMB-87*
Mural painting in Manchester Town Hall

John Dalton, the chemist and inventor of atomic theory, was born in Cockermouth but in 1893 he came to teach in Manchester and was thereafter associated with the city, where his investigations into the behaviour of gases ultimately led to his invention of atomic theory. Brown's mural shows the scientist not in a laboratory or library, but in a pastoral setting that at first seems inappropriate for the only nineteenth-century subject in the series. Dalton is seen stirring up mud in a stagnant pond while a farmer's boy who is assisting him catches the bubbles of gas in a glass jar as they rise, with a saucer at the ready to trap them in the jar. According to Brown's text, the girl in the foreground is telling the little boy fishing that '"Mr. Dalton is catching Jack o' Lanterns" – marsh-fire gas being, when on fire, the substance *the Will o'the Wisp* is composed of.'[38]

The subject, representing modern science, was not in the original list but was adopted after the rejection of *Peterloo*. Brown had been scornful of the visual possibilities, writing that 'Dalton inventing atomic theory could never be anything, pictorially, but one man thinking – unless one might represent him shaking up his atoms, like grated Parmesan, in a bottle.'[39] But Brown seems to have warmed to the idea, perhaps after going further into the life of Dalton and finding that the world-famous scientist had begun his career as an ordinary schoolmaster. The presence of the children in the mural is a reminder of Dalton's humble origins. Brown went on sketching expeditions in Cheshire in search of material, and the half-timbered farm buildings in the right background may have been drawn there, although the pond was drawn from one near his house at Victoria Park, Manchester. He also made studies of brambles for the flowers and foliage behind Dalton (Ashmolean Museum, Oxford),[40] and he consulted portraits of Dalton for the likeness. The child in the one-piece jacket showed the way he himself was dressed as a child.[41]

Although the scene closes the series, it was the ninth to be painted, and the second to be painted in the studio, coming between *Chetham* and *Kay*. It was the last one Brown painted in Manchester. The composition is less crowded than the *Bridgewater Canal*, which precedes it on the wall, and the treatment more tranquil; the smaller size of the figures and the use of curved shapes is less forceful than in the previous murals, and in some areas the handling is tentative. Brown made a small oil study, now untraced, and started work on the canvas in November 1886 but progress was interrupted in December by the Jubilee Exhibition decorations. Work was resumed in May 1887 and finished in December, just before Brown moved back to London.

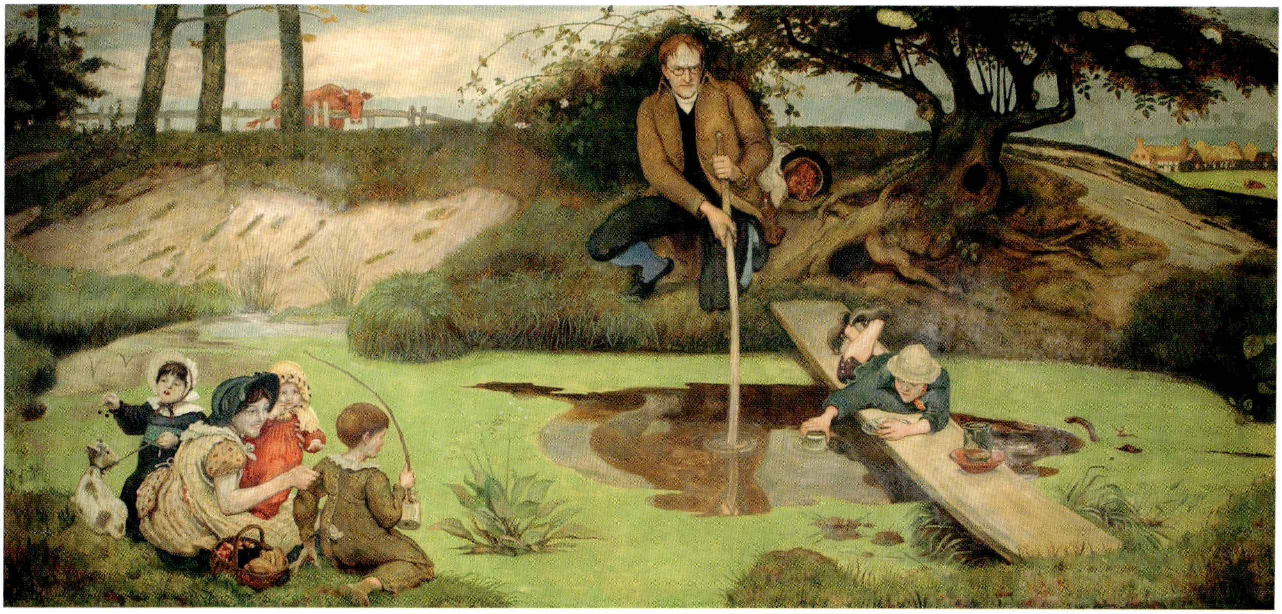

142

MANCHESTER ROYAL JUBILEE EXHIBITION DECORATIONS

A large exhibition of art and industry was held in Manchester to celebrate Queen Victoria's Jubilee in 1887. It was housed in a temporary building in Old Trafford. In November 1886 Brown was asked by the furniture and interior designer George Faulkner Armitage, who was responsible for the interior of the building, to decorate the spaces below the great dome of the central hall. The dome was supported by four arches each spanning 72 feet, creating eight triangular spandrels, each about 36 feet long by 18 feet high. Brown was asked to paint figure groups in each space, but there was not enough time as the exhibition was to open in May, so he devised a simpler scheme: each spandrel would be decorated with a figure representing a Lancashire worker, and to fill the narrower part of the space, each worker would be accompanied by a spirit of Lancashire energy, a winged figure holding a trumpet. Brown included two women workers, *Harvesting the Wheat – Corn* and *Spinning – Cotton*. The other six were men: *The Collier – Coal*; *Shearing the Sheep – Wool*; *The Merchant – Commerce*; *The Fisherman – Shipping*; *The Farrier – Iron and Machinery*; and *The Weaver*.[42] Four of them, *The Merchant*, *The Farrier*, *The Collier* and *The Weaver*, can be seen in a contemporary photograph of the dome (fig. 39, p. 57).

Although there were sixteen figures, Brown's idea ingeniously required him to design only nine, as the spirit of energy would be repeated eight times (four in reverse), and the repetitions could be painted by assistants. The original plan for the figures to be drawn in red chalk set against gold backgrounds was changed; it was felt that red chalk would not have been clearly visible at the height of forty feet, so the figures were painted in oil, but in a reddish colour with gold grounds. Surrounding each figure was scroll-work in ultramarine with white Egyptian lilies, red berries and green leaves; at Armitage's suggestion Brown reduced the scale of the scroll-work so as not to overwhelm the figures. The size of the paintings required a large quantity of prepared canvas, but a sufficient quantity could not be obtained in time, and after a frantic search for a suitable material, the paintings were done on a kind of rough sailcloth, made in Dundee by a manufacturer of floor-cloth. The cloth was primed by an Altrincham coach painter who had a large clean room, before being taken to Brown's house in Victoria Park, where not only the studio, but a spare bedroom and the stable and carriage house at the end of the garden were pressed into service.

Brown employed as assistants William Knewstub, a former pupil and assistant of Rossetti; Thomas, a young decorator from Altrincham; and five Manchester artists: Robert Bruce Wallace, Jessie Kingsley, Fanny Sugars, Isabel Dacre and Florence Monkhouse. The women artists had all studied in Paris. The result was generally praised although the ornamental part of the design was felt to be less successful: 'His symbolical figures are grand … but the scroll-work by which he has surrounded them is – well, not in his line. It is neither sufficiently conventional not natural, but a melancholy growth of the artist's own rearing.'[43]

Even before the paintings were completed, it was reported in the press that it was intended to hand over the series to the city after the closure of the exhibition as 'a valuable memorial of the Jubilee year.'[44] The paintings eventually came into the possession of the Manchester architect Edgar Wood, who in 1926 presented them to the City Art Gallery, where they remain in an unrestored state. Five of Brown's chalk designs for the decorations are shown here.

143
AN ANGEL BLOWING A TRUMPET – ENERGY

(A 124.1)
1886
red and grey chalk over pencil, 16 11/16 × 25½ (42.4 × 64.7)
The Whitworth Art Gallery, The University of Manchester

Brown described these figures as spirits of Lancashire Energy, 'winged but legless'. 'Their long wings would fill the acute angle of the spandrel. Each spirit should bear a trumpet, each trumpet should have a banner, each banner should be inscribed VIS [Latin for energy]. These spirits should be all alike, each blowing up the courage of the Lancashire workers'.

After making this design, Brown painted one of the figures full size as a pattern for the others. 'Mr. Bruce Wallace, of the Manchester Academy of Arts, undertook to repeat these for me in the garden studio. These, with the exception of a few wings and a banner or two, he set to work at with so much courage and "energy", working from six to seven in the morning, that by the day required they were all completed, and when hoisted up looked so like the single original that, had I not known where it was placed, I could not have told it from the others.'[45]

143

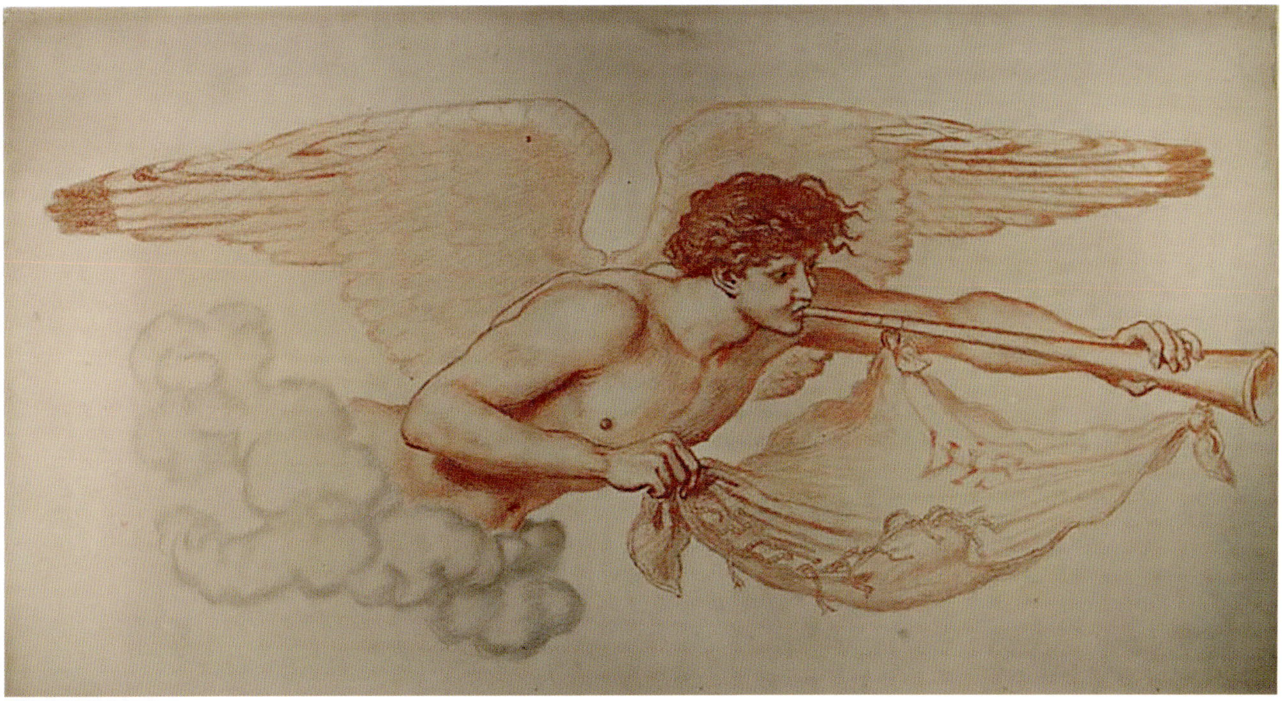

144

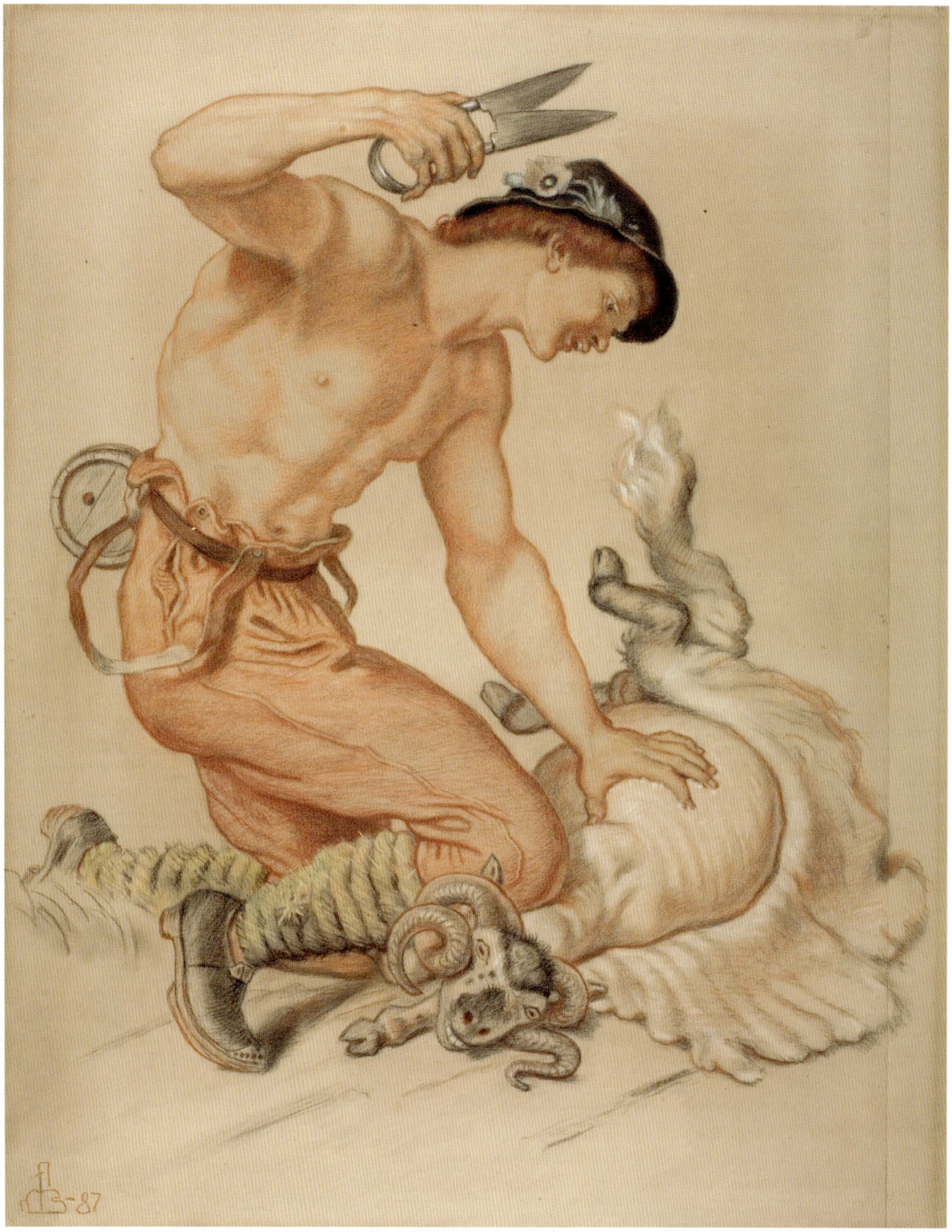

144

SHEARING THE SHEEP – WOOL

(A 126.1)
1886–87
coloured chalks over pencil, 30 1/16 × 23 1/4 (76.3 × 59.2)
signed in monogram and dated: *FMB–87*
The Whitworth Art Gallery, The University of Manchester

145

THE WEAVER

(A 132.1)
1886–87
coloured chalks over pencil, 29 11/16 × 25 3/8 (75.4 × 64.5)
signed in monogram: *FMB–87*
The Whitworth Art Gallery, The University of Manchester

145

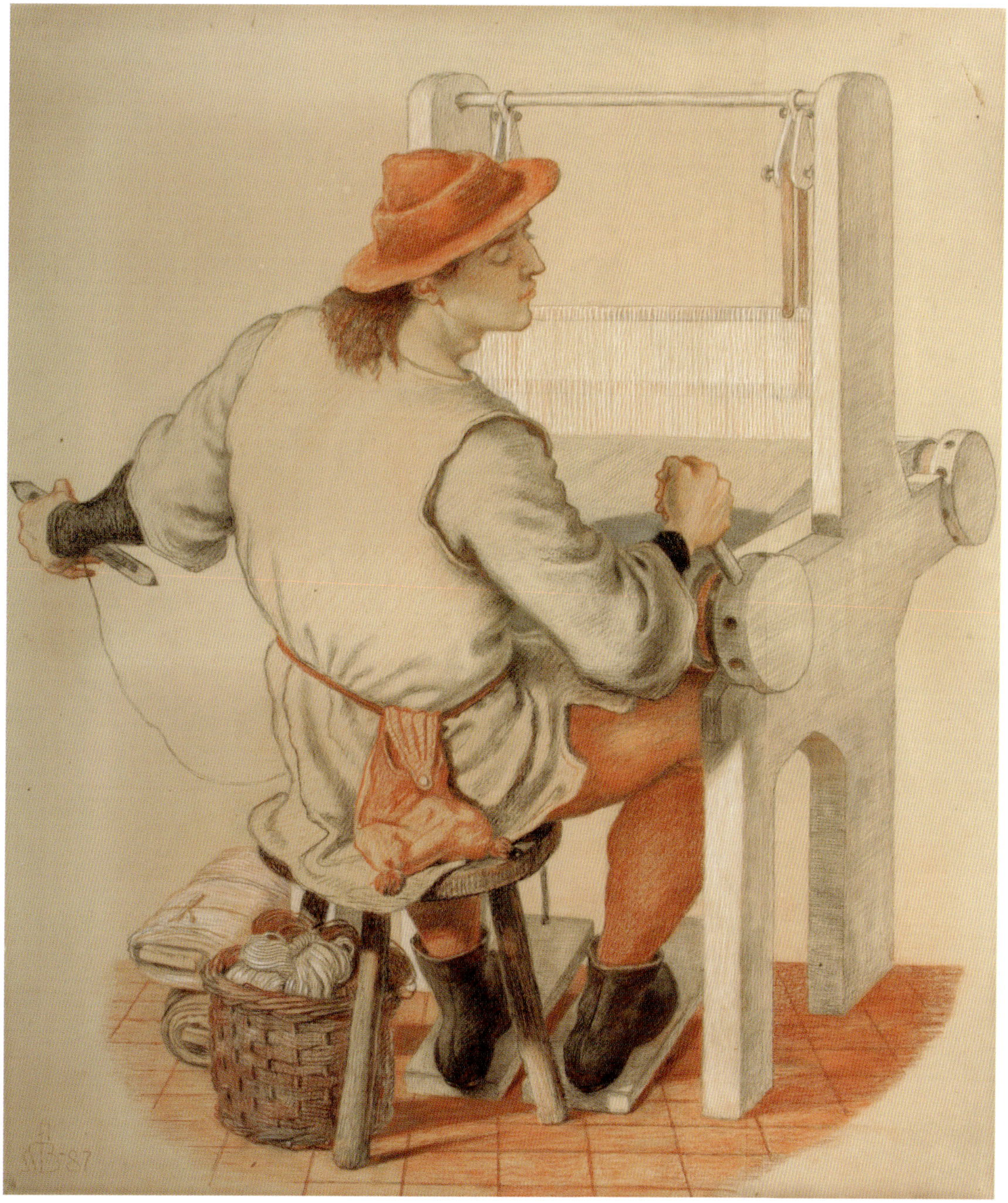

146

THE FARRIER – IRON AND MACHINERY

(A 131.1)

1886–87

coloured chalks over pencil, $30\frac{1}{16} \times 25\frac{5}{8}$ (76.3 × 65.2)

signed and dated in monogram: *FMB–87*

The Whitworth Art Gallery, The University of Manchester

147

THE MERCHANT – COMMERCE

(A 128.1)

1886–87

coloured chalks over pencil, $30 \times 21\frac{11}{16}$ (76.2 × 55.1)

signed in monogram and dated: *FMB–87*

The Whitworth Art Gallery, The University of Manchester

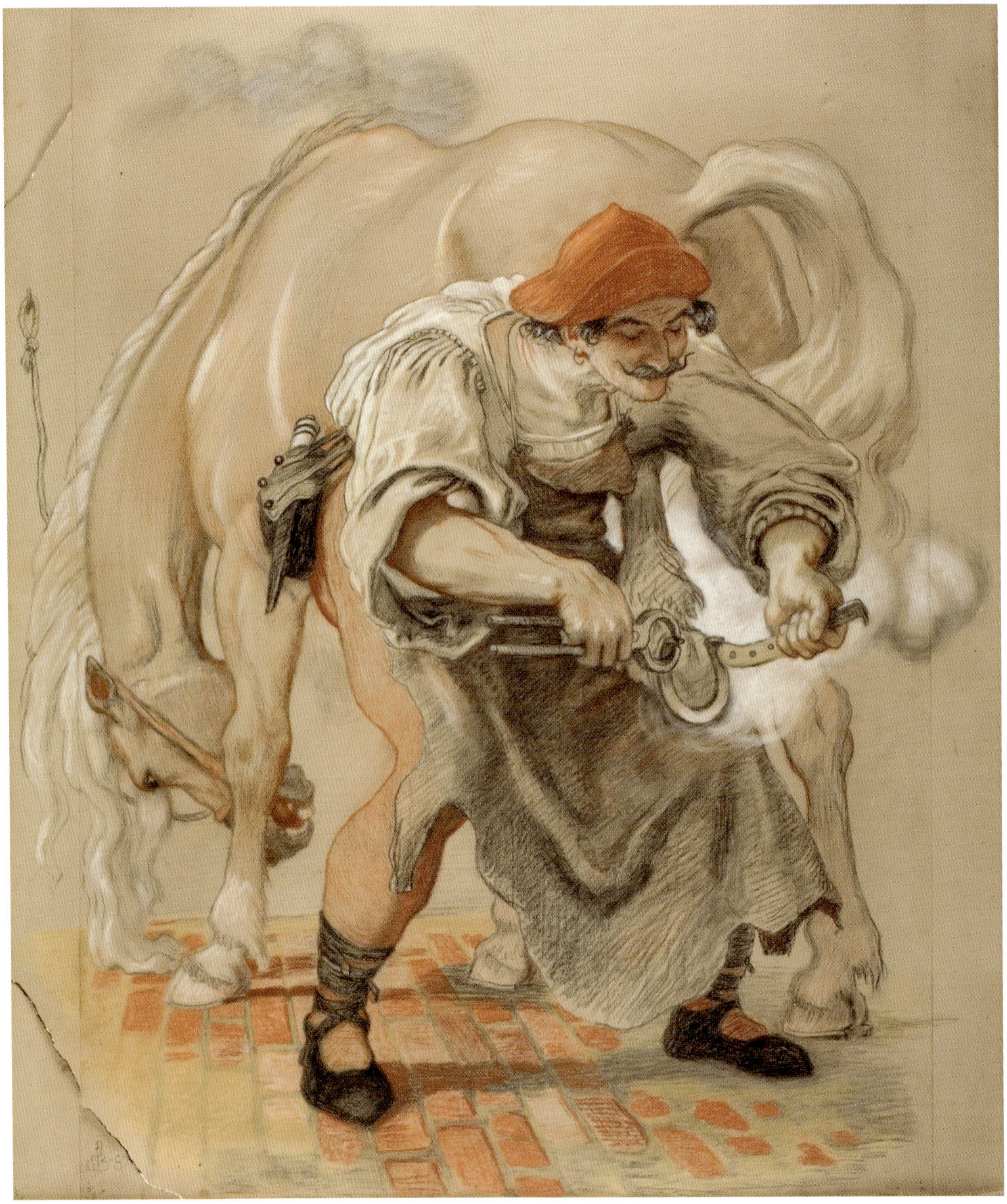

Brown recorded that the designs were 'made 'from nature.'[46] This seems to have included the sheep: 'Knewstub is enlarging a sheep to Brobdingnagian proportions'[47] wrote Brown to his daughter in December and a few days later asked Shields 'Do you think that in London anywhere there is to be got a cast of a shorn *sheep*. I had one in my studio shorn on purpose but he was a Christmas one, and so fat that taking his wool off made very little difference to him or to me. It is the back and shoulders that I want the anatomy of.'[48] The model for the farrier was Brown's assistant Robert Bruce Wallace 'the iron muscles of whose throat and arms I made free with for my figure of Iron.'[49] Brown adapted the weaver from the figures at the loom in the mural *The Establishment of the Flemish Weavers in Manchester* (cat. 122).

Among the artist's bills for materials and other expenses

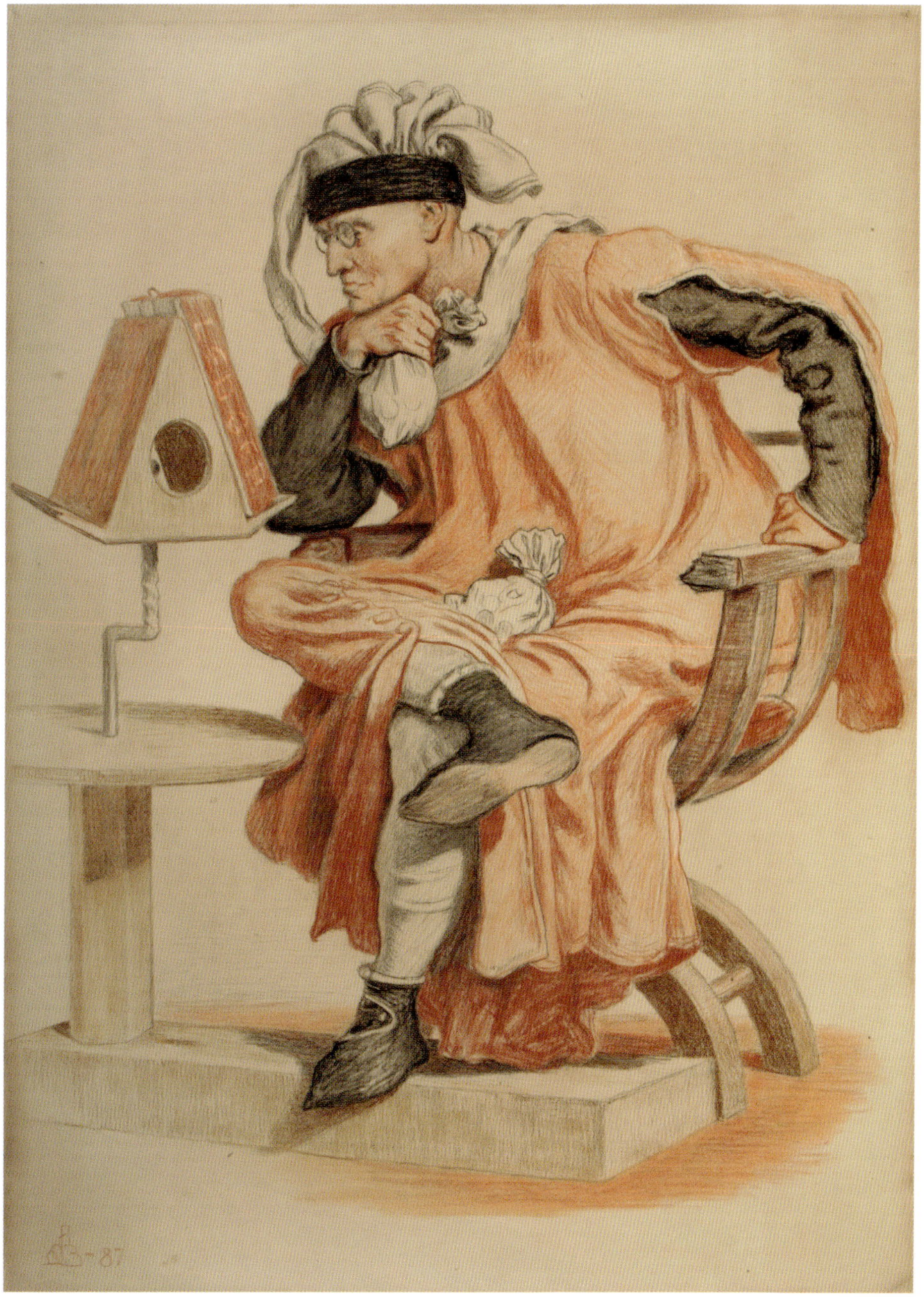
147

connected with the decorations is a bill for a cast of the *Dancing Faun* and several anatomical hands, bought from Alberti, a Manchester plaster statuary maker.[50] The *Dancing Faun* could have been used for the torso of the weaver and perhaps also for the fisherman.

148

MRS. AGNES PYNE

(B 85)
1882
coloured chalks, 21 × 17 (53.3 × 43)
signed in monogram: *FMB to JKP/ 1882* and inscribed
MRS. KENDRICK PYNE JUNR.
Atkinson Art Gallery, Sefton Museums and Galleries, Southport

The sitter was the wife of Dr James Kendrick Pyne, the organist at Manchester Town Hall, who became friendly with Brown (fig. 37, p. 54). In late March or April of 1882 Mrs Pyne modelled for one of the Queen's ladies in the mural *The Establishment of the Flemish Weavers in Manchester*: she is the lady in profile on the right of the royal group (cat. 122).[51]

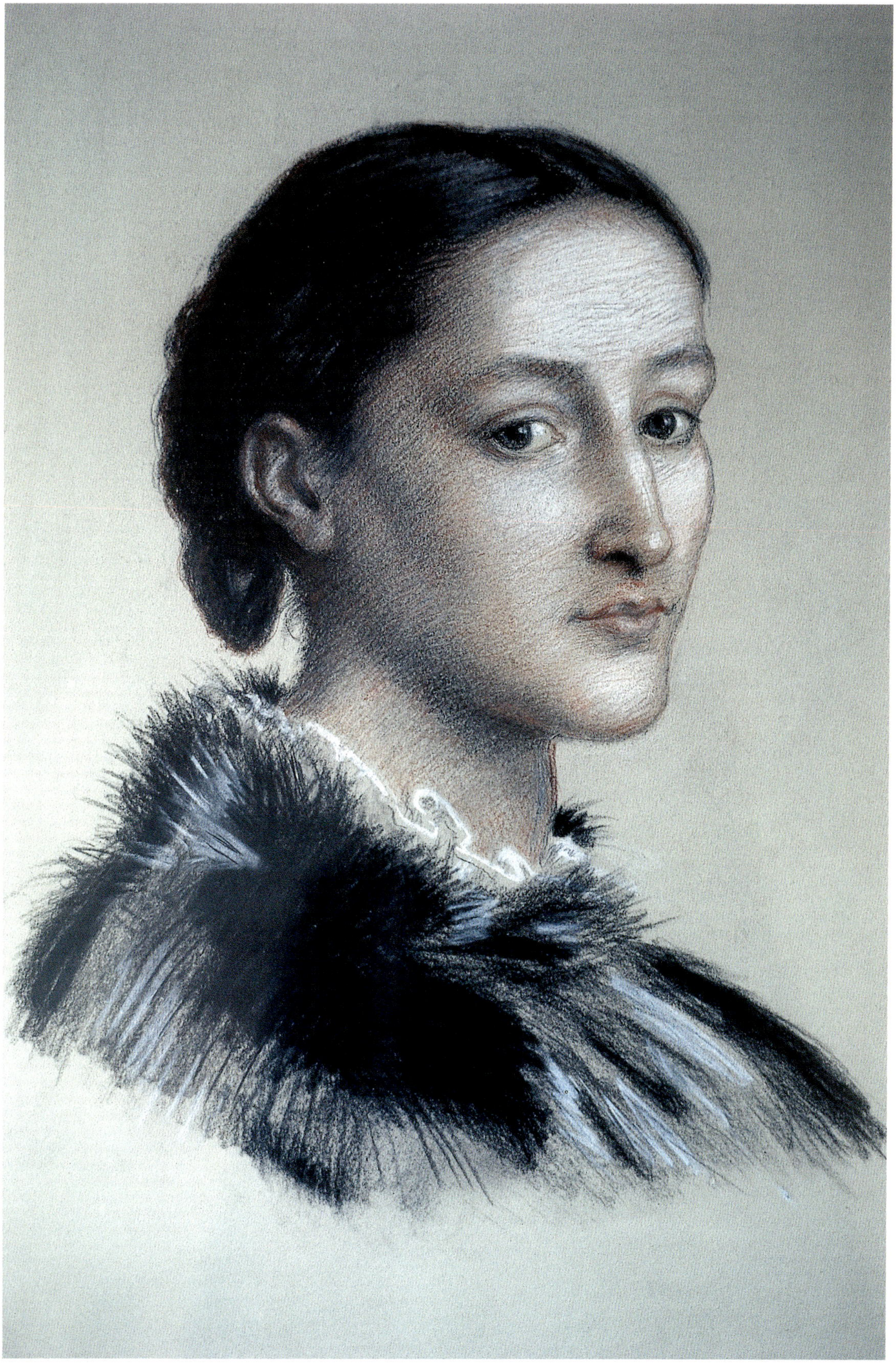

148

149

MADELINE SCOTT

(B100)
1883
oil on canvas, 48 1/16 × 30 7/8 (122.1 × 78.5)
signed in monogram: *FMB–83*
Manchester City Galleries

In this very unusual portrait, Madeline Scott (1876–1958), daughter of C.P. Scott, editor of the *Manchester Guardian* is shown riding a tricycle. She must have been depicted like this because her father was a cycling enthusiast; he used to cycle between his home The Firs, Fallowfield, and the Manchester Guardian offices in the city centre, keeping this up even after his eightieth birthday.[52]

In April 1883 Scott wrote to Brown thanking him for his offer to paint Madeline's portrait,[53] presumably in response to a commission from Scott. Brown went to The Firs to paint her, first making a chalk study of her head (Manchester Art Galleries).[54] In the background of the painting he included a view of the Scotts' garden with a loggia seen through a yew archway. Madeline, aged six or seven, wears an olive green coat with a cape, and holds a spray of apple blossom. 'She is a pretty child' wrote Brown to William Michael Rossetti.[55] The fee for the portrait was 200 guineas, and when sending it to the artist, Scott wrote appreciatively 'You know how pleased my wife and I are with the picture. It will be for us a lasting and delightful remembrance of the childish beauty and simplicity which one deserves never to lose. And this is just what you have caught and what we are so grateful to you for preserving for us.'[56]

A friendship seems to have developed between the Browns and the Scotts, facilitated by the Browns' move from Crumpsall to Victoria Park, which was nearer the Scott's home, in August 1883. In March 1884 Brown showed Scott's children round the murals, which they much enjoyed.[57]

In 1893 Madeline married C.E. Montagu, who had joined the *Manchester Guardian* as a journalist in 1890 and in 1896 became its chief leader writer. The couple were keen mountaineers and went climbing in the Alps and the Lake District. In 1920 Madeline was appointed one of the first female magistrates in Manchester.[58]

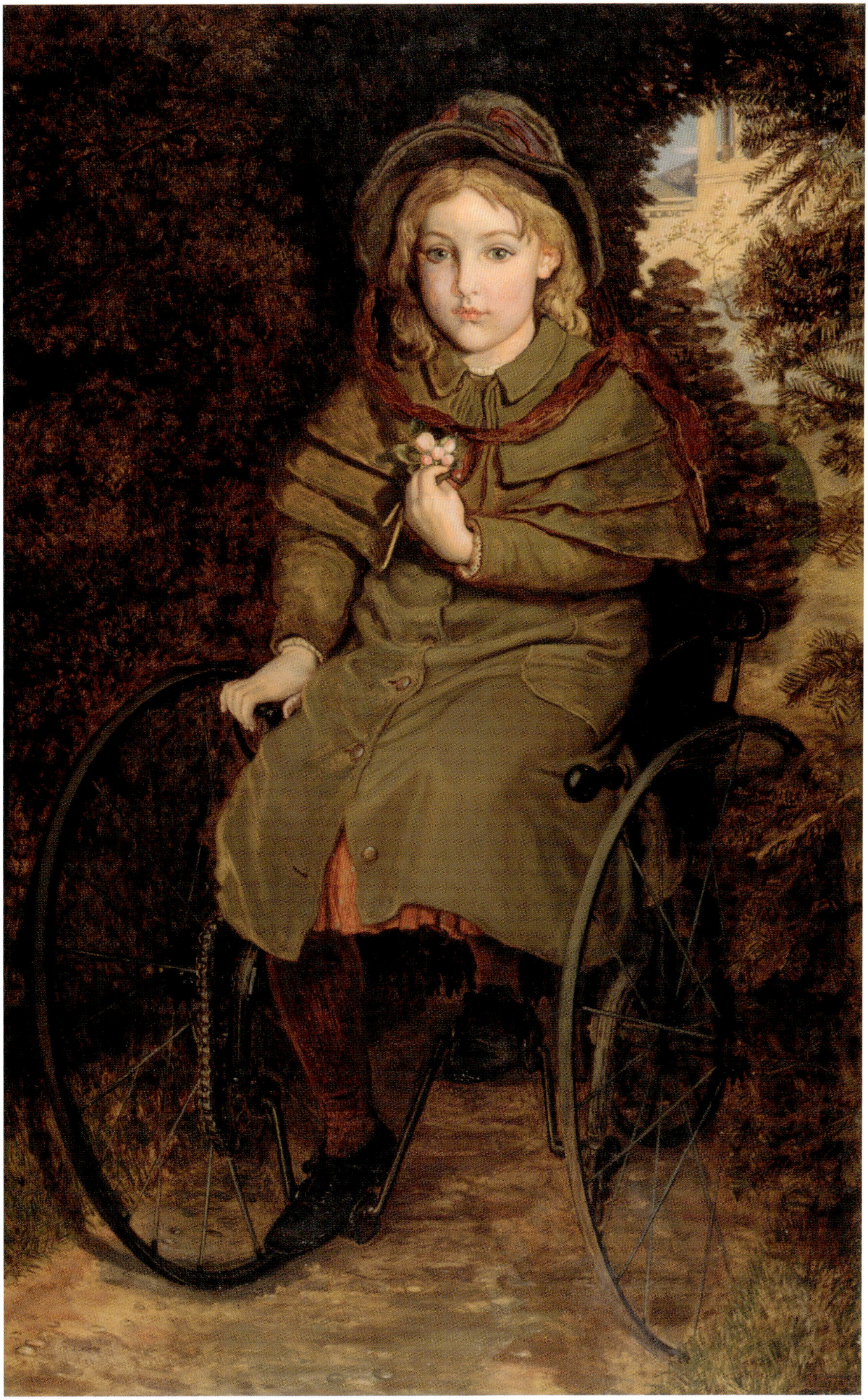

150

CHARLES ROWLEY

(B99)
1885
coloured chalks, 19 3/8 × 17 (49.2 × 43)
signed in monogram and dated: *FMB–85* and inscribed: *CHARLES ROWLEY JUN^R^.*
Manchester City Galleries

Charles Rowley junior (1839–1933) was a leading figure in Manchester art circles: 'He is a self-made and self-educated man, and is not diffident about saying so. Genial, sincere, and zealous for the benefit of the poor, he has, apart from his propensity for punning, only one fault. Like the parrot, he talks too much.'[59]

By trade Rowley was a picture framer, but he was also a social reformer deeply influenced by Ruskin. He became a close friend of Brown, and was one of the artist's principal promoters in the city, helping him obtain the murals commission. The chalk portrait was drawn in 1885 and was shown at the Spring Exhibition of the Manchester Academy of Fine Arts that year: the frame, a standard gadrooned moulding with a gilt oak flat, must have been made by Rowley's firm.

Rowley's father founded a substantial picture framing business, with a shop in Princess Street (later in St. Ann's Street and then Barton Square), and workshops and a timber yard in Ancoats. Rowley junior joined the firm as an apprentice, but by 1874, when the business was registered as a company, he was listed as a shareholder and Managing Director. Rowley's work naturally brought him into contact with artists and his first documented contact with Brown was in 1875, when Rowley bought the monochrome version of *Cordelia's Portion* (begun as the cartoon for cat. 79). The previous December, Brown had lectured in Manchester and this may have been when the pair first met, possibly through the agency of Shields. Rowley visited Brown's home in London in 1876, where he met Brown's friends and family, and soon became a member of the artist's circle.

Rowley commissioned or bought various other paintings by Brown, some, such as the St. Edith stained glass cartoons and the Great Men series (cats. 102–5, 108–10), for presentation to public institutions; the frames he supplied to Brown include the portrait of *Madeline Scott* (cats 149) and his version of *Cordelia's Portion*. He also framed works for Shields and Rossetti. Rowley was proud of his part in securing Brown the murals commission: 'I sat for hands and other things and am in several of the pictures, mostly in my character of a defeated warrior.'[60] This refers to the fallen soldiers in the murals of the *Danes* and *Bradshaw* (cats. 120, 132).

Rowley was a city councillor for the New Cross ward in Ancoats, one of the poorest areas of the city. He campaigned successfully for social improvements for the residents, including the building of a public meeting place, the New Islington Hall, which opened in 1877. This became the base for his efforts to bring cultural enrichment to the working class through the Ancoats Recreation Committee, and later the Ancoats Brotherhood. Activities included free art exhibitions, which included works by Brown from Rowley's own collection and those of other Manchester patrons, also concerts and free Sunday lectures by a range of leading national and local figures – politicians, educationalists, university lecturers, writers and artists including Brown himself. Something of a collector of celebrities, Rowley persuaded many of them to participate in the events at Ancoats: William Morris, Holman Hunt, Canon and Mrs Rawnsley, Canon and Mrs Barnett, Walter Crane and Bernard Shaw all took part. Rowley was also involved in many aspects of art in Manchester: he was a frequent lecturer on artistic subjects, and was active in the affairs of the Art Gallery and the Manchester School of Art.[61]

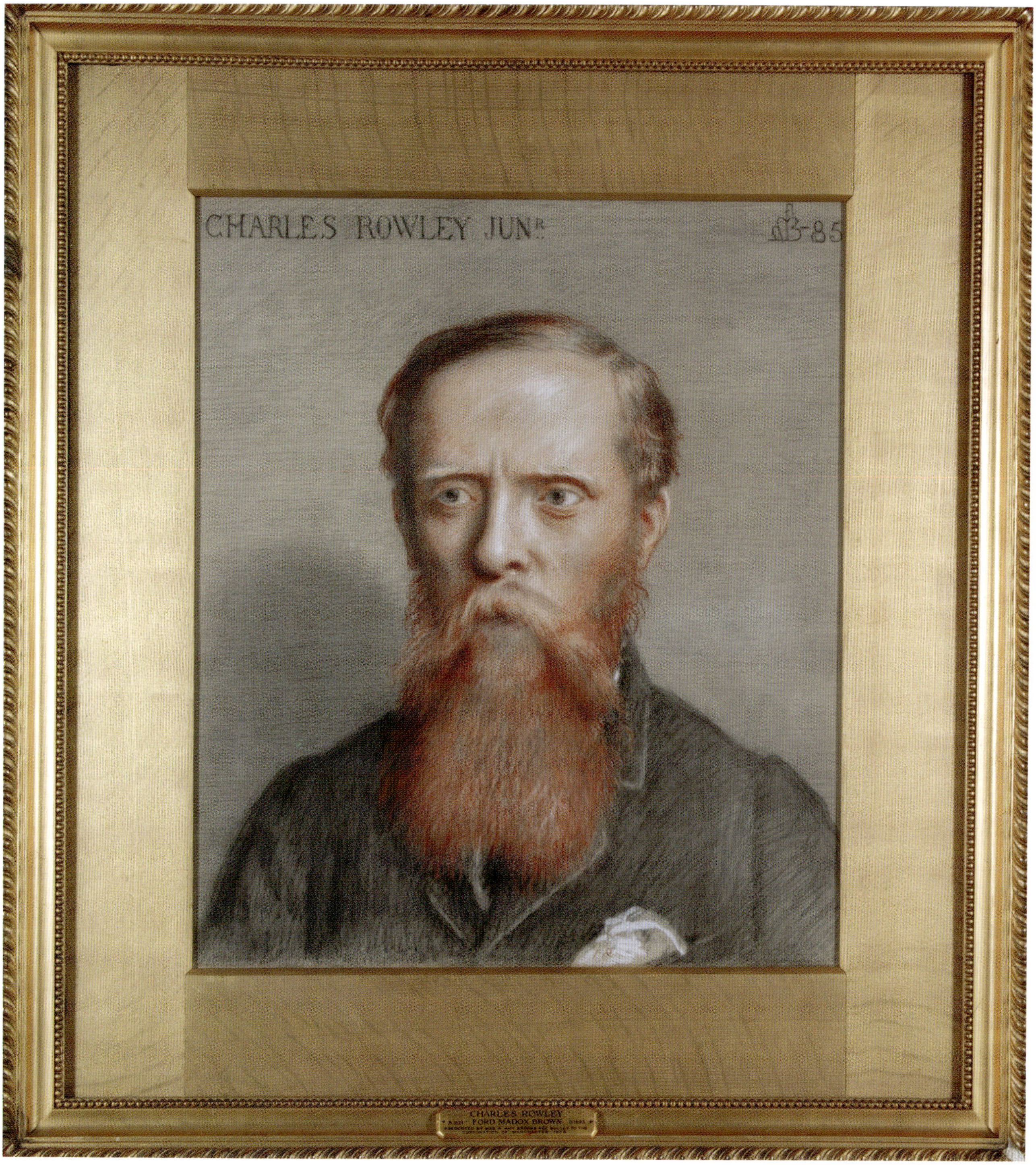

150

151
MASTER DAVID LITTLE

(B78)
1885
coloured chalks, 13 7/8 × 13 15/16 (35.2 × 35.3)
Singed in monogram: *FMB–85*
Manchester City Galleries

Although formerly thought to be a portrait of the artist's grandson Ford Madox Hueffer, Mary Bennett has conclusively identified the sitter as David Little, son of a Manchester eye surgeon Dr David Little. 'I have drawn Master David Little to give to the Queens Park Museum' wrote Brown to his daughter on 8 March.[62] The Littles were neighbours of the Browns and lived in Victoria Park at The Elms, Anson Place.

Brown might have been hoping to attract a commission from the Littles for a portrait or another subject in oils, but he made the drawing to support a specific project, the Horsfall Museum, to which Brown presented it together with his chalk study for the portrait of Madeline Scott (see cat. 149) in 1885. This museum, the brainchild of the philanthropist Thomas Horsfall, was a Ruskinian initiative aimed at bringing art and nature to the people. The museum was initially given space in two rooms of the Queens Park Museum, built by the Parks Committee of City Council in Queen's Park, Harpurhey, but this proved unsatisfactory, partly because there was an entrance charge and the museum was not open on weekday evenings, but also because space was restricted. The Horsfall Museum collection was therefore transferred to Ancoats Hall, where it opened in 1886 under the name of the Ancoats Art Museum. The museum displays were laid out in a didactic manner as 'an illustrated textbook' with labels intended to introduce and explain art and nature to working people. Brown's two chalk drawings of children were part of the display in the 'Mother's Room', later renamed the 'Children's Room', a very early example of a museum display aimed at children. The collections were transferred to the care of City Art Gallery in 1918 but the museum itself continued operating until 1954.[63]

151

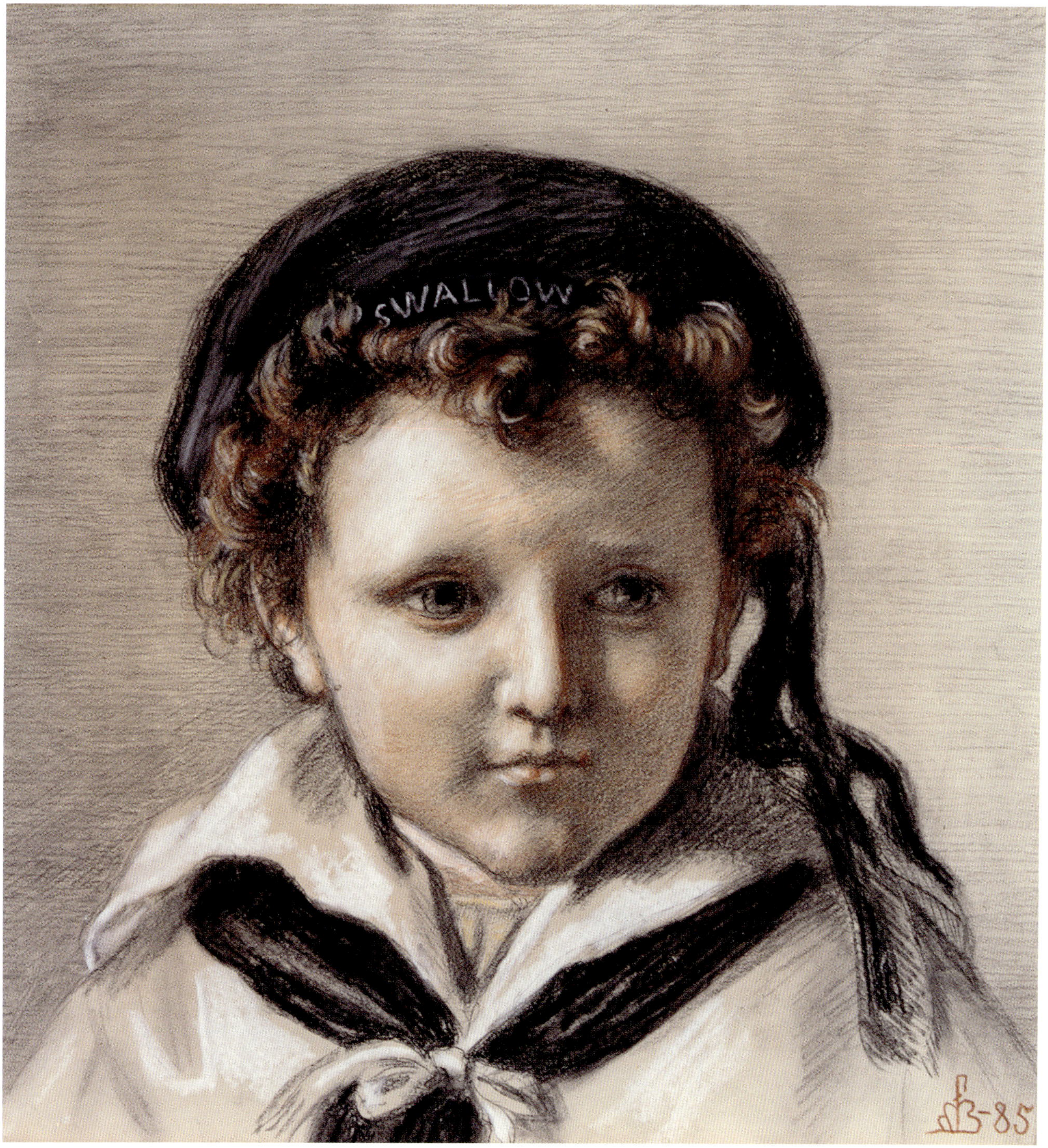

152

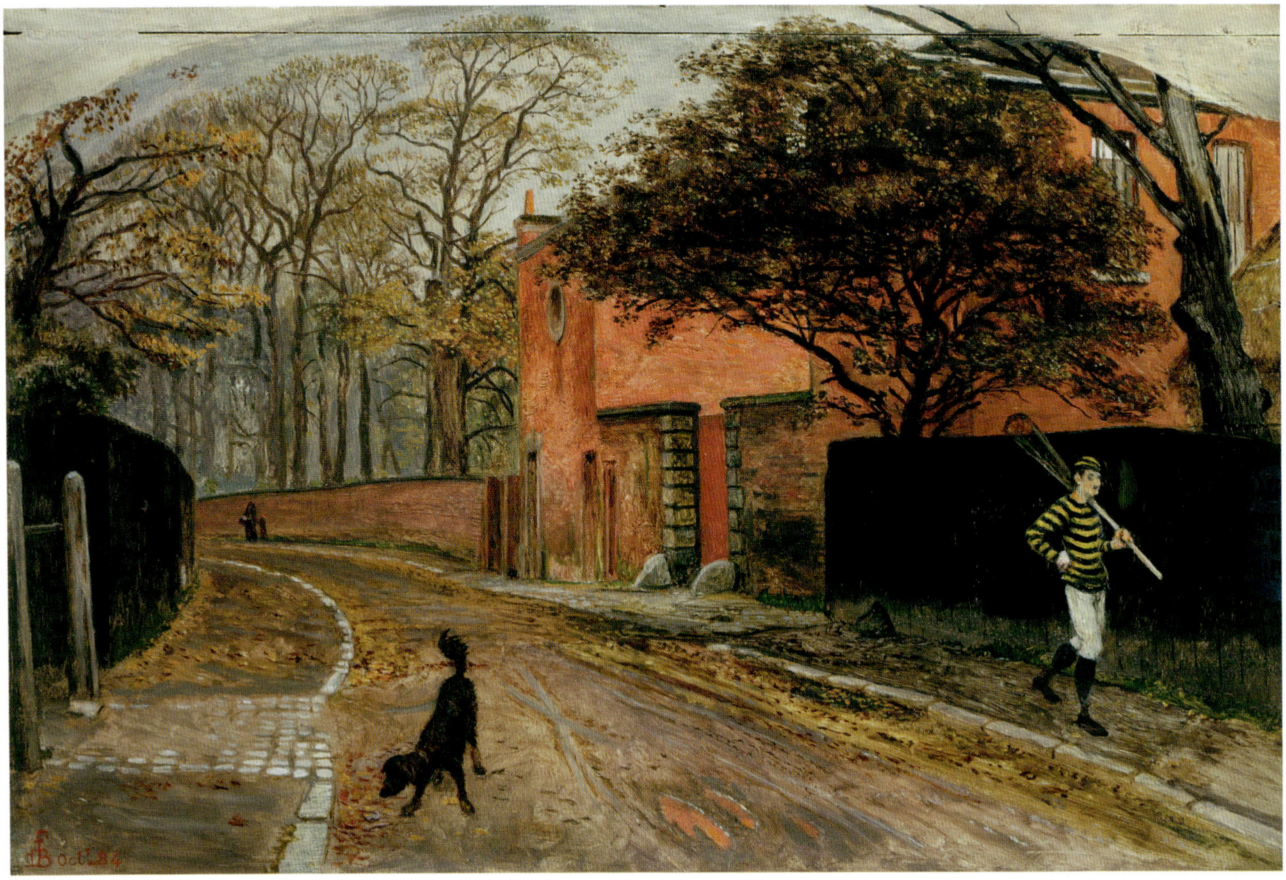

152

PLATT LANE

(A121)

1884, 1886

oil on canvas, 10¼ × 15½ (26 × 39.4)

signed in monogram and dated: *FMB Oc^r – 84*

Tate. Presented by the Art Fund 1942

A study of autumn colours in Platt Lane, Rusholme, not far from Brown's Manchester home in Victoria Park. Brown travelled to the site in a cab, which he used as a shelter when painting the view as Emma explained in a letter to her daughter Cathy written on 2 October 1884: 'Your father is wonderfully well and hearty and is still painting away at his autumn tints in the open air. He has hired a cab in which he sits all through the day. The man drives him there and leaves him, taking the horse away. He brings him back again in the same way, so that your father is sheltered from rain and sun, and Charlotte takes him his lunch with hot coffee every day.'[64]

Brown must have stationed his cab in front of Appleby House, a white stucco building on the north side of Platt Lane, and painted the view looking east towards the Wilmslow Road. The brick buildings and gate-piers to the right, on the south side of Platt Lane, are the outbuildings and the back entrance to the service yard of Platt Hall, the country house of the Worsley family, built by the architect Timothy Lightholer around 1760. The Worsleys sold the house and estate to Manchester Corporation in 1907, and the grounds became a public park. The house and its flanking pavilions still stand but the outbuildings have been demolished. The alleyway in the foreground of the painting is still there, running between Appleby House and a row of mid-twentieth century houses.

Brown described the painting as a study for *Chetham's Life Dream* (cat. 131). The two pictures are not much alike, except that they are both landscapes with trees; he probably went to Platt Lane because there were no trees at Chetham's School. Brown's view of the street in a leafy suburb may have been inspired by similar paintings by Atkinson Grimshaw.[65]

In 1886, following the death in Paris of his student friend Dan

Casey (cat. 43), Brown organised a lottery to help Casey's widow and daughter, the prizes being either a painting by Casey or *Platt Lane*. *Platt Lane* was won by Frederic Shields but the Lottery raised only about £32 for Mrs. Casey. The man with the lacrosse stick over his arm and the poster for the All England Lacrosse game was added by Brown at the time of the lottery in 1886, perhaps to give the painting a topical relevance; lacrosse was introduced to England in the 1870s, and it became especially popular in Manchester where it was played at the Withington ground, not far from Platt Lane.

1 *Manchester Courier* 23 May 1879.
2 MCL, Autograph Letters, FMB to Alfred Waterhouse 1 October 1878.
3 MCL, FMB to Alfred Waterhouse 7 August 1876.
4 Brown, *Mural Paintings*, p. 3.
5 Barlow 1996, p. 91.
6 V&A, Frank O'Donnell to FMB 9 December 1878; *Manchester City News* 2 July 1921.
7 Bennett 2010, 2, pp. 482–84, C115.
8 Bennett 2010, 1, pp. 293–94, A106.7.
9 Rowley 1911, p. 107; UBC, FMB to D.G. Rossetti 16 January 1881.
10 Barlow 1996, p. 93.
11 Bodelian, FMB to F.G. Stephens, n.d. [September/November 1881].
12 Brown, *Mural Paintings*, p. 6.
13 Bodelian, FMB to F.G. Stephens, n.d. [September/November 1881].
14 UBC, FMB to Lucy Madox Brown 22 March 1881.
15 Brown used the spelling Wyclif for the mural in preference to Wycliffe used for cat. 33.
16 Brown, *Mural Paintings* p. 7.
17 Hueffer 1896, p. 374.
18 MAG Committee, 1, p. 274, 17 November 1884.
19 Hueffer 1896, p. 368.
20 Bennett 2010, 1, pp. 321–22, A112.2.
21 Bennett 2010, 1, p. 317, A111.2.
22 The modern spelling is Horrocks.
23 DNB, articles on William Crabtree by Frances Willmoth, and on Jeremiah Horrocks by Wilbur Applebaum.
24 Huffier 1896, p. 349.
25 Bennett 2010, 2, pp. 391–92, B54.
26 DNB, article on Humphrey Chetham by Alan G. Crosby.
27 Bennett 2010, 1, p. 326, A113.2.
28 Rowley 1911, p. 107.
29 Brown, *Mural Paintings* p. 12.
30 Brown, *Mural Paintings* p. 12.
31 DNB, article on John Kay by D.A. Farnie.
32 Bennett 2010, p. 334 reproduces family photographs of Mrs. Boddington and one of her daughters.
33 Brown, *Mural Paintings* p. 13.
34 Reproduced Bennett 2010, p. 338.
35 Soskice 1921, pp. 36–38, 53, 55–56.
36 *Manchester Guardian* 5 May 1892.
37 *The Builder* 14 May 1892, p. 372.
38 Brown, *Mural Paintings* p. 14.
39 *Manchester Guardian* 11 February 1882.
40 Bennett 2010, 1, pp. 331–32, A114.3–7.
41 UBC, 'Account of his Early Childhood', written 25 March 1889 for Henry Boddington.
42 Bennett 2010, 1, pp. 349–65, A124–132.
43 *Cabinet Maker and Furnisher* 2 May 1887.
44 *Manchester Guardian* 26 March 1887.
45 Brown 1888 i, pp. 53–54.
46 Ibid.
47 UBC, FMB to Lucy Madox Brown 1886.
48 Hueffer 1896, p. 377.
49 Brown 1888 i, p. 54.
50 V&A, Box 27.
51 UBC, FMB to Lucy Madox Brown 22 March 1881.
52 DNB, article on C.P. Scott by Trevor Wilson.
53 V&A, C.P. Scott to FMB, 15 April 1883.
54 Bennett 2010, 2, pp. 418–19, B100.1.
55 UBC, FMB to William Michael Rossetti 20 April 1883.
56 V&A, C.P. Scott to FMB, 2 August 1883.
57 V&A, C.P. Scott to FMB, 4 March and 22 May 1884.
58 DNB, article on C.E. Montagu by Keith Grieves.
59 Unidentified press cutting, Manchester Art Gallery files.
60 Rowley 1911, p. 107.
61 Kay 1993.
62 UBC, FMB to Lucy Madox Brown 8 March 1885.
63 Harrison 1993.
64 Hueffer 1896, p. 367.
65 Staley 2001, p. 51.

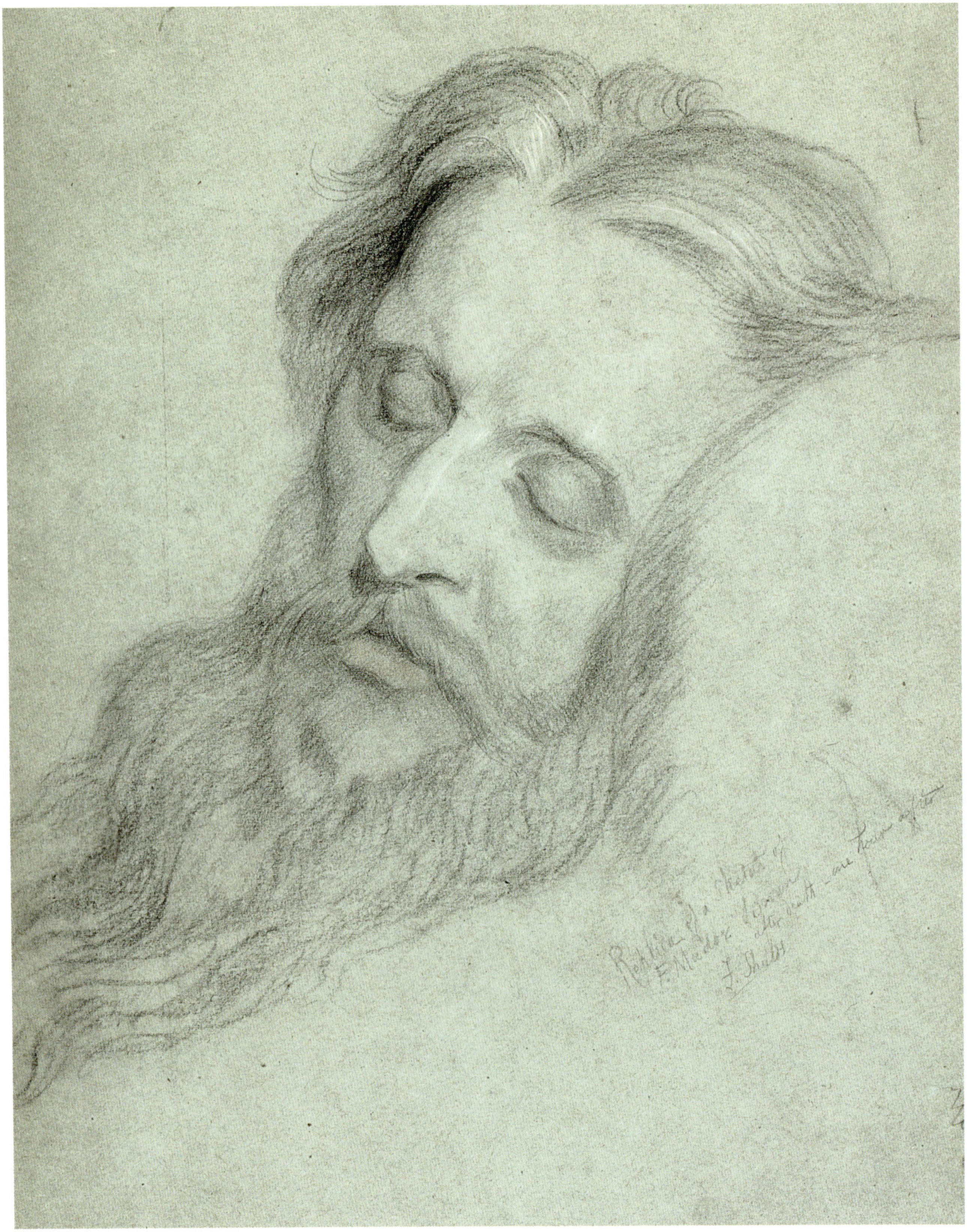

THE END

Ford Madox Brown died peacefully on Friday 6 October 1893, at his home at 1 St. Edmund's Terrace, near Primrose Hill, London. The previous Sunday, after working in the studio on the replica of *The Trial of Wyclif*, he had felt tired and went to bed, saying to Catherine, 'Well, my dear, my work's done now.'[1] On the Tuesday he suffered an attack of apoplexy and remained comatose for three days; on the morning of his death, he briefly regained consciousness but relapsed into a coma and died at 4.30 p.m. The funeral was held in the unconsecrated section of St. Pancras cemetery, East Finchley, where he was buried beside Emma and his two sons Arthur and Oliver; the ceremony was entirely secular, and the address was given by Moncure Conway, the ethical preacher and free-thinker. The mourners included Catherine and her two sons, William Michael Rossetti and his son, Mathilde Blind, Holman Hunt, Arthur Hughes, Georgina Burne-Jones, Lawrence Alma-Tadema, Walter Crane and his wife, Christina Rossetti, Frederick Shields, Kendrick Pyne with his wife and daughter, and Charles Rowley.[2]

153

FORD MADOX BROWN ON HIS DEATHBED

Frederic Shields (1833–1911)
1893
black chalk with touches of red and white chalk,
17¾ × 13¾ (44.8 × 34.8)
signed: *Replica of a sketch of/ F. Madox Brown / after death – one hour after / F. Shields*
Manchester City Galleries

Just after Brown's death, William Michael Rossetti wrote to his wife Lucy, Brown's daughter, who was on the French Riviera for the sake of her health, reporting that 'he died in great peace and assuredly no suffering ... Shields (I learn) wished to get Alma-Tadema to make a drawing of your father's face: but Tadema proves to be out of town and the last thing I saw was that Shields returned ready to do it himself, if Cathy likes. I hardly know whether to prefer this or not. A mould by Brucciani is also to be taken.'[3]

The inscription on Shields's drawing states that it is a replica; it was made for Holman Hunt, as it was presented to the Manchester Gallery by his widow. On the original, which is now lost, Shields wrote 'Drawn by candle-light with an aching heart.'[4]

1 Soskice 1921, p. 73.
2 *Pall Mall Gazette* 11 October 1893.
3 Peattie 1990, p. 568: William Michael Rossetti to Lucy Madox Brown 6 October 1993. The location of the death mask by Brucciani is not known. Shields had previously drawn Dante Gabriel Rossetti on his deathbed (Delaware Art Museum) and had also made several replicas.
4 Soskice 1921, reproduced facing p. 68.

BIBLIOGRAPHY

Ancoats 1880
Exhibition of Works of Art, New Islington Public Rooms, Ancoats [Manchester] 1880.

Arscott 1979
Caroline Arscott, *Social Classification and Pictorial Deconstruction in Ford Madox Brown's 'Work'*, unpublished dissertation, Leeds University 1979.

Banham and Harris 1984
Joanna Banham and Jennifer Harris eds., *William Morris and the Middle Ages*, exhibn. cat., Whitworth Art Gallery, Manchester 1984.

Barlow 1996
Paul Barlow, 'Local disturbances: Ford Madox Brown and the problem of the Manchester Murals', in *Re-framing the Pre-Raphaelites*, Ellen Harding ed., Aldershot 1996, pp. 81–97.

Bendiner 1998
Kenneth Bendiner, *The Art of Ford Madox Brown*, Pennsylvania 1998.

Bennett 1988
Mary Bennett, *Artists of the Pre-Raphaelite Circle; The First Generation. Catalogue of Works in the Walker Art Gallery, Lady Lever Art Gallery and Sudley Art Gallery*, London 1988.

Bennett 2010
Mary Bennett, *Ford Madox Brown. A Catalogue Raisonné*, New Haven and London 2010, 2 vols.

BL
British Library, Papers of Sir Charles Wentworth Dilke, Add. Ms. 43909.

Bodleian Library
Bodleian Library, Oxford, Letters to F.G. Stephens, MS.Don.e.61.

Borowitz 1978
Helen O. Borowitz, '"King Lear" in the art of Ford Madox Brown', *Victorian Studies*, Spring 1978, pp. 309–34

Boyce
The Diaries of George Price Boyce, ed. Virginia Surtees, Norwich 1980.

Bronkhurst 2006
Judith Bronkhurst, *William Holman Hunt. A Catalogue Raisonné*, New Haven and London 2006, 2 vols.

Brown 1848
Ford Madox Brown, 'Modern v. Ancient Art, *The Builder*, 4 November 1848, pp. 530–31.

Brown 1865
[Ford Madox Brown], *The Exhibition of WORK and other paintings by Ford Madox Brown at The Gallery, 191 Piccadilly*, Exhibn. Cat., London 1865 (reprinted in Bendiner 1998 pp. 131–58).

Brown *Mural Paintings*
Ford Madox Brown et al., *Particulars Relating to the Manchester Town Hall and Description of the Mural Painting in the Great Hall*, [pamphlet], Manchester n.d.

Brown 1888 i
Ford Madox Brown, 'Historic Art', *Universal Review*, September 1888, pp. 52–55.

Brown 1888 ii
Ford Madox Brown, 'The Progress of English Art as *Not* shown at the Manchester Exhibition,' *Magazine of Art* 1888, pp. 122–24.

Brown 1889
Ford Madox Brown, 'Self-Painted Pictures,' *Magazine of Art* 1889, pp. 184–89.

Brown 1893
Ford Madox Brown, 'Of mural painting,' *Arts and Crafts Essays*, Arts and Crafts Exhibition Society, 1893, pp. 149–60.

Brussels 2005
Le Romantisme en Belgique, exhibn. cat., Museés Royaux des Beaux-Arts de Belgique, Brussels 2005.

Bryant 1997
Julius Bryant, 'Madox Brown's *English Autumn Afternoon* revisited. Pre-Raphaelitism and the environment, *Apollo*, 146, July 1997, pp. 41–43.

Bryson and Troxell 1971
John Bryson and J.C. Troxell eds., *Dante Gabriel Rossetti and Jane Morris Correspondence* Oxford 1971.

Carlyle 1843
Thomas Carlyle, *Past and Present*, London 1843 (1892 edition).

Carlyle 1845
Thomas Carlyle, *Oliver Cromwell's Letters and Speeches with Elucidations*, London 1845 (1888 edition).

Carlyle 2007
The Collected Letters of Thomas and Jane Welsh Carlyle, Durham and London 2007.

Clark 1960
Kenneth Clark, *Looking at Pictures*, London 1960.

Codell 1998
Julie F. Codell, 'Ford Madox Brown, Carlyle, Macaulay, Bakhtin: The Pratfalls and Penultimates of History' in *Art History*, vol. 21, no. 3, September 1998, pp. 324–66.

Cowling 2000
Mary Cowling, *Victorian Figurative Painting. Domestic Life and the Contemporary Social Scene*, London 2000.
Cruise 2006
Colin Cruise, *Love Revealed. Simeon Solomon and the Pre-Raphaelites*, exhibn. cat., Birmingham Museums and Art Gallery 2006.
Curtis 1992
Gerald Curtis, 'Ford Madox Brown's *Work:* An Iconographic Analysis', *Art Bulletin*, 74, December 1992, pp. 623–36.
Daniels 2004
Stephen Daniels, 'Suburban Prospects', *Art of the Garden*, exhibn. cat., Tate, London 2004.
DNB
Oxford Dictionary of National Biography, online version.
Diary
The Diary of Ford Madox Brown, Virginia Surtees, ed., New Haven and London 1981.
Evans 1985
Stuart Evans, 'The Century Guild Connection', *Art and Architecture in Victorian Manchester* (John H.G. Archer, ed.), Manchester 1985.
Germ
The Germ, The Literary Magazine of the Pre-Raphaelites (reprint), Oxford and Birmingham 1979.
Grieve 1976
Alastair Grieve, *The Art of Dante Gabriel Rossetti. 1. Found. 2. The Pre-Raphaelite Modern Subject*, Norwich 1976.
Hammond 1834
J.L. Hammond, *C.P. Scott of the Manchester Guardian*, London 1934.
Harrison 1993
Michael Harrison, 'Art and Social Regeneration: The Ancoats Art Museum', *Manchester Region History Review*, 7, 1993, pp. 63–72.
Harvey and Press 1991
Charles Harvey and John Press, *William Morris. Design and enterprise in Victorian Britain*, Manchester 1991.
Haydon 1926
The Autobiography and memoirs of Benjamin Robert Haydon, London 1926, 2 vols.
Hueffer 1896
Ford M. Hueffer, *Ford Madox Brown. A Record of his Life and Work*, London 1896.
Huntington
Huntington Library, Dept. of Manuscripts, Holman Hunt Papers.
Hugo 2004
The Essential Victor Hugo. New translations by E.H. and A.M. Blackmore, Oxford 2004.
Hunt 1905
W. Holman Hunt, *Pre-Raphaelitism and the Pre-Raphaelite Brotherhood*, London 1905, 2 vols.
Image 1890
Selwyn Image, 'St. Michael and St. Uriel: Designs by Mr. Ford Madox Brown for Painted Glass: with notes on other Drawings by him for Glass: and some incidental remarks on the Art of Glass Painting', *Hobby Horse* (The Century Guild), 5, 1890, pp. 112–19.
Kay 1993
Audrey Kay
'Charles Rowley and the Ancoats Recreation Movement, 1876–1914', *Manchester Region History Review*, 7, 1993, pp. 43–94.
Laughton 1967
Bruce Laughton, 'The British and American Contribution to Les XX, 1884–1893,' *Apollo*, November 1967, pp. 372–79.
Lethaby 1911
W.R. Lethaby, *Architecture*, London 1911.
Loewinson-Lessing and Nicouline 1965
Vladimir Loewinson-Lessing and Nicolas Nicouline, *Le Musée de L'Ermitage Leningrad*, Brussels 1965.
London 1984
The Pre-Raphaelites, exhibn. cat., Tate Gallery, London 1984
Lushington 1856
[Vernon Lushington], 'Two Pictures', *Oxford and Cambridge Magazine*, 8, 1856.
MAG Committee
Manchester Art Gallery, Art Gallery Committee Books.
MAG Horsfall
Manchester Art Gallery, Horsfall Papers.
MAG MAFA
Manchester Art Gallery, Manchester Academy of Fine Arts Press Cuttings books.
MCL
Manchester Central Library, Archives and Local Studies.
MacCullough 2008
Laura MacCullogh, 'Forgotten Images: The Illustrations of Ford Madox Brown', in *Ford Madox Brown. The Unofficial Pre-Raphaelite*, exhib. cat., Tessa Sidey, ed., Birmingham Museums and Art Gallery, 2008.
Marsh 2005
Jan Marsh, ed., *Black Victorians. Black People in British Art 1800–1900*, exhibn. cat., Manchester Art Gallery, 2005.

Marsh and Nunn 1997
Jan Marsh and Pamela Gerrish Nunn, *Pre-Raphaelite Women Artists*, exhibn. cat., Manchester Art Gallery, 1997.
MCL
Manchester Central Library, Archives and Local Studies.
Meisel 1988
Martin Meisel, *'Pictorial Engagments: Byron, Delacroix, Ford Madox Brown,'* Studies in Romanticism, 27, 4, Winter 1988, pp. 579–603.
NML
Rae papers, National Museums Liverpool, George Rae papers, Lady Lever Art Gallery (on loan to Walker Art Gallery).
Newcastle 1989
Pre-Raphaelites. Painters and Patrons in the North East, exhibn. cat., Laing Art Gallery, Newcastle upon Tyne 1989.
Newman and Watkinson 1991
Teresa Newman and Ray Watkinson, *Ford Madox Brown and the Pre-Raphaelite Circle*, London 1991.
Palgrave 1865
F.T. Palgrave, 'Exhibition of Pictures by M. Madox Brown,' *The Saturday Review*, 25 March 1865.
Parry 1996
Linda Parry, ed., *William Morris*, exhibn. cat., Victoria & Albert Museum, London, 1996.
Patmore 1857
Coventry Patmore, 'A Pre-Raphaelite Exhibition', *Saturday Review* 4 July 1857.
Peattie 1990
Selected Letters of William Michael Rossetti, Roger W. Peattie ed., Pennsylvania 1990.
Plumb 1969
J.H. Plumb, 'The Victorians Unbuttoned', *Horizon*, Autumn 1969.
PRB Journal
The P.R.B. Journal, William A. Fredeman, ed., Oxford 1975.
Princeton
Princeton University Library, Department of Rare Books and Special Collections, Lowes Cato Dickinson correspondence C0152, Box 1.
Rabin 1978
Ford Madox Brown and the Pre-Raphaelite History-Picture, New York 1978.
Robertson 1931
W. Graham Robertson, *Time Was*, London 1931.
Rosenfeld and Smith 2007
Jason Rosenfeld and Alison Smith, *Millais*, exhibn. cat., Tate, London 2007.
Rosenthal 1914
L. Rosenthal, *Du Romanticisme au Realisme*, Paris 1914.
D.G. Rossetti 1856
Dante Gabriel Rossetti, 'Fine Arts. Mr. Madox Brown's Pictures – The Liverpool Academy,' *Daily News* 9 September 1856.
D.G. Rossetti *Correspondence*
The Correspondence of Dante Gabriel Rossetti, William A. Fredeman, ed., 9 vols., Woodbridge 2002–10.
Helen Rossetti 1902
Helen M. Madox Rossetti, *Ford Madox Brown*, London 1902.
L.M. Rossetti 1890
Lucy Madox Rossetti, 'Ford Madox Brown', *Magazine of Art*, London 1890, pp. 289–96.
W.M. Rossetti 1851
William Michael Rossetti, *The Spectator*, London 1851, pp. 19–20.
W.M. Rossetti 1865
William Michael Rossetti, 'Mr. Madox Brown's Exhibition and its Place in our School of Painting', *Fraser's Magazine*, London May 1865.
W.M. Rossetti 1886
William Michael Rossetti, 'Ford Madox Brown: Characteristics,' *The Century Guild Hobby Horse*, 1, 1886, pp. 48–54.
W.M. Rossetti 1895
Dante Gabriel Rossetti. His Family-Letters with a Memoir, William Michael Rossetti, ed., London 1895, 2 vols.
W.M. Rossetti 1903
Rossetti Papers, 1862–1870, William Michael Rossetti, ed., London 1903.
W.M. Rossetti 1906
William Michael Rossetti, *Some Reminiscences*, London 1906, 2 vols.
Rowley 1911
Charles Rowley, *Fifty Years of Work Without Wages*, London n.d. [1911].
Ruskin
The Works of John Ruskin, E.T. Cook and Alexander Wedderburn, eds., London 1903–12, 39 vols.
Sale 1894
No. 1 St. Edmund's Terrace, Regent's Park, A Catalogue of the Household & Decorative Furniture, Works of Art, Books & Effect, belonging to the Distinguished Painter Ford Madox Brown, Tuesday, Wednesday a& Thusday, May 29th, 30th & 31st, 1894, T.G. Wharton, Auctioneers and Estate Agents, 1 Basinghall Street, London, E.C.
Shields 1874–75
Frederick J. Shields, 'The Works of Mr. Ford Madox Brown' and

'On Two Pictures by Ford Madox Brown,' *Transactions of the Manchester Literary Club*, 1874–75, pp. 41–50.
Shields 1912
The Life and Letters of Frederic Shields, ed. Ernestine Mills, London 1912.
Soskice 1921
Juliet Soskice, *Chapters from Childhood*, London 1921.
Staley 2001
Allen Staley, *The Pre-Raphaelite Landscape*, New Haven and London 2001.
Staley 2004
Allen Staley and Christopher Newall, *Pre-Raphaelite Vision. Truth to Nature*, exhibn. cat., Tate, London 2004.
Stammers 1978
M.K. Stammers, *The Passage Makers*, Brighton 1978.
Stansky 1985
Peter Stansky, *Redesigning the World: William Morris, the 1880s, and the Arts and Crafts Movement*, Princeton, N.J. 1985.
Tait 1900
E.M. Tait, 'The Pioneer of Art Furniture. Madox Brown's Furniture Designs' in *The Furnisher*, 3, October 1900, pp. 61–63.
Thacker 2001
Alan Thacker, 'Dynastic monasteries and family cults: Edward the Elder's sainted kindred'. in N.J. Higham and D. H. Hill. *Edward the Elder 899–924*, London, 2001, pp. 248–63.
Thirlwell 2003
Angela Thirlwell, *William and Lucy. The Other Rossettis*, London 2003.
Thirlwell 2008
Angela Thirlwell, *Into the Frame. The Four Loves of Ford Madox Brown*, London 2008.
Townsend, Ridge & Hackney 2004
Joyce H. Townsend, Jacqueline Ridge & Stephen Hackney, *Pre-Raphaelite Painting Techniques*, Tate, London 2004.
Treuherz 1984
Julian Treuherz, 'The Pre-Raphaelites and Medieval Illuminated Manuscripts,' Leslie Parris, ed., *Pre-Raphaelite Papers*, Tate, London 1984, pp. 153–69.
Treuherz 1985
Julian Treuherz, 'Ford Madox Brown and the Manchester Murals,' *Art and Architecture in Victorian Manchester* (John H.G. Archer, ed.), Manchester 1985.
Treuherz 2007
Julian Treuherz, 'Ford Madox Brown, *An English Autumn Afternoon*', *British Vision. Observation and Imagination in British Art 1750–1950*, exhibn. cat., Robert Hoozee, ed., Museum voor Schone Kunsten, Ghent 2007.
UBC
University of British Columbia Library, Vancouver, Rare Books and Special Collections: Angeli-Dennis Collection; James Leathart fonds.
V&A
Victoria & Albert Museum, Ford Madox Brown papers and correspondence, National Art Library MSL/1995/14.
Walker 2006
John Walker, *Work. Ford Madox Brown's Painting and Victorian Life*, London 2006.
Walpole 1786
Horace Walpole, *Anecdotes of Painting in England*, London 1786 (1871 reprint).
Wright 1997
'Suburban Prospects: vision and possession in Ford Madox Brown's *An English Autumn Afternoon*,' M.F. Watson, ed., *Collecting the Pre-Raphaelites: The Anglo-American Enchantment*, London 1997.
Wright 2007
Alastair Ian Wright, 'Ford Madox Brown's "The Body of Harold": Representing England at Mid-Century,' *Nineteenth Century Art Worldwide. A journal of nineteenth-century visual culture*, 6, 2, Autumn 2007 (online).

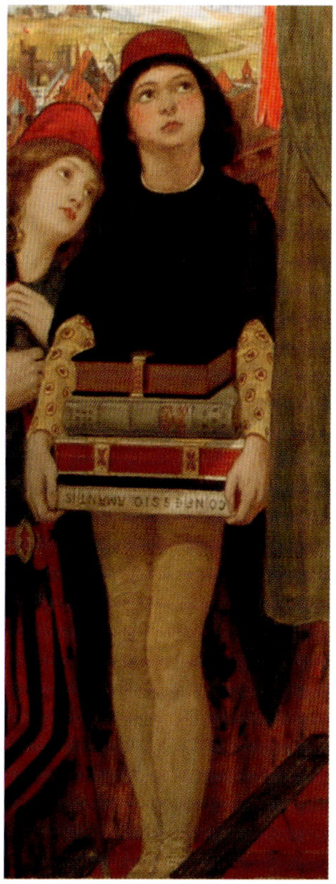

Fig. 110 (Detail of cat. 33), The First Translation of the Bible into English

IMAGE CREDITS

Aberdeen Art Gallery & Museums Collections, Cat. 117
Albert Dawson Trust, Fig. 27
Art Gallery of New South Wales, Sydney, Fig. 53, Fig. 58 (Photo: Carley Wright)
Ashmolean Museum, University of Oxford, Cats.: 32, 67, 93, Figs.: 11, 22
Atkinson Gallery, Sefton Museums and Galleries, Southport, Cat. 148
Clare Bates Photographer, Cat. 29
Bibliothèque Nationale de France, Paris, Fig. 49
Birmingham Museums & Art Gallery, Front cover, Cats.: 4, 5, 10, 38, 39, 40, 41, 42, 43, 44, 45, 49, 50, 55, 58, 74, 80, 83, 84, 96, 124, Figs.: 1, 9, 19, 44, 59, 60, 61, 68, 95
Bradford Museums and Galleries, Cat. 33, Fig. 110
Bradford Museums and Galleries, West Yorkshire, UK / The Bridgeman Art Library, Cat. 98
© The British Library Board, Figs.: 30, 73
© The Trustees of the British Museum, Cats.: 66, 81, Figs.: 24, 29, 67, 80, 82
Mark Chadwick Photographer, Fig. 98
The Governing Body of Christ Church, Oxford, Fig. 55
Donato Cinicolo Photographer, Figs.: 13, 38
Master and Fellows of Corpus Christi College, Cambridge, Fig. 57
© Country Life, Fig. 102
Robin Croft Photographer, Figs.: 99, 100
Delaware Art Museum, Wilmington, USA/ Samuel and Mary R. Bancroft Memorial/ The Bridgeman Art Library, Figs.: 63, 87
By Permission of the Trustees of Dulwich Picture Gallery, Fig. 62
The Forbes Collection, New York, Cat. 26
© Culture and Sport Glasgow (Museums), Cat. 126
Harvard Art Museums, Fogg Art Museum, Bequest of Grenville L. Winthrop, 1943.185, © President and Fellows of Harvard College, Photo: Katya Kallsen, Frontispiece
Harris Museum and Art Gallery, Preston / The Bridgeman Art Library, Fig. 86
James Holland Photographer, Fig. 97
Matthew Hollow Photographer, Cats.: 78, 89
Kelmscott Manor Collection. © Society of Antiquaries of London, Cats.: 112, 113, 114, 115
© National Museums Liverpool, Walker Art Gallery, Cats.: 2, 7, 8, 9, 30, 56, 71, 72, 76, 106, Figs.: 83, 108.

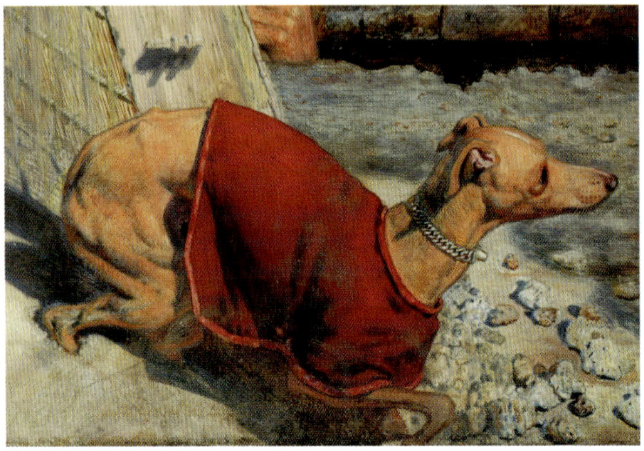

Fig. 111
Detail of cat. 61, Work

© National Museums Liverpool, Lady Lever Art Gallery, Cats.: 47, 79, 87
By courtesy of the University of Liverpool Library, Fig. 12
Maidstone Museum & Bentlif Art Gallery, Cat. 94
Manchester City Council, Cats.: 116, 118, 120, 122, 125, 127, 129, 131, 132, 133, 136, 142, Figs.: 23, 32, 103
© Manchester City Galleries, Back cover, Cats.: 3, 11, 14, 15, 16, 23, 24, 25, 35, 54, 60, 61, 62, 63, 64, 68, 69, 70, 73, 82, 85, 86, 90, 101, 123, 128, 130, 134, 149, 150, 151, 153, Figs.: 4, 8, 34, 35, 36, 41, 48, 50, 64, 70, 71, 72, 74, 75, 77, 78, 84, 92, 101, 109, 111
Manchester Local Studies, Figs.: 37, 39
Courtesy of Manchester Metropolitan University Special Collections. Photo: Tony Richards, Cat. 107
Fraser Marr Photographer, Cats.: 6, 95
Villa Massimo, Rome, Italy / The Bridgeman Art Library, Fig. 54
Musée d'Orsay, Paris, France / Giraudon / The Bridgeman Art Library, Fig. 6
© Peter Nahum, Cat. 1
© The National Gallery 2010, Figs.: 66, 89
By kind permission of the Trustees of the National Library of Scotland, Edinburgh, Figs.: 17 & 18
National Media Museum/Science & Society Picture Library, Fig. 47
© National Museum of Wales, Cats.: 48, 100, Fig. 94
© National Portrait Gallery, London, Cat. 97, Figs.: 15, 69, 90, 106
National Trust, © NTPL/Derrick E. Witty, Cat. 31, Fig. 104. © NTPL/John Hammond, Cat. 88
Art Gallery of Ontario, Toronto, Fig. 51
Parliamentary Archives, London, Fig. 93
Paul Mellon Centre Archives, Cats.: 27 (via Robert Holden Ltd), 46, 108, 109, 110, Fig. 107 (Courtesy of Mary Bennett)
The Pierpont Library, New York. Bequest Gordon N. Ray, 1987. MA 4500. Fig. 10
Princeton University Library, Fig. 45 *(Laurence Hutton Photograph Albums. Manuscripts Division. Department of Rare Books and Special Collections).* Fig. 79 *(Lowes Cato Dickinson Correspondence. Manuscripts Division. Department of Rare Books and Special Collections)*
Reproduced with permission of Punch Ltd, Fig. 76
© Royal Museums of Fine Arts of Belgium, Brussels, Photo: Grafisch Buro Lefevre, Heule, Fig. 3
Sotheby's, Fig. 25
Gemäldegalerie Alte Meister, Staatliche Kunstsammlungen Dresden, Fig. 28
Staatliche Museen zu Berlin, © bpk Berlin/Kupferstichkabinett, Staatliche Museen zu Berlin, Fig. 2. © bpk Berlin/Nationalgalerie, Staatliche Museen zu Berlin/Jörg P. Anders, Fig. 5
State Hermitage Museum, St. Petersburg, Russia / The Bridgeman Art Library, Figs.: 65, 85
© Tate, London 2009, Figs.: 31, 81
© Tate, London 2010, Cats.: 12, 28, 34, 36, 37, 51, 52, 53, 57, 65, 75, 92, 135, 137, 138, 139, 140, 141, 152, Figs. 7, 32
Thomas Fisher Rare Book Library, University of Toronto, Fig. 91
Tullie House Museum & Art Gallery, Cat. 119
© V&A Images/Victoria and Albert Museum, London, Cats.: 77, 111, 121, Figs.: 21, 33, 56, 88, 96
Trustees of the Watts Gallery, Compton, Surrey, UK / The Bridgeman Art Library, Figs.: 40, 42
Palace of Westminster Collection, London, Figs.: 52, 105
The Whitworth Art Gallery, The University of Manchester, Cats.: 13, 17, 18, 19, 20, 21, 22, 102, 103, 104, 105, 143, 144, 145, 146, 147, Fig. 26
William Morris Gallery, London Borough of Waltham Forest, Cat. 99
Yale Center for British Art, Paul Mellon Fund (B1989.11), Cat. 91

INDEX